Secret Body

IN 1989, IN NORTHEASTERN INDIA, JEFFREY KRIPAL HAD A MIND-BLOWING EXPERIENCE THAT CHANGED HIS LIFE FOREVER.

IT WAS THIS EXPERIENCE THAT CAUSED HIM TO DISCOVER THE BIZARRE HIDDEN TRUTH, WHICH UNDERLIES THE HUMAN CONDITION.

FOR DAYS, I HAD BEEN PARTICIPATING IN THE ANNUAL BENGALI CELEBRATION OF THE GODDESS, KALI, IN THE STREETS AND TEMPLES OF CALCUTTA (NOW KOLKATA).

ONE MORNING I WOKE UP ASLEEP, THAT IS I WOKE BUT MY BODY DID NOT.

I COULDN'T MOVE. I WAS PARALYZED, LIKE A CORPSE, MORE OR LESS EXACTLY LIKE THE HINDU GOD, SHIVA...

...AS HE IS TRADITIONALLY PORTRAYED IN TANTRIC ART, LYING PROSTRATE BENEATH KALI'S FEET. THEN THOSE "FEET" TOUCHED ME.

AN INCREDIBLY SUBTLE, IMMENSE PLEASURABLE, AND TERRIFYINGLY POWERFUL ENERGY ENTERED ME, POSSESSED ME, COMPLETELY OVERWHELMED M

Secret Body

EROTIC

AND

ESOTERIC CURRENTS

IN THE

HISTORY

OF

RELIGIONS

Jeffrey J. Kripal

THE UNIVERSITY OF CHICAGO PRESS
Chicago and London

The University of Chicago Press, Chicago 60637
The University of Chicago Press, Ltd., London
© 2017 by Jeffrey J. Kripal
Published 2017
Printed in the United States of America

26 25 24 23 22 21 20 19 18   2 3 4 5

ISBN-13: 978-0-226-12682-1 (cloth)
ISBN-13: 978-0-226-49148-6 (e-book)
DOI: 10.7208/chicago/9780226491486.001.0001

Library of Congress Cataloging-in-Publication Data

Names: Kripal, Jeffrey J. (Jeffrey John), 1962– author.
Title: Secret body : erotic and esoteric currents in the history of religions /
Jeffrey J. Kripal.
Description: Chicago ; London : The University of Chicago Press, 2017. |
Includes bibliographical references and index.
Identifiers: LCCN 2017015351 | ISBN 9780226126821 (cloth : alk. paper) |
ISBN 9780226491486 (e-book)
Subjects: LCSH: Sex—Religious aspects. | Erotica—Religious aspects. |
Occultism—Religious aspects. | Religion—History.
Classification: LCC BL65.S4 K75 2017 | DDC 204/.2—dc23
LC record available at https://lccn.loc.gov/2017015351

♾ This paper meets the requirements of ANSI/NISO Z39.48-1992
(Permanence of Paper).

for David,
who saw the secret body
and guided it, book by book, into form

Without realizing it, the individual composes his life according to the laws of beauty even in times of great distress. It is wrong, then, to chide the novel for being fascinated by mysterious coincidences, but it is right to chide man for being blind to such coincidences in his daily life. For he thereby deprives his life of a dimension of beauty. . . . Synchronicity is a flash moment where you're glimpsing a hidden structure or web of connections. But these can also be little hints that, yes, I am caught in a novel. That can be reassuring or disturbing, depending if you like the novel or not.

MILAN KUNDERA, *THE UNBEARABLE LIGHTNESS OF BEING*

To those who protest that they are not understood, not appreciated, not accepted—how many of us ever are?—all I can say is: "Clarify your position!"

HENRY MILLER, *BIG SUR AND THE ORANGES OF HIERONYMOUS BOSCH*

Contents

Opening: "You Should Write Fiction"   1

CORPUS

1.   In the Land of Oz: Childhood and Adolescence   21
LETTER TO THE EDITOR: *THE BUYER'S GUIDE* (1977)   29

2.   "My Eros Has Been Crucified": Puberty, Asceticism,
and Neurosis   30
ON THE FICTION OF A STRAIGHT JESUS (2008)   37

3.   That Night: Wherein the Knowing Energies Zap Me   46
THE PREFACE THAT I DID NOT PUBLISH (CA. 1994)   53

4.   The Erotic Mystic: *Kālī's Child* and the Backlash against It   56
SECRET TALK: SEXUAL IDENTITY AND THE POLITICS OF
SCHOLARSHIP IN THE STUDY OF HINDU TANTRISM (2000)   65

5.   The Transmoral Mystic: What Both the Moralists
and the Devotees Get Wrong   79
INSIDE-OUT, OUTSIDE-IN: EXISTENTIAL PLACE AND
ACADEMIC METHOD IN THE STUDY OF NORTH AMERICAN
GURU TRADITIONS (1999)   87

6.   How They Really Came to Their Ideas: The Deeper
Roots of Thought and Theory   97
THE VISITATION OF THE STRANGER: ON SOME MYSTICAL
DIMENSIONS OF THE HISTORY OF RELIGIONS (1999)   103

7.   The Gnostic Reversal: The Snake That Bites Its Own Tail   119
     GNOSISSSSS: A RESPONSE TO WOUTER HANEGRAAFF (2008)   127

8.   Wendy's Student: Mythical Paradox and Political Censorship   133
     BEING BLAKE: ANTINOMIAN THOUGHT, COUNTERCULTURE,
     AND THE ART OF THE HISTORY OF RELIGIONS (2010)   141

                              MYSTICUM

9.   That Other Night: The Future of the Body and Evolutionary
     Esotericism   169
     ESALEN: AMERICA AND THE RELIGION OF NO RELIGION
     (2007)   184

10. The Filter Thesis: The Irreducible Nature of Mind and the
     Spirit of the Humanities   192
     AN ISLAND IN MIND: ALDOUS HUXLEY AND THE
     NEUROTHEOLOGIAN (2013)   212

11. The Rise of the Paranormal: And Some Related X Factors
     in the Study of Religion   228
     AUTHORS OF THE IMPOSSIBLE: READING THE PARANORMAL
     WRITING US (2010–2014)   243
     THE MATTER OF MYTH AND THE MYTH OF MATTER (2011)   258

12. *La Pensée Surhumaine*: Paraphysics, the Super Story, and
     Invisible Colleges   261
     FORBIDDEN SCIENCE: A LATE NIGHT CHAT WITH JACQUES
     VALLÉE (JANUARY 24, 2012)   281
     LA MADONNA DELL'UFO (2015)   288

13. Comparing Religions in Public: Rural America, Evangelicals,
     and the Prophetic Function of the Humanities   296
     THE CHESS GAME (FEBRUARY 22, 2015)   308

14. The Super Natural: Biological Gods, the Traumatic Secret,
     and the Future (of) Race   312
     BETTER HORRORS: FROM TERROR TO COMMUNION IN WHITLEY
     STRIEBER'S *COMMUNION* (2015)   331

MEUM

15.   The New Comparativism: What It Is and How to Do It   359
        TRANSMIGRATION AND CULTURAL TRANSMISSION:
        COMPARING ANEW WITH IAN STEVENSON (2017)   376

                Closing: What the New Sacred Is (Not)   399
                        Airport Afterword   423
                    Appendix: The Gnomons   427
                  The Method of All Methods   433
                    Acknowledgments   435
                          Notes   437
                    Index of My Brain   465

OPENING

"You Should Write Fiction"

To see if you will balk against your script.

PHILIP K. DICK, *THE EXEGESIS*

After reading my work, more than a few readers and editors have said to me: "You should write fiction." To which I immediately reply: "But that's what my critics say I've been writing all along."

Still, they have a point (the readers and editors now), and I am finally following their advice in the pages that follow.

Sort of.

What follows is a kind of Reader, in the sense that it attempts to summarize the thought of a single individual through a selection of representative essays, public lectures, experimental pieces, and responses to book reviews, censors, emails, and bloggers. It also participates in the genres of memoir (since this individual happens to be me) and manifesto (since my goal is to express my thought as transparently and boldly as I can). The thing is admittedly more than a little eccentric. The point of this introduction is to explain why and how.

Secret Body is definitely not fiction, but it is also more than straight history or conventional memoir. In other books, particularly *Authors of the Impossible*, I have written a good deal about the literary or narrative dimensions of social and physical reality and how these narrative dimensions can be glimpsed most clearly in paranormal events. The paranormal here is a potential story that wants to be told in and as us, a kind of writing of the real writing us. In the mirror of that weird thought, I have reflected back on my own life as if it were just such an occulted text trying to express itself in the physical world through historical events, uncanny correspondences between subjective states and objective events (living "comparisons"), and gifted readers in whose reflections I have recognized something of my own hidden face. I have written this book as if . . . there is no other way to put it . . . *as if I were a myth become real.*

I mean this quite seriously. The unvarnished truth is that things have been

1

very trippy. Telling it like it is is telling it trippy. In all truth, I have often felt what I imagine the mythical figure of Professor Xavier, or Professor X, in the X-Men films must feel when "mutants"—individuals of various ethnicities, sexualities, and religious backgrounds traumatically transformed by some life event or genetic difference and rejected or persecuted by their families and cultures— come to his secret school for training, advice, and, above all, moral support and human community. Of course, I am not Prof. X. But I do my best to provide this help and community. These people are real. These extraordinary experiences happen. These capacities and gifts are part of our shared world. So are the attempts to deny and shame them, or explain them away as something else. The myth is true.

I am not exaggerating. Because of the books I write and the material I speak openly about in lectures and public media, mutant souls seek me out and, yes, come to my school, where I am indeed a professor. My head bobs in an ocean of intimate reports of human abilities that render any science fiction film or spandex-clad punching brawl banal, ordinary, or just plain silly. These are the real X-Men and X-Women of the world.

Much of what follows could be described as a reception history of the books I have written, were it all not so terribly strange. I am not sure "reception" or, frankly, "history" quite does it. One academic colleague described the books, particularly *Authors of the Impossible*, as psychedelic, as her "gateway drug," and reported strange paranormal effects around reading it. Christine calls this the "*Authors* effect." She should know. She is a professor of rhetoric. Others have described their reading experiences of invisible presences, erotic encounters with a discarnate saint, profound moments of sexual-spiritual healing, poltergeist activity, synchronicities around UFO phenomena, states of hyper-awareness while reading, and new scholarly understandings of previously puzzling historical material. To take just one example of the latter reading phenomenon, during the night of December 17, 2010, "I" showed up, as an *augoeides* or shining etheric body, in the dream of a scholar of Neoplatonism to help him resolve a particular theoretical question with which he was struggling.[1]

Obviously, such reading practices are not simple ones. They are not about moving arbitrary cultural signs around in some neural game in a brain. Rather, they show every appearance of fundamentally changing how such readers receive, perceive, and cocreate the very texture of reality. If our public secular and materialist culture has systematically repressed and denied what I have called the impossible, these reading and writing practices are all about making the impossible possible again.

As a historian of religions who specializes in the study of extreme religious experiences, I take these modern "mutant" forms of esotericism and these reports of strange experiences around the reading of my books very seriously, just as seriously as I would take any other in the historical record. Why wouldn't I? Because the past is more important than the present? Because premodern people are more special than living ones?

To be frank, I think that these super-readers' anomalous responses to my texts are not anomalous at all but point toward some of the most fantastic potentials of reading and writing and, indeed, of consciousness itself. I do not cause these reading events and experiences in my readers. Prof. X aside, I am no super-mutant working wonders in other people's dreams, bodies, and rooms. I am simply an author who takes these dimensions of human nature *as real*, as part of who we all already are, wherever and whenever we are. By acknowledging as much and then exploring the implications of this acceptance, my books give permission to their readers to access and experience these realities for themselves. In effect, the books encourage them to ignore the cultural censor and talk about their experiences openly and honestly. *The readers* make the impossible possible, which, of course, was never really impossible.

Following the lead of these readers and walking the talk of decades now, I have come to read my own essays and books as if these texts were unconscious chapters in an emergent myth, surface signs of something much deeper and stranger. Nietzsche had it just right when he asked: "Do I have to add . . . that all our so-called consciousness is a more or less fantastic commentary on an unknown, perhaps unknowable, but felt text?"[2] I have tried to access, read out, and interpret that occulted text in the pages that follow.

In this true tall tale, this "I" of mine, this "me," is a character who gradually wakes up inside a set of conflicting cultural and religious stories that he himself did not write but that are very much a part of him, indeed, *that have written him*. After realizing this shocking fact, the same character balks at the scripts he has been given and attempts to "step off the page" of his familial, cultural, and professional stories and rewrite himself (and them) anew through another kind of writing—oddly enough, a quarter century of technical scholarship on religion—and, eventually, through a new kind of book: this one. Finally, in the very last pages of the story, this character begins to suspect that he, like everyone else, is not just written or influenced by culture and religion. He begins to suspect that the self itself is a reproduction, a representation, a neurological trick of memory and sensory display, a nonexistent absence (I literally don't believe in myself), but also, paradoxically, a portal of some vast unfathomable presence.

I am the only fiction I will ever write, and I have written it here.

I have taken this mythical turn in my writing practice for a number of reasons. Foremost among these is the conviction that this awareness of being a myth is not simply personal. It is also a deeply social, moral, and political act. As far as I can tell, most of our countless social sufferings and violences arise from the simple fact that we actually believe the social constructions that are our familial, religious, and national identities. We really think we are our masks and language games. We privilege our religious egos over our humanity, our societies over our species, our cultures over consciousness as such. We have it exactly backward. This book is about reversing that reversal. There is no more urgent political project than this.

In my own case, it is my own growing conviction that my social sense of self—this dingbat other people keep calling "Jeff" or, astonishingly, "Prof. Kripal"—is in actual and literal fact a fiction, in short, a "myth" as most people understand that word. "Jeff Kripal" is a little unstable story that I tell myself over and over again (apparently, I need reassuring) from a few bits of memory, which I have selected out of millions of potential bits, that are then strung loosely together to make up a story line or plot that is "me." You are such a myth, too, of course. We all are. As are all our cultures and religions. It's *all* fiction.

But it's enchanted fiction. And that's what makes it myth in the deeper sense of that word. All of this fiction is enchanted in the simple but profound sense that it is authored by forms of mind that are not fictional at all but that can never be known directly by us, not at least as egos or characters in their stories. We are fictional characters on the screen, alter egos thrown up here by a powerful and very real projector "at the back." As hard as we try, we cannot know that projector, not at least as characters on the screen. But this hardly means that it does not exist. For the sake of communication and simplicity, let us refer to this projector of egos in the abstract singular and give this mysterious enchanter, this flickering projector of all the movies of ego and culture, a name. Let us call it simply "consciousness."

Here is the loopy truth. This consciousness is us, and it is not us. There are numerous psychological, neuroscientific, and spiritual expressions of this twoness, many of which I have gathered under my central poetics of the Human as Two. This doubleness is the fundamental structure and central paradox of the present book and, or so I have concluded, of all of my work.

Multiple explanations, qualifications, and nuances will follow. For now, let me keep it brief, if also admittedly enigmatic.

On the professionally acceptable level, this twoness is the basis of the bed-rock insight of modern psychology regarding the ego and the unconscious, from psychoanalysis to contemporary cognitive science. On a more challenging and contested level, this twoness defines the most basic structures of religious prac-tice and experience and so the most basic shape and language of the phenom-enology of religion: this is why "the sacred" is so eerie, so at once strangely fa-miliar, and yet so seemingly Other, so alluring and so terrifying. It's us, and it's not us. This is also what makes the study of religion a paradoxical hermeneutical practice, *in principle*, and why any simple "scientific" or purely "descriptive" or "historical" approach can never get at what makes religion religious. At the end of the day, "religion" is not about objects that can be measured or described or tracked in archives, much less organized and statistically analyzed in a com-puter database. It is about subjects caught in and freed from their own stories.

Put most simply, the Human as Two is finally about the dual structures and existential paradoxes of our mythical existence. We are split in two. We author ourselves, and we are authored. We make things up, and we are made up. We are at once insiders and outsiders to our own stories. So we believe and suffer them, and yet we can see right through them and do not believe them. We *watch* them from some esoteric space that we can never quite locate.

"You should write fiction."

Tell me about it.

TO IMAGINE

Who is doing all of this? Who or what is the "implied spider" spinning all the webs of myth that constitute the history of human culture and religion, includ-ing each of us as actors, agents, and victims in those stories?[3] This is where the negative sense of myth as untruth, coded ideology, or oppressive fiction flips over into its positive, really fantastic, sense as symbolic mediation, translated truth or cosmic enigma. This is the enchanted part. How, after all, can that part of us that authors us speak to that part of us that is authored? How can the author outside the page communicate with the characters on the page? How can the shining projector communicate with the actors on the screen?

If the history of religions means anything, the answer to such questions comes down to this: through symbol and story. Which is another way of say-ing: through the imagination. We desperately need a new theory of the imag-ination (or a revived old one), one that can re-vision the imagination not as simply a spinner of fancy and distracting daydream but also, at least in rare moments, as an ecstatic mediator, expressive artist, and translator of the really real.

Clearly, however, our present dilemma with respect to the imagination is not simply a function of a particular history of ideas. It is also a function of material, biological, and neurological structures. It also has something to do with our double brains—another kind of Human as Two. To speak neuroanatomically for a moment, I think it remains more revealing than concealing, more fruitful than false, to think of mythical thinking or enchanted imagining as expressive of dimensions of mind that are correlated with the right hemisphere of the brain and so are confusing or simply nonsensical to more left-brain ways of knowing. These mythical dimensions of mind cannot speak directly to the ego for a simple reason: ego is primarily a left-brain function. Indeed, these other dimensions of mind cannot "speak" at all, since language as such is also primarily a left brain function. So these presences show us pictures and tell us stories in dream and vision. They possess us. They claim to be gods, or God. They blast us with altered states of energy and pull us, like a magnet, outside our bodies into other worlds and dimensions. They trick us. They mess with us. They seem at once familiar and alien. That's because they are.

We know too much about the brain to take such a duality too simply. Most brain functions are "global" and not restricted to one hemisphere. But the human brain *is* literally split in two (there are really two of you in there). That is a nonnegotiable, neuroanatomical, universal fact. Accordingly, the bi-modal model of human functioning remains heuristically fruitful to address the binaries of any number of human experiences and expressions, including those of the study of religion and what I have hymned as the Human as Two.

The same bi-hemispherical model, I should add, has recently attracted some very sophisticated proponents from the realms of psychiatry and neuroanatomy in order to understand the lopsided, hyper-mechanistic nature of Western culture and the neurological coordinates (not necessarily causes) of mystical states of consciousness.[4] I find the framing of some of this most recent work by historian of esotericism and occultism Gary Lachman especially germane to my goals in the following pages:

> The left cerebral hemisphere deals with language, it is the home of our ego, the verbal "I" with which we identify. Next door to it—or "us"—separated by a bundle of neural fibers called the corpus callosum or commissure, resides, for all intents and purposes, a stranger. This stranger does not speak but commu-

nicates in symbols, images, intutions, hunches, even physical sensations, and may, as some theorists have speculated, be involved in paranormal phenomena.[5]

That is more or less what I think. Both of me. Regardless, I am not bound to the hemispherical model in any slavish way. I am no neurological literalist. It is simply another heuristic device, one of numerous models of the Human as Two that I will be exploring in the pages that follow, from the immortal Self (*atman*) that is not the mortal "I-maker" (*ahamkara*) of ancient Hindu thought, through the divine and human natures of Christ in Christian theology and mysticism, through the modern Freudian ego and unconscious, to the Eliadean sacred and profane, the former shining most brightly as different forms of tranconsciousness refracted through the histories of yoga, shamanism, myth, symbol, and occultism.

All of these speculative engagements are aimed at a larger point, to which I definitely am committed, namely, that we must learn to be more comfortable with these visions, zappings, and apparent entities, no matter how baroque or zany they appear to our rational egos and conventional materialisms. Indeed, in some sense, the more bizarre, the better. *That's* their point. They are not supposed to "make sense" (a phrase, please note, that neatly implies that the human senses have access to all of reality, which is utter nonsense). Indeed, explanation and the language of cause (left-brain functions again) are, in some sense, beside the point (and literally beside the right hemisphere and its symbolic beamings). These religious phenomena are not about mechanisms. They are about meaning. Moreover, although they certainly involve all of these dimensions of who we are, they are also not simply about reason, or cognition, or language, or ego, or anything else that the left brain can count, analyze, explain, or put on a computer chip. They are symbolic expressions of something Other or More. To borrow (and change) a phrase from a historian of mystical literature whom we will meet in due time, they are about "the visitation of the Stranger," a stranger whom, as speaking egos, we seldom recognize or welcome.

"As speaking egos." That is the key phrase, since we are not simply speaking egos. We are not just the ego circuits of our left brains. Consciousness is not just cognition. And, as the history of mystical literature demonstrates in abundance, we *can* intuit and even "know" this Other or More, this Stranger before us. How? Well, for one thing there appear to be other circuits in the brain, neurognostic structures that, in effect, open the veil to other dimensions of mind and reality, a mind and a reality that show every sign of being coterminous with one another.[6]

But there is likely a deeper reason still. We can know these other dimensions of mind and reality because these other dimensions are *us communicating with us*. We are the characters up on the screen. But we are also the projector projecting them. Again, it's *all* fiction up on the screen, but it's fiction enchanted or illuminated by a very real projector at the back of the room, which is us, too. We are the Stranger. *That's* the Human as Two. *That's* the esoteric paradox at the heart of the history of religions that I seek to express and explore here.

TO REASON

But *Secret Body* is not just about coming to terms with the mythical facts of our existence as projected and enchanted egos on the screen of history. It is also very much about public reason, about the primary powers of the left brain, about critical thinking with a professional purpose, about systematization and theory building. Imagine and intuit I will, but, first and foremost, I am interested here in having a public conversation with my colleagues and critics in the study of religion and the interested public at large.

Although I engage in autobiographical reflection, then, in the end the work is not about me. It is about the comparative study of religion as a philosophical, political, moral, and spiritual force in the world of vast, still unseen implications. The secret body emerges from and is an expression of this much larger and much more important professional body and multigenerational project. That is why some of the pieces anthologized or integrated here are not technical essays but public lectures, media pieces, blog responses, and experimental essays. Yes, I want to be a parable, a piece of entertaining fiction. But I want to be a parable for others.

The public work and the personal life are always connected. *Secret Body* is about working through this fact. It is about struggling with what was given to me within a single remarkable event, recognizing that which was given in the mirrors of history and culture, and then shaping these reflections into a set of reasoned arguments that can be discussed, debated, and—most important of all—applied in other historical and cultural contexts.[7] I do not expect you to care about my personal life, much less about my dreams and altered states of mind and energy. But if you have picked up this book, you may well care about the public reasons and the published work, which—and this is my point—was produced by this life and these same strange energies. You don't get the one without the other. That's how it happened. That's what it *is*.

Accordingly, I have systematized and summarized (that is, rationalized) my total body of work in the form of twenty theses or *gnomons*, as I call them. Since all of *Secret Body* points toward these gnomons, some explanation is in order about this term I use: a "gnomon." I first encountered the expression in another writer whom, alas, I have now forgotten. The word has since struck me as perfect for what I am trying to express in this particular context, since it seems to allude to a short aphorism or maxim (Greek: *gnome*) that is "gnostic" in nature. That an entirely different Greek word (*gnomon*) literally means "interpreter" but refers more specifically to the triangular instrument on a sundial, which tracks the apparent movement of the sun (really the spin and orbit of the earth), seems too good to be true. My gnomons, after all, each attempt to track the apparent movement of the sun of consciousness as it casts its shadows over time and history. Finally, that any English reader might also think of a gnome, the little guy with the pointy hat in our gardens, simply makes me smile, as I know this silly piece of popular culture can be traced at least as far back as the occult philosophy of Paracelsus (1493–1541) and originally referred to an earth elemental (Latin: *gnomus*), of which the modern ufological literature is also chockful. For all of these etymological, historical, and eccentric reasons, yes, "gnomon" is just right.

I fully recognize, of course, that these are my conclusions and do not reflect the consensus of the field as it stands now, much less the doctrines and theologies of the religions in question. But I am also convinced that these twenty theses are not just mine; that they are the result of countless swirling currents of pedagogical, social, and hermeneutical interaction; that they accurately reflect powerful and productive currents of thought and experience that have long been an intimate part of the study of religion, even if they are at present suppressed and hushed; and that they constitute a body of public knowledge that can be picked up by others in order to engage different historical materials and cultures to significant and often provocative effect. Indeed, the full implications of some of these theses, if they turn out to be even approximately true, are dramatic beyond measure. If we took them seriously, they would fundamentally reshape our cultures, if not our experience of reality itself. This is another reason that I have labeled them "secret." At this point in time, such sayings cannot be integrated into either the social body or our ordinary conceptual shaping of the real.

Let me immediately add that such gnomons are not offered as certainties, much less as winning arguments. They are not meant to shout over other voices. They are provocations, earnest voices in the corner of the room designed to interrupt the conversation for a moment, perhaps shift it into a new direction someday. Nothing more. But nothing less.

Considering them, then, does not mean that other, much more developed and established voices at the center of the room are unimportant or should not remain central. I consider the established historical-critical, philosophical, sociological, and psychological methods to be the sine qua non features of the field, without which there could be no study of religion. Although I will make my disagreements clear, I do not want to work in a profession in which the thought of such thinkers do not hold a central and distinguished place.

Put a bit differently, I intend to *add* things to the discipline (that were already there), not take anything away. There is no zero-sum game here. When I write about "esoteric currents" in the history of religions, I mean exactly that. These are esoteric currents, and will probably remain so for a long time.

So I will claim. I will complain. I will invoke my defenders. I will answer my critics. I will celebrate. I will polemicize. I will hiss. I will humor. I will tell secrets. I will keep secrets. It is for others to take this thought up and hone it, or to ignore it. In any case, I trust the long arc of the professional and public conversations, wherever they bend. And, of course, I may well be mistaken about any number of things imagined in these pages, including my central speculative suggestions regarding the centrality of consciousness to the future study of religion. But so what? Again, I am writing here to provoke, not to "be right" (what a telling but odd, left-brained expression that is, since the left brain controls the right side of the body).

I have shared this text with many colleagues, and I have received significant critical feedback, much of which I have incorporated, and some of which I have not. The latter criticisms generally boiled down to the earnest request that I return to the rules of the academic game, that I pretend, like everyone else, that I do not really care about transcendence and truth, that I return to the center of the room and sit down. My reply was and remains a simple one: "No. That is not what this book is about. That is not what I am here for, not at least now at this stage of my life and writing. Nor is that really what the intellectual life is about. How else did we get a Freud, a Foucault, or feminism? Certainly not by obeying the established rules of the place and time."

So I say this: if you seek an established, respectable, fully rational, fully defensible program for the study of religion, then go elsewhere. I have none. Put me down. If, on the other hand, you seek an intimate view into the inner workings and future speculative directions of one historian of religions' thoughts on the field and how these esoteric currents might flow out of a much richer history and into a much brighter future, read on.

TO BE READ WHOLE

On another level still, this book is an attempt to understand what it is that I have been trying to say in print for the last quarter century. I have long sensed that there was an unconscious narrative, a knowing dream, a secret body behind all the manifest essays and books, but until recently I could not have articulated what this secret body looks like. I was a dreamer still at work on the dream.

There is another way to put this. I write here first and foremost *to be read whole.*

This aspect of the project is born of a common experience of mine, which goes like this: I receive a letter from a reader or encounter a colleague at another university, after which a conversation ensues about a particular book or essay that I have written. I quickly realize that the reader is reading me through this single topic and not through my total body of work. Rather than a zapped or irradiated historian of religions (which is how I understand myself), I become a harassed or even threatened Indologist (they love that one), or a straight gender theorist writing about gay men (very confusing), or an Aldous Huxley enthusiast (understandable, but far too restricting), or a historian of Western esotericism (close), or a parapsychologist (deeply sympathetic, but no), or a historian of comic book culture (nope), or whatever it is that the person wants me to be.

I become frustrated in these situations, until I ask myself: "But who can read an entire body of work?" This self-questioning is usually followed by an admission in my head: "Well, I suppose it is just a bit confusing what a man might be about who started out writing about Tantric traditions in colonial Bengal and Roman Catholic homoeroticism, ended up writing about science fiction and UFO encounters in Cold War America, and never stopped writing about sex." I mean, really, just *who* is confused here?

This confusion, be it mine or that of my readers, is compounded by the fact that the public responses to my individual books have often been extreme ones. Consider two tall tales.

My first book, *Kālī's Child* (1995), a study of the censored "secret talk" and homoerotic mystical ecstasies of the nineteenth-century Hindu saint Ramakrishna, was the object of both a major book award ("Best First Book in the

History of Religions") and two organized ban movements in India, the second of which went all the way up to Parliament, in the spring of 2001. I was the first American scholar of Hinduism to be blacklisted and targeted for systematic harassment by Hindutva fundamentalists, in both the States and India, in a wave of attempted censorship that has not abated since, twenty years later.

My sixth book, *Mutants and Mystics* (2011), takes a close look at the paranormal currents of American popular culture, particularly as experienced by the authors and artists of the science fiction and comic book worlds. Just such a writer, a screenwriter for one of the superhero films I write about in the book, wrote to me after the book came out. He was sitting on the set of a superhero film shoot between two of my favorite actors, reading my book to them. He then asked for a dozen inscribed copies of the book so that they could be formally gifted to the main cast, director, and producers at their closing party.

So I write a book about the textual history of a censored saint and find that book becoming an object of the same political processes of censorship that I had written about. I write a book about the emergent mythology of "mutants and mystics" and find myself gifting that book to the human backstage of the mythical world I have just written about. What is going on here? I mention these stories at the beginning not to brag or to boast (remember: I'm a myth), but simply to observe that there is something highly unusual about the particular books I have written, something that somehow brings about what they are about.

SECRET BODY

The traditional name for this kind of reading and writing is "magic." Magical language is language that brings about that which it is about. My own expression for this fantastic capacity of language is "secret body." I mean something very specific by this expression. Actually, I mean four specific things.

First, I mean to point to the underlying wholeness of the corpus, which is never made apparent in any single essay or book but that nevertheless produces them all. In this sense, *Secret Body* is a kind of Reader, an attempt to express the whole through a careful selection of its parts.

Second, by the expression "secret body" I mean to point to the fact that the published corpus is a public expression of a paranormal gnosis that, as I will explain in some detail, I received about a quarter of a century ago during an event I have come to call simply "that Night" and have tried, with some success and many failures, to "write out" ever since. *Secret Body*, then, is a linguistic expression of something that, in the end, cannot be fully languaged and to which, let me underline, I myself (again, as an ego up on the screen and not the light at the back of the room) do not have any direct or reliable access. In this sense, such a book is not simply a report on what has been thought. It is also a development and evolution of this thought, a disciplined attempt to nuance and take that Night further still.

Third, these pages constitute a "secret body" in the sense that they express my own physical body and its desires. As such, the book advances again one of my central and long-standing historical arguments, namely, that the male heterosexual body is "heretical" within most orthodox male mystical traditions, particularly when these employ erotic imagery to express the union of the human and the divine. I will explain this comparative thesis in detail below. For now, it is enough to know that the male heterosexual body generally "does not fit" into these theological, spiritual, and liturgical systems. Hence it can only become "secret," heterodox, silenced, and religiously marginalized.

I will speak from and as this secret body once again here, arguing, in effect, that the traditional mystical language of a "marriage" between the human and divine (as evident in the Hebrew prophets and the Christian mystics as in Hindu and Buddhist Tantra) is gradually being left behind for more expansive and queerer languages of an erotic evolutionary impulse and spiritual mutation. Human transformation remains the central concern, but the symbolic and mythical frameworks of this transformation are dramatically morphing.

Fourth, *Secret Body* is a secret body in the sense that I have come to intuit the public work's shape and nature in light of what can only be called an esoteric reception history of correspondence and conversation. "Secret" here refers to the "private," "intimate," and "confidential" contexts of this mirroring, which took place mostly via private email correspondence and, in some cases, through face-to-face meetings. But it also refers to the profound hermeneutical and social fact that I would not have come to an understanding of my own work, or myself, without these secret readers. I literally understood myself and came to be "me" through them.

PARANORMAL READING AND WRITING

Precisely because of the same esoteric reception, I know that the meanings and effects of particular kinds of texts do not lie solely in the past, in the author, or in any single reading. I know that they sometimes appear, like a UFO hovering just above the page, *between* the author and the text, and then *between* the author, text, and reader.[8] They thus speak of self-reflections, doubled selves, parasocial fields, flows of energy, strange synchronicities, and profound human connections in ways that no standard historiography, sociology, psychology, or literary theory has yet been able to capture.

The only places that I have been able to find remotely adequate resources for thinking about such extraordinary processes is in the world of science fiction and in the shared histories of the British psychical research tradition, American parapsychology, and the French *métapsychique* tradition (a specific lineage of psychical research within France that I will engage below). Here, then, is the reason that so much of my later work has been about the paranormal potentials of reading and writing. *That* is my experience of reading, writing and, above all, of being read. *That* is my experience of the secret body.

Along the way, I have become especially intrigued by the semiotic or symbolic function of paranormal events, by which I mean that they often work like texts that are taking expression in the physical world of objects and events. This is the idea with which I opened this opening. I will also close with it.

I have in mind here the ancient Platonic notions of the daimonic or divine sign (*daimonion semeion*), literally the "little daemon that gives signs" that guides the philosopher's life, as we see in the case of Socrates and his guardian spirit or *daimonion*, who famously prevented him throughout his life from making the wrong decisions. As Charles Stang has demonstrated, this notion of a "divine double" that inspires the philosopher in life through signs and leads the soul into the afterlife and into the next life via rebirth is in fact a major theme throughout the Platonic corpus.[9] In a very similar spirit, Peter Struck has explored the ancient Greek birth of the "symbol" as the enigmatic sign or chance meeing on the road that was linked to the experience of oracle, omen, talisman, dream, revelation, and meaningful coincidence, that is, to an order of truth and mind beyond discursive reason. Here were the furthest "limits of the text" in ancient Greece.[10]

These ancient Greek notions of the daimonic sign or uncanny symbol are incredibly important, as they give witness to a collection of human experiences that I believe are also at the heart of the modern American "paranormal." They also give witness to a deep link between paranormal experiences and the life of the intellect (*nous*), that is, to philosophy as a way of life, as a *calling*. Such daimonic signs have certainly functioned as such in my own life and work. Like Milan Kundera in *The Unbearable Lightness of Being* in the opening epigraph, I have taken these as aesthetic calls to "a dimension of beauty" and as "a hidden structure or web of connections" and, accordingly, have followed them at every step and with every book, including this one, as will become evident in what follows to the very last page.

I have suggested that these paranormal signs and symbols have something to do in turn with the ways that "we are written" by culture and religion. In this model at least, paranormal events—at once objective and subjective—can be understood as both little realizations of this "being written" and as inspirational goads aimed at getting us to "write ourselves anew," that is, to conjure other realities out of the cultural texts or inherited stories in which we are presently embedded.

Or *trapped*. Hence two of the most common descriptors of a paranormal experience: "It was as if I were a character in a novel" or "It was as if I were in a movie." Well, we all are, aren't we? We are all characters in those novels and movies we call "culture" or "religion." Here, writing and reading become, in effect, paranormal powers capable of freeing us from our deeply inscripted beliefs and assumptions, be these cultural, religious, or intellectual. We rely on these cultural scripts and languages to become human, self-reflexive, and social. But some of us also grow weary or suspicious of this scripting. We see its dark and dangerous sides. We sometimes write and read, then, *to not be so completely written and read*. We write to balk against our script, as Philip K. Dick came to understand his writing practice after his own experience of Valis, his name for the cosmic mind at the back of the movie theater.

I am hardly the first to become convinced of the paranormal potentials of language. As authors from Mark Twain, Henry Miller, and Stephen King to Walter Benjamin, Jacques Derrida, Nicolas Royle, and, most recently, Jason Josephson-Storm have observed, reading and writing display all sorts of deep resonances with another phenomenon: telepathy.[11] We forget just how utterly strange is the fact that a text created in one place and time can be picked up in another and be reactivated in the mind of the reader, down to minute particulars of mood and nuance. We forget how we write and read one another constantly. Textuality, potentially at least, is telepathy. And telepathy is certainly a kind of textuality. In both the deep act of reading and in the telepathic event, what we have is one form of mind "reading" another, often at a great distance in space-time. Are you are not reading my mind right now? And have I not gotten inside your head?

I am not really "inside" your head, of course. But—and this is the final secret of *Secret Body*—neither are you.

Corpus

Ila prôton anthrôpous tous esomenous theous dei.
Those destined to become gods must first become human.

ISIDORE, QUOTED BY DAMASCIUS (SIXTH CENTURY CE)

Secret Body is divided (and united) into two halves: "Corpus" and "Mysticum," which are then followed by a briefer third section: "Meum." The first two parts attempt to summarize, defend, and develop my published work: each chapter begins with some introductory material that describes a particular period in my life and a specific collection of ideas that absorbed me at that point in time. The voice begins to shift in the second and shifts again in the third, as we move from the past to the present and look to the future. In these second and third parts the memoir gradually morphs into the manifesto. As a result, the autobiographical reflections fade away as the methodological discussions come to the fore. Finally, in the third part, I attempt to sketch in an openly speculative and constructive spirit the future shape of what I am calling a "new comparativism" and a "new sacred"—a future theory of religion. There the book ends.

Here we begin part 1. This first part treats the origins and first half of my published body of work: *Kālī's Child* (1995), *Roads of Excess, Palaces of Wisdom* (2001), and *The Serpent's Gift* (2007). These first three books and these first two decades of research and writing (roughly 1985–2005) focused on the sexual bodies of religion, and more specifically on the profound shaping role that sexual orientation and sexual trauma play within male mystical literature. With the publication of *The Serpent's Gift* and its lead essay "The Apocryphon of the Beloved," I felt that I had adequately answered the questions about sexuality and religion that drove me into the field in the first place. So I stopped. Nothing since then has changed my mind on these particular questions. What follows in the first eight chapters is that story and a summary of its settled answers around these specific aspects of embodiment, male sexual-spiritual orientation, and moral critique.

1

In the Land of Oz

Childhood and Adolescence

Pay no attention to that man behind the curtain!

THE WIZARD OF OZ TALKING ABOUT HIMSELF

One of my early memories, perhaps at four or five, was becoming ecstatic at the bright-colored pages of a library book about dinosaurs.[1] Who knows what ran through my childish mind? My guess is that it had something to do with the monstrous and the fantastic, *which really existed.* I was so happy about that.

Another early memory has me on the living room floor, playing with some tiny little Disney figurines that my mother gave me. I believe they were marketing giveaways, treasures retrieved from boxes of Jell-O powder. I do not remember simply playing with these brightly painted plastic objects, however. In words that I did not possess as a child, I remember relating to them with awe, as if they embodied some special presence or bright power. They were *numinous.* They were little gods.

There were other early hints of my later life, signs that the psyche really is all there early on, that the acorn seed will grow up to become an oak and not a maple tree or a radish. Here's one. When my brother and I were little boys, our parents gave us two kittens. My brother Jerry named his "King Kong" and grew up to become, among other things, a football player, a body builder, and a rock climber. I named mine "Magic." Go figure.

I grew up in a little farming community called Hebron, in Nebraska (population: 1,800, or so). Already we are in the realm of a cultural fusion and a colonial history, in this case the fusion of biblical and Native American histories and the colonizing of the prairies by white settlers. The original town of Hebron, of course, is on the occupied West Bank in Israel. It is most famous for the Cave of the Patriarchs, where Abraham and much of his family are said to be buried. Nebraska, on the other hand, is an indigenous Omaha word for

"Land of the Flat Water," or what the French called the Platte, quite literally, the Flat (River). It is.

My memories of childhood are many and various and reflect, as one might expect, the land and its people. I have two memories of the Native American cultures that spirit and haunt the prairies both where I grew up and just west of there, in Colorado. The first involves my first contact with real religious difference. I still do not know what to make of the second.

As a teenager, I knew an elderly Indian man named Dewey. Dewey was what we called a "character." He was a horse trader who lived on the river road outside of town. He dressed poorly, probably because he was poor, to put it mildly. Most people didn't trust him. He used to come into my parents' hardware store, and I used to visit with him in the town restaurant. He was very fond of my parents, no doubt because they treated him with respect and affection, and he also took a liking to me. Dewey knew that I was interested in the religious life, and so he was always telling me gently critical stories about "the white man's religion" and how different the Native American's notion of "Spirit" is. It never occurred to me to argue with him.

It also never occurred to me to tell Dewey what happened to me in Colorado a few years before our conversations. We were out there on a summer vacation with my cousins, who lived in a suburb of Denver. I believe that we were just outside of Golden, Colorado, visiting Buffalo Bill's grave. The gravesite and memorial sit high up in the foothills, overlooking the city. I wandered away from the group into the trees for no particular reason. Suddenly, something white flew by me—fast. Really, really fast. At first, I thought it was a mountain goat, but that didn't make much sense, since I saw nothing, even immediately after it ran by me. The thing, or so it seemed, just vanished into thin air. Flustered, I ran back to the group and asked my cousins and brother if they had seen anything. I don't think anyone took me seriously. They just brushed it off, as if nothing had happened.

I didn't give the whole event much more thought, but to this day I can't help wondering about the fact that we were at Buffalo Bill's grave, and that seeing a "white buffalo" is a central feature of some Native American mythologies. Whether you can call what I did "seeing" or whether you can call what I saw a "white buffalo," I do not know. I barely saw anything. It could have been an immense white owl as easily as it could have been a small white mountain goat. Or a ghost, for that matter. Still, I cannot quite shake the thought that the thing did not so much run by me, as *through* me or *into* me. Was that the beginning of my weirdness?

Then there was the raw violence of the Nebraska prairies and the manner in which this metereological chaos spun into myth, and into me. Hebron happens to sit in the Little Blue River Valley, otherwise known by the locals as Tornado Alley. The town, which is also the county seat of Thayer County, was pretty much leveled in 1953 by a monster tornado. It took out most of main street, much of the movie theater, the Catholic church, and the high school, and it shaved the roof off the county courthouse building like a crazed boy dismantling his little sister's doll house. Both of my parents were adolescents and remember the event well. So does anyone else there who happened to be alive at the time—it is difficult to forget the back of your car lifting off the ground as you try to escape town on a Saturday night; or your church reduced to rubble with your priest hanging, still very much alive, by a rafter; or the fact that you attended, as I did, a high school that in an earlier version had met its end in the winds earlier in the century.

I was not alive in 1953, but I grew up in the long cultural shadow of this monster storm. This colored, or thundered, everything. I have very distinct memories, for example, of fleeing to my grandparents' storm cellar at the threat of a similar storm. Disturbingly, storm cellars were dug out away from the house, so you had to run through the storm to get out of it.

THEOSOPHICAL OZ

I also remember being scared out of my wits as a little boy watching *The Wizard of Oz*.

The 1939 classic is an adaptation of L. Frank Baum's children's books by the same name, which first appeared in 1900. The movie begins with a Kansas farm and a tornado, that is, with my world. Although I never would have put it this way as a boy, space and time both morph from those opening scenes into one long altered state of consciousness or technicolor dream. As Dorothy famously describes the situation to Toto, "We're not in Kansas anymore." Or Nebraska. And then there were those damned flying monkeys. God, I *hated* those monkeys. They scared the shit out of me. Finally, there was the bumbling, deceptive, and yet somehow still kind and wise Wizard of Oz.

Interestingly, I played the Wizard, not very well, when my elementary school decided to stage the play. I've been playing him ever since, trying to teach young people that things religious are never what they seem to be, that there is a bumbling but profound human nature behind the curtain, and that the "great and powerful Oz" that so frightens us is an insecure fake—a projection on the screen of culture and history. "Pay no attention to that man behind the curtain!" The study of religion follows the little dog Toto and encourages the precisely opposite attitude. "Go ahead," we say. "Pull the curtain back. Take a peek."

I was a terrible actor and remember only one other role in a school play—when I played Hermes, the silver messenger of the Greek gods and the patron deity of hermeneutics, the intellectual tradition with which I most identify today. Go figure.

I have thought a great deal about the shaping influence of *The Wizard of Oz* on my young psyche. Does it have something to do with the fact that Frank Baum was a Theosophist; that, when Baum's family lived in Aberdeen, South Dakota, they held séances in their home; or that Baum even wrote a piece for the Aberdeen *Saturday Pioneer* on the powers of clairvoyants in which he discussed the existence of elementals or nature spirits? Later, he would fill his fairy tales with similar subtle beings.[2] One of these found its way into the Hollywood movie as a conscious ball of light that floats into an early scene and takes the shape of the Good Witch of the East. I would not realize until much later how similar this scene is to multiple reported UFO encounters. Little wonder, then, that when Jenny Randles was looking for an expression to capture the shifts in consciousness that are so common in encounter events, when space and time change shape or speed, or a strange mental tingling signals the activation of a visionary display, she landed on the phrase "the Oz factor."[3]

Baum summed up the basis of his own understanding of Theosophy in the notion that "God is Nature, and Nature God,"[4] not a bad gloss on what I would later call the "super natural." In a similar spirit, Baum portrayed magical powers in his stories as real forces of Nature that we do not yet understand, but will someday, after which we will be able to work true wonders. This same notion would later become the American "paranormal."

As a child, I knew nothing of Baum's Theosophy, of course, but this fictional enchantment certainly worked its way deep into me. I used to have a very distinct kind of lucid dream around four or five. Alas, I was always being chased in my dreams by this or that monster. Oddly, I knew perfectly well that I was dreaming inside the dream, but it was no less scary, and, worst of all, I couldn't get out. Until, that is, I figured out how. Eventually, I learned, still in the dream now, to cover my body with a sheet and tap my shoes together three times. With that, the dream would end, the monster would disappear, and I would wake up in my room, "back in Kansas." Okay, Nebraska. But close enough. It was southern Nebraska, after all.

Believe it or not, it never occurred to me where I had learned this little bit of lucid dream magic. Which is all to say that all this tornado and *Wizard of Oz* stuff was not just about weather and early Hollywood. It was also part of my little psyche. I may have lived in Nebraska just north of Kansas, but I also lived in that Theosophical, ufological dreamworld called Oz.

WONDERS IN THE BACK OF A COMIC BOOK

Television cartoons were really important to Jerry and me. That and sugar-loaded cereal that functioned as a kind of crack cocaine for kids. I still fondly remember getting up early every Saturday morning (the only morning of the week for cartoons), eating five, six, seven bowls of candy posing as nutritious cereal (whose artificial dyes colored the milk in truly unnatural ways), and then sitting in front of the television set, much too close, completely buzzed, for four solid hours watching psychedelic cartoons that neither of us knew were psychedelic, one of which, I kid you not, was called "H. R. Pufnstuf" (1969). The latter marvel featured an evil witch named Witchiepoo, a brightly colored happy dragon named H. R. Pufnstuf (the mayor of the island, of course), a British boy named Jimmy, and a talking magic flute named Freddy, who looked pretty much exactly like a talking penis. Disturbing. Who wrote this stuff? And puff'n on what stuff?

As I grew into adolescence, my enthusiasms shifted from the prehistoric to the superheroic. I imagined myself as an artist. I wanted to draw comic books. No, I wanted to draw *those bodies*. These human forms—both male and female—were glorious, sensuous, and ecstatic. There was also something transcendent about them: they glowed, flew, and disappeared in flashes of energy and light. They also turned me on, whatever that means at the age of eight.

I didn't just want to draw those bodies, though. I wanted to *be* one. Jerry and I would spend countless hours pumping weights in our basement toward this end. We spent one summer month, for example, following the grueling instructions of a poorly produced pamphlet that we purchased (for $4.99, plus $1.25 shipping and handling) from an ad at the back of a comic book. It promised us the secret to putting a whole inch on our biceps. This "secret" basically involved curling dumbbells every other hour all day long until we turned blue and couldn't lift our arms any longer.

It was awesome.

And that was just the beginning of the wonders at the back of those comics. There were the decoders and spy cameras (ordered'em), the Martial arts secrets advertised in martial arts comics (yep—don't mess with me), even underwater sea monkeys (nope—drew the metaphysical line about right *there*). Okay, the latter ads were peddling freeze-dried brine shrimp, but we didn't know that. We thought we were looking at naked monkey people in a fish bowl. We also ordered, believe it or not, Chinese throwing stars. These were basically weapons punched out of cheap steel in the shape of sharp stars. When you threw them at trees or buildings, they stuck. Heaven only knows what they would have done to a neck or a chest. What conscienceless man (it had to be a man), I now ask myself, was punching out deadly weapons in his garage and selling them to kids in the back of comics? And on and on it went, breathlessly, at the back of a single twenty-cent comic.

Depressingly, comic books today sport professionally executed ads that sell respectable things like milk. Not then. Comics were disreputable. They were slightly dangerous (and the throwing stars were *really* dangerous). We felt just a little bit naughty. Most of all, though, the world was magical. Anything was possible. We felt immortal. We felt like minor gods in the making, and those superhero comics were our instruction booklets on how to imagine our own inner superhood into being. We knew, of course, that the stories were "not real," but that's not how our imaginations related to their bright plots, or to the ripped male bodies and busty, leggy female forms arching, aching across the interior pages. No one, after all, had yet told us that our crystalline sense of awareness was just a froth of neurons firing; that we were just biological robots locked into our local language and cultural games; that life is really about money, power, and politics. We didn't know any of this. Not that it would have made any sense.

It still doesn't.

THE FALL

Something else happened in my youth, in the summer of 1971, when I was eight, that has often struck me as potentially significant, perhaps as some kind of neurospiritual opening. I fell out of a tree and landed on my spine and elbow, breaking both. The elbow was obvious enough. It was a compound fracture, and I was rolling around on the ground, screaming in agony. The broken vertebra was invisible and went completely unnoticed until decades later when I visited a chiropractor for some back pain. He took a standard X-ray and commented casually that I had broken a vertebra that had healed.

I have since wondered about this. Was something in my spine "opened up" by that fall and break? I ask this because one of the things that I have noticed in my readings of various mystics and psychics is that they often come to their gifts through some kind of physical injury or neurological event, often involving the head or spine. I do not claim such mystical or psychical gifts, but my life took some very unusual and, by almost any local cultural standards, very anomalous turns shortly after that fall and those injuries. Things got *very* weird. As did I. So maybe it wasn't the white buffalo. Maybe it was the fall.

One manifestation of this weirdness was my odd "nonviolence" in high school football, a sport that up until high school I had loved, if not actually worshipped (my room was a veritable temple to the Dallas Cowboys and my boyhood idol, Roger Staubach). Then, in high school, I became anxious about "hitting," as they called it—a euphemism for putting one's head down and ramming it into the body of another player. Was I unconsciously protecting my spine? I cannot help thinking that I was. This odd football nonviolence was also an expression of another entire psychosexual complex: puberty.

Oh, boy.

We'll return to puberty in the next chapter, and in more detail. For now, it is enough to know that I grew up in a happy and humbly prospering family. Think small-town hardware store, summer baseball, fall football, winter basketball, boyish adventures on the river, and go-kart racing on local dirt tracks with my dad (we had the fastest kart in that part of the state for years—it was a frick'n rocket on wheels). I sensed, on some deep intuitive level, what these odd changes in my flesh meant: they meant that I had to leave, that this utopia would not, could not last. So I did the rational, if never quite conscious, thing: I fought these biological changes. I beat them back. Practically, this meant two things: becoming extremely pious and anorexic. I went to church *a lot* and basically stopped eating. I ate, of course, but never enough. I danced on that line between preserving life and real hunger. The religious and the psychopathological emerged together.

Looking back (from years of counseling and therapy), the unconscious logic was simple enough. Food = body = sex = growing up = leaving utopia. Now that I think of it, it was also oh so biblical, the "fruit" of the Garden being what it was—sex.

Back in 1970s Nebraska, the answer to all of this, again entirely unconscious at this stage, was equally simple, if potentially deadly. No food = stop body = stop sex = don't grow up = stay in utopia. Stay in the Garden. It sounds terribly stupid when I put it like that. It was. But it also appears to have served another more interesting purpose: it knocked me clean off any "normal" secular life path. My dreams as a boy were entirely culture-bound. I wanted to be a comic artist or an NFL quarterback (you know, practical things). None of that was going to happen now. Anorexia and football do not go together very well.

Interestingly, I would remain entirely committed to superbodies and superpowers, but these would not be superheroic or athletic ones now. They would be holy bodies, spiritualized bodies, incorruptible bodies, magical bodies. I began reading, and living, the lives of the Catholic saints. As with my dinosaurs, the fantastic was not the fictional here. It was the real. It was not only possible. It was what we were meant to be and someday would be. I was no longer curling dumbbells. I was fasting and kneeling for endless hours in church as I read about the wonders and terrors of the saints. But the goal was largely the same: *to be changed.*

INTRODUCING THE TEXT

There was a cost to this sublimation from sex to spirit, and it was a very heavy one. My first published piece, reprinted below, speaks to this adolescent battle around sex and the saintly through the earlier genre of my childhood—the superheroic.[5] I was fourteen at the time. It was a letter to the editor of a newspaper, *The Buyer's Guide*, dedicated to the selling of comic books and comic book art, most of which, to this day, is gorgeously sexualized.

The letter is about censorship, which it asks for. It contains an exclamation point that should be a question mark. And it is all about the sexual body. Censorship, claims that should be questions, and erotic superbodies: these themes would all return, with a fury. My first published piece was poorly written, but it was also eerily prescient.

Letter to the Editor

THE BUYER'S GUIDE

(1977)

1977

Jeff Kripal

Hebron, Nebraska

Enclosed is another check for five dollars for another 26 issues of
your *Buyer's Guide*. I really enjoy it, but I have a complaint. I wish
you would censor some of the ads you put in your paper. They really
downgrade your otherwise wonderful paper. They may have a right
to sell underground comics and the such, which are all disgustingly
downgrading the comic industry, but sometimes I wonder if they, or
anybody, has the right to turn your newspaper into an underground
newspaper. And what bugs me even more, *you're* letting them do it!

Now really, there isn't that many of them to really hurt, or for that
matter, dent your huge advertising power. So what's stopping you!

Now, I don't mean to put your paper down as a whole. I love your
newspaper; it's just those few ads you print that sport pictures that
turn your comic pub into a pornography pub! So come on, do something about it. I know I would enjoy your paper more.

2

"My Eros Has Been Crucified"

Puberty, Asceticism, and Neurosis

ὁ ἐμός ἔρως ἐσταύρωται.
"My eros has been crucified."

IGNATIUS, LETTER TO THE ROMANS (EARLY SECOND CENTURY)

The anorexia, which was jet-fueled by a strong genetic OCD tendency on my father's side, got worse and worse. I graduated from high school in 1981, thin as a rail. Karen Carpenter died in 1983 of a similar condition. I do not believe the word was even known in the culture before this, and even after Carpenter's tragic death it was associated with young women, not young men. So I was a double anomaly in the late 1970s. "Weird as hell," as they say in Nebraska.

Naturally, my parents were extremely distraught as they watched their young son inexplicably shrink into a pale frame of skin and bones. Dad is a gifted mechanic and metalworker. We found and bought a professional racing kart (a virtual rocket on four wheels) in a nearby barn that burned up the local racing tracks for years with me behind the wheel, often racing men twice my age. But now I became less and less adept and more and more hesitant on the racing track. I asked dad to put a smaller engine on the cart so I could compete in a slower class. My brother was aghast and, I am sure, ashamed. He had long looked up to his big brother as a star athlete on the baseball, football, and basketball teams. We did everything together as boys. Now he had a religious freak for a brother who could barely play any sport. Worse yet, I had taken up the practice of correcting everyone's vulgar language in the locker room, not exactly a popular move, particularly when most of the language in the locker room is vulgar.

THE SCRUPLES

I was hardly celebrating. It was the worst time of my life, period. I can still remember my green plush bed blanket—it was covered with little dry salt patches from my excessive weeping. I spent most of my days locked into agonizing loops of guilt and fictional sins in my head, a distinctly religious manifestation of OCD. I eventually learned that my Catholic tradition had given this moral torture a name: "scrupulosity," from the Latin for *scrupulus*, which, I was told, is what the Romans called a little pebble that would get stuck in a sandal and make walking painful. Little things become big things. That was an understatement. I well understood why young people commit suicide.

But I also eventually learned that one cannot always trust an emotion or a thought, however convincing or powerful it might be. It was a subtle psychological lesson. I learned how not to identify with these obsessive emotions and thoughts, many of which were moral in nature. *I learned not to feel guilty about my guilt, not to believe my beliefs, not to think my thoughts.* It was an astonishing lesson, really. I eventually came to the conclusion that not only my obsessive thoughts and moral scruples, but also many moral rules, most social customs, and certainly all notions of "purity" are arbitrary things, and often cruel and destructive ones at that. In short, I learned to be extremely suspicious of all that is "right."

But these early suspicions would take a great deal of time to be sufficiently articulated and made fully conscious, and only after much suffering. The situation in high school was not nearly so philosophical. It was pathetic and desperate and sad. And in desperate times people turn to religion. This was complicated, to say the least, as my problems were all being expressed *through* religion. Religion was my problem. Religion was my obsession and neurosis. Religion would also be my eventual solution.

Mom and Dad turned to two priests, one of whom they had known and loved when they were teenagers in Hebron, and one of whom is a monk with whom my father had grown up as a boy in Hebron. The latter saintly monk kept me together through high school and became my first spiritual director through countless hours on the phone and in person. His patience with my obsessive thinking and scruples was simply astonishing.

When I graduated from high school, I enrolled at the monastic seminary attached to the monastery where this monk lived and taught. I wanted to become a monk. A balanced life of prayer, work, and study greatly attracted me. I have told this story in some detail in *Roads of Excess, Palaces of Wisdom*. The barest outlines will suffice here.

I had been an anti-abortion activist in high school. I gave speeches on the moral horrors of abortion on the high school speech team and traveled around the local counties speaking to various church groups.[1] These Catholic moral concerns were honed further in the seminary. There I encountered the riches of Catholic social teaching and the powerful witnesses of figures like the peace and justice activists Dorothy Day and the Berrigan brothers, the martyred Latin American leader Bishop Romero, and the Trappist monk and spiritual writer Thomas Merton. Robust and extensive criticisms of war, of the nuclear arms race, and of capitalism were part of the air I breathed. I registered for the draft (still in place when I turned eighteen in 1980) as a conscientious objector. I worked in a soup kitchen in Kansas City on vacations. I also did what I could whenever I met homeless people, which was fairly often.

One such incident is worth telling, as it reveals how sincere I was, but also how naive. I was working at an amusement park one summer in Kansas City. I was staying in the city at a Hispanic church and driving out to the park every day. On one of these trips, I saw two women standing on the side of the highway. I thought they needed help, so I picked them up. I didn't seem to notice that they were wearing remarkably little. Nor did any of their frank questions to me make a lot of sense to my still completely celibate mind. By the time it occurred to me that I had just picked up two prostitutes, the women had figured out that I was not going to be a paying customer. They were furious.

EAT ME

The seminary was formed around a profound psychospiritual orientation, by which I mean that it insisted on both extensive psychological analysis and what the Catholic tradition calls spiritual direction. The psyche, with all its emotions and complexes, was not ignored for the sake of the spirit. Quite the opposite. The basic working principle was that one could not have a healthy spiritual life without intense psychological work and emotional-sexual honesty. Through countless lectures, sermons, and casual conversations, I was taught that sainthood and neurosis were by no means exclusive, and that not tending to psychosexual issues could well spell disaster down the road. This was the early 1980s. The clerical scandals of the new millennium were still two decades away. If only the Church would have modeled itself on what these monks were already doing then and there.

Everyone was psychologically analyzed, and multiple times, as they moved through the four years of a college education, but the really difficult cases they sent to a monk who was also a psychoanalyst, and as Freudian as they get. He was also our Latin professor. He had a most unusual teaching style. Every other sentence somehow managed to contain the words "fuck" or "damn." It was a marvel of English grammar to see how he did this. I think he did it to loosen us up. So many of us were uptight prudes. I was. All this swearing pushed on that, challenged it.

I entered psychoanalysis with this swearing monk in the fall of my junior year, starving still. He taught me to read my dreams as Freud would have read them—as stories speaking in code. My psyche, already well primed by two years of psychological analysis and coursework, knew how to respond: with Freudian dreams. These were veritable Freudian stereotypes that shouted "Oedipal Complex!" and warned me of the dangers of sexual repression. The same dreams also taught me in explicit and humorous ways how I had linked "sex" and "food" in my unconscious, and how I was refusing the latter to beat back the former. I dreamed of buxom women offering me banana cream pies and milk shakes, which I could not accept despite my furious hunger. By the end of that year, the analyst, the buxom dream women, and I had cured the anorexia.

And I was *really* hungry. I ate everything in sight. I gained about seventy pounds over the next few months. I was a new man at twenty-two. Suddenly, I was also a sexual being.

The seminary community was a hotbed of psychosexual exploration, by which I do not mean anything explicitly sexual, much less genital. I mean that those years constituted a four-year initiation into the sexual roots of the spiritual life and the spiritual roots of the sexual life. The basic point is this: I came into my early psychological awakening and intellectual calling as a confused and repressed straight man in what was, more or less (mostly more), a gay religious community.

Nothing inappropriate happened. The homoeroticism of the seminary community from where I sat (which, as a naive straight skeleton, was pretty darn far away) was a sublimated one, or at least a sublimating one. The gayness of it all (in both senses of that word) would break out at the four annual parties, usually through some comedic skit involving cross-dressing or, in one case I remember, the suggestive handling of a vacuum cleaner hose. But, for the most part, my sense was that everyone was trying the best he could to consider and live a celibate life. It was a supportive and loving community, and I was happy. No tear-stained blankets anymore.

TURNING POINT

There was a dark side to all of this, however, a very dark side, but it did not involve the playful, funny, and affectionate homoeroticisms of the young men

I knew all around me. It involved the Church's teachings about homosexuality, long prejudices which were then being articulated by a future pope, Cardinal Joseph Ratzinger. The dark side expressed itself—or so I am partly guessing—through two suicides and a third attempt that occurred while I was there. A young monk hung himself in the barn. A seminarian blew his head off. And my best friend swallowed a bottle of sleeping pills.

I do not know why the first two men killed themselves, but I know why my best friend tried. He came back, and he was very clear with me about why he did it: he did it because he was gay. He also explained to me that just about everyone else in the seminary was gay. "Didn't you know that?" he asked, with some astonishment. Actually, no, I didn't know that. But, wow, that made *a lot* of sense. In fact, it pretty much explained everything that I had found puzzling, from the sweaty Sylvester Stallone "Rocky" poster on a seminarian's wall, through all the references to *GQ Magazine*, to the sensuous crucifix apparently modeled on the body of one of my classmates that made the seminary officials nervous for reasons I could not quite fathom.

That was a turning point for me. Three things now became obvious. First, these events explained to me why I did not fit into the various cliques of the community. Okay, I was fantastically neurotic, grossly pious, and just plain strange. I also didn't bathe enough (more asceticism), so I probably stank on top of everything else (someone once placed a bar of soap and some deodorant on my books outside of chapel one day—a silent, anonymous act of kindness). But I was also not gay, and that, I could see after my best friend's explanations, made a very big difference.

Second, these events also taught me that a religious tradition's moral position could have broadly destructive, even deadly consequences (read: that a religious tradition's moral position could be *wrong*). I began now to take a much more suspicious position vis-à-vis religious traditions and their self-proclaimed "moralities," especially when it came to anything having to do with sex. My previous struggles with scrupulosity and OCD were signals of this insight, but the attempted suicide of my friend was a full-blown conclusion.

Third, and most importantly of all, these events taught me that there were psychosexual reasons why these particular young men wanted to become celibate priests (that is, not marry women), why so many other young Catholic males did not want to become a celibate priest (that is, why they wanted to marry women), and—and this was the real key—*that it was perfectly possible, indeed likely, that many of these young men would not be aware of these psychosexual reasons.* In simple terms, I had awoken to the fundamental reality of the unconscious.

JESUS AND FREUD

I now had at least two different models for what I would later frame as the Human as Two. There was the daily discipline of the Catholic liturgy, the mind-bending implications of its central ritual of the Eucharist (the god-man become bread and wine, and so us), and endless discussions about Christology and the ancient theological question of the relationship between Jesus's human and divine natures: Jesus as Two. And there was psychoanalysis, its psychodynamic modeling of the unconscious, and its sophisticated readings of dream, slips of the tongue and everyday speech and behavior: the Psyche as Two. Jesus and Freud. Both models were foundational for me. Neither has ever left me.

All of my published work for the first decade or so of writing flowed from fusions of these early theological and psychoanalytic convictions, which, please note, I did not originally learn from any distant book, but from a liturgical and community life and extensive psychological analysis, including a very intense psychoanalysis that cured me of a potentially deadly anorexic condition. There was little "academic" about my explorations and conclusions. As I struggled with my own sexual repressions as a straight man in a loving gay community, these were life-and-death issues. It was either figure it out, or go down trying.

I figured it out. Or rather, to be more precise, something in my psyche figured it out with the help of the monks (and the busty dream women). *All* of this—from living in a sublimating gay community for four years, through Christian incarnational theology, to my own dramatic healing in a psychoanalytic practice—ultimately culminated, years later, in my central thesis about the orthodoxy of sublimated male homoeroticism and the heterodoxy of male heterosexuality within male erotic mystical literature.

My first three books flowed directly out of these same early insights as well. The first book, *Kālī's Child*, was a (failed) attempt to find an exception in Hinduism to the homoerotic comparative pattern that I had encountered in Christianity: Ramakrishna fit the homoerotic pattern beautifully, and once again he was funny and playful, like the seminarians I had known. The second book, *Roads of Excess, Palaces of Wisdom*, was an application of the same homoerotic pattern to Christian, Muslim, Hindu, and Jewish mystical literature. It was in the third book, *The Serpent's Gift*, however, that the theses about the Human as Two and the homoerotic structures of orthodoxy came into sharp focus. There I expressed them as two of my four *logoi mystikoi*, "secret sayings" or, here now, "gnomons."

As I explained above, there are twenty of these now. I will be keeping track of them as we go along. The first two go like this:

1. *Heretical Heterosexuality.* Whereas male heteroerotic forms of the mystical generally become heterodox or heretical, sublimated male homoerotic forms generally become orthodox.
2. *The Human as Two.* Each human being is two, that is, each person is simultaneously a conscious constructed self or socialized ego and a much larger complexly conscious field that normally manifests only in nonordinary states of consciousness and energy, which the religious traditions have historically objectified, mythologized, and projected outward into the sky as divine, as "God" or introjected inward into the human being as nirvana, brahman, or located in some sort of experienced paradoxical state that is neither inside nor outside, as in the Chinese Dao or the American paranormal.

I will resist the temptation to expand on either here, mostly because the rest of this volume is an expression and application of these two basic ideas. I will simply say that Heretical Heterosexuality was the meta-theme of the first half of my body of work (organized here under "Corpus"), and the Human as Two was the meta-theme of the second half of my body of work (organized under "Mysticum").

INTRODUCING THE ESSAY

The following text was delivered on October 9, 2008, at Austin Presbyterian Seminary in Austin, Texas, for a conference in honor of the (now late) psychologist of religion Donald Capps of Princeton Seminary, whom Robert Dykstra, one of his former students, accurately described as "simply the most published and influential pastoral theologian in the history of the discipline."[2] Don had trained my most gifted undergraduate student at Westminster College, Nathan Carlin. After completing his M. Div. under Don, Nate then came to Rice University to study the psychology of religion with Bill Parsons and myself. So there were many intimate collegial connections at play in this event. I felt at home, and I felt welcomed. The audience was predominantly Presbyterian and progressive. The essay treats a whole range of life experiences and intellectual themes, some of which I will treat more fully below. I have anthologized it here, in a slightly updated form, because it is a relatively simple and accessible statement of gnomon 1, and because it treats the time period I have been discussing in the present chapter.

On the Fiction of a Straight Jesus
(2008)

Until we become literal time travelers, all attempts to find the historical Jesus will be steered by instinct and intuition. Appeals to shared criteria may, we can pray, assist us in being self-critical, but when all is said and done we look for the historical Jesus with our imaginations—and there too is where we find him, if we find him at all.

DALE ALLISON, *JESUS OF NAZARETH: MILLENARIAN PROPHET*

"Real Men Love Jesus."

BUMPER STICKER SEEN ON MY COMMUTE
ON THE HIGHWAYS OF HOUSTON

CORRESPONDENCES

I am keenly aware, and deeply grateful, of my status here as an invited guest, as a recent "party-crasher" who has wandered into a lively conversation that has been going on among you all for many years now. So please allow me to begin with a bit of personal introduction, some narcissistic footnotes, and a few correspondences. I will then give my speech on love in the spirit of our "drinking together" (*sym-posium*).

Alas, I have always been the party-crasher here. I first introduced myself to Don Capps in January of 2002. I still have the letters. Remember letters? I had just sent Don my recently published *Roads of Excess, Palaces of Wisdom*, a series of essays on the orthodoxy of male homoeroticism and the heterodoxy of male heterosexuality within comparative mystical literature, including and especially Roman Catholicism, my own native birth tradition.

I do not have my original letter, but I have Don's response to it, dated January 22, 2002. In this initial letter, Don invokes a personal correspondence: our common boyhood state of Nebraska. He grew up in Omaha. In his *Jesus: A Psychological Biography*, Don takes up a boyhood Nebraska memory, of a painting of Jesus driving away the temple money-changers, and employs it as a psychobiographical cipher to understand the prophet's life.[3] The move was certainly an appropriate one, as some of the best New Testament criticism, from

Albert Schweitzer to Dale Allison, has concluded that Jesus was an apocalyptic preacher, a spiritual jihadi, a millenarian prophet who intended by that provocative act to call down God's wrath on the corrupt Temple priests and initiate the beginning of the end of the world as we know it.[4]

Don's memory of the painting got me thinking about my own Nebraska boyhood. I have never quite thought of it this way, but above all of my psychoanalytic reflections on Roman Catholicism looms a similar piece of religious art, a statue this time—the immense crucifix that hangs in my hometown church. This Jesus must be at least eight or nine feet tall. He's huge. Other than his extraordinary size and height, what is so striking about this piece is its super-realistic detail. The art is exquisitely, terrifyingly lifelike in both its sculpted shapes and its painted colors. One can see every drop of blood or sweat, every nail and thorn, and every curve, ripple, and spasm of the tortured male body, a perfect, beautiful male body that is basically naked, except for the traditional loincloth, just barely hanging there, somehow, teasingly. Over the years, I have spoken to a number of individuals, both adults and adolescents, who confess that the statue "creeps me out," that they can't look at it, etc. Others, I suspect, are fascinated in a morbid (and inarticulate quasi-erotic) sort of way.

I certainly was. Don's remarks about his painting have made me realize that this erotic crucifix is without question the artistic source of an adolescent obsessive fantasy of mine. The fantasy involved an ithyphallic crucified Jesus that haunted me for months and foretold my anorexia and my own "crucified" sexuality. Not surprisingly, it is one of the nodal points of the psychoanalytic autobiography that I tell in *Roads*.[5]

The fantasy was constructed out of the symbols of my Catholic culture: I would see a naked ithyphallic Jesus on the cross, with myself and the Virgin Mary standing beneath him. I felt terribly guilty about this fantasy as a boy, but I could never quite shake it, and I certainly did not understand it. Eventually as the years went on I forgot about it, but the problems that it announced shortly after puberty would haunt me for years and in the end would almost take my life. Only years later, in the spring of 1989, as I was returning from India and was in an airport bathroom stall in JFK, to be precise, I finally understood its original meaning and the ominous announcement it was making: at puberty I was about to "crucify" my sexuality for its unresolved oedipal dimensions. The divine erection, I realized, was aimed, if always unconsciously, at (the Virgin) Mother, and for this it had to be crucified; it had to be killed. And kill it I did. For the next six years, from shortly after puberty to my junior year in the seminary, I would engage myself in various ascetic practices, mostly involving different forms of fasting, until my once athletic 6′ 1″ frame was reduced to a skeleton-like 125 pounds, a mere shadow of my former physical self—a modern American case of what Rudolph Bell would call, quite appropriately I think, "holy anorexia."[6]

Don and I would continue to correspond occasionally over the years. Don came to Rice in December of 2003 and delivered a paper on Leonardo Da Vinci for a conference on "The Return of the Repressed," our humble attempt to rejuvenate psychoanalysis within the study of religion after a decade of Freud bashing. Don would also go on to work on numerous projects with one of our PhD graduates, Nathan Carlin, including a wonderful essay on the homosexuality of King James, the gay man who commissioned the translation project that eventually produced the linguistic beauty of the King James Bible.[7]

A SPEECH ON RELIGIOUS LOVE

At this point, I am sure the reader has come to the conclusion that I am curiously obsessed with the issue of homoeroticism and religion. That is correct. Allow me now to explain why. More specifically, allow me to explain why I think this single topic has come to dominate so much of the churches' energies today, and why I think it will continue to do so.

I will not quite speak here in the voice of the professional scholar. I will not back up everything that I state with an arsenal of footnotes, nor will I take safety in a long series of careful qualifications. Those who seek qualifications can go to my books. In any case, I do not seek to argue here. I seek to provoke. I do not mean to debate. I mean to whisper, out loud, a public secret.

There is both an obvious and a more esoteric dimension of my provocations here, both a public cry for justice and a quiet whisper of secret truths. The public cry is widely shared and widely known. Here I simply stand with a multitude, if not yet a majority. The latter, more esoteric position is widely known and commonly debated in academic circles, but it is not so well known outside the academy, and it often comes as a shock or a surprise, if a somehow familiar one, to individuals who have not had their perspectives adjusted in just this way.

The phenomenon of this public secret that comes in and out of focus often reminds me of those immense, awkward, and funny-looking eye machines that one peers into as an optometrist clicks from lens to lens in order to determine precisely what shape of lens is necessary to improve one's own specific ocular distortions: "Now which of these is more sharp and clear. . . ." After dozens of such questions, one realizes that the glasses or contacts one finally puts on are not straight at all, and that it is *precisely* those odd curves and shapes that focus the vision, that "click" into focus a brighter, sharper world, finally allowing one *to see.* Oddly, it is distortion that focuses and gives sight.

On the obvious or public side of my answer, I share the common conviction that the moral issue of homosexuality is a civil rights issue, that it is the "cutting edge" of America's long painful struggle with civil liberties, within which every new American freedom has to be fought for with millions of words and hundreds of thousands of acts of dissent, until it is plain as day to almost everyone (never all) where the moral truth lies. We have come so far. Which of our elected public officials is arguing for enslaving black people now? Which of our religious leaders is arguing that women should not have the right to vote, or that they should not be allowed to speak in public? Who in public policy, the academy, or the media is asserting that blacks and whites should not be allowed to eat together, or sit next to one another on the same bus, or, for that matter, marry, have sex, and bear children? Our grandchildren will look back at these present debates around homosexuality and experience the same set of emotions that we now feel with respect to the troubled, and still troubling, history of American race and gender relations: horror, embarrassment, guilt, condemnation, and repentance.

But this is not the only reason that I think the issue of homosexuality is splitting the churches and dividing the country. Sexual bigotry does not entirely explain the deeper, essentially theological dynamics that are generating this profound crisis. There are, after all, countless good and decent people who work tirelessly for racial justice but who balk at the notion that homosexuality is a civil rights issue. The black churches, for example, are some of the strongest opponents of gay rights. Civil rights, yes. Gay rights, no. Race and sex are related, then, but they are not the same thing. Something else is also going on here.

I understand that the issues are different and distinct in the black churches (where black sexualities have long been the targets of white racist polemics), but there are also historical and theological issues within Christianity that, frankly, transcend any of its specific social or racial locations. That "something else" can best be described as a return of the repressed. All of these controversies, debates, and scandals are so many symptoms or meaningful signs the social body of Christianity is manifesting, and will continue to manifest, because it has not come to terms with its own unconscious conflict, its own secret. That secret boils down to the textual fact that *there is nothing straight about*

the historical memories of Jesus that Christianity has preserved as its canonical
scriptures or New Testament.

Just below all the contemporary talk of "family values" and the bumper stickers that proclaim, with not a shred of intended irony, how "Real Men Love Jesus" lies the scripturally preserved memories of a man who does not appear to have been married, who bore no children, who raised no family, who hung out with sex workers and sinners, who counseled his listeners to hate their parents and leave their families to follow him, who liked to eat and to drink (with people with whom he was not supposed to eat and drink), who objected to much of his own pious Jewish culture, whose most cherished beloved was another man, who encouraged his most devoted male followers to castrate (or feminize) themselves for the kingdom of heaven, who left his disciples the truly scandalous ritual of consuming his own flesh and fluids within a love-meal outrageously modeled after the holiest ritual of his own religion, and who was ultimately executed by the state in the gruesome "electric chair" of the time, that is, by crucifixion. In short, the deepest reason that the churches are so nervous about the issue of homosexuality is the very plausible historical possibility that Jesus himself was a homoerotically inclined man who infuriated both the religious and political authorities of his day.

Jesus's transgressions were many, and I do not mean to reduce all of this to the issue of sexuality. Indeed, I would place Jesus's homoerotic sexual-spiritual orientation and his rejection of the patriarchal family in the same millenarian or apocalyptic worldview that New Testament critics have identified as the key to his prophetic teaching and ascetic lifestyle. A homoerotic sexuality, after all, is a nonproductive sexuality that will produce no children for the end times. It is also perfect for a small band of men preaching a radical message or, as Paul had it, a gospel. Such a spiritual-sexual orientation, moreover, stands not just against the patriarchal family, but, ideally at least, against heterosexuality itself. Hence the (in)famous castration for the kingdom of heaven passage (Matthew 19:12). Not everyone, of course, has ears to hear this, which is to say: not everyone desires like this.

I do not wish to argue that Jesus was "gay" in the sense we speak of and understand that identity today. But neither can I resist the idea that the psychological roots of Jesus's intentional subversion of much Jewish piety, his apocalyptic asceticism, and his radical teachings on love are all fundamentally related to his marginalized and lawfully condemned sexuality (or sexualities). The latter helps explain, indeed requires, the former breaking of the religious law. In short, Jesus's love must obviate the law because Jesus's love could not be fit into the law. *The issue of homosexuality, then, is not some tangential issue or modern perversion within American Christianity. It shines at the very center as the generative force of Christian male sanctity and love and goes back to the god-man himself.*

And little is resolved by turning to the real historical founder of Christianity, the apostle Paul, that Jewish mystic of the Christ who never met the historical Jesus; who was not married either; who bore no children; who preferred his followers remain virgins (the world, after all, was ending); who wanted everyone, men and women alike, "married" to a male god (if that is not queer, nothing is); and who confessed to a famous if never defined "thorn in the flesh" over which he appears to have struggled his entire life.[8] As best I can tell, much of the New Testament and later Christian orthodoxy—literally, the "straight-teaching"— was founded on the lives and loves of a homoerotic divine man and a sexually conflicted apostle, both of whom, if tradition is correct, met terribly violent ends for their transgressive spiritual desires. Ironically, there is nothing straight at all about Christian "straight teaching" or *ortho-doxy*.

This is why the churches are splitting today over same-sex marriages, openly gay clergy, and sexual justice issues. They are struggling, hard, against their own deepest scriptural roots and most fundamental, and most sacred, transgressions. They are setting up psychological and political defenses against their own original genius and power.

There are, of course, also ancient memories and modern cultural constructions of a straight Jesus, but, in a fascinating pattern I have made the centerpiece of my own work, all of these constructions became heterodox or heretical. Some of the early "gnostic" Christians, for example, imagined a Jesus in love with and united to Mary Magdalene. They even appear to have created a secret sexual sacrament around this highest of heterosexual mystical unions— their "bridal chamber," as they called it. But these early Christians were condemned by the bishops and successfully suppressed, no doubt partly because of this same theological and ritual heterosexuality.

One might read the Protestant Reformation in a similar light. Luther's radicalism was not simply theological. It was also sexual. The former friar and professor of biblical studies refused the homoerotic compact of the celibate male Church and married a woman, a celibate nun no less.

There would be others. The great German mystic and visionary Jacob Boehme would imagine Christ, and so the male mystic, "wooing" and wedding Sophia, the female Wisdom of God. William Blake's erotically graphic poems and paintings, which featured any number of transgressive sexual acts as both holy and redemptive, and Teilhard de Chardin's evolutionary mysticism (evolution requires *lots* of sex) also come to mind. But again, all three systems were deeply heretical and profoundly resisted—Boehme was condemned and harassed for much of his life by a local Lutheran minister and even imprisoned for a time; Blake died a nobody, a "mad" poet as they called him; and none of Teilhard's books could be published during his own lifetime. There were many reasons for all of this, of course, but at least some of it had to do with the robust heterosexuality through which all three men imagined and wrote.

Little wonder, then, that there can be no married or female priests in Roman Catholicism. Either move would effectively destroy the male homoerotic structure of the Church that claims to preserve the historical memories about Jesus and Paul. To ordain straight men or any kind of woman and have them serve that originally same-sex love-meal would be to dissolve Roman Catholicism itself, or so is the unarticulated fear.[9]

And I would go further still, for such sexual patterns are hardly restricted to any single denomination or religion. That is to say, there is a comparative pattern here, a central burning idea that we might express this way: in the history of religious literature that employs gendered and erotic language to express a man's union with the divine, *a religiously expressed male homoeroticism tends toward orthodoxy and a religiously expressed male heterosexuality tends toward heresy.* Multiply these sexual orientations, lives, and loves a thousand, a million, a billion times, and the "tends toward" morphs into "becomes." To take the example at hand, how can it be any other way for men in the Christian churches when there is only one God, and that God is imagined as male? What would a straight man need to love the divine as a gay man now can? He would, of course, need a goddess, a divine woman, a female beloved, a Mary Magdalene, a bridal chamber, a Sophia. But that is pure heresy. All we are given in Catholicism is a Virgin, who is our Mother no less. An impossible situation indeed, and oedipal to the core.

"Gay marriage," then, is no modern invention of a perverted American church or a runaway "activist" Supreme Court—it is an integral part of the Christian tradition. The only thing that makes it new is the attempt to move it from the symbolic and the theological realms into the legal and social ones. The controversies arise from making this unconscious secret structure of Christianity fully conscious and public.

Nothing, then, will be resolved by purging the Catholic seminaries of gay men, which is more or less what Pope Benedict XVI, previously Cardinal Joseph Ratzinger, tried to do. Such good men are there for very good, and very historical, reasons (and, if successful, this "solution" would pretty much empty the seminaries—most of those "called to the priesthood" are gay men). Nor will anything positive be gained by scapegoating and imprisoning gay priests whose sexuality has been stunted and tortured by Church teachings. The Church, with its condemnation of homosexuality and the hellish repressions and subsequent pathologies that inevitably result from such a damnation, has essentially produced its own institutional crisis, if not its moral and financial bankruptcy. No, the debates about homosexuality and Christianity will never go away, for the simple reason that Christianity itself possesses a homoerotic secret shimmering at its very historical and scriptural core. The churches can no more avoid this problem than they can deny the savior himself.

Peter once did that. But he at least repented.

ON THE FICTION OF A STRAIGHT JESUS

It is in this same light that I read our present heresies as well. Today, a heretical Christian heterosexuality is carried most effectively not by a reforming biblical scholar and friar marrying a nun, a Lutheran visionary wedding Sophia, a "mad" English poet painting naked men and women in the margins of his poems, or a mystically inclined paleontologist, but by a new kind of gnostic fiction. Think *The Last Temptation of Christ* or *The Da Vinci Code*. Both novels present a heterosexually active, or at least sexually imaginative, savior. Not surprisingly, both novels generated a tremendous amount of nervousness in the churches. The astonishing popularity of the latter novel may suggest that Christians, if not the Christian churches, are more than ready for a new kind of Christian sexuality. Many, it seems, desperately want a return to something like the bridal chamber sacrament the churches condemned and so lost so long ago.

I cannot go into a reading of either novel here. For now, it is enough to voice my amusement at the sexual-theological plot-line of *The Da Vinci Code*, much of which revolves around the idea that the effeminate figure to Jesus's right in Da Vinci's painting of *The Last Supper* is no other than Mary Magdalene, the embodiment of "the divine feminine," as the novel has it. Who else could such an effeminate figure be?

What is being assumed here? What is *not* being asked?

And so, tellingly, the only truly straight Jesus we have today is a fictitious one. The presumed heterosexuality of Jesus has become a bold fantasy, a desperate hope, a sincere wish, a hopeless desire on the part of millions of Christians to have, finally, some theological and historical basis for their own procreative (or simply pleasurable) heterosexual lives. If only Jesus had a child. If only he were sexually active with a woman. If only the effeminate male to Jesus's right were really a woman and Jesus was a real man.

Alas, it's all fiction, all hope. There is little, if any, definitive historical evidence to support this, at least with respect to the historical Jesus (the Jesus of gnostic memory and desire is a very different matter). In the end, we really have no idea what to say about Jesus's sexuality, other than, if we take all the historical memories together, that it was quite queer. No wonder the man chose to speak in parables. His was a love that was not straight, and he knew what such a love would come up against.

It still is.

3

That Night

Wherein the Knowing Energies Zap Me

It seemed to a person that he had a dream, a waking dream, that he was great with
Nothingness as a woman with a child. In this Nothingness God was born.

MEISTER ECKHART, PROBABLY ON HIMSELF

When deeper states begin to manifest themselves and superficial levels collapse, we
panic, fearing that we will be wiped out and, due to this fear, swoon unconsciously,
unable to make use of this most profound state. . . . The fact that the mind of clear
light—which is so awesome when one newly becomes aware of it—is one's own final
nature suggests that the otherness and fear associated with its manifestation are not
part of *its* nature but are due to the shallowness of untrained beings.

JEFFREY HOPKINS, *SEX, ORGASM, AND*
THE MIND OF CLEAR LIGHT

With the help of Freud, then, I realized that my anorexic condition was a symp-
tomatic expression of a repressed sexuality, beat down and fasted away since
puberty. To live I had to learn to read secrets—my own. These secret readings
meant one very practical thing: if I wanted to continue the healing process, I
could no longer repress my sexuality. Celibacy was no longer an option. I did
not conclude from this that celibacy was inappropriate for everyone, but I was
beginning to suspect that Catholic celibacy was not what it appeared to be.
It certainly has not always been a denial or "sacrifice" of sexuality, as is commonly supposed by those outside the intimacies of the tradition. Rather, it has
often functioned as a freedom from a socially enforced *hetero*sexuality and an
affirmation and sublimation of other socially unacceptable forms of sexuality.

Let me explain. Here is a memory. I claim no precision for it, although I
would insist that its lesson is spot on. Groups of Catholics would often come
through the monastery and seminary on retreat or school field trips. I remember one group in particular. It consisted of a number of young high school

women. They were oohing and ahhing over some of the seminarians (the cute ones) and marveling at what a "sacrifice" these young men were making to pursue the priesthood. After the group left, the seminarians were giggling about what they had overheard and how the young women had so wildly misread them. They were not "sacrificing" their sexualities, after all. They were affirming them, sanctifying them, sublimated or no, in the only way their religious tradition allowed. The truth on the inside was the near opposite of the perception on the outside. I was stunned by the contrast, so stunned that I have never forgotten it.

It was all very queer. I was beginning to suspect that male celibacy, male homoeroticism, and male sanctity were all intertwined, like a complicated root system of an ancient redwood tree, in the same biological, social, and spiritual soil. They reached way, way down.

Back in 1985, then, I now had two very good reasons to let go of what I thought might be a traditional religious vocation: (1) I wanted to continue the healing process so dramatically begun within the psychoanalytic framework; and (2) my sexual-spiritual orientation simply did not fit into the male homoerotic models of sanctity and the same-sex institutions of Roman Catholicism. Freud, then, did not just cure me of my anorexia. He cured me of my holiness, of my religion. I was a young man doubly exiled from his own birth tradition. I did not choose this exile. I did not want this.

Still, my spiritual life, whatever that was to be now, remained inextricably intertwined with my sexuality. Sex and spirit had been fused, or, better, realized as two sides of the same coin, and I had no desire to try to pretend otherwise. So what to do? What I really wanted was a mystical life that was also an erotic life. I wanted a male heterosexual mysticism. I simply wanted to fit somewhere, anywhere.

But there was no such orientation available in Roman Catholicism. Such things had been tried, of course, throughout Christian history, but they were always deemed heretical and persecuted out of existence, or just ignored and denied institutional support until they wilted away, as I observed in my lecture "On the Fiction of a Straight Jesus." I saw no other option but to go elsewhere, that is, outside my birth tradition. My first forays here were all imaginative ones in the monastic library, reading countercultural teachers like Alan Watts, Bhagwan Rajneesh, and Swami Muktanananda. I eventually guessed that what attracted me to these figures was something called "Tantra." I decided that I wanted to study that, whatever that was.

CHICAGO

After the usual application trials, I landed in an MA program at the University of Chicago. There I encountered the full force of the contemporary study of religion. I quickly realized that I was out of my league, and that I did not have the background in European and Asian languages that many of my graduate peers and all of my professors had. I was basically a town boy from Nebraska who wanted to be a monk and a saint but had discovered that he couldn't be either, and who was now on a quest for a spiritual life that he wasn't sure even existed.

Feelings of inadequacy aside, Chicago was a great place to be. Ed Dimock was still alive. Ed was the father of Bengali studies in the States and was an expert on Sahajiya Vaishnavism, a tradition dedicated to the worship of Krishna and his lover Radha that is heavily inflected by Tantric themes and practices. Once again, as in the Catholic bridal traditions, the male aspirant "becomes a woman" (usually a milkmaid) to love Krishna, except in the tradition's most heterodox and Tantric forms, where the male aspirant remains a male and "becomes Krishna" to engage his wife or ritual partner (who may not be his wife) as Radha in sexual intercourse. Ed took a few of us under his wings, even though he could barely stand up some mornings. He had advanced cancer of the stomach.

I remember Ed explaining to us what we would have to do if we *really* wanted to understand Tantra: take initiation with a Tantric guru in India. And he meant it. He also regaled us with stories, like the time someone slipped some ganja (marijuana) in his drink during a Durga Puja festival in Calcutta. He found himself sitting on a riverbank watching the celebrations when the colorful statue of the goddess came alive, bent down, and picked him up with her ten arms. He loved that one.

I also studied with Bernard McGinn, a historian of Christianity often, and rightly, called the world's foremost expert on Christian mysticism. A number of us formed a "mysticism study group" and met with Bernie regularly to read an essay and discuss its contents. That group was extremely influential on my early development and thought, as was McGinn's work on the medieval German marvel Meister Eckhart and the whole history of Christian mysticism. I believe this is where I received my Eckhartian convictions.

Wendy Doniger eventually became my main graduate mentor. I say "eventually," because this was not at all obvious in the beginning. Some have imagined that I came to Chicago to study with Wendy, or that Wendy somehow defined my thought and trajectory. These assumptions are false. I knew next to nothing about the history of religions, much less about the study of Hinduism. I came to Chicago because Harvard denied my application. And I was fascinated with sex and gender because of my earlier seminary experiences and psychoanalysis, not because of Wendy. I think Wendy originally saw me as a kind of naive hick from the Midwest, which was true enough.

After studying Bengali for three years, I studied for eight months in Calcutta. There I spent my mornings being tutored and my afternoons and evenings reading the five-volume Bengali classic on the life and teachings of Ramakrishna Paramahamsa (1836–1886) affectionately known in West Bengal as the *Kathamrita*, literally, *Nectar Talk*. I had already worked on this thousand-page text back in Chicago, so I knew parts of it had been bowdlerized or deleted. I now sat down to figure out which parts. I carefully read through the entire text, comparing it line by line to the classic 1942 English translation of Swami Nikhilananda, *The Gospel of Sri Ramakrishna*, which was so influential on the American counterculture and the reception of Hinduism in the US in the second half of the twentieth century. What I discovered was that, more often than not, what had been bowdlerized were Ramakrishna's Tantric practices and teachings. What had been erased or toned down was precisely what I had come to Chicago and Calcutta to study: Tantra.

TANTRA

It is at this point that I am supposed to tell you that the word "Tantra" and what it stands for are famously misunderstood; that what contemporary Western seekers think of and experience as Tantra has nothing to do with classical Indian Tantra; and that all of the sexual charges are untrue or exaggerated. I am supposed to tell you that, but I won't, because I don't believe any of it.

Tantra is not that difficult to understand. The kinds of neurological or spinal lightning-bolt awakenings and erotic out-of-body experiences that contemporary seekers often experience under the rubric, or outside the rubric altogether, are nearly indistinguishable from what we see coded in the medieval Sanskrit and modern Bengali texts. I once compared the modern American abduction literature with medieval Indian Tantra through the prism of Whitley Strieber's contact experience with an almond-eyed, aggressively sexual female being and David Gordon White's playful ufological readings of medieval Tantric yoginis, who are similarly almond-eyed and similarly aggressive.[1] I continue to think that the two cultural complexes are deeply related. As for the supposed fictions or exaggerations, these sexual practices are described, hinted at, and resisted everywhere in the Bengali texts I worked with for ten years, and similar sorts of sexual yogas are practiced to this day, as numerous ethnographers have noted and described. No, these practices are real, and they are practiced. These are not exaggerations.

Tantra is also not that difficult to define. Put very simply, Tantra is a general umbrella term or comparative category—the Sanskrit means "system" or "text," as in "something woven"—that Western and Indian scholars adopted and reshaped from the Sanskrit literature over the last two centuries in order to name and explore some of the most philosophically sophisticated, aesthetically gorgeous, and morally provocative religious systems on the planet. These traditions are in fact globally distributed and are as diverse as medieval Indian Kaula Tantra and Kashmiri Shaivism, various streams of modern and contemporary Shaiva and Shakta Hinduism, numerous forms of Mahayana and Vajrayana Buddhism, the sexual yogas of Chinese Daoism, and the various modern Western chakra systems, evolutionary spiritualities, and kundalini yoga awakenings experienced and described by such figures as Sir John Woodroffe, Sri Aurobindo, Gopi Krishna and Swami Muktananda. *All* of this is "Tantra."

The teachings of these traditions vary widely, of course, and they should not be melted down into some simple essence, but they do seem to orbit around a vast, really cosmic philosophical vision of a bipolar reality that is, deeper down, not-two or "nondual." In the Hindu Tantric systems that I came to study, this bipolar reality is commonly framed as Consciousness (*chit*) and Energy (*shakti*) and mythically expressed as the sexual union of the God Shiva and the Goddess Shakti. The goal of Tantric contemplation and practice here is to realize this fundamental nonduality of all that is, but also to harness the energy or power of Shakti toward human deification (that is, the manifestation of Consciousness as immortal and divine in and as a human being), the realization of the human body as a kind of cosmic portal of divinity, the development of various paranormal superpowers (called *siddhis*), and the desired attainment of practical material and social ends. The latter can range from kingship or political control to magical spells or incantations. The Tantric traditions are also often highly transgressive, that is, they aim to deconstruct the purity codes and social identities of the orthodox system in place. They are, as I have put it, the countercultures of Asia. Hence their popularity in the American counterculture.

Finally, one of the most original moves of these Tantric traditions is their insistence that physical reality is both fundamentally real (that is, not an illusion) and fundamentally divine. Consciousness may be considered absolute, but Energy or Power is a kind of radiation, efflux or manifestation of this Consciousness in and as the material universe. Accordingly, these traditions often insist on the deeper unity or coincidence of spiritual liberation (*mukti*) and physical pleasure (*bhukti*). Hence the famous, or infamous, sexual rites and symbolisms, which seek to reenact and realize this cosmic both-and. As David Peter Lawrence summarizes the situation: "Tantric practitioners variously endeavor to identify with the Goddess, to be ecstatically possessed by her, or to become her possessor . . . [by] identifying with her consort," that is, with Shiva.[2]

There it was. I had found it. A male heterosexual erotic mysticism.

THAT NIGHT

And then it found me.

While I was living and studying in Calcutta in 1989, I was irradiated one night by some kind of conscious energy or personal plasma that engaged me electrically, erotically, and gnostically (it somehow *knew* things). It was during Kali Puja in early November. I was perfectly and immediately aware after the event that my bodily posture during the experience was precisely that of Shiva's as portrayed in the hundreds of beautiful Kali images that dotted the city that same night. He lies prostrate on his back—asleep, in meditation, or dead—underneath the goddess as she stands on top of him and "touches" him with her feet. Exactly as Lawrence describes, I had identified with the goddess's consort. I had "become Shiva."

I have struggled over the years with the meaning of my experience beneath the goddess. I once thought that the purpose of the event was to get back to it, that the experience was about providing me with particular physiological and psychosexual clues, that is, with a yoga (concerning breath retention, erotic arousal, and physical posture) that would enable me to re-create it. But, alas, the experience would never return. Yes, there were little echoes in my body and brain over the years, which came mostly in the nights while I was asleep (once, oddly enough, attuned to a space heater humming in the background). But that was it. It never happened again. Except for that single Night, I am a spectacular genius of non-experience.

Eventually, however, I came to see that the meaning of the event was not in the experience itself, but in what it helped to catalyze. The meaning of that Night is not that Night but the total corpus of work and—perhaps more so, still—the work this corpus does in the world, every hour of every day, around the world, in thousands of readers whom I will never meet. The meaning or "purpose" of that Night is the secret body as text and reception, and, yes, as anti-reception.

I understand, of course, how this might sound arrogant. But I am really not describing the ego named "Jeff." I am describing someone else inside him, or, better, someone coming *through* him (since I really don't think that that someone or something is "in" here at all). I am describing in my own terms what countless writers before me have described in their own terms. This is not a brag or a claim. This is an honest and accurate description of my own creative processes and their constantly morphing phenomenology.

And the accent falls on *morphing*. Over the last three decades, I have come to see that the entire hermeneutical experience of that Night, from its first orgasmic eruption in Calcutta in November of 1989 to the writing of this text here and now, is *alive*. There is no stable meaning of that Night, not at least one that can be languaged or reasoned. Its meanings and energies change or mutate as I engage them in intuitive, rational and literary acts. It is a living hermeneutical process, not a dead historical fact that can be pinned down as "this is what really happened." It is much more a matter of "this is what is still happening" or "this is what wants to happen now."

INTRODUCING THE TEXT

Here is the first polished description of that Night, an event which I have long thought of as the deeper meaning or "secret body" of the title phrase "Kali's Child," much along the lines of the Meister Eckhart quote with which I began this chapter. I am not certain when I actually wrote this particular piece, but it had to be as I was preparing *Kālī's Child* for publication in 1994 or so in New Wilmington, Pennsylvania. This would make it five to six years after the actual event. I think the piece works well alone. The only details the reader may lack are two historical ones. "Narendra" was the beloved disciple of Ramakrishna who became Swami Vivekananda (1863–1902), the first successful Hindu missionary to the West. And "secret talk" is a reference to the *guhya katha* or "secret talk" of the *Kathamrita*, the five-volume Bengali text on the teachings of Ramakrishna that I made the focus of the dissertation and book.

I decided not to publish this preface out of fear that it would distract from the theses of the book and cause trouble. As it turned out, that fear was spectacularly redundant.

The Preface that I Did Not Publish
(CA. 1994)

But *Kālī's Child* is not just a research project. It is also an integral part of my own biography. Looking back, I can see clearly that my methods were not simply linguistic or theoretical; they were also experiential. At one point in my Calcutta researches, shortly after the autumn festival of Kali Puja, what I was studying even entered a waking dream state in a strange and striking way. The safe, comfortable lines between the researcher and the researched dissolved in an encounter that looked—and, so I imagined, *felt*—much like the mystico-erotic states I was then uncovering in the Bengali texts.

Although my body was asleep, resting almost anesthetized on its back, not unlike a corpse, consciousness was lucid and clear, fully awake. Suddenly, without warning, a powerful electric-like energy flooded the body with wave after wave of an unusually deep and uniform arousal. I tried to hold the energies in as *lingams* spontaneously emerged and disappeared in a fluid dream space. At some point, the energies gathered together, as if they themselves were conscious, and erupted "in" in a kind of psychic implosion. As I felt my "I" being sucked up into an ecstasy that felt entirely too much like a death, I watched my legs and torso float uncontrollably toward the ceiling. Quite unaccustomed to death or weightlessness (be they physical or symbolic), I desperately grabbed the bed frame and, in a scene that seemed as bizarre then as it sounds now, instinctively tried to embody the energies in order to bring them "back down" into my physical frame. After much gymnastic twisting and turning and holding on, I finally awoke. Actually, it wasn't a waking up at all, for the "I" had never been asleep, but it was at least a "sitting up," and this with a buzzing body that, thank goodness, was no longer an anesthetized corpse or a floating balloon.

When I later reflected on this powerful, if half-humorous, experience, I often thought of the sleeping but sexually aroused Shiva-corpse lying prostrate under Kali and of the deathlike fear Narendra felt under Ramakrishna's electric foot as the walls dissolved into an "I"-less emptiness around him. As I continued to study the texts, I quite naturally added this strange and yet unmistakably real experience to my otherwise perfectly normal academic toolbox; there was historical criticism, there was philology, there was textual analysis, there was psychoanalysis, and then there was that Night. It didn't seem to fit at all, but there it was. The experience was unimportant and even irrelevant to those aspects of the study that could be established through historical, philological, or analytic methods; dream states, after all, are no substitute for historical knowledge, language study, and theoretical sophistication. But the experience did have methodological implications, for it made me very wary of methods that would reduce Ramakrishna's own mystico-erotic experiences to the "nothing buts" and clinical jargon of classical psychoanalysis. Without that Night, I am quite certain that I would have been quite happy with such reductionisms and would have painted the saint as hopelessly neurotic; that, after all, is what he and his strange states often look like from the outside. But I had been, somehow, "on the inside" of similar states, and I suspected that the neurotic saint I saw was only a half-truth.

This is all to say that what follows possesses, in Eliade's terms, both a discursive, conscious, or "diurnal" dimension, which can and should be judged by normal academic methods, and an intuitive, unconscious, or "nocturnal" side, which I cannot defend but can only state as my own "secret talk."

2017 POSTSCRIPT

That Night has also caught the imaginations of a number of colleagues and readers. The scholar of religion Ann Taves, for example, uses my different accounts of the experience (from the private journal entry composed a few minutes after the original event to my public writing years later) to teach her building-block approach to extraordinary religious experiences at the University of Calfornia, Santa Barbara.

The Stanford anthropologist Tanya Luhrmann also invoked my experience in one of her op-ed pieces for the *New York Times* as a kind of comparative companion to her own experience of a palpable "supernatural power" that coursed through her body while she was studying witchcraft among white Britons as a graduate student. She had ridden on her bike to the train on the way to meet some of the magicians. On the train, she was reading a book they had suggested to her by one of their adepts. In particular, she was pondering this adept's teachings on the "forces that flowed from a higher spiritual reality into this one, through the vehicle of the trained mind." She struggled to understand the book's complicated mix of Christian, Buddhist, and Jewish mystical language and "strained to imagine what the author thought it would be like to be that vehicle." As she did so, Luhrmann felt a strange power "rip" through her. And it wasn't just in her head. A bicycle light in her backpack caught fire and literally melted.[3]

Another reader, Barclay Powers, is an advanced practitioner and teacher of kundalini yoga and Mahayana Buddhism. He is particularly interested in the Buddhist doctrine of *tathagatagarbha* or the "womb of suchness," the Buddha nature that is believed to dwell, already perfect and complete, as the secret core of each of us. Barclay wanted to create a graphic novel based on my life and work. Essentially, he wanted to turn me into an intellectual superhero who had discovered, in his own words now, the "secret elixir of life" or the "golden embryo of enlightenment" at the sexual base of the human body. Barclay and Nancy Hutchison produced the first three pages with artist supervisor Eugene Perez of Octographics. We have reproduced these pages in the interior plates of the present volume.

The text of the graphic novel pages is taken, almost verbatim, from the introduction of *Mutants and Mystics* (2011), where I attempted (again) to remember and re-create that Night. The first two pages are remarkably faithful to the phenomenology of the events. I did not see a mandala machine, but everything else is very close to my memories, particularly the occult sense of energy, the contorted erotic body, and the magnetic ascension. The third page is fiction, of course. I did not get sucked up into a UFO, nor did I mind-meld with some hip blue snake women (not that I would object to either). But this was Barclay's graphic novel, not my autobiography. Still, the last two panels are, again, very close to my own sense of things. Four of my previous six monographs make their appearance in the last panel. The message, however fantastic, is clear and true: the Chicago books were somehow "energized" or "magnetized" by the erotic electrocution of that Night in Calcutta, wherein the knowing energies zapped me.

4

The Erotic Mystic

Kālī's Child *and the Backlash against It*

Both cognitive states and emotional states have the same basic nature, clear light, and thus are not separated off from each other in separate universes; both have luminosity as their core and exist within a continuum. . . . From this [Tibetan Buddhist] perspective, orgasmic pleasure is a type of mind, and the state of orgasm is even utilized to gain realization of the clear light nature of basic mind which is often compared to the sky. . . . In fact, the consciousness that manifests in profound orgasm is deeper than reason, and is its basis.

JEFFREY HOPKINS, *SEX, ORGASM, AND THE MIND OF CLEAR LIGHT*

Now I am telling you something very secret.

RAMAKRISHNA IN THE *KATHAMRITA*

Although I had begun thinking about the dissertation in the few months before that Night, I conceived the structure and mapped out the basic content in the ensuing weeks and months in a kind of creative mania. I was *on fire.* I imagined the dissertation's structure around the iconography of Kali "standing" on a sleeping or entranced Shiva, that is, around the Consciousness and Energy fusion I had known within my own waking sleep. In effect, I re-created that Night as an electromagnetic book.

I returned to Chicago from Calcutta in the spring of 1990 and wrote the dissertation "out of that Night" over the next three years, completing it in the spring of 1993. The text was published as *Kālī's Child* in 1995. Much could be said at this point about the book's explicit content, its attempt to put Shakta Tantra and psychoanalysis into deep dialogue, its Tantric focus on bio-energies and the material world as divine, its understanding of trauma as a trigger or "cracking open" the human psyche to transcendent forms of Mind, and its conclusions about the homoerotic superstructure of the saint's ecstasies and esoteric community or inner circle. I will glance at these various key ideas below but focus on the reception issues.

How to write about the most painful part of my story? I do not want to dwell on the controversies of the 1990s, which, it must be pointed out, have never really ended. To this day, I continue to receive angry letters whose jingoistic contents have been culled from hate sites on my work that grotesquely twist and distort my thought. But I also do not want to deny these voices or wish them away. I want to honor my cruelest critics, since they honored me in some twisted way. Even if the central dialectic of my hermeneutic—the way I read the religious texts on multiple sexual-spiritual levels—completely escaped them, they did understand, incoherently but truly, what was at stake. They, at least, saw, and saw clearly, how powerful and challenging scholarship on religion can be.

I also do not want to wish the controversies away for another reason: because they made me. That is to say, they radicalized me as a public intellectual. They taught me—emotionally, existentially, and politically—that there is no way that the robust critical study of religion can be comfortably aligned with religion itself. There is a vast abyss between the professional study of religion and the religious traditions themselves. Anyone who denies this gulf or seeks to bridge it too quickly is compromising the intellectual freedom and robust analysis that are the very lifeblood of the modern academy and its precious forms of knowledge.

So what to say? The first thing to say about the *Kālī's Child* affair is that it was not about me. It was about the rise of Hindu nationalism in India, as Martha Nussbaum has documented and keenly analyzed with respect to my case and a number of other more important ones.[1] The book became a pawn in a public political chess game. I was the first American scholar of Hinduism to be targeted by these conservative ideologues. Many other scholars, American and Indian alike, would be targeted after me. Two decades later, my graduate mentor Wendy Doniger would become the new favorite target, primarily for her *The Hindus: An Alternative History*. Her "offenses" involve crimes like privileging suppressed voices in the tradition (women and outcastes) and writing beautiful prose about the stunning diversity and rich sexual complexity of the Hindu traditions. Numerous Indian intellectuals and media outlets came to Wendy's defense. *The New York Times* printed robust pieces. And the book quickly sold out in India. The court-ordered "pulping" of all the remaining copies thus never happened, since there were no books left to pulp.[2]

None of this happened with *Kālī's Child* in the 1990s. My critics would claim that I had offended "millions" in India, but I knew, from the press reports I receive each summer, that the book had sold no more than a few dozen copies in all of India, ever. Alas, this was only the beginning. Many have suffered since, and far worse. Twenty years later, dozens of scholars, bloggers, and professional writers have been similarly targeted, labeled, vilified, and silenced, even, in some cases, murdered for their honest questions and writing.

HOUSE OF MIRRORS

The critics were many, and I do not want to lump their specific criticisms together. But one of the earliest and most consistent lines of criticism focused on my alleged translation errors. In its fullest form, this approach was developed and published by a swami of the Ramakrishna Order. Swami Tyagananda claimed that my knowledge of Bengali was slight, and that, worse yet, I had willingly manipulated the texts to fit my perverse readings. These assumed willed errors were collected into a document that was distributed both at the annual meetings of the American Academy of Religion and online. These later became the basis of a book that he published with Pravrajika Vrajaprana, a nun of the same tradition.[3]

I had already responded to Tyagananda's early document in a long essay in the inaugural issue of an Indian journal, *Evam*, pointing out that most of the "errors" were not errors at all but my own clearly marked glosses or interpretations, which he had misread as literal translations for reasons that still escape me. I also pointed out that even the few genuine errors he had located, which were all minor, had no effect on my readings. Finally, I also pointed out that in the second edition I had already apologized for and happily corrected the errata of the first edition I knew about (some of which had been pointed out to me by another swami), and that I would happily do so again in any future edition.[4] I apologized once again for the genuine errors that Tyagananda had found with his microscope but calmly pointed out that the majority of the accusations were unfounded. They were simply false.

Later authors confirmed this.[5] Indeed, two would also advance sexual-spiritual readings that I had not seen or made, that is, they would take my erotic hermeneutic further still. Enter William Schindler's autobiography, *God's Dog: Memories, Confessions, Dreams & Revelations of a Modern Mystic*, and Rajagopal Chattopadhyaya's *Kali's Child and Lover.*

Schindler provides a fascinating look into the reception history of my work within the Ramakrishna tradition from the perspective of a contemporary American gay man. His comments on *Kālī's Child* are mere moments in his rich memoir, but they are also especially insightful. These comments were critical of my rhetoric and language but also advanced learned extensions of my homoerotic thesis out of his own sexual-spiritual orientation, a knowledge of the nuances of the Bengali language, and his long personal involvement in the tradition. As a straight man, I had simply missed some of these linguistic nuances.[6] Like Chattopadhyaya, he found little to argue with in my translations: "I checked every reference and found Kripal's translations credible."[7] He even describes some dramatic erotic mystical states involving his own subtle body, a heavenly scent and taste, and the presence of an invisible bearded Lover climbing on top of him that were triggered by his reading of *Kālī's Child* on two consecutive days.[8]

For his part, Chattopadhyaya systematically and nearly exhaustively tackled the translation criticisms of Tyagananda. He declared in print what I always knew and had pointed out in my own responses numerous times, namely, that the vast majority of what Tyagananda and the polemicists have advertised as my "errors" were simply interpretive glosses, and that the errata that were genuine mistakes were superficial and minor and added up to nothing of substance. This had always struck me as patently obvious. If, after all, this were not the case, how is it that other scholars, both English speakers trained in the language and native Bengali speakers, had come to more or less the same conclusions that I had both before and after me?[9]

Chattapadhyaya even crunched the numbers. According to his count, I was correct in 156 out of the 191 cases Tyagananda listed in the earlier, widely distributed internet document.[10] He also points out, with a refreshing obviousness, that thirty-five translation errors in a book of literally thousands of referenced passages is neither unusual nor significant. As any writer, editor, or press knows, *every* book published contains such errors—they are simply unavoidable, regardless of how carefully one looks for them or tries to correct them before the manuscript goes to print.

One would think reading Tyagananda that I am some sort of linguistic idiot or, worse yet, a pathological liar. One gets the exact opposite impression reading Chattopadhyaya. As a native Bengali speaker born into the language (Tyagananda is not), Chattopadhyaya praises both my intuitive grasp of Bengali culture and my translation choices as deeply, sometimes uncannily, insightful. The most striking of the latter moments involves my Tantric-phallic readings of Ramakrishna's foot, moments in which his foot was ecstatically placed in the lap of a young male disciple in a devotional trance or became the oral object of sexually aggressive women. My critics railed against these as particularly outrageous markers of my own Freudian "Western" perversity. Not so,

Chattopadhyaya answers. He takes up one of these readings, locates the original source text behind the passage I was working on, and demonstrates that my reading was even more accurate than I imagined: the "toe" of the text (being sucked by a Tantric woman) that I had interpreted as a symbolic phallus, it turns out, was the saint's "organ" (*indriya*) or penis in an earlier source text of which I was not aware.[11] *That* is how dramatically wrong my critics have been.

Having said all of that, I should add that I have never claimed fluency with the Bengali language. I was not born into the language. I had to learn everything from scratch in my adult years, and I never learned to speak the language with any even remote adequacy. The reading facility I did achieve took me ten years of hard work, all, it turned out, so that I could focus on the *Kathamrita* and write a single book, which is to say: out of love for a single text and its electric saint.

I once thought I would correct the minor errata of the second edition for a third edition, but I no longer see this as necessary or desirable. For one thing, I left the study of Hinduism almost two decades ago now and no longer possess the linguistic skills or, frankly, the emotional will to carry such a project through. The other simple truth of the matter is that *Kālī's Child* is now a historical document as well as a work of youthful scholarship. Other future scholars can wrestle over the translation details (and they have Chattopadhyaya's text as their guide here). I have not changed my mind about any of its conclusions and remain calmly convinced that its assumed errors add up to exactly nothing.

THE EROTIC

So the translation issue was a house of mirrors, a stratagem of distraction. From what? From the book's basic ideas, which many readers, including many Hindu readers, found extremely plausible and often very attractive. The most fundamental of these was the book's thoroughgoing refusal to separate spirituality and sexuality and its refusal to draw any final ontological separation between the forms of consciousness and bliss glimpsed in sexual arousal and orgasm and the forms of consciousness and bliss known more fully in some types of mystical ecstasy. I also argued that Ramakrishna's particular form of erotic mysticism was homoerotic in structure (gnomon 1) and speculated about the psychosexual connections between his adult states of ecstasy and what I read as some likely early sexual trauma. We have already encountered the homoerotic hypothesis, and we will return to the link between trauma and transcendence below (gnomon 17). For now, it is enough to focus on the relationship between what I called the erotic and the mystical.

I was hardly being original here. As we have already seen, this deeper unity of Consciousness and Energy or Mind and Matter is the fundamental claim of many of the Hindu Tantric traditions. It is also the fundamental claim of *Kālī's Child*. Whatever we choose to call the two poles—body and soul, sex and spirit, Shakti and Shiva, Corpus and Mysticum—they appear to be two poles of a deeper super-reality. Following Plato and his notion that eros is a divine or semi-divine force, I framed this dialectic very early under the banner of "the erotic." The idea can be framed most simply this way:

3. The Erotic Mystic. There is a profound connection between the mystical and the erotic.

This gnomon is intentionally open-ended, as I really do not claim to understand how these two poles of human experience—the sexual and the spiritual—might be related. I am only convinced that they are connected, if not actually identical on some deeper bio-spiritual level. Over the years, I have explored different ways to turn these "two sides of the same coin" into a floating sphere. Consider these three models.

First, there is the ancient Platonic "remembrance" model that explains how the descended or reincarnated philosopher remembers some eternal experience of Beauty and his companionship with a god (Zeus, for example) in the mirror of the beloved boy and the desire and pleasure the beloved's body invokes in him. Here the erotic state recalls the philosopher's prebirth existence in the world of the gods and so can be used to return to that same world in philosophical and erotic contemplation. This was Plato's model in classic dialogues like the *Phaedrus* and the *Symposium*, where the pleasures and intensities of sexual desire (ideally unconsummated) remind the advanced soul of the eternal world of spirit and "wing" him for ecstatic flight to the eternal world of the Forms or Ideas. As I pointed out in *Kālī's Child*, this is also essentially what we see in the case of Ramakrishna and his various mystico-erotic relationships to his young male disciples, some of whom he treated as manifestations of Krishna, that is, as a god or as God, with himself as Radha, Krishna's lover.

Second, there are the numerous "hydraulic" models that work from the assumption that there is some bio-energetic or fluid current connecting the genital and brain regions that can be spent outward (through orgasm), built up and magnified (through celibacy and meditation), even literally reversed or "turned around" back into the brain and into the beyond (through yogic sexual techniques involving "locks" and body postures, or through spontaneous irruptions of transcendence in and around sexual activity). Hence the various esoteric physiologies and chakra models of the Hindu, Buddhist, Daoist, and Western Tantric traditions. Again, this is what we see in some of the "secret talk" passages and censored visions of Ramakrishna. In one such passage, the saint sees a miniature version of himself arousing vagina-shaped lotuses with his tongue as he moves up the central spinal channel of the yogic Tantric body.[12] And, no, I did not mistranslate or invent that passage.

As I pointed out in *Kālī's Child*, the Freudian and Tantric models share the same basic hydraulic insight into the sex of the spirit but draw the direction of that relationship in opposite directions: whereas the reductive Freudian model assumes sex is an entirely natural force that can be "sublimated" into (illusory) experiences of spirit, the Tantric models understand natural sexual energies to be sleeping or unactualized spiritual forces that can be realized as forms of *shakti* or real superconscious energy. Both insist on the unity of the mystical and the erotic, but each prioritizes a different member of that pair as more ontologically basic or ultimate.

Thirdly, there are also the various "resonance" models. Most of these are implicit models, that is, they are not theorized as such. Most of these also depend on some kind of "filter," "transmission," "contraction," or "reduction" understanding of the brain-mind relationship. The latter see the physical brain not as the producer of consciousness (as we have it in the conventional neuroscientific picture today) but rather as the *reducer* of consciousness, that is, as a kind of transducer or transformer that "steps down" the high voltage of cosmic Mind into a localized body-brain interface in order to create the low-voltage hum or glow of a personal ego (much more on this later).

In these resonance models, extreme states of sexual arousal can be understood in at least two different but related ways. Most simply, they can be understood as means to temporarily shut down, blind, or outshine the filter of the ego interface and so let other ever-present transcendent forms of Mind rush in. More complexly, the same erotic states can be interpreted through the extremely common metaphysical languages of frequency, vibration, magnetism, and attunement. Here, aroused erotic energies and the trance states they induce can be understood to somehow activate neuro-electric currents or magnetic fields in the human body that can then "tune" into the higher frequencies of consciousness, as we see, for example, in the healing and often clairvoyant trance states of Mesmer's "animal magnetism" and as I knew firsthand in that Night.

Note that in this third set of models the erotic states do not cause or produce the mystical states in any hydraulic or otherwise direct fashion. Rather, they *remove* something that is in the way (brain states or cognitive function); or they set up a kind of cellular conductivity or magnetic all-body polarization that can pick up the always present signal of Mind. (Obviously, I am speculating here, but out of the remembered magnetized state of that Night.) In any case, it is not a matter of "preserving" or "reversing" bio-energies through hydraulic techniques, as we have it in the Tantric yogic techniques, or even "sublimating" them into cultural forms, as we have it in the Freudian models. It is more a matter of "striking the tuning fork" or "changing the channel" on the body radio.

This is why I call them resonance models. They imagine a state of sexual arousal as setting up an entrainment or resonance with some cosmic form of Mind, but they imply no simple, direct, or causal relationship between the two. The metaphor of resonance nevertheless does imply a real relationship. The radio may not "produce" the radio wave, but the radio was made for the radio signal, and vice versa. They cannot be understood apart from one another.

Obviously, these three models of the relationship between the mystical and the erotic are not mutually exclusive of one another.[13] Nevertheless, they do provide different nuances. When I wrote *Kālī's Child*, I leaned toward the hydraulic models. Today, I am more inclined toward the resonance models. At the end of the day, the relationship between the erotic and the mystical is still a very open question. If we add to this situation the oft observed pattern that parapsychological abilities and an openness to "abduction" or "contact" experiences appear to run in families, that is, possess a genetic component, we can see even more clearly that we have barely begun to plumb all of those altered states of energy and consciousness that we so clumsily lump together under the simplistic banners of "sexuality" and "mysticism."

INTRODUCING THE ESSAY

The creative fact that all my books in some way go back to this first one—or at least to the Night in which it was mystico-erotically conceived—renders the *Kālī's Child* affair particularly powerful, and particularly poignant, for me personally. After all, what is at stake here are the psychological, really parapsychological, wellsprings of my writing practice and gnostic thinking. Accordingly, I wrote no less than a dozen responses to my many critics and haters. Some of these responses were delivered as formal public lectures or were published in technical academic contexts, including in India. Others were written at the request of individuals or colleagues, while still others were published and remain online.

I am anthologizing this particular response piece because it does a good deal of work for us in the context of the present book. It lays out the autobiographical context of my early dissertation work on Ramakrishna at the University of Chicago. It describes the religious reasons I was so attracted to the Hindu Tantra. Finally, it summarizes some of the conclusions that I reached early on as I processed some of the censorship campaigns that were spiking all around me as I taught at Harvard Divinity School in 2000–2001.

Many of the themes and ideas of the present essay, slightly shortened and edited here, will be familiar to the reader by now, as they have already been treated above in the previous chapters. But repetition is good. Such details take on a new life and context here, as they cease to be simply a response to my own birth tradition and become the intuitive basis of a new comparative erotics. I smile now when I read it, as I realize that it ends with a story from my mentor Wendy Doniger about clairvoyant or precognitive dreams, which she herself has had (more on that later) and which would become a major focus of mine later in life (much more on that in part 2). I also realize, only now, that the essay encodes the earliest expression of another major theme that would not become apparent until much later: the way that a deeply engaged reading practice might hermeneutically activate or create anomalous states and claims in the reader and, by extension, in the larger cultural world. Here, I begin to approach this idea through a discussion of the ways the Ramakrishna of the Bengali texts is hermeneutically divinized by the listener's and then reader's answers to the saint's honest questions about his own mysterious double nature: reading as deification, if you will. The earliest and faintest glimmers of the secret body were beginning to shimmer at Harvard around the turn of the millennium, as I taught *Kālī's Child* and finished writing *Roads of Excess*.

Secret Talk

SEXUAL IDENTITY AND THE POLITICS OF SCHOLARSHIP

IN THE STUDY OF HINDU TANTRISM

(2000)

When I was a student at seminary, there was something I just didn't understand. I knew that much of the Christian mystical tradition drew on the Song of Songs from the Hebrew Bible as the preeminent source of its theological speculation and mystical doctrine. From Origen in the third century to Bernard of Clairvaux in the twelfth to Teresa of Avila and John of the Cross in the sixteenth, the Song was employed and commented on in order to imagine the feminized Church or human soul wedded to Christ in a variously conceived mystical marriage. Because I was born within the Catholic tradition, was living in a Catholic seminary rich in monastic culture, and wanted to participate in the Church's most intimate forms of community and experience, I tried my best to pray with the Song while I read these mystics. But it didn't work. How, I asked myself, was I supposed to imagine myself as a woman and, even more puzzling, as one married to another male? This was no good at all.

Teresa of Avila? Now she made sense to me. Here, after all, was a woman who could quite naturally encounter a male divinity, or so I thought in my box-like gender categories. But John of the Cross and Bernard of Clairvaux? What were they doing? And how was I supposed to make sense of whatever it was they were doing? It was as if there simply was no genuinely established place in the Catholic tradition for a modern heterosexual male who desired to use erotic language to effect and express his embodied religious experience. That, after all, would require some kind of feminine divinity. But, doctrinally speaking, there was one God, and he was definitely male. Or so said the scriptures, the liturgical language, and all the statues and holy cards I had ever seen. Consequently, every male is feminized in relationship to Him—we are all brides, or, in the biblical language of Paul, are are all "virgins for Christ."

While I was puzzling over the mysteries of gender, sexual orientation, and mystical language, I was also reading in the seminary's library, where I encountered beautiful art books on Hinduism, accounts of modern gurus (especially Krishnamurti, Swami Muktananda, and Rajneesh) and something called Tantrism. The latter particularly intrigued me, as here, finally, was a tradition that allowed the male mystic to be heterosexual and approach the divinity as female, that is, as a goddess. I was intrigued and hopeful that I might be able to find something in Hinduism that seemed to exist nowhere in my own Catholicism. Consequently, after I graduated from the seminary, I decided to study the history of religions with a special focus on Hindu Tantrism and the comparative study of mysticism at the University of Chicago. Because I knew that Tantrism in the form of Shaktism was especially popular in Bengal, I began to study Bengali and, three years later, found myself living in Calcutta.

SEEING FROM THE WEST

It is wise to define one's perspective precisely up front, to name one's voice. With some rather clear psychoanalytic convictions and concepts, I see from my own specifically Western cultural and historical perspectives. Unlike the two major theorists of the same subfield, Sudhir Kakar and Gananath Obeyesekere, both of whose lives in South Asia (Kakar grew up in what is now Pakistan, Obeyesekere in what is now Sri Lanka) render them remarkably familiar with these cultures "from the beginning" and "from the inside," I came to these same cultures much later in life, or, to put it much more precisely, *they came to me* later in life in the culturally translated forms of New Religious Movements— and particularly North American guru traditions—within the historical context of late twentieth-century American culture. I thus write, certainly not as a South Asian commenting on my own culture or even as an anthropologist with extensive ethnographic experience commenting on someone else's (I claim neither theoretical voice), but as an American historian of religions trying to make sense of American religious pluralism and the profound effects it has had and continues to have on our contemporary understandings of religion, mysticism, and Western Hinduism, not to mention my own postmodern plural self.

In many ways, then, my situation is the mirror opposite of that of someone like Gananath Obeyesekere, who has so eloquently written of the Western influences and anthropological training that permanently alienated him from his own indigenous village culture: "I felt increasingly drawn toward understanding [Sinhalese] village culture," he once wrote of his early youthful researches, "thereby hoping (futilely, I soon learned) to abolish my own alienation."[14] Like Obeyesekere, I too became alienated early from my own indigenous village culture (we call them "small towns" in America), but not primarily because of any Westernizing influence or intellectual training (although these too no doubt played important roles); rather, it was again the radical religious pluralism of American culture, and particularly my contact with the beauty, power, and sheer otherness of Asian mystical traditions, that rendered my indigenous worldviews no longer completely tenable. There simply was no way to hold on to the comfortable Catholicism of my youth after Advaita Vedanta, Theravada, Mahayana and Vajrayana Buddhism, and the Indo-Tibetan Tantric traditions (although the iconographic and liturgical riches of my Catholic heritage allowed me to see and appreciate facets of these traditions that other perspectives might have closed off).

The intellectual discipline of the history of religions, much like Obeyesekere's anthropology, became a way for me both to make sense of this personal alienation and to confront the mesmerizing otherness of these Hindu and Buddhist mystical systems, which, I must add, I still feel personally drawn to on levels I can only begin to explain (with Kakar, I could well describe my worldview as a kind of liberal, rational agnostic mysticism).[15] I have written of these autobiographical dimensions in some detail elsewhere and will not repeat myself here, except to make clear the deeply personal, essentially religious place from which I write about these Tantric traditions of indigenous and cross-cultural extremes.[16]

While living in Calcutta, I was surrounded by a Bengali saint named Ramakrishna (1836–1886) smiling at me from the posters and calendars that decorate the shop stalls, homes, and public spaces of that remarkable city. Because of my Bengali training at the University of Chicago, I was already familiar with the primary text on his life and teachings, Mahendranath Gupta's magisterial five-volume *Kathamrita*, better known to English readers in its 1942 New York incarnation, *The Gospel of Sri Ramakrishna*.[17] As I worked my way through the five volumes in Calcutta, I began to notice something significant: the English translation was both incomplete and, in at least some places, heavily bowdlerized. In particular, there were places in the text in which Ramakrishna or the narrator would announce some "secret talk" (*guhya katha*), after which something both Tantric and sexual was usually recorded. It was these passages, among many others, that were inevitably either bowdlerized or completely omitted in *The Gospel*. I also noticed another pattern: Ramakrishna would consistently take on feminine identities to engage both male deities and disciples in relationships that were often encoded in language that was simultaneously religious and emotionally charged, if not sexually suggestive. Following Neoplatonic and Christian mystical discourse, inspired by the dialectical ontologies of the Tantric traditions themselves, and insistent on avoiding the reductionistic tones of classical Freudian readings, I decided to call this *coincidentia* of the palpably sexual and the genuinely mystical "the erotic."

I also noticed that Ramakrishna adamantly refused to engage women sexually, either within his own marriage or, more to my point, within the Tantric ritual universe in which the male mystic was expected to sexually engage the goddess in the form of an actual female ritual consort (Ramakrishna's female Tantric guru attempted to force him into these rituals but inevitably failed). As I encountered more and more of these gendered and consistently sexualized scenes, I began to develop a thesis. Ramakrishna's mysticism, I realized, cannot be adequately understood without positing some kind of culturally and historically distinct homosexual orientation in the saint, since both his mysticism and his charisma were homoerotically structured around mystico-erotic encounters with male deities and highly charged devotional encounters with male disciples.

Certainly, he would have had no access to any kind of homosexual social identity as we do now, thus I did not argue that the saint was "gay" or even "a homosexual" (such solid nouns are completely absent from my dissertation and first book), as such expressions imply a socially constructed identity stabilized in language and institutionalized practice rather than the fluid, polymorphous movement of desire, energy and ecstasy that we find in the Bengali texts. Human beings, it appears, can express (and create) themselves only in the idioms and symbols with which their historical cultures provide them. Ramakrishna was no exception. He expressed his own energies (rather marvelously, I might add) through the religious languages of his culture and then transformed them through ritual, symbol, and vision into powerful mystical experiences.

More specifically, he was deeply influenced by the Hindu Tantra and used its dialectical understanding of the mystical and the sexual to transform his culturally illicit homoerotic desires into profound visionary and religious experiences, but because the heterosexual structure of Tantric ritual seriously violated the homosexual orientation of his own desires, Ramakrishna was torn, troubled, and conflicted about this same tradition. Whereas I had been a heterosexual aspirant in a homoerotically structured religious world (Catholic bridal mysticism), he had been a homosexual mystic in a heteroerotically structured religious world (Hindu Tantrism). We were both in very similar structural dilemmas, if for exact opposite reasons. I understood him precisely because I was *and* was not like him.

After three years of formal Bengali study at Chicago and an academic year in Calcutta, I returned to the States in 1990 and began to write my dissertation on the saint. I would later publish the thesis as *Kālī's Child: The Mystical and the Erotic in the Life and Teachings of Ramakrishna* (University of Chicago Press, 1995). Things were relatively quiet for the first year. Then Blake's creative hell broke loose. In the fall of 1996 the book was awarded the American Academy of Religions' History of Religions Prize, and appreciative reviews began to appear in academic journals. A few months after the award ceremony, in January of 1997, the book was vilified in a major polemical review in a Calcutta English newspaper (the review began by comparing my Ramakrishna to an American drag queen and ended with the words "plain shit"). This "review" predictably exploded into a three-week-long flood of letters to the editor (none of whom showed any signs of having ever seen the book) that finally elicited a special plea from the paper to end the deluge: no piece in recent memory had elicited such a response, they claimed.

But the debates continued. Soon a ban movement was announced in national newspapers, at least once on the front page. The central government created a special file on the book, and the work was examined by the CBI (India's FBI) to determine whether or not it should be banned (it was not). Just this last fall the book made headlines again when some individuals noticed that *Encyclopedia Britannica*'s online article on Ramakrishna included a Barnes and Noble link that listed *Kālī's Child* as its first book. Disturbed by this, they initiated a letter-writing campaign that was announced on the front page of *Anandabazar Patrika*, Calcutta's largest Bengali newspaper. Unlike the earlier movement, these individuals were not asking that the book be removed, much less banned. Rather, they wanted it moved down the list, and they wanted the primary texts (like Gupta's *The Gospel*) listed above it. Aware of the complexities of this situation, with the production of knowledge and the interests of capitalism coming together in a no doubt imperfect alliance, I was and remain sympathetic to such concerns.

During all of this, positive reviews continued to appear in America, England, France, and Australia, as I heard from a broad spectrum of professional disciplines and existential perspectives. Indologists, Buddhologists, playwrights, artists, a novelist, psychiatrists, psychologists, philosophers, theologians, devotees of different prominent gurus, Sufis, Tantrikas, Ramakrishna devotees, and gay activists all wrote or spoke to me about their personal readings of the book, almost all of which were deeply appreciative, warmhearted, and grateful. I even learned of a contemporary American guru tradition (Adidam) that highlighted the book in its own publications with a warm blurb from the guru himself, who put *Kālī's Child* on a special list for his disciples to read and called on them to move beyond the prudery and homophobia of the past and grapple openly with the issues of sexuality and repression in their own devotional and mystical practices.

I have struggled almost continuously for the last four years to make some sense of both the obvious anger and the equally apparent gratitude, even love that have greeted my work and (just as often) my imagined persona. These years have been at once humbling, satisfying, embarrassing, manically creative, and utterly confusing. In terms of the embarrassment, precisely because of the book's obvious potential to offer a radically new perspective on the saint, it has come under intense, indeed microscopic scrutiny from those heavily invested in the traditional perspectives. Not surprisingly, such attention has uncovered a number of genuine errors, all of which I deeply regret, most of them involving translation points or hermeneutical slips that I will now happily correct (all of which, I should add, can easily be addressed without altering either the form or basic argument of the book), precisely as I did in the second edition of the book.[18]

In terms of the broader and more important reception issues, I can make no claims to full insight, and I am quite certain that I do not understand many, if not most, of the political, ethical, and cross-cultural intricacies into which I have wandered. Still, exactly four years after the initial Calcutta controversy, I would like to offer the following reflections in the hope that others, including and especially my harshest critics, might find something helpful to think about here.

Kālī's Child presented itself as a study of secrets. Beginning with the assertion that the English translation (Nikhilananda's *The Gospel of Sri Ramakrishna*) of the central text of the tradition (Gupta's *Kathamrita*) bowdlerized and even completely omitted aspects of Ramakrishna's "secret talk," I proceeded in the body of the book to translate, interpret, and contextualize in considerable detail these same secrets. The facts that Ramakrishna's Tantric culture was itself coded in esoteric terms and was practiced within secret antinomian rituals made such an approach more than appropriate. Indeed, Ramakrishna himself spoke in excited, revelatory terms and so invited his listeners (and now readers) to enter this same esoteric discourse, "Listen! Now I'm telling you something very secret. . . ." Interestingly, the Ramakrishna of the texts also often asks his listeners to help him interpret his visions, explain his ecstatic states, and even tell him who he is; it is as if he does not know and needs the interpretations of others—listeners and now readers—to come into meaning. The hermeneutical patterns of the text are thus open-ended, dialectical, still in process, and they extend into the present of the text before the reader, who has become Ramakrishna's audience through the magical acts of reading and interpretation.

What I attempted to do in my own text is re-create and extend these esoteric and hermeneutical processes, imaginatively enter them (as the Ramakrishna of the texts invites us to do), and understand them anew with our own contemporary categories. To do so, however, I had to address some very intimate details of the saint's life. That is, after all, why the passages were coded as secret. The rhetorical result was a kind of intellectual transgression that participated in the esoteric structure of the Bengali texts and, by so doing, imaginatively relived the Tantric revelations and occultations of Ramakrishna's life and teachings, sexual details and all. There is a certain excitement, a hint of danger, a note of awe in any such enterprise. Who, after all, does not want to hear a secret? Is not this the very logic of secrecy, a seductive telling that one is not telling everything and thus an invitation to listen for more? We all bend our ears.

Still within this same discursive field, readers and hearers of such secrets are naturally inspired to speak their own. Hence one of the most serendipitous aspects of the book's reception was the consistent pattern, repeated over and over again in the letters, of readers spontaneously sharing their own secrets with me. Having read the book as a sympathetic treatment of Ramakrishna's secrets, they assumed, and reasonably so, that I was open to such things, that I would try to understand. And so they re-created and extended Ramakrishna's "secret talk" in their own. I thus read and heard about powerfully erotic, if emotionally conflicted visions of Kali, of parental sexual abuse linked to later adult trance states, of the emotional sufferings of those with culturally vilified sexualities, of transsexual and psychedelic experiments with the goddess, and of ecstatic and dream experiences catalyzed by the reading of *Kālī's Child*. The rhetorical patterns and emotional tones of such contemporary secret talk quite accurately echo and extend, if in distinctively modern or postmodern voices, the secret talk of both the Bengali texts and *Kālī's Child*. A kind of hermeneutical union has thus been realized between the subject of the study (Ramakrishna), the author of the study (myself) and the readers of the study (the readers) within a single esoteric discourse shared orally and now textually across cultures and times.

Psychologically speaking, such secret talk was made possible by what psychoanalysts call transference phenomena, that is, the transposition of emotional associations and reactions originally connected to some figure or event of one's past onto an analogously perceived figure or event of one's present. Many, if not most, of my religiously inclined correspondents, for example, responded positively to *Kālī's Child* precisely because of its ability to speak to their own psyches and souls. In effect, they saw their own struggles with gender issues and mystical states reflected in my own. Here, because the transferences were positive, the tones were enthusiastic and trusting.

Similar but significantly darker transference phenomena showed themselves in the negative receptions. This process was encouraged somewhat by the fact that my Czech surname also happens to be popular in northern India, where it is usually associated with the Sikh tradition (in a new twist on the story, this summer I learned that family oral tradition traces our roots back to East European gypsies, who immigrated from—where else?—India). "Jeffrey J. Kripal," then, strikes the Indian eye as an unusual amalgamation of Western-Christian (Jeffrey) and Indian-Sikh (Kripal) traditions. Accordingly, I was vilified in one American-Hindu cartoon as a secular, liberal Sikh (complete with turban) teaching in a godless American university. In other contexts—for example, in the letters to the editor of a major Calcutta newspaper or in personal correspondence—I have been portrayed as a sinister gay man, as an NRI (Non-Resident Indian), or as an ill-trained pseudo-scholar who just made it all up, as it were. Now none of this is true. I am not gay. I am not a Sikh. I am not an Indian living abroad. (Although I fail utterly to see what is wrong with any of these identities.) Nor am I a dilettante. All of this name-calling, then, is an unfortunate collection of emotionally charged transferences, personal and cultural complexes projected onto the blank slate that was "Jeffrey J. Kripal."

Such negative transferences are complicated further by a very difficult colonial and now postcolonial history. Certainly common Indian perceptions of "the West" as materialistic, morally dissolute, and antireligious and "the East" as spiritual, moral and religious—that is, the typical orientalist constructions—played into these cross-cultural reactions. Our contemporary global culture, the hermeneutical powers of critical theory, and the philosophical realities of the postmodern world may promise to reduce all such binarisms to virtual nonsense. Still, because of the colonial and Christian missionary legacies, which are all too filled with gross distortions of Hindu practice and belief and disturbing acts of cultural and theological arrogance, any perceived encroachment on the part of a Westerner, however well intentioned or appropriately trained, is almost immediately coded—and so effectively fended off—as another example of Western neocolonialism.

To make matters even more precarious, 150 years of Victorian and colonial sexual prudery have, with other cultural forces, attempted to efface the ancient and exquisite eroticism of much of Indic scripture, art, and mystical practice, making it difficult at best to address these remarkable cultural legacies openly without offense (a particular colonial offense which does not seem to be historically indigenous). In such a difficult atmosphere, knowledge of any kind can easily and facilely be reduced to a form of intellectual imperialism. A hermeneutical method like psychoanalysis that wants to critically examine universal themes across cultures and times, and this through an open discussion of the intimacies of sexuality, becomes particularly problematic, even when its history is defined by a fantastically rich literature, a radically critical approach to *all* religion, including and especially Western religion, genuine cross-cultural dialogue, the constant adjustment of its categories, and the eloquent presence of gifted South Asian practitioners (the Indian analyst Sudhir Kakar and the Sri Lankan born anthropologist Gananath Obeyesekere come immediately to mind).

I believe that such criticisms have seriously misread both the intentions and the trajectories of religious studies in America. Among many other matters (like the very different cultural and political histories of America and England), what such criticisms fail to take into account is the fact that often scholars, far from taking up the psychoanalytic, anthropological, or historical-critical pen to "imperialize" another culture, do so, in effect, to understand and interpret their own now postmodern "colonized souls." In some genuine sense, *they* are the converted ones. Certainly this was true in my own case. I was born in the 1960s and grew up in an American society that was post-Christian, radically pluralistic, and increasingly global in worldview. Within such a cultural context, religious forms migrate with great ease across national boundaries through books, higher education, and now the internet (recall that I first encountered Hinduism in a Catholic seminary). That I chose as a topic of study the Hindu tradition that had had the most impact on my own American culture was certainly no accident. I was simply trying to make sense of something that had permanently altered the religious, philosophical, and even ontological landscapes of my psyche and soul. Far from participating in any kind of Christian missionary activity in India, what I was actually doing was trying to respond positively to Hindu missionary ventures in my own American backyard.

To frame such a willingness to step out, if not actually leave, one's own indigenous religious tradition in order to sympathetically and critically understand another's as an act of colonial oppression or intellectual imperialism is hardly fair; in psychoanalytic terms, it is a false and ultimately dysfunctional transference of a past cultural event (colonialism) onto a present one (the practice of religious studies within a global culture) whose dynamics must be made conscious and worked through if any genuine dialogue is to take place. Certainly there are features and patterns of the latter that are analogous to those of the former (for colonialism, globalism, and religious studies were and are driven largely by Western intellectual forces), but to collapse the two into a single process seems simplistic at best, and to blame individuals who spend much of their professional lives teaching the integrity and beauty of Hinduism among largely Christian populations for this borders on the baffling. What we have here is an inherited and mutually constructed history to work and think through, not an accurate measure of personal intentions or individual moral character.

This same orientalist critique, moreover, is often implicated in the very cultural essentialisms it so rightly seeks to overcome and transcend, as if there were such a thing as an unproblematic "West" or "Westerner." It is no longer a matter of being either this or that but of being both this *and* that. This is our postcolonial world become postmodern world. In this same spirit of merging identity-rivers, we could say that the moment Swami Vivekananda (Ramakrishna's most famous disciple) opened his mouth and uttered his justly famous speeches at the Parliament of World Religions in the Chicago of 1893, any and each American's work on Ramakrishna or his tradition became both eminently legitimate and culturally creative, for at the moment this particular tradition entered American culture it became subject to this culture's own traditions of public, religious, and academic discourse.

Moreover, it has been argued many times that it was Vivekananda's trip to Chicago and America that made him into "Swami Vivekananda," and it is now a truism of Indology that modern, global Hinduism is a creative synthesis of traditional Indic thought and Western, post-Enlightenment social, religious, and political philosophies. Seen in this historical light, I see no reason why the cross-cultural dialogue between Bengali and American religious cultures must somehow stop in the nineteenth- or early twentieth-century, and why we, as contemporary American scholars living in what is essentially a global post-modern village, are not perfectly authorized, indeed *called*, to continue this important task of cultural criticism, self-understanding, religious transformation, and public debate. The cultural rivers flow on and into one another, and creatively so.

In the end, it seems apparent to me that any remotely fair analysis of *Kālī's Child* and its reception must explain two seemingly contradictory events: the book's fantastically warm reception among certain intellectual, artistic, and religious circles *and* its passionate rejection among many, if not most, devotees and officials of the Ramakrishna tradition (and please note that this binary pattern cannot be mapped onto some simplistic East/West or insider/outsider dichotomy, as if there have been no real critics here or genuine supporters in South Asia and within the tradition).

How *does* one explain an award-winning book that has been hailed as both a "disturbingly delightful celebration" of Ramakrishna's spirituality and as a detestable "bloated bladder of lies" worthy to be banned? Are we talking about the same book? There are many issues here (including the fact that the latter phrase was penned by a person who had never read the book), some of which I have attempted to map above, but the most important of them, I believe, is the ethical status of homosexualities within our religious traditions. Put differently, it is my own conviction that the "contradictory" receptions of *Kālī's Child* are not really contradictory at all. Those readers who do not fear or condemn homosexualities read the book exactly as it was written—as a warm, deeply sympathetic portrait of a remarkable Hindu Tantric mystic, a "disturbingly delightful celebration" indeed, filled with those very things that graced Ramakrishna's historical presence: loud laughter (some of it quite bawdy), sexually suggestive religious visions, and moments of ecstatic joy in the presence of beloved human beings. Those readers, however, who reject homosexualities as somehow aberrant, impure, or "Western" project their own fears and hatreds onto the book (and me) and so read it as something it was not, is not, and never will be—an "attack" on Ramakrishna or, more bizarrely still, on Hinduism itself. What is genuinely contradictory, then, is not the book itself but the moral sensibilities that its different readers bring to it.

At some point, my critics will have to explain why, if I am wrong, other scholars, both Western and Bengali, have come to virtually identical conclusions or to analogous, powerfully sexualized readings. Malcolm McLean, for example, translated the entire *Kathamrita* and concluded, among many other things, that Ramakrishna's homosexuality was central to understanding his relationships with his male disciples.[19] Sumit Sarkar, the great Bengali social historian, has suggested similar homosexual patterns in his "The Kathamrita as a Text."[20] More recently, Parama Roy has used postcolonial and queer theory to write about Ramakrishna's erotic feminine identification, his simultaneous worship of women and gynophobia, his rejection of sexuality as a rejection of (hetero)sexuality, his erotically charged relationship to the young Narendra (Swami Vivekananda), and Vivekananda's subsequent transformation of Ramakrishna's mysticism into a hyper-masculine heterosexual nationalism.[21] All of these patterns fit *seamlessly* into the homoerotic hermeneutic of *Kālī's Child*. And then there is the important work of Narasingha Sil, who has published three volumes so far on Ramakrishna and Vivekananda, all of which profoundly sexualize (if in quite different directions) both the guru and the disciple.[22] Even more recently, Brian Hatcher, a historian of religion specializing in Bengali religious history, traveled to Calcutta to do fieldwork on the reception of my work there, found support for it among Bengalis, and returned to some of the more controversial passages in the Bengali text only to come up with virtually identical readings.[23] Indeed, now reversing our temporal focus, if we count the unexplained "scandalous interpretations" that one Bengali text records Ramakrishna's own contemporaries advancing when his temple manager gave him women's clothes and a wig to wear in the manager's presence, we could easily argue that the homoerotic thesis is both indigenous to Bengal and about 150 years old now.

Clearly, even such a brief history of scholarship as this exposes the "controversy" of *Kālī's Child* for what it is: a function neither of my assumed moral character (or are all of the above scholars equally suspect?), nor of my alleged translation disabilities (for Bengali speakers have come to virtually identical conclusions), but of our contemporary debates about gender, homosexuality, and religion. *There* is the controversy.

If an adequate comparative history of male erotic mysticism is ever to be written, the implied presence of culturally and historically conditioned homosexualities in the texts and their specifically gendered symbolic structures (and I fully realize that the latter do not necessarily imply the former) is an issue that we will have to address more directly than we have so far. Homophobic denials, anti-Freudian diatribes, and identity politics will no longer do. Of course, there are many more important reasons to address homosexuality as a religious issue, foremost among them the sexual bigotry and social injustice that render the lives of millions of human beings compromised at best and terrorized at worst. Unfortunately, our religious traditions have contributed more than a little to this social and sexual suffering. Many of our Christian communities (from Rome to the Southern Baptist Convention), for example, recently seem bent on making such suffering a virtual dogma of the faith. Solid, critical, public scholarship on these traditions and their handling of sexuality and gender seems central to any adequate response to such a situation.

What we will find, if I may be allowed a prediction (which, I must add, I owe largely to the brilliant work of the Catholic historian and theologian Mark Jordan[24]), is that the very religious traditions that condemn homosexual practices and public identities are themselves filled with fantastically rich, if still deeply ambiguous, resources, particularly in their mystical dimensions, for homoerotic religious experiences and even identities. The irony of this is both glaring and tragic, and it needs to be addressed directly and, above all, publicly. Only then can the secret talk be truly spoken and adequately understood. Only then can we stop vilifying the messengers and listen with open hearts and minds to that which was once whispered and is now being spoken out loud.

I want to end these reflections with a story that my mentor at Chicago, Wendy Doniger, likes to tell her graduate students. She borrowed it from Heinrich Zimmer, the great German Indologist, who no doubt borrowed it from someone else, and so on. It is about the Rabbi of Cracow, and it goes like this. A rabbi from Cracow once dreamed that he should go to Prague to find a hidden treasure buried under a bridge there. In Prague, far away from home, he found the bridge guarded by a Christian, who laughed at him for believing in dreams; he, after all, had had a similar dream, which told him to go to Cracow, where he would find a treasure buried behind the stove of a rabbi named Isaac, son of Jekel. The rabbi said nothing but hurried home, for he was Isaac, son of Jekel, and the treasure he had sought in a distant land was in fact buried in his very own home. But—and this is the key to the story—such a treasure could only be discovered and fully appreciated by a trip to a distant land and its foreign (in this case, Christian) culture.

This, I would suggest, is the story of many of us who have studied the history of religions as a specifically comparative and essentially religious enterprise. For my own part, I began with Roman Catholicism and a fascination with erotic forms of mystical literature that somehow spoke, and yet did not speak, to my own modern psychosexual patterns and identities. Much like the Rabbi of Cracow, my thoughts and dreams led me to a foreign culture and its religion, where I found much beauty and wisdom and, eventually, a road back home. Still on this road, I am presently working on a study of these same mystico-erotic themes in the Western monotheistic traditions and, even closer to the stove, in the lives and works of twentieth-century scholars of mysticism. Perhaps it is finally time that we tell our own stories, share our own dreams, even recount our own mystico-erotic experiences, for there is undoubtedly more behind our sooty stoves than we realize, even if we need a Christian guard (or a Hindu saint) to tell us as much.

5

The Transmoral Mystic

What Both the Moralists and the
Devotees Get Wrong

For he makes his sun rise on the evil and on the good.

MATTHEW 5:45

As I wrote the dissertation and then suffered the backlash against *Kālī's Child*, a number of my friends in the field and more senior colleagues were also writing about Tantric figures and ideas, many of them in that impressive historical wave of charismatic power and presence that was Swami Muktananda (1908–82). Muktananda had toured the US in the 1970s as one of the spiritual stars of the late American counterculture. Many of my colleagues were either still part of this community and tradition, or were just emerging from it. Actually, "emerging" is not quite the right word, as some had left out of deep hurt and sadness when rumors of the guru's sexual relations with young women began to circulate before he died.

I found myself in the middle of all of this, or standing just to the side. In any case, I was too close. I was struck by how similar this all sounded to the nineteenth-century Bengali materials that I had worked on. The sexuality being described, of course, was very different (the alleged sexual objects in Muktananda's case were young women, not young men). It was the sociology of censorship and the psychology of denial that struck me as so disturbingly similar. That I had by that time become the object of other people's censorship and devotional denial only made this particular topic more pressing for me.

Looking back, I can see now that my work was very much an expression of this historical period and its religious traumas. I mean, what does it mean that *Kālī's Child* appeared in the middle of a decade (1995) that saw, or followed by just a few years, not one or two, but *dozens* of sexual scandals involving spiritual teachers from various Asian religions who had been teaching in the West? And more, of course, would follow. If we add to this the fact that my next book, *Roads of Excess, Palaces of Wisdom* (2001), which treated the homoerotic structures of male mysticism from Roman Catholicism to Kabbalah, appeared just before the clerical scandals of the Roman Catholic Church exploded in the spring of 2002, we can easily see that these first two books do not stand alone as eccentric gestures of a delusional mind. They stand amid a very large crowd of observers, journalists, scholars, and deeply wounded believers.

We can also see that these charismatic dynamics are by no means restricted to Hindu and Buddhist spiritual teachers. They can be seen nearly everywhere we find charisma, including in the life of Jesus as recorded in early Christian literature and debated in modern scholarship. One can find these in sources ranging from the controversial "Secret Gospel of Mark" fragment involving what looks, to me anyway, like a nocturnal homoerotic initiation rite ("and in the evening the youth comes to him, wearing a linen cloth over his naked body. And he remained with him that night, for Jesus taught him the mystery of the kingdom of God"[1]) to the very canonical Gospel of John featuring, of course, the "man Jesus loved," that is, the beloved disciple. Of course, none of our own American legal decisions and cultural assumptions around sexual maturity (at eighteen years of age) were relevant in first-century Palestine. I am not taking any positions on these particular textual-historical debates here. I am simply noting that the same kinds of controversies around charisma and eroticism are present in both early and present-day Christianity. No tradition of any scope or breadth is likely immune from them.

All of this eventually crystallized in my work around the relationship between mystical states of consciousness and social ethics. One of my friends in graduate school was Bill Barnard, who now teaches at Southern Methodist University. Bill had lived in Swami Muktananda's ashram in Ganeshpuri, India, and had almost taken *sannyasa* (a formal vow to become a monk or renunciate). In the early 1970s, when he was a young teenager in Florida, Bill had had a profound spontaneous mystical opening in which he felt he "woke up" and briefly, yet ecstatically, experienced himself as a Consciousness without limits. On another occasion, this earlier opening blossomed into a full-blown awakening when he came to know the utter transcendence of the Self (*atman*) and the illusion of the suffering ego in the presence of Swami Muktananda, in this case at the touch of the latter's ritual peacock feather: "I remember laughing, realizing on some level of my being that my previous identification with my body and my ego was a cosmic joke, knowing that I never was just an ego and I never would be just an ego, recognizing in the core of my being that, contrary to what I'd always believed, I never had suffered and I never would."[2]

These two experiences, which fundamentally changed Bill's life, in turn entered the study of religion in a number of ways. Bill, for example, wrote about his first mystical opening in an essay engaging the work of the philosopher of religion Wayne Proudfoot and Proudfoot's classic study *Religious Experience.*[3] Ann Taves engaged this dialogue and Bill's initial experience in turn in her own *Religious Experience Reconsidered.*[4] I have also long featured Bill's transcendent opening before Swami Muktananda in both my teaching and, most recently, in my textbook, *Comparing Religions*. Bill's spiritual awakening is now a part of the literature of the study of religion.

After the scandals erupted, Bill entered graduate school, partly to try to make some sense out of it. It was there that we had countless friendly debates about whether or not mystical experiences are related to morality and ethics, or what we might call, following Plato, the Good. Bill's thought was (and still is) nuanced and careful here. He recognized, of course, that religious prodigies often engage in troubling behavior and advance social or ethical norms that many of us in the modern West would find appalling, but he argued that deep mystical experiences have a strong tendency to lead to moral behavior, love, and compassion, since they are expressions of the real, which is fundamentally good and loving. I was (and still am) much more reluctant to link the moral and the mystical. I was more of the opinion of Jesus, or at least my eccentric reading of him: the sun of consciousness "shines" on (and in) the good and bad alike; morality is important for our social lives but probably not translatable into this other realm. Bill would agree, and then I would try another line of argument: I would explain how sometimes really bad things (like sexual or physical trauma) can open us up to really good things (like mystical experiences). The relationship between the moral and the mystical is *complicated*. Bill would agree. This is how we went on. At some point, we decided to turn our friendly sparring into an edited volume.[5]

Earlier in my writing, I characterized this theme as the "amoral mystic." I still find that useful and accurate, say, on Mondays, Wednesdays, and Fridays. On Sundays, Tuesdays, and Thursdays, though, I am persuaded by my interlocutors—colleagues like Bill again, but also Elliot Wolfson—and would prefer to speak of the "transmoral mystic."[6] (On Saturdays I am simply confused and don't know what to think.) We can crystallize this open-ended discussion as gnomon 4:

4. The Amoral or Transmoral Mystic. There is no necessary or simple connection between the mystical and the ethical.

There are many complexities involved here, which I have addressed at length at different points in my corpus, including one that we will meet below as the "traumatic secret" (gnomon 17). For now, perhaps it is enough to explain briefly what distinguishes an "amoral" mystic from a "transmoral" one.

Most simply, the adjective *amoral* signals a "no" or "not," that is, it signals that there simply is no connection between those realms of mind accessed in mystical states and the moral concerns and customs of a particular society. Hence any attempt to relate or join them will only produce confusion. One might as well turn to the mathematical behavior of subatomic particles to make a decision about whom to marry or vote for.

The adjective *transmoral*, on the other hand, signals a "yes/no," that is, it signals that there is a deep connection between the mystical and the moral (the "yes" part), but that the moral codes of society and religion are finally not what we think they are (the "no" part). The key idea here is transgression, that is, the conscious or intentional breaking of a moral code or purity system toward some transcendent or transformative end beyond that system (hence the "trans" part of transmoral).

The issue here is fairly simple: to get the "power" or "punch" of a transgressive act, one needs a moral system or purity code to transgress. Such transgressive acts, then, are not technically amoral, much less immoral (although they will be perceived as such by those still embedded in and committed to the moral system in place). Such transgressive acts are in fact deeply moral ones, since such individuals are dramatically engaging dominant moral systems in an attempt to launch or explode beyond them toward some truth or state that transcends the social system in place: they are being "transmoral."

These are only the beginning of the complexities. The simple truth is that profound spiritual transformations, healings, philosophical insights, and paranormal effects are commonly experienced around religious prodigies, who are also engaging in behaviors (often of a sexual nature) that can be profoundly destructive. There is something about spiritual charisma that is explosive, something that honors no stable personal boundaries.

In my more nuanced moments, I sometimes think that the dilemma of the immoral or transmoral saint is simply a function of the (false) presumption that the mystical or paranormal effects experienced around a charismatic prodigy are being directly or completely "caused" by the spiritual teacher himself or herself. Today, I doubt that this is the case. These effects are more likely arising from a shared and highly "magnetized" social field, which is somehow being activated or focused into a laser beam because of the presence of a charismatic prism. Eric Ouellet has proposed a new parasociology—that is, a study of how societies interact with psychical and paranormal phenomena—to model and begin to understand something of these force fields and special effects.[7] I think that this is the right direction to go.

In any case, such real-world special effects displays—which range from poltergeist and other physical psychical phenomena, including light forms and materializations, to profound states of bliss, freedom, and experiences of eternity or timelessness—may well be *correlated* with the presence of the charismatic prodigy, but they need not be *caused* by him or her. This, of course, would immediately remove the seeming contradiction of the saint behaving badly, since the mystical states and the immoral behavior would be issuing from different forms or levels of agency—one parasocial or collective (the magnetic and the mystical), one personal or egoic (the ethical or unethical). This is all speculation on my part, but it is speculation that can make some better sense of the historical record, which simply makes no sense in the ordinary moral terms that most of us take for granted.

I would also observe that my position—that there is no necessary or simple connection between the mystical and the ethical—need not involve any profound undersanding of the nuances of the amoral or the transmoral, since it is nothing more, and nothing less, than a basic moral sensibility that insists on listening *to everyone*. Once one puts aside one's own assumptions and listens in a sufficient way, two things become patently obvious: (1) numerous human beings experience life-changing energies and altered states of mind in the presence of or at the touch of these "electric" spiritual teachers; and (2) the same spiritual teachers often sexually engage their disciples in ways that many disciples and most religious communities today would find deeply problematic. It is as if the energies of charisma, once released, cannot be shoved back into the moral boxes of society and ordinary life. It is as if the spiritual and sexual energies overflow *together*.

All of the "debates" and "controversies" follow from these two simple observations. The debunkers of these amoral, immoral, or transmoral mystics affirm only (2). They are correct about that, but they ignore or misrepresent (1). The denying believers or censoring disciples affirm only (1). They are correct about that, but they ignore or misrepresent (2). The solution is very simple: affirm both (1) and (2).

The intellectual and moral benefits of such a double move are considerable. Such a double vision, after all, not only allows us to observe and describe the profound religious effects that these charismatic teachers have on other human beings. It also allows us to advance ethical criticisms for the behaviors (on the part of the spiritual teacher) and cover-ups (on the part of the community) that our own moral sensibilities consider destructive, dangerous, and, more often than not, outrageously hypocritical. We can do *both* because we are no longer confusing or conflating the two separate psychic orders. We can affirm the realm of the larger conscious field or Mind even as we can criticize the actions of the social ego through which such a Mind temporarily shines. Gnomon 4, in other words, is another expression of gnomon 2 on the Human as Two.

SECRET READERS

The genesis of my thinking here was not simply the public scandals of the 1980s, 1990s, and new millennium. There was also a more private process going on that involved my readers and students, who were now approaching and writing me with the most astonishing stories. It was this esoteric reception of *Kālī's Child* that really helped me to finalize my thought around the mystical, the ethical, and the traumatic.

But which stories to tell here? Should I tell, for example, the story of the elderly American woman whom I knew in Calcutta as a prominent Ramakrishna devotee, who, after my book came out, wrote numerous letters to an English Calcutta newspaper under various fake names so as to give the impression of an angry flood of mail? Should I stop there? Or should I go on to tell how this woman's adult daughter, a woman named Kate, later wrote me long, kind, supportive letters from Lincoln, Nebraska, explaining how her mother used to do the same when she was younger, usually on one-woman campaigns against this or that state senator? Should I stop there? Or should I go further still and explain how Kate told me that her mother had been sexually abused by her father in her own childhood and how she in turn had abused and ignored her two daughters, including Kate, when they were growing up in a small rural community in Nebraska, not far from where I grew up? Just how much of the truth can we take? Do we *really* want to talk about a Calcutta censorship campaign against a book that was about the links between erotic mysticism and sexual trauma that was partially led by an American woman who had been sexually traumatized and had in turn abused her own children? The ironies here are as obvious and familiar as they are sad. I should add that Kate ultimately found my work healing and redemptive.

As did many others. Should I tell their stories? What about all the students and correspondents who found in the book a rich and warm resource for negotiating their own existential embrace of Tantric spiritualities and personal awakenings?[8] What about all the students and correspondents over the years who found in the same book the tools to process what they always knew but could never positively articulate, namely, that there was a real connection between the sexual trauma of their early years and the ecstatic mystical experiences of their later years? They understood my deeply sympathetic discussions of the saint's sexual trauma perfectly well, and so they could now see that there is no obvious causal reason to reduce their later mystical experiences to the former God-awful traumas. Trauma, as I explained in *Kālī's Child*, may well be what cracks open the door to mystical states of consciousness. But what is inside the house need not have *anything* to do with how one got in. A door is not a house. The ethical (or unethical) is not the mystical.

THE TANTRIC TRANSMISSION

My interactions with the North American guru traditions led to another meta-theme in my work. Technically speaking, this idea would not really take shape until the *Esalen* project and my history of the human potential movement after the turn of the new millennium, but its roots nevertheless lie here, in the hysteria around *Kālī's Child* and the larger questions around the moral behavior of Tantric gurus both in the historical past and in the American present. It was through such events that I began to understand the more recent American reception of the Asian religions in a new countercultural light.

Born at the very end of the Baby Boom, in 1962, I had long felt that my generation was riding a "wave" that had crested just before us, in the 1960s and 1970s. We were surfing on this cultural crest. I wanted to better understand the motion and physics of that wave. I wanted to theorize the counterculture. I eventually concluded that the countercultural wave was the cultural filter that determined what aspects of the Asian traditions would be embraced and celebrated in the youth movements of the 1960s and 1970s (read: the countercultural Tantric and erotic ones) and what aspects would be quietly ignored or rejected (read: the orthodox and ascetic ones). Briefly, that history was defined by what I came to call the Tantric transmission. It goes like this:

5. The Tantric Transmission. In terms of the twentieth-century American translation of Asian religions, we can see a fairly clear "flip" around 1950. Before that date, the Asian systems and practices that drew the most attention tended to be ascetic and dualistic in practice (think Advaita Vedanta and

Theravada Buddhism). After 1950, with the rise of Beat culture and the subsequent counterculture, they tended to be much more Tantric and erotic in
practice (think Tibetan Buddhism, kundalini yoga, Shakta Tantra, Kashmiri
Shaivism, and a general Daoism).

Such a Tantric transmission into the West in turn would have a profound effect on the shaping and formation of the study of "comparative religion" in the
1960s and 1970s. More on that later, when we get to gnomon 9.

INTRODUCING THE ESSAY

One of my earliest statements on the amoral or transmoral mystic and, implicitly at least, the Tantric transmission thesis appeared in the journal *Religious
Studies Review* in 1999.[9] I anthologize the core of the essay below, because
(a) it is my earliest published statement on these meta-themes; (b) it provides a
few helpful case studies; (c) it is brief and to the point; and (d) it silently draws
on the energetic transmission or zapping (*shaktipat*) I had known in "that
Night." The same review essay also functions nicely as a transition piece to
our next gnomon, as it deals with a theme that dominated my thought during
this same period: the fundamental inadequacy of any clear division between
the "insider" and the "outsider" positions in the study of religion (gnomon 6).

If I had anything to add today it would be a deeper and more sympathetic
understanding of the complex political and religious dynamics in which my
colleagues in the Siddha Yoga tradition were working. I regret if I caused them
any pain or suffering with this review. Obviously, when I wrote about their
self-censorship, I was also writing about my bitter experience of being censored for writing about another North American guru tradition. We were all
struggling with some very difficult and very personal issues as best we could.

Inside-Out, Outside-In

EXISTENTIAL PLACE AND ACADEMIC METHOD IN THE
STUDY OF NORTH AMERICAN GURU TRADITIONS
(1999)

The study of North American guru traditions is particularly poignant. On the one hand, critics not particularly disposed to the religious experiences of gurus and their disciples commonly attack the guru figure as a charlatan or a despot of a religiously toned totalitarianism or theocracy. On the other, disciples constitutionally allergic to the insights of psychologists, anthropologists, historians of religions, and sociologists often claim omniscience, doctrinal infallibility, and moral perfection for their gurus (a task made immeasurably easier if the guru in question is safely dead).

The situation is especially complicated, if not positively topsy-turvy, for the scholar who refuses both of these dualisms and chooses instead to stand (if that is the right word) somewhere in the middle. This middle is no doubt in fact a spectrum of existential and theoretical choices, all of which have some merit but some of which, I think, are more theoretically useful than others for the academic study of religion. Of particular interest to me are the existential places and theoretical practices of scholars who imaginatively allow their own worldviews to be turned "inside-out" by the traditions, even as they turn the traditions "inside-out" through critical theory and rational discourse. Ideally in such a situation (and there are few, if any, "ideallys" in the world of religious studies), a mutual transformation takes place, and both the scholar and the tradition find themselves transcended in a moment of understanding that is neither here nor there, neither clearly inside nor quite outside, bad news perhaps for the dogmatist (whether devotee or theorist) but a positively giddy experience for the imaginative and open-minded.

Such is the ideal anyway. The actual is, as always, a glorious mess, both "glorious" and "messy" in the way that Mary Douglas defined the ambiguous, fearful possibilities of "pollution," "impurity," and "dirt"—a fertile chaos, a liminality awaiting birth. I have chosen to review three books below, partly to examine and work through my own chaotic experiences studying the historical roots of a prominent North American guru tradition, but mostly because they raise for all of us questions and concerns about these traditions that must be publicly addressed "on the outside." There are quite enough family secrets "on the inside," both in the guru traditions themselves and in the academy. What follows flows from the assumption that we will understand neither the traditions nor ourselves until we begin to speak such secrets—openly, honestly, respectfully, and fearlessly.

I begin with an author whose existential place is already both an inside and an outside. I will then proceed to authors who inhabit places progressively further and further "in."

INSIDE-OUTSIDE LOOKING OUT AND IN

Jeffrey Rubin's *Buddhism and Psychotherapy* is refreshingly balanced and, precisely because of this, theoretically useful. Both a practicing Buddhist and an experienced psychotherapist, Rubin refuses, like a good Buddhist, to give either of these "subject-positions" absolute autonomy or epistemological priority.

This is a repetitive book, but one with a message well worth repeating, namely that, taken alone, both the psychoanalytic and the Buddhist perspectives are limited, partial, and, at points, potentially dangerous. Rubin employs a whole host of metaphors to flesh out this basic thesis. He criticizes, for example, both the "Eurocentrism" of psychoanalytic models of the self, which tend to restrict human potential to the mundane compromises of a functioning and ultimately disintegrating ego (a narrative that Rubin identifies as "tragic"), and the "Orientocentrism" of Buddhist practitioners, who operate with a far more open and hopeful vision of human potential (which Rubin identifies as "romantic") but who also insist on treating Buddhist culture as sacred and thus beyond reproach. Buddhists are described as "near-sighted," minutely attuned to the "microscopic" complexities of consciousness but quite unaware of the developmental, psychodynamic, and pathological concerns of the psychotherapist, whereas psychotherapists are "telescopic" and "far-sighted," skilled in the exquisite psychoanalytic mappings of self-deception and defense but rather unprepared to address the life-affirming, life-changing truths of Buddhist meditation.

There is no absolute perspective, Rubin tells us, and any choice entails consequences that must be acknowledged and dealt with. Whereas various psychotherapies tend to "cut off" the self in an unnecessarily limited vision of the human being that can leave a person depressed and disenchanted, Buddhism tends to avoid subjectivity altogether, leaving the meditator in a psychological position that must fear the "return of the repressed" (in this case, the ego) and in a sociophilosophical stance that renders any real social concern tangential at best.

Related to Buddhism's avoidance of subjectivity are the troublingly consistent moral failures of contemporary American Buddhist communities, failures that Rubin suggests flow at least partly from the traditions' refusal to confront the realities of social agency and embodiment, cross-cultural differences, and the authoritarian structure of the guru-disciple institution. The latter point is especially relevant for the present discussion. Rubin points out that in 1983 "five of the six most esteemed Zen Buddhist masters in the United States, who presumably were selected by an enlightened teacher abroad to teach, were involved in grossly self-centered and conspicuously unenlightened behavior."[10]

Rubin also refuses to dichotomize or hierarchize spiritual development and psychopathology, insisting instead that profound religious experience and real psychopathology are often found together. In this same vein, Rubin shows a genuine appreciation for the therapeutic, aesthetic, and religious benefits of meditation, even as he calls into serious question the possibility of total enlightenment. Here Rubin refuses the absolute answer and suggests instead that "the emperor of enlightenment may have no clothes," or in a more analytic mode: "The vast knowledge gained by psychoanalysts about the ubiquity of self-unconsciousness casts grave doubt on Buddhist claims about permanent and irreversible self-transformation and wisdom."[11]

The end result of all of these dialogic reflections, therapy vignettes, and philosophical discussions is a basic, eminently reasonable proposal, namely, that we take seriously both the Buddhist and the psychoanalytic narratives and create out of their mutually conflicting, mutually complementary worldviews a new "contemplative psychoanalysis" or "analytic Buddhism" that might provide postmodern humanity, not with the absolute solutions of guru traditions or the depressing conclusions of Freud, but with a more reasonable and hopeful "civilization with less discontent."[12]

INSIDE LOOKING IN AND OUT

Stephen Butterfield's *The Double Mirror* is a beautifully written, hilarious, touching, and shockingly honest "skeptical journey into Buddhist Tantra" (the book's subtitle), functioning, not unlike Vajrayana Buddhism itself, as a kind of bizarre meditation on death and emptiness that allows its readers no stable place, be it "outside" or "inside," devotional or academic. The utter freedom— emotional, rhetorical, religious—of this text is simply astonishing. Indeed, so impressed was I with the inside-out "double-mirrored" vision of this book on the Vajrayana lineage of the Buddhist teacher Chogyam Trungpa, that I decided, halfway into it, to call the author. "I'm looking for Professor Butterfield," I told the college operator. "He's dead," she said. I hung up the phone, saddened and confused. "And that," I said to myself quietly, "explains the utter freedom of his prose." As I read further, I noticed Butterfield's repeated references to his sarcoidosis (a potentially life-threatening disease of the lungs). Like the Joker in "Batman" who lost his life in a bath of acid only to be miraculously reborn as a legendary antihero, Butterfield had apparently already "died" to himself and so had nothing to lose; he could thus speak (and laugh) his truths freely.

The book begins with three disconcerting images of death that shocked Butterfield out of the stupor of naïveté: a room "that resembled a stage prop for a TV sitcom," where somber meditators counted their beads, meditated, and pulverized the auspicious bones of their recently deceased guru (Trungpa) to mix with jewel dust in golden amulet statuettes; a troubling conversation Butterfield had with Osel Tendzin, Trungpa's chosen successor, as Tendzin made fun of a television talk show on AIDS that they were watching at an airport (a year later, as noted above, the Buddhist world would learn that Tendzin had AIDS at the time of this conversation, intentionally kept it secret, and infected one of his male lover-disciples); and the suspicious death of Jamgon Kongtrul, whose car accident, Butterfield suggests, was connected to a political struggle around the installation of the seventeenth head of the Karmapa sect.

By page nine, Butterfield's poor head is spinning, and he must admit: "I no longer knew how to reconcile my inner experience of the dharma, which had been nothing less than life-giving, with my distrust of its outer organizational forms." "Selective coverage of Buddhist events is propaganda," he concludes, "resulting in a credibility gap between the public face of the Buddhist institution and its hidden undercurrent."[13] The result? He stopped practicing. The remainder of the book is Butterfield's brave attempt to balance both the life-giving "inside" and the suspect "outside" of Trungpa's Vajrayana, to see "whether you can make a Buddhist journey and yet stand outside the experience and study it."[14] Appropriately, in doing so, Butterfield turns both himself and the tradition inside-out.

But only with the delightful help of his central rhetorical figure, Doubt, who appears throughout the text as Mother Wit, as the third face of enlightenment, as a mocking court jester, and (my personal favorite) as a hick farmer chewing a grain of straw and donning the proverbial John Deere cap:

> "How much did those thingies there cost ya? Wow, I guess you gotta have money to be a Buddhist, huh? Somebody must be making some bucks off it. . . ."
> I turned to him and began to chant: "Om, O Sovereign you are the nature of all. You are beyond any mark of arriving or departing. Yet, like the moon in water, you manifest wherever thought of. . . ."
> "You're weird," he replied.
> "Thank you." I said.[15]

This Doubt may be nothing but "rat shit" to Trungpa, but to Butterfield it is a manifestation of the individual's pristine and original sanity, that mystery in the human being that will not allow itself to be controlled completely by anyone: "To write and speak freely as an individual is a difficult, precious act, one which is generally devalued by religious and political orthodoxies," Butterfield tells us. "But the individual voice keeps faith with a moral code greater than any other commitment: to make an authentic response to our world."[16] Butterfield, like no other author I have read, remains unabashedly faithful to this most precious and priceless of intellectual codes.

Throughout the book's twenty chapters, Butterfield can be seen flipping a coin and standing it, every time, on its edge, as he ruthlessly analyzes the intimidation, cultlike corruption, dysfunctional secrecy, anti-intellectualism, authoritarianism, betrayal, financial expense, and blatantly theocratic nature of the guru-disciple relationship ("He [Trungpa] looked like a Tahitian king who had finally subdued the British Empire"[17]), even as he recounts in beautiful detail the psychological wonders of his ritually transformed perceptions within the "double mirror" (his defining traditional metaphor for the nondual experience of the perceptual field-neither "in" here nor "out" there), the intellectual force of emptiness, the magic of synchronistically stopping clocks and inexplicable rainbows at Trungpa's death and funeral pyre, the strange black-cat omens that punctuated his devotional life, and the absolute necessity of the guru—even one who "smells of saki"—to get beyond the ego self. Such a journey, although a fiction, is absolutely necessary, for without it there can be no transformation: it is at once "fate, faith, and fraud." Or again, it is "just like a blind man finding a jewel in a heap of dust."[18]

It is Butterfield's uncanny ability to find this jewel in the dust, to see his faith as a fraud and this fraud as his fate that sets *The Double Mirror* apart and makes it an outstanding example of what I have called the "inside-out" position. Appropriately, Butterfield ends where he began, insisting on the nondual truths of the double mirror and the spinning coin standing on its paradoxical edge. "There is no such thing as master and student," he tells us, and "this is why the relationship works."[19]

INSIDE LOOKING IN

The last book, *Meditation Revolution*, is in some ways the most interesting and important of the three. The title is derived from a saying or "mission statement" of Swami Muktananda ("My work in this world is to start a meditation revolution"). The book is divided into two parts: history (chap. 1) and theology (chaps. 2–9). The first part consists of a single long chapter written by Swami Durgananda (a female renunciant of the tradition) on the history of the Siddha Yoga movement, which she divides neatly into the careers of the tradition's three central gurus: Swamis Nityananda (d. 1961), Muktananda (d. 1982), and Chidvilasananda (b. 1955). The story Durgananda tells is a succinct and helpful one, but it is also a history that merges imperceptibly into simple hagiography at times. Except for the author's courageous treatment of the familial and religious crises surrounding the succession of Chidvilasananda (Muktananda had named both her *and* her brother as his successor), the essay lacks almost completely that "thick description," sociopolitical complexity, and earthy psychological detail that we have come to recognize as human history.

My overwhelming impression while reading this massive volume was that I was not so much reading a critical treatment of the history of the movement as I was witnessing the actual construction of that history; that I was witnessing not a discussion about canon but the actual formation of a canon; that I was encountering not a group of scholars writing about *shaktipat* (the "descent of power," a particular energetic transmission from guru to disciple) and kundalini yoga but a group of colleagues who had actually experienced the awakened energies of this "descent of power" and were now offering their testimonies "from within" that gnoseological or gnostic perspective (even though none of them actually discuss their own experiences); and finally, that this is not a historical-critical book about the Siddha Yoga lineage at all—it is a scholarly legitimation, systematization, and canonization of the Siddha Yoga lineage, the tradition made text.

Personally speaking, I have no doubts about the transforming psychological and physiological effects of the experiences discussed at such length and so eloquently in this volume; in many places, I found myself deeply moved by the overwhelming sincerity of the testimonies. The body electric of the guru, who induces vision, ecstasy, and transformation in the disciple by a mere touch, is a phenomenon with which I am quite familiar in my own work on Rama-krishna, who was, like Muktananda, able to grant *shaktipat* with a touch of his hand (or foot); I have never doubted the psycho-physical reality of such experiences, and this volume only confirmed, deepened, and enriched that conviction.

What concerns me here, though, is that the emotionally overwhelming psycho-physiological effects of those energies and—even more significantly— the institutional, devotional, and interpersonal channels through which they flow tend to discourage, suppress, and even censor any open, interpretative discussion about the rather obvious psychological, physical, cultural, and so-cial dimensions of those same energies and the traditions in which they are experienced. There is no Stephen Butterfield here. No Mother Wit to make us laugh. No Farmer Doubt to ask us pointed, unsettling questions and call us weird.

None of this, of course, would be a problem if the authors did not explic-itly present themselves as historians of religions and their essays as acts of both scholarship and devotion, thus leaving readers who are scholars but not devotees feeling very uncomfortable with the tones and—more importantly— with the silences of their texts. To take one particularly significant example, these scholars are very much aware that kundalini yoga and the energies of *shaktipat* (the Tantro-yogic foundations of Siddha Yoga practice and self-understanding) are closely related to human sexuality, a fact amply docu-mented by historians of religions and embedded in the Indic traditions' own erotic symbolic and ritual encoding of these concepts. Muktananda's own statement is unambiguous and, I think, psycho-physiologically correct: "The source of power to give Shaktipat is this *urdhvaretas*, the rising of the sexual fluid."[20] Indeed, as scholars, the essayists rightly return to this theme of sexual sublimation more than once. Yet there is a consistent denial, always implicit and at times explicit, that anything really sexual is going on.[21] I am sure that Brooks is right about reading the *published* and *official* literature of the line-age as "right-handed" in its Tantric orientation (that is, restricting its use of Tantric eroticism to the metaphorical).[22] But what about the unpublished and unofficial traditions, both written and oral?

Take, for example, the very convincing evidence that Muktananda engaged in numerous "left-handed" (that is, actual) sexual encounters with a number of female devotees, many of them quite young, toward the end of his life, most likely, as one theory has it, in a Tantric attempt to reinvigorate a waning *shakti* or "spiritual power."[23] Such well-known incidents, which no contributor to this volume even hints at, raise a number of important and unanswered questions: Where or from whom did Muktananda learn such techniques? And when? What role did they play in his own practice, seminal sublimation (*urdhvaretas*) become *shaktipat*, and enlightenment? Are we to believe that these were isolated incidents, mere quirks of fate at the end of an otherwise perfectly celibate life? What can we say about the agency and integrity of the young women involved, that is, why not read at least some of these scenes as abusive? Perhaps most pressing for our present purposes, why do these components of Muktananda's person and practice find no legitimate place in the textual constructions of his life as presented in this volume? Not unlike the "unstruck sound" (*anahata-nada*) that liberated yogis are said to be able to hear or the silent "background noise" that pervades our once exploded universe, the deep silences of this volume are at once haunting, deeply meaningful, and disturbing.

In *Meditation Revolution*, then, we have a fairly clear case of a group of distinguished insiders "looking in" but refusing, or being prevented from, "looking out." The result is an admittedly valuable and welcome self-description of a historically important guru tradition but one that answers few of the questions that outsiders always ask. The theoretically powerful "inside-out" approach has become a less ambiguous, more devotional "outside-in" approach, with the "outside" virtually swallowed up by the "inside." We are thus back to a way of writing Indology that denies the unabashedly Tantric elements of the tradition and the plethora of problems that Tantric ritual (as practiced rather than as idealized or imagined) presents to the modern, Western individual.

CONCLUDING REFLECTIONS: TOWARD A METHODOLOGICAL NONDUALISM

What do these three books teach us overall? I think that they help us acknowledge that gurus, of whatever stripe, are complex human beings with equally complex motivations and intentions, not all of which are conscious or apparent to them.

Take Rubin's helpful metaphor of the shortsighted and farsighted lenses. Too often scholars parrot the obvious truth that every method, every (Western) cultural perspective, distorts and limits what we can see about another culture. This, no doubt, is true. But why must every concave and convex curve

THE TRANSMORAL MYSTIC || 95

in our vision distort? Why is this metaphor always used to pathologize or deny a scholar's perspective? Concavity and convexity, after all, can also be used to correct vision, and lenses can focus and magnify just as easily as they can distort. The metaphor, in other words, like Rubin's book, "cuts" both ways. Perhaps our cultural distance, our otherness, our farsightedness give us a focus, a vision that the Other does not, cannot have, just as the Other's own nearsighted focus gives it a similar, if very different, advantage.

Or consider for a moment the "descent of power" of the Siddha Yoga lineage. In describing the phenomenology of the *shaktipat* experience, the electrical analogy seems apt, not just because Siddha Yoga devotees commonly refer to their *shaktipat* experiences as "getting zapped," but more importantly because the final dynamic of these energies appears to be nonmoral. Getting touched by the guru is rather like getting brushed by a live wire. As the essayists rightly point out, it often does not matter if one "intends" or "deserves" this shock of grace, or—I would add—through what ritual or personal channels, tender or abusive, the electrical charge flows. It just flows.

Any attempt to understand such experiences, then, would do well to abandon the simplistic dualisms of ethical norms upon which we, as social agents and actors, must inevitably base our social and institutional lives. Mysticism is not morality, at least in this case, and we can unequivocally affirm the utter reality and genuineness of these experiences without insisting that their manifestations conform to our own, equally genuine, social, personal, and moral needs.

If, on the other hand, we insist that the mysticism of such gurus must be moral in our social sense of that term, then we are left with only two options: we either declare gurus such as Muktananda fakes (which flies in the face of overwhelming testimonial and textual evidence) or scapegoat authors who point out to us uncomfortable and important facts about them. I suggest that we throw out an obviously faulty assumption (mysticism must be moral) rather than deny the obvious (e.g., that Muktananda was a great mystic) or commit the reprehensible (e.g., scapegoat authors).

Putting it differently, one might say that the superior hermeneutic is the one that can encompass and understand and even at times explain the most data, not the one that insists on denying, censoring, or reducing that which it cannot (in the case of the secular scholar) or does not want (in the case of the devotee) to see. More specifically, I am proposing: that we not fear to see the truly sexual in the genuinely spiritual, with all this implies about the roles that gender, sexual orientation, and human physiology play in religious experience; that we not assume that states of "enlightened" consciousness and psychopathology are mutually exclusive; that we not lock mystical experience away in some airtight categorical safe (like "purity" or "perfection") to protect it (and ourselves) from the moral, cross-cultural, and political issues of antinomianism, authoritarianism, nationalism, sexual abuse, and censorship that appear in these guru traditions; and that, finally and most importantly, we challenge the dichotomy between "insider" and "outsider" and not assume either that the historian, psychologist, or anthropologist who seems to be on the outside—and in many senses truly is—does not also know and appreciate something of the shimmering truths of which the insider so passionately speaks or that the insider, however devoted to an ideal, cannot also see clearly and bravely something of the actual. Scholars are not religiously inept, and disciples are not dumb.

Perhaps in the end, as many of the guru traditions themselves teach, there really is no "inside" or "outside," no nirvana or samsara (the cycle of birth and death), no either-or on which to hang our dichotomous categories and concerns. Perhaps everything, as Butterfield so eloquently put it, really is a reflection in the double mirror of ourselves and the perceived world, each reflecting the other in a world turned doubly inside-out by the gazes of the mystic and the scholar.

6

How They Really Came to Their Ideas

The Deeper Roots of Thought and Theory

1. Man has no Body distinct from his Soul; for that call'd Body is a portion of Soul discern'd by the five Senses, the chief intlets of Soul in this age.
2. Energy is the only life, and is from the Body; and Reason is the bound or outward circumference of Energy.
3. Energy is Eternal Delight.

"THE VOICE OF THE DEVIL," IN WILLIAM BLAKE'S
THE MARRIAGE OF HEAVEN AND HELL

I was now at once energized and haunted by those initial controversies in India and the States. Those experiences radicalized me as an intellectual in the simple sense that I had now abandoned the notion that the study of religion could (or should) be made palatable to the religions themselves. I had accepted my own subversion and necessary "offense." This did not mean, of course, that I now believed that every form of scholarship or every scholar must be offensive. It was simply that I realized that some forms of scholarship (particularly those that attempt to analyze race, gender, or class) will be deeply disturbing to and will be resisted by particular religious communities, especially conservative majority ones in power.

The reasons for this inevitable offense are not difficult to discern. Social systems are held together by elaborate systems of power, the unequal distribution of resources and opportunities, various forms of hierarchy, and, in my own American context, white privilege. It naturally follows, then, that any method or lens that focuses on these particular subjects will inevitably expose the rules of the game, demonstrate their historically constructed natures, and expose their injustice. The writer or teacher engages in intellectual transgression here not to be immoral but to push the system toward some fuller expression of human flourishing and justice.

This, or so it seems to me, constitutes the powerful "prophetic" dimension of the humanities (more on this in chapter 13). This is also, of course, the deep moral impulse that turns so many of us into the dreaded "liberal" voices that we in fact are. This is how a word derived from "free" has become a hated label or blunt club in conservative American discourse. It is time to take our liberalism back, and to celebrate this freedom, this intellectual prophecy, and these moral acts of transgression.

But, in doing so, we should never underestimate what is at stake: pretty much everything. To take just one example, if *any* major religious system abandoned its gender inequities, and in every area now (institutional structure, authority, symbolism, scripture, images of deity, and so on), the tradition would look nothing like it does now, if in fact it could exist at all.

My next two books were expressions of the realization and radicalization around gender, sexuality, and the study of religion: *Roads of Excess, Palaces of Wisdom* (2001) and *The Serpent's Gift* (2007). Significantly, both books were written under the aegis of the dissenting English poet and artist William Blake. Both featured beautiful Blakean pieces on their covers. *Roads* displayed a plate from *The Marriage of Heaven and Hell* (one of my favorite books of all time) that features a prostrate male with a flaming female form hovering over him, an image which, for me personally, invoked the erotic and mystical energies of that Night. *The Serpent's Gift* carried a painting of a winged Satan hovering over Eve, like some Blakean Batman, that reversed the gender dynamics of the first Blakean painting/cover. These two books developed a number of comparative arguments around gender and male sexuality that were rooted in my seminary experiences and moral and spiritual awakenings described above.

RESONANT COMPARISONS

Another major argument of both books was the camouflaged mystical or gnostic background of thought and theory in the study of religion. In *Roads*, this was articulated through the observation that scholars of mysticism sometimes employ the memories and embodied intuitions of their own anomalous encounters to tune into the anomalous states and teachings of the texts with which they work. It is in this way that a kind of deep hermeneutical resonance is set up that allows them to "see" things in the texts and traditions that others cannot generally see, particularly connections, comparisons, and correspondences. Comparison, here at least, is no random anything-goes shebang, as is often claimed. It is the expression of a deep psychospiritual or on-

tological resonance between the interpreter and the interpreted. Those outside such a resonance, of course, can only suspect or reject such comparative
acts, as they really have no access to these deeper currents of comparison and
correspondence.

Allow me to describe a relatively simple example in order to show how this
works. Readers will recall that the phenomenology of that Night was defined
by a temporary bodily paralysis that lasted through the entire event until I
could sit upright, an intense electric-like energy that was also deeply erotic,
and a resulting experience of floating or flying outside the body. Later, in *Mutants and Mystics*, I would describe the intense "vibrations" and "magnetic"
sense of this same event. There I would also implicitly identify this event as
the origin of my thoughts around the Human as Two. Those are the barest
outlines.

Now consider a classic text in modern American metaphysical literature:
Robert A. Monroe's *Journeys Out of the Body* (1971). This is the author and text
that brought into popular use the phrase "out-of-body experience," previously
known as "traveling clairvoyance" or, in its Theosophical (and ancient Neoplatonic) form, "astral projection." Monroe was a businessman and engineer who
underwent a long series of spontaneous out-of-body experiences beginning
in 1958. He eventually founded the Monroe Institute of Applied Sciences in
Virginia in order to pursue the study and technological catalyzing of psychical
phenomena.

In chapter 1, "Not with a Wand, Nor Lightly," Monroe describes how he
first stumbled upon his magic. He describes a number of states that visited
him while he was resting or sleeping (a bit humorously, always it seems on a
Sunday, while the family was away at church). During these states, his body
would feel as if it were shaking violently or "vibrating," even though, he points
out, he could see no external signs that it was shaking. One of these unusual
states appeared to be initated by a beam of light from the sky "to the north at
about a 30 degrees angle from the horizon."[1] During the latter event, he was
"powerless to move," that is, he was temporarily paralyzed: "As I slowly sat
upright on the couch, the shaking and vibration slowly faded away and I was
able to move freely."[2] He compared the "vibration" to "an electric shock running through the entire body without the pain involved," and explained how
sometimes the "surge" would begin in his head and spread from there.[3]

Soon, these states developed further and he found himself, completely
shocked now, observing the bodies of his wife and himself in bed from the
ceiling. It was very confusing: he was "down there," and yet he was also "up

here." When he asked a psychologist friend whether he might be going crazy, the friend responded with a comforting "no" and an encouragement to look into yoga and Hindu philosophy, where, the psychiatrist insisted, he would find very similar experiences described and explored.

Toward the end of the opening chapter, Monroe describes another flight that was cut short by an "overwhelmingly strong sexual drive," as if sexual expression and astral flight drew on the same occult energies and so were mutually exclusive of one another. Later, after five more episodes, he would discover "the secret of such control" and the immense importance of sexuality in the induction and maintaining of such out-of-body flight.[4] All of this would shatter his scientific materialism and lead him to explore over the next decades what he called "the Second State" and "the Second Body."[5]

Now here is my point. Before that Night, I am certain that reading these pages of Robert Monroe would have been very confusing to me. They would have sounded like gobbledygook. After all, I would have completely lacked any lived referent or existential context to which to compare them and so understand them. But *after* that Night, they all make, well, perfect sense. Indeed, they sound pretty much exactly like the bizarre energies, sexual sublimation, and floating to the ceiling that I knew that Night. Their precise correspondences and patently physical sensations of "vibration" or "energy" also make me seriously wonder if there is a real but unknown physics at work here, some subtle, living form of electromagnetism, for example.

In any case, this is what I mean by "resonant comparisons." The interpreter possesses a memory of some previous event or experience that resonates perfectly with the set of expriences being recounted in the text or tradition. Note that the utter strangeness of the events being related in the two cases to be compared only *adds* to their comparative punch, to the conviction that, despite the differences, "something is going on here, and it's the 'same' thing." Note also that none of this establishes the ontological status of such experiences nor requires any particular local framework. Nor does it result in the location of any cause or explanation. It does nothing more, but also nothing less, than set up an uncanny comparative correspondence that the interpreter in question simply cannot reasonably ignore.

These were the kinds of experiential or anomalous roots of scholarly interpretation that I explored in *Roads* through five case studies of five different major scholars of mysticism. I framed the project somewhat differently at the time, mostly through the poetics of weird Will Blake. I would now frame it, admittedly somewhat more anemically, this way:

6. Resonant Comparisons. The works of scholars of comparative mystical literature are often catalyzed by the mystical or anomalous experiences of the intellectuals themselves. These autobiographical roots set up intuitively obvious resonant patterns between the interpreter and the interpreted, patterns which are then camouflaged in their texts and secreted in their theories of religion.

I understand, of course, how this gnomon might be read as elitist. Maybe it is. So is practically every other form of specialized knowledge. I also understand, of course, how such methods can be used poorly and result in imprecise or simply misleading comparisons. But a badly used idea is not the same thing as a bad idea, and the fact remains: much of the most influential scholarship on mystical literature possesses precisely this kind of noetic or gnostic background. Moreover, the same is true in other areas of related research. I cannot count the times I have read or heard a parapsychologist or ufologist recount the reason she or he entered the field: because of a deeply personal experience of the phenomonen in question.[6]

One memory stands out for me here. I can still vividly recall Jacques Vallée reflecting back on his early scientific and historical passions for ufology and how they stemmed back to a sighting that he had as a teenager in France. He and a friend saw separately (the friend with binoculars), in broad daylight no less, a classic disk with a cupola on top floating over a neighborhood of Paris. I recall him saying to us something like this: "I am sorry, but *it was a flying saucer*." And this from a successful capital investor in the highest echelons of biomedical and space technology with an MA in astronomy and a PhD in computer science.

INTRODUCING THE ESSAY

What follows is a slightly condensed version of the first essay I published on the scholar of religion as closeted mystic, that is, on gnomon 6. Some of this material, on Louis Massignon, would find its way into *Roads*. Much of it, on Mircea Eliade and Gershom Scholem, would not, mostly because I decided that others had written a great deal about these two figures, and that I could make more of a contribution by focusing on others.

Still, I was especially intrigued with the case of Eliade, his dissertation work on Tantric yoga and his later paranormal novella *The Secret of Doctor Honigberger*, in which a fictional character named Zerlendi "wakes up asleep" and becomes fascinated with the *siddhi*s or paranormal powers of Indian yoga. I, too, of course, had "woken up asleep" in that Night, and I too would soon become similarly fascinated. Did Eliade have an experience like that Night? It sure looked like it to me. And, if he did not, how could he write lines about it in a work of fiction that read like precise phenomenological descriptions of what I had actually experienced? I was beginning to read Eliade in a mirror. I was intuiting the resonances between his life and my own. These comparative resonances would return, and then deepen, as we will see.

One figure I did choose to look at in *Roads* was the contemporary Kabbalah scholar Elliot Wolfson. I did not know it then, but Elliot would become one of my closest colleagues in whose thought, immeasurably more sophisticated, I nevertheless consistently recognize my own. Like Eliade, Elliot too would become a kind of mirror for me. His books are filled with paradoxical or "reversing" statements like this one: "to attribute human form to God is to attribute divine form to humans."[7] The line can be traveled both ways. The reduction can be reversed.

The Visitation of the Stranger

ON SOME MYSTICAL DIMENSIONS OF THE HISTORY OF RELIGIONS

(1999)

During my youth . . . I would imagine that I got up in the middle of the night and
stopped time; and while the universe hung suspended, I would read *War and Peace*
or learn to play all the Bach fugues or teach myself Chinese. . . . Perhaps this Faustian
fantasy drove me to seek in the study of Indian yoga many of the things that Eliade
had sought there before me, and many others will seek after me.

WENDY DONIGER, "TIME, SLEEP, AND DEATH IN THE LIFE, FICTION,

AND ACADEMIC WRITINGS OF MIRCEA ELIADE"

INTRODUCTION: SKEPTICISM AND MYSTICISM
IN THE HISTORY OF RELIGIONS

The Indologist, mythologist, and historian of religions Wendy Doniger has
written in numerous contexts about "myths lived by scholars who study
myths,"[8] always careful to point out that the relationship between art and life,
scholarship and biography, is never clear-cut, resembling as it does a set of
mutually reflecting "fun-house mirrors" that both distort and smooth out
the features of the "real" scholar who stands caught between the mirrors of
art and life.[9] Here I would like to extend Doniger's project from the study of
mythology to the study of mysticism and discuss the role of subjective mystical and ecstatic experiences in scholars who study mysticism. Put differently,
I want to address the twentieth-century study of mysticism as itself a kind of
mystical tradition, with its own unique history, discourses, sociological dynamics, and rhetorics of secrecy (for this, after all, is what the mystical always comes down to—something "secret" [*mustikos*]). I will do so through
brief analyses of three prominent twentieth-century historians of eligions: the
French Arabist Louis Massignon, the comparativist Mircea Eliade, and the
Kabbalah scholar Gershom Scholem.

The history of religions is an academic discipline with a distinct history in
Western forms of thought and experience. Born in the nineteenth century as

a means of ordering the numerous religious worlds that Europe was encountering in her political, economic, and missionary ventures, it has remained to this day a distinctively academic way of making sense of the foreign, the eccentric, and the strange. The historian of religions, almost by definition, it seems, is someone who deals in the exotic. Shamanic identifications with totem animals, ecstatic trips to the world of the dead, mystical unions with God, with the cosmos and with the Self, macabre visions of dismembered gods and disemboweled holy men, ascetic practices that seem to alternate between the horrible and the ridiculous, erotic spiritual experiences, myths of blood-thirsty goddesses, of godmen and of monsters neither human nor divine—these are the spiritual realities that the historian of religions seeks out in the texts, rituals and myths of the world's religions in order to experience and understand them "from within."[10]

What happens to someone who willingly enters this confusing "labyrinth"[11] of strange beings and mythological presences? Much, it seems, depends upon who that someone is. Many scholars of religion, no doubt, remain relatively unaffected, protected as they are by a thick skin of skepticism, objectivity, relativism, and religious doubt. Perhaps another layer of bitterness, anger, or cynicism protects them even further. They have a "chip on their shoulder," so to speak. They are out to prove religion wrong, to reduce it to psychological, social, or economic forces that can somehow be captured in a laboratory or traced on a computer chip. But other scholars harbor no such grudges against religion and possess, at the same time, unusual powers of imagination, receptivity, discipline, and experience. For these scholars, academic method and personal experience cannot be so easily separated. "Objectivity" is transcended, not in a shallow subjectivism that yields little more than private experiences (however profound) and personal fantasies, but in an interpersonal communion with the object of their study that produces, among other things, powerful insights into the nature of religion that stand up to the test of time and the criticisms and researches of the larger academic community. There is something genuinely "mystical" about the work of such scholars, for their interpretations and writings issue from a peculiar kind of "hermeneutical union." They do not so much "interpret" religious "data" as they unite with sacred realities, whether in the imagination, the hidden depths of the soul, or the very fabric of their psychophysical selves. Their understanding, then, is not merely academic. It is also transformative, and sometimes salvific. In a word, it is a *gnosis*.

Here I want to look at this "hermeneutical union" or academic gnosticism as it manifests itself in the lives and works of Massignon, Eliade, and Scholem.

In doing so, I will argue, not that these scholars were "mystics" in the traditional understanding of that term (they were not), but rather that their work was driven by explicitly religious concerns, and that, at certain points in their researches, their encounters took on powerful, and sometimes genuinely mystical, dimensions. I will argue, moreover, that at such moments the understanding of these scholars went far beyond the bounds of academic study or speculation. In its subjective pole, their understanding became personally transformative; in its objective pole, it produced genuine insights into the nature of the phenomena under study. It was a type of understanding that was at once passionate and critical, personal and objective, religious and academic. Finally, I will close my essay with a few thoughts on how such encounters, genuinely mystical and yet rigorously academic, might act as models for us in our own attempts to assimilate the religious truths of foreign worlds.

THE PASSION OF LOUIS MASSIGNON (1883–1962)

In the words of Herbert Mason, Louis Massignon was a man "of profound and eccentric desire."[12] Massignon's writings certainly support such an evaluation. Composed in a style that Mason describes lovingly but honestly as "herky-jerky,"[13] they move back and forth—usually with little warning—from rigorous historical prose on the most mundane and ordinary of topics to impressive flights of lyricism and mystical insight. At numerous points in his oeuvre, especially in his later "minor works," the Arabist abandons the scholarly objectivism and didacticism of "the orator who is more or less an actor playing the God of modern biblical exegesis" (whom he obviously scorns) and returns to a more intimate, and for him more natural, "testimonial" style.[14] In such deeply personal testimonies, Massignon writes openly, lyrically, passionately of what he called the "axial event"[15] of his life, his conversion in the desert of Iraq before "the visitation of the Stranger." That event would determine everything that came after it, *especially* the research and writings of the now stricken scholar. Indeed, in many ways, Massignon's dazzling oeuvre can be seen as flowing directly out of that mysterious visitation. Let us begin, then, with this experience and then turn to some of the ways it defined both the structure and content of the writings that followed.

The year was 1908. Massignon, now twenty-five, had decided to write his doctoral thesis on the tenth-century mystic and martyr of Islam, al-Hallaj. While returning from an aborted research mission in Mesopotamia, he was put under surveillance on a Turkish steamer, partly because he was suspected of espionage, but also because his increasingly erratic behavior threatened his own and the other passengers' safety (he had pointed a gun at the captain and then at his own head, swallowed three lit cigarettes, and would later become delirious, perhaps in part because of a case of malaria). When the boat stopped near the ancient ruins of Ctesiphon, Massignon, fearing for his life, tried to escape but was captured again. Back on the steamer, utterly exhausted and morally distraught over "four and a half years of amorality,"[16] Massignon tried to commit suicide with a small knife for some unspecified "horror"[17] he felt about himself, a barely veiled reference to his homosexual tendencies, about which he would speak with such candor later in his life.[18] But he was not to die that day, for around 2:30 p.m. the despairing Massignon, bound hand and foot in the captain's cabin, was suddenly struck down by what he would later call "the lightning of revelation."[19] There are numerous passing references to this event in his writings. The most beautiful and certainly the fullest account occurs in his piece, "Visitation of the Stranger: Response to an Inquiry about God":

> The Stranger who visited me, one evening in May before the Taq, cauterizing my despair that He lanced, came like the phosphorescence of a fish rising from the bottom of the deepest sea; my inner mirror revealed Him to me, behind the mask of my own features. . . . The Stranger who took me as I was, on the day of His wrath, inert in His hand like the gecko of the sands, little by little overturned all my acquired reflexes, my precautions, and my deference to public opinion.[20]

"Like the phosphorescence of a fish rising from the bottom of the deepest sea . . . like the gecko of the sands": the Ocean and the Desert paradoxically meet in the passage as the tinyness of God rising in the waters of Massignon's soul becomes the tinyness of Massignon himself, now fearfully cupped "like the gecko of the sands" in the awesome hands of God, "on the day of His wrath."

But there is another, more important, polarity hidden within this account, that between the Stranger and the Friend. Since He is utterly transcendent, God is "the Stranger" for Massignon: when "He comes into our midst, it is as a Stranger who interrupts our normal life, like a moment of rest from work, and then passes on."[21] These visits of the Stranger carry (homo)sexual overtones for Massignon, and, sometimes, hints of scandal. The Virgin Mary, "Mary of Nazareth, who offered herself to the Stranger, becoming an object of suspicion all her life,"[22] seems to be the scholar's model here. Writing in a long tradition of Christian mystical thought,[23] Massignon claims that the soul too must become such a virgin: "Before the Lord who has struck the blow, the soul becomes a woman (*l'âme se trouve femme*). . . . She starts only to commemorate in secret (*en secret*) the Annunciation, viaticum of hope, that she has conceived in order to give birth to the immortal." She has been visited by "a mysterious Stranger whom she adores" (*un Étranger mystérieux qu'elle adore*).[24] Mystical experience thus carries a definite (homo)sexual structure for Massignon, with God as the active, if invisible, male Presence or "Stranger" and the soul as a feminine creature, "who intends to remain passive, in the embrace of the real, in order to conceive it."[25] The homosexual element that seems to have helped initiate Massignon's original visitation experience is thus carried over into his later discussions of the mystical.

But this Stranger, who "penetrates" the "one single Virgin" of our hearts,[26] is balanced in Massignon's account of things by the figures of the Guest and the Friend. These figures would enter deeply into Massignon's thought to the point where he would later claim that one gains access to Semitic mysticism "only through perfect hospitality."[27] Friendship, religious experience, and research thus became virtually indistinguishable in his thought.

But there were also other friends present at the conversion, invisible friends that Massignon somehow sensed in his soul: "I felt with certainty a pure, ineffable, creative Presence suspending my sentence through the prayers of invisible persons, visitors to my prison, whose names disturbed my thought."[28] According to Massignon, these disturbing names belonged to five people, four of whom Massignon knew personally and one of whom had been dead for almost nine hundred years—al-Hallaj himself: "I would write my doctoral thesis about him begun then in Cairo."[29] Research flowed naturally out of religious experience, as if Massignon, the woman, had conceived that night in May. "Discovery antecedes theory," he would write, "commotion precedes denomination."[30] That is to say, the experience of the scholar, however confused and at first unbelievable, nevertheless constitutes the seed of all that grows out of it. And more *must* follow, for such a believer must not only become a woman and conceive God in the secret "virginal point"[31] of the soul; unlike the woman, who conceives "blindly," this believer must also "explain the notion one has of Him."[32] In other words, it is not enough to have the experience, however profound. It is not enough to conceive "blindly." One must also strive to articulate it, to express it, to make it known, for language itself, if handled properly, can draw the reader "toward the real author of the article beyond the personality of the one who signs it,"[33] and the proper technical terms, gleaned from the biographies of the mystics, can enable the researcher "'to enter into the presence' of the One whom no Name *a priori* dare evoke."[34] Such "inspired" articles and mystico-linguistic studies began for Massignon shortly after the visitation of the Stranger. They would continue to flow for over fifty years, the varied fruit of the scholar's mystico-erotic "conception."

Behind many of these writings was Massignon's deep conviction that somehow a tenth-century mystic had reached across history and helped effect his conversion. Indeed, Massignon believed that all five invisible intercessors had the power of reaching across time and space through their "transmissive compassion"[35] and prayers. Nor were they alone in their powers. According to Massignon, there is an elite corps of human beings who by their willing assumption of "the blind anguish of living multitudes" understand the efficacy of vicarious suffering and announce "its transcendental glory." It is this line of hidden saints that constituted for Massignon "the secret of history."[36] Al-Hallaj, "who died crucified for the pure, inacessible love of God"[37] and in order to unite his fellow Muslims in the Unity of God, was one such hidden ruler of history. Certainly he was the most important and influential presence in Massignon's life, a fact to which the scholar's immense magnum opus on the mystic and martyr amply testifies.

Massignon admitted that such a claim might seem "queer"[38] to those who have not experienced its reality, but he nevertheless continued to apologetically[39] share in print with his fellow historians of religions the strange instances of his own "premonitorial dreams"[40] and experiences of this transmissive compassion and continued to insist that such cases of vicarious suffering possess a real "parapsychological genuineness."[41] Clearly he was speaking out of his own experience of that desert May night of 1908. Years later, as if still struggling to find a vocabulary with which to "conceive Him," he would stammer out whole paragraphs filled with words drawn from disciplines and fields as disparate as Sanskrit symbolism, parapsychology, modern cosmology, Greek theology, and Jungian depth psychology in order to communicate this deepest of his convictions:

> Here lies the ford, the wade (*tirtha*), for crossing—from paraspychological research to the invisible realm. Here we get on from the "orderly" material world, through a distortion (Einsteinian) of Space *and* Time to an "overorderly," chrono-grammatically personalized "constellation" of human events: no longer casualized, but as Jung says, "synchronized" by their intelligible meaning; which

appears *apotropaic*, i.e., transmissible—not genealogically, but as a chain of spiritual rings.[42]

"A distortion of Space *and* Time": Massignon intentionally underlines that "and," for he knows and proclaims that the single most significant presence of his life is a man who has been dead for over nine hundred years: "I do not pretend that the study of his life has yielded to me the secret of his heart, but rather it is he who has fathomed mine and who fathoms it still."[43] The researched had become the researcher, the "reader of hearts" who knew Massignon across the centuries and now guided his life.

This mystical "correspondance"[44] over time, with which Massignon simultaneously plumbed both his own biography and that of Hallaj, constituted the secret of his lifelong research on the "Passion of al-Hallaj." Certainly the very title of Massignon's magnum opus speaks of this "hermeneutical union" between the researcher and the researched. For al-Hallaj's "Passion" was not only an "essential, insatiable, transfiguring divine Desire" (*le Désir divin, essential, insatiable et transfigurant*)[45] that united his soul to the divine Beloved; it was also an anguished suffering, a literal crucifixion, that by its very intensity and mystical efficacy somehow united the mystic to Massignon himself across the farthest reaches of space and time. Such an event, Massignon writes, fulfills "the 'hope against hope' of a miracle appearing in the center of the universe, which could change our hyperextension through an involution, and unite us as freedmen of a Hidden Guest, half-veiled as before dawn."[46] With this miracle, this "hole" in the fabric of space and time, the goal of Massignon's "mystical hermeneutic" had been reached. The Stranger, through a Friend, had become the Guest.

MIRCEA ELIADE'S TANTRIC YOGA (1907–1986)

When we turn to the life and writings of Mircea Eliade, we see a similar dialectic between method and experience, but here the initial "axial event" was structured around themes profoundly different from those of Massignon's "visitation of the Stranger." If Massignon's experience in the deserts of Mesopotamia, with its constant stress on purity and absolute transcendence, was preeminently Muslim,[47] Eliade's experiences in India, to the extent that they fused the transcendent and the phenomenal worlds in a paradoxical unity, were preeminently Hindu, and to be more precise, Tantric.

Eliade's defining experiences occurred, like Massignon's, away from home in the strange land of his doctoral research—in his case, India. But before we get to his discoveries in India, we must first look, however briefly, at his researches in Rome a few years before. He had spent some time in Italy in 1927 and 1928 doing research on his master's thesis on Renaissance Italian philosophy. It was in Rome that he first encountered the *coincidentia oppositorum* doctrine of Nicolas of Cusa, who postulated that God was best defined as a "union of opposites." Later Eliade would explain how Cusa's doctrine acted like a catalyst on his thought. Certainly it would follow him to India where he encountered a Hindu version of it in the mystical texts of yoga and discovered, through many personal trials and painful failures, that it was his destiny to embody and live out its truths in his own paradoxical life.

In 1928, shortly after his discoveries in Rome, Eliade traveled to India to study Indian philosophy with Surendranath Dasgupta, at that time the world authority on the subject. With the Bengali pundit he would discover the Tantric texts and their insistence on "the possibility of a blessed and autonomous existence, here on earth and in Time."[48] Unlike the Upanishads and the tradition of Vedanta, whose doctrines Eliade knew but found lacking,[49] Tantric yoga sought to transform one's psycho-physiological experience of the world through bold, alchemical-like physical disciplines and sacramental rituals of a deeply sensual, and sometimes sexual, nature. For Eliade, Tantra was a tradition that "exalts incarnate existence as the only mode of being in the world in which absolute freedom can be won."[50] From the very beginning, catalyzed by Cusa's *coincidentia oppositorum* and his own ethnic roots in the "cosmic religion" of ancient European folklore, Eliade seems to have been attracted to such a dialectical vision. Certainly he tried to realize it, both in his practice of yoga in India and in his romantic encounters, first with Dasgupta's daughter, Maitreyi, and then with a certain "Jenny" in Shivananda's Himalayan ashram. He seems to have been much more successful at yoga than romance, for whereas he would later "camouflage" his own mystical experiences of yoga, which he claimed were quite genuine and real, in his novels, his romances proved to be disastrous. Dasgupta, with whom he was living at the time and who had more or less adopted him as a beloved son, sent him packing when he learned of his student's affair with his own daughter;[51] just a few months later, as if reliving a pattern, Eliade would have to leave his newfound Himalayan ashram after his nightly Tantric experiments with Jenny were discovered.[52]

But these "failures" themselves taught Eliade an important lesson: "I could not know it then, but eternal *maya*, in her blind wisdom, had set those two girls on my path in order to help me find my true destiny."[53] Eliade explains:

What I had tried to do—renounce my Western culture and seek a 'home' or a 'world' in an exotic spiritual universe—was equivalent in a sense to a premature renunciation of all my creative potentialities. . . . To believe that I could, at twenty-three, sacrifice history and culture for 'the Absolute' was further proof that I had not understood India. My vocation was culture, not sainthood.[54]

By his own confession, Eliade did not have "a mystical vocation,"[55] for it was his "destiny" to live "paradoxically," "to exist concurrently in 'History' and beyond it. . . . Not *les extremes me touchent*—but *coincidentia oppositorum*." Such an existence, "camouflaged in biographical incidents and creations of a cultural order," was, as he discovered, his "religious mode of being in the world."[56] It was his experiences in India, both mystical and romantic, that taught Eliade this basic truth about himself and his world. We might speculate that he came to such a vocation through his dreams as well, for, like Massignon, Eliade believed in the role of premonitorial dream visions in deciphering one's destiny: "I believe that in such dreams, which I can sometimes recall very clearly, one is being given an autorevelation of one's own destiny."[57]

As for his experiments with yoga, they would prove to be very significant for him, for they taught him "the reality of experiences that cause us to 'step out of time' and 'out of space.'"[58] Since he doubted that he would be able to describe in "scientific prose"[59] the nature of such experiences, he would later "camouflage" them in his literary writings, and particularly in his novella *The Secret of Doctor Honigberger*. Eliade explains:

In describing Zerlendi's Yoga exercises in *The Secret of Doctor Honigberger*, I included certain pieces of information, drawn from my own experiences, that I omitted from my books on Yoga. At the same time, however, I added other, inaccurate touches, precisely in order to camouflage the true data. . . . [The reader] would then be led to conclude that all the rest is invented— imaginary—too, which isn't the case.[60]

There is much in Zerlendi's experiences that is classically "mystical." Consider, for example, the following passage, on the "waking sleep" of the yogi, a common theme in mystical literature in both the West and the East. The narrator of the story, a Romanian Indologist (obviously Eliade!), is reading the secret journals of Zerlendi, a Romanian doctor who had literally "disappeared" while experimenting with the occult practices of yoga. Trying to figure out exactly what happened, the narrator comes across the following passage in Zerlendi's cryptic journal:

> I really don't know how it happened, but after some time I woke up sleeping, or, more precisely, I woke up in sleep, without having fallen asleep in the true sense of the word. My body and all my senses sank into deeper and deeper sleep, but my mind didn't interrupt its activity for a single instant. Everything in me had fallen asleep except the clarity of consciousness.[61]

Whether such an account, and many others like it, are "pure fiction" or are accurate, if "literary," reflections of Eliade's own yogic experiences is difficult to say. Eliade's camouflaging technique prevents us from ever truly knowing. Art and life merge imperceptibly here. Certainly, however, the novella as a whole and Eliade's admitted camouflaging technique witness to Eliade's genuine experiences of at least the preliminary stages of yoga.

Drawing on the conviction born in these states and working out of his discovery of his own *coincidentia oppositorum*, Eliade would use, however consciously, these experiences as models to write about the Tantric yogi in his doctoral thesis and later, in his more theoretical books, about the nature of religious experience in general. In his famous *Yoga: Immortality and Freedom* (the published version of his dissertation), for example, Eliade wrote about Tantric yoga and its own "conjunction of opposites." Expressed both symbolically and ritually through sexual union, such a state effects a "non-conditioned existence"[62] in which one becomes conscious that "the ultimate nature of the phenomenal world is identical with that of the absolute."[63] According to Eliade, a similar "paradox of opposites" is found at that base of every sacred form:[64]

> The paradox of opposites is found at the base of every religious experience. Indeed, any hierophany, any manifestation of the sacred in the world illustrates a *coincidentia oppositorum*: an object, a creature, a gesture becomes sacred—that is, transcends this world—yet continues to remain what it was before: an object, a creature, a gesture; it participates in the world and at the same time transcends it.

Such a notion, which he first came across in Nicolas of Cusa and then "realized" in his own Tantric experiments, he would later employ as an overarching methodological principle in his morphology of religious forms, evident in such works as *The Sacred and the Profane* and *Patterns in Comparative*

Religion. His early work (and experience) of Tantric yoga and his later morphology of religious forms, in other words, were united through the common category of the *coincidentia oppositorum.*[65] The category may have had its historical roots in the theology of Nicolas of Cusa, but, as Eliade used the term, it clearly carried with it the psychological structures and personal lessons of Eliade's own yogic experiences and (by his own confession) illusory romances.[66]

Both Eliade's *Yoga: Immortality and Freedom* and Massignon's *The Passion of al-Hallaj* were originally dissertations in which the researcher and the researched were "united" in unusually powerful ways. Like Massignon's *The Passion,* moreover, Eliade's *Yoga* contains within its very title the key, at once experiential and categorical, to much that followed. Whereas in Massignon's case the emphasis was unmistakably on the word "passion," in Eliade's case, it rested squarely on the term "freedom." For Eliade, Tantric yoga was interesting, not because it insisted on some transcendent "liberation" *from* the world, as did Vedanta and most of classical Indian religious thought, but because it promised a "freedom" *within* a divinized world.[67] "Everything depends upon what is meant by freedom," he would write in the very last line of his *Yoga.*[68] For Eliade, at least, "freedom" harked back to the paradigmatic mystical state of the Tantric yogi, "liberated in life" (*jivanmukta*), who does not deny incarnate existence but seeks to "magically" transform it into a new, essentially dialectical unity of "formal existence and the nonformed."[69] This strikingly Tantric state, itself highly suggestive of the *coincidentia oppositorum* around which Eliade would structure his morphology of religious forms, is what Eliade would seek to realize in his own life to the very end, even if, as he would say, it had to be "camouflaged in biographical incidents and creations of a cultural order." How fitting it was, then, when Wendy Doniger chose to read the last pages of Eliade's *Yoga,* those devoted to this "freedom," for the scholar's memorial service.[70] The end of Eliade's life thus coincided with the end of his *Yoga* and its hard-won conclusion: "Everything depends upon what is meant by freedom."

GERSHOM SCHOLEM'S MOUNTAIN (1897–1982)

Moshe Idel has described Gershom Scholem, the father of modern Kabbalah studies, as a "theoretical mystic," a theorist of both Kabbalah and the mystical experience who once practiced Kabbalistic techniques but who nevertheless was something of a "failure qua mystic." Yet he was, Idel tells us, "one who longed for mystical experience."[71] Scholem was also a scholar who could speak of "a kind of inner compass" that guided his spiritual quest,[72] and he was not above describing his academic studies in deeply emotional and explicitly religious terms: "this field, the study of Kabbalah and Jewish mysticism," he once confessed to an audience, "drew me like a magnet, so that my involvement therein involved rather less wisdom or reflection and rather more enchantment, magic, and love."[73]

But perhaps nowhere does this complex mix of desire and failure come out more clearly than in an unusual letter that the scholar wrote for the sixtieth birthday of his friend, the publisher Zalman Schocken. Scholem titles the letter "A Candid Word about the True Motives of My Kabbalistic Studies." I quote portions of it below:

> And perhaps it wasn't so much the key that was missing, but courage: courage to venture out into an abyss, which one day could end up in us ourselves, courage also to penetrate through the symbolic plain and through the wall of history. For the mountain, the corpus of facts, needs no key at all; only the misty wall of history, which hangs around it, must be penetrated. To penetrate it was the task I set for myself. Will I get stuck in the mist, will I, so to say, suffer a "professorial death"? But the necessity of historical criticism and critical history cannot be replaced by anything else, even where it demands sacrifices. Certainly, history may seem to be fundamentally an illusion, but an illusion without which in temporal reality no insight into the essence of things is possible. For today's man, that mystical totality of "truth," whose existence disappears particularly when it is projected into historical time, can only become visible in the purest way in the legitimate discipline of commentary and in the singular mirror of philological criticism. Today, as at the very beginning, my work lives in this paradox, in the hope of a true communication from the mountain, of that most invisible, smallest fluctuation of history which causes truth to break forth from the illusions of "development."[74]

Scholem's desire to penetrate "through the wall of history" and his fear of an academic stagnation, a "professorial death," are both evident here. And yet he also insists on combining the mystical and the intellectual, the historical and the transcendent, for the nature of revelation demands it. History, the place of revelation, is a paradoxical sort of affair for Scholem, since, although "fundamentally an illusion," no real insight "into the essence of things" is possible without it (here we are reminded of Eliade's *coincidentia*). Thus that atemporal mystical truth "whose existence disappears particularly when it is projected into historical time" only becomes visible to the scholar in "the legitimate discipline of commentary and in the singular mirror of philological criticism." It is only in language, in doctrine reflected in the "singular mirror of philological criticism" that the mystical world of the Kabbalist (or any mystic) can be understood and experienced. Like Moses, the scholar must climb back up the "mountain of facts" that is history and language in order to witness the revelation of God.

Scholem's unique blending of the mystical and the academic reveals itself in other contexts in his rejection of "experience" as an adequate criterion of religious truth, in his absolute insistence on the rigors of philology and historical criticism, and in his defense of scholarly "distance." Scholem was particularly critical of Martin Buber's emphasis on "primal experience" (*Urerlebnis*) and "intense emotional experience" (*Erlebnis*) as adequate sources of religious truth, for such subjective states were elusive and all too devoid of content.[75] Moreover, although historical criticism is "not the key that opens all of the locked chambers" and "there are intuitions and reflections that penetrate (or claim to penetrate) to the depths,"[76] the genuinely esoteric, metaphysical truths to be learned within history can only be uncovered and revealed with the tools of historical criticism; they can only be found by "going to the sources" (*zu den Quellen gehen*), that is, by learning Hebrew.[77] Indeed, historical criticism is doubly important, for "it protects us from the illusions and self-deceits that we all love so much," and it establishes a solid foundation upon which to build any future mysticism: "Whoever denies the methods of historical criticism holds in contempt its conclusions or attempts to avoid them, builds his structure upon quicksand, and will in the end pay the price for his alienation."[78]

Finally, very much related to this scholarly stubbornness was Scholem's defense of academic "distance": "I am actually of the opinon that whosoever identifies fully with his subject loses a certain scholarly measure without which there can be no research. A scholar is not a priest; and it is a mistake to attempt to make a priest out of a scholar."[79] Scholarship, in other words, is *not* mysticism and has its own integrity.

Still, Scholem was far from discounting the possible mystical dimensions of scholarship, even of a "distant" scholarship. "Profound philology can have a genuine mystical function," he would write in another context.[80] Here we are reminded immediately of Massignon's conviction that the technical terms of Muslim mysticism were not borrowed or created but were "discovered" by the early Muslim mystics and "minted" into "anagogical" realities[81] that could take the mystic, and the researcher who properly meditates on them,[82] to the very heights to which they allude. But "philology," as it was for Massignon, is more than a study of words for Scholem. It is also a study of the *history* of technical terms and myths.[83] Trained in the *Religionsgeschichteschule* or "History of Religions School" of late nineteenth- and early twentieth-century German scholarship, Scholem continually sought to trace the "transfer of certain mythological topoi from one particular religious tradition to another."[84] The main instrument of this search for patterns and "major trends" was philology. Perhaps it was in this sense, at once terminological, mythical, and historical, that Scholem claimed that "philology" can have a genuine mystical function.

In the end, though, Scholem was melancholy and dubious about the possibility of a renewed Jewish mysticism in our time in the sense of a series of "awakenings of individuals leading to new forms of mystical teachings or to significant movements in public life."[85] Certainly there have always been and always will be "wild flourishings of private mysticism of which we know nothing and which existed without leaving a trace in the living literature and tradition."[86] But such private, subjective experiences—so commonly talked about today in popular and academic discourse—have no real historical significance, for, lacking a solid grounding in sacred text and tradition, they fail to nourish community with new interpretations of history and faith.

It is thus unlikely that there can be a "new Kabbalah" today. Why? Ironically, because of the same historical criticism that Scholem insisted must be central to any modern Kabbalistic experience. As Scholem points out, the basic assumption upon which all Kabbalah is based is "the acceptance of the Torah, in the strictest and most precise understanding of the content of the word of God."[87] And Scholem is quite clear—in our modern period, in which the potential mystic's "path has become clouded by history and historical criticism,"[88] such an "absolute belief" can only become an "absolute obstacle": "We do not believe in Torah from heaven in the specific sense of a fixed body of revelation having infinite significance. And without this basic assumption one cannot move."[89]

Modern religious people are thus left with the ultimate question of "whether there is any hope of creating public forms of fundamentally mystic inspiration even in the absence of any positive dogmatic basis."[90] Scholem is not particularly hopeful here—he ends the speech by acknowledging that he has been "unable to bring any concrete tidings"[91]—but he does provocatively invoke the American poet Walt Whitman and Richard Bucke's "cosmic consciousness" as possible hints of a future "secular mysticism." "These are things," he concludes, "which may perhaps allude to the possibility of a mystical embodiment in nontraditional forms."[92] Perhaps. In the meantime, historical-critical research has clearly opened up a "door," a door "leading to a hidden chamber, and we do not know what else is hidden there."[93] The mystical as "the hidden" and "the secret" thus returns in Scholem, if not in the present or in the future, at least in possibilities of solid scholarship.

To sum up, we might say that, unlike Massignon's "passion" to desire a male God, suffer for others, and communicate with a temporally distant mystic and Eliade's dream to effect a Tantric "union" (*yoga*) of the transcendent and the imminent, Scholem's life was driven by a search through the "misty wall of history" for "a true communication from the mountain." The suffering and passionate martyr of Massignon and the paradoxical Tantric yogi of Eliade are here answered by the ironic, modern Jew, straining to witness the revelation on the sacred mountain in a secular age disturbingly devoid of true tradition.

CONCLUSION: SEEKING THE STRANGER TODAY

I have presented the cases of Massignon, Eliade, and Scholem as models for what a modern, intellectually rigorous, and yet genuinely religious approach to the world's religions might look like. If these three lives do not offer us religious certainty on any particular doctrinal isssue, they most certainly offer us hope, for each of them tried, and to some extent succeeded, to understand and experience the depth and variety of human religious experience. Certainly each of them conceived their disciplines "as part of the struggle for regaining a new and adequate spirituality."[94] In this struggle, their theoretical programs and their religious experiences became mutually intertwined through the weavings of innumerable biographical, intellectual, sexual, psychic, and, as Massignon would say, even parapsychological threads. At some points in their quests, moreover, both theory and experience took on genuinely "mystical" qualities, for in such moments the researcher and the researched were united in ways that far surpass ordinary academic methods and models. Moreover, all three engaged the esoteric rhetorics of the mystical traditions they studied: Massignon provocatively ignored them, sharing often his most intimate sexual and mystical secrets; Eliade, on the other hand, in a more classically "mystical" vein, camouflaged his ecstatic experiences in his fiction; finally, Scholem, like the Kabbalists he studied, found the secret revealed in the sacred texts and their hermeneutical deciphering.

I have presented these three unusually rich and complex lives with the hope that they might function as models for us in our own attempts to understand

and critically appropriate our own religious histories. More specifically, I would hope that their examples might help prevent us from wandering into at least two mistaken fronts. For religionists, they might suggest that the facile anti-intellectualism into which they sometimes slip is both sterile and a bit unbelievable—scholars, after all, are sometimes also mystics. Moreover, and perhaps more importantly, as Scholem never tired of pointing out, any modern tradition built on a rejection of historical criticism is a house built on quicksand. It can only sink, and sink quickly, with time. For historians of religions, on the other hand, such examples might remind them of the genuinely mystical, if submerged, dimensions of their own discipline and lead them to ask if objectivity and relativism are really the best ways to understand human religious experience. In a world such as ours, we cannot afford a sanctity devoid of intellectual integrity and discipline, but neither can we endure an intellectualism intolerant of the essentially religious nature of human being.

Finally, perhaps it is not too bold of me to suggest that the lives and works of these three scholars offer us genuine hope in our own individual religious quests, for they suggest that we too, under the right conditions and with the proper intellectual, imaginative, and religious training, might someday "step 'out of space' and 'out of time'" or understand the "mystical function" of profound philology. Perhaps we might even experience a "visitation of the Stranger" and come to realize with Massignon that even the most fearful Stranger can sometimes become a Friend.

7

The Gnostic Reversal

The Snake That Bites Its Own Tail

> We are not human beings having a spiritual experience; we are spiritual beings having a human experience.
>
> SAYING ATTRIBUTED TO TEILHARD DE CHARDIN

I would soon pursue a history of contemporary "secular mysticisms" and their various expressions of a "mystical embodiment in nontraditional forms," of which Scholem wrote with reference to Walt Whitman's panerotic "spirituality" and Richard Maurice Bucke's vision of an evolving "cosmic consciousness." But that would all come later. I saw none of that as I was writing *Roads of Excess* (2001) and, a bit later, *The Serpent's Gift* (2007). These two books were focused intensely on the study of religion itself, which is to say: on other professional intellectuals.

The Serpent's Gift took the project of *Roads* one step further. It was a self-conscious attempt not just to write about scholars as closeted mystics, but to walk the talk and *write mystical literature as scholarship*. It was an act of coming out of the closet. It was an act of setting aside most of the academic conventions in which I had been trained, instead speaking my mind more or less as it spoke, or hissed, to me. What are articulated in the present volume as gnomons 1 and 2 constituted the majority of the hissing there. The book was in fact my first attempt to systematize my thought in four such gnomons, which I called *logoi mystikoi*.

THE SERPENT'S GIFT

The book began with the central trope of my first two books: the erotic. Rhetorically speaking, *The Serpent's Gift* was a retelling of the biblical story of Adam and Eve, this time from the perspective of the snake as I imagined this wisdom figure to be embodied in the modern study of religion and its erotic, humanistic, mystical, and esoteric forms of gnosis.¹ It was a strange tale, with the usual protagonists and antagonists reversed. Inspired by early gnostic Christians who could not help noticing just who in the story was graciously bestowing knowledge (the serpent) and who was jealously and rather pettily trying to prevent it (God), I took the ancient gnostic myth as a powerful and ultimately positive parable for all of us who would wish to "grow up," leave the garden of our sexual and religious innocences, and venture forth into larger, if admittedly more ambiguous, visions of the world, ourselves, and the divine.

I began the book by pointing out that early Jewish and Christian commentators often interpreted the story in sexual terms. Indeed, these were so common that Augustine (354–430) found it necessary to argue against the symbolic equation of "tree" and "sexual intercourse" in his *The Literal Meaning of Genesis*.² I also pointed out that modern American English use has its own similar insights, even if we do not always recognize their connection to these first few chapters of the Bible. English speakers, for example, speak jokingly of how "he knew her" (with a very heavy and winking accent on *knew*), of "carnal knowledge," and of so-and-so being "forbidden fruit"—all transparently sexual innuendos that take us back to the garden story. One of the many local erotica and pornography stores in my Houston neighborhood bears the licensed logo of the national franchise: "Adam & Eve." Obviously, whether we admit it or not, we already know that the forbidden fruit of the tree of knowledge of good and evil that God forbid the beautiful couple to eat was sex—sweet, delicious sex.

Well, sort of. Actually, the fruit was clearly not just "sex," as we use that word much too loosely today. Rather, the fruit functions in the story as a type of erotic gnosis that was understood to effect, immediately, both moral awareness and the partial divinization of the human being. The fruit of the knowledge of good and evil that the knowing serpent offers the couple to eat, after all, is understood by the myth to be both a kind of partial divinization and a preparatory stage to the couple awakening more fully to their own immortal natures. Indeed, God states quite clearly that the couple has already "become like one of us" through the act of eating the fruit (which implies that sex is divine), exactly as the serpent promised, and later points out that, should the couple manage to eat of the second tree of life, they would live forever, that is, they would become gods.

In a rather tragic way for Western religious thought, then, the story seems to suggest that God stands against our own moral maturity, against sexuality, and against the divinization of human nature through the acquisition of knowledge and sensual pleasure. It also insinuates that we all die because our first parents "knew" each other within the intimate gnosis of sexual intercourse. Because they fucked, we're screwed. Through this troubling logic, the serpent's gift was turned into an ancient curse and the gracious giver into the Devil himself.

The modern study of religion, I argued in *The Serpent's Gift*, can help us to recognize the wise snake, the lovely loving couple, and the angry, jealous god among us. The fruit still hangs before us, and the serpent still hisses its promised gift. And it is up to us now what comes next, that is, how we tell the story from here.

THINK THE THIRD

I had my own way of telling the story from here. I proposed that we move "beyond reason" and "beyond belief" into a more radically reflexive epistemology that I chose to label "gnostic." I was inspired here by the work of Gilles Quispel, the Dutch historian of gnosticism and friend of C. G. Jung who once noted that there are three major strands of Western culture: *faith*, a way of knowing the world and oneself via religious doctrines, themselves dependent upon divine revelation and the authoritative creeds of the religious communities; *reason*, a form of knowledge deriving, at least in the West, from Greek philosophy and logic that relies on analytic and linear thought, empirical sense data and doubt to arrive at the objective truth of things (it is this form of knowledge, of course, that resulted in the scientific method); and, finally, *gnosis*, a form of intuitive, visionary or mystical knowledge that privileges the primacy of personal experience and the depths of the self over the claims of both faith and reason, traditionally in order to acquire some form of liberation or salvation from a world seen as corrupt or fallen.[3] As Greek reason morphed into modern science, could ancient gnosis now morph into the study of religion? Has it already?

Here I observed that whereas the public faces of the study of religion have alternated back and forth between visages of faith and reason, the field in fact encompasses, and has always encompassed, faith, reason, *and* gnosis in both its history and philosophical structures. Is this not what I was trying to get at in *Roads* with the mystical lives of the scholars of mysticism? I wanted to extend and develop those readings now. I wanted to read the study of religion as a gnostic project that cannot be properly appreciated, much less fully realized, without engaging its deconstructive, apophatic, and implicitly mystical dimensions.

In other words, without in any way denying the relationship of the discipline to the history of faith, or for that matter to a deeply ambiguous history of colonialism, or its central reliance on reason and doubt as methods of inquiry, I wished to emphasize its positive, transformative, experiential, intuitive, and gnostic powers. What I was *not* doing was rejecting the reductive methods and social-scientific scholarship of the contemporary academy. Nor was I suggesting a simple resolution of the tension between faith and reason via gnosis.

In the model I worked out in the book, the gnostic intellectual is the one who privileges knowledge over belief, who knows that she knows, *and* knows that what she knows cannot possibly be reconciled with the claims of any past or present religious tradition, including the ancient gnostic Judaisms and Christianities, whose common radical dualisms and consistent rejections of the body, sexuality, and the physical world render any simplistic mimicking of these elaborate mythological systems quite impossible and hardly desirable. To borrow an expression from Elaine Pagels, such a gnostic epistemology or way of knowing is quite literally "beyond belief."[4] It is also, however, quite "beyond reason," at least if we restrict reason to the reductive sociopolitical Marxisms of much humanities scholarship, the quantitative models of the social sciences, or the extreme relativisms of so much postmodern thought.

THE GNOSTIC REVERSAL

Again, I was not attempting some kind of futile return back to the symbolic and ritual worlds of the third century or the Nag Hammadi library. I was attempting to name a particular kind of intellectual reflexivity, a "reversal," "flip" or "reflexive rereading," whereby one used reason to reduce the divine—that is, all religious experience and expression—back to the human, only to discover that the human overflows any and all purely rationalist or materialist models; that it is, in effect, "divine." I wanted us to acknowledge the moral ambiguity and human suffering of the first tree, but not to forget about the distant promise of the second tree.

And why not? Once we locate a line between religious experience and human nature (and we, of course, have accomplished this a hundredfold over the last two centuries), we can travel *either way* along that line. We can travel in one direction along that line and reduce the religious "down" to the human, but we can also reverse direction and travel from the human back "up" to the religious. The reduction can be reversed or transduced, exactly as we saw Elliot Wolfson doing at the end of the last chapter's introduction: "to attribute human form to God is to attribute divine form to humans."

Here is how I would now summarize the same academic gnoseology:

7. The Gnostic Reversal and Reflexive Rereadings. The study of religion possesses both Enlightenment and Romantic roots. Both together can form gnos-

tic epistemologies that employ robust rational models to "reduce" the religious back to the human only to "reverse" or "flip" the reduction back toward theological or mystical ends. These are what we might call reflexive rereadings of religion.

I did not arrive at this "reversal method" through any logical cognitive process. I arrived at it through broad reading in philosophy and the history of the study of religion (particularly Feuerbach's "reversal method") in an attempt to understand the structures of my own thinking, which, I began to notice, consistently took on this "loopy" reflexive structure, no matter what subject or historical material I was examining. I became very curious about this hissing consistency. I began to suspect that it stemmed back to that Night, that—to invoke the computer metaphors that everyone seems enamored with these days—what I was seeing in my writing and thought were multiple applications of a common "operating system" that had been put in place through a kind of rewiring or reprogramming effected by the noetic energies that had beamed into me that Night. This anyway had now become my personal mythos, my way of understanding the structure and consistency of my own thought, which I did not quite think but which thought me.

This "flip" was most obvious in the robust forms of reductionism I commonly employed, mostly of the Freudian sort but which were also deeply informed by feminist, Foucauldian, and Marxist thought. As they now thought me, they always insisted on a "something left over" that could not be explained away by such reductionisms and rationalisms. Such a dialectical method was already explicit in *Kālī's Child* (1995), even if it was not fully articulated as such. There it was framed in the South Asian epistemologies of Tantra, where spirit is experienced and expressed through sex, but where sex is also sublimated into spirit. Indeed, as we have already seen, the yogic hydraulic techniques that are designed to sublimate the sexual fluids or energies from the genitals up into the brain are sometimes referred to as the "reversal" method, and the ascetic is sometimes called an *urdhva-retas*, that is, one whose semen is "reversed" or "turned up." There is an energy line or subtle channel in the body here, *and it flows both ways.*

What I did in *Kālī's Child* was put these two ways in conversation—I related the reductive methods of Western psychoanalysis to the sublimating methods of Indian Tantra, and vice versa. I gave the Tantric yogic methods an intellectual form, turned them into an academic theory—a kind of Tantric yoga of reading, as it were. It was in this way that I got the thing flowing both ways. If there are potential erotic dimensions to the mystical, then there are potential mystical dimensions to the erotic.

But again, I was not fully aware of all of this when I wrote *Kālī's Child*. I was just a graduate student. It was a dissertation, a first try. It was only in the next two books that this reflexive reversal and the gnostic outlines of my thought began to take on some clear shape. And now I was very much aware of what was happening, and I was trying my best to cooperate. The secret body was making itself known. I was learning to speak, or hiss, for myself.

THE DEEPER ROOTS OF COMPARISON

There were other arguments in *The Serpent's Gift*. One was that the professional study of religion displays all sorts of deep historical and conceptual resonances with ancient gnostic and mystical thought. Here I isolated four basic shared resonances or meta-themes: eroticism, humanism, comparativism, and esotericism.

To take just one here, I suggested that comparativism can be practiced on many levels and in many modes, but that, historically speaking, some of its most sophisticated expressions have been aligned with what we now call mysticism. More specifically, they have been aligned with apophatic mystical literature, that is, philosophically informed literature that deconstructs or "says away" (*apo-phasis*) the most basic cognitive, cultural, and religious assumptions of the reader in order to reveal deeper and more universal states of mind and energy.

Here, for example, we have the general Neoplatonic superstructure (think the influential corpus of Pseudo-Dionysius) of so much of Jewish, Christian, and Islamic mystical literature. Here also we can comfortably place numerous forms of non-Western thinking, from the Hindu Upanishads ("Not this! Not this!") and the Buddhist category of "emptiness," with its elaborate philosophical expressions, to the Chinese Dao ("The Dao that can be spoken is not the Dao").[5] In each case, the culture in question engages in profound comparative acts, affirming the surface cognitive, egoic, and cognitive structures, but also denying them for deeper, and more universal, forms of mind and being. These traditions of thought and practice are not the same, but they are *counter-coherent*, that is, they are similar in the nuanced ways that they deconstruct or "say away" their local cultural and cognitive constructs in order to realize some deeper reality.

Here is how I would now put that basic conceptual and historical thesis ("mystics" here, by the way, refers to both historical human beings but also to the double discipline of deconstruction and affirmation, as in "physics"):

8. Comparative Mystics. The deepest roots of critical theory in the comparative study of religion lie in apophatic mystical literature, which is to say that they lie in the nature of consciousness itself before and beyond any local cultural shaping of that same consciousness.

I implicitly made this argument about the mystical roots of comparativism in both *Roads* and *The Serpent's Gift*, but it would soon become much more explicit as I worked on the counterculture and came to see the deeper historical pattern more clearly. And it would become a major theme in my textbook, *Comparing Religions*, which began with this famous line from the medieval Sufi philosopher Ibn al-'Arabi: "Be then, within yourself, a receptacle for the forms of all beliefs, for God is too vast and too great to be confined to one belief to the exclusion of another, for indeed He says, 'Wheresoever ye turn, there is the Face of God.'"

INTRODUCING THE ESSAY

The Serpent's Gift garnered a number of responses. Probably the most significant was from the Dutch historian of Western esotericism Wouter Hanegraaff. I deeply admire Hanegraaff's work and thinking. And, like the work of Elliot Wolfson, if in a very different key, I recognize my own thought in the mirror of Wouter's much more erudite books. I have worked closely with Wouter over the years on a number of projects, including four annual symposia on the history of Western esotericism at Esalen and a volume on esotericism and eroticism that came out of one of these symposia.[6] As will become obvious in part 2 of this volume, his thought has become more and more central to my own projects.

Wouter was the first to use the word "oeuvre" to describe my work, in a review essay of *The Serpent's Gift* in 2008 (to which this chapter's anthologized essay is a response). After summarizing the controversial reception history of my early books, he wrote this: "Kripal is evidently not just writing books, but working on an *oeuvre* in the true sense; his writings do not stand apart from one another, but should be seen rather as parts of a larger intellectual gestalt, which is organically evolving and taking shape as its author is working out the implications of certain germinal ideas."[7] In many ways, the present volume is a result of Hanegraaff's naming. It is an attempt to work out the implications of those "certain germinal ideas."

But Wouter and I also have our real differences. He is the scholar's scholar, the exquisite historian committed to the intricate and precise study of history as a kind of numen or sacred presence. His apartment contains an entire wall of technical journal essays (in I don't want to know how many European languages), all carefully collated and numbered in a hundred or so three-ring binders. I am more the cross-cultural comparativist, the hermeneut, the intellectual provocateur, the intuitive interpreter who is willing to say what it all means. Or might mean. And my home study contains no journals or three-ring binders. As one of my former students put it, it looks like a UFO crash site. Seems about right.

Wouter is committed to keeping the "emic" (roughly, the insider's perspective) and the "etic" (roughly, the outsider's perspective) apart in scholarship. I am so committed to not doing this that I write review essays with titles like "Inside-Out, Outside-In," and to this day I am not entirely sure which is which, that is, I get the emic and the etic confused, or reversed. I am positive that I do this because I have unconsciously (or just consciously) blocked this easy distinction out of sheer stubbornness. In any case, we disagree about these things, and we are comfortable in these differences.

Wouter's fairly long review essay on *The Serpent's Gift* was both appreciative and critical. I encourage the reader to go and read the full review, since, as with all of his writing, it is extremely rich and rewards the careful reader. What follows is my response to it, with a few minor cuts to avoid repetition in this volume. I am including it here because this little essay contains a brief but accurate description of the "ouroboric" nature of my thinking (the *ouroboros* is an ancient esoteric symbol from Greek culture—a snake biting its own tail). Here is another version of the "flip" or reflexive rereading practice again.

Perhaps most importantly, the response to Hanegraaff signals very clearly the basic philosophical question and subsequent suspicion that would animate and drive the second half of my work—the question of the Human as Two, now reframed as the relationship between mind and matter or, if one prefers, the nature of embodied consciousness. One can begin to see here the clear lineaments of my growing suspicion that materialism and scientism are inadequate answers to this question of all questions. Put differently, I was beginning to see that the underlying materialisms of the university are gradually killing off the humanities and need to be robustly resisted.

I still think this.

Gnosisssss

> The new sensibility does not threaten a regression from rationality to superstition; rather, it allows for expansion beyond the one-sided worldview that scientism has provided us over the last three hundred years. We should never forget how utterly unsophisticated the tenets of eighteenth-century rationalism have left us, believers and unbelievers alike, in that complex arena we blithely dub "spiritual." Even as we see all too clearly the kitsch of much New Age religiosity and fear the rigidity of rising fundamentalism, we remain alarmingly blind to our own unconscious tendencies in this same direction. . . . We forget that Western culture is equally about Platonism and Aristotelianism, idealism and empiricism, *gnosis* and *episteme*, and that for most of this culture's history one or the other has been conspicuously dominant—and dedicated to stamping the other out.
>
> VICTORIA NELSON, *THE SECRET LIFE OF PUPPETS*

I read the review essay of Wouter Hanegraaff on my recent hissings with a mixture of admiration, gratitude, and respectful difference.[8] As an author who has been grossly misread and misrepresented on more than one painful occasion, it is an especially meaningful experience to be read this well and, most of all, *this fully*. To my knowledge, Hanegraaff is the first major scholar to state in print what I have felt for some time but have never had the courage to say in public, namely, that my different books appear to represent a developing oeuvre. Whether these texts finally constitute a meaningful whole that is greater than its individual parts is not for me to decide. I can only admit to such a bold hope, and confess that, if it is true, I am not yet conscious of the lineaments and implications of this still potential corpus. I suppose that is one reason I continue to write: to see what will appear. Like a novelist, I want to see what these characters will do. Hence my deep gratitude for a thoughtful review like this one, which helps me to see the bigger picture and intuit the larger plot.

This is the point in a response when the author moves into that predictable "But. . . ." But I will not do this. Not yet anyway. There is still too much that

Hanegraaff gets exactly right. He understands, for example, that the professional traumas of *Kālī's Child* immunized me, forever, from the naive assumption that truly robust scholarship on religion can, or should, simply "represent" a faith tradition. He also understands that the same experience led me to a long consideration of that profound disjunction between what many scholars think and what the believing public thinks about "religion." It is this epistemological, ethical, political, and professional abyss between what we might call the academic esoteric and the public exoteric out of which the serpent of this book slithers to hiss his deepest worries, and his most poignant truths. Finally, I can only agree with Hanegraaff's final conclusion that there are real and important differences between American and European models of scholarship. Our only apparent difference on this point is that I am just fine with those differences. This is not a zero-sum game for me, as if Hanegraaff must be wrong for me to be right, or vice versa.

Okay, but what do I think he misses about my hisses? There are places in the review that go to the very heart of the hiss, and then miss it. There are two such kinds of places: (1) those places where Hanegraaff fails to read me dialectically or ouroborically; and (2) those places where he fails to follow his own advice and read my books together, that is, as a whole.

To take some examples of the first slip, Hanegraaff associates me with the writings of the New Atheists like Dawkins and Dennett and writes that I claim that "spiritual entities or metaphysical realities are illusions." I am indeed probably too dismissive of independent spiritual entities in the book. The truth is that I think most "objective" religious experiences are in the end forms of our own mind-blowing consciousness revealing itself to itself. I accept Hanegraaff's critique on this point. But I certainly do not think that metaphysical realities are illusions, and I cannot possibly see how I can be classed with the New Atheists. I appreciate their robust rationalism, but they would reject my thought as far too friendly to religion.

What I *do* think is that all linguistic, cultural, and historical mediations of metaphysical realities—whatever they are—are local and historical, and so relative. To the extent that these religious events are absolutized, dehistoricized, or literalized as universal truths, they do indeed become illusory, false. This is usually obvious to almost anyone not completely embedded within that shared cultural experience, hence the gnosis of "the outsider" that I explore in the book. To the extent, however, that these events are handled as psychically mediated actualizations of some more fundamental potential, they can be approached as reality posits, that is, as crystallizations of consciousness become culture. *Both* moves of this dialectic—denial and affirmation, reduction and symbolization—constitute the ouroboric nature of my comparativism (chapter 3). And the same biting-tail phenomena is evident in my mystico-erotic criticism (chapter 1), whereby the sexual and the spiritual are always changing places, and in my mystical humanism (chapter 2), whereby religious phenomena are "reduced" to a human nature that turns out to be irreducible and immeasurable.

Anyone, then, who attempts to characterize my thought as either simply reductionistic (as some of my Hindutva critics have done with respect to my mystico-erotic criticism) or as simply religious is half-right, but also half-wrong. That is, my real hiss boils down to the fact that I am committed both to the most robust rational-critical methods *and* to the metaphysical reality that is the object (really, I suspect, the subject) of religious experience and expression. On the whole, Hanegraaff clearly understands this, and his category of the "religionist" scholar, to the extent that it preserves this critical-sympathetic dialectic, is not inappropriate to describe the basic contours of my thought.

As an example of the second slip, Hanegraaff leads the reader to believe that my essay on the erotics of the gospels is a function of some idiosyncratic selection of a few particularly provocative scholars, and that any other sufficiently scholarly reading would be equally convincing. He also claims that I have not weighed the pros and cons of the different positions. He fails to note a number of facts here: first, that this essay is presented as an experimental apocryphon, a little secret book, certainly not as a standard work of scholarship; second, that I discuss why my homoerotic reading is "counter-coherent" with both the New Testament texts and a large body of modern scholarship, which *is* more or less exhaustive and upon which I rely; third, that I have indeed weighed the pros and cons of different models of Jesus's sexuality through thirty years of reading, four years in a monastic seminary, and seven years of intense and nearly deadly anorexic sexual suffering (all of which I have openly discussed and analyzed in print); fourth, and finally, that I offered this first essay as a single expression of a much larger pattern in the history of religions, about which I have theorized in hundreds of pages, particularly in *Roads of Excess, Palaces of Wisdom*, a book which Hanegraaff obviously admires.

That comparative pattern is expressed in *The Serpent's Gift* this way: "*Whereas male heteroerotic forms of the mystical generally become heterodox or heretical, sublimated male homoerotic forms generally become orthodox*." This, I would propose, is a real piece of knowledge in Hanegraaff's scholarly sense. It originates in historical criticism. It can be rationally expressed and openly discussed. And it can be applied in different historical and cultural contexts. I cannot possibly explain, much less defend, these ideas here, nor discuss their qualifications. It is all in my books for anyone who cares to look, who cares, as Hanegraaff proposes, to read me whole.

I understand that Hanegraaff has dedicated his professional life to the study of Western esotericism, and that his empirical-historical method generously leaves open the question of the metaphysical status of such historical phenomena. And I agree, completely, that our "first and foremost task is to *study* religion," and precisely in the terms Hanegraaff sets out. I am all for what he calls the relativizing of one's own birth culture (I certainly left my own because of that study), his call for humility before the other, and his call to historicize. *But then what?* Hanegraaff suggests that the study of religion will lead us to ask new questions about religion and ourselves. Okay. But the new questions I am led to ask after this empirical-historical study are precisely the questions Hanegraaff won't let me ask as a scholar.

Must we *all* restrict ourselves to historical issues? Must we *never* venture beyond historical criticism and ask the philosophical questions every sophomore in our classrooms is already asking? Does not profound historicism force on us profound questions about the nature of reality, which, amazingly, appears to be experienced very differently in different periods and places? And who can seriously study psychical phenomena and not ask metaphysical questions about mind-matter interaction? Why be bound by the historicism and materialism of our present culture? If our historical methods can show us the relativity of all of this—and I think they can—why be bound by such artifice? Does not the very power of our thought lead us out of this thought?

Hanegraaff would argue that such questions are indeed worth asking, but that any answers must remain fundamentally speculative, hence we cannot possibly write about them as scholars of religion. There is much truth here, but it is absolutely binding only if we define the intellectual life along strict historical and materialistic lines. I am no longer willing to do this. Having said that, I also think that we must be very clear with both ourselves and our readers when we are representing a religious tradition (faith), when we are advancing historical-empirical knowledge (reason), and when we are developing an always speculative academic gnosticism (gnosis). These indeed are different projects, and we would do well to articulate this professional truth in as clear and as precise a way as possible. At the same time, however, I also think that we must admit that these three forms of thought are manifestations of the same human consciousness, and so there are constant and deep exchanges between them that we would also do well to recognize and theorize.

* * * *

I began this response with an epigram from Victoria Nelson's *The Secret Life of Puppets*, partly because I think it captures beautifully the project of the study of Western esotericism that Hanegraaff has done so much to nurture and develop, but also because Nelson's critique of modern intellectual culture mirrors my own. "The greatest taboo among serious intellectuals of the century just behind us," she writes, "in fact, proved to be none of the 'transgressions' itemized by postmodern thinkers: it was, rather, the heresy of challenging a materialist worldview." Not that we can go back to any premodern answers. We cannot. But we possess our own wisdom. "We are in a better position than our ancestors to integrate the wisdom of the transcendental if we make use of the profound wisdom of the psychological," Nelson observes.[9]

She then goes on to give us a brilliant study of the modern demonization of the soul as puppet, robot, or cyborg and the bracketing (really repressing) of the deeper questions of human consciousness within contemporary intellectual culture. What was once a sacred grotto has become the grotesque. For her, this demonization is born of an exaggerated and unbalanced scientism, an Aristotelianism that she sees us now moving beyond within a new, still submerged, Platonic Renaissance, witnessed, for example, in the "sub-Zeitgeist" of science fiction, comic books, film, and fantasy, much of which are fundamentally gnostic. Although I had not yet read Nelson when I wrote *The Serpent's Gift*, this is without doubt the deeper cultural context of my concluding essay on the X-Men as an apt metaphor for the study of religion. Mythically speaking, we are indeed mutants, nervously poised between the believers and the reducers as we think and write our way to a new gnosticism we ourselves do not yet understand.

Or so I have heard the serpent hiss as he bites his own tail.

2017 POSTSCRIPT: THE BRIDAL CHAMBER

One of the focal points of *The Serpent's Gift* was the "bridal chamber," which, in some readings at least, appears to be an early sexual sacrament of some gnostic communities that approached the conjugal bed as a sacred "mystery" through which the couple could access their angelic doubles and so help reunite their souls with divinity. Such thoughts, I believe, helped to catalyze a most remarkable synchronicity that is worth relating here.

After I became chair of the department at Rice University in 2004, I began to explore how we might attract April DeConick, an expert on early Christian gnosticism, to our department. I was finishing *The Serpent's Gift* at this time. As part of my recruiting strategy, I invited April down to Houston, where she delivered an essay on the bridal chamber sacrament at Christ Church Cathedral, in downtown Houston, as part of a lecture series that I organized on "Hidden Histories." We walked to my car after the lecture event. It was probably 10:00 p.m. or so. We were in the car, with the city rising up around us, in the middle of an empty parking lot, and ready to drive away. As we spoke, a bridal couple emerged from the darkness as if out of nowhere. They were in full dress: a tuxedo and a long flowing white wedding gown. The couple walked across the parking lot in plain sight. "See," I exclaimed to April. "See that! That means something." What I really meant was, "See! That means that you will soon be at Rice."

We hired April a few years later. She now chairs the department. Together with our collegues, April and I would build our GEM collective, a community of faculty and graduate students dedicated to studying gnostic, esoteric and mystical currents in the history of religions.

8

Wendy's Student

Mythical Paradox and Political Censorship

The structure of myth is a dialectic structure in which opposed logical positions are
stated, the oppositions mediated by a restatement, which again, when its internal
structure becomes clear, gives rise to another kind of opposition, which in its turn is
mediated or resolved, and so on. . . .
"Mediation" (in this sense) is always achieved by introducing a third category which
is "abnormal" or "anomalous" in terms of ordinary "rational" categories. Thus myths
are full of fabulous monsters, incarnate gods, virgin mothers. This middle ground is
abnormal, non-natural, holy.

WENDY DONIGER O'FLAHERTY QUOTING THE STRUCTURALIST
ANTHROPOLOGISTS CLAUDE LÉVI-STRAUSS AND
EDMUND LEACH IN *ŚIVA: THE EROTIC ASCETIC*

Looking back now, I can see that the snake of thought that bites its own tail
is not simply a reflection of my lifelong immersion in gnostic, esoteric, and
Tantric literature. It is also a distant echo of the Eliadean *coincidentia oppositorum* or "coincidence of opposites," which, as we saw above, functioned as a
kind of deep ontological baseline for the comparativist. More immediately,
such tail-biting thought is a reflection of my intellectual training under Wendy
Doniger and her own indebtedness to the structuralist anthropology of figures
like Claude Lévi-Strauss, Edmund Leach, Victor Turner, and Mary Douglas.

These structuralist influences are apparent throughout Wendy's corpus, which
is so often about the play of binaries or doubles, but perhaps it is most apparent
in her first book, *Śiva: The Erotic Ascetic*. Here she homes in on the mythologies
of the god Shiva and locates the two "opposite" value systems of Hindu culture
expressed in them: ascetic withdrawal or release from the cycle of birth and
death, and erotic desire leading to procreation, family, and social engagement.
She then demonstrates how these two life orientations play out within the mythologies in a millennia-long attempt to resolve the binary. The basic tension
is never really resolved in any single myth or figure, but that is of the essence
(or "structure") of cultural creativity.

Hence Shiva is the fiercely chaste yogi who lives in the cremation ground, sits in yogic repose, smears his body with cremation ash, and vaporizes the god of love, Kama, with his third eye. But he is also the ithyphallic god whose yogic repose is stirred by the same Kama, who seduces the wives of the Pine Forest sages, and who is the consummate lover of the goddess Parvati. The two forces—the ascetic and the erotic—are seen by the myths as two sides of the same psychological and ontological coin. They are not really opposites. They are two forms of energy or "heat," one expressed sexually (*kama*), one expressed ascetically (*tapas*).[1] In ascetic or yogic practice, the erotic forces are concentrated, preserved, and finally sublimated until they explode into the realizations of mystical illumination: "he is a yogi *because* he is a lover."[2] Hence we get the paradoxical icon of the *lingam*, the central symbol of Shiva that is both an erect phallus (it sits in a *yoni* or "vagina") and a sign of absolute transcendence.

We read a lot of structuralist anthropology at Chicago in the late 1980s and 1990s. Looking back, I can see now that my own early work on the mystical and the erotic in comparative mystical literature—in essence on the "erotic mystic" to match Wendy's "erotic ascetic"—was deeply informed by these same structuralist instincts. My later work on the paranormal as a "nondual signal" of the real, as a temporary collapse of the binary structures of self/world and subjective/objective into the anomalous and the monstrous, would be even more indebted to structuralist (and now post-structuralist) thought. More on the latter in due time.

ANSWERING THE POSTCOLONIAL
AND HINDUTVA CRITICISMS

My work was also bound to Wendy's structuralist Shiva in another, perhaps even deeper, sense: looked at through this particular anthropological lens, the *Kālī's Child* affair is nothing more, and nothing less, than yet another chapter in this millennia-long mythological tension or structural contradiction between the erotic and the ascetic. The erotic mystic *is* the erotic ascetic in another key.

It is one thing to collapse a binary in structuralist thought. It is quite another to do so in public, and with a beloved saint or god no less. Not surprisingly, both of us would struggle with the same Hindutva or fundamentalist censorship campaigns, I in the mid-1990s and into the new millennium, she a decade or so later.

In truth, I was always answering these critics. In books like *Roads of Excess*

(2001) and *The Serpent's Gift* (2007), I sought to do many things. One of those things was answer my critics. Specifically, I sought to answer those scholars who wanted to claim that the comparative study of religion is a kind of intellectual colonialism or imperialism, that it must unduly privilege European culture at the expense of every other culture, and that it needlessly "exoticizes" other cultures for the sake of its own ideological ends.

Having grown up in the Midwest and sensing intensely that everything about comparativism and the history of religions was aimed directly at the heart of my own birth culture's ethnocentrism and religious nationalism, I found this argument to be less than satisfying, to say the least. I also knew that the forms of subjectivity and mind that I had privileged in my work (because I had received them in that Night?) found their closest cultural analogues in Hindu and Buddhist epistemology and philosophy of mind; they were anything but white and Western.

The question, then, became how to answer a set of nuanced criticisms that were in fact half-right, that is, that got some things very right but missed others in spectacular and troubling ways. On the simplest of levels, of course, it is perfectly true that my thought is informed by colonialism. So is everyone else's, including and especially the writings of the Hindu nationalists and postcolonial theorists. I see no way around this. We are all historical beings situated in a very particular global moment, and we are all thinking and writing "after colonialism." It is also perfectly true that the comparative study of religion was first institutionalized at the height of British colonialism in Europe (although a beginning is not an ending). So, yes, indeed, the postcolonial hermeneutic is an appropriate and valuable one.

I can go further, though. As I explained in "Secret Talk," the essay anthologized above on the early anti-reception history of *Kālī's Child*, I can observe through the postcolonial lens the historical roots and social psychology of my conservative Hindu critics, whose vehement denials of the eroticisms of Tantra are very much a product of a colonial mindset that stems from the nineteenth century, when bourgeois Hindus largely accepted and then incorporated Christian missionary screeds against Tantra and the polytheistic dimensions of the Hindu traditions as all that is darkest and most corrupt about Hinduism. Ironically, then, what the postcolonial hermeneutic can show us is that it is my critics who are "colonizing" when they so vehemently condemn or anxiously deny the historical importance of Tantra.

What I was doing in *Kālī's Child* was uncovering the older Tantric roots of the saint's teachings and experiences *before* they were successfully censored, disciplined, and finally rejected by the British and Indian colonized minds of the late nineteenth and early twentieth centuries. I was also tracking how the colonial processes were suppressing and, literally, erasing the Tantric passages and secret teachings. I was engaging in a kind postcolonial criticism without knowing it.

So that is the half-right part.

Here is the difficult, and much more personal, part. I fully recognized how rich and subtle postcolonial criticism can be. But I could not also help but notice that the postcolonial card was played again and again by right-wing Hindu nationalists in their censorship campaigns against my work and the work of my colleagues. I could not help but notice that any critical scholarship on Hinduism that cannot be fit into some extremely dubious notions of history and culture was (and still is, to this day) framed as "colonizing." This is a clever rationalization for engaging in vitriolic harassment of working intellectuals and active censorship of important scholarship.

Moreover, the same rhetorical ploy works extremely well for audiences who are completely ignorant of the history, scope, and radicalism of the study of religion and so do not know that the exact same critical methods have been applied first and foremost (and to a much greater extent) to the Jewish and Christian traditions for over two centuries. For every essay or book there is on the erotics of some aspect of Hinduism, there are a hundred, or a thousand, on the Bible or Christiainity. (So, no, no one is "picking on" Hinduism.) At the end of the day, these rhetorical strategies do little more than polarize people, trump up a set of false moral charges, and shut down the conversation, which, of course, is the real goal here. We need to call these rhetorical tricks and this aggressive bullying what they in fact are: an attempted repression of religious studies, a real danger to intellectual freedom, and a propogandistic religious campaign against scholars of India.[3]

So the conclusion was difficult for me to avoid: postcolonial criticism and Hindu fundamentalism are not the same thing, but they can be aligned in suprising and disturbing ways. This is the real, and very personal, source of my abiding suspicion of postcolonial criticism: in my own experience and observation over the last quarter century, this particular discourse has mostly functioned to constrict or even prevent conversations that many of us wanted to have. It did not encourage or nurture these conversations, much less inspire them. Quite the opposite. The postcolonial functioned as a heavy sign over the door that read "Thou Shalt Not!"

CONSCIOUSNESS BEFORE CULTURE

But I would also take my response to the postcolonial criticisms in a second direction, which I articulated early on in the essay anthologized below. I began to argue that, if we want to be robustly historical and apply the same micro-contextualization to ourselves that we attempt to apply to every other historical figure and movement, we will have to acknowledge that much about "comparative religion," at least as it is practiced today in departments of religion across the US, is much more indebted to the American counterculture than it is to British colonialism. That is, we have to take much more seriously our own immediate historical context, and not just the obvious distant colonial ones that were in full force a century ago.

I have never met a colonialist, but I have met a great number of individuals who found real revelation and life-changing inspiration in the counterculture of the 1960s and 1970s and then fanned that initial spark into a blazing flame through a lifetime of scholarship and teaching. Some of the most recent and influential roots of comparativism do not just lie in the psychosexual and mystical lives of prominent scholars of religion, as I had argued in *Roads of Excess*. They lay in the Asian, occult, magical, psychedelic, and paranormal enthusiasms of the American-European counterculture.

According to the historian who coined the expression "counter-culture" in 1968, Theodore Roszak—and this is the key—such a counterculture can be simply described as *that broad social, artistic, spiritual, and philosophical project that sought to privilege and prioritize consciousness over culture.* Consciousness over culture. Consciousness before culture. That is the psychic foundation of comparison across cultures. It was also the psychic foundation of the American-European counterculture as articulated by intellectual muses like Aldous Huxley, Alan Watts, and Allen Ginsberg, all of whom were deeply drawn to Hindu and Buddhist forms of mind and thought because of this same privileging of consciousness over and before culture.

Although it is clearly morphing again now with robust immigration patterns and large influxes of indigenous scholars into the fold, for about three decades (roughly 1960–1990) the comparative study of Asian religions was very much a countercultural phenomena. There was Huston Smith and his first psychedelic revelation on New Year's Day, 1961, with Timothy Leary, which both terrified him and split him wide open to the multiple dimensions of the real. Is this how and why he saw five flying saucers in broad daylight, outside the

Dean's Office at the University of Washington, with his dean no less? As the latter put it: "Well, Huston: I'm a dean and you're in religion; they'll never believe us."[4] There was also Mircea Eliade's flag-planting essay "History of Religions and a New Humanism" (1961 again), poised firmly against Western ethnocentrisms, European provincialism and strictly rationalist notions of the human, and the countless countercultural celebrations of his *Yoga* and *Shamanism* books (both became countercultural classics, not to mention how-to practice books). And then there were, of course, all of the Hindu Tantric gurus, Tibetan lamas and Japanese roshis who dominated the Western reception of the Asian religions in the second half of the twentieth century—the Tantric transmission again.

The conclusion is an obvious one—the study of Hinduism and Buddhism as they were secretly inspired in the 1960s, 1970s, and 80s, had *far* more to do with LSD, the Summer of Love; and the Beatles' trip to an Indian ashram than anything that happened in British India or the Middle East. Indeed, the latter colonial influences, which I would never want to deny, simply paled in comparison to the influence of the former countercultural ones. When George Harrison sang "My Sweet Lord" (to Krishna), he was not enacting an implicit colonial trope. He was expressing a genuine and heartfelt religious conversion. He was really singing to Lord Krishna. He was *also* trying to sell albums. Real devotion and real commodification are by no means exclusive, as my former PhD student Andrea Jain has argued with such eloquence with respect to modern American yoga traditions.[5]

It was in this same countercultural space that tens of thousands of Western youth took a "journey to the East." Most of them traveled with extremely naive and idealistic visions of the cultures they were exploring. Many were disappointed or disillusioned. Many were inspired, illuminated, even enlightened. And why not? A civilization like that of India (or Tibet, or China, or Japan) really is different, really is special, really does offer something that Western civilization does not and, apparently, cannot.

The truth is that there is a good deal of truth to the orientalist trope of a "spiritual" or "mystical" India. No, of course, Indian culture cannot be framed as simply spiritual, any more than Western culture can be framed as simply materialistic. But it does not then follow that Indian culture does not possess a rich vein of philosophical discourse and psychophysical practice around idealist, dualist, and nondual forms of consciousness that is without peer in the history of religions. India does possess all of these remarkable things, and in astonishing abundance. This is the real reason so many modern intellectuals and seekers are so attracted to Indian civilization: India *is* special.

Allow me to crystallize these different arguments in this way:

9. It's about Counterculture, not Colonialism. The most significant and immediate historical roots of critical theory in the comparative study of religion do not lie in colonialism; they lie in counterculture and its insistence on the primacy of consciousness over culture.

The last two gnomons (8 and 9) would take many forms in my work, but the basic point would remain the same: colonialism was one historical instance or context of comparativism, not its necessary social base or inherent cultural logic, and certainly not its necessary ideological end or political conclusion. Quite the precise opposite: the deepest historical and intellectual impulses of comparativism are apophatic, cosmopolitan, and countercultural, not colonial and imperial.

Finally, at the risk of getting ahead of myself here, allow me to observe that the postcolonialist allergy to "exoticizing" culture is equally myopic. With respect to my own case, the truth is that I have always been an equal exoticizer. I would, after all, exoticize the study of religion itself, myself, and my own American cultural surround in far more excessive ways than I ever did with Ramakrishna in *Kālī's Child*. I am thinking here of my focus on the mystical (and erotic) experiences of scholars of mysticism in *Roads of Excess* and my writing on the paranormal in Western intellectual history, American popular culture, and individual experiencers in books like *Authors of the Impossible, Mutants and Mystics*, and *The Super Natural*. You think writing about a Hindu erotic mystic is "exotic"? Try writing about a Catholic boy from San Antonio who grew up to become a horror writer and was abducted by "aliens." In truth, the history of religions *is* exotic because *consciousness itself is exotic*. The attempt to deny or damn exoticism in the academy is just another symptom of the banal materialism and base denial of consciousness that controls the humanities to this day. Enough.

INTRODUCING THE ESSAY

The essay anthologized below in a slightly condensed version functions well as a kind of transition piece from part 1 to part 2. It continues my engagement with the mystical roots of the comparative study of religion, as I had begun in *Roads of Excess* and *The Serpent's Gift*. It honors the Blakean inspirations of the same. It treats some of the controversies around *Kālī's Child*. It also looks forward to the second half of *Secret Body* and its focus on the primacy of consciousness over culture in the American counterculture and the Tantric transmission.

I wrote this piece for a Festschrift for Wendy Doniger that David Haberman and Laurie Patton put together entitled *Notes from a Mandala* (2010). It witnesses silently to Wendy's intellectual and pedagogical generosity. As anyone who knows Wendy knows, she is no fan of the counterculture or California. Still, as with so many of her other students, she granted this one his own passions and eccentriticities. As I explain below, she gave us *space* to be ourselves.

Being Blake

ANTINOMIAN THOUGHT, COUNTERCULTURE, AND

THE ART OF THE HISTORY OF RELIGIONS

(2010)

> Both read the Bible day and night; but you read black where I read white.
>
> WILLIAM BLAKE, "THE EVERLASTING GOSPEL"

It is always a tricky matter to fathom one's intellectual, aesthetic, literary, and spiritual lineages, to understand how one came to think and see and write what one thinks and sees and writes. This task is trickier still when one's thought is essentially antinomian, that is, "against the law"—poised to counter what most people consider to be true, real, and right. One hesitates to name others as accomplices in one's own crimes, even if in one's own mind these are not crimes at all, but acts of painful beauty, liberating insight and positive wisdom.

In truth, Wendy is responsible for none of my crimes. I learned my Freud in a Benedictine seminary, dying of anorexia and a hundred dreams that I did not understand, *that I could not read.* Freud taught me how to read these nocturnal stories I was telling myself, how to interpret them, how to reveal their secrets, how to trace the lineaments of my own sexual desires through faith and family. He taught me, with the monks who trained me with such care and concern, that food and sex and mother and father and religion are all apiece. That bit of wisdom—it is really more than a bit—saved me. Literally. I would have died in my youth from obsessive fasting were it not for that core insight. The same monastic community taught me, by silent example if not by word, that much of male religious behavior is homoerotic in structure, and that this is nothing to fear, that there is holiness here, even if it is a holiness that effectively "exiles" heterosexuality and renders it heretical. I knew all of this—in my bones, as we say—before I ever set foot in Hyde Park. I carried around my theory in my body. My written work has thus always been an intimate expression of my sexual body. It's all one corpus.

Wendy helped me to articulate what was still "unconscious," as it were, in that erotic body. She, with Sudhir Kakar, Gananath Obeyesekere, and Paul Ricoeur, also taught me to think with Freud outside the boundaries of my own little birth culture, my own tiny tribe. She taught me that the stories I knew from my own heritage could be found, in different forms, in other cultures and times, that other cultures also had other completely different stories, and—most of all—that our stories had much to learn from their stories (and vice versa). Perhaps most radically of all, she taught me that, although we might all have different stories, we all have "the same body," and thus it is the human body that can ground responsible thinking about religion across all clime and time. Wendy, that is to say, taught me about the comparative study of myth and religion, where reality and illusion, sex and sanctity, self and other, body and soul, male and female, classical and popular culture are always trading places.

Having grown up in a religious culture that had me daily consuming the flesh and fluids of a beautiful male deity and collecting holy cards that looked more than a little like superhero comics, those were all vaguely familiar themes, but I had never encountered them put in just this way, that is, I had never encountered a scholar of religion *who could write like this.* Whatever it was that Wendy was communicating, transmitting, in her books, it was not a purely rational truth. Stories and images, after all, are as central to her books as linear arguments and structuralism. There was also what I would now call a certain moral spaciousness. Much like the Freud I had encountered through my swearing monastic psychoanalyst (a classicist who was more than a little fond of the "F" word), there was no fear in Wendy's approach to sex and religion. There was no censorship, no repression, no denial. As we say in the farmlands of Nebraska, there was no bullshit. And I had stepped in plenty of the latter, so I knew what it felt and smelled like. How it squished around one's shoes. There was none of that here. One could run through this pasture with joy, not fear.

But it is not quite this lack of fear or absence of repression that I want to address here, not directly anyway. I want to address that other quality of Wendy's writings, that uncanny ability of hers to do theory through story, to combine image and words in ways that provoke one to think in radically new ways about assumed truths that can no longer be assumed. I want to write a few words that can reflect something of her aesthetics, something of the fact that her living and working spaces—the ones I have seen anyway—are filled with the sculpted forms and painted images of Hindu and Buddhist deities she so obviously loves, and with works of art, both very high (Picasso) and very kitsch (that effeminate Jesus knocking at that silly door).

On a more theoretical plane, I want to suggest that the history of religions can be as much an art as a rational discipline, and that there is something essentially antinomian about the art we call comparison. Comparison, after all, denies each and every local truth for a greater human truth that is never really reached. Paradoxically, comparison denies culture in order to affirm humanity. Sometimes this affirmation is a bit too clear (as in some forms of perennialism). Done well, however, it need not be this way. Wendy, I would suggest, does it well, really well, partly because she communicates what she has to say not through dogmatic statements about inaccessible but certain religious truths, but through a uniquely playful and humorous combination of story, theory, and image. Put most simply, Wendy is an artist.

BEING BLAKE

Which brings me to a particular obsession of mine: the illuminated poems of William Blake. These have long struck me as particularly central to what I do as a historian of religions. I am not entirely sure why. I do not believe I encountered Blake in any serious way until graduate school, and then only on my own. Chronologically speaking, it was Jesus, then Freud, then Blake. And who could say which of these men's thought is more antinomian? Two of my published books feature Blakean covers, and one, which I will get to in a moment, is explicitly Blakean in structure and argument. It was thus with some delight that I encountered the following passage from Walter Capps a few years ago in his textbook on religious studies:

> Consider . . . what turmoil William Blake's insights would create for the methodological conceptualization of standard religious studies. How could any of them be fitted into any coherent scheme, or, if they were, would they remain what they were originally? Why is the mentality of the technician sanctioned in religious studies while the attitude of the artist is treated with suspicion?[6]

I have long felt the same. And as a student of Wendy's, I have always tried to be as much the artist as the technician. When I was writing *Roads of Excess, Palaces of Wisdom* in the late 1990s, for example, I imagined composing the text within what I called "a Blakean spirit," by which I meant that I consciously intended the book to transmit something of the deep poetic, erotic, and noetic energies I had sensed within my own aesthetic engagements with the seer's corpus. On a more public and less esoteric level, *Roads* was also an attempt to reread the history of comparative mystical literature—from Europe and India, to Oxford and Harvard—through the poet's *The Marriage of Heaven and Hell*, a text which has functioned as a kind of personal Gospel for me over the years and that I have long affectionately called "Blake's English Tantra."

With my own text, it was not that I was interested in mechanically applying Blake's mythological categories to the history of religions: Urizen here, Luvah there. It was more that I was interested in "being Blake," that is, I desired to re-imagine and so re-create something of the Blakean gnosis into modern critical theory. Such a desire was hardly tangential to the book. Indeed, in many ways, that desire *was* the book. My central thesis, after all, was that scholars of mystical literature often undergo profound shifts of consciousness and energy while absorbed in mystical literature and then encode these altered states in their subsequent theory building and interpretive work. In this way, I suggested, the modern study of mysticism can function as a kind of modern mystical tradition. This, of course, implies that some types of scholarly writing can also function as modern mystical literature, that at some point one might cease, for example, to write about Blake in order to "be Blake."

Now this, to say the least, was an eccentric thesis, and I was not at all sure how it might be received. (Indeed, I am still not sure how it was received.) I begin with this personal note, not to sound like a résumé, but to set the context for the triple thesis that I want to suggest (without quite developing) here, namely, that the American counterculture of the 1960s and 1970s (which was really as much a British performance as an American one) performed its own transmission of Blake into modern Western society, that the comparative study of religion is in some way indebted to this history, and that we all now stand in the waning light of the various political, ethical, and spiritual advances of that brief antinomian moment.

This is not simply a fantasy on my part. It is also a historical observation. Our own present political realities, after all, are not so different than those in which Blake lived. In the poetic scholarship of David V. Erdman and E. P. Thompson, Blake was a "prophet against empire" and a "witness against the Beast" whose weird mythological visions constitute, on one level at least, radical political critiques of both imperialism and monarchy,[7] and, I would add (for our own time now), of the imperialism and monarchy of Religion. It is not for nothing that Blake's genius erupts in *The Marriage of Heaven and Hell* (1793) immediately after "the Eternal Hell revives" as the American and French revolutions. It is not for nothing that his burning spirit of revolution, Orc, may be etymologically related to the creative freedom and fiery passion of the testicles (Greek *orcheis*).[8] And it is not for nothing that the poet suffered throughout his life from what he himself described as an exaggerated "nervous fear" over censorship, sedition charges, and possible government action.[9] This is why the historical birth of democracy and Western liberalism become, in Erdman's reading, an event of mythological proportions that Blake's poetry and illuminations can prophetically announce to the world only in coded form: "The revolt of Energy against the restraining Reason of kings would open all the gates to Paradise and to the perception and creation of Eternal Delight," Erdman writes. "The dialectic of Contraries was now at work, and now was "the dominion of Edom, & the return of Adam into Paradise."[10]

We are still, it seems, very much in this dialectic of Contraries, lost in a slow birth (or is it a death?) that is now no longer simply American or French or British, but truly global. It might, then, do us well to remember Blake again, to see and hear again what he might teach us. It might also do us well to remember our own recent Blakean past, not to romanticize or idealize it, but to take better stock of our present. I would suggest anyway that it is precisely this dominion of Edom, this antinomian or countercultural stance vis-à-vis both church and state, this Orcian political-sexual revolution, that made Blake such a powerfully attractive figure to the American-British counterculture of the 1960s and 1970s. This, after all, was the era of the civil rights movement, of the beginnings of both feminist and gay consciousness, of what Wilhelm Reich had earlier (already in the 1920s) coined as the "sexual revolution,"[11] of the definitive entrance into Western consciousness of the Asian religions, often, it turns out, in highly eroticized or "Tantric" forms, and of the definitive birth and development of the comparative study of religion in the universities (the AAR was created in 1964). In the words of Theodore Roszak, the American historian who coined the expression in 1968, this was a true "counter culture."[12] Which is to say that antinomianism was the order of the day.

FROM THE HISTORICAL BLAKE TO THE COUNTERCULTURAL BLAKE

In his own time at least, Blake was a relatively unknown, deeply eccentric, and highly marginal figure whose status in Western culture has nonetheless grown with every passing generation. Certainly the latter fame could not have been guessed by his real-life reputation. Some of his own contemporaries considered him "an absolute lunatic" and "a saint amongst the infidels & a heretic with the orthodox." Here indeed was a man who "said many things tending to the

corruption of Xtian morals" and who "outraged all common sense & rationality."[13] The charge of madness was a common one in his own day, and it can still
be heard occasionally in ours, even as a veritable industry of elite scholarship
sifts through and debates every detail of his personal mythology and largely
hidden life. If Blake was once a relative nobody of very humble means, he is
now a veritable icon of high Romantic and Gothic art whose weird works sell
for millions of dollars and draw adoring crowds at places like the Metropolitan
Museum of Art in New York, the Tate Gallery in London, and the J. Paul Getty
Museum in Los Angeles. Blake has arrived, as we say, but alas, as someone
long dead.

As E. P. Thompson has convincingly argued, the deep structure of Blake's
art and thought is fundamentally antinomian, literally "against (*anti-*) the law
(*nomos*)," not in a simple legal or criminal sense (although Blake was charged
with sedition and put on trial in a series of events that terrified him), but in a
culturally creative or prophetic one. It is certainly important that Blake seriously considered himself to be a prophet in the same line as the biblical figures
of Isaiah and Ezekiel, and that many of his later works are titled, quite literally,
"Prophecies." This prophetic quality, this rage against social injustice and the
mediocrities of any stable culture, certainly contributed to the antinomian tradition in which Blake participated.

Perhaps, then, it is hardly surprising that Blake's vision was poised against
the hegemonic discourses and common-sense assumptions of his (and our
own) social order, be that order framed as church or state. The art bore within
itself a vision of fundamental challenge and change. As our opening epigram
makes starkly obvious, Blake was no friend of established religion or the state,
even and especially if he was intensely religious and deeply engaged with the
politics of his own place and time. He was a contemporary, after all, of both
the French and the American revolutions, and he wrote or "prophesized" passionately about each. If there is a figure, then, who demonstrates in an especially dramatic way why it is so important to pay very close attention to "antisocial" eccentrics, "weirdo" artists, "mad" poets and other radically dissenting
personalities, William Blake is that figure. Indeed, within the historical period
I wish to treat here (American artistic and intellectual culture of the 1950s and
1960s), Will Blake approaches the status of a kind of patron saint of all such
ignored but prophetic weirdos.

This "countercultural Blake" is no accident, I would suggest. And the secret
of this particular moment of popularity lies again in the nature and structure
of his antinomianism. After all, to identify with a particular social order, *any*

social order, is to guarantee one's own eventual irrelevance and historical relativity. To stand against social and religious order as such (anti-nomos), however—that is, to see the constructed and relative nature of all "common sense" or "decent" belief systems and to locate the truth of religious claims in the person rather than in the tradition—is to become perennially relevant.

Hence that wonderful bit of conversation an aging Blake had with his old friend, Crabb Robinson, in December of 1825, not long before he died: "On my asking in what light he viewed the great question concerning the Divinity of Jesus Christ," Robinson reported, "he said; 'He is the only God.' But then he added—'And so am I and so are you.'"[14] This is a perfect example of what I am calling antinomianism: the language of the nomos or religious order is adopted, but only to reverse or invert its orthodox meaning. One needs a "law," after all, before one can transgress that law. One needs a religious projection or emanation ("He is the only God") before one can withdraw the projection and return it back to its mystically inflected human source ("And so am I and so are you").

This is the countercultural or counter-coherent attraction of gnostic forms of religious thought I have explored in another context: it is the "counter-part," not the "-cultural part," that speaks to us across the centuries, crystallizes through the comparative imagination, and eventually forms into new categories like "mysticism," "gnosticism," and "esotericism." It is all too easy to dismiss such abstractions as modern constructions (for that is what they are), or to recoil against their popular pieties and common naïvetés (for there are many of both); it is not so easy, however, to dismiss their power to challenge, to counter, all hegemonic systems, including and especially our own.

Still, I fear I have already misled. I fear I have suggested that I am somehow interested here in developing another political or spiritual archaeology of the historical William Blake. This is not so. Others have done that for us with impressive, if also impressively different, results. Kathleen Raine, for example, has given us a Neoplatonic mystic uncannily learned in the Western esoteric traditions; E. P. Thompson a political radical deeply resonant with the Muggletonian faith of radical dissent and the Western antinomian traditions; Sheila Spector a master of language and myth and a mature poet of the Christian Kabbalah; and, most recently, Marsha Keith Schuchard an erotic mystic with fantastically tangled roots in Moravian sexual-spiritual vision, Swedenborgian contemplative sexuality, and even a hint of Asian Tantra.[15]

All of this work, it turns out, is relevant to my task here, but not directly so. I am, after all, not interested in the historical Blake. I am interested in how the historical Blake's Neoplatonic, antinomian, Kabbalistic and sexual-spiritual thought was picked up by American countercultural actors in the 1950s and 1960s in order to help form the antinomian base for what, by any measure, was a remarkable period of social reform, political dissent, and culture creativity, including the creation of the comparative study of religion.

From its radical literary and poetic beginnings in the late 1940s and 1950s, through its psychedelic and sexual transgressions of the 1960s and early 1970s, to its final denouement in the depoliticized spiritual longings of the New Age movement and the AIDS crisis of the 1980s and early 1990s, this counterculture was defined by any number of altered states of history that were Blakean in character and often in actual name. Epigraphs, songs, private journal entries, underground newspaper art, public book covers, and high intellectual titles: there are far too many of these to list, much less to analyze and compare. Blake in this era, it turns out, was rather like the Christ of his own little ditty, "His Seventy Disciples sent/ Against Religion & Government." That is, he was everywhere. For the sake of space, I cannot, of course, treat all Seventy Disciples, as it were. Three will have to do: Allen Ginsberg (in 1948), Aldous Huxley (in 1953–1954), and Theodore Roszak (in 1968).

A BLAKEAN POSSESSION AT COLUMBIA (1948)

In 1948, Allen Ginsberg was a twenty-two-year-old college student at Columbia University.[16] Since he was subletting an apartment from a Columbia theology student, he was also subletting a significant library of theological and philosophical books, among them many works of Western mystical literature: Blake, Yeats, John of the Cross, Plato, and Plotinus in particular. Ginsberg, it turns out, was especially drawn to Blake.

And a little masturbation. Lying in his bed, in what his biographer Michael Schumacher describes as "a sort of dull postorgasmic blankness resulting from his having read Blake's poetry while he was idly masturbating,"[17] Ginsberg stared out his window onto East Harlem and experienced a satori, or Buddhist enlightenment, event that would change his life. Specifically, he heard a voice reciting Blake's "Ah Sunflower":

Ah Sunflower! weary of time
Who counts the steps of the sun.
Seeking after that sweet golden clime
Where the traveller's journey is done.

But it was a strange voice, for although it was clearly his voice, somehow it was also just as clearly Blake's, speaking to him through the long corridors of eternity. Ginsberg's consciousness now shifted and he could, with Blake, see eternity in time, not in the famous grain of sand, but in the much larger gray Harlem sky and rooftops: "In one shudder of illumination," Schumacher writes, "Allen reached the understanding that poetry was eternal: A poet's consciousness could travel timelessly, alter perception, and speak of universal vision to anyone attaining the same level of consciousness."[18] In the poet's mind at least, Blake and Ginsberg had shared the same consciousness, mediated through the visionary poetry on the page. Words were alchemy. Texts could transform. A kind of hermeneutical union was thus effected between Ginsberg the young aspiring poet and Blake the seemingly dead visionary.

Ginsberg responded to this momentous, if utterly bizarre, event in two ways. The first thing he tried to do was communicate the experience directly to unsympathetic listeners, that is, to people who had not had similar experiences and were not particularly keen to hear about them. More specifically, Allen climbed out onto the fire escape of the apartment building, tapped on his neighbors' window, and tried to tell the two women living next door that "I've seen God!"

The women were not impressed. Frightened maybe, but definitely not impressed. They slammed the window in his face.

Next he tried to call his analyst on a public pay phone. Perhaps he would appreciate what had happened. The psychiatrist refused to accept the charges.

Ginsberg's second response was more successful. He went back to his room's theological library and began paging through other visionary texts: "I immediately rushed to Plato and read some great image in the *Phaedrus* about horses flying through the sky, and rushed over to Saint John and started reading fragments . . . and rushed to the other part of the bookshelf and picked up Plotinus about The Alone—the Plotinus I found more difficult to interpret. But I immediately doubled my thinking process, quadrupled, and I was able to read almost any text and see all sorts of divine significance in it."[19] A few days later he had a similar experience in a bookstore. He sensed that everyone in the bookstore somehow knew the same cosmic consciousness, so utterly at peace with itself, so eternal, but that they preferred to hide it from themselves so that they could go about their daily banalities. Perhaps, however, this was for the better, he reasoned, as, should they all decide to give their immediate attentions to it at once, daily life as we know it would no doubt collapse.[20]

The mystical was somehow everywhere and in everything, and yet its full force was quite incompatible with the mundane workings of social life. Put simply if also somewhat anachronistically (we are presumably dealing with eternity here, after all), Allen saw that *reality itself is countercultural,* that it cannot be easily reconciled with the practicalities of daily life. In essence, the cosmos revealed itself to him as a kind of hyperdimension that was both fundamentally antisocial and metaphysically antinomian. The young poet could hardly remain in such a state, and he saw the wisdom of letting others, and even himself, go on with their petty illusions. Still, at least the memory of such a cosmic consciousness could remain with him without too much violence.

And it did, guiding Ginsberg's poetry and art for the next fifteen years. The post-orgasmic Blakean possession, it turns out, became the origin point of his vocation as the "howling" muse and prophet of the counterculture. Indeed, it was in 1957, during the obscenity trials of Ginsberg's famous 1955 poem, *Howl,* that the image of the Beatnik was definitively born. And Ginsberg was very clear that this obscene poem was inspired by none other than William Blake: "I'd had a beatific illumination years before during which I'd heard Blake's ancient voice and saw the universe unfold in my brain," he wrote.[21] A Blakean possession in 1948 had thus led to the birth of the Beatniks, who would in turn lay much of the poetic and literary groundwork for the coming counterculture.[22]

This is all significant enough. But there is more here, I think, that deserves at least some passing comment. Allen Ginsberg, after all, was not the first great American poet who came to his genius with his hand, that is, through manual masturbation. Walt Whitman's "Song of Myself" appears to be similarly inspired. Hence what Harold Bloom has aptly called the poet's "masturbatory Muse," that is, Whitman's explicit insistence that he was inspired by autoerotic arousal: "A touch now reads me a library of knowledge in an instant," the poet claimed.[23] Bloom at least is clear that the Whitmanic "headland" is both an apt metaphor for autoerotic arousal and the originary sign of America's literary genius: "'I went myself first to the headland' is Whitman's crucial beginning as the New World's bard, however uncomfortable this may render some among us."[24] And Whitman's polyamorous, often homoerotic sexuality, of course, could not possibly be fit into any heterosexual box or "straight teaching" (*ortho-doxy*). Very much like the later Ginsberg, Whitman was one of our many "gay" American poets. Hence, again, his genius to see beyond the social order into something deeper, into something fundamentally cosmic, the transcendent witness Self beyond and within all the world's egos.

So too was Ronald Johnson, another American countercultural poet of the mystical and the erotic, again similarly indebted to Blake. In his *Radi Os*, a stunning poem constructed by taking Milton's *Paradise Lost* and deleting letters to form the poem (hence Milton's "Paradise Lost" becomes Johnson's "Radi Os"), Johnson invokes Blake's belief that Milton had entered him through his left foot (in order to inspire Blake's own *Milton*) in order to express his own belief in a similar poetic possession. The image is a familiar one by now: *Radi Os*, Johnson claims, was "the book Blake gave me (as Milton entered Blake's left foot—the first foot, that is, to leave Eden), his eyes wide open through my hand."[25]

The decent reader might object that such sexual details are entirely tangential or too speculative, or at least quite beside the point. Obviously, it is best not to try to picture such things in one's head, I mean, Allen on a Columbia couch reading Blake or Walt with his hand in some field imagining God only knows what.

I beg to differ. Profoundly, antinomially. Such contemplative sexual acts can alter consciousness in dramatic ways, and, perhaps more to the point, a homoerotic orientation must put an individual in profound and irreconcilable conflict with the normative social constructions of practically any society, almost all of which are formed around some form of procreative heterosexuality (hence the common hysterical prohibitions against entirely non-procreative masturbation). The homoerotic man or woman thus knows what it feels like to stand "against the law" (*anti-nomos*) of culture and society not abstractly, but physically, biologically, ontologically. He or she thus also possesses special gifts of transcendence, insight, and social criticism that are not easily won by those deeply embedded in the heterosexual order, by those who "do not have ears to hear." This is why, I would suggest, the ranks of intellectuals, artists, and prophetic religious figures (from Jesus to Nietzsche, as it were[26]) are filled with homoerotic figures who saw through and transgressed the social and religious orders of their day. Such was their being. They could do no other precisely because they could *be* no other. Quite literally, they did not "fit in."

No, Allen Ginsberg's homoerotic orientation and masturbatory calling are not beside the point. Nor were Walt Whitman's or Ronald Johnson's. They *are* the points.

BLAKE ON MESCALIN: ALDOUS HUXLEY'S *THE DOORS OF PERCEPTION* (1953–1954)

The coming American counterculture, of course, would need more than a single poem, however howling in its rage "against the law." And it would have it.

In the spring of 1953, shortly before Ginsberg published his "obscene" poem, the British-American writer Aldous Huxley swallowed four-tenths of a gram of mescalin in the hills above Los Angeles in the company of his wife, Maria, and under the supervision of his psychiatrist friend, Humphry Osmond. Huxley swallowed the mescaline in order to explore the mystical potential of the hallucinogen, for, as he wrote a bit later, "short of being born again as a visionary, a medium, or a musical genius," how else "can we ever visit the worlds to which, to Blake, to Swedenborg, to Johann Sebastian Bach, were home?"[27] In short, Huxley wanted to know "from the inside" those altered states of history from which the mystics, artists, and musical masters had been writing, painting, and composing their visionary works. He didn't want to write about Blake, Swedenborg, and Bach. He wanted to *be* Blake, Swedenborg, and Bach.

What the writer expected from the drug was an elaborate visionary show within the solipsistic confines of his own chemical brain. What he got instead was an apocalyptically tinged revelation of the external world and the creative genesis of a little Blakean tract, *The Doors of Perception* (1954). It was Huxley's fortieth book, written during one of the most conservative and repressive moments in American history. Eisenhower was in office, the races were violently segregated, conservative gender roles were fixed and unquestioned, and McCarthyism would dominate the political imagination of much of the decade. It was in this political and social context that Huxley penned a text that would become a true cult classic for the 1960s counterculture, inspire a generation of writers on the mystical, and provide, in the process, a catchy name for a popular rock band (The Doors).

But Huxley was not thinking about the 1960s, much less rock music, at the time. He was thinking about ancient Greek philosophy, Platonism to be exact, and medieval German Christian mysticism. Much of *The Doors of Perception*, however, concerns itself, not with any of these things per se, but with Huxley's speculations on what it all might mean. Huxley wonders in particular whether the brain's function might be primarily eliminative, filtering out every sensation and bit of information that is not important to human physical and social survival. Through mystical or psychedelic experience, however, something Huxley calls Mind at Large "seeps past the no longer watertight valve" and "all kinds of biologically useless things start to happen."[28]

Among these useless things revealed in the psychedelic state are an apocalyptic entrance into reality itself beyond the cozy symbol and linguistic sign and a subsequent indifference to human relationships and social concerns. Such mystical states, Huxley admits, cannot be reconciled with active charity and practical compassion.[29] Under the influence of mescalin, then, Huxley confesses that he knew contemplation "at its height, but not yet in its fullness."[30] In the end, a more dialectical position is needed, one that knows the ontological ground but can still insist on the integrity, even holiness, of the individual and human reason:

> But the man who comes back through the Door in the Wall will never be quite the same as the man who went out. He will be wiser but less cocksure, happier but less self-satisfied, humbler in acknowledging his ignorance yet better equipped to understand the relationship of words to things, of systematic reasoning to the unfathomable Mystery which it tries, forever vainly, to comprehend.[31]

Huxley, in other words, recognized very early that the altered states of mescalin could be both mystically profound *and* morally wanting. He understood that the psychedelic is not the ethical, and he was wise enough to make room for both human concerns in his broad humane worldview. Rather like Ginsberg's insight in the bookstore, Huxley came to understand that the metaphysical revelations of mescalin cannot be easily reconciled with the mundane workings of the world, that is, that there was something fundamentally antisocial about the room into which the doors of perception now opened. He would extend these concerns and articulate them again in a second Blakean tract two years later entitled *Heaven and Hell*, again obviously indebted to Blake's *The Marriage of Heaven and Hell*.

Two iconic figures are worth mentioning in this same psychedelic context: the Harvard psychologist (Richard Alpert) turned Hindu guru, Ram Dass, and the comparativist of religion, Huston Smith. Dass recounts the following experience at the beginning of his countercultural classic, *Be Here Now*:

> At one point I had been in the meditation room in the community house we had in Newton, and I was for four hours in a state of total homogeneous light, bliss, and then I recall starting to "come down" and this huge red wave rolled in across the room. It looked like a cross between a William Blake (that picture of the wave) sketch and a Hieronymous Bosch painting, and it was all my identities, all rolling in over me. I remember holding up my hand and saying, "NO! NO, I don't want to go back." It was like this heavy burden I was going to take on myself. . . . "Oh, here I am again—Richard Alpert—what a drag!"[32]

Once again, the Blakean antinomian revelation is catalyzed by a psychedelic substance and set directly against the socialized ego. It is a drag to be a little self with a little name.

Ram Dass was an eloquent voice in the counterculture, but he was not a trained philosopher, nor was he particularly fluent in the world's metaphysical systems. Huston Smith, however, was both. Hence the importance of his session report of his first mescaline experience (on New Year's Day, 1961) under the auspices of Timothy Leary and the Center for Personality Research at Harvard University. Not surprisingly, this little report became something of a key text in the underground American mystical tradition that quickly developed around these sacred substances. Smith, for example, reprinted this same session report to lead off his recent *Cleansing the Doors of Perception* (yet another obvious Blakean moment in the history I am recounting here).

The session report's value for us lies in its keen awareness of a kind of metaphysical horror that was also stunningly meaningful. "The world into which I was ushered," Smith wrote, "was strange, weird, uncanny, significant, and terrifying beyond belief." Much like Huxley before him, Smith gathered from this multidimensional state of consciousness that the conscious mind "screens out" most of reality and smelts "the remainder down into a single band we can cope with." The brain's primary function, then, is to be a filter, that is, to *protect* us from the full brunt of reality and our own cosmic consciousness. We are back to Ginsberg's bookstore. For his own part, Smith traces this epistemology back to Henri Bergson's notion of the brain "as a reducing valve."

But it was Rudolf Otto's notion of the sacred as a *mysterium tremendum et fascinans*, that is, a mystical order at once terrifying and fascinating, that spoke to him the most clearly and accurately. "It should not be assumed from what I have written that the experience was pleasurable. The accurate words are significance and terror." Hence he warned Leary afterward about the mortal dangers of such states. People, he insisted, really and truly can be scared to death. He, at least, felt like he had barely survived the experience.[33]

It is important to note that Huston Smith did not employ a category like antinomianism to explicate his experience, and indeed, many of his concerns were moral ones surrounding the issues of cultural and religious pluralism. It is also important to note that Smith's comparativism has generally been uncomfortable—and that is probably an understatement—with many of the hermeneutics of suspicion that have driven the Chicago school of the history of religions. For example, he strenuously resisted my own use of psychoanalytic categories to understand the life and teachings of Ramakrishna.[34] Still, it is not difficult to see in his first mescaline experience the lineaments of an empirical metaphysics that is profoundly, terrifyingly, "against the law" (*antinomos*), at least in the sense that it ushered him into a hyperdimensional order of consciousness against whose terror the social order (not to mention the human brain) is designed, precisely, to protect us. Suspend the filter of the human brain, and you suspend the *nomos* of human society.

And soon enough, of course, the sacramental substances through which figures like Huxley, Alpert, Leary, and Smith entered these antinomial realms would be literally, legally, against the law. Leary—who also, of course, loved Blake ("Take it [LSD] yourself and read Blake," his old friend, Frank Barron, had counseled him[35])—would pay the dearest for this coming criminality. Indeed, he would spend much of his life in prison for his brash, beautiful, outrageous, foolish, sincere attempts to pit reality against society.

Reality always loses those battles. The filter always falls back into place. It has to. How else could we go on in our bookstores?

ANTINOMIAN ASIA AND THE MAKING
OF THE COUNTERCULTURE (1968)

In Blake's mind, at least, those now famous doors of perception would finally be opened not by some Mexican mushroom, but "by an improvement of sensual enjoyment." This was Blakean code for a kind of metaphysically grounded eroticism, an eros as mysticism, if you will (or even if you won't). This, it must be admitted, was not Huxley's (or Smith's) strong point. Indeed, Huxley explicitly warned Timothy Leary "not to let the sexual cat out of the bag," that is, not to reveal in his published writings the fact that LSD often fantastically magnifies sexual pleasure and effectively mythologizes the erotic into unbelievable forms and heights (Leary, by the way, spectacularly ignored this advice, giving a very famous *Playboy* interview on this very subject playfully titled, I kid you not, "She Comes in Colors"[36]). Moreover, Huxley's ascetically tinged Advaita Vedanta—which tended to see the phenomenal world in illusory terms and so privileged ascetic lifestyles and models of sanctity—worked directly against this same sexual cat, indeed tended to deny its very existence.

But Huxley was a complex and learned man whose knowledge of Asian religions extended well beyond the abstract metaphysics of Advaita Vedanta. Thus when he imagined his own utopia called Pala in *Island* (1962) toward the very end of his life, this utopian island looked much more like a Tantric commune than a Vedantic monastery. The Palanians, after all, consumed a

psychedelic drug called "Moksha" (the normative Sanskrit word for "liberation" or "release" from the karmic cycle of birth and death) and engaged in
sexual practices that looked remarkably like those Huxley would have encountered in the literature on Hindu and Buddhist Tantra. Indeed, the Palanians even used another Sanskrit word for their contemplative sexual practices,
maithuna (literally, "sexual intercourse"), taken directly from the famous Five
M's of Indian Tantra, that is, those five antinomian acts or transgressive substances (meat, fish, wine, parched grain and sexual intercourse, all beginning
with "M" in the Sanskrit) that constituted the sacramental heart of many forms
of Indian Tantric ritual, at least those reported in the scholarship of the time.

This, no doubt, was the "fictional" or Palanian context in which Huxley introduced Timothy Leary to Tantra in a letter dated February 2, 1962—probably one
of the definitive entry points of the term into the coming (in colors) American
counterculture. In this letter, Huxley suggested to Leary that Tantra's paradoxical,
Zen-like ideal of "enlightenment within the world of everyday experience" was
"the highest possible ideal," in the sense that it sought awareness "on every level
from the physiological to the spiritual." More practically, he encouraged Leary to
read Indological and Buddhological scholarship, specifically Sir John Woodroffe
(the Calcutta High Court judge and early pioneer of Tantric studies, most all of
whose Sanskrit translations were actually ghost-translated by a Bengali pundit
named Atul Behari Ghosh[37]), Heinrich Zimmer (whose influential chapter on
Tantra in *Philosophies of India* was actually written by Joseph Campbell), Mircea
Eliade, and Edward Conze.[38]

Leary and, through him, a whole host of other writers and enthusiasts would
run with such advice. In other words, the groundwork of at least this dimension of the counterculture was laid by our own Indological and Buddhological
ancestors. As a result, much of the psychedelia of the 1960s was heavily eroticized precisely along Tantric lines. Blake's "improvement of sensual enjoyment" was back, now in "new" Asian-inflected forms whose antinomian and
transgressive implications merged nicely with the Western antinomian tradition of the Ginsbergian Beatniks and Huxley's mescaline-inspired Blakean
Bible.[39] It was the "countering" or antinomianism of the Tantric traditions, of
course, that allowed them to speak so deeply to the counterings of the Beatniks and the psychedelics.

One of the first persons who noticed both the heavily eroticized nature
of the 1960s and the shift in American fascinations with Asian religion from
ascetic traditions like Advaita Vedanta to eroticized or complexly antinomian
ones like Zen Buddhism and Hindu Tantra was the American historian who

brought the term "counter culture" (first, as two separate words) into broad public use in 1968: Theodore Roszak.[40] Here is what Roszak had to say about the counterculture's appropriation of Asian religion:

> The amorality of Zen, as one might imagine, was rapidly given special emphasis where sex was concerned. And in this respect, the latest European-American journey to the East *is* a new departure. The Vedantism of the twenties and thirties had always been severely contemplative in the most ascetic sense of the term. One always has the feeling in looking through its literature that its following was found among the very old or very withered, for whom the ideal swami was a kindly orientalized version of an Irish Jesuit priest in charge of a pleasant retreat. . . . But the mysteries of the Orient we now have on hand in the counter culture have broken entirely from this earlier Christianized interpretation. In fact, nothing is so striking about the new orientalism as its highly sexed flavor. If there was anything Kerouac and his colleagues [the Beat poets] found especially appealing in Zen they adopted, it was the wealth of hyperbolic eroticism the religion brought with it rather indiscriminately from the *Kama-sutra* and the tantric tradition.[41]

Such a counterculture was not simply youthful, orientalized, and eroticized, as Roszak explicitly argued, however. It was also, as Roszak implicitly suggested, fundamentally Blakean. This is already signaled by the textual fact that Roszak's *The Making of a Counter Culture* begins and ends, quite literally, with William Blake. Roszak, in other words, was inspired to create what were essentially Blakean bookends for the text that would effectively introduce the term "counterculture" into the English language.

The book thus begins with a Blakean epigraph on "the New Age"[42]: "Rouse up, O Young Men of the New Age! Set your foreheads against the ignorant Hirelings! For we have Hirelings in the Camp, the Court & the University, who would, if they could, ever depress Mental & prolong Corporeal War." And it concludes with a very Blakean chapter entitled "Eyes of Flesh, Eyes of Fire," which begins with this question: "What are we to say of the man who fixes his eye on the sun and does not see the sun, but sees instead a chorus of flaming seraphim announcing the glory of God?"[43]

Roszak dismisses the usual reductive, literary, and historical answers: the man was mad; he was a poet gifted with the lyrical turn of phrase; he was a religious eccentric influenced by the writings of Swedenborg, and so on. No such reductive rationalisms or strictly historical explanations will do for Roszak, who saw that what drove both Blake and the American counterculture could not, finally, be reduced to the technocratic and rationalist terms of modern society, that is, to the "Eyes of Flesh." No, these were "Eyes of Fire" that were finally seeing something completely different, that is, a mystical re-visioning of reality itself, a utopia, an eschaton, a gnosis beyond both the faith of the churches and the reason of technocratic modernity:

> This, so I have argued, is the primary project of our counter culture: to proclaim a new heaven and a new earth so vast, so marvelous that the inordinate claims of technical expertise must of necessity withdraw in the presence of such splendor to a subordinate and marginal status in the lives of men. To create and broadcast such a consciousness of life entails nothing less than the willingness to open ourselves to the visionary imagination on its own demanding terms. We must be prepared to entertain the astonishing claim men like Blake lay before us: that here are eyes which see the world not as commonplace sight or scientific scrutiny sees it, but see it transformed, made lustrous beyond measure, and in seeing the world so, see it as it really is.[44]

Certainly much of modern critical theory—and particularly that applied to religion and sexuality—is a rationalized expression or cultural sublimation of this same visionary imagination, of this same countercultural mysticism. Hence it is probably no accident that race, class, and gender have come to define the study of the humanities and particularly the study of religion. These, after all, were precisely the concerns and passions of the American counterculture. To the extent, then, that we still place these concerns and passions at the heart of our scholarship and political life, we still inhabit what is essentially a countercultural state of consciousness. We have transmitted something of Blake into the present. We have conjured Orc and have engaged in intellectual battle with Urizen. We have become Blake.

* * * * *

It was in this way—through masturbation and poetic possession, mescalin and psychedelic vision, Asian religion and a modern Tantric imagination—that the American counterculture translated Blake into some specifically contemporary forms of consciousness and energy, including at least some of us. Whether this was a faithful translation of the historical William Blake is not for me to say, at least with any final certainty. If, however, Marsha Keith Schuchard is correct about eighteenth-century Asian diffusions into European culture, about their

fusion with Christian Kabbalah, and about their subsequent impact on the esoteric cultivation of erotic trance in Zinzendorf, Swedenborg, and Blake—and
I suspect that she is correct, if not in every speculative detail, then certainly
in her overall argument about "the sexual basis of spiritual vision"—then what
the American counterculture accomplished in the second half of the twentieth
century was quite remarkable. It somehow already knew, unconsciously, gnostically, what the historical scholarship is only getting around to now via reason
and archival work. It knew that sex is one of the deepest secrets of religion, and
that to alter the sexual body is to alter the social body.

As a whole, that Blakean moment called the counterculture constitutes one
immense cultural argument about the linking of political oppression and sexual
repression ("Make love, not war"), about the ethical centrality of race, class, gender, and sexual orientation in any liberal society, about the beauty and power of
cultural pluralism, and, yes, about the sexual basis of spiritual vision. What the
era did, essentially, was resurrect William Blake. Its bad trips and human trag-
edies were many, and it finally lost much of its political and ethical radicalism
in what became the New Age movement—let us admit as much. But its deepest
intuitions, its gnosis, its eroticization of the spiritual life, and the New Age's
refusal to submit to any single tradition or jealous god, appears to have been,
let us also admit it, an eerily accurate resurrection of Blake's spirit and art. Thus
Will Blake lived again among us, if only for a moment.

Oh, were we to have him back again now. Perhaps, though, we do have him
back again, somewhere, in the words we write, the stories we tell, and the images we so lovingly put in our books. That is my hope anyway. May we be Blake.

2017 AFTERWORD

Two stories are worth telling here, as they both involve Wendy and both function nicely as transitions into our next chapter and the paranormal subjects
of part 2. One took place at the Esalen Institute, the topic of our next chapter
and the epicenter of the second half of my corpus. The second took place in
Jerusalem and Chicago but was told to me by Wendy when we were in Big Sur
together.

The first story played out the week of June 1–6, 2007.[45] I had invited Wendy
to an Esalen symposium entitled "From the Supernormal to the Superpower."
Most of the participants there were from the comic book or film industries.
Some, however, were involved in various psychical or parapsychological projects, including Dean Radin, the well-known parapsychologist and head scientist

at IONS, the Institute of Noetic Sciences in Petaluma, California, founded by the Apollo 14 astronaut Edgar Mitchell, who was deeply committed to parapsychological research and all sorts of paranormal topics, including the UFO and abduction phenomena.

Dean showed us an eerie film clip that was typical of the conversations and that brought the two main topics that week (science fiction and the paranormal) together in one story. It was an interview with actor Alec Guinness, who played Obi-Wan Kenobi in *Star Wars*. Guiness told the story of how he met actor James Dean at a restaurant in 1955 and warned him, just out of the blue and with no forethought, not to get into his new sports car lest he be dead within a week. Dean got in, of course. He was killed in the same shiny sports car exactly a week later.

Also present was Russell Targ, the laser physicist who led one of the remote viewing programs for the US intelligence community in the 1970s with fellow physicist Hal Puthoff. I have written about remote viewing elsewhere.[46] Remote viewing is essentially an attempt to operationalize and technologize what used to be called clairvoyance for intelligence gathering purposes. Many have called it "psychic espionage," and that is not inaccurate. Russell—a gentle man of impressive height, bottle-thick glasses (he is nearly blind), sparkling humor, and an unwavering conviction in the superpowers of the human mind and spirit—gave us a demonstration of how remote viewing works.

He had hid an object in a brief case before the event. He gave us the most basic protocol for how to remote view it. We all did this together. Only one of us drew the object, which turned out to be an aluminum apple corer: Wendy. It was difficult to deny. What she drew looked pretty much exactly like the apple corer. She was very happy about that. So was I. (I drew something that looked like Flash Gordon's ray gun, or a penis. Typical.)

The impossible conversations sparked something in us, as it so often does at these Esalen symposia. Wendy told me a related story, this one about her beloved dog Bill. She was in Jerusalem on a lecture circuit when she had a disturbing dream about Bill, whose paw had been cut off in the dream. Upset, the next morning she called a graduate student who was watching Wendy's home for her and, of course, Bill as well. The student confirmed her concerns. Bill had accidentally shut himself in the kitchen pantry. He had tried to claw his way out under the door and in the process had seriously cut his paw. The graduate student had already taken him to the veterinarian for stiches.

Wendy had no trouble at all with admitting the obvious, namely, that she had somehow "dreamed" the truth (or something very, very close to the truth), thousands of miles away. Her deep bond with animals, in this case a beloved human dog, is also apparent in the story. And why not admit the obvious? The clairvoyant dream fit perfectly with her earlier mind-bending writing on uncanny shared dreams, nested realities, dreams that come true, and the complex metaphysics of illusion (*maya*) and the deeper nature of consciousness (*atman*) and its identity with the cosmos (*brahman*) in Hindu mythological and philosophical thought.[47]

Which brings us to part 2. . . .

Mysticum

The vague and fleeting intuition with which a writer on religions often begins first appears to me, at least, as an unidentified flying object hovering about my materials: a UFO, for short. As a glimmering origin of a piece of religiohistorical writing, this intuition appears as neither a mirror nor a lamp but has something of the properties of both. . . . It is the act of reporting on these unidentified flying objects—trying to point them out to others, to convince those around us of their existence—that may be the most crucial event in changing our own understanding of their reality. Once publicly described, they become less unidentified; as their identity becomes established, they are less liable to fly away.

DANIEL GOLD, *AESTHETICS AND ANALYSIS IN WRITING ON RELIGION*

The initial inspirations of my thinking and writing, then, were three: the psychosexual crisis of anorexia, the discovery of the unconscious within a psychoanalytically savvy monastic seminary, and the comparative erotics of mystical literature, first applied to my own Christian tradition, then to a Hindu Tantric saint, then to the Western monotheisms as a whole. Once the first crisis around the anorexia was resolved through the second psychological awakening, I could turn to the third, comparative erotics, which is what I did for two decades (roughly 1985–2005). The figure who towered over all of this was Freud, even if my own ontological leanings were anything but Freudian.

By the time I was finishing *The Serpent's Gift* toward the end of this period, I felt like I had answered to my satisfaction most of the questions with which I entered the field—those around male sexual orientation and comparative mystical literature. I felt closure. I am sure this also had something to do with the biology of middle age and the natural waning of testosterone levels, that is, I am certain my early work on the erotic was itself erotic, a sublimation of the sexual into the textual. As these natural bio-energies waned, so did my interest in this particular subject. For all of these reasons, I felt done with all of that, intellectually, spiritually, and biologically.

It was around this same time that I began turning from the study of historical traditions and figures to the study of the contemporary ones via a decades-long engagement with the California human potential movement. It was here, in the present, that I began to encounter story after story of exotic anomalous experiences, from the parapsychological to the ufological. These in turn began to change how I read my historical materials. Confronted with the exotic in my friends, readers, and acquaintances, I could no longer simply brush aside the anomalous in my historical sources as "legendary" or as "mythical accretions." I also became extremely suspicious of the oft-heard charge that so-and-so is "exoticizing" a particular historical text or recorded experience: "Uhhmm, it *is* exotic." The comparative logic was a simple one: if such-and-such exotic thing could happen in Palo Alto, California, or Yahoo, Nebraska, in the 1960s or 1970s, why on earth couldn't it have happened in first-century Palestine or nineteenth-century Calcutta? And what does *this* mean for the study of religion?

This, in a nutshell, was the "What if?" thought experiment of the second half of my published body of work (roughly 2005–2015). "Mysticum" treats this material, which, very generally speaking, has focused on the nature of consciousness as a presence and power that is not in the final analysis reducible to Enlightenment rationalisms, mechanical materialisms, neurological correlations, or even the limitations of space-time (read: history). Looking back now, I would say that I was attempting to reimagine and reenact transcendence for the study of religion. I wanted to give the discipline a vertical dimension and so "lift it off the page" from its present two-dimensional Flatland, something like Dan Gold's UFO hovering off the page that requires our hermeneutical engagement and intellectual labor to become real.

The next five books—*Esalen* (2007), *Authors of the Impossible* (2010), *Mutants and Mystics* (2011), *Comparing Religions* (2014), and *The Super Natural* (2016)—look quite different than the first three, and, in many ways, they are. For example, with all five I made a conscious effort to cross over into a broader readership, to write for more people. I had wearied of writing for fifty people in the world, twenty-five of whom hated me.

Still, I was also very aware that my mind continued to work like it had long worked, that is, dialectically or ouroborically against the dualisms of our cognitive software. Whereas I had once written to collapse the binarism of "sex and spirit," I was now writing to collapse the binarism of "mind and matter." If my first three books went after the deep-seated Western assumption (drawn from the Garden again) that "sex is sin," my next three books explored the Darwinian cosmology that, actually, "sex is selection" and, ultimately, the driver of human evolution, which—I could not shake off the intuition—appears to have something, maybe everything, to do with consciousness.

My thinking and writing were returning again and again to the same themes and ideas, no matter what I wrote about. It was as if I were a spy satellite orbiting some distant gnostic planet. I began to suspect that my choices about what to look at were hardly random or accidental. It was not so much that I was choosing the subjects. It was more that the subjects were choosing me. The Human as Two took on yet another layer of meaning: it now served as an extremely accurate description of my experience of the creative writing process. I was not writing. I was being written. By whom or what I did not know.

Somewhere around 2008 or so, I think at the encouragement of the literary critic Victoria Nelson, I read about Philip K. Dick's experience of Valis, his name for a kind of cosmic mind that beamed into him in the winter of 1974 and through whose plasmic pink light he came to understand his entire writing career as a kind of occult evolutionary practice leading up to the Valis revelation he called simply "2–3–74" (for February and March of 1974, when it shone in). My own experiences were much humbler and quieter than Dick's (thank God), but the sci-fi master gave me a new language and a new confidence through which to express my own little Valis event, as it were. I began to suspect that I had been "reprogrammed" that Night, that something very real and very knowing had been downloaded into this Midwestern townboy. I decided that the best thing I could do was let it speak. I removed as many of the self-censoring academic filters as I could. I stepped aside and let go. And why not? Whatever this presence or thing was, it was way smarter than me. And it was on a roll.

9

That Other Night

The Future of the Body and Evolutionary Esotericism

Tantric traditions resonate with contemporary cultural theories in conceiving *embodiment* as integral to human identity. They do not, however, celebrate the status quo experience of the human body. For them, rather, the ordinary experience of the body is an extremely limited and inadequate realization of much greater possibilities. . . . [One text] proclaims that all that is observable (*drisya*), that is, the universe is one's body.

DAVID PETER LAWRENCE, *THE TEACHINGS OF THE ODD-EYED ONE*

Michael Murphy, the cofounder of Esalen Institute, called me late one night in the early summer of 1998, at the very nadir of the *Kālī's Child* affair. He had just finished the last page of *Kālī's Child* in a San Rafael restaurant, armed, as he likes to tell the story, with a glass of red wine in one hand and a cell phone in another. He was ecstatic about the book, primarily for its focus on the Tantric teachings of Ramakrishna and the manner in which these expressed a panentheistic vision of the Self as divine and the material world as the energetic radiation (*shakti*) or vibratory emanation of this same transcendent Consciousness (*chit*). Here, the entire universe is indeed one's true body, as David Lawrence captures the core teaching of the Tantric traditions above.

Cosmic body or no, though, Mike was also calling very late, as it did not occur to him that there was a three-hour time difference between our two coastal time zones. I remember the call at around 11:00 in the evening, but others push it toward midnight or even later. In any case, it was late. To mythically mark the event, Mike often calls himself "Nightcaller" in our conversations, a humorous allusion to one of my favorite X-Men characters: Nightcrawler, a über-pious Catholic teleporter who happens to be blue and looks a lot like a traditional demon but is not (hey, I can relate).

If one were to measure the eventual effects of this single call during "that Other Night" on my spiritual and professional lives, the mythicization seems more than appropriate. Through that late-night call and the countless conversations that followed over the next two decades, Mike effectively pulled me out of the emotional foxhole that I was hiding in and eventually set me on a new path, one that would come to shape, really define, the second half of my body of work.

Never underestimate the power of a friend in a foxhole.

I first visited Esalen at Mike's invitation the week after Thanksgiving in 1998. Many other invitations and visits followed. A few years later, around the turn of the millennium during and just after the one-year stint at Harvard, I began to engage in a long-range historiographical project on the place and the human potential movement that it had helped birth. I would work on this project for about seven years. *Esalen* (2007) was the eventual result.

As I slowly began to realize, Esalen and the human potential movement are powerful examples of my earlier thesis that comparativism and mysticism are historically, psychologically, and philosophically linked. This is almost ridiculously obvious in the history of Esalen. Both founders (Michael Murphy and Richard Price) were inspired by Frederic Spiegelberg, a professor of comparative religion at Stanford University, whose comparativism was founded on his apophatic notion of the "religion of no religion," which was in turn inspired by his reading of Latin medieval mystical theology and a cosmic experience of his own as a young man in a wheat field (more on this below). Esalen, in short, was inspired by a professor of comparative religion whose comparativism was deeply linked to his mystical life—a perfect exemplum of my earlier theses in *Roads of Excess* and *The Serpent's Gift* about the intellectual generativity of the mystical experiences of scholars of mysticism and the apophatic and mystical roots of "comparing religions."

ESALEN BODIES

There were other previous conclusions at work in the *Esalen* project. The "body," for example, remained central to my thought, but it was now morphing, shape-shifting, mutating. The body now overflowed any and all ordinary notions of embodiment that we find in the academy or the biomedical world. The human potential literatures are replete with various esoteric notions of the body's cosmic energies, geo-spinal alignment, sensory awakening, memories "buried" in deep tissue and organs, the consciousness of cells, and, of course, the various "subtle bodies" and chakra systems of Tantric yoga that had migrated into Western culture in the twentieth century and, in turn, were transformed there—largely, it turns out, at Esalen—into their present New Age forms.[1]

To take just one example of such esoteric bodies, the Reichian "orgone"—*so* influential and *so* generative in these human potential worlds—is believed to be present in the human body, but Reich also believed it to be present in the microbiological world, the atmosphere, and even the stars. Indeed, he even saw the orgone at work in the UFO phenomenon.[2] In the end, the orgone is *cosmic*, not simply sexual or instinctual, and it is anything but a metaphor, as the libido became in classical psychoanalysis. The idea also possesses mystical roots in a transcendentally tinged sexual experience Reich had as a young soldier with an Italian peasant girl in 1916: the mystical as the erotic, or the erotic as the mystical, or just "orgone."

I did my best to treat all of these different notions, but I was especially drawn to Mike's vision of "the future of the body," mostly, I think, because of a common Tantric lineage that we both shared. My relationship to Mike and Esalen flowed directly out of *Kālī's Child* and the Tantric teachings that it attempted to describe and interpret for the contemporary reader. Mike's lifework was inspired by the Bengali spiritual teacher and philosopher Sri Aurobindo, born as Aurobindo Ghose (1872–1950). Ghose was immersed in the same Shakta Tantric streams of thinking and practice that Ramakrishna was, except that he had added Darwin and Nietzsche to the mix, utterly transforming their ideas in the process.

Indeed, as his two-volume *Record of Yoga* makes more than obvious, Aurobindo was deeply involved in various yogic practices designed to access and develop the *siddhi*s or "superpowers" of the Tantric yogic traditions: capacities known in the British psychical research tradition (with which Aurobindo was familiar) as telepathy, precognition, telekinesis, levitation, and clairvoyance. Astonishingly, Aurobindo provided *hundreds* of Sanskrit names, distinctions and nuances for each of these abilities and attempted to perfect them for himself in his Pondicherry ashram room. He also theorized them within a grand evolutionary vision and looked for a common species-wide metamorphosis that he wrote about under the banners of a descending Supermind and a coming Superman.

Mike has pursued the *siddhi*s in his own way in Big Sur and the Bay Area for over a half century now, mostly through the hosting of hundreds of symposia on topics like the physics of consciousness and the personality's potential survival of bodily death. Most of all, though, he has sought to support a community of practice that might function as a catalyst for some broader cultural acceptance, integration, and stabilization of these superpowers. Like Aurobindo recording his super practice of the *siddhis* in his ashram room, Mike is not just interested in talking or thinking about such things. He is also interested in people *doing* them.

ESALEN AND THE X-MEN

It is an interesting autobiographical fact: I tend to self-censor myself at the end of a book project, but then I inevitably use this same censored material as a kind of "seed" for the next book project. Unknowingly, I began this practice when I self-censored the original foreword to *Kālī's Child* (on that Night) but then developed it into my second book: *Roads of Excess, Palaces of Wisdom*.

The same thing happened at the very end of the *Esalen* project, this time with an appendix. I originally wrote an appendix entitled "Esalen and the X-Men: The Human Potential Movement and Superhero Comics," in which I played out the striking similarities between Michael Murphy's vision of Esalen and the mythical figure of Prof. Xavier and his private school for young mutants in *The X-Men* comic books of my youth.[3] The similarities are difficult to miss. Both figures think and live out of a vast evolutionary vision of humanity's secret supernature. Much like Prof. X, Mike has long sought out and nurtured the supernormal powers and thoughts of real-world X-Men and X-Women wherever he can find them (and invite them). The two American stories, moreover, began within a few months of each other: in late 1962 (Esalen) and early 1963 (X-Men). It was as if the West Coast was putting into actual practice what the East Coast could only imagine. An American mysticism (the Esalen Institute) and an American mythology (the Xavier Institue) answered one another, co-inciding across the country on the two opposite coasts.

Once again, I would take this text out of the book for which it was originally intended, and once again it would reappear as a new book: *Mutants and Mystics*. The original appendix became a chapter on the early esoteric roots of the X-Men mythology entitled "X-Men before Their Time." In it I observed the simple historical fact that all of the "mythical" features of the X-Men narrative were already well established as "mystical" potentials long before the 1960s. The Aurobindonian inspirations of Mike's Esalen were obvious examples, but, as we shall soon see, there were many, many others, and they stretched back all the way to the beginning of evolutionary biology in the 1850s and 1860s, and indeed well before that if we are willing to count pre-Darwinian examples. I would eventually collect these under the rubric of evolutionary esotericisms.

In 1992, Mike would publish his magnum opus on his own evolutionary esotericism: *The Future of the Body: Explorations into the Further Reaches of Human Nature.* If we wish to continue our mythical referents, this would be the central textbook used for the curriculum of the Xavier Institute. This would be the book that provides young mutants with a history, a theory, and a model of practice for their supernormal gifts. They better be willing to do some serious reading, though. It is 785 pages long. And it is technical stuff. Prominent cosmologists and evolutionary biologists are extensively engaged alongside the histories of comparative mystical literature, psychiatry and psychotherapy, religious art, fantasy literature, science fiction, meditation, creativity, psychical research and parapsychology, the extraordinary capacities of disabled people and the whole literature of savant phenomena (a kind of paranormal disability studies), hagiography, adventure, the martial arts, and sport. The book is a curriculum all to itself.

Such a "future of the body" is rooted deeply in evolutionary biology and natural history (the book emerged from decades of close conversations with professional biologists, physicists, and cosmologists at Esalen), but such a body also clearly transcends the biomedical body. In a word, the human body is *cosmicized* here. Much as we have it in the medieval and modern Tantric systems, the universe is the true body. Theologically expressed, the universe is God's body, visible nature is hidden God, and the evolutionary process is a long, multibillion-year journey of divinity "waking up" within and as an already super natural world.[4]

This, in a nutshell, was the real-world X-Men school that I set out to historically trace and describe in the *Esalen* project.

THE SECRET HISTORY OF EVOLUTION

It would take me almost a decade to begin to get some sense of the esoteric currents into which I had dipped my intellectual toes in the *Esalen* project. I am still trying to fathom those depths and follow the directions these whirling currents have taken me. What follows are some working thoughts, nothing more. More thoughts will follow in the following chapters and, no doubt, in future work, always in conversation with colleagues who have written insightfully about similar esoteric currents before me.[5] I claim no particular clarity here.

How could I? We are not even close to grasping the scope and meaning of these evolutionary esotericisms. The academic world barely acknowledges they exist at all, and when it grudgingly does so, it immediately brushes them aside as marginal and dilettantish, despite the facts that (a) they go all the way back to one of the two founders of evolutionary theory (Alfred Russel Wallace); (b) they are often written or spoken by elite scientists and are vibrantly present today among some of the most successful scientists in the world, if always in the "invisible colleges" of confidentiality and private conversation; and (c) the basic outlines of many of these evolutionary esotericisms are indistinguishable from central scientific discoveries and theories. Apparently, it is not what is being said. It is who gets to say it.

Let me give one telling example of the third pattern. Let me say that I am openly annoyed when a respectable astrophysicist like Neil deGrasse Tyson can wax poetically about "the most astounding fact," that is, his scientific vision of human nature as an expression of the fourteen-billion-year evolution of the cosmos, whereby the cosmos comes to know its own workings in and as that human subject and its science.[6] This *is* astounding. Why, then, when the same observation is made by a modern spiritual writer or evolutionary mystic is it immediately denigrated as "New Agey"? This looks to me like nothing more than pure prejudice. It is also, I dare add, very bad history.

Here is the situation. The history of science has taught us a great deal about the precedents, autobiographical contexts, and reception histories of Darwin's revolution, signaled by his two most famous texts, *The Origin of Species* (1859) and *The Descent of Man* (1871). We can now read endlessly of earlier philosophical and Romantic intutions of nature's transmutations, of Darwin's own diaries and motivations, of various nineteenth-century Evangelical resistances, of the American Scopes Trial and its cultural aftermath (still with us), of the American creationist movement of the 1980s, or of the Intelligent Design movement of the 1990s (still with us).

We now have, for example, an elegant study of how Darwin's demolition of the Adam and Eve myth opened up inebriating possibilities for other understandings of gender and human sexuality and inspired early generations of feminist thinkers to create a new Darwinian cosmology of female agency, non-essentialist models of gender and sexual desire, biological transmutations and a shared human-animal continuum. As Kimberly Hamlin has demonstrated, Darwin was no feminist, but his work made feminist visions possible in new and exciting ways, much like Freud's work did, I would add.[7] We also know a great deal about Darwin's clear stand against "polygenesis," or the doctrine that the different races are different species, his insistence on "monogenesis," or the doctrine that all human beings evolved from common ancestors, and the latter's implications for racism and the practice of slavery. We are one species, and we enslave ourselves.[8] These *moral* impulses of Darwin's thought and its reception are worth emphasizing, particularly since it is often assumed that the only social effects of Darwinism were of an ethnocentric and colonial nature, that "evolution" must somehow translate into an assumption of the superiority of European or Western culture.

While this nuanced scholarship proceeds, our public cultures continue to be mired in all the simplicities of the religion and science wars, as if our only options were the silliness of "creation science" (subsume the science into literalist religion), the straw-man of Richard Dawkin's "God delusion" (science eliminates all religion) or—only slightly more sophisticated—the schizophrenic truce of Stephen Jay Gould's "non-overlapping magisteria" (keep science and religion entirely apart, thank you very much).

What we seldom, if ever, hear about in the history of science literature or the public conversations are what I want to call *evolutionary esotericisms*. Such an expression encompasses a wide range of philosophical positions, from traditional religious faith to atheism, and a wide variety of genres, from autobiography, memoir, and poetry, to philosophy, theology, and science writing. Significantly, some of the most influential early voices were queerly gendered (I am thinking in particular of the American poet Walt Whitman, whose *Leaves of Grass* is a gorgeous expression of an evolutionary esotericism, and the British spiritual writer Edward Carpenter, who brought the phrase "cosmic consciousness" into the English language, first as "cosmical consciousness" in 1889, then as a report of a conversation with a South Indian Hindu holy man that he published in 1892[9]). It is also significant that some of the most recent voices have been professional scientists and philosophers. What defines these evolutionary esotericisms, what such writers share across the board (and so why I am grouping them together in this way), is a desire to read evolution in terms that are not strictly materialist or mechanistic. The latter position, as we will see, is also what renders these systems finally "esoteric."

Sometimes these esotericisms are the expression of some dramatic encounter with an intelligent "highly evolved" force or presence in the environment. Let us call these *esotericisms of contact*. Sometimes these esotericisms are theoretical visions about the spiritual advance of a particular individual or, much more common, the entire species. Let us call these *esotericisms of advance*. Sometimes these esotericisms are strictly theoretical or intellectual in nature and presume neither contact nor advance on the part of the author or any other historical individual. Let us call these *esotericisms of thought*. Often, of course, a particular text or author might participate in all three categories.

There is no single orthodoxy about the science-and-religion relation in such a literature. As numerous writers have commented, the borders or boundaries between science and religion are fluid and constantly shifting ones. They are not stable or particularly clear.[10] This is patently evident in the evolutionary esoteric literature, which in some ways is all about those borders and boundaries.

Certainly, the elaborate mystical theologies of Sri Aurobindo's *The Life Divine* (1914–1919) and Teilhard de Chardin's *Hymn of the Universe* (1969) are expressions of evolutionary esotericism. But so are the extraterrestrial Overlords, the Overmind they serve, the "paraphysical powers latent in mankind," and the supernormally evolved children whose "apotheosis" definitively ends the species' childhood of faith, and human history itself, in Arthur C. Clarke's sci-fi classic *Childhood's End* (1953);[11] the black monolith that mysteriously guides primate evolution in Stanley Kubrick's film adapation of another Clarke classic, *2001: A Space Odyssey* (1968), itself, by the way, inspired by Nietzsche's *Thus Spoke Zarathustra*; the playful but serious "stoned ape" theory of human evolution of Terence and Dennis McKenna in books like *True Hallucinations* (1994) and *The Brotherhood of the Screaming Abyss* (2012), whereby human consciousness first emerged when early primates consumed psychoactive mushrooms; the Kathmandu encounter of writer Grant Morrison with mercurial fifth-dimensional "antibodies" that showed him the universe "from the outside" in the "AllNow" or "Supercontext" of a "higher unfolding reality," visions and experiences that he wove right into his celebrated *The Invisibles* (1994–2000); and the predatory invisible species posited by cell biologist and atheist feminist critic Barbara Ehreneich to explain her own teenage mystical encounter in *Living With a Wild God* (2014). So are *countless* modern personal accounts of mystical, out-of-body, near-death, and abduction experiences.

Obviously, the complexity and plurality of this literature frustrates any and all stereotypes. To take just one common misunderstanding, such texts seldom engage in the kind of ethnocentric evolutionism into which they are commonly lumped and condemned. Far from leading to arrogant notions about the pinnacle of one's own culture or religion, such contacts more often lead to profound states of humility, confusion, even despair. Again and again, an encounter with a superintelligent presence forces the realization that the egoic awareness of the social present is grossly limited, a mere blip (or burp) in the cosmic scale of things. We are not "more advanced" in these views. We are stupid hairless primates, with dangerous religions, guns, and nuclear bombs on the brink of an ecological global disaster.

It is also important to understand that there were numerous precursors of such evolutionary cosmologies in the history of religions. These are never, of course, "evolutionary" in the Darwinian sense of natural selection and blind mechanism, much less in the contemporary sense of genetic mutation, but they nevertheless often resonate with these scientific models in provocative ways. As Olav Hammer has noted, reasonable interpreters have split on how to read and relate these older models of progress to the newer evolutionary ones.[12]

Consider, for example, the French theoretical physicist Basarab Nicolescu and his study of Jacob Boehme, the humble German cobbler and yarn and glove peddler before whom the "gate" of the cosmos opened one day in 1600 in the gleam of a pewter vase and blew his mind wide open with streams of information that he could not process, a noetic download that would take him twelve years to fashion into the weird form of his first mystical text, *Aurora* (1612). In the words of Joscelyn Godwin, Nicolescu's thesis is that "Boehme, through some faculty of supersensory vision, was able to behold the principle behind the creation and evolution of the cosmos."[13] This, of course, is an evolutionary reading "looking back," but its suggestive force remains in place for the physicist. For my own purposes, such a reading constitutes Nicolescu himself as a modern esoteric evolutionary visionary and, through him, Boehme.

There are other commonly cited historical precedents, including numerous Christian apocalyptic visions, like Joachim of Fiore's (1135–1202) three progressively more spiritual historical stages or Ages of the Father, Son, and Holy Spirit. But probably no precedent is more important than the ancient Neoplatonic worldview, whose central feature was an immense cosmic cycle of emanation from and return to the One. Here is one of the major sources for what Hanegraaff calls "cyclical" and "closed" models of evolutionism, since the process returns to the source of its own beginning. There is no open-ended or "linear" development here.[14] There is rather a return to an original state of perfection, which in a tradition like Neoplatonism is always present and perfect throughout the cosmic process.

We might also include here any number of transmigration beliefs toward some kind of final salvific, liberated, or enlightened state, with reincarnation now functioning as the soul's mechanism of "spiritual evolution." Historically speaking, as in the Neoplatonic case, these were almost all of the "cyclical" and "closed" type in the Asian traditions, with some kind of state of perfection posited as both telos and source. Still, reincarnation systems throughout

Asia do often possess their own developmental impulse (there *is* progress of both an ontological and cosmological sort), and rebirth ideally occurs through and across all species and life-forms, lending these systems a strange quasi-Darwinian accent.

Partly historical accident, partly theological resonance, these traditional Asian models made a dramatic entry into European culture just after Darwin, that is, in the second half of the nineteenth century with Europe's transformative encounter with Asia and the meteoric rise of movements like Spiritualism and Theosophy. Then and there, they quickly fused with general "evolutionary" sensibilities and cultural beliefs in the States and Europe, but also in Asian cultures like India.[15]

Reincarnation beliefs, it should be noted, were hardly new to the West. Transmigration had long been a standard feature of the ancient Neoplatonic systems and had also long been present in esoteric traditions like Kabbalah and some forms of Sufism, both of which were deeply indebted to Neoplatonism again. We can find evolution-like beliefs, for example, in heterodox Sufi literature, where we ecounnter the story of humanity's cosmic voyage from the simple elements into the perfect human being or realized saint, more or less as we find it in so much contemporary New Age spiritual literature. Hence the genre of Turkish Sufi poetry known as *devriyye*s, mostly penned by the poets of Alevi-Bektashi movements from the sixteenth century on.[16]

What Rebecca Stott calls "Darwin's Ghosts" or "the secret history of evolution," then, is far older and far more complex than is normally suggested.[17] These secret histories in turn possess complex, but by no means simple or direct, relationships to non-Darwinian, nonmechanistic models of evolution that have long been present but are now abundant in mainstream professional biology.

The latter models range from various contemporary observations of "convergence" in the paleontological record (the emergence of life or a particular sensory organ, like the eye, in multiple ecological and historical contexts, thereby challenging the supposed "chance" or "randomness" of evolution), to the more speculative "semiotic" or "semantic" models of Code Biology (by which cells and organisms are not simply mechanistic physico-chemical systems but are also semiotic, information-sharing organisms that work through translation, meaning, and message). We also now find serious reservations about "junk DNA" (almost certainly not junk) and very sophisticated revisionings of evolutionary theory in the light of epigenetics (the study of how environmental factors, including presumably social and religious practice, can switch on and off particular gene expressions) and the quantum biology of extraordinary natural phenomena, like the eyes and beaks of migratory birds using quantum processes to "see" and "read" the geomagnetic field in order to navigate across the globe.[18] Even in conventional science now, quantum processes are *not* restricted to the subatomic realm, as many would like to think, presumably to push back on the profound, and profoundly strange, implications of quantum theory. Quantum effects and proccess play major roles "up here" as well. I will return to this idea below in order to observe the provocative quantum-like structures of paranormal events and processes in experiencers—my own quantum-navigating birds, so to speak.

I pretend no adequate knowledge of these sciences. I invoke them to observe two things: (1) first, that the days of some simple mechanistic-materialist Darwinian model that works in a strictly linear, local, and causal fashion after old-fashioned Newtonian physics appear to be numbered; and (2) second, that the old and new vitalistic, holistic, semiotic, and quantum models are already providing experiencers and authors with new forms of plausibility and new sources of metaphor, with a new *imaginaire*, through which they have been creating new spiritual worlds. These spiritual orientations, which have been forming for about two centuries now, I want to call the new evolutionary, paraphysical, and extraterrestrial esotericisms.

WHAT'S SO SECRET, ANYWAY?

Since these three complexes will focus much of my attention moving forward from here, both in this book and in a subsequent trilogy on the same, it is important to define the substantive noun they all have in common: *esotericism*. It is also important to answer up front and immediately a single question: What makes such systems "esoteric"?

I think there are many psychological and social reasons for keeping secrets in these realms, from the simple incommunicability of anomalous experiences that other people do not and cannot share to the severe professional penalties paid by individuals who choose to step in front of the firing squad of scientific materialism. Witness the veritable heresy trial that the much admired American philosopher Thomas Nagel suffered when he published *Mind and Cosmos* in order to observe the obvious, namely, that a theory of evolution other than the neo-Darwinian materialist one is going to be necessary to explain the fact of consciousness, that is, us.[19] Such observations were immediately, and bizzarely, branded as "antiscience." Or, worse yet, they were implicitly aligned with fundamentalist design arguments and Evangelical creationism. Basically, they beat him up.

But I do not want to focus on these psychological and social reasons here. I want to home in on what I consider to be the much deeper, and much more important, cultural backstory. Such intellectual witch hunts are not new, after all. Indeed, in a previous era, a figure like Nagel may have suffered far worse. In Western intellectual history, these intellectual armies have focused their guns since the sixteenth century on categories (and people) like "paganism," "Papists" (read: Catholics), "superstition," "enthusiasm," and "mysticism" (the latter two inevitably feminized), all Protestant and Enlightenment code words for what Wouter Hanegraaff has aptly called "rejected knowledge."[20]

For Hanegraaff, whom I am following here, an esotericism is, by definition, a rejected form of knowledge. This does not mean that such a knowledge is correct or true, of course, only that its social and professional rejection mark it as "esoteric" for the purposes of writing a history of Western esotericism. Hanegraaff has also pointed to the key theological fights behind this history of rejected knowledge in the West, fights, it turns out, that bear directly on the philosophical structures of the new evolutionary, paraphysical, and extraterrestrial esotericisms. Here he has highlighted the debate between Christian models of *creation* and pagan models of *emanation*.

Creation models imply a theistic worldview and a certain distance or distinction between God and nature: God creates the world, but God is not his creation. These understandings became normative and orthodox, particularly with the establishment of the doctrine of *creatio ex nihilo*, that is, "creation from nothing," a nonbiblical expression whose purpose was to keep God and the created order distinct. If, after all, God creates the natural world "from nothing," then that natural world cannot be God. Certainly these most basic assumptions about "God" and "creation" now function as the religious common sense of most of Christian America.

Emanation models work differently. They carry a "pagan" pedigree (that is, a non-Christian origin, often traced back to Hellenistic Egypt in Late Antiquity) and a more intimate relationship between what the Neoplatonic traditions calls "the One" and the physical cosmos. Here the One does not "create" or "cause" the material cosmos. The One effortlessly "emanates" or radiates the cosmos from itself, like rays from the sun, all the while remaining transcendentally itself, entirely unaffected by such a shining. These models imply a fundamental identity between the One and the cosmos. Here, as in the Tantric traditions of

Asia with which we began this chapter, "the universe is one's body," or better, the universe is the One's body—the ultimate "secret body." These models and convictions became heretical and so "esoteric" in Western history. Nevertheless, they exerted a tremendous influence on Jewish, Christian, and Islamic mystical thought, particularly through the central figure of Plotinus and his philosophy of the One.

It is important to understand that such pagan emanation models are in turn rooted in particular claims (and no doubt incommunicable experiences) of mystical "gnosis." Here are the epistemological roots of the "rejected knowledge" of Western intellectual and theological history. Again, with a word like "gnosis," we are not referring to any form of discursive, descriptive, objective, or simply rational knowledge, nor to any Christian heresy (which is how the category of "gnosticism" formed). We are referring to what Hanegraaff has summarized as "a much broader and variegated movement or type of religiosity 'characterized by a strong emphasis on esoteric knowledge (gnosis) as the only means of salvation, which implied the return to one's origins.'"[21]

The key phrase here is "return to one's origins," since in the emanationist models the origins to which one returns are divine. To "know" in this way, then, is not only to know the divine nature; it is also to know the deeper source and origin of human nature, which emanates from and so *is* divine (recall the "flip" of gnomon 7). Here is Hanegraaff on this theological logic: "Emanationism implied that human beings could return to God by attaining direct experiential knowledge of their own divine nature, by means of 'ecstatic' states of mind, and this was clearly equivalent to the quintessential gnostic heresy of auto-salvation and deification by means of a salvational gnosis."[22]

The new evolutionary, paraphysical, and extraterrestrial esotericisms often fit Hanegraaff's model of a Western esotericism in strikingly precise ways. They often express just these kinds of gnosis and just these kinds of claims of deification. These same literatures are also obvious examples of what Hanegraaff has identified as esoteric attempts to find a middle ground or "third way" between scientific rationalism and traditional religious orthodoxy.[23] They thus point to the interplay between the histories of the natural sciences and Western esotericism.[24] Moreover, because they inevitably adopt some model of evolution that is more emanationist or transmissive than creationist or causal, they implicitly side with the Egyptian and Greek pagans against the Christian theologians, Protestant polemicists, and Enlightenment materialists. This is how and why they became "esoteric" in the first place and remain so to this day.

EVOLUTIONARY ENERGY

A single example might help here to illustrate the key issues that Hanegraaff has so precisely isolated for us, but also to observe that the evolutionary, paraphysical, and extraterrestrial esotericisms inform one another and are by no means distinct and to acknowledge how these esotericisms are not exclusively Western and are now a global phenomenon.

Consider the autobiography of the Indian civil servant and spiritual teacher Gopi Krishna (1903–1984), the countercultural classic *Kundalini: The Evolutionary Energy in Man* (1967). The book, it turns out, is introduced by none other than Frederic Spiegelberg, Michael Murphy's Stanford mentor, who links the text directly to the evolutionary philosophy of Aurobindo and what he calls "the world of Tantra."

While meditating one morning as a young man, Krishna experienced a dramatic uprush of the *kundalini*, a bio-physical-spiritual energy that in many Tantric traditions is believed to be asleep at the base of the spine, but that can be activated by a realized guru, by specific yogic practices, or by accident, as in Krishna's case (or in mine, during that Night). What is so interesting about Krishna is the way he identifies this very traditional Tantric force with "the evolutionary energy in man." Such an energy is not an abstraction or metaphor for Krishna. It is a real biochemical process that he firmly believed should be scientifically studied and someday established as the secret driving force of evolution itself. Hence his dialogues with professional scientists, including the German quantum theorist Carl von Weizsäcker. Here, in Krishna's realist understanding of a mystical-material "energy," the evolutionary and paraphysical esotericisms merge.

For Krishna, it is this same energy that drives evolution forward, that spikes in human genius, sainthood and various paranormal powers (*siddhis*), and that wreaks havoc in psychopathological states when it flows wayward or awakens in an individual who is insufficiently prepared. Perhaps most striking of all, however, are Krishna's extraordinary claims about the energy's noetic qualities, how it is coded with information and potential knowledge:

> On every occasion I am made to feel as if the observer in me, or speaking more precisely, my lustrous conscious self, is floating, with but an extremely dim idea of the corporeal frame in a vividly bright conscious plane, every fragment of which represents a boundless world of knowledge, embracing the present, past, and future, commanding all the sciences, philosophies, and arts ever

known or that will be known in the ages to come, all concentrated and contained in a point existing here and everywhere, now and always, a formless, measureless ocean of wisdom from which, drop by drop, knowledge has filtered and will continue to filter into the human brain.[25]

In light of our discussion above about creation and emanation models, it is also worth observing that Krishna's cosmology is a strongly emanationist one, even if in his Indian case such a cosmology is entirely orthodox (his is clearly indebted to Kashmiri Shaivism and its understanding of the physical cosmos as the *spanda* or "vibration" of the absolute Consciousness that is Shiva). From this same "real, interpenetrating and all-pervasive ocean," he can thus write, "the entire existence, of which my body and its surroundings were a part, poured out like radiation, as if a reflection as vast as my conception of the cosmos were thrown out upon infinity by a projector no bigger than a pinpoint, the entire intensely active and gigantic world picture dependent on the beams issuing from it."[26]

Had he somehow witnessed a film in a movie theater, Plotinus could have easily written those lines.

INTRODUCING THE ESSAY

The following essay was originally written for *The Chronicle of Higher Education* in 2007. In May of 2015, the HBO hit series "Mad Men" aired its final episode, which ended at Esalen, or at least at a place that looked and felt exactly like Esalen (the institute, it turned out, had denied them filming rights on property for a variety of practical reasons, so they went just down the road and re-created Esalen there). *The Daily Beast* contacted me for a piece on the history of the institute and why it might have served as the location for the finale. I dusted off the *Chronicle* essay, changed a dozen words to bring it up to date, and gave it to them. Here it is, more or less in that second version. It functions well as a crystallization of the much larger book and fleshes out some of the ideas discussed above, including Prof. Spiegelberg's mystical awakening in the wheat field and his subsequent comparative practice of the "religion of no religion."

Esalen

AMERICA AND THE RELIGION OF NO RELIGION

(2007)

The kingdom is inside you, and it is outside of you.

GOSPEL OF THOMAS 3

I once had the pleasure of teaching for a year at Harvard Divinity School. My office was on the same floor and just three doors down from the little chapel where the American Transcendentalist Ralph Waldo Emerson delivered his famous Divinity School Address on July 15, 1838. In this sermon, originally read to just six graduating students, their families, and faculty members, Emerson denied the unique divinity of Christ, affirmed the divinity of the "infinite Soul," and celebrated the inspiration, indeed revelation, of contemporary religious experience. He called on his listeners to "live with the privilege of the immeasurable mind" and to refuse the temptation of traditional authority: "Let me admonish you, first of all," he exhorted the graduates, "to go alone; to refuse the good models, even those which are sacred in the imagination of men, and dare to love God without mediator or veil."

Emerson was inviting his listeners and readers to move beyond "historical Christianity," an institution whose perverse mythologization of Jesus as the only divine human being and whose slavish reliance on the Bible as somehow final and complete he found particularly odious. More positively, what he wanted was a democratic, individualized form of spirituality that is fundamentally open to present and future revelations, not just past ones. The goal of the religious life for Emerson was not Christianity. It was consciousness, or what he would later call the Over-Soul. "Man is a stream whose source is hidden," he wrote in another essay. "Our being is descending into us from we know not whence."

Despite charges of impious offense, atheism, and blasphemy following Emerson's speech, his mystical humanism and transgressive individualism were never effectively silenced, and they have since had a long run in American religious history: most immediately among Emerson's own Transcendentalist circles, but also among countless individuals who have lived under the broad, generous sky of what the historian Catherine Albanese has called "metaphysical religion," that immense swath of mystical, gnostic, and esoteric traditions that encompasses everything from the early Swedenborgians, the Mesmerists, Spiritualists, Christian Scientists, and Theosophists, to the contemporary human-potential and New Age movements. There is more, it turns out, to American religious history than Evangelical fervor and denominations.

"I am spiritual but not religious." The phrase has become a well-worn platitude. It is often dismissed as superficial, vacuous, and narcissistic. In truth, it is none of these things, not necessarily anyway. It is, after all, fundamentally Emersonian and deeply American. This was brought home to me when I wrote and published a cultural history of the Esalen Institute in Big Sur, California, one of the undisputed meccas over the last six decades of the human-potential movement, the counterculture, and the American translation of Asian religions into new, democratic forms that have taken root and spread throughout American society.

When people hear mention of Esalen now, if they have heard of it at all, they often dismiss it as "New Agey"—lacking in substance and rigor at best, flaky and irrelevant at worst. But Esalen is much more than a stereotype. It holds a legitimate place in America's religious history and spiritual landscape, offering a kind of secular mysticism that is deeply conversant with democracy, religious pluralism, and modern science. In the process, Esalen has had a profound, albeit subtle and indirect, influence on American culture over the last half century. Many of the practices and ideas the institute stood for, virtually alone, at its inception in 1962—from meditation and yoga to the synthesis of evolutionary biology and theology—are now common features of public culture and discourse.

Esalen, a kind of retreat center and alternative think tank where permanent residents, visiting guests, and invited intellectuals participate in a wide variety of personal-growth programs and symposia, was founded in the fall of 1962. It was not a child of the counterculture, as is often assumed, although it did predict much that the counterculture would come to embrace. Its deepest intellectual, spiritual, and psychological roots reached back to the 1950s, in the initiatory experiences of its two founders, Michael Murphy and the late Richard Price. Both men were Stanford graduates. Both were dedicated to the contemplative practice of meditation—Murphy's more Hindu in accent, Price's more Buddhist. Both had experienced intense, life-changing events in the mid-1950s.

Murphy returned from a sixteen-month trip to India, where he had lived in the ashram of Sri Aurobindo, a psychically gifted metaphysical writer and guru. Murphy envisioned a kind of intellectual ashram where East and West, science and spirit could meet and merge. Price had suffered through a psychotic break and enlightenment experience (paradoxically woven together) that was shut down by brutal psychiatric intervention, including electroshock. He sought a kind of breakout center, a safe space where those who had been similarly abused by the medical establishment could come and be healed through a more humane integration of body, mind, and soul. These two men, in both their deep friendship and their real differences, would come to define the dynamism and debates of Esalen's culture.

Above all, though, Esalen would be about something called "the human potential." The phrase was coined as a movement in 1965 by the writer George Leonard and Michael Murphy. The terminology, though, goes back to a lecture Dick Price had heard Aldous Huxley give in 1960 about accessing latent "human potentialities" within a contemplative educational practice he had dubbed the "nonverbal humanities." Both ideas were behind Leonard and Murphy's "human potential movement." The phrase captures a broad band of ideas and practices whose basic claim is that human beings possess immense, untapped reserves of consciousness and energy that cultures have repressed in different ways but that we now can actualize and develop into a more integral vision of an evolving human supernature. Explorations in psychology, psychical research, and psychedelics dominated the institute's earliest seminars; eventually Asian religions, mind-body relations, Cold War, and now Middle Eastern citizen diplomacy, environmentalism, the food movement, and political activism all would enter the stream that became "Esalen."

Through all of this, Esalen has demonstrated a quite remarkable synergy with the broader culture and its actors. Consider, for example, what happened in the summer in 1962, just before the little institute got its start. Murphy had bought the staff copies of Abraham Maslow's just published book *Toward a Psychology of Being*, which they were discussing together as a kind of visionary reflection of their own goals. That same summer, Abe and Bertha Maslow were driving down the winding curves of Highway 1 looking for a motel, in the dark. They pulled in to Big Sur Hot Springs, the motel establishment on the cliff that would, within weeks, begin its seminar series. Abraham Maslow appeared at the front desk to check in. It was as if the staff had somehow magically conjured the psychologist through their reading and enthusiasm. Maslow was as shocked as they were, and as deeply moved. He would embrace Esalen as a model of what he was trying to say in his own writings on self-actualization, the peak experience, and the psychology of being. If Huxley gave Esalen its language of human potential, it was Abraham Maslow who taught its early founders and students how to think about actualizing those potentials.

Although Esalen was not a product of the 1960s counterculture, it emerged in tandem with it and sought to further many of its goals. Both were reactions to the fear and stunted staidness of what the writer Henry Miller had called "the air-conditioned nightmare" of American society in the 1950s. That decade's racial segregation, unquestioned gender roles, McCarthyism, conformism, and backyard bomb shelters gave way, in the 1960s, to the full bloom of the civil rights movement, the rise of feminism and gay rights, the sexual revolution, psychedelia, a creative explosion in popular music and the arts, and a widespread fascination with Asian religions. Certainly Esalen played a role, usually behind the scenes, in many of these cultural upheavals, mostly as a place where people gathered to explore, develop, and experience new ways of being, knowing, interacting, and creating. Huxley's nonverbal humanities again, with a vengeance.

The institute received its share of sensationalist media attention, especially in the late 1960s. Such attention almost always missed Esalen's deeper intellectual and religious roots, but the sensationalism was not entirely unearned. It is indeed a sensational place. The institute is perched on magnificent cliffs overlooking the Pacific Ocean, and it understands its mission as revolutionary and catalytic—nothing less than the eventual integration of consciousness and energy, soul and body, mind and matter. People of all ages come from all over the world to learn, heal, explore, chant, dance, drum, massage, and meditate, and many of them eventually find themselves bathing together in outdoor, cliff-top hot tubs in full view of the sea—swimsuits optional. A parade of colorful characters have written, talked, thought, and sang their way through the Esalen story, people like Henry Miller, Aldous Huxley, Alan Watts, Jack Kerouac, Hunter S. Thompson, Joan Baez, Fritz Perls, Ida Rolf, J. B. Rhine, and Terence McKenna (a modern-day shaman who advocated the use of psychotropic plants), to name just a few. So it is not difficult to understand the sensationalism.

But it is the activist, intellectual, and metaphysical dimensions that have struck me as both the most significant and, oddly, the least known aspects of Esalen's story. Esalen has always been a place of gnosis where the intellectual and experiential have intersected and coexisted, giving birth to new ideas and practices. Through its role as a kind of research center for human potential, Esalen played a catalytic role in gestalt and humanistic psychology in the early 1960s, educational reform in the late 1960s, the embryonic alternative-medicine movement of the early 1970s, and the development of citizen diplomacy with the Soviet Union in the late 1970s, 1980s, and 1990s. The institute has also been an active player in the environmental, conscious business, and food movements.

Esalen's diplomatic adventures in the Soviet Union comprise a particularly surprising story. In 1979, after years of excursions "behind the Iron Curtain" to explore psychical research being conducted there on telepathy and related matters, the institute's leaders attended the International Symposium on the Problem of the Unconscious, in Tbilisi, Georgia. The conference sought to address the problematic status of Freudian psychoanalysis in Russian history and culture. As it turned out, the conference functioned as a kind of cultural cover for other, alternative interests—such as sports performance and creativity studies—many of which were captured by the phrase "hidden human reserves." Of course, Esalen leaders immediately recognized this notion as a clear analogue to their own "human potential." It was precisely in these hidden and potential realms that the Esalen actors were able to engage their Russian colleagues and hosts.

In 1989, the institute, now well known among top-ranking Soviet and American officials, was chosen to sponsor Boris Yeltsin's trip to the United States. Throughout that trip, his communist stereotypes of "imperial America" fell like so many zapped flies, until they were burned to a crisp before the fruits, meats, and vegetables of a Houston grocery store and the simple answers of a random female shopper. Yeltsin's biographer, Leon Aron, tells the story of what happened. In response to his polite question, the woman told Yeltsin that she spent $170 a week of her family's $3,600 monthly income on groceries. Her answer shocked and angered him, as average Soviets were spending about 56 percent of their income on food of poor quality and limited availability—about three times what the American shopper was spending on abundant groceries of extremely high quality. Yeltsin returned the the Soviet Union, quit the Communist Party, and was standing on a tank before the Russian parliament two years later to face down an attempted regressive Communist Party takeover. He would later sign the declaration dissolving the Soviet Union.

Esalen's multiple interests and activist pursuits can all be traced back to the metaphysical commitments of its founders. Many streams fed into those commitments—too many to recount here—but one flowed directly out of academe and became a kind of preview for American culture's "I am spiritual but not religious" sensibility.

Murphy and Price both studied with Frederic Spiegelberg, a refugee from Nazi Germany who taught comparative religion and Asian religions at Stanford University. During his lectures at Stanford and elsewhere—often to immense, spellbound crowds—he advanced what he called "the religion of no religion."

That potent little phrase was based on a mystical encounter with the natural world Spiegelberg had experienced as a young theology student. He was walking in a wheat field on a bright, spring day when his consciousness suddenly shifted, and he found all of nature lit up from within by the palpable presence of what he understood to be God. He was stunned. When he later encountered a gray church on this same life-changing walk, he was horrified. How could such a boring building claim to contain the awesome, conscious, cosmic divinity he had just personally experienced in the sky, poppies, and birds? Could such a being be contained in any building, in any tradition, in any religion? From that experience came his notion of the religion of no religion, a ground of being both within and beyond all its local cultural expressions.

Spiegelberg's religion of no religion is profoundly resonant with Emerson's insistence on the individual's ability to experience the divine directly, "without mediator or veil." Spiegelberg's religion of no religion, along with Murphy and Price's own experiences of a reality that seemed to transcend what their normal senses could perceive, provoked them to create a place they hoped could change the rules of the religious game. Essentially, they wanted to reject the dogmas and literalisms of all religious systems and replace them with a deeper spirituality of transcendent consciousness and transformed flesh—an enlightenment of the body—that, like Spiegelberg's walk through the wheat, could unite God, humanity, and the natural world in a single integral vision.

The natural world was central to this vision, and Esalen fervently embraced matter and the human body as the most potent sites of mystical experience. No churches or priests are required for this democracy of the soul. This is a secular mysticism that is distinctly American because it encodes in theological form one of the core principles of the American Constitution—the separation of church and state. In America, anyone can be religious precisely because there is no official religion. The religion of no religion is not just a theological expression of one man's mystical experience, then. It is also the metaphysical ground of our constitutional and legal polity with respect to religion.

Seen in this light, "America" becomes a truly subversive mystical ideal, and thus not a surprising foundation for Esalen's iconoclastic vision. Precious few religious traditions, with the possible exceptions of groups like the Quakers and the Unitarians (that is, Emerson's lot), seem to be aware of what such an America could mean. Few realize that the deepest psychological, social, and spiritual implications of democracy are far more radical than any society—including our own—has yet realized. What sense does it make, really, to speak of the integrity of the individual, of human rights, of personal freedoms, and then obediently bow down to an imagined King, Lord, or Father in the sky? Alas, our religions appear to be more or less (mostly more) stuck in monarchical notions of hierarchical authority and patriarchal power. Put another way, our political ideals have far outstripped and embarrassingly outdated our scriptural traditions. Hence in his Divinity School address, Emerson bemoaned "this eastern monarchy of a Christianity" that dwells so noxiously, so slavishly, on the person of Jesus instead of the divinity of the one mind, of the infinite soul shared equally by all.

On some level, Esalen actors have always understood this historical mismatch or anachronism that defines so much of the modern world. They have thus offered what might be called an Emersonian spirituality, a vision of the infinite Over-Soul that is radically democratic, rooted in a much beloved nature, and profoundly committed to new revelations in the here and now. Perhaps most relevant of all is the fact that Esalen authors have turned to modern psychology and natural science to catch a glimpse of these potentials of the human spirit. Evolutionary biology, for example, has always been central to the founding vision of Michael Murphy. Evolution is not a "theory" here to debate alongside creationist fantasies. It is both a biological fact and a cosmic spiritual process through which God wakes up in and as the universe, in and as *us*.

Here, in the Esalen gnosis, we can glimpse a third option beyond the dualisms of the intelligent-design movement, where faith demands that reason fit its biblical literalisms, and the antireligious polemics of the new atheists, whose otherwise refreshing reason and justified moral concern too often slide into their own kind of troubling fundamentalism. Esalen's tertium quid or "third thing" beyond all of that certainly finds deep roots in the history of science itself. Alfred Russel Wallace, who co-proposed the theory of evolution by natural selection with Darwin, was both a great field biologist who cared little for the orthodox faith of his century and a psychical researcher who attended séances, performed mesmeric experiments on his students, and asserted the postmortem survival of our mental and spiritual natures. Jonathan Rosen, in the *New*

Yorker, quotes him as speculating that "there yet seems to be evidence of a Power which has guided the action of those [evolutionary] laws in definite directions and for special ends."

What the history of Esalen finally suggests, to me anyway, is that there are always more than two options, that we need not choose between our sexual bodies and our spiritual lives, between our heads and our hearts, between matter and metaphysical mind. Like Ralph Waldo Emerson, we can choose to be concerned about consciousness, not religion, the Over-Soul, not the religious ego. We are indeed a stream whose source is still well hidden from even our best science (and our best religion): "Our being is descending into us from we know not whence." Certainly Esalen's religion of no religion, which simultaneously affirms and denies each and every religious tradition, has given witness to this hidden source of mind and energy. Its turn to the universal and yet ever-particular evolving mind-body makes Esalen one of America's most sophisticated metaphysical expressions. Even if its consciousness has not yet become culture, even if it remains only a utopian hope or a still-unrealized potential, such a vision prophetically counters precisely that which we now suffer: religion itself.

10

The Filter Thesis

The Irreducible Nature of Mind and
the Spirit of the Humanities

The suggestion is that the function of the brain and nervous system and sense-organs is in the main *eliminative* and not productive. Each person is at each moment potentially capable of remembering all that has ever happened to him and of perceiving everything that is happening anywhere in the universe. The function of the brain and nervous system is to protect us from being overwhelmed and confused by this mass of largely useless and irrelevant knowledge. . . . An extension or modification of this type of theory seems to offer better hopes of a coherent synthesis of normal and paranormal cognition than is offered by attempts to tinker with the orthodox notion of events in the brain and nervous system *generating sense-data.*

C. D. BROAD, "THE RELEVANCE OF PSYCHICAL
RESEARCH TO PHILOSOPHY"

If God did not exist nor would I; if I did not exist nor would He.
HEGEL QUOTING MEISTER ECKHART IN *LECTURES
ON THE PHILOSOPHY OF RELIGION*

The early December day that I left Esalen on my first visit in 1998, a Harvard-trained neuroscientist named Ed Kelly drove me to the airport. My first symposium had just ended. Ed's was about to begin. Ed would become the leader of what would eventually be dubbed the Sursem group, "Sur" standing for "Big Sur" or, for some, "Survival," since the central topic of the meetings would be the scientific evidence for the personality's survival of bodily death.[1] Ed was coming from the University of Virginia, where a psychiatrist named Ian Stevenson had spent decades studying what he dubbed "CORT," or Cases of the Reincarnation Type, that is, young children who remember previous lives. Ian refused to come to Esalen himself. He considered the place too dicey, not sufficiently respectable. He sent a small team of his colleagues in his stead, one of whom was Ed's wife, Emily Williams Kelly, who had written her dissertation on the psychology of Frederic Myers, one of the key founding figures of the

British psychical research tradition to whom we will return below. Ed, as he likes to put it, was only there "to carry the bags." He was not expecting much. He could not have been more wrong. Esalen would change Ed's life. Sursem would run for roughly a decade and a half, producing two iconic volumes under Kelly's editorial leadership: *Irreducible Mind* (2007) and *Beyond Physicalism* (2015). No idea was more important to these two volumes and this Sursem group than the filter thesis. Already evident in figures like Myers, William James, Henri Bergson, and C. D. Broad, the idea's most eloquent spokesperson was probably a figure whom we have already met above: Aldous Huxley.

This is significant, as there was probably no single figure who was more intellectually influential on early Esalen than Huxley. His writings on actualizing "human potentialities" (again, he coined the expression), on "psychedelics" (another word he helped coin, this time with Humphrey Osmond in playful correspondence), and on psychical research and mesmerism (a particular fascination and practice of his) were all profoundly influential, if not actually prescient when it came to the history of Esalen and the later counterculture.

The further facts that Aldous's grandfather was T. H. Huxley, "Darwin's bulldog," one of the members of the "X Club" (a small, quasi-secret collective of intellectuals committed to pushing evolution into the public square), and the coiner of the term "agnostic," and that Aldous's brother was Julian Huxley, the cosmopolitan biologist and "evolutionary humanist" who was a friend of Teilhard de Chardin and used words like "transhumanism," only made Aldous's presence at the origins of Esalen more foundational. Here was a man of exquisite scientific pedigree who was trying to imagine and put into words a new mysticism of science. Or was it a scientific mysticism? In Aldous's own terms, he was an agnostic striving to be a gnostic, but a gnostic without any dogmas or unquestioned beliefs. If ever there was an intellectual who advanced an explicit intellectual gnosticism, it was Aldous Huxley.

THE FILTER THESIS
(OR SOMETHING GOOD ENOUGH)

Central to Huxley's vision was the filter thesis, also sometimes called the transmission or reduction thesis.[2] Basically, the filter thesis is a type of objective idealism in the sense that it posits the existence of Mind outside and independent from any brain processes. This Mind at Large, as Huxley called it, need not be personal, much less human, but it is conscious, if not superconscious, on its own level or in its own dimension.

One thinks of Eliade's references to "transconsciousness" and "absolute free-dom" in his dissertation and first book on Indian yoga. And why not? We can find inummerable analogues of the filter thesis in the history of religions, espe-cially in the Asian religions. The "Buddha nature" and *alayavijnana* or "store-house consciousness" of Mahayana Buddhism come immediately to the com-parativist's mind, as do the cosmic Self and *brahman* of the Hindu Upanishads beyond the body-brain-ego, or the Shiva/Self of Kashmiri Shaivism that ema-nates the entire physical universe as an energetic or vibratory reflection of itself. And, of course, Gopi Krishna's description above of a "formless, measure-less ocean of wisdom from which, drop by drop, knowledge has filtered and will continue to filter into the human brain" is a nearly perfect expression of the filter thesis, here in the same Shaiva code of North India.

Similar models can easily be found in the West as well. Here we encounter any number of examples of what Charles Stang has called the figure of the "di-vine double," whereby the human self or ego is, in effect, a distant function or reflection of transcendent Intellect (*nous*), and the human form is seen as an inverted plant, with its "roots" in the upper intelligible world of Mind. In these Platonic models, mind is not an emergent fragile property of brain processes, as we have it in conventional neuroscience. The truth is actually the "flip" or "reversal" of this (gnomon 7). Rather, the physical brain is the result of Mind growing, like an upside-down plant, out of its own transcendent state "down" into the material world, "as though," Plato explains in the *Timaeus*, "we are plants grown not from the earth but from heaven." Not a bad intuitive meta-phor for the rootlike structure of the neurons and their countless connections. Stang comments on this same Platonic doctrine through the prism of the *dai-mon* or divine double that guides the individual philosopher or soul: "Our kin-ship is in heaven, and we experience our *daimon* pulling us homeward, up from the very summit of our bodies. Except that our experience is upside-down: we are in fact not ascending from earth to heaven, but instead *descending*. We are inverted plants, and the *daimon*, our 'divine part' (*to theion*), is our root."[3]

These are ancient philosophical examples, but the point remains the same that Huxley was trying to make. Mind is not a function of brain. The brain is a function of Mind. The materialist has it exactly backward or, better, upside down.

Huxley was hardly alone in his enthusiasms for this idea. William James, for example, ended his life with a speculative conviction along the same lines. In a late essay entitled "A Suggestion about Mysticism," published just a few months before he died in 1910, the philosopher-psychologist asked rhetorically: "Is . . .

consciousness already there waiting to be uncovered and is it a veridical revelation of reality?"[4] In another late text, his Hibbert Lectures that became *A Pluralistic Universe*, he had already suggested the existence of a Sea of Consciousness or an Ocean of Mind from which little dribbles drip into space-time as human personalities and into which these same human egos dissolve again at death. Gopi Krishna again.

James could never quite commit to the survival of the human personality (egos in heaven), and the filter thesis clearly does not require this, but he found that positing the existence of such an objective superpersonal Mind fit well the psychical data he had struggled with for so many decades. Huxley felt the same.

The filter thesis would become a major meta-theme of the second half of my body of work, perhaps *the* meta-theme. It is now the philosophy of mind through which I speculatively and tentatively reconstruct both the dynamics of the "impossible" phenomena of the history of religions and envision a new comparativism. The filter thesis is what makes the impossible possible. It is also what allows us to compare states of consciousness across vast reaches of space-time. It goes like this:

10. The Filter Thesis. Mind exists independently of the brain, into and by which it is filtered, transmitted, reduced, particularized, and translated through all of the neurological, cognitive, linguistic, cultural, and social processes that we have identified in the humanities, sciences, and social sciences. The filter thesis does not require that we deny any of these hard-won knowledges—only that we "flip" our interpretive perspective and see these processes as reductions rather than as complete productions of consciousness.

The filter thesis is not a purely psychological or subjectivist idea. Quite the contrary, the thesis carries profound collective and physical dimensions that bear on the very nature of social being and the texture and behavior of society and, indeed, of reality itself. I will try to flag these as we proceed.

The thesis is deeply resonant with Immanuel Kant's famous philosophy of mind, particularly his ideas about the noumenal realm and how the real can only be known by us through the a priori cognitive categories of space, time and causality, that is, through phenomenal experience and the human brain. Even Kant, after all, was deeply impressed with the empirical accuracy of the clairvoyant powers of the Swedish seer Emmanuel Swedenborg (1688–1772) and said as much in his private letters, despite his politic dismissals in print.[5]

Where the filter thesis parts company with Kant—and certainly where I part company with him—is in a discomfort with his ironclad position that the nou-menal realm can *never under any circumstances* be known as such. This feels to me entirely too much like a piece of European provincialism, since so much of Hindu and Buddhist philosophy and practice is about directly knowing re-ality as it really is, the very "suchness" of things, as the Buddhists have it. And reality for these traditions is often identified with consciousness as such, be-fore and beyond all attention, sensory processing, cognitive function, or egoic contraction.

This is why I am suspicious of the Western epistemological dogma—as evi-dent in the contemporary physicalist philosophies of mind as it is in Kant—that consciousness is always consciousness *of* something, that all forms of con-sciousness are by definition "intentional." Most are, of course. All of mine cer-tainly are. But I do not know how to make any sense of the Hindu and Buddhist philosophical and contemplative traditions that I spent my early life studying (Advaita Vedanta, Shakta Tantra, Madhyamika Buddhism) without leaving the door wide open to the possibility that human beings can and do experience (or non-experience) consciousness as such before and beyond all that we think of as "human." We can be suspicious of such claims, of course, but I do not see how we can simply take these traditions off the table and dismiss their claims from our own a priori epistemological (and very Western) assumptions. Kant was Kant. He was not God. Nor is Europe or the US.

The filter thesis, at least imagined here, takes the Asian claims very seri-ously and so leaves the door open to these noumenal experiences and their gnostic truths, even if it also recognizes, and indeed emphasizes, that ordi-nary subjective experience *and* every expression or memory of a mystical or noetic event are everywhere and always filtered, reduced, particularized, en-cultured, languaged, and so on. Indeed, it goes further still. It is not just that our everday experience is filtered. Rather, it is the case that our everday selves *are* filters. As dark brains and cavernous bodies, we are not in Plato's Cave. We *are* Plato's Cave.[6]

I should finally add that, although I am not at all happy with the dualistic con-notations of these metaphors (more on this just below), I think that something like the filter thesis is true. I am not agnostic about it. I am not exactly gnostic about it either, since I have never myself directly experienced Mind at Large. But I simply do not know how else to make better sense of the comparative literature I have read and thought about for three decades, from Calcutta to California. It is simply the working model that captures the most data for me.

THE WORLD SPLITTERS

Any theory of mind is also a theory of matter and the alleged mind-matter interface. So too here. One such theory of the mind-matter relation has been slowly emerging from quantum physicists and their engagement with the history of mystical literature, depth psychology, and psi phenomena. I had been reading about these literatures since the seminary in the early 1980s, interestingly in two books whose Esalen connections and origins I later wrote about in my history of Esalen: Fritjof Capra's classic *The Tao of Physics* (1975) (after which Capra taught at Esalen) and Gary Zukav's *The Dancing Wu Li Masters* (1979) (which literally begins at an Esalen symposium). But such interests were deepened and nuanced through extensive interactions with a number of physicists at Esalen in the Sursem meetings.

Inspired by these conversations, I moved closer and closer to the metaphysical position of dual aspect monism, that is, the position that ultimate reality is neither "mental" nor "material" but somehow both and neither that then "splits off" within the sensory and cognitive systems of our ordinary perceptions to become self and world. We are not only filters and caves. We are also world splitters.

In this model, reality as such is ontologically or fundamentally "one" but epistemologically or experientially "two." This is why someone can "become one" with the cosmos in a mystical state when the reality-splitting ego temporarily collapses or disappears (since everything really is already one outside the phenomenal experience of the ego); or how one can dream about a future or distant event (since the flow of time appears to be a function of our own neurological and biological systems and not a feature of the real itself). In truth, the mental and material dimensions of the real are not really separate. They only appear so in our sensory and cognitive processes, which are designed to accomplish exactly this split.

We do not normally sense and think that oceanic vastness, then. We are but filters and reducers. We are caves. We are splitters. And so our job is to reduce the immenseness to banality and the cosmic sameness to cultural, social and individual difference. That is what we do. That is who we are as social egos, as evolved sensory systems tuned into adaptation and survival. But that is not all we are. There is another field of cosmic sociality and consciousness. There is an occulted nonlocal world in which we are already embedded, and of which we are local historical particularized expressions. The splitting we do, the splitting we *are*, is only momentary. Difference is us, for sure, but Sameness is also already and always the case.

Let me play this out a bit more. The Swiss quantum theorist Harald Atmanspacher, who was a central participant in the Sursem gatherings at Esalen, has written extensively about such dual aspect thinking in different figures, including Wolfgang Pauli, C. G. Jung, Bertrand Russell, David Bohm, and, most recently, David Chalmers.[7] His clear thought has been particularly influential on my own. Harald is an expert on the collaboration and correspondence of the depth psychologist C. G. Jung and the quantum mechanics pioneer Wolfgang Pauli. He has summarized the Pauli-Jung variant of this dual aspect monism in the form of a simple diagram that looks like this:

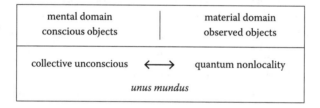

Note that, as long as we are thinking or perceiving above the horizontal historical line (there is no historical time as such below the line), the mental domain cannot be derived from (or reduced to) the material domain. Nor can the material domain be derived from (or reduced to) the mental domain. They appear to be independent. But they are not. So, although both an absolute materialism or absolute idealism give us something important, neither can ever be adequate, as each speaks to only half of our experience (and experiential splitting) of the real. Rather, both the mental and material domains are understood to have "split off" the deeper One World (*unus mundus*), which can be approached psychologically and mythically (Jung's collective unconscious) or physically and mathematically (Pauli's quantum nonlocality).

This dual aspect model, please note, is radically at variance with the metaphor of the filter (if not, I think, with the impetus or general direction of the filter model), and the two should not be equated or confused. In dual aspect monism, the horizontal line does not "filter" something greater into something less of the same quality or nature. Rather, the passage from the One World into the human mental and material domains fundamentally changes the ontological status of what is below the line into the epistemic or phenomenal aspects above the line. There is a "splitting" or "symmetry break" of reality, not a filtering of a lot into a little.

Note also that, with such a heuristic in place, one can also begin to understand and appreciate the critiques of "experience" in figures like the philosopher of religion Wayne Proudfoot and the Buddhologist Robert Sharf. Experience, of course, presumes a dual structure of subject and object "above the line," that is, an experience *of* something. Dramatic religious experiences happen all the time and are integral features of the general history of religions, of course, but they cannot, in principle, reveal the nature of the deeper strata of reality. And they can always be deconstructed as historically constructed, since every historical human subject is in fact so constructed above the line. Once one moves below the line, however, there can be no "experience" as such, since there is no longer any subject or object. We are, in effect, in the nondual logic or "emptiness" (*shunyata*) of Sharf's Madhyamika Buddhist philosophers. Or, if you prefer a Western language, we are in the realm of the apophatic mystics, "saying away" (*apo-phasis*) anything and everything that a subject can say or think about the divine as a presumed object or Other. None of this works anymore.

But if no experience above that horizontal "flat" line can fully reveal the true nature of our cosmic condition, some events might still point to or gesture toward the One World from which our ordinary phenomenal experience has split off. Indeed, we would expect exactly that. Here is where I stand in fundamental disagreement with the religious traditions that either dismiss or demean various miraculous, magical, and paranormal phenomena as somehow unrelated to the nature of reality, as distractions on the spiritual path, or, worse yet, as literally demonic. None of these judgments can hold here. Indeed, within a dual aspect monism, something like a paranormal event is no longer a shocking event. It remains extraordinary in relationship to ordinary experience, for sure, but it is still perfectly normal. In any case, it does not upend. It inspires and reveals. It is nothing more and nothing less than a mental-material event that points back to our actual cosmic condition by displaying the two aspects of the One World together, that is, within a "correspondence" or "co-incidence" that emerges from this deeper quantum substratum (or superstratum). Hence all the paradoxical "physical meanings" of paranormal events, where material objects—like flying objects in a poltergeist event or a burned lawn in a UFO encounter—function as semiotic signs or symbolic traces that signal the *relations* between the mental and material domains. If such events are squeezed into a purely materialist framework, where they appear to violate physical laws, or into a purely mental, subjective, or hallucinatory framework, where they bear no relationship to the real, they can only be misunderstood and so misread.

There are other, more traditional and more esoteric ways to say such things. For example, we could say with Jacob Boehme that no spirit (the mental realm) exists without some kind of body (the material realm), and that spirit realizes itself only through embodiment. In a dual aspect monistic world, this makes good sense.

On the simplest of levels, of course, there is something fundamentally dual about how we normally experience the world, that is, as a subject looking out onto an objective world. Hence the utter reasonableness and persuasiveness of scientific materialism and its "objectivity": this is in fact the ordinary structure of our experience *as ego filters and world splitters*. There is also something fundamentally two about, say, a dream or psychological symptom speaking to us from "the unconscious," or a religious vision or voice manifesting to us from "God." The world as we experience it *appears* to be dual in different ways (since we are always splitting it in two, both consciously and unconsciously, by our very existence), but this is actually not the case. An epistemological dualism sits perfectly well within an ontological monism. Within human experience anyway, things are "two" and "one" at the same time.

Seen in this light, my constant evocation and performance of paradox, non-duality, poetic allusion, and symbolism are not some fatuous gestures meant to confuse or impress. They are necessary and unavoidable expressions of the facts that we all normally inhabit a psychic space "split off" from the One World, and that our primitive language and cognitive systems are simply not set up to express or understand our true cosmic condition, which occasionally erupts into our lives as fantastic forms of nondual, imaginal, or paranormal experience.

WHAT "EVOLVES"?

Ideas like the filter thesis and dual aspect monism allow us, in different ways and with different nuances, to think through some of the complexities of the evolutionary esotericisms introduced in the previous chapter, and indeed of the paraphysical and extraterrestrial esotericisms that we will get to as well. If, after all, mind is fundamental to the universe and not simply a temporary function of neuronal activity in a biological organism, then such a cosmically distributed mind would become the matrix through which a minded individual organism could tap into and encounter the cosmos as an evolving living being (evolutionary esotericism), as a mathematically structured, nonlocal, timeless and potential reality populated by conscious forms of energy (paraphysical esotericism), even as a nonhuman or exoplanetary life-form (extra-terrestrial esotericism). Such a shared mental matrix would make *all* of this possible.

There are other intellectual gifts here. For example, many of the complexities of an evolutionary esotericism can be illuminated by taking up the filter thesis and asking a single question: "What evolves?" The question, like most questions, is not an innocent one. It all comes down to that word *evolves*. As is often noted, the word "evolution" was controversial from the beginning, since its Latin etymology implied not a random process but a "rolling out" or "unfolding" of something that already exists. Here are the famous last lines of *The Origin of Species*, where it appears for the first time in its modern meaning as the very last word of the epic book:

> There is grandeur in this view of life, with its several powers, having been orig-inally breathed by the Creator into a few forms or into one; and that, whilst this planet has gone circling on according to the fixed law of gravity, from so simple a beginning endless forms most beautiful and most wonderful have been, and are being evolved.[8]

What is so interesting about this passage is that it actually encodes two kinds of rollings or circlings, one living and divinely animated "breathed by the Cre-ator," and one material, even mechanical "according to the fixed law of gravity." It thus encodes, from the very beginning, the tensions between vitalism and materialism, between theism and mechanism, between creation and emana-tion that have haunted the idea of evolution from day one.

Those tensions remain. I cannot go into all of these complexities here, as they would take us far afield into present discussions on the limits of neo-Darwinian materialism, the rise of quantum biology, and the possible role of consciousness in evolution, the "new materialisms," and ancient philosophical and theological debates on the relationship between God and world, time and eternity, and his-tory and transcendence. But note again the emanation/creation divide discussed in our previous chapter. Notice in particular the differences between "what evolves" in each theological system.

In the orthodox theistic creation model, "what evolves" is the material world. The theist might understand evolution as the mechanism through which God causes and creates, but neither evolution nor its results are divine here. In the unorthodox emanationist model, on the other hand, "what evolves" is, in some very real sense, the divine, since there is no ultimate or final separation between the One and its "lower" or more "distant" emanations, vibrations, or transmissions, even if the One (at least in the ancient Greek and Indian systems) also remains entirely itself and completely unaffected by this cosmic process—another paradox or both-and, now on the grandest of scales.

With such distinctions in place, we can see quite easily that the present cultural wars around evolution have sidelined or simply ignored the esoteric emanation models (as did Darwin, as the above quote makes clear) for a battle-to-the-death between the theistic creation models and the mechanistic materialism models. And this despite the facts that (a) the word "evolution" itself seems to imply some kind of unfolding or rolling out that is much more in line with the ancient emanation models, and (b) the same nondual emanation metaphor sits in between the two exclusive options of theistic creation (a kind of dualism) and mechanistic materialism (a kind of monism) and so could act as a more satisfying mediating position were it adopted and updated. All of the "emergence" models of mind from matter seem particularly relevant here.

There are other distinctions (or warnings) to render here. Consider this. Because we are clearly in the heuristic realm of the Human as Two with the filter thesis, there are at least two ways to talk about "what evolves" within the symbolisms of contact and advance of the evolutionary esotericisms: (1) one focused on the filter, and (2) one focused on that which is filtered.

In the first approach, a focus on the filter, we might say that what "evolves" is the body-brain, that is, the neurobiotechnology that becomes more and more capable of tuning into or resonating with Mind at Large. Here the filter or transmitter "evolves" or changes, but that which is filtered or transmitted need not change or evolve at all, very much like the Plotinian One or the *chit* or transcendent Consciousness or Shiva of Kashmiri Shaivism again.

In the second approach, a focus on that which is filtered or transmitted, we might notice that, after Darwin, any human contact with a form of cosmic Mind could easily and understandably be framed as a contact with some "highly evolved" being, that is, with what was traditionally conceived as a god or God. This does not mean, of course, that this being, god, God, or Mind *has* evolved, only that it is experienced as an entirely different species or form of life that warrants, indeed that demands some language of radical advance. Here, obviously, the language of "spiritual advance" is applied metaphorically to that which initiates contact, not to the human contactee.

Such a thought experiment is obviously imperfect. Consider, after all, what would happen if we simply insert the metaphor of emanation into this same filter narrative. Here there *would be* an ontological relationship between the filter and that which is filtered, between the transmitter and that which is transmitted, since the filter or transmitter has emanated or evolved from the same source that it is now filtering or transmitting. It would be as if the world evolved a television set to pick up its own signal, or, better, as if it evolved both a television set and a signal together, since, obviously, a television set and its signal are mutually dependent. There would be no way of denying any absolute distinction here, since none has ever really existed. (We will see something like this when we get to Hegel's evolving *Geist* or Spirit below).

There are still other issues that such imperfect metaphors help us to think through. Consider, for example, how easy it would be to conflate or equate that which is coming through with that through which it is coming, that is, consider how easy it would be for a human receiver to honestly think that he or she has *become* the received. Hence what our secular psychological age likes to call the "narcissisms" or "ego inflations" of charismatic prodigies, but which we might just as well recognize as common experiences of "deification." Hence also all of the cultural and personal traumas of the North American guru traditions we looked at briefly above, many of which boil down to this single problem of confusing a teacher's ego with those transcendent forms of Mind coming through the spiritual teacher's ego.

Notice, however, how the emanation metaphor provokes us once again here. After all, if it we take it seriously, we might conclude that the human receiver *has* truly become divine in some very real sense, since he or she is now simply intensely aware of what has always been the case for everything and everyone. The radical mystic, deified guru, incarnation of God, or charismatic prodigy may be socially dysfunctional in a particular social setting (or in all of them), but this does not exclude the real possibility that such a subject is telling us the truth when he or she says, "I am God." If the emanation model is correct, we all are. Hence lines like this one from Saint Catherine of Genoa (1447–1510): "The proper centre of every one is God Himself. . . . My *Me* is God, nor do I recognize any other *Me* except my God Himself."[9]

At the end of the day, our metaphors are just metaphors. We cannot forget that. But we must also realize that it matters very much *which* metaphors we choose. I may use the filter or transmission metaphor because they help us to query our present assumptions and understand better what might be going on within a mystical or paranormal event, but this does not mean that I "believe" them. Actually, I do not believe the filter metaphor, since the metaphor remains an expression of the splitting ego. To the extent that it points to the One World before and beyond any such temporary ego split, it is provocative and useful, but nothing more.

RESTORING THE HUMANITIES
TO CONSCIOUSNESS

Something like the filter thesis and its extended cosmic mind, particularly when it is linked or applied to evolutionary forms of esotericism, invoke for many the spirit of Hegel, since the center and goal of Hegel's philosophy are an Absolute Spirit or Mind (*Geist*) evolving into its own realization through the different "forms of consciousness" (*Gestalten des Bewusstseins*) of social, political, religious, and philosophical history. Accordingly, some have detected in my writing on the filter thesis and evolutionary esotericisms a certain Hegelian current.

I understand these readings and accept them to a certain extent. I observe this with some trepidation, however, because I have read very little Hegel, but also because I know that to be called a Hegelian in any sense is a difficult thing these days. But, as the present text strives for clarification to the point of transparency and seeks to come to terms with my critics and colleagues and, indeed, with my own thought, allow me to follow this particular current here.

I think there are at least three separate issues at work: (1) Hegel's infamous understanding of cultural or social development whereby all of human thought and civilization culminates in his thought and his German culture, really his philosophy, which finds no place in my work or intentions but which, as I will explain below, I recognize as a common problematic pattern in the history of religions that, in turn, might suggest to us something important about Hegel's system; (2) Hegel's understanding of *Geist* ("Spirit" or "Mind") and how this was passed on into the German hermeneutical tradition and general humanistic milieu in which I was trained at Chicago; and, finally, (3) the deeper Hermetic or mystical roots of Hegel's thought, which, yes, extend well into the soil of my own project and its particular understanding of the history and importance of comparativism. Let me treat each of these in turn.

1. Hegelian History. I do not think that my thought or my culture, much less my nation (audible groan), is in any way the pinnacle of human thought and civilization. Indeed, as I have already pointed out above, my working assumptions about central philosophical subjects like the nature of consciousness or, as we will see below, the transtemporal complexity and fundamental plurality of human subjectivity (read: reincarnation phenomena) are far more indebted to Indian and Asian traditions than European or Western ones. Moreover, my insistence on the comparative method is fundamentally about decentering, destabilizing and denying Western provincialism, American exceptionalism, and religious nationalisms of all kinds. Period.

Having said that, it is indeed true that I do not think of cosmic history as some random meaningless process. The fundamental forces of the universe show every sign of being "rigged" for life and consciousness, and I have never encountered a mental or cultural expression that was not a product of intelligence and intention. I simply find it dishonest to deny the presence of intelligence and agency in *both* the physical *and* mental realms (and my dual aspect monism requires both, since both realms are split off from a shared superstratum).

Clearly, it is the teleological or goal-oriented implications of Hegel's thought that most offends secular intellectuals today. I do not accept his particular reading of that intention and goal (his own philosophy), but I recognize in such an outrageous claim a very old problem and very stable pattern in the history of religions, namely, the way that charismatic prodigies, heretical mystics, and deified human beings commonly conflate their own thought and person with those forms of cosmic mind that appear to be beaming through them (gnomon 10). I read Hegel, as it were, as a kind of European self-deifying philosophical guru, and as with the North American gurus of my early career, I do not confuse the mystical or philosophical genius apparent in the man with his moral and ethnocentric faults, none of which we need adopt to read and appreciate his work. I simply do not conflate the two (gnomon 4). Period.

2. *The Spirit of the Humanities.* It is Hegel's understanding of *Geist* and, subsequently, what the Germans would call the *Geisteswissenschaften*, literally, the "Sciences of Spirit" (more or less equivalent to what the English call the humanities), that are more relevant here. My training at the University of Chicago was rooted in the latter German expression. "History of Religions" is a very imperfect English translation of the German *Religionswissenschaft*, or the "Science of Religions." Rooted deeper still in the hermeneutical philosophy of Wilhelm Dilthey (1833–1911), such an intellectual project understands cultural and religious expressions to be forms of mind refracted in and through texts, art objects, religious architecture, mythical narratives, ritual systems, and so on. To seriously engage such a crystallization of consciousness is, in effect, to reactivate the form of consciousness that first encoded it.

This is precisely what Eliade meant by his phrase "creative hermeneutics." He meant a type of deep engagement with a religious text or symbolic world that brings it to life, that *awakens* the form of consciousness it encodes; he meant a kind of conjuring. This is also how I understand what we too casually and humbly call "the humanities." Here is how I have defined these forms of knowledge both in public essays and in the textbook *Comparing Religions*:

11. The Humanities Are the Study of Consciousness Coded in Culture.

Humanist intellectuals, of course, do not study consciousness directly, nor do they generally claim to know what consciousness is. They study consciousness as it is reflected and refracted in cultural artifacts, like texts, art objects, architecture, languages, ideas, rituals, and social institutions. They are never, like Plotinus, "turned around" by Athena to contemplate Mind or Intellect (*nous*) directly. They never, like Hegel, claim to know Absolute Spirit as it is. The eyeball never sees itself, not here, anyway. But that does not mean that it cannot, only that it has not in these particular historical forms of knowing.

Is this really such an outrageous suggestion? Consciousness is the fundamental ground of all that we know, or ever will know. It is the ground of *all* of the sciences, *all* of the arts, *all* of the social sciences, *all* of the humanities, indeed *all* human knowledge and experience. Moreover, as far as we can tell at the moment, this presence is entirely sui generis. It is its own thing. We know of nothing else like it in the universe, and anything we would know later we would only know in, through, and because of this same consciousness. Many today, of course, want to claim the exact opposite, namely, that consciousness is not its own thing, is reducible to warm wet tissue and brainhood. But to this day no one has come even close to showing how this might work.

Probably because it doesn't.

Still, with such autobiographical observations and philosophical convictions, I am only confessing influence and the general intellectual milieu in which I was trained. I am claiming no erudition or even remotely adequate knowledge of the Hegelian system. What I *can* observe is that I have learned my Hegel through a kind of collegial osmosis in conversation and correspondence with a contemporary Hegelian philosopher: Glenn Alexander Magee.

3. *A Hermetic Hegel.* It is Magee's specific Hermetic reading of Hegel that has most influenced my own thought. By "Hermetic," Magee means to point to all of the uncanny ways that Hegel's writings appear to point back to some direct mystical knowing of truth or gnosis that lies at the ancient Greco-Roman Egyptian roots of the West's "counter-tradition." He is thinking of texts like the *Corpus Hermeticum* and later traditions and figures like medieval German

mysticism, alchemy, Kabbalah, Jacob Boehme, Renaissance occultism, Bruno, Paracelsus, Agrippa, Rosicrucianism, German speculative pietism, and German Romanticism.

Magee isolates a single theological idea as the key to Hermetic thought, a "middle position" between theism and pantheism that he summarizes in this way: "Hermeticism is a middle position because it affirms both God's transcendence of the world and his involvement in it. God is metaphysically distinct from the world, yet God needs the world [and especially the human] to complete himself." The latter doctrine of the "circular" relationship between God and world is what makes the Hermetic position "utterly original" for Magee and what sets it apart from systems like Neoplatonsim (in which the One is unaffected by human contemplation) and ancient gnosticism (in which the physical world was often demeaned and denied).[10]

Such a Hermetic panentheism in turn is rooted in a certain "evolutionary" impulse, which goes back to the familiar figure of Jacob Boehme: "This is the core of Böhme's Hermeticism: the conception of God not as transcendent and static, existing 'outside' the world, impassive and complete, but as an active *process* unfolding within the world, within history."[11] As David Walsh puts it succinctly: "Böhme is the herald of the self-actualizing evolutionary God."[12] But, and here is the Hermetic punch, such an evolutionary God needs to "other" itself to know itself. Such a God needs a human knower to self-actualize. This is human potential language, cosmicized. This is an evolutionary panentheism before its time, deeply resonant with Michael Murphy's *Future of the Body* and my own writing on "authors of the impossible," that is, on us writing the paranormal writing us.

Obviously, with such ideas we are in the presence of another snake biting its own tail. Hegel's architectonic system is an attempt to speak this snake and so to slither into the Western tradition its own hissing counter-tradition. Mentored by Magee's writing and erudition, I now think of Hegel's philosophy as the rationalization of a massive noetic "download," rather like what Jacob Boehme "knew" instantly and completely before the gleam of the pewter vessel but then took the rest of his life to express, quite imperfectly, in mythical-mystical narratives like *Aurora* and *Six Mystical Points*; or what Philip K. Dick gnostically "knew" in the two months after the gleam of a golden necklace on a girl's neck catalyzed in him a massive revelation event, which he spent the rest of his life trying to express, quite imperfectly, in mythical-mystical narratives like *Valis* and *The Exegesis*.

This is by no means an eccentric or original suggestion. Indeed, Hegel's idealism has been consistently read by both disciples and opponents as an intellectual transformation of German mysticism and German Romanticism.[13] Cyril O'Regan has gone so far as to suggest "massive structural correspondences" between Hegel and Boehme, an observation with which Magee agrees.[14]

Again, I possess none of the Hegelian erudition of writers like Magee and O'Regan. Perhaps as a kind of compensation, I am reminded here of something William James once noted. He observed that while he was high on nitrous oxide (how or why he was on the gas he chooses not to tell us), James understood Hegel perfectly well. It all made sense. He "got it." Once he came down from the psychoactive gas, however, Hegel, alas, no longer made any sense at all.

I do not think this is just a Jamesian joke. I think there is something to this. I think that Hegel's system is a gnostic one that can only be properly understood from states of consciousness similar to those that first produced it. Given the hermeneutical understanding of the text as a form of crystallized or coded consciousness, this in fact makes good sense. None of this need imply that Hegel had a "mystical experience," as we understand that expression, but neither does it exclude the possibility. Magee certainly offers no such evidence or argument.

Still, laughing gas or no, it is certainly difficult to read Hegel and not get the sense that the rising Gothic cathedral and flying buttresses of his philosophical system are all built around some such noetic or gnostic revelation. Magee begins his *Hegel and the Hermetic Tradition* pointing out that the philosopher was not claiming to simply think about Absolute Knowledge. He bluntly claimed to *have* it. Perhaps that is why he explicitly equated "speculative" philosophy with the older "mystical" philosophies and insisted that true speculative wisdom is a kind of recollection or mirroring (*speculum*) of Absolute Spirit or absolute consciousness.[15] Indeed, as Magee points out and features on his cover, even Hegel's doodles were Hermetic.[16] Such Hermetic interests, moreover, were no passing fads or youthful excesses.[17] These Hermetic passions lasted the philosopher's entire life and intensified at the end during his years in Berlin, much as similar esoteric currents of thought became more explicit in the much later cases of Mircea Eliade at the end of his life in Chicago (with respect to the evolutionary and paraphysical esotericisms—more below) and Jacques Derrida in Paris at the end of his (with respect to the deconstructive reality of telepathic phenomena—more below).

Many of the patterns discussed in the present book—from the importance of the paranormal to the highest reaches of the filter thesis—are also present in Hegel's philosophy. Consider, for example, how Hegel conceived the three forms of Spirit or Mind (*Geist*) that he believed were progressively developing in world history: Subjective Spirit, Objective Spirit, and Absolute Spirit.

By "Subjective Spirit" Hegel meant to refer to the most basic, preconscious, even prehuman expressions of mind in the world and human nature. Very significantly, Hegel turned to a very specific type of human experiences to plumb these depths, what he called "magnetic phenomena." These included clairvoyance, precognition and premonitions, dowsing, spontaneous forms of healing, and what we would today call "remote viewing." He even recounts a case of the latter that replicates in eerie detail some of the weirdest moments of the US secret remote viewing program that I described in *Esalen*. I am thinking of the story the laser physicist Russell Targ often recounts, when Pat Price "saw" a CIA target at a swimming pool in Palo Alto not as the site stood then but as it stood in 1947, with a water tower that had long been torn down.[18] The same thing occurs in Hegel, when the philosopher recounts a particular visionary who "saw" his own street not as it was, but as it stood in an earlier era.[19] Another resonant comparison.

Hegel developed his own theories of the paranormal. Interestingly, he privileged sexuality in the production of such states, which is to say that he recognized the importance of the erotic in the paranormal: "the function exercised by the brain in the waking state of the intellectual consciousness is taken over by the reproductive system during magnetic somnambulism."[20] More fundamentally (but not unrelated), he explained such phenomena as the result of Subjective Spirit sinking into the primordial World Soul, which he thought of as a singular "natural soul" that manifests itself in an infinite multiplicity of individual souls.[21] Once the individual soul has become one with the singular World Soul, the barriers of space, time, and individuality no longer exist. Hence the utter reasonableness of clairvoyance, telepathy, and magical influence in such a transtemporal, nonlocal state of *Geist* or Spirit.

Hegel, then, like other German idealists (including Kant and Schelling), was utterly fascinated by such paranormal subjects and thought them philosophically significant. He did not idealize them, and some of his thought is deeply problematic by our present standards. Indeed, he often considered these phenomena in regressive, pathological or ethnocentric terms, with less developed peoples (like the Scottish Highlanders, Italians, or Spaniards) having more access to these more primordial or basic states of Spirit. Still, he took them very seriously, and he was completely convinced of their reality. Indeed, he went so far as to claim that his ability to theorize and explain magnetic, magical, and paranormal phenomena—all completely impossible in the fixed conceptions and causal and mechanistic categories of ordinary reason (what Hegel called the Understanding)—constituted an empirical proof of his own speculative philosophy. He was right because he could explain *this*.

After and above these forms of unconscious mind or Subjective Spirit are all of the cultural artifacts and practices of Objective Spirit, that is, all those forms of *Geist* that have taken on material reality or have been embodied in some social practice. These forms of Objective Spirit are preeminently displayed in human endeavors like law, politics, art, literature, religion, and, finally and most fully, philosophy. My own framing of the humanities as the study of consciousness coded in culture can quite comfortably be placed here, as it assumes a similar objectification or materialization of the human spirit in artifacts, texts, social institutions, and thought forms.

Thirdly, there is what Hegel called "Absolute Spirit" and its "Absolute Knowledge." Today, we might reframe such an Absolute Spirit as "consciousness as such." Hegel did: "We usually suppose that the Absolute must lie far beyond; but it is precisely what is wholly present, what we, as thinkers, always carry with us and employ, even though we have no express consciousness of it." It is the goal of Hegel's philosophy to remedy this ironic situation and effect "the liberation of absolute consciousness."[22]

Finally, there is the ultimate Hegelian, Hermetic, or hermeneutical insight: God or the Absolute becomes complete only when it is known by a Hermetic adept or gnostic intellectual, who in turn finally knows his or her own secret nature in this same God. It is in the mirror (*speculum*) of philosophical or mystical speculation that what we call "God" achieves self-awareness. This is all coded in Magee's book in the very first lines, an epigraph from Hegel's *Encyclopedia of the Philosophical Sciences*: "God is God only so far as he knows himself; his self-knowledge is, further, a self-consciousness in man and man's knowledge *of* God, which proceeds to man's self-knowledge *in* God." As Meister Eckhart put the same idea (better) in one of his mind-blowing sermon sound bites: "If I had not been, there would have been no God."[23]

At the risk of getting ahead of myself (that is, ahead of chapter 12), here, I dare add, is the ultimate quantum object that requires an observer to come into being. In these weird paradoxical moments, yes, I am a Hegelian, but I am also an Eckhartian, a Boehmian, and a Philip K. Dickian. It all depends on how far one wants to go back, or forward, within these swirling and shared esoteric currents.

And what would "the humanities" become if they were about more than just the cultural, artistic, textual, philosophical, and material expressions of Objective Spirit? What if they also ventured "down" into the magnetic or paranormal phenomena of Subjective Spirit and "up" into the mystical mirror of Absolute Spirit or consciousness as such, where the actualization of God relies on us? What then?

INTRODUCING THE ESSAY

The following piece articulates the filter thesis in Aldous Huxley's thought and how such a philosophy of mind became aligned late in his life with his understanding of the nondualisms of Buddhist and Hindu Tantra. Parts of it appeared in different forms in my history of Esalen, in an illustrated essay commissioned for *The Chronicle of Higher Education*, and finally in a volume in honor of Sudhir Kakar. I am anthologizing the core of the essay that bears directly on the discussion at hand.

An Island in Mind

ALDOUS HUXLEY AND THE NEUROTHEOLOGIAN

(2013)

> "But who are the grown-ups?"
> "Don't ask me," she answered. "That's a question for a neurotheologian."
> "Meaning what?" he asked.
> "Meaning precisely what it says. Somebody who thinks about people in terms, simultaneously, of the Clear Light of the Void and the vegetative nervous system. The grown-ups are a mixture of Mind and physiology."
>
> ALDOUS HUXLEY, *ISLAND*

AN AMERICAN PRESENT

In 2008, David Brooks, a conservative columnist for the *New York Times*, wrote an essay called "The Neural Buddhists." In it he called the still fashionable arguments about the existence of God with professional atheists like Christopher Hitchens and Richard Dawkins easy, predicting instead that the real challenge would "come from people who feel the existence of the sacred, but who think that particular religions are just cultural artifacts built on top of universal human traits." He continued: "In unexpected ways, science and mysticism are joining hands and reinforcing each other. That's bound to lead to new movements that emphasize self-transcendence but put little stock in divine law or revelation." "Divine law" and "revelation," of course, are code terms for the Western monotheisms, and his essay's title had already given away what he meant by his preferred modes of "mysticism" and "self-transcendence." He meant Buddhism. More specifically, what Brooks was referring to here was the now well-developed dialogue between Buddhists and neuroscientists around the nature of consciousness, its relationship to brain processes, and whether human beings can have some access to the real outside the assumed parameters of scientific materialism and mechanism.

I will leave aside for the moment the problems and promises I see in the latter dialogue. I will also leave aside—after bitterly complaining about it for a few sentences—Brooks's apparent ignorance of the professional study of religion in its rich historical, textual-critical, anthropological, and psychological modes, which created the very category of "mysticism" and most of which has been organized for two centuries now around the working thesis that "particular religions are just cultural artifacts built on top of universal traits." Certainly the latter phrase can also be accepted, with little or no tweaking, as the base assumption of classical psychoanalytic models of religion and culture. The neural Buddhists, then, are in historical fact very late to the game and are simply the latest players in a centuries-long inquiry, and what struck Brooks as a shocking "unexpected" thesis is in fact a well-established consensus, and has been so for a very long time.

Professional self-esteem wounds aside, Brooks is an expert and reliable purveyor of American culture and politics, and he is onto something here. He has correctly identified and named an increasingly strong current within American religious thought. His phrase "neural Buddhists," after all, calls up a long history of debates and discussions around the nature of mind in the mirror of comparative mystical literature and—never to be underestimated—the actual mystical experiences of the researchers and writers themselves. Such discussions, moreover, are part of a much broader interest in what we have come to call the "spiritual" (as distinguished from the "religious") or, in a slightly different register, what Brooks calls "mysticism." Significantly, the modern resonances of both of those terms—spirituality and mysticism—arose in the middle of the nineteenth century at more or less the exact moment that science, in the form of an ascending Darwinism, was first seriously challenging institutional religion. One of the first distinctions between the religious and the spiritual, for example, can be found in Ralph Waldo Emerson's early essays, after which it blooms in Walt Whitman's ecstatic poem-prophecy *Leaves of Grass* (1855) and eventually finds a very explicit expression in *Democratic Vistas* (1871).[24] Similarly, "mysticism" was invoked by Emerson as early as the 1830s, but it did not really come into positive use until the first decades of the twentieth century, after the seminal work of the American philosopher and psychologist William James, on the academic front, and the British writer and Anglican spiritual director Evelyn Underhill, on the religious. The categories, in short, were created and honed by intellectuals for radically liberal visionary, intellectual, and ecumenical projects.

LOOKING BACK . . .

These were the projects inherited by Aldous Huxley (1894–1963). Huxley was an iconic literary figure who embodied many of the tensions of our contemporary intellectual scene, particularly those orbiting around those warring twin Titans, science and religion. On the scientific side, Aldous's older brother was Julian Huxley, a well-known evolutionary biologist, science activist, and ecological visionary. Julian and Aldous were the grandsons of Thomas Henry Huxley, the biologist, great English defender of Charles Darwin, and the man who coined the word "agnosticism." Other than Darwin himself, T. H. Huxley probably did more than anyone else to lay the cultural foundation for our present scientific worldview. The results, as is well known but not always admitted, were devastating for traditional religious belief in the West. W. H. Mallock captured the tone in 1878: "It is said that in tropical forests one can almost hear the vegetation growing," he wrote. "One may almost say that with us one can hear faith decaying."[25] One can only guess what Mallock would say now.

This kind of high-minded dismissal of human idealism and belief is evident in Huxley's most famous and oft-read novel, *Brave New World* (1931). The story revolves around a future civilization that produces happiness through a regime of high biotechnology in which humans are genetically engineered in test tubes on a conveyor belt and then socialized into a rigid caste system. The regime includes abolition of the nuclear family, establishment of a free sexuality decoupled from procreation, a systematic hatred of nature, and a constant government supply of "soma tablets"—named after the mysterious ambrosia of ancient Indian Vedic seers—that deliver mindless happiness or, in higher doses, sound sleep. Motherhood is obscene in this brave new world, and all genuine individuality is socialized away. The novel depicts a scientifically savvy but superficial monoculture that accomplishes its day-to-day tasks through social stratification, the systematic suppression of individualism, and an unlimited supply of free sex and drugs. Constant distraction makes the system work.

Huxley's vision would not remain rooted in this kind of pessimism, however. Inspired by comparative mystical literature and his discussions with two friends, the writer-philosopher Gerald Heard and Swami Prabhavananda of the Hollywood Vedanta Society, he would move on to a much brighter and deeper worldview. Huxley outlined the basic features of his new worldview in his *The Perennial Philosophy* (1945), which appeared just as World War II was ending. His minimum working hypothesis, as he called it, involved positing four basic theses: (1) the existence of a divine ground of being that is (2) both immanent to and transcendent from the physical world of phenomenal and sensory experience; (3) the claim that human beings are ontologically connected to this ground of being and so can know it experientially and directly as the "Supreme Identity" of the human condition; and (4) the moral position that the ultimate purpose of human life is to know reality in this way so that, once aligned and grounded with it, humanity can find personal and social peace.

His primary inspiration, at least early on, seems to have been Advaita Vedanta, a classical Indian nondual philosophy that, historically speaking, was rooted in Indian asceticism and monasticism. Strongly idealist in orientation (with ultimate reality defined as "being, consciousness, and bliss" and the phenomenal material world framed as a paradoxically existent-but-nonexistent *maya* or "illusion"), Advaita Vedanta captured the attention of European intellectuals trained in German idealism in the nineteenth century. It also captured much of elite Hindu thought and practice in the same century and subsequently heavily influenced the reception of Hinduism among American intellectuals and artists in the first half of the twentieth through figures like Swami Vivekananda and, later, Swami Prabhavananda. Huxley was one of these intellectuals. Like many before and after him, he took the basic metaphysical insights of Advaita Vedanta but left behind or politely ignored the cultural artifacts of its original Indian institutions and cultic expressions, which he obviously considered relative and nonessential.[26]

What is almost always overlooked is the fact that Huxley would move on from this early Advaita-inspired, vaguely ascetic worldview as well. Indeed, his worldview in 1963, the year he died, was radically different from his worldview in 1945, when he published *The Perennial Philosophy*. There were many influences here. Huxley became profoundly interested, for example, in psychical research. The botanist turned parapsychologist J. B. Rhine of Duke University was a good friend, as was the Irish superpsychic Eileen Garrett. Huxley was also intensely interested in animal magnetism and Mesmerism, which he would sometimes practice at home, even on an occasional baffled guest; in various alternative therapeutic practices, which he was driven to because he was half-blind; and, perhaps most famously, in the spiritual potentials of mind-altering plants and drugs. In the latter interest, Huxley remains to this day an unquestioned and much revered pioneer. His correspondence with his psychiatrist friend Humphrey Osmond, for example, produced the English neologism "psychedelic" (literally, "mind-manifesting"), and he wrote one of the earliest, and probably still the finest, pieces of literature on the mind-manifesting potentials of psychotropic plants and chemicals—that beautiful little Blakean book *The Doors of Perception* (1954).

It must be remembered that in 1954 substances like mescaline and LSD were not legally prohibited. The challenges they posed were theological, not social. Basically, the question was this: How can what looks very much like a genuine experience of the divine be caused by a little mushroom or, worse yet, a man-made chemical originally designed to address menstrual bleeding? Huxley's answer was as simple as it was provocative: the mushroom or chemical does not cause the experience of God; it suppresses and messes with brain function to the extent that mystical forms of mind, which are always present, always "there," can get into the brain and so manifest as a human experience. More precisely, something like mescaline, Huxley speculated, could suppress the brain's "filter," thus allowing what he called "Mind at Large" to bleed through into the individual's experience. Most succinctly put, psychotropic substances do not cause Mind at Large; they allow us to become aware of it; *they let it in.* In this way, Huxley sought to explain how the mystical states so often reported during psychedelic sessions could be related to their obvious chemical catalysts in an associative but noncausal way. It was a brilliant move.

But not an original one. He inherited this model directly from the psychical research tradition, and more specifically, from the British psychical researcher Frederic Myers, William James, the French Nobel Laureate Henri Bergson, and the British philosopher C. D. Broad. Drawing on such men, Huxley consistently argued that consciousness was filtered and translated by the brain through incredibly complex neurophysiological, linguistic, psychological, and cultural processes, but not finally produced by it. We are, *of course,* cultural egos, conditioned historical actors, socialized persons, and neurological robots. But we are also something else, something More, as James had suggested in *The Varieties of Religious Experience.* In the end, Huxley suggested in so many ways, we are not who we think we are. Or better, who we think we are is only a temporary mask (*persona*) that a greater Consciousness wears for a time and a season in order to "speak through" (*per-sona*). That old English bard had it just right, then: the world really is a stage. We are acting.

It is very important to realize that the use of psychedelic substances to manifest this More or Mind beyond brain and outside of ego was no whim or passing phase for Aldous Huxley. He was so impressed by and so committed to the sacramental potential of such substances that he literally ended his life on LSD, on November 22, 1963. Huxley's second wife, Laura, in her lovely biography of her husband, *This Timeless Moment* (1975), published a facsimile of the very last sentence Aldous shakily wrote a few hours before he died: a self-prescription for a hundred milligrams of LSD to be delivered intramuscularly. His friend Timothy Leary delivered the final sacrament to the Huxley home. This was the door through which the writer departed our stage. This was the way he left us.

And, again, he departed the stage a very different being than he came onto it. Indeed, by the early 1960s, Aldous Huxley, now transformed by his psychedelic revelations, had clearly abandoned both his early philosophical pessimism as expressed in *Brave New World* and his ascetic, world-renouncing Vedanta as expressed in *The Perennial Philosophy*. The world and the body were no longer a materialist prison to endure or a paradoxical illusion to renounce, nor was sexuality something to mock and make fun of, as it almost always was in his earlier novels. No longer. No more. The world, as he put it in his very last novel *Island* (1962), was now a place of "luminous bliss," the very context in which to experience Supreme Identity. The means, moreover, of experiencing this bliss and this Supreme Identity was the human body, and especially the sexual and psychedelic body. As he put it, Huxley had finally aligned himself with a deep stream of unorthodox doctrine and practice that he found running through all the Asian religions, which, he proclaimed was a "new conscious Wisdom . . . prophetically glimpsed in Zen and Taoism and Tantra."[27]

"Tantra." The word is everywhere in *Island*.

This new conscious Wisdom—which Huxley also linked to ancient fertility cults, the study of sexuality in the modern West, genetics, and Darwinian biology—emerged from the refusal of all traditional dualisms; that is, it rejected any religious or moral system that separates the world and the divine, matter and mind, sex and spirit, purity and pollution (and that's rejecting *a lot*). It also clearly linked Asian Tantra, contemplative sexual practice, and psychedelics in ways that would prove astonishingly prescient. Numerous human potential, countercultural, New Age, and pop-cultural traditions would soon follow, all drawing on different elements of Huxley's writings and vision.

Island appeared in March of 1962, just one month after Huxley had introduced a still unknown Timothy Leary to "the ultimate yoga" of Tantra. The novel celebrates Tantric eroticism and harshly criticises ascetic forms of spirituality, which, in a most astonishing and most psychoanalytic move, Huxley now explicitly links to sexual repression, a guilt-ridden homosexuality and aggressive militarism. Even Freud returns. Huxley was now openly suggesting that the common ascetic strategies of what the novel calls Purity, Brahmacharya (celibacy), and thinking "of Woman as essentially Holy" are, at root, expressions of a conflicted male homosexuality anxious to avoid any and all heterosexual contact.[28] It is much better, the novel now suggests, to think of the erotic union of man and woman as holy, that is, to see the sacred in the sexual and the sexual in the sacred. Hence the novel's celebration of "the cosmic lovemaking of Shiva and the Goddess."[29] In short, late in life Huxley appears to have been moving away, fast, from his earlier ascetic Vedanta, so prominently featured in *The Perennial Philosophy*, toward a new psychologically and sexually inflected Tantra.

It should be stressed that, like his embrace of psychedelics, this was no fanciful fluke or last-minute change of mind on Huxley's part. Indeed, Laura Huxley shared with me that she considered *Island* to be her husband's final legacy, the place where he put everything he had learned. When I asked her about the novel's obvious focus on Tantra, she was quick to point out that Aldous was not particularly friendly to traditional religion, and that he considered Tantra to be a technique, not a religion. Everything written in *Island*, she insisted, had been tried somewhere. The novel thus laid down a real and practical path to follow, not just a dream or another impossible religious claim. The novel was Aldous's blueprint for a good society, even, Laura pointed out, if that "island" is one's own home or private inner world. It can be done. That is the point.

The story itself involves a jaded Western journalist, Will Farnaby, who lands by accident on a forbidden island called Pala. Palanian culture had been formed a few generations earlier by a pious Indian adept in Tantric forms of Buddhism and Hinduism and a scientifically enlightened Scottish doctor. Pala's Buddhism, we learn, came from Bengal and Tibet, which meant that it was "shot through and through with Tantra."[30] Through the Indian adept and Scottish doctor, the culture thus embodied both a literal friendship between and a consequent synthesis of Tantric Asia, with its lingams, deities, and yogas, and Western rationalism, with its humanism, psychology, and science.

Farnaby quickly learns that Pala's two principal educational practices involve a contemplative form of sexuality called maithuna (the Tantric term for ritual intercourse) and the ingestion of a psychedelic mushroom the inhabitants called moksha (the traditional Sanskrit word for spiritual liberation). The practice of maithuna is explained through two Western models: Freud's psychoanalysis and John Humphrey Noyes's nineteenth-century Oneida community. The latter utopian community practiced something called Male Continence, which was essentially a form of extended sexual intercourse without ejaculation. Such a sexual practice functioned as both a contemplative technique and as an effective means of birth control (many reports suggest that the women of the Oneida community were generally happy, empowered, and successful). There was more, though. The goal of maithuna on the mystical side amounted to a spiritual form of what Freud had called a polymorphous sexuality. "What we're born with, what we experience all through infancy and childhood, is a sexuality that isn't concentrated on the genitals; it's a sexuality diffused throughout the whole organism. That's the paradise we inherit. But the paradise gets lost as the child grows up. Maithuna is the organized attempt to regain that paradise."[31]

Then there was the moksha, that is, the mushrooms. The psychedelic practice initiated the young islanders into metaphysical wisdom, that is, into the empirical realization that their true selves could not be identified with their little social egos, which were understood to be necessary but temporary "muddy filters" of a greater cosmic consciousness.[32] The doors of perception again. Mind at Large.

The novel meanders lovingly through and around both this maithuna and this moksha—which are manifestly the real point and deepest story of the novel—as the Rani or Queen Mother of Pala and her sexually repressed homosexual son, Murugan, take the utopian island further and further toward Westernization, industrialization, capitalism, and a finally violent and murderous fundamentalism organized around notions of "the Ideal of Purity," "the Crusade of the Spirit," and "God's Avatars" (the pious Queen liked to capitalize things). The ending is as predictable as it is depressing: the forces of righteousness and religion win out over those of natural sensuality, pantheism, and erotic wisdom.

But not before Huxley has his say. "We have no established church," one of the islanders explains, "and our religion stresses immediate experience and deplores belief in unverifiable dogmas and the emotions which that belief inspires."[33] Hence the prayer of Pala humorously mocking the Lord's Prayer: "Give us this day our daily Faith, but deliver us, dear God, from Belief."[34] The islanders even integrated this religion of no religion into their agricultural affairs: the scarecrows in the fields were thus made to look like a Future Buddha and a God the Father, so that the children who manipulated the scarecrow-puppets with strings to scare off the birds could learn that "all gods are home-made, and that it's we who pull their strings and so give them the power to pull ours."[35] As for prayer, well, "if prayers are sometimes answered it's because, in this very odd psychophysical world of ours, ideas have a tendency, if you concentrate your mind on them, to get themselves realized."[36]

Science, particularly what would become neuroscience, was a key part of Huxley's mature vision as fully expressed in this final testament-novel. What Huxley was really proposing here is a fusion of Tantric or Tibetan Buddhism and neurophysiology, a proposal captured in the figure of the "neurotheologian," identified as someone "who thinks about people in terms, simultaneously, of the Clear Light of the Void and the vegetative nervous system."[37] This Buddhist neurotheologian was in fact a fictional embodiment of Huxley's own personal philosophy of mind, that is, of the filter thesis.

How far Huxley had come! Indeed, in almost every way, *Island* was the mirror opposite or photographic negative of *Brave New World*. The last novel, which was essentially the author's utopian answer to his own dystopian legacy, answers the authoritarian monoculture of *Brave New World* point by point. Biotechnology is present, for example, but as a kind of ecologically wise agricultural system. Family planning is in place too, but through genetically gifted frozen sperm and the disciplined practice of maithuna that allows Palanians as much sex as they wish without the constant burden of pregnancy. The nuclear family has been abolished on Pala, but only to increase human attachment among all its inhabitants and share the responsibilities of childrearing among multiple couples and families. Soma tablets have been replaced by "moksha-medicine," which initiates the taker into a direct experience of cosmic consciousness—that is, Mind at Large. Finally, just as *Brave New World* ends with the despairing suicide of the rare and true individual, *Island* ends with the political murder of the enlightened island doctor, as Pala is invaded by a foreign power hungry for the island's oil reserves and morally supported by the Rani's fundamentalist state religion.

Things do not quite end there, though. The novel really ends, exactly as it began, with the island's mynah birds repeating the mantra they have been trained to mimic over and over again: "Attention." Constant attention to the here and now is the key to the island's contemplative culture, even and especially when it is being invaded by a military power bent on oil and aided by ignorant notions of Purity and God.

. . . TO LOOK FORWARD

I find it strange, and more than a little depressing, that, despite all of this well-known biographical and metaphysical material, Aldous Huxley is best known today for his dystopian novel. Countless American high school students, for example, read *Brave New World* in their literature classes. No one, as far as I can tell, ever assigns *Island*. Why? Why is a man who had so much to say about the synthesis of science and spirituality and the deeper dimensions of human consciousness known primarily for a novel about the authoritarian horrors and technological dead ends of the modern consumer state? Why is this consummate individualist, this psychedelic voyager, still almost completely identified with a story of moral despair and quasi-fascist political control?

Obviously, part of the answer is because *Brave New World* was so incredibly accurate. As a culture (I speak of American culture now), we are in the midst of a vast, decades-long repression and forgetting of Huxley's utopian island Pala, where consciousness is literally cosmic, where the body is mystically erotic, where consumerism is dead, and the earth is alive. Politically anyway, the counterculture of the 1960s and 1970s was challenged and beat back by the Religious Right of the 1980s and 1990s. An emerging nature mysticism was replaced by an unhinged capitalism. Until now, we have chosen to enact Huxley's "brave new world," a mechanical world of advanced science, unsustainable consumerism, looming nuclear apocalypse, and impending ecological disaster. Alas, as of this writing, the only thing we in the States have enacted from *Island* is precisely that which destroyed the island: a politics dominated largely by religious fundamentalism wedded to a violent, hysterical, rightwing nationalism.

But Huxley did more than diagnose the disease of modern Western culture; he also provided what he thought of as a realistic treatment in *Island*. What was that treatment? And is it still applicable today? The answers to such questions, of course, are extremely complicated, but let me sketch out an answer of sorts through three very brief lines of thought: (1) on the psychology of belief; (2) on the intellectual discipline of the modern mystical life; and, finally, (3) on the state of contemporary neuroscience vis-à-vis the profound philosophical questions Huxley wanted to ask. All of these lines come together, it turns out, in Huxley's notion of the neurotheologian.

1. THE PSYCHOLOGY OF BELIEF. I am first of all struck by Huxley's vibrant critique of religion, and more particularly religious literalism, fundamentalism, and belief itself, in a novel like *Island*. "In religion all words are dirty words," the Old Raja's little green book declared. Hence the novel's ideal of the "Tantrik agnostic" (Aldous's grandfather returns) and its scorn for that "Old Nobodaddy." The Old Nobodaddy (the expression is pure William Blake) is Huxley's scornful term for the common public conceptions of God as an objective super-parent in the sky. This Daddy is a Nobody. That's because he doesn't exist. He is pure nonsense. Pure projection. This, of course, was precisely Freud's thesis in *The Future of an Illusion*. He was right. And he's still right.

Huxley in fact had already said much the same thing eight years before *Island*, in a preface to the first book of one of his close friends, the Indian philosopher and education reformer Jiddu Krishnamurti, with whom he started a school for children in Ojai, California. Huxley felt that Krishnamurti, who was famously dismissive of "religion," actually had realized the Supreme Identity of unity with the ground of being. In this preface to *The First and Last Freedom* (1954), Huxley wrote that man is an amphibious creature who lives in two worlds at the same time: the world of sensory data and the world of symbols. Symbol-systems, he went on to point out, can be highly advantageous for the survival and flourishing of a social group, since they can preserve knowledge and allow us to manipulate our existence in an at best chaotic world. They can also be extremely dangerous, if not actually deadly. Why? Because "belief inevitably separates." That is, every belief system is, at base, an exclusionary system that privileges one group of human beings over another. Every belief system is also always encouraging human beings to take symbolic statements literally, as if the beliefs were perfectly true, as if they matched reality as it is. They never do, of course.

And so Huxley turns to his favorite authors: mystical ones. "And why," he quotes Meister Eckhart now, "why do you prate of God? Whatever you say of God is untrue." So too with the wisdom of Mahayana Buddhism: "the truth was never preached by the Buddha, seeing that you have to realize it within yourself." Words are just words. Beliefs are just beliefs. They are abstractions. They are constructions. At best, they are pointers to the real. They are not, and never can be, the experience of the real. To the extent, then, that symbolic systems—*any* symbolic system—claim to speak either for all of humanity or reality itself, they are by definition lies. Consequently, for Huxley, the man who has resolved his relation to the domains of science and religion, to "the two worlds of data and symbols," is "a man who has no beliefs."[38]

In his biography of Huxley, Dana Sawyer sums all of this up by suggesting that Huxley's work can fruitfully be read as a lifelong attempt to answer his grandfather's call for modern people to adopt the stance of agnosticism with respect to all religious claims. The truth is that Huxley was not an agnostic with respect to radical mystical sensibilities, for he had actually experienced Mind at Large, and many times. But he was most certainly an agnostic, and then some, with respect to all traditional religious claims about that great Nobodaddy in the sky. "I remain an agnostic," Huxley wrote, "who aspires to be a gnostic—but a gnostic only on the mystical level, a gnostic without symbols, cosmologies or a pantheon."[39] In the end, his was a religion of no religion.

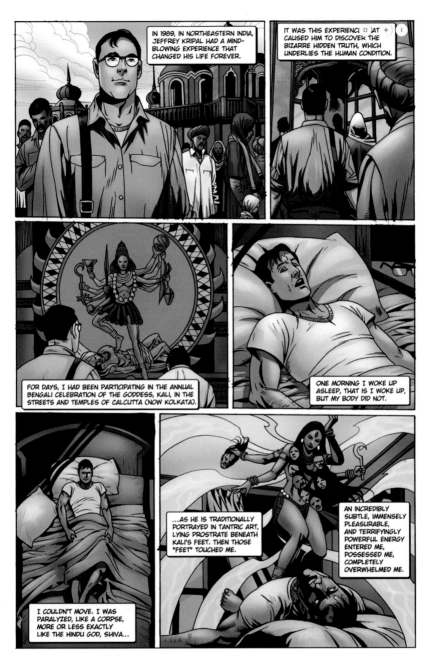

Apocalypse of Glycon by Golden Elixir Productions, producers Barclay Powers and Nancy Hutchison, artist supervisor Eugene Perez of Octographics, p. 1.

Apocalypse of Glycon by Golden Elixir Productions, producers Barclay Powers and Nancy Hutchison, artist supervisor Eugene Perez of Octographics, p. 2.

Apocalypse of Glycon by Golden Elixir Productions, producers Barclay Powers and Nancy Hutchison, artist supervisor Eugene Perez of Octographics, p. 3.

Madonna and Child with the Infant Saint John the Baptist, attributed to the "Maestro del Tondo Miller," late fifteenth century. Palazzo Vecchio, Florence. Courtesy of De Agostini Picture Library.

2. THE INTELLECTUAL DISCIPLINE OF THE MYSTICAL LIFE. At least with respect to American culture, many of Huxley's interests were both prescient and pioneering. Certainly it would be difficult to name a figure who had more influence on the American and British counterculture than Aldous Huxley. Which is not to say that the counterculture and Aldous Huxley were the same thing. They were not. At all. Personally now, I sometimes wonder if the counterculture of the 1960s and early 1970s, for all its long-term positive transformations, social progressivism, and artistic accomplishments, also had the unfortunate effect of delegitimizing the mystically inclined Huxley in the broader culture. Certainly many of the counterculture's shortcomings and casualties arose not from following Huxley through the doors of perception, but from *not* following him closely enough. In particular, the counterculture lacked Huxley's intellectual discipline and his high regard for the arts of reading, writing, and thinking.

Huxley was an accomplished British-American literary figure, a gifted intellectual product of Eton and Oxford, and a member of England's cultural aristocracy. And he remained so, even in his psychedelic explorations, which were neither casual entertainments nor public parties, but profound and private philosophical considerations. Moreover, he clearly rejected the idea that such powerful substances should be made available to everyone. Quite the contrary, he argued that they should be carefully controlled and more or less restricted to professional writers, scientists, artists, and intellectuals who would use them responsibly as catalysts for their creative work. At one point, he complained of his good friend, Timothy Leary, whom he feared was messing it up for everyone: "I am very fond of Tim—but why, oh why, does he *have* to be such an ass?" He also told Leary to "go about your business quietly" and, whatever he did, never, never "let the cat out of the bag" that psychedelic states could amplify sexual experience to unspeakable dimensions. Never was a piece of advice more spectacularly ignored.

3. THE NEUROTHEOLOGIAN OF TOMORROW. For Huxley, we might recall, a neurotheologian is someone who thinks about the human condition from the double perspective of neurophysiology and the Clear Light of the Void, that is, from the brain and Buddhism, or what we might reframe here more generally now as neuroscience and philosophically sophisticated forms of mystical experience.[40] This, it seems to me anyway, remains a very live option for us today, as long as—and this is a crucial proviso—the phenomenology of mystical experience, as elaborately coded in the history of comparative mystical literature and

minutely analyzed by trained scholars of religion, is treated with equal authority and respect within the inquiry and not simply shoved into the philosophical assumptions (and they really are assumptions) of classical materialism and
reductionism.

Sadly, this is exactly what too often happens today. When neuroscientists
treat mystical experience at all, they inevitably treat the subject superficially
and with little, or no, adequate training in the deep epistemological, philosophical, and ontological issues involved. They appear to assume that humanists,
literary scholars, philosophers, and theologians have nothing to teach them,
that only measurable replicable objects are real, and that only the scientific
method can grant any knowledge worth having. At the end of the day, theirs is
not a serious intellectual dialogue. It is a dogmatic and often frankly ignorant
monologue.

I am exaggerating. But not much.

There are also, of course, bright moments in the neuroscientific literature
as well. I might briefly mention three such moments here: Sam Harris on parapsychology; Jill Bolte Taylor on her "stroke of insight"; and David Eagleman
on the inadequacies of reductionism and the need to keep our philosophical
options open with respect to the true nature of mind.

Sam Harris is a neuroscientist and one of a handful of contemporary New
Atheist writers who has reached a broad and educated audience with what is
essentially a vigorous, morally driven, and sometimes thoughtful materialist
rejection of religion. Three other writers are usually named in this context:
Richard Dawkins, Daniel Dennett, and Christopher Hitchens. From the perspective of the professional study of religion, a field in which none of these
four writers possess a shred of training, there are numerous and serious problems with their handling of religion.[41] Many of these boil down to a bad habit
of implicitly or explicitly conflating the nature of religion with its most intolerant, literalist, and violent forms. For them, religion appears to equal fundamentalism or literalism, full stop.

But not always. Harris is most interesting here for at least three reasons:
first, because he is on record as admiring the contemplative wisdom of Buddhism (while firmly rejecting the Buddhist faith); second, because he unam-
biguously asserts that contemplative practices have transformative effects and
mystical states have something to teach us about the mind; and third, and
perhaps most interesting, because in his *The End of Faith* he has famously left
the door open (in an endnote) to the possible importance of two totally taboo
subjects—children who remember previous lives (as evidenced in the im-

mense corpus of the late University of Virginia psychiatrist Ian Stevenson) and parapsychology. Even when criticized for this endnote by his atheist compeers, Harris did not back down, insisting that parapsychology has been treated badly by professional science. In his own words: "My position on the paranormal is this: While there have been many frauds in the history of parapsychology, I believe that this field of study has been unfairly stigmatized. . . . It seems to me that reasonable people can disagree about the data."[42] There is an open mind.

Jill Bolte Taylor is a neuroanatomist who, while working at Harvard in 1996, experienced a massive stroke in the left hemisphere of her brain. Her book *My Stroke of Insight* describes in detail her stunned realization—through the traumatic shutdown of her rational, linguistic, and egoic capacities—that there is an entirely different order of consciousness and being hiding within her, and that it has nothing to do with ego, language, culture, or even, most shockingly, space and time.

Taylor's language is careful and ambiguous throughout the book on the question of whether she is describing the still material mind of her right brain or an entirely independent, self-existing order of consciousness, in effect, a Mind at Large. It is difficult, however, not to detect the latter in places, for example, in her description of the brain-body as "a portal through which the energy of who I am can be beamed into a three-dimensional external space"; or in her framing of the body as "a marvelous temporary home." She even marvels at how she could have spent so many years unaware of this, never really understanding "that I was just visiting there."[43] This does not sound like your typical neuroscientist. This sounds like your typical mystic.

Finally, there is neuroscientist David Eagleman and his recent *Incognito: The Secret Lives of the Brain*. The book is a marvelous tour through the "most complex material we've discovered in the universe," that is, the human brain. The message is as simple as it is provocative: our day-to-day consciousness is like the emperor of a giant kingdom. He may take credit for what goes on in the countless interactions in his land each day, but it all goes on without and beyond his control. His monarchy is an illusion.

The human brain, *your* brain, contains hundreds of billions of neurons and glia, which are "connected to one another in a network of such staggering complexity that it bankrupts human language and necessitates new strains of mathematics. A typical neuron makes about ten thousand connections to neighboring neurons. Given that there are billions of neurons, this means there are as many connections in a single cubic centimeter of brain tissue as there are stars in the Milky Way galaxy."[44] And you—and this is the punch line—you are aware of *none* of this. Obviously, the king is not in charge. The monarch has been dethroned.

After treating the neuroscience of perception (the brain actively constructs its reality rather than passively receives it), the universalisms of sexual attraction (yep, hip to waist ratios and breast size matter), the manner in which evolutionary pressures have determined what we can, and cannot, think (try thinking in five dimensions, or sexually desiring a frog), and the largely fictional nature of responsibility and free will (big problems for the courts and conservative political philosophies), Eagleman turns at the very end of the book to the question of soul. Here he advances a vigorous critique of reductionism, that is, the idea that we can understand something, like mind, by reducing it to its constituent parts, like neurons and chemicals. Nope, Eagleman concludes. In a most refreshing move, he also rejects promissory materialism, that is, the commonly heard claim that, although we don't yet know how to explain mind through material processes, we eventually will. Maybe, Eagleman concludes. Maybe not.

It is extremely unlikely that we just happen to be living at the moment when all things will soon be explained. Previous scientific generations claimed that, and they were all dead wrong. The more likely scenario, Eagleman observes, is that the more we learn about the brain and consciousness, the more things will get stranger and more wonderful, not simpler and tighter. Here is where his final thought experiment comes in. A parable of sorts:

Imagine that you are a Kalahari Bushman and that you stumble upon a transistor radio in the sand. You might pick it up, twiddle the knobs, and suddenly, to your surprise, hear voices streaming out of this strange little box. . . . Now let's say you begin a careful, scientific study of what causes the voices. You notice that each time you pull out the green wire, the voices stop. When you put the wire back on its contact, the voices begin again . . . you come to a clear conclusion: the voices depend entirely on the integrity of the circuitry. At some point, a young person asks you how some simple loops of electrical signals can engender music and conversations, and you admit that you don't know—but you insist that your science is about to crack that problem at any moment.

Assuming you are truly isolated, what you do not know about, of course, is radio waves, electromagnetism, distant cities, radio stations, and modern civilization. You would not even have the capacity to imagine such things. And even if you could imagine such things, "you have no technology to demonstrate the existence of the waves, and everyone justifiably points out that the onus is on you to convince them." You could convince almost no one, and you yourself would probably reject the existence of such mysterious, spirit-like waves. You would become a "radio materialist."

The parable's "radio theory," of course, is identical to Huxley's filter thesis. "I'm not asserting that the brain is like a radio," Eagleman points out at the very end of his book, "but I *am* pointing out that it *could* be true. There is nothing in our current science that rules this out."[45] This is where the neurotheologian steps in. There is, after all, massive evidence in comparative mystical literature that rules the radio theory in, that sees the human brain as a kind of transmitter or receiver of consciousness. An island in Mind.

11

The Rise of the Paranormal

And Some Related X Factors
in the Study of Religion

> Some time after he had begun work at the library he experienced a long, dramatic
> dream. . . . There was one detail in particular he remembered: in the aftermath of his
> electrocution [by lightning], his mental activity anticipated somewhat the condition
> men will attain some tens of thousands of years hence. . . . In short, I'm a mutant, he
> said to himself on awakening. I anticipate the post-historic existence of man. Like in
> a science-fiction novel, he added, smiling with amusement.
>
> DOMINIC MATEI IN MIRCEA ELIADE'S *YOUTH WITHOUT YOUTH*

The first half of this excessive, eccentric autobiography was dramatic enough.
I mean, I was run into by an invisible white buffalo, or something. I almost
died of years of adolescent and teenage starvation. I was saved from my own
self-torture by the grace of a Christian community of monks and the psychoanalysis of a Jewish atheist. I was erotically electrocuted by God(dess). I wrote a
dissertation on a Hindu saint that many of my academic seniors hailed as pioneering, after which I was pretty much run out of an entire country and then
a professional field. If that were not enough, I told you that Jesus and Paul
were queer men, which pretty much makes the present conservative Christian
positions on homosexuality and gender look idiotic.

One will look in vain for such public drama in the second half of my career
(thank God). Things settled down, at least on the surface. But the story continued. The drama simply went inside. I continued to "have" all kinds of excessive
impossible experiences, but these were now those of others. These were those
of my historical subjects, my reader-correspondents and my professional colleagues. The latter would pull me aside at conferences, lectures, and dinners
to tell me one crazy story after another, all of which, I have no doubt, are true.
As I explained in the very first lines of this book, I began to feel like Professor X
of the X-Men. It was as if there were "mutants" everywhere, living in the mar-

gins of our flatland materialist culture but afraid to speak, afraid to come
of the closet, not even sure how to talk about the inbreakings and impossib
powers that had turned their lives inside out.

I know why they sought me out. From about 2007 on, I began to lecture in
public and publish on paranormal themes and histories. By doing this, I unin-
tentionally gave such closeted mutants an intellectual way to talk about these
things without feeling stupid or embarrrassed. I made them feel safe. As I listened to their stories year after year, this same effect became my own conscious
goal. I now wanted "to make UFOs sound Ivy League," as one academic colleague described to another the accomplished intent of one such public lecture.
UFOs, and a whole lot of other things. I was now out to fashion a new intellectual language or way of speaking that could take the paranormal seriously and
reinsert these key phenomena back into the heart of the study of religion, from
which they first emerged and to which they really belong.

As things turned out, I did not have to invent too much. Most of it was already
there in the intellectual histories that the academy had forgotten, repressed, or
simply ignored. I set out to recover and write about these not as historical artifacts or "superstitious" things that we have left behind in our materialist maturity,
but as signs and signals of some future form of knowledge and culture.

Surprisingly, I received very little pushback from the academy. I am often
asked why. I have two different answers. The first is what we might call "the professional closet." The simple truth of the matter is that every other anthropologist and scholar of religion knows darn well that these are real events and real
experiences, and they very much want a new way of thinking and talking about
them. This anyway was my experience again and again as I lectured on the topics in the US and Europe. The second reason is more personal. We might capture it under the banner of "street cred." I suspect, but I cannot prove, that many
of my senior colleagues allowed me these eccentricities because I had been beat
to hell by Hindu fundamentalists, and I had stood my ground. They watched
all of that. They knew I am a very serious intellectual, and that I do not hesitate
to speak and write of difficult things. They also know how much I admire their
work and insist on its centrality to the discipline. For all of these reasons, I think
they gave me a kind of "free pass" here with the paranormal, at least for a time.

Having said all of that, I am certain other forms of resistance are still coming,
and I have already seen early signs of this.[1] One does not openly challenge the
deepest philosophical assumptions or operating system of a culture without that
culture responding in some immunological way. One is treated like an invading
virus or disease.

STRUCK BY COMPARISON

t "Prof. X" meeting a "mutant," one of many who changed,
irection and content of his thought and writing.

., I was working on, among other things, Mircea Eliade's
. ..nout Youth, which begins with an aging academic struck by lightning on Easter night behind a church in the rain while he holds an umbrella.
As Dominic heals in the hospital, he also mysteriously grows younger. His
old teeth fall out and new ones take their place. His skin grows young. The female nurses marvel and giggle at his body's reaction when they bathe him. But
the lightning strike has brought more than youth. It has brought strange new
powers. Dominic dreams little snippets that play out the next day. He begins
to manifest all sorts of new capacities, including telekinesis and the ability to
absorb books by simply passing his hand over them (every aging academic's
dream!). He begins to wonder whether he might be some kind of mystical
mutant.

About that same time, I met Elizabeth Krohn at a symposium on near-death
experiences here in Houston. I was asked to respond to her at the event.[2] In 1988,
Elizabeth was walking across the parking lot behind her Houston synagogue
(not three blocks from my office at Rice) to attend a service in honor of the first
anniversary of her beloved grandfather's death. She was holding an umbrella
in one hand and the little hand of her two-year-old son in the other. She had
just spent an inordinate amount of money on new clothes and some very ex-
pensive shoes. She had no idea why. Then it struck her. Literally. The lightning.

She kept walking anyway, right into the synagogue. She realized, though,
that something was not quite right. She looked down and noticed that her
feet were floating a few inches off the ground. She looked back into the parking lot and saw her body lying in the rain and her two-year-old screaming his
head off. His eardrums had burst, her new shoes were fried, and the umbrella
was still on fire in the rain, smoking. An extremely elaborate NDE followed
that involved a moving conscious light, a speechlessly beautiful garden and
fantastically colored alien landscape (with multiple moons or planets), a body
and skin grown young, a sense of absolute unconditional love, and a long telepathic conversation with a presence she experienced as her grandfather but
that she suspected was really God. The total experience lasted two weeks. Here
on earth it lasted maybe two minutes.

I will not get into all of the details, as these are hers, not mine, and we
are presently working on a book together about her total experience and the

teachings that emerged from it. I will simply say that
as she healed in bed from the burns on her feet, Elizabe
side out by the appearance of new psychical capacities,
tive nightmares of major plane crashes, tsunamis, and e
whose empirical accuracy she later learned to confirn
emails to herself immediately after she awoke from the n

As with other paranormal prodigies, the mental and
often mixed or traded places in unbelievable but socially confirmed empirical ways. On one occasion, the phone rang at 3:30 a.m. Never a good sign. Her husband insisted she answer it. It was her dead grandfather. After a brief conversation ended (about a very practical matter involving her mother), the couple watched in disbelief as the room filled up with a strange smoke and a red laser-like light appeared at the end of the hallway. Then it was just gone.

I asked Elizabeth what she thought of all of this. She complained that the precognitions only brought her suffering. What was she supposed to do with a plane crash precognition? Call the FAA? The FBI would be at her door the next day. She also commented on how these particular abilities really had nothing to do with her. She *hates* them. Her sense was that she received them, "like a readjusted radio." She did think that the new capacities have something to do with "energy," which she understands as intelligent or conscious and believes has something to do with the fundamental nature of the universe—hardly unreasonable suggestions, given the fact that it was the plasma of a lightning bolt that initiated her into her NDE, precognitive dreams, and so much else.

I explained the filter thesis to Elizabeth and how such a model allows us to understand how traumas like hers might "crack open" the psyche so that other forms of Mind can rush in. I told her that the radio metaphor is often used as an analogy, exactly as she had intuitively used it. That made perfect sense to her. At some point in my conversations with her, I kept thinking of Eliade's *Youth Without Youth.* It seemed too close to her experiences to be real. I gave her my copy. She went home and read it. The next time we met I asked her what she thought of the book. Her reply was immediate and firm: "That's not fiction."

It is not difficult to understand her reaction. Like Dominic, Elizabeth had been struck by lightning holding an umbrella behind a religious building and subsequently developed various psychical capacities. As in Dominic's case again, the cloudburst was an exceptionally odd, even "symbolic" one: it appeared to be restricted to the small space over her. Indeed, it was sunny out in other parts of Houston. Like Dominic again, one of the first powers to emerge

ognitive dreams.[3] It is an odd experience reading about yourself in
one else's novel.

"That's not fiction." There is the crunch. The novel, after all, is a piece of
fiction. Or is it? As we have already seen, Eliade was very clear that he "camouflaged" real experiences, both his and no doubt those of others he had been
told, in his literature of the fantastic. So what is real here? And what is imagined? And how are we to distentangle the threads of the real and the imagined
in extreme religious experiences like Elizabeth's, or in Eliade's life and work for
that matter? It is difficult to avoid the conclusion that Elizabeth's irradiation
changed her, "in the blink of an eye," as the title of our public event had it. It is
also difficult to avoid the conclusion that her new abilities had something to
do with altered states of energy and what we want to call "the imagination," as
if we somehow know what that means. Many of her precognitions, after all,
occurred within dream states, and dreams are products of the imagination.

Aren't they? When is a dream not a dream? When is something imagined
not imaginary? How does the imagination become temporarily "empowered,"
to use Jess Hollenback's felicitous phrase, and so access *empirical* knowledge
entirely outside the ordinary sensory channels, and indeed outside the normal
parameters of linear time or "history" itself?[4]

Elizabeth is always perfectly aware in her nocturnal precognitions that
what she is seeing is not just a dream. She knows what a dream feels like, looks
like. These are no dreams. She scoffs at the word "dream," but she doesn't have
another word to describe what she is in during those nocturnal visions. Our
spiritual stupidity and crude worldview have failed her.

I would submit that it is the job of writers to help change this situation. It
is our job to help write reality anew. I would also submit that this work must
begin with the category of the imagination. Here we arrive at the first and
most important of the X factors of the study of religion, a kind of black box
that is seldom, if ever, opened these days. For what it's worth, I suspect that
the deepest roots and reaches of the imagination are the roots and reaches of
consciousness itself, and that this consciousness is also an exotic "energy" that
has its own super-physics, one that is not bound by what our primate brains
have evolved to cognize as space and time. But I am getting way ahead of myself here, so let me back up (or back down) very quickly and make a few, much
more humble, observations.

Here is one: our difficulty in accepting and understanding historical events
like Elizabeth's irradiation, both as a scholarly profession and as a public culture, is largely a function of the fact that we lack a sufficiently robust and nu-

anced model of the human imagination. We may not have an adequate theory of the imagination, then, but at least we can see the intellectual and cultural effects of not having one.

We were not always so blind. Enter the category of *the imaginal*, that is, the empowered functioning of the imagination that cognizes and symbolizes events and realities that do not appear to be imaginary, cognitions and visions that seem, well, "super." Enter also the category of *the paranormal*, that is, the experienced collapse of the mind-matter split via the irruption of events in the physical world that uncannily correspond to the subjective or unconscious states of a focal agent—a semiotic or meaning-soaked manifestation of Pauli and Jung's One World. The paranormal, it turns out, is a turn-of-the-century French transformation of a slightly earlier English Victorian category: *the supernormal*. If the philosophy of mind of the filter thesis is the first, the imaginal and the paranormal (or supernormal) are the second and third X factors upon which I have built my theory of religion. It's Xs all the way down. Or all the way up. I am not quite sure.

THE RISE OF THE IMAGINAL

The category of the imaginal is usually associated with the French historian of Iranian mystical literature Henry Corbin. Corbin understood the imaginal to be a noetic organ that accessed a real dimension of reality whose appearances to us were nevertheless shaped by what he called the "creative imagination" (which he borrowed from Jung, who in turn borrowed it from Théodore Flournoy—more soon). This was the intermediate world of the *mundus imaginalis*, the "imaginal world," which for Corbin is the "place" where myth and symbol happen, where they are true, where visions occur and the spiritual body is resurrected.

Corbin's imaginal, it should be stressed, was deeply informed by his own Christian docetic Christology, that is, his convictions that the doctrine of the Incarnation should be interpreted symbolically and not literally: divinity cannot become literal flesh for Corbin, ever. It only "appears" to have done so. This is terribly important when interpreting Corbin's use of the imaginal, since Corbin used the expression both to keep apart and to mediate the material world of the flesh and the transcendent world of the spirit. This dualism could be mediated through symbols and paradoxical mystical doctrines, but it could never be truly transcended or completely overcome for Corbin.

Corbin's understanding of the imaginal, it should also be stressed, assumed the presence of paranormal phenomena, as is evident in his repeated and rather matter-of-fact treatment of clairvoyance, mind reading, telepathy, even materialization and teleportation in the life and teachings of the great Islamic mystical philosopher Ibn al-'Arabi.[5]

But Corbin did not in fact originate the term "imaginal." Not even close. It was already in use by one of Jung's mentors, the Swiss psychiatrist Théodore Flournoy, who employed it in *From India to the Planet Mars* (1899), his classic study of a Swiss medium named Élise Müller, who claimed to be both the reincarnation of an Indian Hindu princess and a regular visitor to Mars. Flournoy's lively novelistic retellings of the medium's various personalities and channeled adventures made his book an instant hit. In the process, Flournoy also helped to revolutionize the study of mediumship and trance formations through a relatively new tool: hypnosis. This is quite significant, I think, for the history of extraterrestrial esotericisms, as the same technique would later play a major role in the production of the alien abduction literature in the 1960s, 1970s, and 1980s—"to the Planet Mars" again, as it were.

Flournoy was both devastatingly skeptical and deeply sympathetic when it came to the imaginal contents of Müller's visions and channelings.[6] Hence he could demonstrate how Müller's claims to speak a Martian language, to remember a past life in India, and to communicate with dead spirits were no such things. They were creative imaginative products of the medium's present-life memories that she had forgotten and unconsciously wove back together in her various sittings with the hypnotist. Still, Flournoy marveled at the astonishing unconscious creativity of this process: it was like being present for the inspiration and production of some serially published Jules Verne novel. He referred to this productive ability of the human mind as *l'imagination créatrice.*

Like Corbin after him, the psychiatrist thought of the imaginal and the paranormal *together*. Although he was extremely suspicious of the mythical content of Müller's mediumship, Flournoy took very seriously what he called the "supernormal appearances" of her life. By "supernormal" (an adjective he borrowed from an earlier author whom we have already met above with the Sursem group and the modern origins of the filter thesis, Frederic Myers), Flournoy meant things like telepathy and telekinesis, which he concluded were likely real. His final conclusion? That the common assumption that one must choose between the "brutal alternatives" of Spiritualism (the medium was really talking to dead egos) and materialism (there is nothing to any of it and human life ends at the grave) "is surely puerile."[7] That is to say, childish and stupid.

Flournoy would have none of this either-or thinking. Nor, though, would he jump to conclusions about what it all meant and where it was all going. He refused to take a position about whether these imaginal visions and supernormal abilities were "forerunners of a future evolution" (which is what Myers thought), or evolutionary survivals from some previous condition (which is what Freud would later suggest), or "whether they are purely accidental" and so meaningless.[8] He just did not know, and so he left it at that.

But Flournoy did not originate the imaginal either. He borrowed it from Myers. As in Corbin and Flournoy, for Myers the imaginal and the paranormal (or what he called the supernormal) were more or less the same thing. He defined *"Imaginal"* this way: "A word used of characteristics belonging to the perfect insect or *imago*;—and thus opposed to *larval*;—metaphorically applied to transcendental faculties shown in rudiment in ordinary life" (HP 1.xviii). He was thinking of entomology when he wrote such lines. An imago is the final adult form of an insect's metamorphosis during which it attains wings and becomes sexually mature. This final stage is also sometimes called the imaginal stage. The insect's immature or adolescent feeding form is called the larval stage. Just as the larval stage of an insect looks nothing like the imago of its adult form (which indeed appears "bizarre" or alien-like in comparison to the larval slug), so too the functioning of the human imagination can metamorphize into extremely strange but astonishingly effective forms, which Myers called "imaginal," after his beloved bugs.

Eerily, these exact same insectoid, telepathic, and future human themes would later show up, in spectral form now, in the alien abduction literature, where gigantic telepathic humanoid bugs are extremely common.[9] For reasons that I cannot fathom, the modern abduction visions replicate, in precise and eerie detail, the imaginal of Frederic Myers. What was an entomological metaphor in Myers has become a literal visionary form in the alien abduction literature. The larval stage of the human being has morphed into the future stage of the imaginal, which appears to the present human mind as a super-insect with the exact paranormal power that Myers himself first named: telepathy.

THE EMPIRICAL AND THE SYMBOLIC

As I have worked with experiencers like Elizabeth and her precognitive dreams, I have also worked explicitly with Myers's category of the imaginal and found it necessary to offer a distinction of my own: that between the empirical imaginal and the symbolic imaginal.

I use the expression the *empirical imaginal* to name those moments when the dream or waking vision corresponds closely (but not always exactly) to an event in the objective or historical world. There is a definite *realist impulse* here (much more on this later). Here at least the imagination is not the imaginary. It is a super-sense for detecting and responding to historical events in the physical world, and it is of immense adaptive and survival advantage. The "veridical hallucination" of Myers and his colleagues, for empirically accurate telepathic communications (generally, of the time and nature of a loved one's death), falls into this type, as do Wendy Doniger's dream of her recently wounded dog across the ocean and Elizabeth's precognitive "dreams that were not dreams" of plane crashes. Here the human imagination is, in a word, "clairvoyant." It seems to work like a camera or video projector: it "sees" and then projects to a viewer or visionary what is happening at some distance along the space-time continuum. Little or no interpretation is needed in this type of the imaginal event. The visionary knows instantly what the vision is about. The vision is about what it says it is about. Finally, note that there need be only one world or order of being in play here—the material-historical world, even if it is not quite playing by the usual materialistic and historical rules.

The *symbolic imaginal* works very differently. I use this expression to name those moments in which the dream or waking vision is experienced as mediating some other world or hidden reality. Here the content of the dream or vision can be quite baroque, bizarre, or fantastic. The sense is that these images and narratives are functioning as ciphers of some other form of mind or dimension of the real. Here the human imagination is not so much clairvoyant as it is an organ of revelation: it is *not* clearly seeing and projecting in any one-to-one fashion. Rather, the imagination is intuiting or sensing something Other and then translating or picturing what it has known to a human psyche, but always in code. Hence interpretation is necessary. Elizabeth's telepathic conversation with her grandfather who she suspected was actually God is a good example of such symbolic imaginal material. Note that there are at least two worlds or orders of being at play here—the subjective or material-historical world of the person and the "other" occulted world being mediated or translated.

I must immediately add that we cannot treat this dual typology as a literal or exclusive one. These two modes of the imaginal, after all, clearly overlap and are probably functions of some deeper human capacity still—perhaps consciousness itself. Accordingly, Bertrand Méheust has noted that a certain "inimitable mixture" of metaphor and veridical accuracy often constitute oracular or prophetic speech.[10]

I have seen the same, up close and personal, in my work with the contemporary channeler and medium Paul Selig. I taught with Paul for a month at Esalen (a course on the history and practice of mediumship and channeling), immediately after which I wrote a foreword for one of his books in which I recount my first meeting with him in Greenwich Village.[11] There and then, at my wife's earlier request to me, Paul "tuned into" Julie in Houston, whom he had never met or seen, and uncannily took on her most unique facial features in a way that almost made me fall off my chair. It was *her*, but in a man 1,600 miles away. Paul's subsequent reading of her (note the literary or semiotic metaphor) was accurate but mostly in a more metaphorical and symbolic way. Subsequently, as we taught together at Esalen years later, I witnessed again and again the empirical imaginal and the symbolic imaginal fuse effortlessly in his trance states and channeling work.

It is also worth noting in this same context that, as is often seen in cases of robust precognition, the visionary or medium often misses this or that detail of the event or adds others that are not accurate. It is as if the imagination is filling in details that the transmission or telepathic cognition does not supply, much, I should add, as we see in ordinary sensory processing. As has been noted in the neuroscientific literature, the "movies" we see in dream and in everyday sensory awareness are not entirely different, and everyday sensory consciousness can be thought of as a kind of dream that is constantly controlled and guided by sensory input from the external environment.

So we need to be careful here. Very careful, since *all* of our sensory preceptions are illusory. It's *all* constructed. As the film critic Roger Ebert saw right before he died, even our sense of linear time is "an elaborate hoax." What Ebert reported to his wife, Chaz, was "a vastness that you can't even imagine." He was witnessing, entering a space "where past, present, and future were happening all at once."[12] Such a vision, of course, is impossible within the parameters of our sensory materialist worldview. If, however, we begin with the data of precognition and clairvoyance, like Elizabeth dreaming the future or Paul somatizing a woman halfway across the country, Ebert's deathbed vision of all space and time happening at once is not only possible; it is entirely predictable. What such an ontological order would mean for writing "history" is an entirely different matter, one that we have not even begun to imagine.

For now, we might summarize all of this in the form of another gnomon:

12. Sometimes the Imagined Is Not the Imaginary. The category of the imaginal draws attention to those moments of energetic influx or empowerment

in which the human imagination appears to have become a cipher of the real either as the empirical historical world of events toward some adaptive or survival advantage (as in a precognitive or clairvoyant event) or as some other dimension of being (as in a visionary or revelatory event). We might refer to the former as the empirical imaginal and to the latter as the symbolic imaginal.

The payoffs for the student or scholar of religion are considerable here. We can be both more precise and more generous with such a dual typology in place. We can be more precise because we can distinguish between two very different types of imaginal function. We can be more generous because we can recognize the necessity and importance of the most baroque or fantastic imagery. We need not shy away from visionary phenomena that are bizarre or strange simply because they appear absurd or outrageous to our rational egos and social selves. Indeed, we might well expect that this absurdity is their point, that the symbolic imaginal is calling us to see these forms not as literal truths but as coded constructions and communications of some other nonhuman or superhuman form of consciousness.

THE PARANORMAL IS A STORY

The most confusing (and so theoretically productive) aspects of imaginal events are the ways that they combine the mental and the material, the subjective and the objective. It is the empirical imaginal that most offends. It is this nondualism of the mental and the material within an imaginal event like a precognitive dream or clairvoyant vision that I have called "the paranormal," a technical term first coined by French scientists and researchers at the turn of the twentieth century (in 1903, to be precise) to locate mind-over-matter phenomena in a hermeneutical framework that did not rely on supernatural or dualist notions to make sense. As I explained in *Authors of the Impossible* (2010), the category was a central one for many of the founders of the study of religion, but it was gradually eclipsed—like a brilliant noonday sun behind a temporary passing moon—over the last century as the field turned to more and more social scientific models until it too became a kind of X factor, a black box.

The core idea of *Authors of the Impossible* is that paranormal experiences are *semiotic events* that erupt between two forms of mind as a series of coded signs that must be read and interpreted—the oracular "symbol" of the ancient Greeks again, or, if you prefer, the symbolic imaginal. Paranormal experiences are also often deeply *social events*. They tend to appear or manifest in moments of personal or social crisis, as if to signal the inadequacies of one personal or cultural narrative and the beginning of another. They appear in the interstices, gaps, and breaks of a social system or psychism. Generally speaking, they are meant to confound (the earlier narrative or subjectivity) and inspire (a new one). As such, they work through ontological shock and, as such, carry the potential to change the fundamental structure and behavior of the real within the experience of a person or community.

This is why paranormal events will never be understood with the mechanistic thinking and causal models of the sciences as they stand now, or any other kind of rational reductionism. They will never be understood in mechanistic terms because they are not about mechanisms. They are about *meaning*. They are about narrative or, if you prefer, "myth." They are about realms and dimensions of sociality and collective life about which our classical social theories and secular flatland ontologies have barely a clue.[13] As such, they constitute the first building blocks of a future sociology of the impossible.

We might capture the core argument this way:

13. The Paranormal Is a Kind of Story. Paranormal experiences tend to organize themselves around narrative, language, even playful puns and metaphors. They are, as such, expressive, goal-oriented, and inherently meaningful phenomena within which we are both authorial agents and fictional characters.

This, of course, is the same sensibility with which I opened *Secret Body*.

THE PARANORMAL AS ANTI-STRUCTURE AND DECONSTRUCTION

There are other ways to articulate the paranormal. I have already mentioned the deep structuralist influences on my thought through the work of my mentor Wendy Doniger and her teaching of figures like Claude Lévi-Strauss, Victor Turner, and Mary Douglas. I have also briefly addressed the ontological structures of the paranormal through Harald Atmanspacher's model of dual aspect monism. These same intellectual currents have carried over into my engagement with the paranormal as structural anomaly, uncanny co-incidence, intellectual paradox, and—soon enough—spectral monster.

I have been deeply inspired here by the work of George Hansen and his *The Trickster and the Paranormal*. Hansen is an engineer, an eloquent skeptic and a rigorous parapsychologist who is convinced that psi (the parapsychological shorthand for the presumed force or mechanism underlying all things psychical) is real, that it is primarily social in nature and function, and that psi events can best be approached as manifestations of the liminal spaces that exist between the binaries of a particular social system: self/world, inside/outside, presence/absence, human/nonhuman, and so on. The function of psi events is to collapse or to confound such binaries as artificial and relative. Hence paradox is the normal mode of the paranormal. Psi events, Hansen has observed, also routinely spike in times of great social upheaval (like the 1960s counterculture) and manifest "demonic," transgressive, or absurd qualities that are classically expressed in the comparative mythology of the trickster figure.

These trickster qualities, it should be underlined, are not functions of our lack of knowledge for Hansen; they are not something that we will eventually understand, solve, and explain (away). They are integral to psi itself. A rational model of psi is an oxymoron for Hansen. And this, he points out, is why fields like parapsychology or ufology have never successfully integrated themselves into the institutional structures of the academy: they cannot be so integrated, because they are working with a force or agency that only appears in the gaps and that is, by definition and function, anti-structural and anti-institutional. It is that which confounds every neat categorization or assumed essence. It is born from a fracture or temporary dissolution of the ordinary self-world relation, that is, of the assumed structure of us. As such, psi lies outside any and all rational or institutional structures. That is what it *is*—the gap, the break, the hesitation, the doubt, *the other of every discourse, every system, and every reason.*

And it gets worse (or better). As Hansen has also observed, it is not just that paranormal phenomena are liminal, paradoxical, and trickster-like by their very nature. It is also the case that different psi phenomena are hyper-connected within the liminal realm from which they erupt. Paranormal phenomena cannot be artificially isolated from one another. Moreover, their imaginal and spectral forms are often outrageous. UFO encounters routinely display telepathic phenomena (as do psychedelic experiences) and even, believe it or not, humanoid or cryptid sightings (think Bigfoot). The phenomenology of near-death experiences often eerily resembles that of UFO encounters, which in turn uncannily mimic Marian apparitions. The dead routinely appear in alien abduction accounts. And so on. As I have repeatedly stressed, as one moves further and further into these forests, things do *not* get more and more reasonable. They just get weirder and weirder. And then they get weirder.

This "bleed-over" or hyper-connection of psi-related events and mythical phenomena is an especially embarrassing fact that often confounds interpreters who want to explain a particular phenomenon (say, the UFO or the NDE) with some single and simple explanation, say, "It's about extraterrestrial craft" or "It's about heaven and Jesus." Such easy explanations just never quite work, as the point of the paranormal is to *confound* any and all neat cultural categorization, including spaceships and Jesus.

Little wonder, then, that psi events are so commonly pathologized by psychiatrists and debunkers ("this is madness"), and that some of the most eloquent voices on them have come from the realm of clinical psychology, that is, from therapists trying to help people integrate anomalous traumas back into their lives.[14] Little wonder that a classic post-structuralist philosopher like Jacques Derrida was so attracted to the mind-bending implications of telepathy and precognition and his own multiple personal experiences of the same. As Derrida well understood (and as I explore below), psi phenomena dramatize and radicalize his "deconstruction" in ways that nothing else can. Indeed, they deconstruct pretty much everything that we take to be real, from "self" and "other" to the locality of space and the straight arrow of time. With all due respect, every other form of criticism or deconstruction is mere child's play before *this*.

We can express all of this philosophically through dual aspect monism again. It would look something like this:

14. The Paranormal Is a Nondual Signal. A paranormal event is one in which a material event corresponds more or less precisely to a subjective event or mental state, thereby collapsing the assumed subject-object dualism of our ordinary cognitive and sensory experience and suggesting some deeper super-reality that is neither simply mental nor material but somehow both.

I recognize, of course, that this is confusing. The confusion, of course, lies with the rational ego or filter self, which naively thinks it is all there is or can be thought. The splitter is not aware that it is splitting. It just splits.

INTRODUCING THE ESSAYS

Here I will anthologize two brief pieces instead of one longer one. The first piece introduces in a very basic form a number of key elements in my work, foremost among them the storied nature of the phenomenology of the paranormal and a call for the theoretical significance, really centrality, of the same in the study of religion. This is a public lecture that I gave multiple times in both the US and Europe. The second piece is lifted directly from the introduction of *Mutants and Mystics* entitled "Origins." It demonstrates in a particularly clear way what phrases like "the paranormal is a kind of story" or "the paranormal is a nondual signal" feel like and appear like in an individual human life—in this case, my own. This story will return at the very end of this book, too, as if it wants to make sure it is heard.

Authors of the Impossible

READING THE PARANORMAL WRITING US

(2010–2014)

It became clear to me that writing was the controlling factor. It appeared that the energy I used for [automatic] writing had previously been used for causing poltergeist
disturbances.

ENGLISH HEALER MATTHEW MANNING, *THE LINK*

Impossible anticipation, it is always from there that I have addressed myself to you
and you have never accepted it. You would accept it more patiently if something
wasn't telling us, behind our backs and in order to subject us to it, that this place, it,
knows us, forecasts our coming, predicts us, us, according to its code.

JACQUES DERRIDA, "TELEPATHY"

In my most recent work, I have sought to challenge the epistemological and
ontological structures of the humanities as they are practiced today, that is,
those largely taken-for-granted models of how we know (epistemology) and
our assumptions about what reality is (ontology). We generally assume in our
language and social interactions that each of us is a kind of skin-encapsulated
ego (as Alan Watts had it), an "I" or knower locked inside the brain-box,
which through the medium of the senses is perceiving an objective world "out
there." There are thus two dimensions to our everyday experience: a material
dimension, which is external to our sense of awareness, and a mental dimension, which is internal or intrinsic to that same sense of awareness. These two
dimensions are mediated, supposedly faithfully, by what we call the senses,
which we normally close down at the number five.

Our philosophical and historical training, moreover, tell us that we can
never truly know the world out there as it is. We can only know it as it appears
to us through these five senses, the taken-for-granted categories of cognition
(things like space, time, and causality), and the taken for granted categories of
our specific culture (things like language, history, social custom, family, and
religion). In short, we more or less assume in the humanities that appearance,

cognition, and culture are all there is, and that even these are always mediated, constructed, and so relative. In essence, our methods and our discipline lock us down tight to the cave floor of our brain and its box. We are seeing shadows, reflections, appearances, but never ever the real.

We also generally assume, following standard orthodox science, that the only thing there really is in the universe is (dead) matter, and that this matter is organized in causal chains controlled by unchanging mechanical and mathematical laws. These laws of physics lead to the bonding patterns of chemistry, which in turn lead to biology, which in turn leads to the evolution of life and, eventually, to you and me. After fourteen billion years of cosmic evolution, we remain and are nothing but complexly organized matter. To the extent that we believe we are mind or soul, we are simply mistaken. Mind is a function, emergent property, or accidental product of dead matter in this view. End of story.

Science, by far our most successful means of knowing the world out there, has resulted in us knowing about just about everything, except, embarrassingly enough, the knower of all of this stuff. The best science can do when it comes to the nature of mind or consciousness is tell us that there is no such presence, and that our own obvious awareness that there is in fact such a presence is a delusion created by loop-like circuits in the brain. This is not very helpful. Actually, it is more than a little stupid, though no one will quite say that.

I have argued that the modern study of religion could well function as a most potent challenge to this stupidity, but that it has failed to do so. The discipline, I suggest, has failed to act as a philosophical tonic precisely to the extent that it constantly encounters historical phenomena that subvert *both* this dualism *and* this materialism and then refuses to consider such things in any truly serious and sustained way, no doubt because they cannot be slotted into these same dualist and materialist assumptions. I am thinking of what we now call psychical and paranormal events, or what in a previous era would have been described as magical or miraculous events. It is my own conviction that "we have the goods," that is, that we work with material all the time that could revolutionize not just the humanities but the sciences as well, if only we could take this material more seriously and not simply engage in endless "bracketing" and other polite and politic forms of noncommittal.

I sometimes think of these historical phenomena as one immense elephant standing right smack in the middle of our professional living room. Many scholars of religion bump into this giant from time to time. The general response is either to simply look away and walk on, or to deny it is there. If it is not there, after all, we do not need to think about it, and we certainly do not need to rethink our most basic assumptions about knowledge and reality. But it's there. It's definitely there.

I want to talk about that elephant.

OPENINGS: ANSWERING LOGOS WITH MYTHOS

But how? How does one talk about an elephant that one's interlocutors claim is not really there? How does one speak about impossible things without appearing to one's peers as, well, impossible? I have learned over the years that it is quite futile simply to argue with individuals who are committed to resisting such historical phenomena out of their own quite reasonable commitments, many of which I share. Pure reason here gets one exactly nowhere. What finally melts the ice of rationalism is not more rationalism, but story. What finally pushes beyond logos is not more logos, but mythos.

In this mythical spirit, let me begin, then, with a deceptively simple claim. Let me claim that *the paranormal is a kind of story*.[15] By "story," I do not mean "just a story." I do not mean a simple work of fiction. By story, I mean "what really happened," which then becomes a story that is inevitably more polished or clean than the original event but which nonetheless exists only because of the original historical empirical event. By "story," I mean to refer to what has traditionally been called "myth," which I understand, at least here, as a narrative expression, partly empirical, partly symbolic, of a real event that overflows and exhausts any rational explanation.

Here are two concrete examples.

Consider first the American writer Samuel Clemens, otherwise known as Mark Twain. Twain's life was riddled with bizarre events and strange coincidences. "History," he wrote, "may not repeat itself, but it rhymes." Life, in other words, is not simply linear, temporal, and causal. It is also organized around meaning, metaphor, and poetry.

And dream. Sam and his brother Henry were working on the riverboat *Pennsylvania*. The night before they embarked, Sam dreamed of Henry's corpse in a metal casket dressed in his older brother's suit with a large bundle of white roses on his chest and a single red rose in the center. The dream was so real and so disturbing that it took a walk outside to convince Sam that, yes, "it was just a dream." Unfortunately, it was not just a dream. Sam was transferred to another ship, and Henry was killed in a boiler explosion on the *Pennsylvania* a few days later. Robert Moss describes the funeral:

246 || CHAPTER 11

When Sam entered the "dead-room" of the Memphis Exchange on June 21, 1858, he was horrified to see the enactment of his dream: his dead brother laid out in a metal casket in a borrowed suit. Only one element was missing: the floral bouquet. As Sam watched and mourned, a lady came in with a bouquet of white roses with a single red one at the center and laid it on Henry's chest.[16]

Who would not be permanently marked, at once inspired and haunted, by such a series of events? And who of us, if this were *our* dream and *our* brother, could honestly dismiss it all as a series of simple coincidences? Twain certainly could not. He was obsessed with such moments in his life, of which there were all too many. In 1878, he wrote a few of them out in an essay. But he could not bring himself to publish it, as he feared "the public would treat the thing as a joke whereas I was in earnest."[17] Twain then offered the essay to the *North American Review* on the condition that they publish it anonymously. They refused to do so. Finally, Twain published this material in *Harper's* magazine in two separate installments: "Mental Telegraphy: A Manuscript with a History" (1891) and "Mental Telegraphy Again" (1895).[18]

The expression "mental telegraphy" captured Twain's core conviction that some types of psychical events can be thought of as special types of writing and reading. Biographically, Twain's own understanding was related to the fact that he had repeatedly noticed the phenomenon of "crossed letters." This involved a person writing, say, a long-lost friend or family member only to find a letter from that same individual arrive in the mail a few days, or a few hours, later: the letters had "crossed" in the mail. After experiencing some very dramatic examples of this phenomenon, Twain came to believe that minds somehow send out signals, like a telegraph, and that it is the intention that manifests the resulting effect. One need not even necessarily send the letter. Twain would thus often joke about saving the postage.[19]

Twain told a most dramatic case of such crossed correspondence in his first *Harper's* essay. On a particular 2nd of March, Twain explains how a "red-hot new idea" for a book about the Nevada silver mines came blazing into his mind. He wrote down the book's details, order, and sequence in the form of a letter to a colleague whom he thought was best poised to write this book, a certain Mr. Wright. But he never mailed that letter. When, though, he received a letter in the mail from Mr. Wright just a week later, on the 9th of March, after years of silence between the two friends, he knew already the date of the letter's signature (the 2nd of March) and what it contained (the outline of the book on the Nevada silver mines that had come to him, as if out of nowhere). Twain did not stop here, though, with this internal conviction. As a little experiment, he described this all in detail to a cousin, who happened to be present, before he opened the envelope. He was correct on every count. "I could not doubt," Twain wrote, "that Mr. Wright's mind and mine had been in close and crystal-clear communication with each other across three thousand miles of mountain and desert on the 2nd of March."[20]

Note here that a paranormal event is not simply structured like a story. It *is* a story.

Ah, you say, that was the nineteenth century. They were obsessed with Spiritualism and séances. Those things don't happen anymore. Really? Consider a CNN story from 2011.[21] It opens with a New Jersey hairdresser named Nina de Santo, who one Saturday evening saw a longtime customer named Michael standing outside her beauty shop. She met him at the door. Michael was smiling, but he was in a hurry and could not stay long. He had been going through a very difficult divorce and had lost custody of his kids. He just wanted to thank Nina for all the times she was there to listen. And then he left. The next day Nina received a phone call from one of her employees. Michael had committed suicide, nine hours before she met him in front of her shop the evening before.

The Twain and de Santo stories capture beautifully the impossibility and poignancy of the paranormal. I am especially interested in such histories because I have come to think that very similar psychical phenomena lie at the core of the history of religions, right behind what we have traditionally called "myth," "miracle," and "magic." As such, these phenomena have the potential to revision and renew the study of religion, to make it miraculous and magical again, if only we can stop thinking about these phenomena in the naively subjectivist ways of the debunker (it's entirely subjective) *or* the naively objectivist ways of the true believer (it's all literally true and as factual as that chair over there). In essence, I am suggesting that we reject these subjectivisms and objectivisms for a more nuanced and paradoxical vision of things, one that can render what we now consider to be impossible possible.

Toward this end, I want to crystallize these wildly various phenomena into a single offensive word—*telepathy*. The remainder of my lecture will proceed in three parts. In the first part, I will discuss (1) *the traumatic technology of telepathy*, that is, the technological metaphors and emotional dynamics of what the early writers often intended through phrases like "mental telegraphy" and "telepathy." In the second part, I will discuss (2) *telepathy as text and the text as telepathy*, that is, the dual manner in which paranormal events tend to look a lot like texts and texts themselves can function as paranormal events. And third and finally, I want to bring the material home, as it were, and discuss (3) *telepathy and the study of religion*. Put most simply, I want to talk about how the humanities, and particularly humanistic approaches to textuality, can help us make good sense out of paranormal events, which are generally misunderstood, or simply disappear, if slotted into scientific ways of knowing.

1. THE TRAUMATIC TECHNOLOGY OF TELEPATHY

Most of us in the professional study of religion read at some point, usually in graduate school, a single book by William James, *The Varieties of Religious Experience*. *The Varieties* consists of a series of lectures James gave at the University of Edinburgh in 1901 and 1902 and then published later that same year. The book has since been quoted and debated endlessly. What gets lost in much of this discussion, and certainly got lost in my own graduate training, is the fact that this book is deeply embedded in the psychical research tradition.

Through much of *The Varieties*, James is in fact drawing on the work of his close friend and colleague, Frederic Myers, who was the leader of this tradition. It is also worth observing that James himself wrote over fifty essays and reviews out of his own extensive work with mediums. Indeed, an entire volume in the Harvard edition of his complete works is dedicated to these psychical writings.[22] We did not read this William James in graduate school. Nor were we ever introduced to the micro-histories of the technical terms that the psychical research tradition produced with such care in the late nineteenth century. Three such terms come to mind: "psychical," "telepathy," and "paranormal." Contrary to popular assumptions, none were born in the tabloids. All three were coined by scientists and intellectuals, and all three are nuanced.

Psychical. The English expression *psychical* goes back to around 1871, when Sir William Crookes, the pioneering British chemist, created a sensation by publishing the results of a series of experiments he had performed with the Scottish super-medium Daniel Dunglas Home in the *Quarterly Journal of Science*. Home was known for all sorts of extraordinary abilities, from playing musical instruments without touching them to levitating in front of multiple witnesses. Astonishingly, none of this was ever proved to be fraudulent.

Crookes was convinced that Home was the real deal. Here he described what he called "a New Force" unknown to science. Since this New Force was obviously connected in some way to the human mind, "Psychic" was quickly added to "Force" and a new episteme was born. "Psychic" and "psychical" commonly changed places in the literature here. What the words referred to, however, remained stable, that is, *an assumed but still ill-understood power of the human mind to manipulate the immediate physical environment or access information that is otherwise unavailable through the normal sensory channels.* The adjective "psychical" encoded this baffling both-and provocation particularly well: to the ear, the word "psychical," after all, alludes at once to both the "psyche" and the "physical." Yes.

Crookes's later collection of essays, *Researches into the Phenomena of Spiritualism* (1874), would come to play a major role in attracting other intellectuals to the subject. In the winter of 1882, some of these intellectuals, many of them connected to Cambridge University, formed the London Society for Psychical Research. Alfred Russel Wallace, the co-creator of the evolutionary thesis with Darwin, attended the first official meeting on February 20, 1882. Wallace had already attended multiple séances and witnessed full-blown materializations before various physical mediums.[23] He saw the phenomena of Spiritualism as evidence for a separate, nonphysical line of moral or spiritual evolution. An American branch of the S.P.R. was founded three years later, in 1885, around William James of Harvard University. By 1885, in other words, the term "psychical" was embedded in a global intellectual network that stretched between two elite establishments—Cambridge and Harvard—and had been linked, as it remains linked to this day in popular culture, to evolutionary biology.

Telepathy. The word "telepathy" was coined by Frederic Myers in 1882 as part of this same psychical research tradition. Myers was a classicist, and so he was always coining new words from the Greek and Latin. This was one of them. The word had nothing to do with predicting the stock market or the next horse race. It was much more serious than that. It had everything to do with suffering, trauma, and, above all, the horrors and agonies of death. Put more positively, it had everything to do with human emotion, human bonding, with some fantastic trans-spatial and trans-temporal sociality. It had everything do with *love.*

Here is how it came to be. At this point, Myers and his colleagues had put ads in the newspapers asking for letters about strange occurrences around the death of a loved one. They received thousands. They sifted through these, selected out what they considered to be the most interesting, and then backchecked the facts through interviews, coroner reports, obituaries, and so on. They discovered a number of comparative patterns through this process. For one thing, they noted that the subject would often receive extremely accurate information about the death of the loved one in a dream or waking vision, regardless of how distant he or she was from the event. Even more bizarrely, often this information would come *before* the event actually occurred, exactly like we saw with Mark Twain's dream of his brother's impending funeral. It looked very much like a form of communication was occurring outside the normal parameters of space and time. Myers coined the term "tele-pathy" to describe these communications.

The word means, literally, "*pathos* at a distance." This was the key. What Myers intended to communicate here is that such communications outside the reaches of the normal sense channels appeared to depend upon two fundamental processes: (1) an extreme emotional state, often connected to serious danger, physical trauma, or actual death; and (2) a level of the human psyche that is not bound by the normal parameters of space and time.

Myers called the latter dimension of the psyche the "subliminal Self." The word "subliminal" was Latin again, this time for "under the threshold." It was Myers's central organizing idea and, as such, did a great deal of work for him. He suggested, for example, that the subliminal Self is the source of intellectual genius and literary creativity through moments he called "subliminal uprushes." He also became convinced that individuals commonly receive telepathic communications from their loved ones below the same threshold of awareness. Such regions, however, cannot speak to the conscious self directly, and so they generally emerge into consciousness indirectly through a dream image, a waking hallucination, or an overwhelming intuition. In short, the subliminal Self speaks to the ego through signs.

Paranormal. We might recall that neither Twain nor Myers used the expression "paranormal." There is a reason for this. It did not yet exist. This new word, which seems to have morphed from Myers's earlier evolutionary concept of the "supernormal," was coming into use just as Myers lay dying, that is, just after the turn of the century, this time among French scientists. The first published occurrences of the paranormal appear to be in Joseph Maxwell's *Les Phénomènes Psychiques* (1903).[24] Most later uses early in the same century are derivative of Maxwell, who was in turn probably simply translating Myers's "supernormal."[25]

After Renaud Évrard's mining of the original French text, it is clear that Maxwell's uses of the adjectives *paranormal(e)/paranormaux* were not tangential or minor ones. They are used extensively throughout his study.[26] He defines "paranormal phenomena" as those that lie "outside" or "to the side" of the habitual rules of experience.[27] He is thinking in particular of phenomena like telekinesis or psychokinesis (PK), that is, mind-over-matter effects.

In another place, he defines paranormal phenomena as those that imply the existence of some mode of perception that is "estranged" or foreign to the "normal personality." He is thinking of things like clairvoyance, clairaudience, and telepathy (and here he cites the British researchers, including Myers).[28] The same author will also use "supernormal" (as *supranormal*) as a synonym and will isolate the single most stable character of paranormal phenomena as their irregularity or upredictable nature.[29]

All the dials are set right here. The adjectives *paranormal(e)/paranormaux* referred to some natural but ill-understood force that could extend from the mind into the physical environment and have real physical effects there. In essence, it referred to a correspondence or connection between a mental state and a physical event, but it carried no necessary supernatural or religious connotations.

Noisy Ghosts and Sexual Spirits

This transition from the supernatural to the super natural can perhaps best be seen in the history of the poltergeist, whose story we can now finely trace thanks to the careful historical work of Christopher Laursen.[30] Such a "noisy ghost" first appears in Martin Luther's *The Misuse of the Mass* (1522) as *die polter geyster*, "ghosts that bang about." Luther had personally experienced these weird forces—things like strange noises behind the stove or flying hazel-nuts. He associated them with the Devil and considered the common Catholic interpretation of such occurences (that they were poor souls in purgatory asking for prayers and masses) to be one of the many "abuses" of the Catholic Church. The German expression and its demonic reading thus begin as a piece of Protestant polemic aimed at the doctrine of purgatory and the ritual efficacy of the Mass.[31]

The poltergeist was first introduced into the English language by Catherine Crowe in her influential *The Night-Side of Nature* (1848). Crowe called for scientific study. By the early twentieth century, researchers were beginning to suspect that classic poltergeist phenomena (things like knocks, scratches, pops, and falling or flying objects) were not the results of a departed soul, much less the Devil misleading good Lutherans into Catholic abuses, but were somehow related to the emotional suffering of a living human being.

Such thinking can clearly be seen in the books of Charles Fort (1919–1932), who often observed the marginalized or troubled status of the person around whom occult bizarrarie exploded. About the same time, in 1921 to be precise, Hereward Carrington began to notice that the phenomena tended to manifest around pubescent boys and girls. This intuition was formalized in the middle of the century, when Carrington and the psychoanalyst Nandor Fodor explicitly related these forces to the Freudian concept of sexual repression in *Haunted People* (1951). The American parapsychologist William Roll formalized this line of thought around 1958 with his concept of RSPK, or recurrent spontaneous psychokinesis. The parapsychologist Hans Bender carried the same line of thought forward in Germany. It was in this way that the modern writers and researchers naturalized the supernatural by locating the angry ghost squarely in the emotional energies of the sexually maturing human being, even if this was now a human nature whose sexual and spiritual potentials appeared, well, fantastic.

The new paranormal worked like the slightly older supernormal. Just as the dying loved one appears to send out subliminal signals through her intense suffering or fear within a telepathic event (Myers's supernormal), so too the subject of paranormal activity appears to be manifesting these powers out of his own intense emotional or sexual states. Hence the poltergeist commonly reported to this day around emotionally conflicted adolescents or within highly troubled family networks.

It is difficult to avoid the suspicion that rare types of sexual energy are being deployed in at least some of these cases. Consider, for example, the Sauchie Poltergeist case in Scotland of 1960–61, involving eleven-year-old Virginia Campbell and a poltergeist she affectionately dubbed "Wee Hughie." Pillows rotated, sheets rippled, the linen chest moved back and forth eighteen inches, and strange knocks and sawings were heard at night, often as Virginia went into a trance and expressed thoughts in a strange voice "with a lack of normal inhibition." At other points, the girl's pajamas were pulled off and her nightdress was pulled up—ghostly pranks that suggest a childish but still innocent sexual play. During the day, school desks vibrated and levitated slightly off the ground, a blackboard pointer and a bowl of bulbs moved on their own, and the lid on her desk raised on its own (as she tried to hold it down). The many witnesses found all of this "awe-inspiring" but not particularly scary, and they identified Virginia as the source of the exotic energy. Her school teacher, Miss Stewart, took careful note of the dates of the occult happenings in her classroom, which she witnessed up close, and identified a fifty-six-day interval between them, that is, exactly two lunar months, "a very suggestive figure," Cambridge mathematician and poltergeist researcher A. R. G. Owen notes, "if the phenomena are related to physiological happenings associated with a quasi-menstrual cycle occurring as a result of exceptionally rapid pubescence."[32] Whether in bioenergetic actuality or in cultural memory, human sexuality has become a kind of unconscious superpower here. If exaggerated and rendered more fearful, these are scenes that could have come right out of a Stephen King novel or an X-Men movie. It was King in fact who popularized the work of Fodor, Carrington, and Roll in his thriller *Carrie* (1974).

2. TELEPATHY AS TEXT AND THE TEXT AS TELEPATHY

So telepathy as an experienced reality was expressed early on through the technological metaphor of the telegraph, which was understood to send out its signals via the emotional sufferings and physical traumas of dying human beings, as if the human being is the "battery" of the psychical technology. These dramatic stories were then recorded and transmitted within another form of telepathy: the published text. Here the act of reading and writing become the privileged site of the paranormal.

The American horror and science-fiction writer Stephen King has written about his occult understanding of the craft of writing, which he understands as a form of effective telepathy whereby one's mental state comes to transcend not only space but also time through the magical medium of the published text. A published story, for King, is a narrative state of mind "caught" in a text and waiting to be precisely reactivated—word for word—two, ten, even twenty years later down the space-time continuum.[33] Writing and reading stories for Stephen King, in other words, mimic or replicate paranormal processes.

In a different but related vein, the literary critic Nicholas Royle has written extensively about what he calls the "telepathy effect," by which he means to remind us that a modern genre like narrative fiction requires an imitation of telepathy to work at all. That is, the author's omniscient view whereby he or she describes in great detail to the reader the contents of the minds and hearts of the novel's characters is, in effect, a replication of telepathy.[34] Royle is drawing on Derrida here, who was similarly fascinated with the rhetorical links between telepathy and human communication and wrote an essay on the subject in the summer of 1979.

The essay reads like a dream, by which I mean, it reads as if one were caught inside the logic of a dream, by which I mean, it is really, really confusing.[35] There are a few clear moments, however, like the time his female interlocutor asks Derrida what is changing in his life. "Well," he answers, "you have noticed it a hundred times recently, it is the opposite of what I foresaw, as one might have expected: a surface more and more open to all the phenomena formerly rejected (in the nature of a certain discourse of science), to the phenomena of 'magic,' of 'clairvoyance,' of 'fate,' of communications at a distance, to the things said to be occult."[36] Although he will frustrate any easy answer here, his conversion appears to have been the result of personal experiences: "Remember and we, we would not have moved a step forward in this treatment of the dispatch . . . if among all these tele-things we did not get in touch with Telepathy in person. Or rather if we didn't allow ourselves to be touched by her."[37] Less enigmatically, he relates the intimate details of at least four cases of what Mark Twain would have immediately recognized as cross-correspondence involving things like a postcard from his son seemingly responding to a dream Derrida had about a childhood scar, which he playfully describes for the knowing as a "trace."[38]

The essay's dream logic violates the usual straight arrow of time: "Something shoots! Something hits the target! Is it me who hits the target, or the target who shoots me?"[39] Or again: "Imagine that an anachronism resembling no other shifts us, out of phase, it lifts or displaces the blocks, brakes or accelerates as if we were late with respect to that which has already happened to us in the future."[40] I do not claim to understand this essay, but it very much appears that Derrida is writing about the experience of being written, from the future no less.

I mention this theme here because one of the most common descriptors of a paranormal experience in my most recent subjects—artists and authors of American popular culture—is precisely this, that is, the experience of being written from the future. They also commonly describe their paranormal experiences with some version of the phrase: "It was as if I were caught in a novel." In short, paranormal events commonly replicate literary processes.

Weirder still, literary processes can sometimes herald paranormal events. For example, professional writers commonly report paranormal effects spinning out of their writing practices. I have written about two of these instances, that of the comic book writer Doug Moench and that of the science-fiction writer Philip K. Dick. Both men wrote stories that they thought were fictional only to have them play out in real life shortly afterward. In Moench's case, a comic-book scene of a violent burglary in a *Planet of the Apes* story played out within seconds after he wrote it, in his own home no less; in Dick's case, he allegedly met a woman in real life who matched in uncanny ways the character in a novel that he had written months earlier. So it is not simply the case that truth is stranger than fiction. Fiction may in fact *be* the truth of things.

3. TELEPATHY AND THE STUDY OF RELIGION

This, of course, is all impossible. That is to say, such stories and claims make no sense in the present terms in which we understand the world in both the humanities and the sciences. Reality is not made of words and stories. It is made of matter and numbers. Reality does not work through metaphors and symbols. It works through mechanisms and causal chains. These things cannot happen by those rules, hence they do not happen. Period.

Unfortunately for our assumptions, they do happen, and all the time. Which is all to say that such impossible things are part of history too. How, then, are we to make sense of them as students and scholars of religion? How might we recover and revision our central categories of myth, miracle, and magic? Or are denial, suppression, and polite neglect proper historical methods?

The problem here, I want to suggest, is not the historical events themselves, but our present philosophical assumptions about human consciousness. As we saw in the very beginning, these assumptions pretty much understand the human subject as an illusory froth of neurons firing in complex loops and circuits inside the bony box of the skull. The specific firing of this froth, moreover, is largely determined by the social and historical surround, by language, by child rearing, by social practices, and so on, which essentially acts as a kind of software on the hardware of the neurological system. In this model, any visionary or paranormal experience is a purely subjective affair occurring inside that bony cave. As such, such an event has no reference to reality "out there." It is simply an illusion or misperception. Basically, in this view, we are biological robots locked down into our local cultural and social contexts and trapped inside our skulls. Like Data on *Star Trek: The Next Generation*, we may desperately want to be human, to be More, but we never can be. We are biological robots, and our circuits are showing now. We cannot escape this hardwired neurology or this local cultural software, and we certainly can never know anything beyond them. Transcendence is a ruse, or a power grab. The soul is a bygone fancy. Those are the rules of the materialist game.

Derrida had it just right when he wrote that "everything, in our concept of knowledge, is constructed so that telepathy be impossible, unthinkable, unknown."[41] The same is true, I would suggest, of myth, miracle, and magic. These are all impossible, unthinkable, unknown within our reigning epistemologies. It is not that we do not understand them. It is that we *cannot* understand them with our present rules of the game.

All these rules, moreover, come down to a single meta-issue: how we are thinking of consciousness, that sui generis elephant in the middle of all of our living rooms. Is consciousness really a product, in toto, of brain matter and can it really be conflated with cognition, as we have it in so much brain science? Or with culture and context, as we have it in so much of the humanities? Or is it something much, much more, as we have it suggested in the data of psychical and paranormal phenomena? Obviously, this last question is a rhetorical one. My answer is: Yes, it is more, way more.

Derrida notes that Freud ends his own essay on "Telepathy and Psychoanalysis" with a vision of the figure of Saint Denis walking and holding his own decapitated head, as portrayed, for example, over the entrance of the Cathedral of Notre Dame in Paris.[42] It is only the first step that is costly, Freud wryly observes, "but what a step beyond it would be," adds a paraphrasing Derrida.[43] That is to say, it is only the presupposition that we are locked down into our heads, that we *are* only those heads, that needs to be overcome. After that, the field is open, wide open, and many of those things that are now impossible will not only become possible; they will become predictable. It is precisely this presupposition, for example, that something like telepathy challenges, calls into question, subverts. Telepathy is, after all, only possible if communication can take place *between* heads separated at great distances in space and time. As Derrida so accurately puts it, telepathy is "outside-the-subject."[44] It is also, I might add, outside-the-skull. If telepathy really happens, then, we are obviously not just our heads, and mind cannot be reduced to brain or local culture. Telepathy, in effect, beheads us. If telepathy happens, we are all Saint Denis.

I want to close with Nina de Santo's impossible encounter with an already dead Michael. What are our options here? One option is to look for mistakes or distortions in the transmission of the story. Perhaps we could go and interview Nina and see what she says now. Perhaps we would find that the original event was not this extraordinary. Perhaps. That would be a relief.

Whatever we would find, do not such stories tell us many things about how religious belief arises and develops? Doesn't her story look more than a little like the encounters of the disciples with the resurrected Jesus? In one we have an executed criminal and in the other a suicide victim, but both are basically dead guys appearing in remarkably good form. Aren't those gospel stories supposed to be legends? Tell me, then, if this can happen in New Jersey and show up on CNN last fall, why couldn't it have happened in first-century Palestine and have shown up in the gospels? And—the really subversive question—what does it mean, what *can* it mean, that what is supposed to be a single, unique historical event is not so unique after all? What do we do when the resurrection shows up in our own back yard as the paranormal, amid a suicide no less?

What should we say? Where should we stand? All we are allowed to do at the moment within the professional study of religion is historicize, relativize, and so disempower such stories by locking them down tightly to a specific religious or political identity and to a specific time and place, to a "context" or a "text," as we so safely say. Such methods are necessary beginnings, but they are hardly sufficient. In the end, they will not produce a historiography that is truly adequate to the history of religions, much less to the modern lived experience of the paranormal. For this, we will need something more along the lines of what Robert Orsi has called an "abundant historiography," that is, a way of writing history that allows modern experiences of transcendence to challenge, radically and really, one's own assumptions about history and time itself. In Orsi's terms, such a historiography is "the effort to write abundantly about events that are not safely cordoned off in the past but whose routes extend into the present, into the writing of history itself."[45]

This is a very fine description of what I have tried to show, in my own stumbling ways, with the paranormal experiences of contemporary individuals and these events' intimate relationship to writing and reading, semiotics, and yes, the writing of history itself. I have tried to reimagine the historian of religions as someone who does not shy away from myth, magic, and miracle, who, more importantly still, allows these actual events to call into question our deepest and most fundamental assumptions about the real, about time, and about history itself. If such a project has any hope of finding some cultural traction in the future, we will need new forms of knowing, new models of reality, and, above all, new ways of reading and writing history. We will need authors of the impossible.

The Matter of Myth and the Myth of Matter
(2011)

Beginnings are particularly important for writers of all sorts. So too in the superhero comics. Often the superhero acquires his or her powers from some sort of accident or trauma: the alien Superman crashes onto planet earth from Krypton; Batman, struggling with the horrible memory of the murder of his parents, learns the martial arts and dedicates his life to fighting crime; scientist Bruce Banner is radiated by an atomic bomb test—that sort of thing. Every superhero, it turns out, needs a story about how he or she came to be different, how he or she became *super*.

But I am not the potential superhero here. You are. It is my hope anyway that this book might function as a crash-landing or radioactive blast for at least some of its more imaginative super-readers. In any case, this particular book possesses its own Origins story. It goes like this.

In the fall of 1962, two Stanford graduates, Michael Murphy and Richard Price, founded a little visionary community on a remote cliff in Big Sur, California. It would come to be known as the Esalen Institute. The intentions of the two founders were multiple, but on Murphy's side all of the deepest ones boiled down to an evolutionary vision that understands psychical and paranormal experiences to be "evolutionary buds" witnessing to the future occult form of the species, what Murphy calls "the future of the body."

We will get into some of the details of this particular story later on. For now, it is enough to note that I spent the first seven years of the new millennium researching and writing a history of Esalen and, while doing so, found myself, with no little embarrassment, becoming more or less obsessed with the comic-book mythologies of my adolescence. At first, this simply puzzled me. But the obsession would not go away, so I began to quiz it, ask it questions, talk to it (yes, I do this sort of thing). Eventually, the obsession turned into an intuition, an idea-in-the-making. I began to realize how eerily similar Murphy's evolutionary mysticism is to the mythology of the X-Men. Indeed, the similarities border on the uncanny. I would go even further. Murphy's evolutionary mysticism not only looks very much like the X-Men. It *is* the X-Men. To add insult to injury, the evolutionary mystical school that would become Esalen was founded in Big Sur in the fall of 1962, that is, one year before Stan Lee and Jack Kirby dreamed up a similar occult school in Westchester, New York, for their X-Men. This strange resonance between East Coast mythology and West Coast mysticism, between mutants and mystics, I decided, was the probable source of my embarrassing midlife obsession with superhero comics.

Then, like all things paranormal, these mythical musings literally entered my physical world in the summer of 2006. I was walking out of the cave of a cool dark movie theater after watching *X-Men 3: The Last Stand* and feeling especially perplexed, again, about how close this popular mythology was to Murphy's evolutionary mystical system, about which I had been writing and thinking all that same summer. As I watched these strange ideas appear and disappear "in here" and approached my minivan in the hot parking lot after the movie, something suddenly appeared "out there," something golden and shining in the painfully bright sun. I couldn't possibly miss it, as it was lying immediately below the van door, as if it were waiting just for me. At first, I thought it was a Christian cross (I live in pious Texas, after all). It turned out on closer inspection to be a cheap piece of costume jewelry in the perfect and unmistakable shape not of a cross, but of an "X."

That was the final straw that broke this rational camel's back. That was the moment I decided to write this book. The pages that follow are an imperfect record of what happened when I picked up that X, decided to trust whatever it was that it represented, and write the present seven meditations on what Chris Knowles has so aptly called "the X factor" of superhero comics. I found that X factor—literally.

I am not, of course, asking the reader to be particularly impressed by that cheap piece of costume jewelry in that extraordinarily ordinary parking lot picked up by this particular dingbat. I certainly would not be if its sudden appearance did not correspond perfectly with my internal hyper-creative state. I recognize, fully, that the force and meaning of such a minor event can be appreciated only by the person experiencing it. I am not, then, asking the reader to experience my experience. I am asking only that the reader know that what

260 || CHAPTER 11

follows is a creative expression of *both* the bright movie screen *and* the hot parking lot. Put a bit paradoxically but not at all inaccurately, the Super-Story I am about to tell you is unquestionably a myth, but it is a myth made of matter.

Or a piece of matter made of myth. I'm not really sure.

In any case, you're holding it.

Good luck with that.

12

La Pensée Surhumaine

Paraphysics, the Super Story, and Invisible Colleges

Hydrogen is a light, odorless gas that, given enough time, turns into people.

ANONYMOUS, IN DAVID CHRISTIAN'S *MAPS OF TIME: AN INTRODUCTION TO BIG HISTORY*

When everything is human, the human is an entirely different thing.

EDUARDO VIVEIROS DE CASTRO, *CANNIBAL METAPHYSICS*

Recall that Frederic Myers brought the expression *the imaginal* into modern English in order to describe those empowered or electrified forms of mind, telepathic communications and precognitive dreams that he believed express a more highly evolved form of the imagination and give witness to the early signs of our still-evolving supernature. He described these highly evolved future forms of human functioning with a new adjective: *the supernormal*. Recall also that the supernormal would morph around the turn of the century, through the French researchers now, into what we today call *the paranormal*. All three categories were advanced within a general cultural milieu, the late nineteenth and early twentieth centuries of Europe, that was heavily inflected by various esoteric understandings of human evolution, contact with discarnate or invisible beings (Spiritualism) and spiritual and moral progress.

Things got much stranger in the twentieth century. On the cosmological front, while the biblical creation stories and the Adam and Eve myth contined to be severely challenged (including in the American courts), the new "Big Bang" and cosmic expansion stories exploded. They are still exploding, even if we don't yet have them quite right. There is an understatement. At the time of this writing, we are being told that we have very little right, since *all* of our physics and *all* of our science applies to only about 5 percent of the cosmos. The rest, now mysteriously dubbed "dark energy" or "dark matter," is a complete blank spot on our scientific maps. We know virtually nothing, it turns out. Even worse (or better), cosmologists have learned more and more about the fine-tuning of the universe's most basic forces, from the force of the original Big Bang itself to the strong nuclear and gravitational forces, all of which appear to be eerily set just right. In the words of astronomer Bob Berman, there are in fact "more than two hundred physical parameters within the solar system and universe so exact that it strains credulity to propose that they are random—even if that is exactly what standard contemporary physics baldly suggests. These fundamental constants of the universe—constants that are not predicted by any theory—all seem to be carefully chosen, often with great precision, to allow for the existence of life and consciousness."[1]

And then it got stranger still. The rise of quantum mechanics shortly after the turn of the twentieth century effectively shattered (at least for philosophically aware physicists) all familiar notions of materialism, objectivism, temporality, even causality itself. This was accomplished through formal mathematical models and confirming laboratory experiments. It was all unspeakably strange. And it wasn't strange because we poor laypeople cannot understand it without knowing the exquisite mathematics. It was so strange because *no one can understand it*, math or no math. It simply makes no sense, nor is there any way to make it make sense to our primitive primate imaginations. As physics bad boy Richard Feynman famously observed: if you think you understand quantum mechanics, you clearly don't.

PARAPHYSICAL ESOTERICISM AND
AN OVERLORD IN A LIBRARY

Professional debunkers (I refuse to call them skeptics, because they are anything but[2]) often lazily label comparisons between the new physics and mystical literature "New Age woo woo," their cruel code for everything that offends their materialisms. But in fact these rhetorical sneers are, at best, partial and, historically speaking, simply wrong, since it was the physicists themselves who first made the case for some haunting resonances between the philosophical implications of quantum physics and the reported experiences of mystical literature.

The quantum theorists are hardly alone in their observations. Similar employments of mathematics and physics to explore, even God forbid explain, a whole spectrum of anomalous experiences are apparent throughout the modern period. Mathematical Platonisms (whereby mathematical structures

preexist their discovery or remembrance by the mathematician in some esoteric space or transcendent reality), hyperdimensional or hyperspace models
(whereby the positing of further dimensions beyond the three of our primate
imagination are invoked to naturalize "magical" and "miraculous" events), and
the positing of exotic states of living energy or conscious plasmas (whereby
the soul or a god is understood to be some form of "energy") are all examples
of what I want to call the paraphysical esotericisms.

Allow me a simple illustration. Some of the many curious phenomena of
near-death experiences involve their effects on visual and temporal perspective.
Subjects routinely report being able to see inside things or bodies, or having
their vision reversed, as in a mirror, or experiencing all time at once. They also
sometimes report a striking 360-degree perspective, as if they can somehow
see in all directions at once, "like a sphere."[3] This, of course, is all impossible
within our ordinary visual experience in three dimensions and linear time, but
all of this would be quite ordinary were we to "pop out" into a hyperdimensional
space. And it would often take only one more such dimension, hence Edwin
Abbott's classic *Flatland* (1884), in which he imagined how the natural perspectives of three-dimensional beings, such as ourselves, would appear godlike and
"miraculous" to two-dimensional beings living on a flat surface. The beauty and
simplicity of this reimagining are simply remarkable.

In any case, this is what I mean by *paraphysics*—a rethinking of the paranormal in light of physics and mathematics and, I dare add, a rethinking of
physics and mathematics in light of the paranormal. I borrow the expression
from the novel *Childhood's End* by Arthur C. Clarke, who was in turn drawing on the British psychical research tradition. By such expressions Clarke intended some fusion of parapsychology and physics that constituted the "Pan-
dora's Box" of human knowledge. Indeed, what we learn at the very end of the
novel is that the Overlords, extraterrestrials who look exactly like the devils
of world mythology, have been appearing in our histories in service of the
Overmind to guide our evolution and prevent us from opening this very box,
to check "all serious work on paranormal phenomena." Why? So we would
not prematurely destroy ourselves, or worse. "The physicists could only have
ruined the Earth," explains the Overlord Karellen over a million radios that
he has taken over to speak to the planet, but "the paraphysicists could have
spread havoc to the stars."[4]

As dangerous as such a gnosis might be to an unprepared human species,
it is also their destiny and eventual apotheosis. As humanity begins to understand its own history under the tutelage of the Overlords, it simply lets go of

its long childhood of faith: "Beneath the fierce and passionless light of truth, faiths that had sustained millions for twice a thousand years vanished like morning dew."[5] But something more profound still is happening to the children. Their minds, not yet closed down and particularized by human culture, explosively metamorphize and mutate, like some sudden Zen enlightenment on a global scale.[6] They will be the last generation. At the very end, they literally float into the sky like so many balloons, as they rise to the stars to join the Overmind and so end human history. Earth itself dissolves in a flash of light, "growing brighter, brighter, blinding."[7]

This is science fiction, of course, but it is science fiction that expresses the grand spirit of a century of psychical research and parapsychology and includes some beautiful passages on the filter thesis and telepathy.[8] I borrow the expression *paraphysics* from the special library of the story that so absorbs the Overlord Rasheverak, who spends much of the novel reading through its fifteen thousand volumes in an attempt to separate the truth from the nonsense and so figure out what the human race has already realized, already knows, already *is*. Even the Overlords do not possess this kind of potential.

I intend no eschaton with my own use of the paraphysical, but I do intend to signal any number of literatures that fuse the parapsychological and the physical in order to suggest that consciousness is primary and primordial and not some random afterthought or accident. I also intend something of the importance Rasheverak attaches to the paranormal library, despite the constant mocking of others, and something of the sublime awe that the reader feels as the deified children rise into space and the Earth disappears in a flash of light. The implications of the paraphysical ideas, after all, are so great that they really could "end the world," if not quite so literally or apocalyptically.

PHYSICS AND MYSTICS

Probably the most well-known genre of the paraphysical literatures is the quantum literature and the physics-to-mystics resonances that it routinely posits. These resonances, it should be stressed, have often been overplayed, and many of them are a function of one important but by no means established interpretation of quantum mechanics, what is called the Copenhagen interpretation, so named because it was first developed by Niels Bohr and his German assistant Werner Heisenberg in Copenhagen. In lay terms (all I have), such an interpretation states that a quantum state does not take on a distinct property until that property is measured and the probability "wavefunction" of the quantum event "collapses." The most controversial element of such an interpretation is the apparent centrality of consciousness in the theory. It is as if, deep down, physical reality depends on being observed or measured to take on any particular state. Before that, or so the interpretation suggests, quantum reality exists only in a kind of statistical blur, neither here nor there.

The physics-to-mystics resonances should not be denied *or* exaggerated, then. Like the quantum itself, they seem to exist and not exist at the same time. That is why I prefer to describe these resonances as "hauntings." They seldom appear in conventional physics discussions, and they are commonly repressed or simply made fun of, but they also will not go away. They appear throughout the history of physics, like ghosts, often outside the formal science in the personal lives and secret passions of the physicists themselves. Consider Werner Heisenberg, Niels Bohr, Erwin Schrödinger, Wolfgang Pauli, and Carl Friedrich von Weizsächer.[9]

Werner Heisenberg (1901–1975) was a passionate reader of Plato's dialogues.[10] He also nutured a lifelong interest in India, so much so that he was nicknamed "the Buddha."[11] Niels Bohr (1885–1962) put the *yin-yang* symbol of Chinese Daoism on his coat of arms, in most readings as an expression of the paradoxical wave-particle behavior of quantum reality (a quantum event will behave as a particle or a wave, depending on how one sets up the experiment). Erwin Schrödinger (1887–1961) was an avid reader of Schopenhauer's idealist philosophy as well as the scholarly literature of the time on Buddhism, Hinduism, and Advaita Vedanta.[12] He also stated bluntly that he thought there was only one Mind in the universe, with the implication, of course, that our individual minds participate or plug into it—a pure expression of the filter thesis, from one of the founders of quantum theory no less.[13] Wolfgang Pauli helped C. G. Jung come to his idea of synchronicity or acausal correspondence. These same ideas were in turn heavily refracted through Pauli's paranormal experiences, primarily of a telekinetic or poltegeist nature. Basically, when he walked into a laboratory of a colleague, or even got near one, things would break or malfunction. The latter bizarrarie, well known in the physics community, entered the history of science as a kind of joke under the safe anemic cover of "the Pauli effect."[14] It was no joke to Pauli, though. Another kind of haunting of quantum physics, and another kind of attempted repression.

These are all well-known biographical facts, easily available in the literature. A much lesser-known but equally fascinating figure was Carl Friedrich von Weizsächer (1912–2007), whom we have already met briefly above as the physicist with whom Gopi Krishna, the Indian evolutionary mystic, interacted. Weizsächer studied with both Bohr and Heisenberg and was the director of the Max Planck Institute for Research into the Essentials of the Scientific-Technological World. The title reflects his self-understanding as "a politically active professor of philosophy trained as a physicist."[15] All of this is on display in his *The Unity of Nature* (1971), an immensely learned book that ends with a full-chapter comparison of "the One" of the ancient Greek philosophers Parmenides and Plato and modern quantum theory. Here the physicist homes in on the paradoxes of the ancient Greek mystical aphorism *hen to pan*, or "One is All," that is, the totality of the world that was said to be "comparable to a well-rounded sphere." He reflects on Parmenides' noetic insistence that "it is the same to [know] (*noein*) and to be (*einai*)"[16] and writes openly of "the mystical experience."

But most originally of all, von Weizsächer observes how everything that Parmenides taught about "the One" (that it has no beginning, no center, no end, no shape, no location, no rest, no motion, etc.) makes perfectly good sense if one approaches it from quantum theory (really, the Cophenhagen interpretation of quantum theory) and thinks of the totality of the universe, that is, the One, as one immense quantum mechanical object. Since no one can measure or observe this Unity from the outside, it in fact could not take on any such properties. If I may put in my own terms, such a singular quantum object would be "non-experienced" within a mystical event exactly as Parmenides describes such an event—as a "One" with no shape, location, rest, or motion.[17]

Here the incommunicability of mystical experience is more or less identified with the problem of measurement and observation in quantum mechanics. Whatever one makes of such comparisons (and that, at the end of the day, is what they are), one closes the book with the distinct impression that, for von Weizsächer, Parmenides and quantum theory are saying something similar, if in radically different cultural codes: one poetic, mystical, and philosophical; and one mathematical, formal, and scientific.

As even such a brief discussion makes very clear, such physics-mystics comparisons are clearly not pseudoscientific inventions of the uninformed, nor have they gone away.[18] They are a central, intimate, and stable part of the history of science. Indeed, in the case of Pauli the Poltergeist, they are intimate physical expressions *of the scientist himself.*

BEAUTIFUL COMPARISONS

The question remains what such correspondences between the mathematical formalism of the physics and the experienced unity of the mystics might mean. This is a rich modern comparison fraught with obvious risks and contagious possibilities. The quantum mechanics, after all, does not "prove" the mystical experience any more than the mystical experience "proves" the quantum mechanics: we cannot get from one to the other in any naively direct or causal way. Knowing the mathematics will not make one a mystic, anymore than a mystical experience can make one a mathematician or quantum theorist. So it is simply bad comparison to claim that the Upanishads, Daoism, Neoplatonism, or any other premodern mystical system somehow "knew" or "predicted" quantum mechanics, or that quantum mechanics is saying "the same thing" as the mystical traditions.

But none of this, please note, means that the comparison or correspondence itself is necessarily wrong or inappropriate. Atmanspacher's dual aspect monism and the Jung-Pauli conjecture outlined above gives us an efficient and elegant way forward here. Once we move to such a thought experiment, we can see immediately that such correspondences might mean that the mathematical formalism of matter and the mystical experiences of mind have split off from some deeper super-reality, and this is why the material mechanisms and the mystical experiences "up here" naturally co-incide, correspond, mirror one another. It is not, then, that one leads to or is the other, but that both point back to some deeper third or ground of which they are two very different expressions. That would be my own position, my own comparative move, anyway.

I also happen to think that the quantum esoteric literature serves at least two other purposes. I think that such a literature is providing classical mystical tropes (unity, eternity, transcendence, paradox, indeterminacy, etc.) with (1) new metaphors; and, more fundamentally still, (2) new plausibility structures.

The new physics offers new metaphors, new images, and a new comparative aesthetic. There is a rare symmetry and simplicity at work in the best moments of this literature. I am thinking of moments like the pure symmetry of Atmanspacher's dual aspect monism or von Weizsächer's striking realization that the cosmos would take on all the features of a classic mystical experience were it encountered as a simple quantum object or indeterminate One. The comparisons can be quite pleasurable and surprising, not unlike the intellectual elegance of a mathematical formula or proof suddenly understood.

But there is more. What the quantum theorists, and indeed the paraphysical esotericisms in general, also offer us are *new reasons, new forms of plausibility* that render what we once considered impossible (instant communication across space and time, radical unity, the transcendence of time) not only possible, but thinkable, even predictable. The impossible becomes possible; the metaphysical becomes mathematical. Here, I strongly suspect, is the real "punch" of the paraphysical esoteric literature. Suddenly, the historian is no longer dealing with strange, purely anomalous, simply anecdotal experiences of no philosophical import or scientific interest. Suddenly, one is dealing with human expressions of the fundamental, irreducible strangeness of reality itself, right down into the mathematical structures of the subatomic realm.

MYSTICISM AND MATHEMATICS

It is not simply the case that there are beautiful correspondences between quantum physics and mysticism. It is also the case that the two often work together in the history of science and end up producing real scientific results. As I will explain further below in my discussion of "invisible colleges," I have spoken to professional scientists and engineers who matter-of-factly credit their extremely lucrative scientific and technological discoveries to spectral encounters and anomalous experiences. Those are the kinds of things for which we simply have no adequate model. We will not even talk about them. The colleagues who share these things with me certainly cannot talk about them in public, and so they do not. Again, another kind of haunting from the corner of the eye or in the middle of the night.

But such encounters are only the beginning. Consider the philosophy of mathematics. There is probably no greater evidence for real correspondences between the human and the cosmic than mathematics, that entirely formal practice that can be created in purely abstract terms in the mind of a human being but that turns out to have everything to do with the structure, behavior, and history of the physical universe itself, down to completely invisible subatomic particles and all the way back to the Big Bang. How this mind-to-matter correspondence is possible at all no one can quite say, but this occultism—and that is what it is—is the very foundation of modern science. Perhaps to protect ourselves, we have forgotten the utter weirdness of the situation, not to mention the practice's original mystical origins in figures like the ancient Greek shaman-seer Pythagoras.

Similar transformations of mysticism into advanced mathematical theory can just as easily be found in modern figures, like the Russian theorization of set theory and infinity that was inspired by a heretical mystical practice called "Name Worshipping" within Russian Orthodoxy in the early part of the twentieth century.[19] An even more dramatic case can be seen in the South Indian mathematical prodigy Srinivasa Ramanujan (1887–1920). Ramanujan's mathematical gifts were nurtured early on through basic high school and college instruction (the latter he failed out of, multiple times, because he refused to study anything other than mathematics), but none of that comes close to explaining what this man accomplished and somehow "just knew." Over the course of his short life, he was able to re-create approximately 3,900 mathematical formulas, particularly in number theory and infinite series. Significantly, Ramanujan also interpreted dreams, was attracted to paranormal phenomena and Hindu mystical literature, and attributed his mathematical discoveries not to any simple cognition or problem solving but to his family deity, the goddess Namagiri of Namakaal, who would write formulas on his tongue and bestow mathematical intuitions in his dreams.[20] Note again how the symbolic imaginal and the empirical imaginal mix and meet. Ramanujan captured this fusion of the metaphysical and the mathematical in a single sentence: "An equation for me has no meaning unless it expresses a thought of God."[21] He was entirely serious. God, Zero, and Infinity were all somehow related for him.[22]

And this is all before we even get to what Einstein famously resisted as "spooky action at a distance," that is, the famous "entanglement" of particles and what would eventually become Bell's Theorem. The latter predicts that two particles that are once "entangled" or have interacted will always be connected, no matter where they end up in the universe. Space and time are both irrelevant, and "communication" is instant. Quantum reality, in a word, is *nonlocal*. No physicist puts it this way, but the implications of Bell's Theorem are clear enough: deep down, matter, and so the entire material world itself, is nonhistorical.

Once again, the history of a major quantum idea is deeply, well, entangled with mystical and, in this case, parapsychological interests. MIT historian of science David Kaiser has called the physicists who kept this model alive through the 1960s and 1970s the "hippie physicists." While their established colleagues were dismissing Bell's Theorem and being told to "shut up and calculate" (largely, to do more efficient work for the military complex and their bombs), these out-of-work quantum theorists were enthusiastically embracing the same theorem and exploring its philosophical and existential implications, which they believed (correctly) were mind-blowing.[23] Kaiser points out that the same countercultural physicists were deeply interested in mystical and psychical phenomena, including and especially telepathy, since that it is precisely what entanglement looks like, if now on a literally cosmic scale.

Kaiser's story is also Esalen's story. After all, many of these same physicists, including and especially one of Kaiser's main historical subjects, Nick Herbert, were at Esalen during the same period and took part in the physics of consciousness seminars there. Nick is a dear friend. He is also a delightful wizard of a human being who found his materialist and mathematical arrogance shattered by a powerful LSD experience in 1963. The experience convinced him "that I didn't know *fuck* about the world." This was no formal abstract proof. This was a spiritual revelation of the most dramatic sort. "I was plunged into an abyss of consciousness. Everything seemed to be made of mind. Nick Herbert was gone. There was this huge vastness. Consciousness was full of all of these details that I could barely receive, but I was in them and was them." Nick's conclusion? "Wow! *Wow!* Physics is such a trivial enterprise. *Consciousness* is where it's at."[24] Nick would go on to write a number of books, including an acclaimed introduction to quantum mechanics and another on "elemental mind," his own unique argument for consciousness as a fundamental in the cosmos and not simply a function of brain matter—in short, the filter thesis.[25]

Once again, I observe such mystics-to-physics correspondences not to argue a point about quantum physics, but to make a simple point. It is not necessarily true that entanglement is telepathy, but it is *certainly* true that entanglement provides us with a model and metaphor of the real world that would make something like telepathy (communication at a distance between entangled loved ones) not only plausible but predictable.[26] We would *expect* to see exactly this, and so we would go looking. And we would find much evidence for this, if only we looked.

In this very practical way (a new metaphor *inspiring* or *guiding*, not determining, a new research agenda), something like "entanglement" would render the impossible possible. In such a world, of course, people's common telepathic experiences would cease to be dismissed as mere "anecdotes" or demeaned as "woo-woo" and would instead become precious clues and real data for a new scientific humanism or humanistic science. In the reverse direction, we might also take note of the profound apophatic "indeterminacy" of classical mystical experiences (how they cannot be described, located, or languaged) and how these mirror or resonate with the indeterminacy of unmeasured quantum states. With such states and experiences in mind, we might even stop insisting that quantum effects always "decohere" and so disappear as they scale up into our level of reality. That would change everything, including how we write a history of anomalous experiences, whose fleeting hauntings do indeed look, well, rather quantum-like. *That's* my point.

Entanglement, by the way, has been repeatedly confirmed in the laboratory. The loopholes are closing, fast. It is looking more and more certain: physical reality is "telepathic." Or, if you prefer Einstein's complaint, the universe is one immense "spook."

TOWARD A SUPERHUMANISM

I have imagined a new set of mythologies emerging from such scientific developments and their intellectual gifts of new metaphor and new plausibility structures. I call this broad, centuries-long remythologization process the Super Story. In *Mutants and Mystics* (2011), I sketched out seven mythemes that I detect within its constant retelling in American popular culture and located the creative origins of some of the most successful and famous pop-cultural versions in the paranormal experiences of specific authors and artists.

Such a Super Story is not a religion or institution, not at least as we normally think of "religion," and it may never be one. But it does appear to be an emergent mythology, a new worldview coming through the floorboards of both elite and popular culture, whether we are ready for it or not. We can frame the situation this way:

15. The Super Story. Modern science (willing or not) has inspired and guided in an intimate and often secret dialogue with the anomalous experiences of individuals (including and especially those of scientists) a new narrative of where we have come from, who we are, and where we are going, in short, a new evolutionary or cosmic humanism. This future humanism takes a strikingly empirical and experimental approach to what were once considered to be "religious" or "supernatural" experiences.

In books like *Authors* and *Mutants*, I began to trace this emergent meta-mythology, mostly with respect to the North American scene, recognizing all along that the North American story is a part of a much larger emergent mythology that is genuinely global in scope, not unlike the sciences upon which it seeks to base its worldview and claims.

How to describe such a project in terms that are nevertheless respectable and so can be heard? For example, can such a project be tucked away in some already established box, say, a postmodern, transhuman, or posthuman one? I doubt it. These currents of thought have all contributed something to the developing Super Story, but they are, in the end, too ontologically timid. I think we are closer to some kind of superhumanism.

I do not quite intend my superhumanism in the Nietzschean sense, not at least in the ways in which he is generally read, that is, as mad, as a nihilist, as a proto-fascist, or as a simple atheist. There are resonances, for sure, more than I can address here, actually. I am thinking of the ways that I have insisted on separating the mystical and the ethical (perhaps an echo of the philosopher's famous "beyond good and evil"); the manner in which Nietzsche understood himself as Two ("I am a *Doppelgänger*, I have a 'second' face in addition to the first"[27]); his still mysterious philosophy of the future Superman or Preterhuman (*Übermensch*), and his related block-universe-like vision of time as "eternal return," a revelation which he spoke of to friends in awed whispers and considered "the most scientific of hypotheses"[28]; his invocation of the "omen" or "miraculously meaningful coincidence," particularly around the writing of his books;[29] his understanding of his books as communicating not information but *states* that require the proper "ear" to hear (as he put it, to understand six sentences from *Zarathustra*—that is, "to have really experienced them—would raise one to a higher level of existence than 'modern' men could attain"[30]); and, "strangest of all," as he himself puts it, his very clear sense of what I have called in *Authors of the Impossible* the semiotic nature of paranormal events, that is, the way the physical world sometimes speaks and signs with things and objects ("It actually seems, to allude to something Zarathustra says, as if the things themselves approached and offered themselves as metaphors").[31] Yep. I've got ears to hear that.

Closer still are the ways Nietzsche bluntly located the origins of his theory and thought in nonrational moments and embodied mystical states, much as I have insisted and performed in books like *Roads* and *The Serpent's Gift*. A case in point is the explicitly revelatory origins of *Zarathustra* and its core idea of the eternal recurrence, what he described as "this highest formula of affirmation that is at all attainable."[32] Nietzsche received this revelation in August of 1881 along the lake of Silvaplana near Sils Maria, Switzerland, "6,000 feet above man and time." This was no moment for false humility or qualifying footnotes: "This is *my* experience of inspiration; I do not doubt that one has to go back thousands of years in order to find anyone who could say to me, 'it

LA PENSÉE SURHUMAINE || 273

is mine as well.'" So too, his precise psychological and physiological descriptions of the experience of inspiration: "If one had the slightest residue of superstition left in one's system, one could hardly reject altogether the idea that one is merely incarnation, merely mouthpiece, merely a medium of over-powering forces." He goes on to describe these same "facts": that he never had any choice in these inspirations; that something "becomes *visible*, audible, something that shakes one to the last depths and throws one down"; that such a "rapture" results in "a flood of tears," that there occurs "the distinct consciousness of subtle shudders and of one's skin creeping down to one's toes" (many would say "vibrations" today), a "superabundance of light," and a "gale of a feeling of freedom, of absoluteness, of power, of divinity."[33] Such lines indeed match very well the embodied expression, experienced twoness, and sheer intellectual wonder of what I am calling a new superhumanism: "I speak no longer with words but with lightning bolts."[34]

And this is all before we get to moments like Nietzsche's thirteen-year-old precognitive dream, in 1851, that he had of his recently deceased father emerging from a grave, going into a church, and returning into the grave mound with a child in his arms: "On the day that followed this night, little Joseph [his younger brother] suddenly fell ill, seized by severe cramps, and after a few hours he died. Our grief knew no bounds. My dream had been fulfilled completely."[35] What is the reasonable philosophy of *that*?

Still, I am no more a Nietzschean than I am a Hegelian (see chap. 9) or a Kantian (see chap. 10). Rather, I consciously intend my superhumanism in the terms of my own actual intellectual influences. Here, at least, the expression is much more indebted to the late-life conclusions of William James, who wrote of "a superhuman life" with which we may all be unknowingly co-conscious, and the independent French philosopher and modern sage Aimé Michel, who invoked the superhuman to make sense of the mystical, parapsychological, and ufological materials with which he worked with such originality and genius. It was Michel who influenced in turn the French astronomer turned American computer scientist and UFO writer Jacques Vallée, and the French sociologist Bertrand Méheust. Without quite knowing it, I was writing in this same American-French lineage when I wrote *Authors*, which features full chapter studies of Fort, Vallée and Méheust and a briefer discussion of Michel himself. I know Vallée and Méheust and consider them both friends and colleagues.

Aimé Michel sits quietly at the center of all of this, as a largely unrecognized genius of twentieth-century religious and philosophical thought. Through numerous books and countless essays, Michel advanced his own evolutionary notion of what he called the *surhumain(e)*, the "superhuman." Extremely well read in the natural sciences and philosophy, Michel turned his gaze on subjects like the history of Christian hagiography and mysticism, contemporary ufological phenomena, and the strange stuff of *la métapsychique*, the uniquely French version of what the British had called "psychical research" and the Americans would bring into the controlled laboratory and name "parapsychology." The result was an especially sophisticated, and especially eerie, vision of the human.

Michel's total thought is impossible to capture in a few lines. Happily, it has been generously collected, mapped, edited, and anthologized by Bertrand Méheust and Jean-Pierre Rospar in two major French volumes.[36] For our purposes here, brief as they are, it would not be inaccurate to observe that Michel intuited in the histories of hagiography, parapsychology, and ufology some future or super-evolved mentality attempting contact with our own hopelessly inadequate religious and rational forms of thinking. In my own categories, there is a kind of fusion of "contact" and "advance" at work in his evolutionary estericism, since the intelligence making contact is sometimes (not always) posited to be human, or superhuman.

Michel (well before the contemporary posthumanists and transhumanists) referred to the effects of these other mentalities in a human subject as *la pensée surhumaine ou non-humaine*, that is, "superhuman or nonhuman thought" (there again is that fusion of advance and contact, in five words, no less). He compared the epistemic abyss that yawns between these other mentalities and our present humanities to the situation of a man trying to communicate with his pet dog. (William James had made the exact same comparison well before Michel, in his case, as we shall see below, in the figure of a cat in the library and with respect to apparent psychic communications from the dead.) Michel also compared our situation to modern humans trying to communicate with chimpanzees.

The latter image is the closer analogy, he believed, since what appears to separate *la pensée surhumaine* from *la pensée humaine* of the present is an evolutionary transfiguration within a related branch of a species. This, of course, appears to have been Nietzsche's point (minus the evolutionary accent), with his famous enigmatic lines about the present human condition positioned between the ape and the future Superman who will overcome or surpass us as a mere laughingstock or embarrassment, just as we now mock and laugh at the ape.

The comparative strategy at work in such thinking seems simple enough: imagine "back" along the evolutionary scale in order to imagine "forward." Such superhuman or nonhuman thought carries immense implications for how we view ourselves and our own cognitive and cultural functioning. The results are in essence double, since such thinking implies that we are *both* historically relative, transitional beings *and* capable of some future metamorphosis or transfiguration. It is utterly humbling, and yet cosmically optimistic. It is this double edge of humility and optimism that cuts at the core of the evolutionary, paraphysical, and extraterrestrial esotericisms, each of which Michel imagined and wrote about.

INVISIBLE COLLEGES

Some of this superhuman thought was inspired by Michel's entrance into what he calls a "global secret society" of scientists and intellectuals interested in subjects like parapsychology and flying saucers after his 1954 book on the saucer phenomenon appeared.[37] Vallée would later invoke a similar community of inquirers with his notion of a new "Invisible College." What both men meant by their expressions was a close-knit community of intellectuals who took paranormal phenomena seriously in an academic world that did not but eventually must if it was to be truly serious about solving the deepest enigmas of science and philosophy. Both men wanted *to have a conversation that should be happening but is not.* Michel's basic sensibility here was that the historical facts are there via the witnesses, that none of this amounts to scientific proof, but that the phenomena in question should, can, and secretly do guide and inspire scientific curiosity and research among more than a few.[38]

For what it is worth (probably a lot), I have witnessed the same with contemporary scientists and their private, often quite intimate relationship to paranormal phenomena. Such loosely knit, decentralized, confidential Invisible Colleges carry on to this day. For example, I have personally met two professionals, a geneticist and a rocketry and metallurgy expert, both at the very top of their fields. The geneticist is convinced that we are genetically directed, rewritten. He also wants to find out how we can redesign our neurological circuitry to better enable or disable contact with non-terrestrial intelligences, which he is convinced from personal experiences are very real (and not always welcome). The rocket scientist and metallurgist, who intentionally interacts with a contactee whom I have also met, notes that the toroidal-shaped DNA could emit an electromagnetic signal in the same general range as that identified by astrophysicists as the cosmic range.

Again, I do not possess the scientific training to judge any of these statements. That is not my point. My point is that these versions of the transmission or filter thesis, here imagined in neurobiological terms, are being advanced by individuals from within the very heart of modern genetics and rocketry, *but secretly*. And these individuals are careful to point out that their colleagues are often not dismissive but utterly fascinated by these same topics. In many private professional exchanges, it is all their scientific colleagues want to talk about, even if they know that they cannot talk about such things in public or in their publications. Hence the genesis of more evolutionary esotericisms not on the fringes, please note, but in the very heart of cutting-edge science and technology.

MIRCEA ELIADE AND THE FANTASTIC MUTANT

Significantly, one of the intellectuals who explored something very much like Aimé Michel's *la pensée surhumaine* was none other than Mircea Eliade. I have already addressed some of the camouflaged mystical currents in Eliade's early life and scholarship above. The evolutionary esoteric currents to which I refer here were more apparent in his later life and final creative writing, especially in books like *Occultism, Witchcraft and Cultural Fashions* (1978) and *Youth Without Youth* (1988). I return to the latter novel now and will do so again in my conclusions, since I believe it encodes in a barely fictional form the deepest secret convictions of the scholar, secrets in which I can see something of my own thought mirrored and doubled.

The main point I want to make here is that one can follow a fairly clear current of thought in Eliade's publications from the "new humanism" that he famously announced on the first pages of the first volume of the flagship journal the *History of Religions* in 1961 to his fictional exploration of a "new humanity" in his late paranormal novel *Youth Without Youth*, which he finished in Paris at the end of 1976.[39] This current might be best described as a gradual metamorphosis from a strictly academic framing of the comparative study of religion that could function as an antidote to European provincialism and Western materialism into a full-blown, if still safely fictional, evolutionary esotericism that expressed a form of *la pensée surhumaine et non-humaine* through literary personas, like the lightning-struck scholar Dominic Matei become fantastic mutant in *Youth Without Youth*, whom, of course, we met above in conversation with Elizabeth Krohn.

The principal characteristic of this future "new humanity" is "the structure of its psycho-mental life," by which is meant a radical new *anamnesis* or Platonic knowledge-through-remembrance. Through such a remembering or direct knowing, "all that has ever been thought or done by men, expressed orally or in writing, will be recoverable through a certain exercise of concentration."[40] This was the primary effect of the lightning strike on Dominic Matei. For no particular merit of his own, Dominic had experienced a "mutation" and was "gifted with a universal erudition such as will become accessible to man only many thousands of years from now."[41] He did not have to learn new languages and sciences. He somehow just *knew* them. Such moments of all-knowing were "the experiences of a mutant that anticipate the existence of post-historic man."[42]

This appearance of an extreme form of the filter thesis in a fictional figure would not be so strange, were it not more or less identical to the claims of the quite historical Gopi Krishna recounted above about "a boundless world of knowledge, embracing the present, past, and future, commanding all the sciences, philosophies, and arts ever known or that will be known in the ages to come." Perhaps Eliade read *Kundalini: The Evolutionary Energy in Man* and was fictionalizing its central idea here via a lightning bolt. This would make more than a little sense out of some of the odd details of the novel. Hence the vaguely mystical description of the lightning strike as an "explosion of white incandescent light" and Dominic's sense that "he had been sucked up by a fiery cyclone that had exploded at some mysterious moment on top of his head."[43] This is not a bad literalization of a classic *kundalini* awakening through the portal-like opening at the top of the skull (the *brahmarandhra*), which, of course, Eliade had written about in his dissertation-book on yoga and Tantra.

It is my own sense that Eliade held some kind of evolutionary esotericism in his private thinking and confessed as much in this late piece of occult fiction, even if he could never own such a bold idea in his public scholarship.[44] I think it is significant that the figure of Dominic Matei is the figure of an aging academic who is experiencing the loss of his intellectual abilities and fears he will die before he completes his one great work. Wendy Doniger has described the novel as the most autobiographical of Eliade's novels.[45] What I think is this. I think that Eliade told us what he really thought in this final novel, even if he could only bring himself to do it through the voice of Dominic and, indeed, even more so in the voice of Dominic's uncanny double, who shows up throughout the novel to do things like materialize roses or utter enigmatic statements, as Dominic's interior thoughts, about parapsychological matters that are never followed up on. I think Dominic and his double are both Eliade, transformed and explored in the *littérature fantastique* of Eliade's gifted literary imagination.

Such a posited transformation in Eliade's writing from a "new humanism" to a "new humanity," from the history of religions as an academic discipline to the fantastic mutant of his most autobiographical work of fiction, took place over the exact time period that I have identified above as the key historical influence on the contemporary comparative study of religion in the US: the countercultural period (gnomon 9). One can debate when such a countercultural moment began and ended, but the height of Eliade's career at Chicago, say, from 1961, when the "new humanism" essay appeared, to the end of 1976, when he finished *Youth Withouth Youth* in Paris, would work very well as defensible bookends just outside the period, hugging, as it were, all those countercultural books and young people.

CONCERNS AND RESISTANCES

I am well aware of how such thinking is traditionally received in academic circles. Almost any embrace of evolutionary thinking applied to esoteric ideas is traditionally received as some kind of simplistic Hegelian Absolute floating through history and culminating in whatever culture the theorist happens to inhabit. Or, worse yet, it is read as a colonizing social Darwinism or regeneration of the Übermenschen or fascist supermen of German Nazism, as if a particular misreading of Nietzsche were the only historical influence here. Such rhetorical moves are designed to derail and so end an otherwise fantastic conversation through a shared, and entirely justified, sense of moral horror at German Nazism, white racism, and Western colonialism.

And such moves usually work. They work because they contain historical truth. Hegel's massively influential philosophy does contain troubling ethnocentric forces and, in Hegel at least, some bizarrely ethnocentric conclusions. There were occult dimensions of German Nazism, as the classic work of Nicholas Goodrick-Clarke has taught us.[46] And evolutionary forms of thinking have supported various European and American projects of social Darwinism, colonialism, slavery and out-and-out racism. Finally, a figure like Eliade did have fascist friends and connections in his Romanian youth. Moreover, he was well aware of how a figure like Dominic Matei, the fantastic mutant, might be read. That is no doubt why Matei has to have surgery to change his physical appearance and spends most of the novel in hiding, trying to avoid the Gestapo and the clutches of Dr. Rudolf, the Nazi scientist who wants to study him.

The problem with fascist, racist, and colonialist readings is not that they are wrong, then. The problem is that they are partial. Other readings are always possible with other lenses and, above all, with a more generous historical canvas. As just two quick brush strokes toward this larger view, consider the moral and poltical commitments of two of the most significant evolutionary visionaries in these histories: Frederic Myers and Henri Bergson.

Myers spent his days reforming the English educational system and arguing for the education of women. When he coined "telepathy" and wrote of it as the early sign of an evolving "supernormal" capacity, he was not thinking of human domination and violence. He was thinking of human love and poignant loss (hence the *pathos* of telepathy). Bergson was probably the most famous philosopher of his time. He became the president of the Society for Psychical Research in 1913. He saw mystical and psychical capacities as hints of our future evolution and won the Nobel Prize for literature in 1928 for his assault on mechanism and works like *Creative Evolution*. More to my present point, he refused the Vichy government's title "Honorable Aryan." Instead, he stood in line in the cold rain to register as a Jew and died two days later, of pulmonary congestion, at the age of eighty-two.[47]

INTRODUCING THE ESSAYS

The following two unpublished essays imaginatively sit in the "Invisible College" of Aimé Michel and his students. They treat different moments in the history of the extraterrestrial esoteric literature. The first involves one of the students of Michel, Jacques Vallée. Jacques has taught me as much as anyone about the scope and power of folklore and mythology, mostly through their eruptions within the visionary experiences of contemporaries who have been transformed or traumatized (or killed) by an encounter with a UFO. I wrote the first piece after a phone conversation with Jacques about the late Harvard psychiatrist and abduction researcher John Mack, whom I was reading at the time. I think it captures fairly well my thoughts about trauma, trance and transcendence, which we will encounter again below in my engagement with Whitley Strieber. This piece also frames my growing sense of the central importance of trance induction in the psychological and cultural creation of new mythologies.

I wrote the second piece after a trip to Florence, mostly because I was so annoyed by the certainty of the male museum guard and so irritated by the simplicities of the art historians. I think this was the first piece in which I decided to own and name what I had in fact been proposing for many years: a new comparativism. Unsurprisingly, it was in a private piece that I wrote for myself and a few close colleagues as a kind of thought-experiment.

Forbidden Science

A LATE-NIGHT CHAT WITH JACQUES VALLÉE

(JANUARY 24, 2012)

Historical references suggest that in the absence of claims of unknown aerial phenomena that amazed and inspired their people, Pharaoh Amenophis IV would not have taken the name Akhenaton and introduced the cult of the Sun Disk into Egypt and Emperor Constantine might not have established Christianity in Rome in AD 312. Ancient chronicles assure us that beings from mysterious realms . . . were responsible for telling Mary she would bear the son of God, for instructing Japanese emperor Amekuni to honor the Supreme God, for inspiring Mohammed to found Islam in Medina in 612, [and] for saving the life of a priest named Nichiren shortly before his execution in 1271. . . . Joan of Arc was inspired to take the leadership of French armies and drive the English out of France after getting her instructions from beings of light in 1425; Christopher Columbus saw a strange light as he approached America; and the claim of an apparition in Guadalupe was responsible for converting millions of Mexican Indians to Catholicism in 1531.

JACQUES VALLÉE AND CHRIS AUBECK, *WONDERS IN THE SKY:*
UNEXPLAINED AERIAL OBJECTS FROM ANTIQUITY TO MODERN
TIMES (2016 DELUXE EDITION)

I am reading John Mack's *Abduction: Human Encounters with Aliens* (1994). I am particularly interested in the book because of Mack's use of Eliade and the history of religions school as one means of trying to understand the "abduction" phenomenon (obviously, already a loaded word). Mack compares the abductee to a kind of unconscious shaman, whose out-of-body experiences and visions he then contextualizes within humanity's long history of encounters with beings from the sky. His view of the "alien" was fundamentally positive. He saw the entire phenomenon as a kind of ontological shock campaign, as an attempt to right a worldview (our materialist scientific culture) that has blinded itself to the larger cosmic and metaphysical realms in which we are embedded and now, because of this same unseeing, threatens to do tremendous damage to the ecological system, to the Earth itself.

As a trained Harvard psychiatrist with an interest in nightmares and an author of a Pulitzer Prize–winning book on T. E. Lawrence, Mack was more than aware of the powerful projections of the human psyche. He understood perfectly well how the "alien" was culturally shaped, but he also was honest and courageous enough to recognize that these psychological dynamics do not come close to explaining the full UFO phenomenon. In the end, Mack was deeply suspicious that the reality of the same phenomenon could ever be established with the scientific method, since such a method requires the very "split" between measuring subjects and measured objects that these events so often clearly frustrate, or simply obliterate altogether. He basically threw his hands up before the question of what they are. He didn't know, and he knew he didn't know, but he also suspected that *that* was part of their point and one of their most important functions. They were here to humble, boggle, and provoke us, to push us beyond our present assumptions and values.

I never knew John Mack, although I believe I was at a lecture with him once while I was teaching at Harvard in 2000–2001. Sudhir Kakar was visiting and lecturing on some aspect of Hindu mystical literature. A stately gentleman stood up in the Q and A session afterward and asked Sudhir about the alien abduction phenomenon. It was an impassioned question, and it struck me at the time as a bit out of place, if also issuing from a place of deep conviction. I think that was John Mack.

So I am reading *Abduction*, puzzling over the material, and remembering this chance encounter, which may not have been an encounter at all, and I do what I often do in these situations: I write Jacques Vallée. I dedicated a chapter study to his corpus in *Authors of the Impossible*, and he has made it a practice since of sending me the most recent volume drafts of his privately published journals, entitled *Forbidden Science*, and his work with Chris Aubeck and an impressive team of internet sleuths on UFO-like reports before 1880, entitled *Wonders in the Sky*.

It is in the former journal pages that Jacques really tells his story and often describes historical figures in striking and disarming detail. It is in the latter pages that he does with Aubeck and their team what I have seen him do so many times in person: take what looks like an established story in the UFO literature, trace it back to its historical sources (often in the medieval or premodern past with the help of classicists and historians), and demonstrate beyond a shadow of a doubt how it is based on some historical hook (say, a war, a locust invasion, or a particular text) but is itself at the end of the day a mythical transform, a garbled memory, or a simple hoax.

From Jacques, I have learned a deep and abiding skepticism about UFO reports that float on the internet and appear in published books, "90 percent of which never happened," as he puts it. Even as he displays all the joys of a humanist scholar employing the archival resources and linguistic tools of source criticism, historical contextualization, and reception history, it is that other 10 percent that so intrigues him as a human being and philosopher. As my opening epigraph makes clear, the entire history of religions looks different once once applies the comparative lenses of glowing "disks," beings made of light, and unknown aerial phenomena. To take just one telling example, Akhenaton did not just introduce the cult of the sun disk (which resembles a flying disk), after all. He was also the first historical promoter of an unambiguous and robust monotheism. It is this same combination of deep skepticism, humanist learning and honest, unblinking assessment of an enigmatic core or irreducible remainder that causes us to look anew at what we thought we knew that so attracts me to Jacques' work and thought.

I knew Vallée would have some real insight into Mack. He did. But he didn't want to write about it. He wanted to talk about it. So we set up a time to chat, which happened to be late last night.

The hour-long discussion revolved around the use of hypnosis and, more particularly, Jacques' witnessing of some professional psychiatrists working with an individual whom he had brought to them for help. Jacques was struck by the differences between the careful practice of these psychiatrists, whom he clearly admired, and what he knew about the hypnosis practices of Budd Hopkins, the late New York artist and UFO researcher, and historian David Jacobs, who together played such an important role in mythologizing the alien phenomenon in the 1990s as a dark and disturbing "abduction," often toward some kind of hybrid breeding program or genetic experimentation.[48] Interestingly, Mack acknowledged the sexual components and wrote a good deal about the reproductive aspects of the phenomenon as well. He did not look away, even when it came to the most difficult topics—in this case the sexual and erotic ones.

A personal sidenote. Hopkins and Jacobs have a real point. Alien-human hybridity and sexual themes are indeed everywhere in the modern abduction accounts. They are also everywhere in the history of religions, from the Greek hero Herakles to the man-god Jesus, to the avatar of God Ramakrishna. My point here is not to deny this hybridity (on the contrary, the present book can be read as a theorization of it via the poetics of the Human as Two). My point is to paint the modern abduction reports on a much larger historical canvas, and to observe that they are not always dark, much less conspiratorial. As with so many encounters with the sacred elsewhere in the history of religions, abduction phenomena and their apparent genetic interests can be as terrifying as they can be transcendent, as much a rape as a rapture. The real question for me is how this is all taken up by various psyches and practices and so transformed into very different cultural narratives or myths.

Jacques related to me on the phone how he thinks that the alien phenomenon as portrayed and professed by Hopkins and Jacobs is largely a mythical narrative that is implanted into the subjects through unprofessional hypnosis sessions. It then becomes a "real" memory for them, but its narrative and meaning is largely imposed from without. These subjects, of course, have probably gone through some very real trauma, even had some anomalous experience in some cases, but the memories around these events are often unconscious and vague until the hypnosis sessions shape them into the standard mythos. Narratives that emerge that do not fit this standard mythos, or flatly contradict it, are rejected, explained away, or simply ignored and not published.

Jacques thus told the story of one woman who had been visited by friendly little creatures for much of her life. This does not fit the standard narrative. So an abductee researcher attached his own orthodox narrative to her experiences via hypnosis. Thereafter she experienced the friendly little creatures as threatening demons.

Similar kinds of demonizations, I must note, appear to be active on a very grand scale in American culture as well, particularly with the ways elite Evangelical Christians have demonized the UFO phenomena and transformed these—via the military and the film industry—into an endless stream of paranoid "invasion" fantasies and end-of-the-world Armageddons, which fit their own fundamentalist ideologies and military interests but dangerously and grotesquely misread the phenomena themselves as initially experienced and reported by individuals. Just go watch an alien invasion film like *Battle: Los Angeles* (2011). It is practically a full-length feature advertisement for why a young man or woman should join the Marines.

The question then becomes to what extent Mack's therapeutic work with contactees and abductees played into a similar mythologization process. There are different positions on Mack at this point.

Vallée certainly does not read Mack in the same way that he reads Hopkins and Jacobs, but he nevertheless worries about Mack's use of hypnosis. Ralph Blumenthal, longtime *New York Times* writer and present biographer of Mack, takes a somewhat different position. He points to the very real differences between Mack's vision of the alien phenomenon in books like *Abduction* and *Passport to the Cosmos* and the books of Hopkins and Jacobs. Mack acknowledged the frightening aspects of the phenomenon that Hopkins and Jacobs rightly pointed out, but his views were finally more complex, as he also focused on the positive, cosmic, and specifically religious aspects. Blumenthal also observes that Mack was a trained Harvard psychiatrist, that he studied and practiced hypnosis as a professional, and that he adamantly denied that the abduction accounts were simply products of false memories planted through hypnosis. For Mack, there was simply too much evidence outside of any hypnosis to the contrary. He would point here to things like the simultaneous sightings of UFOs by multiple witnesses, physical evidence such as scoop marks on bodies and flattened grass in fields and yards, accounts from children as young as two, conscious recollections outside of hypnosis, experiences in broad daylight not associated in any way with sleep or sleep apnea, the wholly convincing affect of experiencers recounting their encounters, and the universality of accounts from people the world over (no, it is not just an American phenomenon).[49]

So Mack remains an ambiguous paradoxical figure, not unlike his paradoxical subject matter: a Harvard psychiatrist studying and, to some extent, affirming the reality of alien abductions.

I have my own tentative thoughts here. What I see in the abduction phenomenon, and particularly in the use of hypnosis as a generator of the narratives, is a dramatic model not of aliens and little gray humanoids, much less of some future extraterrestrial assault on planet Earth, but of the irreducible complexities and projections of religion itself. In this model, religion begins with these same kinds of apparitions, light forms and aerial phenomena and the subsequent traumas and trance formations that they catalyze in human subjects. These traumatic trance narratives are then shaped and policed through public narratives, rituals, and institutional structures. In this view, the history of a major public religion is one immense, state-sponsored trance formation, which is given a fantastic shape and direction through the hypnotic powers of myth and ritual, which in turn builds on the profoundly plastic and suggestive nature of the human psyche. A religion is a fantasy that an entire culture is living in, more or less.

I should quickly add that I also suspect that some profound encounter, anomalous event, or altered state of consciousness often lies at the origin point of all of this, but that its interpretation or meaning is probably always open-ended and pliable. On the relatively gentle end of things, I cannot help thinking here of the practice of spiritual direction with its "discernment of spirits" that I knew intimately in my seminary days, whereby spiritual experiences or religious convictions that do not fit the orthodox narratives are actively resisted, discouraged, or simply ignored. On the extreme end, there is, of course, the whole dark Western history of heresiology, heresy hunting, and burnings at the stake. Culture and religion write us, and when we write something that doesn't fit in, they write over us, or just write us out.

My interest in the ufological literature, then, does not stem back to the question of whether the UFO and the alien presence are real or not, that is, whether they exist outside our own mind spaces and materializations. My interest stems back to the conviction that, *whatever they are*, they have something profound to do with the history of religions and all of its descending sky gods and tricky demons. If we can better understand these modern appearances and mythologies, we will better understand the history of religions.

In other words, I am not interested in aliens as aliens or ships as ships, none of which I personally believe in as they appear in the popular mythologies. I am interested in what aliens and ships—*whatever* they are (reality, illusion, or something in between)—can teach us about "religion." In the end, of course, they may turn out to be real in some sense that we cannot yet grasp. They may work through some unknown exotic physics, or through some biotechnology that interacts with a cognitive and sensory system that our own primitive primate system cannot conceive. Technologies, after all, are always extensions of the sensory and cognitive systems that created them and only work for those same systems. What would a dolphin do with a car or a computer? Or they may turn out to be unreal in ways that we can grasp but that will nevertheless surprise us: poltergeist-like materializations, for example. In *any* case, we win intellectually, that is, we better understand our own situation and our religious productions.

2017 POSTSCRIPT

I have continued to read and talk about Mack since this late-night conversation with Jacques. Two moments seem significant.

First, I have learned that there is an Esalen connection here. Mack, it turns out, was taking holotropic breathwork sessions with Stan Grof in the early 1990s at Esalen. Holotropic breathwork sessions induce altered states of consciousness through breathing techniques and music. Mack spoke to Keith Thompson at Esalen. Keith told me. Keith wrote a very thoughtful book on the UFO phenomenon, much along the hermeneutical and ontological lines that Mack later would.[50] Mack also spoke to Michael Murphy about "beginning my journey in the Big House," that is, in seminars with Grof in the original Murphy vacation home. Such Esalen connections no doubt played some part in the psychiatrist's turn to a serious exploration of the abduction phenomenon.

Second, as noted above, I have also corresponded with the *New York Times* journalist Ralph Blumenthal, who wrote a fair and fascinating piece on Mack for *Vanity Fair* entitled "Alien Nation: Have Humans Been Abducted by Extraterrestrials?"[51] Ralph has explained to me that Mack allegedly appeared to many of his friends and colleagues after his death in order to tell them about the painlessness of death and the reality of the afterlife. Ralph's essay ends with an alleged postmortem communication with Mack, who—and this is significant—may be speaking about the nature of death *or* the alien abduction phenomenon: "It is not what we thought."

Be it death or the alien (or both), that is almost certainly true.

La Madonna dell'UFO
(2015)

We are part of a symbiotic relationship with something which disguises itself as an extraterrestrial invasion so as not to alarm us.

TERENCE MCKENNA

On Sunday, December 14, 2014, I stood in the Hercules Room of the Palazzo Vecchio, or the Medici Superhero Room, as I prefer to call it.[52] Well, that is what it is. I was not there to look at the Greek hero and his superhuman labors brightly illustrated, like some Renaissance graphic novel, on the ceiling for the Florentine rich and famous. I was there to view a minor early sixteenth-century painting entitled simply "Natività" (1510–20). The painting appears to depict a "UFO" hovering in the sky.[53] A man and his dog stand on a hill, both staring up at the sky, the man's hand shielding his eyes, apparently puzzling over the same object that the viewer of the painting is. In the foreground, the Virgin, with her back to the thing in the sky, smiles reverently at the two holy cousins: baby John, who will become the Baptist, and the infant Jesus, who will become the Christ.

It is hardly a major piece of art. I had to ask two museum guards to locate it in the palace and could find no reproduction of it in the bookstore. One of the female museum guards described it to me, with a big smile, as the "la Madonna dell'UFO." She seemed delighted with the modern renaming of the painting and the new, if quirky, appreciation that this new designation signals. Another museum guard, this one male, said, with a gentle arrogance, "Well, of course, you know it's not a UFO. It's a standard Renaissance representation of the Holy Spirit."

"Really?" I answered silently in my head. I didn't have the courage to ask him what the Holy Spirit was doing in a scene that had nothing to do with the Annunciation, or why a man and his dog are staring at the thing hovering in the sky, whereas the Virgin seems completely unaware of it. I never knew the Holy Spirit was an *object* that could be seen by any passerby (or pet), but not by the Virgin. Dogs, by the way, feature prominently in contemporary UFO

encounters—they commonly see the things, too, and react with the same astonishment and fear that human hairless primates do.

Still, the male guard had a point. It is true that the Holy Spirit is sometimes
depicted in similar ways in paintings of the Annunciation and, more rarely, of
the Nativity. It is also true that the shepherd shielding his eyes from the "glory
of God" can be found in other pieces as well. Still, there is something about
this Holy Spirit or glory of God that is different. The glowing object is just too
similar to what is described today in the ufological literature. The comparison
is *eerie*.

One skeptical commentator, Filomena D'Amico, describes the object as an
ellipsoidal or "lead-colored disk that is tilted to the left and that has a kind of
turret dome very similar to descriptions given by traditional science fiction to
extraterrestrial spacecraft."[54] That is fair and generous. D'Amico nevertheless
thinks that the artist intended to portray an angel in the form of a luminous
cloud—an extremely rare artistic choice, but again not entirely unknown. Another online art critic, Diego Cuogi, agrees, observing that artists of the time
consulted the apocryphal *Protogospel of James*, which contains a reference to
a cloud of light. This material reference apparently proves for Cuogi that it is
not a UFO, that it is "only art."[55]

I understand the art-historical precedents, of course, but I doubt that they
really explain the Madonna of the UFO. My reasons are textual and historical. After all, one hardly needs an obscure apocryphal text to find a textual
reference to the luminous cloud of the painting. The cloud filled with light or
lightning is very biblical. The "glory of God" is described in similar terms, for
example, at key moments in Exodus (16.10 and 24.16). Much more damning
for Cuogi's reading, however, is the fact that the same motif appears in the first
lines of Ezekiel, where the prophet describes a vision of a bizarre something
that looks and sounds remarkably like a modern UFO encounter. The biblical
text even describes weird "wheels," how the thing floats, roars, and gleams like
some kind of electric metal,[56] and how the prophet was "abducted" or lifted
up by the spirit of God and taken to another physical place (Ezekiel 1.1–3.15).
David Halperin, the historian of ancient Judaism, author of a psychoanalytic
study of Ezekiel, and easily one of the most astute interpreters of the modern
UFO phenomenon, has observed the obvious: the vision looks genuine (that
is, based on an actual phenomenological event), and, yes, it looks like a modern UFO.

Halperin goes on to comment on the typical move that biblical scholars
make, which is the same typical move that art historians make, that is: restrict

the phenomenon in question to a very particular time and place and so create an existential fire wall between it and us. That simply does not work here:

Bible scholars pooh-pooh such notions, insisting that what Ezkeiel saw must be interpreted in terms of Ezekiel's own time and culture (early sixth century BCE). But the traditional tools of exegesis get us only so far in understanding the Bible's strangest, most numinous text. There's a sense in which Ezekiel really did see a UFO: something unidentified, beyond Ezekiel's categories and our own, capable of being culturally pigeonholed as "visions of God" (Ezekiel) or as a spaceship. The truth transcends both.[57]

The conclusion here is as simple as it is important: Cuogi's reductive historicizing attempt to explain away the luminous cloud by citing a textual precedence backfires, since *the texts themselves may well have been expressions of actual sightings and encounters.* The classical text of Ezekiel is a powerful case in point.

But I am finally skeptical of the skeptics for another simpler reason, namely, that modern UFOs are also commonly reported as hiding in or appearing as luminous clouds that look, well, like the object hovering, as if out of place and out of time, in the Renaissance painting.[58] Michael Lieb calls those who witness (and ride) such things the "children of Ezekiel" and the "new riders of the chariot." "They are moderns, the prophets of the New Age. Theirs is the religion of the New Age, the religion of the modern through which earlier forms of devotion, archaic modes of worship, discover a new outlet."[59]

These resonances between the Renaissance art and the modern ufological literature, moreover, quickly multiply, if one knows where to look. Numerous contactees, for example, have experienced the "alien" as a kind of technological "angel." So the art-historical explanation that "It is a representation of an angel" only digs the hole deeper. It does not get us out of it.

And this is before we get to the really weird stuff, like the point-by-point identities between the history of modern Marian apparitions and the ufological materials, down to tiny, utterly bizarre details: like the falling of "angel hair" (a strange weblike substance that falls from the sky around Marian and ufological apparitions, often only to dissolve or disappear before the stuff hits the ground) and the "falling-leaf" pattern of the descending flying saucer and the silver spinning "sun" or disk that thousands of people reportedly witnessed falling from the sky in the most famous Marian event of all time, the "Miracle of the Sun" of October 13, 1917, in Fatima, Portugal—predicted with perfect precision, by the way, by three shepherd children *months* before it happened. A fantastic and utterly impossible Marian ufology could be developed here for hundreds of pages—the Madonna of the UFO, indeed.

This broader historical and comparative context is what makes me so uncomfortable with *both* the art-historical response ("It's a common Renaissance representation of the Holy Spirit") *and* the UFO enthusiast ("It's an extraterrestrial space ship"). Halperin had it just right, it seems to me: "The truth transcends both."

Why, after all, privilege one relative historical moment and cultural framework over another? Perhaps the artist did intend the object as a representation of the Holy Spirit or an angel, but so what? Modern contactees commonly describe their encounters in remarkably similar religious terms. I see no reason why sixteenth-century Italians could not have seen the same damned things that twenty-first-century Americans (or Italians, or Belgians, or Brazilians, or Japanese) see every other week. Nor can I imagine a single good reason why some Italian artist (or the author of the *Protogospel of James*, for that matter) would not have taken these "things seen in the sky" as appropriate figures through which to depict the Holy Spirit or an angel.

Perhaps the artist saw one himself. Obviously, he did not intend to represent a "UFO" in his painting. Such language and the modern scientific cosmology, along with the Big Bang, galaxies and space travel that it encodes, were simply not available to an early sixteenth-century Florentine artist. And that's a gross understatement. Another Italian, the Dominican Giordano Bruno, would be burned in a Roman public square a few decades later, partly for claiming the existence of other planets or "worlds" within an infinite universe with no center. Simply because the artist dressed his own experience or a reported vision in the codes of his own local religious culture, then, does not mean that the object's nature was significantly different from that of those encountered today. It simply means that these were the cosmological codes available to him. What else *could* have he intended?

In the end, of course, we must admit that there is no way to come to a firm conclusion, a rock-bottom experience or singular event behind these art-historical processes. If there was one (or, much more likely, a thousand), these are now lost to us in the centuries and their silences. Or are they? I suppose this is the other point I want to make. Why *not* use the modern luminous clouds, to which we have some fairly direct (if never completely direct) access via the contemporary UFO witnesses, in order to tentatively read the Renaissance luminous cloud, to which we have no reliable access?

What I think we have to interrogate here is what is at stake in the art-historical denials of this popular comparative practice. I think the reason the art historian is so troubled by the ufological comparison is the same reason that the conventional scholar of religion is so troubled: both the art historian and the scholar of religion are ideologically committed to a purely materialist history in which there can only be political, institutional, textual, and material influences but never, ever, interventions out of space and out of time. It is "only art." Or it is "only power and politics." Or it is "only the texts." Or it is "only in the scholar's imagination." So let's go find an obscure text that can explain (away) what we otherwise see in the painting. Let's do *anything*, other than entertain the simple idea that sixteenth-century Italians may have been like us and may have responded religiously to what tens of thousands of contemporary people see today and narrativize in very different mythological and cosmological codes.

The comparativist, on the other hand, can see clearly that both the art historian and the modern UFO enthusiast are falling into some remarkably unsophisticated readings—one stuck in Renaissance Catholic culture (or positivist historicism), the other in twentieth-century sci-fi culture. I think they are both wrong. I think we need an entirely new language and imaginaire, a new way of seeing the history of religions that is neither bound to the symbolisms and theologies of the religious past nor hypnotized by our present technologies and military violences. In terms of the latter, the "UFO" is an early 1950s military acronym designed to turn an anomaly in the sky into an enemy on radar. I doubt very much that these paranoid Cold War origins of the UFO—and the whole history of the US military and intelligence communities' involvement in shaping, suppressing, and distorting the public representations of the UFO—have much of anything to do with what these apparitions are really about.[60]

"Really about." Those are strong words, and completely inappropriate ones in our present intellectual climate. But that climate will pass, as all academic orthodoxies eventually do. And, yes, I think these presences possess their own intentions and agencies, which we are in no position to understand or essentialize at this point in our cultural evolution. This same exact point has recently been made by the atheist and feminist social critic Barbara Ehrenreich, struggling with her own mystical experience, which she can no longer deny and whose cultural impossibility and intellectual embarrassment she compares to an alien abduction experience.[61] (More on the Ehrenreich encounter with some kind of invisible energy species in due time.)

None of this, of course, has much to do with what one sees as one walks around Florence today. This city and its religion were once dominated by the immense wealth and power of the Medici family and the public theology, art, and architecture of Roman Catholicism, whose churches literally tower above the cityscape. Such public religions of power, politics, and men have been one of the primary objects of the professional study of religion. As well they should be. I have nothing against this project.

But must we all only do this? Why not build something new on these historical-critical foundations? Or must we just keep digging the basement, deeper and deeper into the dirt? Why not build on these foundations a more radical project still? This would be a new comparative project that focuses on the paranormal present in order to better understand the magical and miraculous past; that does not assume the "only" of "It is only art" or "It is only power and politics" or "It is only in our scholarly imagination"; a project, finally, that is as skeptical of our own present materialist and subjectivist ideologies as it is of the religious and institutional ideologies of the past. For the sake of a conversation, let us call this the new comparativism. Until we can begin such a project, the Madonna of the UFO will continue to mock us.

As well she should.

In the end, we have no answer for her. I think we should just say that and stop pretending that we do. Much better to begin reimagining the history of religions as a long and complicated series of real (as in "really experienced") contact events, followed by a countless number of personal mystical communions and public communications (including artistic ones), all disciplined, filtered, and shaped by material history, all the way down to our neurology and biology. *Of course*, everything about "religion" is constructed, but everything is constructed *upon* something—something really seen, really experienced, and something still unidentified.

Perhaps, as J. Z. Smith has famously argued, "religion" is indeed a construct of our scholarly imaginations, but—I am very sorry—these sorts of experiences/events are not. They are not just scholarly constructions. They are not just texts. They are not just power ploys. They are not just subjective illusions. They happen, often in striking empirical and publicly perceivable ways. And we cannot explain them with our social-scientific and historicist methods, or just ignore their obvious ontological provocations, as Smith does in an essay on the modern UFO phenomenon.[62] That is much too convenient, and frankly suspicious.

Perhaps, you will say, this is much too grand of a proposal to build on such a dubious case study. Maybe you are right. Maybe the Madonna of the UFO is no such thing. Perhaps the object-out-of-place in the sky was intended and viewed as a simple symbolic convention. I doubt it, but okay.

But do we really need such a painting for the new comparativism I am imagining? Similar "new" comparative observations could be made around Brent Landau's work on *The Revelation of the Magi*, a third-century Christian text that, as Landau has honestly observed, contains strikingly modern "ufological" themes, including the famous "star" or intelligent ball of light that leads the magi to the nativity scene, distorts the sense of time for the magi (exactly as contemporary UFO encounters often do), and then morphs into a small luminous humanoid, that is, into the infant Jesus, who is never named as such in the first-person section of the text. The same anonymous "star," by the way, also utters mystical teachings that are indistinguishable from modern perennialist and New Age convictions. In Landau's own terms, the text presents us with "a sentient ball of light who can take the form of a little humanoid and who tells his witnesses that he has appeared to many other individuals throughout human history."[63] Nor would this be the last such story. Stars and balls of light turn into angels and humanoids throughout Western history up to and including the present day.[64]

The art historian or textual critic, of course, could note that the traveling star theme is reliant on an earlier textual source, the Gospel of Matthew, and, of course, that is correct. But, again, so what? Note how little this explanation explains. The star from the East in the gospel story does not distort time or morph into a small humanoid, nor does it preach a clear form of perennialism, in the third century no less. We are in the same situation here as we are with the Renaissance painting in Florence. Yes, we have precedents and symbolic conventions, but they explain very little in the end. Something is "out of place" and "out of time" here.

If an unmarried Jewish teenager ever scandalously conceived a god-man with the help of a spirit or an angel (or a luminous cloud), it no longer matters so much, at least as some singular historical event. The same conscious spheres of light and transphysical beings are engaging women and men from the depths of human sexuality (and so from the depths of human genetics and evolution) by the thousands now, and probably have always been doing so.

In the meantime, there is the Madonna of the UFO, eerily uniting the religious cultures of the European pasts and the emergent mythologies of the

American present. How this resonance is possible at all is the real question. But who is asking it? Who is ready to re-vision the history of religions as a material history haunted by real contact? Who is ready to affirm both the all-too-human and the nonhuman (or the transhuman) within a new comparativism? Who is ready to smile, like my female museum guide, instead of sneer, like my male museum guide? Who is ready for "la Madonna dell'UFO"?

13

Comparing Religions in Public

Rural America, Evangelicals, and the Prophetic Function of the Humanities

Jesus said to them, "A prophet is not without honor except in his own town, among his relatives and in his own home." He could not do any miracles there, except lay his hands on a few sick people and heal them. He was amazed at their lack of faith.

MARK 6.4–6

Religion protects man as long as its ultimate foundations are not revealed. To drive the monster from its lair is to risk loosing it on humanity.

RENÉ GIRARD, *VIOLENCE AND THE SACRED*

The easiest way to dismiss an interest in evolutionary esotericisms is to suggest that they are carriers of cultural superiority, as Darwin's natural selection was for Western colonialists and Nietzsche's Superman was for German fascists. Never mind the countless evolutionary thinkers who were neither colonizing nor fascist, who detected in the evolutionary impulse a beneficent cosmic play or purpose. The moral insinuation is that any historian interested in such religious phenomena must think that his or her own culture is somehow on the leading edge of humanity's evolutionary advance.

God, I hope not.

TOWN AND GOWN

I go home to rural Nebraska every year. For decades now, I have been deeply struck, if not emotionally wounded, by the immense moral abyss that separates my university community from the general culture of rural America. Those key intellectual practices and central moral values that we simply take for granted in the university culture and strive to achieve as positive ideals are held in deep suspicion in vast swaths of the Midwest.

I am thinking of practices and ideals like self-reflexivity (the ability to step away from one's own cognitive and emotional responses and *watch* them, to not think one's thoughts, to not believe one's beliefs); historical consciousness (the ability to see present beliefs, values, and social institutions as relative products of long historical trajectories); religious pluralism (the simple fact that there are, and always will be, many religions, that such plurality is a good thing, and that no single religion should be privileged in any public institution); gender equity (the genders, of which there are more than two, should be treated equally); racial and sexual diversity (human beings and bodies are different and should be affirmed and valued as such); environmental sustainability (we are shitting in our own living room, which is getting really hot now, and, yes, it's because of us); the importance of privileging empirical data and thoughtful debate over received opinion and blind propaganda; and, above all, a secular public space that guarantees both freedom *of* and *from* religion (not to be cleverly identified with some nonexistent "attack on Christianity").

I go home to rural Nebraska grateful for my family and birth culture and return to the city depressed about the seeming futility of explaining to my loved ones why I think so many of their beliefs are built on dangerous half-truths (or just falsehoods) and ultimately unsustainable values. These beliefs and values may work for them in their own individual lives and in their own isolated communities, and Midwesterners may be among the nicest people on the planet, but—and here is the catch—the politicians and policies they routinely vote for will result in suffering for others, including their own descendants. Their own grandchildren and great-grandchildren, who will grow up in a more diverse and ecologically fragile world (if not a polluted, melting, and dying one), will almost certainly pay a heavy price for the long-term effects of their collective choices. Apparently, they either cannot see these long-term effects, or they simply do not care about them. I have heard evidence of both in my conversations.

I am not the first to have felt this kind of frustration. Even Jesus felt a version of it, as the verses from the Gospel of Mark above give witness. I think something similar applies, in very different terms, to scholars of religion and their hometowns. I am not claiming that any of us are prophets individually, but the humanities possess radical forms of knowledge that could serve a genuine prophetic function in American and global culture if we could but see and say this, out loud.

I sometimes joke that the American Academy of Religion should host a panel on a single question: "So, what does your family think of what you think?" The

298 || CHAPTER 13

answer would often come down to this: "Not much" or "Very little" or "We try not to talk about it." I predict a vast therapy session would follow.

In my own experience, the cognitive dissonance has been extreme. At the time of this writing, the general beliefs of rural America as I have repeatedly heard them include: a fundamental denial of climate change and environmental crisis (all "liberal fictions"); a profound and pervasive anti-intellectualism (with thinking people and investigative journalists demonized as "elites" or as the "liberal media"); intolerant and ill-informed views about sexual orientation and gender camouflaged as positive "family values"; unconscious and conscious racist attitudes toward African Americans and utterly bizarre statements about President Obama's presidency that make no sense unless one simply translates them as "there was a black man in the White House"; seriously distorted views of Muslims, Mexicans, immigrants, and religious plurality in general, again all rationalized as measures to "protect our Christian country," a sensibility which is in turn linked to the military, which must always be supported, apparently without a shred of critical thought, as if every war were a good and just one. Taxes for schools, universal health care (you know, taking care of people), and national and local infrastructure are "wasteful." Taxes for the military are never ever questioned.

Émile Durkheim and the sociologists are right: religion is society worshipping itself, here under the banner of an unimpeachable "God, faith, country." Bruce Lincoln and the radical critics of religion are right: religion is ideology working insidiously through religious narratives or myths that are played out endlessly, and largely unconsciously, in everything from the Sunday worship of an imaginary King in the sky, through the constructs of religious identity itself, to the endless fighter jets, fireworks, and American flags on display at NFL games.

In essence, "God" is a word in contemporary America that rationalizes for many why they (whom God loves) live and flourish while so much of the rest of the world (whom, apparently, God does not love) suffers in poverty and dies in misery. "Real" Americans deserve health care, wealth, trade, and happiness, but forget about the disadvantaged, the poor, the marginalized, the political refugee, and certainly any human being who happened to be born south of an imaginary line we call "the border." They are not us. Why should we care about them? That sounds harsh, but that *is* the underlying logic of this worldview, of this American exceptionalism, of this grotesque conflation and confusion of God and nation.

This is difficult for me to see and to say, but it is so. And it is here that I see another red thread running through my life. Here is another glimpse of what I have called the secret body of my work. This same tragic confusion of God and country was one of the reasons I left my birth culture in the first place, even if then I framed these unbearable moral dissonances in religious terms. I fought this fake "God" with what I believed was the real God, the God of Jesus who taught his disciples to bless the poor, tend to the sick, turn the other cheek, and love their enemies.

I was especially upset by my culture's quiet disdain for the poor, who were (and still are) considered "lazy" and so somehow underserving of help. But I was equally upset with my culture's militarism and, above all, with the nuclear arms race. When I registered for the draft in 1980, I registered in protest as a conscientious objector, despite the fact that there was no active draft. The poor local Postmaster didn't have a clue what to do with me. Nor, frankly, did I. The truth was that I was completely alone in my hometown in my convictions and my concerns.

They're back. Indeed, in many ways, the situation is much worse today than it was in the 1970s and early 1980s. At least then the American Catholic bishops spoke up against the insanity of the nuclear arms race and the injustices of neoliberal capitalism. At least then the public did not equate the message of Jesus with its exact moral opposite: the right-wing political extreme.

My emotional reaction to the Trump election flowed directly out of this personal history. The election did not surprise me. It felt familiar, too familiar. The implicit racisms of American culture were now explicit and on display for all to see. And it was ugly. I cannot read hearts. But I can read the news, and I know that anyone who voted for Donald Trump voted for a man who openly and repeatedly expressed racist, misogynist, hate-filled, and factually false views over and over again. That is not up for debate. It is simply the case.

I think that these developments felt all too familiar to me because I had *always* been fighting against this kind of bigotry and prejudice, from the day I entered the monastic seminary to follow Jesus to my long struggles with the Hindu Religious Right in India and the US in the 1990s and early millennium. The right-wing Hindu ideologues sounded exactly like Trump before Trump. Unsurprisingly, the anxious fear I feel in my body at the beginning of the Trump administration as I write these lines feels much like the anxiety I felt then.

I should add that I am not without cautious hope. I suspect that much of this is temporary and will be addressed with the changing demographic patterns and with the gradual urbanization of American culture. The cultural debates that the old white male politicians rage over in an insidious "bait and switch" technique ("Oh, the shame of gay marriage! Oh, the horrible fate of our once pure Christian nation! Now vote for me and let me make the rich richer and the poor poorer and pass laws that hurt those not like us") are simply over among the younger generations. And they are settled on the left, not the right.

I am also hopeful because I believe in the fundamental goodness of the people with whom I disagree. Such a belief is not naive or misplaced. I can see fundamental changes in the Midwest I know, where young people who come out of the closet are commonly shunned but are also commonly embraced (unsurprisingly, such young people inevitably move "to the city," that is, they leave rural America for urban America). Moreover, I have seen the very same people twist up their faces at the mere mention of gay marriage but warmly and affectionately engage individuals whom they know are gay. Such contradictions go uncommented on. The truth is that these are good, decent, loving, complicated people, and that Midwestern culture is ambivalent, shifting, thinking, moving. The truth is that Midwestern families are caught and conditioned by a set of cultural, religious, and historical scripts that they did not write. As individuals, they are not the problems. Those unconscious scripts are the problems. Or better, the problem is that these otherwise good and decent people do not know that they have been programmed. They are unconscious of the scripts, and so they identify almost completely with them. They think the scripts are themselves.

But they are not.

BECOMING HUMAN ONCE AGAIN

And there, in this near total conflation of a cultural script with personhood and community, is the most basic problem of all. It is this same problem that intellectuals can most effectively address, if only they will. Here anyway is my own answer to our present political climate and its moral disasters. Here appears what I want to call the prophetic function of the humanities.

Intellectuals in the humanities make a number of fundamental philosophical assumptions that often go unspoken but are nevertheless active and important. Such assumptions have been increasingly questioned and nuanced in recent decades, particularly in postmodern and postcolonial thought, but they are nevertheless worth acknowledging and describing, since (a) they continue to exert tremendous influence and are, at the end of the day, both defensible and plausible even after the criticisms; and (b) they will *have* to be acknowledged, reemphasized, and re-visioned if we are going to have any effective public voice and political influence moving forward. The new political realities have forced the issue and have demanded new, or renewed, responses from us.

Consider this. Humanists commonly assume *in principle* that all human beings share a common human nature and that, therefore, their cultural productions can be studied with similar methods and tools within a common field, be it history, anthropology, art history, literary study, or the comparative study of religion. They also assume that any and all religious identities are secondary, are "constructed" upon the deeper and more fundamental facts of human nature— our most fundamental forms of awareness, our sensory system and kinesthetic orientation in the world as upright bipeds, our ability to manipulate vocal and visual symbols to communicate with each other in language and (much more recently) writing, our social capacities to organize, our biological need to reproduce and raise children, our shared genetic pool, and so on.

We may not ever be able to get to that shared human nature, and it is a morally fraught enterprise to try to describe whatever that shared nature might be (since we will always be tempted to confuse our own local experiences and cultural assumptions for some universal "human being"), but the disciplines, by their very existence, assume that there is such a shared human nature. Otherwise, the disciplines make little or no sense. What would be the point of, say, a department of anthropology or religion if such assumptions were not made? In other words, intellectuals can say that there is no shared human nature, no "psychic unity," to use the old anthropological phrase, but the existence of departments suggests otherwise.

But here is the catch. Religious people often assume the exact opposite. They reverse the fundamental assumption or moral principle of the humanities. They value their religious identities over the human species. They assume that their religious identities are primary and that their humanity is secondary. That is why such communities or individuals will express hatred or act unjustly toward other human beings who are outside their religious fold. That is why they will sometimes even kill other human beings who do not share their belief systems or religious affiliations. Such acts of intolerance, injustice, and violence follow logically from a set of simple assumptions, which we might put in our own terms like this: religious identity is primary, more fundamental, and more important than any other human marker; religious identity is not a construction—it is who a person really is.

Many of the religious traditions do not speak or think like this, of course. They use their own local religious languages about being "saved," or being "chosen," or being a "believer," or possessing some proper "essence," or belonging to some special community or ethnic group. This sounds different, for sure, as it seems to draw on modernity's unspoken contract to respect any and all religious expression, but the underlying logic remains the same. The moral problems of such speaking are simply hidden behind a thin screen of relative religious egos and historically constructed cultures. Basically, a form of intolerance is papered over with a form of political correctness: the political correctness of respecting religious belief, even when it is functioning as a dehumanizing form of exclusion that would be condemned and rejected were it expressed in any other nonreligious way.

If we as intellectuals can demonstrate, in public, how every cultural and religious identity is in fact a historical, relative construction built upon a deeper shared human nature, whatever that deeper nature turns out to be (and I will offer my own answer below, in my final gnomon), we will have an important and central voice moving forward. We will become a collective prophet. If we cannot, or will not, do this for whatever good reasons, we are likely in for some difficult times, both inside and outside the academy. The choice is ours. The pivot is there to make, but we will have to make it. We will have to model for our families, our cultures, and our world how to *turn around* from any and every political or religious ego and look at the looker, watch the watcher, and so become human once again.

THE IMPORTANCE OF HISTORY

This will not be easy. There is so much to address and work through. Take the sadness. I sense a poignant sadness in the fear of difference and the insistence on returning to some lost golden age so evident in American culture today. People are mourning the gradual disappearance of a cultural world—their own. We should be honest and forthright with them about this: they are correct to sense such a loss. The broader culture *is* changing; globalization will continue to roll on; America will continue to become more, not less, diverse; and the world they grew up in will soon be no more, for better and for worse.

What they are mistaken about, of course, is the assumption that their cultural world, or any cultural world for that matter, should remain unchanged. The world is *always* ending. The world they grew up in was not the world their parents grew up in, which was not the world their grandparents grew up in, and so on. What such an insight requires, of course, is a fairly developed sense of history, which such communities simply do not possess. They do not possess such a historical sense because they have not studied history.

My Catholic family, for example, simply does not know that the same fear-filled logic that now wants to wall off the Mexican and deny political asylum to the persecuted Muslim refugee as dangerous and as somehow contaminating the "purity" of America is the *exact* same logic that once targeted our own Catholic ancestors, our grandparents and great-grandparents. They do not know that Protestant haters once burned down Catholic churches and crudely painted immigrant Catholics as lazy, dangerous religious others who idolatrously worshipped a foreign despot (the Pope), who were out to steal their jobs and who would certainly compromise the biblical purity of Protestant America.

How many times do we have to repeat these mistakes before we realize that they are mistakes? As long as we do not study history. Until then, good and decent people will misunderstand the deeper historical nature of religious intolerance and racism. They will continue to think that religious intolerance and racism are conscious attitudes that they do or do not have, or that these attitudes are reasonable because of some recent terrorist act or crime. Seen in the light of history, religious intolerance and racism are much more like invisible magnetic social fields that arrange all of the filings (that is, us) and make those filings feel like they have chosen their particular positions and actions. The filings *do* choose, but their choices are profoundly influenced by the (really bad) choices of those who have gone before them. In short, the filings are *caught*, and they will mostly stay caught until those invisible fields of force are exposed for what they really are—historically conditioned, unnecessary, and profoundly unjust. Only then will the terrible magnet weaken. Only then will more of the filings break free.

NOT BY A VOTE

I engage in such personal reflections not to dwell on my own Midwestern culture, nor to criticize the people whom I love and from whom I came. I dwell on these things because I think these values are representative of a large segment of the American, indeed global, population with which the professional study of religion has failed to engage in any direct and effective way. I have certainly failed in my own attempts. I write from pain, loss, confusion, and shame here, not from any sense of achievement. There is no happy ending. There is no resolution in sight.

Why have professional scholars of religion not engaged these local populations more, and more publicly? Is it to protect ourselves from the personal and political backlash that will inevitably follow? Perhaps. Is it because of the liberal mistake of not wanting to sound "elite," as if we do not think that such views are dangerously and demonstrably wrong, and that we are more or less correct in our analyses? These reasons no doubt capture something, but I think there may be a deeper reason still. I am thinking of the opening epigraph from René Girard. I think many of us fear that if we publically expose the social and political foundations of religion, if we really show the monster for what it is, we will in effect loose this same monster on the world, and on us personally and professionally. Better not to drive the beast from its lair. Better to stay silent, or retreat into language that is so technical that no one will read or understand it.

We may be right about that. But what are the risks of staying silent or remaining siloed in our professions? And have the truths that the humanities are about *ever* been won by a popular vote? New ideas are seldom friendly to old established ideas. Ideas are dangerous to the received order, that is to say, to any and all forms of conservatism. That is why universities, and especially schools of humanities, are bastions of liberalism. There are always exceptions, of course, but for the most part, *thinking is inherently and irrepressibly liberal.* Unsurprisingly, then, the kinds of truth the humanities are about— interpreting texts, decoding cultural scripts, and deconstructing ideologies— are inevitably poised against the public consensus, whatever that consensus happens to be. That is why right-wing politicians hate us and want to defund us. That is why demagogues and dictators begin their reigns by eliminating or demonizing the intellectuals. That is why scholars around the world are routinely harassed, imprisoned, censored, and killed. That is why my own state, Texas, passed a law in 2015 to allow students at state universities to bring concealed weapons *to class*: to intimidate us.

We should not look for agreement or popularity, then. Nor should we equate the value and importance of what we do with winning a particular election. That is not the point. The point is that someone, anyone, needs to stand up for the pursuit of truth (in any and all of its forms) and the affirmation of our humanity, however imperfect or incomplete those truths and however undefinable that shared humanity may turn out to be.

CLASSROOM INITIATION

Of course, the main social space in which an academic engages the public is the classroom. I have thought and written about the classroom for some time, particularly around the pedagogy of comparison and the existential costs that comparative acts commonly carry for young people. It began in the mid-1990s, when I was teaching at Westminster College. Bryan Rennie and I both taught the introductory course to the study of religion there, more or less every semester. After teaching the course for a few years, I was growing increasingly disturbed by a particular pattern I was seeing.

I was teaching the course in the fall. I was giving these young people powerful new methods to think about religion, particularly their own religions, which was usually some form of Protestant Christianity or Roman Catholicism. The end result was often massive confusion, if not full-blown existential crises. And then the course just ended.

And then we sent them home for Christmas.

That seemed irresponsible, if not actually a bit perverse. Not that I wanted, or want now, to have students leave the introductory course comfortably confirmed in their religious *or* secular heritages. But I came to think that we needed some way to help them come to some personal closure for the course. That did not need to be a final closure, of course. I wanted them to see the educational process as ongoing, but also as not simply deconstructive, much less as destructive.

Bryan suggested that we use the anthropologist Victor Turner and his model of initiation to structure a course. Turner, as is well known, had picked up on earlier anthropological work to write eloquently about a three-stage process that can be seen in countless initiation rituals around the world: (1) the recognition or acknowledgement of a pre-initiation identity; (2) a deconstructive "liminal" stage in which this earlier social identity is taken apart and "killed" or dissolved through some symbolic or ritual means; and (3) the social recognition of the new post-initiation identity. College, of course, is American culture's one widely shared initiation cycle. If a college classroom could not be turned into an initiatory space, I concluded, then nothing could be. I thought that Bryan's suggestion was a wonderful idea.

It worked. I used this method at Westminster College throughout the late 1990s and into the new millennium. When I wrote *Comparing Religions* (2014) with three of my PhD students, I adopted the same tripartite structure, now in conversation with what I considered to be the various consensus positions of the field. The fundamental move that I made in the text was foregrounding the intellectual act of comparison as a universal cognitive function and backgrounding the religions themselves. I also took it as one of my goals to explain how and why absolute "difference" has been overemphasized and fetishized over the last four decades, while "sameness" has been denied and tabooed as some kind of horrible intellectual sin.

COMPARISON IS JUSTICE

I did not reverse the fetishization, fetishizing sameness over difference now. Rather, I offered a comparative model that could balance the two poles of comparison instead of using one to beat up on the other. I wanted to show that comparative thinking is involved in pretty much everything human beings do, from the histories of polytheism and monotheism to the birth of evolutionary biology, from how the media thinks about ethnicity and religious identity to our deepest yearnings for social justice, which makes no sense at all without some intuited or assumed sense of sameness, and which can be defined simply as "a demand for sameness in difference." *Comparison done well is justice. Comparison done poorly is injustice.*

Humanist intellectuals need to recognize that their fetishization of difference also carries serious political costs, and that our exclusive emphasis on difference over any and all sameness has backfired. Again, we must pivot now. If we cannot emphasize our shared humanity as much as our local important differences, we will have nothing effective to say to our publics, and we will continue to retreat into smaller and smaller silos. We will be scattered.

It is also worth reminding ourselves: simply because scholars decide not to compare religions (again, for whatever perfectly defensible historical and philosophical reasons) does not mean the rest of the world will suddenly stop doing it. Quite the contrary, they will just keep comparing religions. Human beings *must* compare to make sense of anything. And without any input from professionals with sophisticated historical and reflexive methods, they will usually do it badly, which is to say, without a sufficient historical consciousness or any adequate degree of critical reflexivity. They will assume the eternal, unchanging truth of their own religions and use these relative measuring sticks to "compare" every other religion. They will privilege their ethnic or religious ego over a shared global humanity. When professional intellectuals refuse to compare religions, for whatever reasons, what they are also doing is handing the public shop over to these same unsophisticated, and often extremely dangerous, voices.

It is time to stop doing that. We can now see where that got us.

INTRODUCING THE ESSAY

I have not only tried to engage the publics of family and classroom. I have also tried to engage Evangelicals, as they have carried so much political force in recent decades. I have debated two Evangelical intellectuals in public at Rice University, both of Fuller Theological Seminary: Prof. Marianne Meye Thompson in 2012, on the nature and person of Jesus;[1] and Dr. Richard Muow, on religious tolerance and religious pluralism. The brief piece anthologized below is the text I delivered during my debate with Dr. Muow for an event on "Shutting Heaven's Door," that is, on Christian theology and religious exclusivism. This event was sponsored by Rice University's Boniuk Institute for the Study and Advancement of Religious Tolerance.

In a much more extensive and personal fashion, I have also engaged Frank Schaeffer, a well-known and especially eloquent counter-voice who emerged from the Evangelical community. Frank is the son of Francis and Edith Schaeffer, two extremely prominent Evangelists and political activists in the 1950s, 1960s, 1970s, and 1980s. Frank broke with his family's Evangelical faith as a young man and has since written a number of eloquent memoirs detailing the inner workings of Evangelical politics and why these are so dangerous and dysfunctional. He should know. He was there.[2] It is Frank who has taught me about the "paradox" of American Evangelicals (and so also about Midwestern Catholics)—wonderful people and neighbors who vote disastrously in large blocks. It is also Frank who has pushed me to see that the academy's exclusive emphasis on difference and its near total neglect of human sameness have backfired and, in effect, silenced us in the public square. I think he is right about both points, and about so much else. It is time for all of us to pivot, to turn around, and "to be frank."

The Chess Game

(FEBRUARY 22, 2015)

I am most interested this evening in having a conversation with Prof. Mouw, not hearing myself blab about this or that. Having said that, I do think it is important to get some ideas on the table right away so that we can have a rich conversation. I will speak autobiographically and bluntly, as I think that this will best serve our conversation this evening.

I grew up in a small rural community in Nebraska among German immigrants. When my maternal grandmother left her Lutheran church for my grandfather's Catholic church in the 1930s, it was a terrible scandal. By the time I graduated from high school, Catholics and Lutherans married all the time.

I did my undergraduate work at a Benedictine monastic seminary in the early 1980s. I wanted to be a monk. There I was trained in the rich intellectual traditions of Roman Catholicism, the same intellectual tradition that eventually birthed the university itself in the thirteenth century: hence the monastic gowns that we wear every graduation day. I learned that the Church had long held a strong *exclusivism* on matters of faith. This was captured in the Latin sound bite *nulla salus extra ecclesiam*, "Outside the Church there is no salvation." This all changed in the 1960s with Vatican II, when the Church abandoned this exclusivism for a clear *inclusivism*. Now we were told that there *is* salvation in the other religions. Judaism was recognized as the mother faith of the three Abrahamic monotheisms, and Islam was a treasured member of the family. Moreover, profound truths were recognized in the devotional, philosophical, and contemplative traditions of Buddhism and Hinduism. Still, the full truth resided in the gospels and the ancient deposit of faith that is Roman Catholicism. All the other religious truths, including the other Christian denomination truths, were "rays" of this same universal light.

That seemed like a giant step forward, but it also seemed like a halfway house. I could see no good moral or rational reason to raise the accident of anyone's birth culture, including and especially my own, to the full truth of final divine revelation, into which all other people's faiths must be somehow "included." It all seemed suspiciously convenient.

I graduated from the seminary and took up the comparative study of religion at the University of Chicago to pursue these questions. By the time I had my PhD, I had adopted a new set of metaphors and a new *pluralism*, that is, I now believed that each of the religions was a kind of filter or prism of the sacred, and that each filter was blocking out as much of the divine light as it was letting in. None were absolute. None were perfect.

In the new millennium, I found myself working with various modern mystical movements in California. Again and again, I encountered profound people who had found their own birth traditions painfully lacking and had decided to step out on their own, as it were, into a new world, a future faith in which religious experiences of all kinds could be embraced but none would be taken absolutely. This orientation would eventually morph into our present "spiritual but not religious" demographic, a deeply American tradition that does not go back to the New Age movement of the 1980s, or the counterculture of the 1960s but to the Bostonian Transcendentalists of the middle of the nineteenth century and, beyond that, back centuries and millennia to countless mystics and visionaries around the world.

So that has been my spiritual journey. What would I say now? I would probably not describe myself as a pluralist any more. I have grown frustrated with the clunkiness of this way of thinking. Pluralism too easily suggests that there is a single objective goal, a mountaintop "out there" that we are all walking up from different directions. After thirty years of studying religion, I am no longer convinced that this is the case. I think we are walking up different mountains, and that there are *a lot* of mountains, none of which can say with any convincing argument, "I am the highest!" Each of these different mountains, moreover, gives us *different* things.

There is something else I came to. I came to think that all of these mountains emerge out of the earth of our own humanity, that is, *out of us*. I have never encountered a religious experience, vision, out-of-body experience, scriptural text, or revelation that was not experienced and expressed by a human being. Clearly, if the gods exist, they need us to speak. In truth, I think the gods *are* us, but that we are not ready to see this yet. I think they are the unconscious, unintegrated part of us speaking to the conscious integrated part of us.

If I had to name my present position, I would describe it as a *secret humanism*. I think that it is our own secret humanity that lies behind and within all of the planet's religions. If the revelations of these traditions mean anything at all—and I think they do—I think that they mean that we are not who we think we are. We are not just our religious egos, our conscious selves, our families, our languages, our genders and races, our customs. We are More. There is something transcendent, some secret divine spark, something More out of which all revelations emerge. What that secret More is I do not know and so cannot say. Nor do I think any ego here can know or say. The filter cannot speak for that which is filtered. The prism cannot speak for the light. It can only refract and reflect it.

A secret humanist, then, does not ask, "Which religion is true?" That is the wrong question. She does not pit this religion against that one in a never-ending story of conflict. She sees the history of religions as a centuries-long chess game, with different communities moving different pieces around on a shared, and quickly shrinking, global table. At some point, she simply stops identifying with *any* of the pieces on this chessboard, stands up from the table, and asks a simple question: "Just who is playing this game?" And, perhaps more radically still, "Is there not another game to play?" "Do we *really* have to keep playing this one?"

Religious believers, and particularly exclusivist religious believers, of course, often operate with the exact opposite assumptions. They don't see the game. They see life-and-death issues of absolute meaning and import. They see the eternal fate of their souls at stake. Accordingly, they assume that one is primarily a Christian, a Hindu, a Muslim, or a Jew and only secondarily a human being, a global citizen, a member of a species. They do not generally put it this way, of course. Rather, they use their own religious language to claim that one cannot be "saved," be "twice born," become a "believer" or "chosen" unless one is a member of a particular religious community—their own, of course. From my own perspective, this is the exact reverse of things. It is also suspiciously convenient.

There *is* a profound truth hidden (and distorted) in the religious claims, though. It is indeed the case that human beings need culture, language, and community to become fully human, and probably to become fully conscious. An infant boy abandoned to wolves does not grow up speaking elegant British English and always looking bathed, like Mowgli of the Disney film. He grows up dirty, mangy, and acting, howling, and eating like a wolf, if he grows up at all and is not eaten. We might say, then, that human beings do not need a *particular* culture or community to become fully human (which is what the religions commonly assert), but they do need *a* culture or community. Moreover, it clearly does matter through which culture one chooses to become human. There are many mountains, not one, and where you end up in your life will depend largely on which path you start the climb on, whether or not you understand that you are really already there, that the individual mountain you are climbing for a time has been pushed up out of us all.

14

The Super Natural

Biological Gods, the Traumatic Secret,
and the Future (of) Race

There lay the Overmind, whatever it might be, bearing the same relation to man as man bore to amoeba. Potentially infinite, beyond mortality, how long had it been absorbing race afer race as it spread across the stars?

ARTHUR C. CLARKE, *CHILDHOOD'S END*

The Negro is a sort of seventh son, born with a veil, and gifted with second-sight in this American world,—a world which yields him no true self-consciousness, but only lets him see himself through the revelation of the other world. It is a peculiar sensation, this double consciousness, this sense of always looking at one's self through the eyes of others, of measuring one's soul by the tape of a world that looks on in amused contempt and pity.

W. E. B. DU BOIS, *THE SOULS OF BLACK FOLK*

My attempt to engage different publics was not restricted to the textbook project and the classroom. Nor did I just want to open a conversation with my Midwestern Catholic and Protestant culture and Evangelical Christians. I also wanted to talk to that immense swath of individuals who are fascinated by anomalous phenomena but would wince at the notion that these events have anything to do with religion. I wanted to engage what Eliade called the camouflaged sacred, which is nowhere more apparent today than in the fantastic worlds of science fiction and film, television, and the graphic novel.

The lens can be reversed. I began to read the history of religions as the original and ultimate collection of movie scripts and special effects. I resonated deeply with the sociologist of religion Martin Riesbrodt, who suggested that religion can well be seen as "a legitimate form of science fiction," as "a complex of practices that are based on the premise of the existence of superhuman powers, whether personal or impersonal, that are generally invisible."[1] The sacred art and architecture of the world, from the pyramids of Mesoamerica through the stained glass windows of Europe's cathedrals to the sculpted gods, goddesses, and Buddhas of Asia began to look like so many 3-D virtual reality machines in which exquisite art, careful ritual, and trance induction have long brought to life those imaginal worlds we now call "religions." The same sci-fi reading seemed even more appropriate with the visions, apparitions, levitations, and materializations of the religious prodigies whom this art and ritual honored, and, in many cases, literally worshipped. Indeed, the visionary projections and paranormal displays of the history of religions began to look *exactly* like special effects.

Are they?

I spent four days with the biochemist and Nobel Laureate Kary Mullis, his wife, Nancy, and a group of intellectuals studying different aspects of the UFO phenomenon in the fall of 2016. We listened to Kary explain in rich detail the context and specifics of his abduction experience near his cabin in northern California.[2] The event was initiated by the appearance of a glowing raccoon that he encountered on the way to the outhouse. "Good evening, doctor," it said to him. The next thing he knew six hours had passed and he found himself walking down a road toward the cabin as the sun rose. Kary could not shake the feeling that the absurd display, "the little bastard and his courteous greeting," was some kind of projected hologram.

Was it?

In a similar spirit, Jacques Vallée has often commented, both in his books and in person, about how UFO encounters look "staged," hoaxed, as it were, but hoaxed by some nonhuman or superhuman force. Both *Authors* and *Mutants* were forays into similar ideas about the sacred as performance, theater, entertainment, and what I called the "trick of the truth." I ended *Mutants* with a chapter study of the science fiction writer Whitley Strieber.

Like Jacques, Whitley has taught me a great deal about the UFO phenomenon and the extraterrestrial esotericisms, if in a different key. Jacques is the astronomer, computer and information scientist, and iconic field investigator. Whitley, on the other hand, is the classic experiencer, novelist, radio host, and public bard of the whole UFO phenomenon. His book *Communion* (1987) is probably the most influential, and easily the best written, account of a contact event ever published.

Communion is not just a book. It is also a mirror. And a hypnotic gaze (as the cover). When Kary Mullis read it, he immediately recognized his own abduction experience in the book's eerie narrative. As he was reading, the phone rang. It was his daughter, calling him to ask if he could read a particular book:

Communion. She recognized in it the outlines of a similar experience she had had at the family cabin, unbeknownst to her father. Both father and daughter, it turned out, had independently encountered something strange on the family property: the daughter was "gone" for three hours, as her fiancé screamed and frantically searched for her on the grounds. Both father and daughter "awoke" walking in the same direction on the same road near the cabin. When each encountered *Communion* separately, both knew instinctively what Strieber was writing about.

If I hear and read him correctly (and I am reading the written tradition off the oral one), what Whitley is proposing in his total body of work is the real presence of intelligent light forms or conscious plasmas in our shared cosmic environment, their long historical interactions with human beings, and their subsequent very real effects on human civilization, particularly through story and symbol, or what historians of religions call "myth." He possesses no certainty about the source or nature of the lights and energies. He has learned instead to focus on their practical and spiritual effects on individual human beings and communities. His approach, in short, is a profoundly humanistic one.

Or superhumanistic one. His conception of human nature overflows any ordinary secular notions. He thus thinks of a human being as an "incredible interdimensional entity" and suspects that what we normally think of as a person is only one form of human being. Here he tells the story of how he once asked one of the spectral presences who visited him regularly in his nightly meditation practice to show itself, not in yet another symbolic projection or movie special effect, but in its true form. Something that resembled a small luminous star, about the size of a basketball, appeared outside his cabin. Laser-like beams shot out in every direction. When these beautiful rays struck him, he felt/tasted/perceived/knew the presence of a person in ways that he never had before. This, he realized, was a human being in another form. This was one of us, or what we might yet become.

One of the most powerful and long-lasting effects of such encounters is the inspiration and eventual production of new cultural stories, which we now call religions. Here is where his deep skepticism appears. Such light stories, after all, have led to the institutional structures and psychological intolerances of religion and belief, and the latter Strieber clearly abhors: "Do we have to go there yet again? Do we have to create yet another religion out of these things? Have we not suffered enough?" This deep and abiding suspicion of religion and belief, this turn to the human, or the superhuman, as the proper locus and meaning of the contact experience, this notion of the soul as a kind of star or humanoid light form, render all of this deeply "gnostic."

I had vaguely known about Whitley's books on the "visitor" phenomenon, his careful language for the recurring mythological pattern of an often diminutive, and usually mischievous humanoid that morphs through the centuries via the various culturally inflected forms of the angel, demon, jinn, sylph, fairy, troll, elemental, and now the alien or gray. But I did not actually read anything Whitley had written until around 2008 or so. I was deeply impressed when I did. I contacted Whitley through a mutual friend. From many years of conversation and a number of Esalen symposia emerged our 2016 book, *The Super Natural*.

The book is conversational and, by intention, nontechnical. It attempts a number of things, but foremost among these is what we called a "shift in the conversation." We wanted to demonstrate that an experiencer and an academic could have a serious conversation about the most baroque aspects of something like the UFO phenomenon. We were trying to carve out a third space that was open to the ontological shock of such spectral events, but that did not immediately push the buttons of psychological reduction or religious belief. We were trying to fashion a new gnostic mind space. Basically, I was just being myself. So was Whitley.

THE SUPER NATURAL

I had explored this third space beyond the frameworks of science and religion before. In *The Serpent's Gift*, I had dubbed it an "intellectual gnosticism." In *Authors of the Impossible*, I had called it "science mysticism." These were somewhat clumsy expressions, but the basic point was correct enough. They were beginnings.[3]

In *Comparing Religions*, I tried again with a new phrase: "the super natural." This was another attempt to translate "the paranormal," but it was also a conscious updating and re-visioning of Eliade's "hierophany." The latter is a deeply dialectical notion that has been largely misunderstood and so misrepresented by those who want to insist that the man was some sort of naïf, some kind of simple believer in an unchanging floating absolute. As best I can see, there is no pure manifestation of the sacred, no simple transcendence, in the Eliadean hierophany. Rather, the sacred manifests itself in and through human nature or some other natural phenomenon, which remains perfectly "natural" even as it reveals something Other or More. Hence my reworking of the hierophany as the super natural.

I used the category of the super natural again with Whitley's corpus to explore how the visitor or contact experience, along with a whole range of other anomalous experiences, might well be perfectly natural, as long as we expand our notions of the natural beyond the present materialisms in which it has been temporarily imprisoned. This, I pointed out, is precisely what the French researchers and scientists meant when they first coined the language of the "paranormal" around the turn of the twentieth century. They meant the super natural. Hence my next gnomon, itself another echo of my dual aspect monism (gnomon 13):

16. The Super Natural. The paranormal is the super natural not yet fully understood or sufficiently modeled. It is the natural world behaving in a "super" way, that is, beside or before our sensory and cognitive capacities split and so reduce it to a human experience.

Once we frame the paranormal as the super natural, we can immediately see why the sciences have been so important to its formations, and why one really cannot separate religious phenomena and scientific discoveries. The creationists are wrong: science cannot be denied for the sake of some naive literalist religion. The new atheists are wrong: religion cannot be denied for the sake of some naive materialist science. Stephen Jay Gould is wrong: science and religion cannot be kept apart. It is One World. Or, if you prefer, it is the One.

EXTRATERRESTRIAL ESOTERICISM

In the foreword to Jacques Vallée's *Dimensions* (1988), a book that appeared just a year after *Communion*, Whitley wonders out loud whether the visitor phenomenon "may simply be what the force of evolution looks like when it acts on conscious creatures."[4] Here, of course, is another evolutionary esotericism, but one expressed in the symbolic imaginal framework of the extraterrestrial.

"Extraterrestrial," I must immediately add, is a leap. As already noted, Strieber himself generally avoids the language of the "alien," preferring instead the more neutral "visitor." He encourages his readers to leave the door open to some extraterrestrial possibility (since there is much about the encounters that suggest as much), but he cautions them against assuming it, much less believing it.

Still, his visitor corpus is one modern expression of a much larger literature that we might well call both "extraterrestrial" and "esoteric," since it posits contact with beings from other worlds and reveals the result of this contact as a series of secret truths.

The secrets are not just spiritual ones, either. Consider the modern history of one major branch of this literature, the ufological literature. On June 24, 1947, American businessman and pilot Ken Arnold spotted nine silver somethings whizzing over the mountains near Yakima, Washington, in perfect formation and at incredible speeds. As a good patriot, Mr. Arnold immediately reported what he saw. It was, after all, 1947, and it was widely believed that the Soviets might try to invade or fire nuclear missiles from the northwest. It was Arnold's description of these things as moving across the sky as if they were skipping over water, like a pie plate or saucer, that gave us the word "flying saucer" through a journalist on the scene later that same day named Bill Bequette (despite the fact that Arnold did not report seeing saucer-shaped objects—they looked more like stingrays). The story was then supercharged two weeks later, when the Air Force announced that it had recovered a flying disc near Roswell, New Mexico, where some of our nuclear bombers were stationed. A retraction the next day did nothing but fuel the fires further, now with the gasoline of a cover-up.

It was the same US Air Force that coined the expression "UFO" a few years later, in the early 1950s, largely for defense reasons. The acronym in its origins is a Cold War expression. It names something that *we need to defend ourselves against*. Ever since, the UFO phenomenon has been central to American popular culture—morphing, fascinating, and baffling anew as each decade ticks by. We are still defending ourselves against it, especially in the academy.

I am extremely suspicious of the mythology of invading extraterrestrials that was the eventual result of all of this. Born in the military secrets of the security state and its intelligence apparatus, fueled by Christian fundamentalist military professionals who believe that flying saucers are demonic presences that we need to defend ourselves against, and literalized (and demonized again) by countless Hollywood movies for the last seven decades, such a paranoid mythology now obscures far more than it illumines.

Good historiography can correct our lenses here, though. Take Ken Arnold's so-called flying saucers. Arnold himself seems to have thought of them more in esoteric than technological terms. In a recent interview with Paolo Leopizzi Harris, Kim Arnold, Ken Arnold's daughter, has stated very clearly that one of the "hidden secrets" of her father's literary remains is that he witnessed the flying objects "pulsating with a blue-white light," like a heartbeat. He eventually concluded that the stingray shaped objects were "not mechanical in any sense at all," that is, that they were alive; that they could change their density; and that they came from another dimensional world, which is the same one we enter when we die. In our own terms, we might say that Ken Arnold's original flying saucer vision was not about technology at all. It was about eschatology.

Such an observation is supported by the visitor corpus of Whitley Strieber, who saw individuals within his abduction experiences who he knew to be dead or, stranger still, who had died without him knowing about it. Anne Strieber, who sifted through hundreds of thousands of letters that her husband's *Communion* elicited, and cowrote a book on a select core of these—*The Communion Letters* (1997)—has repeatedly observed the common presence of dead loved ones in the abduction experiences of the letter writers. The abduction experience, she concluded, "has something to do with what we call death." Again, it's about eschatology, not technology. It's about spirits, not spaceships.[5]

Kim Arnold has also spoken about the telepathic gifts and reincarnation beliefs of her mother and what a historian of religions would recognize as a Theosophical framework in which her father and mother understood these historical sightings and their cultural aftermath. Kim Arnold has spoken at length about how the events stressed and strained their family, mostly because of the way her father's experiences were mangled by the media, by Hollywood, and by the debunkers, but also because of the endless phone calls and some ten thousand letters that her father received. She has also noted how her father was threatened by a government agent and warned not to speak about what he saw. Kim describes in some detail how both of her parents spent the rest of their lives in fear of being killed by the US government, whose intelligence community appears to have manipulated and harassed the Arnolds for its own security purposes.[6]

And there we have it. A vision of living beings in the sky emerging from some other dimension misreported and misperceived as flying machines likened to a little plate for your tea or coffee and immediately mixed up with the Air Force, Cold War intelligence, the politics of the security state, Christian fundamentalism and an entire new Hollywood demonology of invading extraterrestrials. Where to start? Where to begin anew?

BIOLOGICAL GODS

Arnold's understanding was in fact not new. It is sometimes called the "space animal" theory, since such a theory posits the existence of invisible species living in the atmosphere. Charles Fort clearly articulated this idea already in the 1920s, and many others, since him, have offered different versions of the same basic idea. Strieber's turn to conscious light forms can be read within this same current of esoteric thought. Here the language of the natural sciences—particularly the physics of plasma and electromagnetism and the analogical imagination of evolutionary biology (with different species at different scales or branches of evolution)—are employed to approximate some adequate description of dramatic encounters with spectral presences in the physical environment.

And Strieber is hardly alone here. I have been collecting cases of this emergent religious imagination under the banner of the new "biological gods," a kind of subgenre that spans both the evolutionary and extraterrestrial esoteric literatures. I am thinking of figures and texts like Philip K. Dick's *Valis* (1981), Strieber's *Communion* (1987), and Barbara Ehrenreich's *Living with a Wild God* (2014). In each of these three cases, we see how a professional writer describes a life-changing encounter with what any earlier culture would have recognized as a deity or demon. Each author engages these earlier religious interpretations but finally moves outside of them to posit highly evolved invisible species in the environment that interact with human beings at their own whims and for their own interests, perhaps, the authors speculate, to "feed off" of human emotion or to tame, domesticate, or evolve us via sexual communion and interspecies symbiosis. The result is a new set of evolutionary animisms or biological polytheisms that pose a challenge to the reigning materialisms and projection theories of conventional science and the humanities. The result is a new mythology of "biological gods" deeply imbued with evolutionary and extraterrestrial esoteric convictions.

We have already met Dick and Strieber. Allow me to play this out a bit with the case of Ehrenreich.

In early May of 1958, seventeen-year-old Barbara Ehrenreich went skiing on Mammoth Mountain in northern California. On the way home, something would happen to her on the streets of a little town called Lone Pine that would eventually upend her entire philosophical worldview. Her 2014 memoir *Living with a Wild God* is her profound and hilarious look back on her science training and this life-changing "epiphany," as she calls it.

Ehrenreich studied theoretical physics at Reed College and earned a PhD in cell biology at Rockefeller University. She grew up in a passionately atheistic family, a fact signaled by stories like the time her dying grandmother threw a crucifix across the room when a local Catholic priest tried to give her the last rites. Trained in these family ways of fighting against all forms of authoritarianism,

Ehrenreich would spend her professional life as a take-no-prisoners writer, a social critic concerned about health care and poverty, and a social activist picketing and meeting for various feminist and economic justice causes.

Lone Pine continued to haunt her, though, even if she effectively suppressed it for most of her life. As she writes, she had known "an event so strange, so cataclysmic, that I never in all the intervening years wrote or spoke about it." What was she supposed to say? She knew what she would sound like. She would sound like Whitley Strieber:

> So what do you do with something like this—an experience so anomalous, so disconnected from the normal life you share with other people, that you can't even figure out how to talk about it? I was also, I have to admit, afraid of sounding crazy. Try inserting an account of a mystical experience into a conversation and you'll likely get the same response as you would if you confided that you had been the victim of an alien abduction.[7]

What was she so afraid to speak about? Back to May of 1958 and the skiing trip. The group was heading back home on a long road trip. She had slept the night before in a car with her fellow teenage travelers. She had also eaten little. In a state of sleep deprivation and hypoglycemia—that is, "in the kind of condition that the Plains Indians sought in their vision quests"[8]—the young woman woke up and took a walk through the little town of Lone Pine. Or tried anyway. The world suddenly burst into living fire. She invokes the biblical "burning bush" to describe what she knew then, but there was little biblical, much less monotheistic, about the experience. And, indeed, Ehrenreich makes it crystal clear throughout the book that she despises monotheism as a form of "deicide" that insists on killing the gods and leads eventually to modern science, which kills everything else.

But nothing was dead on the streets of Lone Pine on that fateful morning. Nothing. *Everything* was spirited. *Everything* was alive, even the teacups and toasters in the shop window of a secondhand store. Here are a few lines. Notice the basic dual aspect monism of the passage, that is, the way that it collapses "inside" and "outside" or "subject" and "object":

> The world flamed into life. . . . This was not the passive beatific merger with "the All," as promised by the Eastern mystics. It was a furious encounter with a living substance that was coming at me through all things at once. . . . Nothing could contain it. Everywhere, "inside" and out, the only condition was overflow.

Again, what could she say? "That I had been savaged by a flock of invisible angels—lifted up in a glorious flutter of iridescent feathers, then mauled, emptied of all intent and purpose, and pretty much left for dead?"[9]

Living with a Wild God is an attempt to contextualize and describe this flock of mauling angels. She explores a number of implications and possibilities encoded in her own mauling. Two are very much worth highlighting here: the "wild" amoral nature of the Other that overwhelmed her; and its possible biological nature.

In terms of the amoral, she enacts very clearly what I have performed above as the separation of the mystical and the ethical (gnomon 4). The mauling sacred Other is *not* moral, is *not* social, is *not* even really religious. "Mysticism often reveals a wild, amoral Other, while religion insists on conventional codes of ethics enforced by an ethical supernatural being. The obvious solution would be to admit that ethical systems are a human invention and that the Other is something else entirely."[10] Or again: "Whatever I had seen *was what it was*, with no moral valence or reference to human concerns."[11] Exactly.

So what was it? She proposes that it was, in my own terms now, a kind of biological god. As such, it is neither malevolent nor benevolent. It is what it is. Here she turns to the same text that I turned to for my notion of a paraphysics or paraphysical esotericism, Arthur C. Clarke's *Childhood's End*, where she finds the fully developed theme of "an über-being that uses humans for its own inscrutable purposes . . . an unseen 'over-mind' of remote extraterrestrial provenance, which sends its agents to essentially domesticate humankind." Really, what the Overlords do is "seek out the more mystically adept members of humanity, who are eventually recruited into a kind of trance culminating in mass spiritual unity with the over-mind."[12] The result is the end of history and the end of the Earth, as the Overmind presumably moves on to another planet and another species to bond with and subsume.

Ehrenreich knows that this is a novel, but she thinks that Clarke, "an avowed atheist with a background in physics and rocket science," may well be onto something here, and that this something deserves further research and study: "Science could of course continue to dismiss anomalous 'mystical' experiences as symptoms of mental illness, but the merest chance that they represent some sort of contact or encounter justifies investigation."[13]

She has in mind not only her own Lone Pine event, but also the Valis experience of Philip K. Dick. Dick, Ehrenreich points out, sensed that Valis was a *living creature*. His own metaphysical opening was experienced as what he described and what Ehrenreich now affirmingly quotes as an "interspecies symbiosis."[14] Ehrenreich entertains the same notion, wondering out loud to what extent that what overwhelmed her on that skiing trip was a biological species of some kind. She even asks out loud if such invisible beings "feed" on our forms of consciousness, as they do in science fiction. This is a *very* common thought in the abduction literature as well, where it is also an experience and where it is extended to our emotions and the bio-energies of our sexual arousals. This would be "a being no more visible to us than microbes were to Aristotle, that roams the universe seeking minds open enough for it to enter or otherwise contact."[15]

In the end, Ehrenreich confesses that, thanks to her reading of history and theology (that is, the study of religion), she can no longer deny and repress what she had seen in the mountains, nor can she brush it all aside as "unverifiable and possibly psychotic." She is now ready, and has been ready for nearly a decade, "to acknowledge the possible existence of conscious beings—'gods,' spirits, extraterrestrials—that normally elude our senses, making themselves known to us only on their own whims and schedules, in the service of their own agendas." "In fact," she goes on, "I began to think, edging to this conclusion bit by bit and with great trepidation, that I had seen one."[16]

HORROR AND TRAUMA

Ehrenreich's Lone Pine experience was hardly a happy simple event, much less a claim for some kind of individual evolutionary advance. It looks much more like a violent spiritual assault. Hence her language of being "mauled" and "left for dead."

Similarly, I do not think it is an accident that Whitley Strieber is a horror writer. Horror writers commonly and consistently report a broad range of paranormal experiences.[17] That is one major reason they write horror: they have been horrified, mauled, assaulted, transformed, inspired. We even have a very strong case of the monster movie pioneer Forrest J. Ackerman engaging in all sorts of playful puns, synchronicities, and jokes "from the other side," that is, dead, more or less exactly like he did when he was still alive.[18] The constructivist, of course, would argue that the supernatural experiences of horror writers are products of their horror reading and writing. Yes, and no. The line of influence often flows both ways: the horror writing, after all, can also be an expression of an original super natural experience or overwhelming intuition. Another kind of gnostic reversal or reflexive rereading.

Very much related to this genre of assault and horror is another theme that came up often in my engagement with Whitley's visitor experiences: trauma as a catalyst of experiences of encounter, possession, and transcendence. Again and again, Whitley would insist that he was "cracked open" by early childhood trauma, and that it was these traumatic events that provided the psychological doors for the visitors to enter many years later.

This was hardly a new theme for me. Indeed, this was a theme that had first appeared on the condemned pages of the last chapter of *Kālī's Child*, where I read "the House" of Ramakrishna's adult ecstasies as mystical states that, psychosexually speaking, were entered through a "Door" cracked open by early traumatic experience of a sexual nature. The traumatic theme would return again much later with the paranormal materials, as we have already seen above in the "Authors" lecture with the traumatic technology of telepathy.

All of these thoughts would come into sharper focus until I finally landed on the expression "the traumatic secret." The occasion was an essay I was asked to write about the influence of the French philosopher George Bataille on my thought.[19] The traumatic secret goes like this:

17. The Traumatic Secret. The paranormal event or altered state of consciousness appears to be "let in" through the temporary suppression or dissolution of the socialized ego, which was opened up or fractured (either at the moment of the event or earlier in the life cycle) through extreme physical, emotional, and/or sexual suffering, that is, through what we would today call trauma. The trauma here is the trigger, but not necessarily the cause.

By the traumatic secret I mean to signal a number of related ideas. I mean to signal the observation that in many cases the mystical event or psychical cognition occurs in a state of grave danger, illness, or near-death. I also mean to signal that such states and cognitions often serve obvious adaptive purposes, since any "trauma" implies something survived. As such, they are dramatic expressions of an evolutionary function (the writer and blogger Eric Wargo has helped me to see this). Such a model does not reduce the mystical event to the traumatic fracture, but rather understands the trauma as a psychological correlate or catalyst of the mystical state of consciousness.

Which is not to deny that the state of consciousness "let in" is also laced with all sorts of cultural, linguistic, historical, and psychological details. It almost always is. These, after all, are precisely the features of the biological and

324 || CHAPTER 14

cultured medium through which the state of consciousness manifests itself: the individual human being. The traumatic secret, then, is another expression of the filter or reduction thesis.

I am perfectly aware that most forms of trauma are simply destructive and result in no experience of transcendence whatsoever. I do not wish to romanticize trauma. I am also perfectly aware that some experiences of transcendence display no traumatic features. I do not wish to issue inappropriate generalizations. I am simply observing that sometimes, and remarkably often in the mystical literature, these two modes of human experience appear to occur *together*. They appear to be correlated.

Three further points here.

First, again, I am very aware that my multiple invocations of the superhuman could be read as idealizations of some perfect impenetrable male body, some simplistic humanist univeralism, or some elite white subject. As with the dominant queer, nonnormative male bodies of my histories of comparative mystical literature, the truth is the opposite. The traumatic secret suggests that the superhuman will often manifest precisely in and around the disabled body, the sick or dying body, the psychedelic or psychoactively assaulted body, the mentally ill body, the abducted body, the tortured body, the haunted or repressed body, and so on.

Second, the traumatic secret comes with a hidden gift. Any theory of religion, particularly one that leans so heavily on extreme or anomalous experiences (as mine certainly does), must not only provide a model for those extreme experiences at the beating heart of the theory. It must also provide a model for their ordinary lack or utter absence in normal human life and so for the honest doubt and skepticism that surrounds their invocation. Together, the filter thesis and the traumatic secret do exactly this. They not only explain why extreme religious experiences tend to occur in dangerous or traumatic circumstances and why they are so common (people suffer a lot). They also explain why the rest of us might find them unbelievable or impossible, particularly in the modern West where our lives are so privileged and relatively secure—because we have not sufficiently suffered, because we have not been cracked open.

Third, a very speculative but serious sidenote. I happen to think that the trigger of transcendence is often a traumatization of the left hemisphere of the brain, where the ego and language primarily reside: hence the trope of the secret beyond all speaking, beyond all language, beyond all stable sense of self. To enter the kingdom of "the right" one must often suffer and die "on the left." One must be *pushed* into the right. There is, in other words, a likely neuroanatomy of the mystical at work in these histories.

Consider this. Whitley once described in a radio interview we did together that after one of his visitor experiences he literally could not speak. He could hear himself speak, but it made no sense. He had temporarily lost the capacity to understand language. This, of course, is precisely what we would expect to happen were we to temporarily shut down the left hemisphere and move to or prioritize the right. This is also what happened to the neuroanatomist Jill Bolte Taylor during her own "stroke of insight" and subsequent experience of nirvana: she could hear herself and others speak, but everyone sounded in her own brain like golden retrievers, that is, they sounded like barking nonsense. As Taylor's stroke began and her consciousness began to shift over to her right brain, moreover, she witnessed her own hands as long and clawlike, which is precisely what people (including Whitley Strieber) often see when they see an "alien."[20]

If I might extend such inappropriate comparisons further still, it seems worth noting that the right hemisphere of the brain focuses on the eyes of the face and, for the most part, cannot process anything below them.[21] If, then, we were to imagine what a "right brain" encultured in the West might see were it temporarily empowered over the ordinary dominance of the left brain, we would expect to see a face with large eyes and almost no nose or mouth. Which is to say: we would expect to see an alien gray.

THE FUTURE (OF) RACE

The motifs of evolution, biological gods, and trauma invoke the critical issue of race for the contemporary intellectual. If the paranormal, moreover, most commonly appears in the margins, gaps, or fissures of a particular social system, one might expect that such phenomena would spike and flourish among marginalized communities and individuals. This, in fact, is what one finds, if only one looks.

As the above autobiographical narrative makes clear, I had given my professional life to the related categories of gender and sexuality. As I worked on the contemporary American materials in the new millennium, I was also working closely with my colleague Anthony Pinn, who works in the areas of black religion, theology, critical race theory, and humanism and whose central humanist notion of black religion as the search for complex subjectivity before the historical terrors of the Middle Passage, chattel slavery, lynching, and the absurd social conditions of being black in America echoes the "double consciousness" of the opening epigraph from W. E. B. Du Bois (a student, by the way, of William James).[22] Here is another form of the Human as Two, this time generated by gross social injustice, immeasurable human trauma over multiple generations, and the irreducible, Sisyphus-like absurdity of human existence performed and analyzed by the novels and essays of Albert Camus, one of Tony's favorite authors.

I was also helping to train a number of Tony's graduate students. One such former student, Stephen Finley, works on esoteric currents in African American religion and, in particular, ufological themes. These colleagues and this body of work in the department have influenced me deeply and will no doubt play key roles in my future thought. On a deeply personal level, these black esoteric currents also make me wonder again about that Night under Kali, whose very name, after all, means "Black." Was this some imaginal encounter with an occulted racial Other?

Or with some occulted shared "race"? As genetic anthropology has shown us, the human species first evolved in Africa. We are all, in some profound sense, Africans. We are primordially, ontologically black. And yet most of us are no longer such. We are, and we are not. This double history, yet another form of the Human as Two, encodes itself in the English expression "race," which can function as a marker of bodily characteristics (that is, as a term of difference) or as another expression for "species" (that is, as a term of sameness).

None of this, of course, is irrelevant to esoteric thought and experience and their various contemporary sci-fi expressions. There is in fact a large Afrofuturist literature that is rich in sci-fi esotericisms, including evolutionary, paraphysical and extraterrestrial ones.[23] There is an even larger and deeper history of African American magical practice, conjure, and esotericisms, which have barely been plumbed and seldom integrated into the scholarly discussions.[24] These currents are especially important to the Super Story, since any honest esotericism that attempts a long view and reaches down into deep historical (which is to say, evolutionary) questions will inevitably end up expressing both deep anxieties around "race" and positive hopes around some "future race."

This is patently, almost ridiculously, obvious in the ufological literatures and extraterrestrial esotericisms. Consider, for a start, the foundational American narrative of Barney and Betty Hill, the mixed-race couple whose remembered abduction event on the night of September 19–20, 1961, and reports of "lost time," large eyes and sexual experimentation entered the public culture through a series of psychiatric hypnosis sessions and John G. Fuller's subsequent *The Interrupted Journey* (1966). These trance narratives became the basis for the first major abduction story that "set the dials" on nearly every such account that followed in the US.

Numerous authors, including most recently the Canadian sociologist Eric Ouellet, have pointed to the likely social-emotional base of this first iconic case: the civil rights movement, in which both Barney and Betty were active, and the attending anxieties around being a mixed-race couple, particularly on Barney's part as a black man married to a white woman. Hence the sexual experimentation themes of the trance narratives that emerged from the hypnotic regressions and their implied theme of racial hybridity: semen was extracted from Barney; and Betty was given pregnancy and skin tests. Moreover, and perhaps most tellingly, the famous alien "gray" is named after its color: a combination of "black" and "white" (in a different but equally obvious racialized code, the large eyes of the gray are often described as "oriental").

Ouellet even sees Barney's drawing of the UFO he recalled in the regression therapy, with single red lights on the front and back, as a dreamlike transformation of the similarly lighted buses that were used by the Freedom Riders, civil rights activists who rode buses across the South in public protest of the racist segregation rules that declared where black people could sit on a bus. In essence, what he saw was a "flying bus," a Freedom Bus in the sky.[25]

None of this, please note, need look away from the multiple paranormal or mythical-physical dimensions of the historical events, including the strange magnetized marks on the Hills' car, the couple's earlier interest in and experiments with telepathy, or Betty's family's history of paranormal encounters.[26] Ouellet, for example, spends nearly as much time on the apparent "substantive spontaneous psi effects" of the events as on their racial symbolisms. Such a parasociological reading displays the classic both-and structure of the gnostic intellectual and not the simple either-or choices of the traditional rationalist.

And this may not have been the first black case in the history of the American UFO. Although we presently lack a clear textual trail and so cannot say for certain, one of the first American ufological traditions may well be the teachings of an important black religion: the Nation of Islam. As Stephen Finley has observed, the origins and secret teachings of the Nation appear to be related to various Shiite, masonic, Theosophical, esoteric, and science fiction currents.[27] At the center of these esoteric teachings spins what "every member of the Nation calls the 'Wheel' or the 'Mother Plane' or 'Mother Wheel.' "[28] The phrases go back to the founding prophet Master Fard Muhammad, who spoke

328 || CHAPTER 14

of a mysterious "Mother Wheel," "a destructive dreadful-looking plane that is made like a wheel in the sky today." It was described as "a half-mile, by a half-mile square" and as a "a humanly built planet."[29]

This extraordinary teaching of the Nation was then developed by Master Fard's successor the Honorable Elijah Muhammad, whose son Wallace in turn attempted to suppress it as part of "all this spiritual spookiness."[30] The teaching survived, though, and was professed again by the Honorable Minister Louis Farrakhan, who made the Wheel central to his mission and described his own dramatic encounter with it at a press conference on October 24, 1989, in an address entitled "The Great Announcement: The Final Warning." Here are a few lines from that press conference:

> In a tiny town in Mexico, called Tepotzlan, there is a mountain on the top of which is the ruines of a temple dedicated to Quetzalcoatl—the Christ-figure of Central and South America—a mountain which I have climbed several times. However, on the night of September 17, 1985, I was carried upon that mountain, in a vision, with a few friends of mine. As we reached the top of the mountain, a Wheel, or what you call an unidentified flying object, appeared at the side of the mountain and called to me to come up into the Wheel.[31]

Farrakhan goes on to describe how he was carried up into the Wheel by a beam of light and heard the voice of Honorable Elijah Muhammad speaking to him through a speaker. As the prophet spoke, Farrakhan saw a scroll that was "a projection of what was being written in my mind" (such beaming transports and mind-to-mind or telepathic communications are extremely common in UFO encounters). Such a vision is absolutely central to Farrakhan's sense of vocation and mission: "I am telling America that wherever I am the Wheel is!"[32]

As scholars like Michael Lieb and Finley have described these African American esoteric currents, the Mother Plane functions in the Nation of Islam in ways similar to how the divine "chariot" functions in the biblical book of Ezekiel and the later chariot mysticisms of Kabbalah: as an awesome mystical technology, as a shockingly real *spiritual thing*, revealed as a secret teaching to the prepared and the elect. In Lieb's powerful phrase again, these are the "new riders of the chariot." In Ezekiel, this technology mesmerizes, abducts and inspires the prophet Ezekiel. It also functions as an expression of the awesome military power of the Lord of Israel. In the Nation of Islam, the Mother Wheel or Mother Plane is a military weapon that floats above all earthly injustice, is directed against racial oppression and will eventually descend to destroy this unjust world and usher in a new millennium of black peace and flourishing (the FBI files on Elijah Muhammad give this destructive nature of the Mother Plane a good deal of attention[33]). It is also embedded in a disturbing anti-Semitism (particularly in the speeches of Minister Farrakhan) and an elaborate cosmology and mythology in which blackness is coded positively as divine, original, and cosmic, and whiteness is coded negatively and as a secondary creation (of a lower black god-scientist named Yakub or "Big Head") that is of "the devil." Such mythical referents shock, but they also give accurate and honest witness to what can only be called a centuries-long white terrorism waged on African Americans and their communities.

In a much more positive, if equally provocative direction, in the same Nation of Islam theology, God is a human being: Master Fard Muhammad. Here we have another deification of the human, what I would call a black superhumanism.

And the Nation is just the beginning. There is Prophet Yahweh: Seer of Yahweh, "who claims to be have seen UFOs and to have an intimate relationship with them, so much so that he can impart secret knowledge to others through his UFO Summoning School." There is the United Nuwaubian Nation of Moors, "whose religious narratives of alien beings and vehicles frame the ultimate religious narrative for their community." There are the UFO twins, "two African American women who claim to have been abducted by what they call the 'Galactics' and encountered beings who looked like 'black women.'" And on and on we could go, if only we would look and make these robustly positive black ufologies and evolutionary esotericisms part of the scholarly discourse.[34]

Why haven't we? As Finley describes the situation, scholars have yet to come to terms with the fact that for many African Americans, "UFOs are indispensable in their quests to make sense of the world." Finley pushes the point further, now into the the histories of West Africa, the Middle Passage, and the auction block of American chattel slavery:

> What I am arguing is that African Americans are descendants of alien abductees. Indeed, their ancestors on the continent of Africa encountered an alien presence from another world, who showed up in "ships" between the 16th and 19th centuries to abduct bodies and whisk them away to another world. In this new world, they became the alien presence, the other.

Such an alien presence of the abducted at the heart of American society took on deep religious significance, both for those who were abducted and those who did the abducting. Hence, in this reading at least, the haunting historical memories of chattel slavery in the spectral presence of the abducting alien "gray."

Finally, I want at least to mention in this context a rich contemporary lore around American Indian UFO sightings, which are commonly linked to traditional folklore around sky beings, star people, shamans, and spectral shapeshifters.[35] The Native American ufological lore is quite extensive, if also relatively untheorized and insufficiently analyzed. What should the professional scholar do with such indigenous comparative practices around the omnipresent UFO? And what to make of these particular ufological cosmologies and the ways that they both integrate and resist American colonialism and Western technology? Already in 1923, Charles Fort had compared those who were reporting "super-constructions" in the sky to "savages upon an island-beach" gazing out at three ships in the bay on October 12, 1492.[36] The modern American Indian ufologies reverse this dark galactic colonialism and interpret the ships in the sky as fantastically positive presences, as signs of the return of their ancestors, the star people.

INTRODUCING THE ESSAY

The following essay was originally commissioned for a special issue of the academic journal *Social Research* on the subject of "horrors." I then reused most of the material in *The Super Natural*, for a chapter called "Context in the Sky." I would add only one historical detail if I had it to write again, namely, that the Hudson Valley (the original home of both Charles Fort and Whitley Strieber's initial visitor encounters explored in the essay) sits on the eastern boundary of the famed "Burned-Over District" or what Joscelyn Godwin has more recently, and more appropriately, called the "Upstate Cauldron."[37] This is the geographical area of north-central New York state that generated so many new religious movements in the nineteenth century, from the angelic contact and golden plates of Joseph Smith and Mormonism to the community erotics or "free love" of John Humphrey Noyes and the Oneida community.

Better Horrors

That I am in direct mind-to-mind touch with extraterrestrial intelligence systems has
been obvious to me for some time, but what this means is not in any way obvious . . .
these are new words to describe ancient experiences. . . . Basically this is a religious
experience, but also it is more because we are no longer a religious world.

PHILIP K. DICK, LETTER TO CLAUDIA BUSH, NOVEMBER 26, 1974

No, the visitors may very well be real. Quite real. But what are they, and what in their
context does the word *real* actually mean? I do not think that this is a question that
will in the end admit itself to a linear and mechanistic answer.

WHITLEY STRIEBER, *COMMUNION*

REAL MONSTERS

I cannot watch horror movies. I do not read horror novels. And yet I am constantly drawn to thinking about horror. As a student of the history of religions,
how can I *not* be? How can I not think about the classic religious emotions of
fear, terror, and dread, about the hair-raising phenomenology of eeriness and
the uncanny, about the ghost, the possession, and the haunting, about the
centrality of death, dissociation, and dissolution in religious symbolism (and
experience), about the cosmic violences of comparative eschatology, and—we
cannot possibly avoid the fact—about the horrific spectacles of contemporary
religious terrorism? Clearly, as Greg Mogenson has put it recently, for whatever else deity is or is not, "God is a trauma."[38]

Historians of religion have long known, at least since Rudolf Otto's still
unsurpassed *The Idea of the Holy* (1917), that the experience of horror often
functions as a kind of potential or camouflaged numen. We have long known
that the holy and the horrific are cut from the same phenomenological cloth,
and that the experience of sacred terror can "flip over" into a whole range of
ecstatic and visionary experiences. Literary critics and historians have more

recently engaged horror from a somewhat different angle. Enter "monster theory," which looks at the narratives and images of the monster throughout Western history as a kind of recurring deconstruction and reconstruction of cultural and social categories. Here the monster is taken seriously, but only, as far as I can tell, as an unconscious Foucauldian discourse, Derridean deconstruction, or postmodern materialism. That may not be quite fair (and it certainly reveals my own intellectual frustrations), but it is not too far from the truth.

I am also, of course, deeply interested in discourses and deconstructions, but I want to take them much further. Are we willing, for example, to consider Derrida's striking late in life acceptance of telepathic phenomena, which, as he quite correctly noted, effectively "behead" us by demonstrating that consciousness is something "outside-the-subject" and not localized in a skull?[39] *There* is a deconstruction of the most radical sort.

Or, closer to the present essay, are we willing to listen to the scholar of religion Carl Raschke, who observed that that UFOs resemble "ultraterrestrial agents of cultural deconstruction," cognitive tricksters issuing from "outside the very matrix of space, time, and matter" with a mission "not to provide our civilization with a jeweled capstone to the grand edifice of secular science, but to undo the very architecture itself"?[40]

Or how about the American sci-fi master Philip K. Dick, who describes how he was radiated over a three-month period in the winter of 1974 by a plasmatic linguistic entity from the future, a cosmic Mind he called Valis (for Vast Active Living Intelligence System)? For the rest of his life, Dick was in awe of this revelation event as he struggled (for some eight thousand pages) to understand it. He never did. But in the process he came to see how we cannot understand "the deepest core of meaning at the ontological heart of reality," not because it is not there or because it is somehow intentionally "creating mystery," but because our neurological and conceptual filters are simply inadequate to its transtemporal reach. Like some immeasurable kabbalistic structure, all of reality is really made of letters, words, thoughts, in short, of a writing mind, but we only catch glimmers of this Logos, this Meaning of all meaning. As a result, we are not the writers but the written. "We are not the artists but the drawings."[41] And so we submit to the inherited scripts of our ancestors—so many fake worlds, unreal identities, and simulacra. Dick gave all of these constructions and discourses a name: the Black Iron Prison.

And what of *real* monsters? By "real," I do not mean to point to some future biological taxon. I do not think that we will someday shoot a Sasquatch or

net the Loch Ness Monster. By real, I mean quite simpl·
I mean "phenomenologically actual." I mean to remind
cluding many modern people, have experienced mᴄ
or as cultural "deconstructions," but as actual incarnate,
incarnate beings. It would be difficult to exaggerate just how w
tling, this monster literature can be. As a way of getting at this hiₜ
ness, here is a single example sure to offend pretty much everyone's inteli
tastes.[42]

Biochemist Colm A. Kelleher and investigative journalist George Knapp
have written about a monstrous presence that stalks a particular section of the
American Southwest. Enter the Skinwalker, so named after the local Navajo
folklore about a shape-shifting super-witch believed to inhabit this part of
the Utah wild. The whatever-it-is certainly shape-shifted its way around the
scientific team that Kelleher led, and this despite eight years (1996–2003) of
intensive, high-tech monitoring and testing. Kelleher and Knapp tell the story
in the aptly named *Hunt for the Skinwalker*. "It's as if," they write, "some cosmic puppet master had written a laundry list of every spooky phenomenon
of modern times and then unleashed them all in a single location, resulting
in a supernatural smorgasbord that no one could possibly believe, even less
understand."[43]

Indeed. The reader, from the very first page, confronts scene after scene
that could not have possibly happened, which happened. Among other (im)pos-
sibilities, we encounter: a giant (prehistoric?) gray wolf who trots out of the
trees in full daylight before multiple witnesses, tries to pull a screaming calf
through a fence, is shot multiple times at close range to no effect, and then
trots back into the trees, never to be seen again; prized cattle mutilated in the
fields with surgical precision; local Bigfoot sightings, often seen around UFOs
or even accompanying ufonauts; multiple UFO sightings in the surrounding
areas, one resembling a giant floating gray manta ray that may have been "a
creature or a craft," another estimated to be *five miles* across; an orange tear
or "tunnel" in the sky through which the rancher who owned the property
could see into another world and through which he watched a black triangular
craft fly; multiple basketball-sized, bright blue orbs filled with an incandescent blue liquid energy that cracked with static electricity and provoked a kind
of primordial terror in witnesses; beloved ranch dogs incinerated by a flying
orb into a pile of biological goo; weird magnetic anomalies; and an immense,
four-hundred-pound, six-foot-tall, black creature climbing out of a kind of
wormhole or tunnel of light in the sky.

ist such a panopoly of bizarrarie not to believe them. I am no fan of the stemology of belief. I list them here to immediately "monstrosize" this essay, hat is, to put it well outside any comfortable religious or rational episteme— including yours, and including mine. If you think that you have an adequate theory about what I am about to discuss, I would humbly but firmly suggest that you simply have not read far enough into this literature.

The religious episteme can only handle such historical narratives through the traditional strategies of literalization and demonization, and this despite the curious fact, in this case at least, that the Skinwalker displayed a stable moral sensibility, consistently distinguishing between the human and the nonhuman in its various violences and abuses. The demonization strategy also represents a dualistic and frankly naive understanding of the sacred, since it fails to treat the already noted fact that sometimes sacred terror "flips over" into profound religious experience: the demon becomes an angel. Exactly as Otto explained with his famous Latin sound-bite definition of the holy (as a *mysterium tremendum et fascinans*), the mystical reveals a kind of double nature in the history of religions—at once fascinating (*fascinans*) and terrifying (*tremendum*). A holy horror.

The rational or scientistic episteme is little better, and just as dualistic in its equally naive insistence on materialistic or mechanistic explanations. Indeed, the Skinwalker case could easily function as a moral tale (or just a bad joke) about the hopeless inadequacies of science and its objectivist epistemologies. The technology and scientific protocols of the NIDS team failed, utterly, to collect any definitive evidence (except for some magnetic anomalies), and this despite the indubitable fact that the members of the team witnessed many of the occurrences up close and personal. Tom Gorman, the former rancher (he sold the property after the thing, or things, haunted the crap out of him and his family), suspected strongly that the very presence of the scientific team provoked the presence into a cat-and-mouse game. Knapp has noted that it was this relational, intelligent aspect of the horror that was its most puzzling feature.[44]

But the historian of religions is not at all surprised by any of this. Quite the opposite. What the discipline, following Otto and Durkheim, calls the sacred is understood to be not a stable "thing" "out there," but a kind of living energetic presence, power, or effervescence interacting with(in) a particular individual or community. Hence its fundamentally paradoxical structure at once "inside" and "outside," at once "mental" and "material." Clearly, when we are dealing with the monster as a paradoxical manifestation of the sacred, then, we are not dealing with pure evil, simple destruction, or unmitigated chaos. Nor are we dealing with zoology. Nor are we dealing with ordinary fantasy, projection, a cultural discourse, or any other academically correct subjectivism or relativism. Since when does such a discourse carry away your livestock or a subjective projection melt your dog? Have you ever sold *your* dream ranch in fear of a construction?

I ask again, then. What are we to do with monsters, *real* monsters?

BETTER HORRORS

There can be no serious intellectual engagement with the monstrous sacred without encountering those human beings who have known such presences up close, either in the historical record or in person. This essay works out of the latter personal approach.

Whitley Strieber is a professional writer, mostly known for his horror and science fiction but also a prolific writer of nonfiction books as well. He is also arguably the twentieth century's most famous "abductee," due, largely, to a single dark and beautiful book, *Communion* (1987). The latter book, which is the focus of the present essay, ranges widely in time, indeed all the way back to his childhood in San Antonio in the 1950s and up to the book's present in the mid-1980s, but the central narrative of the text involves a series of overwhelming events that transpired on a single evening, that of December 26, 1985, while the Strieber family was vacationing in their secluded cabin in the Hudson Valley region.

Although Strieber clearly and consciously remembered a set of bizarre happenings earlier that October in the same cabin (including a powerful light outside and a loud explosion near his head) that heralded what would happen a few months later, Strieber remembered little of the events of December 26 when he awoke the next morning, except for the uncanny memory of a barn owl staring at him in the window during the night. But he knew that there was no barn owl (he checked the snowy window sill). Moreover, he felt extremely anxious, felt pain in the anal region, and quickly developed an infection on a finger. He wrote a haunting short story to "cope" with all of this the next day. Entitled simply "Pain," the story is about a prostitute named Janet O'Reilly who teaches the protagonist, a married man named Alex, that he is not the body, that "the cup is not the wine." Through Janet's instruction and physical tortures, Alex learns that pain "breaks down the barriers of ego, of personality, of false self. It separates us from ourselves and allows us to see deep."[45] This theme of trauma as transcendence would return in *Communion*, as we will soon see.

The author could not simply write out the pain, though. He sought medical and soon psychiatric help. Two hypnosis sessions followed on March 1 and 5, 1986, under the care of Dr. Donald F. Klein, Director of Research at the New York State Psychiatric Institute. Anne Strieber, who did not share the full scope of her husband's experiences but, like others, did experience various physical anomalies around them, also underwent a series of hypnosis sessions on March 13 and 21 under the care of another psychiatrist, Dr. Robert Naiman. The transcripts of these four hypnosis sessions, of a husband and a wife, form the heart of *Communion*.

Through these "trance texts," if I may call them that, a terrifying but fascinating story emerges. It involves different types of strange beings, including a "good army" of short and stalky troll-like blue creatures that carried Whitley off paralyzed and screaming, lifted him up above the trees, presumably to a waiting craft, and submitted him in an oddly cluttered and messy room to various disturbing medical procedures, including a needle inserted into his brain and an ugly instrument inserted into his anus, he assumed to collect fecal matter but that was also accompanied by an erection and ejaculation, with the semen collected into a little tube held by one of the willowy gray figures.[46] This "good army," which Strieber would relate to the *kobold* or underground troll folklore of Germany (etymologically related to the discovery of radioactive "cobalt" in German mines), appeared to be commanded by another figure, one more striking in appearance: a thin, almond-eyed, magnificent being whom Strieber related to as feminine. Her immense black eyes and humanoid face, painted by Ted Jacobs on the cover, was what, in effect, cemented the iconic form of the alien face in the public imagination in 1987, when the book hit the best-selling charts. Strieber has since observed that the actual being whom he encountered did not look as human as the cover painting, that she was less human than this. As we have seen, he would also wonder out loud whether the alien is how the living force of evolution appears to a conscious creature like us. Whatever or whoever she was, her image would endure in the public imagination.

Cover icon aside, Strieber studiously avoids or heavily qualifies the term "alien" in the text itself. He prefers to call the beings simply "the visitors," as it was not at all clear to him what they were or where they came from. He in fact entertains multiple hypotheses both in *Communion* and in a series of books that would quickly follow it. These included a striking hypothesis about a special "power within us" that can materialize its content in the physical environment (for example, anomalous lights outside the cabin, a loud explosion during the previous October, a UFO reported in a local newspaper around the December abduction, and different sightings of the visitors by friends in and around the cabin). They also included—in a very different direction—numerous reductive hypotheses, from neurological and psychological explanations, like temporal lobe seizures, to possible chemical or electromagnetic causes.

And he did not just speculate. Strieber had the temporal lobe tests done (negative), along with an EEG, a CAT scan of his brain, an MRI, and a battery of standard psychological tests too numerous to list or explain here. He also attempted to have an implant removed from his ear (positive: it crawled up further into his ear when a doctor attempted to surgically remove it[47]). He tested the water near his cabin for pesticides and the air in his basement for radon gas, and he wondered about the possible geomagnetic effects of the iron-laden subsurface of the area around his cabin. One is struck by the profound *physical* nature of Strieber's approach to all of this.

None of the easy causal explanations panned out, however. This is why Strieber eventually moved to more fluid, interactive models. He is very clear, for example, that what he experienced that night was partly a product of his own psyche, and that the visitors interacted with him through his emotional past and fears like some kind of bizarre team of occult therapists, complete with a kind of silver wand. This interactive nature of the events is all perfectly obvious to any careful reader of *Communion*.

I once witnessed Whitley speak to a group of academics whom I had convened at the Esalen Institute for a private symposium on the paranormal and popular culture. One evening, he explained to us that he was perfectly aware that his visionary experience of the visitors was deeply informed by the bad sci-fi B movies that he had seen in such numbers as a kid in the Cold War 1950s in southern Texas, but he was also perfectly aware that something else and more was behind these visionary displays. And then he went further. He said that, if it is in fact the case that the bad sci-fi films have shaped the reception, understanding, and even experience of the visitors, it follows that what we need to do now is make better science fiction movies so that future abduction experiences will be more positive and productive.

Strieber was, in effect, calling for "better horrors." That is, he was asking us, as a public culture now, to search for new ways to engage sacred terror more intelligently so that this horror might "flip over" more often into something not terrible but terrific, into a kind of profound mutuality and spiritual transformation that he calls "communion." This is the basic message of the present essay.

Strieber has paid a price for this subtle position that the visitors are real, that our experience of them is inevitably mediated through our own elaborate

338 || CHAPTER 14

historical, pop-cultural, political, psychological, and neurological filters, and
that it is our task now to deepen and even advance our relationship with
whatever-or-whoever-this-is. Such an open-ended, fiercely questioning both-
and appears to be as offensive to the pure rationalist as it is to the conservative
religious believer. The intellectual left and the media (including the animated
series "South Park") mocked him, and still mocks him. The religious right sent
death threats.

He is hardly alone in his strange experiences, of course. "There has been a
lot of scoffing directed at people who have been taken by the visitors," Strieber
observes. "It has been falsely claimed that their memories are a side effect of
hypnosis. This is not true. Most of them started with memories and under-
took hypnosis to attempt greater recall. Scoffing at them is as ugly as laughing
at rape victims."[48] The analogy is not another careless male feminist faux pas.
Many of the abductees, after all, have been women who have reported terrifying sexual encounters and even missing fetuses. Moreover, abductees of both
genders commonly report forced sexual acts, gestures, or visions suggestive of
hybrid children, the removal of semen and sexual fluids against their wills, and
extreme highly unusual states of erotic arousal. Indeed, the very first modern
abduction on record, that of the Brazilian farmer become lawyer Antonio Vila
Boas in 1957, already contained all these features. Strieber has also repeatedly described his abduction as a rape. When he went to see a doctor for the
multiple symptoms that developed immediately afterward, including pain in
the anal region, the doctor found perianal contusions and treated the case as a
potential crime scene. Again, not your typical "construction" or "discourse."

I share neither the demeanings of the intellectual left nor the demonizations
of the religious right. I am a historian of religions interested in comparative
erotic mystical literature. If *Communion* is not a piece of modern erotic mystical
literature, then I do not know what it is. I consider Whitley Strieber and his most
famous text to be, in effect, litmus tests for my field. If we cannot take this text
seriously, if we cannot exegete it in some satisfying fashion, if we cannot make
some sense of this man's honest descriptions of his traumatic-transcendent experiences, then we have no business trying to understand his spiritual ancestors
in the historical record. We either put up here, or we shut up there.

But how to put up? Strieber's corpus is immense, so there is no hope of offering some comprehensive reading. I will restrict myself to four very basic tasks:
(1) I will summarize Strieber's implicit theorization of terror in *Communion*;
(2) I will historically and geographically contextualize Strieber's abduction experiences; (3) I will struggle with Strieber's most difficult suggestion, namely,

that what he had encountered was another actual species; and, finally, (4) I will conclude with some thoughts on his central notion of "communion" as the final transformation of terror into a new state of consciousness that is not horrible but humorous, not fearful but joyful, not painful but loving, and finally cosmic.

THEORIZING TERROR IN *COMMUNION*

I think it is fair to say that Strieber's theory of fear or horror is built on a general psychoanalytic foundation. Strieber's theorization of terror is Freudian in the sense that it relies on the psychodynamics of repression, amnesia, and various dreamlike symbolic processes that transform the unthinkable or impossible into the thinkable and the possible, like barn owls or sci-fi scenarios. Hence Strieber's invocation of Freud's notion of screen memories. The basic idea here is that when the human mind encounters something too far outside its expectations or abilities to process, it will reflexively handle this impossible situation through repression, forgetting, and amnesia. It will self-censor. It will deny. It will shut down. Hence lines like this one: "Something was hideously wrong, so wrong that my mind went blank."[49] Let me add here that the later public rejections of the impossible event on rational or religious grounds—the media shamings, the hate mail, and the threats—function as further means of repression, censorship, and fear. They extend the horror and the internal censorship processes into the public sphere and, of course, make it all worse. They ensure that we will never really understand the horror or the holy. They make us spiritually dumb.

There is another way of saying this: if we take the entire phenomenon of *Communion* into account, we can see that terror and horror operate on multiple private and public levels, including and especially unconscious ones. The latter processes are abundantly demonstrated in the text through passages like the ones in which Strieber describes how, since the original events in October, he had been inexplicably searching under beds and in closets, he had bought a shotgun to defend the cabin, he had installed a burglar alarm system, and he had quite suddenly wanted to move the family back to Texas (and almost did). None of this behavior made any sense, unless one reads it through a kind of unconscious terror. The same model is implied again, of course, in the psychiatric practice of hypnosis—a practice that makes no sense at all without some model of the unconscious and its relative access through induced trance states.

But there is also a deeper dimension to fear in Strieber's *Communion*, and it involves what we can well call the religious. Exactly as Otto argued with respect to the horrific and the holy, extreme fear or terror in *Communion* can and does function as a kind of portal into other states of being. Extreme overwhelming fear alters Strieber's state of consciousness so radically that he becomes something, or someone, else. This is especially clear early on in the book when Strieber writes about the "extreme dread" of the December abduction: "the fear was so powerful that it seemed to make my personality completely evaporate. This was not a theoretical or even a mental experience, but something profoundly physical."[50] He was separated from himself "so completely that I had no way to filter my emotions or most immediate reactions, nor could my personality initiate anything. I was reduced to raw biological response."[51] Terror erases the ego and splits the human in two.

Finally, before we move on, it is very much worth noting that in Strieber's theorization fear is understood to flow both ways, if for different reasons. We might be afraid of the visitors because they are "impossible" or nonhuman, but they are also afraid of us because of our astonishing individuality and agency, which they, as a group, appear to lack and so fear. The beings he encountered seemed choreographed. They moved automatically, almost robotically, as if they were responding to some sort of communal or hive mind. We, on the other hand, operate as free individuals, and this scares them, makes us dangerous. "My impression is that these people, if they exist, are more than a little afraid of us. They are deeply afraid."[52]

A CONTEXT IN THE SKY: HUDSON VALLEY, 1909–1986

Academics are very good at insisting on the historical context and nature of every human experience, and rightly so. But many of us balk when that historical nature and those contexts offend our own metaphysical commitments, which are more often than not materialistic and secular in orientation. Then we are very good at ignoring both the history and the contexts, since they no longer support our assumptions about the world.

Consider the broad and immediate contexts of the events recounted in *Communion*. I am certain that many a reader of this essay has assumed that Strieber's experiences are anomalous or "anecdotal" (as the debunkers love to say), which is to say "meaningless," since specific meanings are always generated by some broader context, theory, discourse, or grammar. But this is simply not the case here, whether we look at the big picture or the little picture.

Take the big picture. The visitors, of course, possess *countless* precedents in the general history of religions. That is an understatement. I do not think it is too much of a simplification to suggest that the entire history of religions can be summed up this way: weird and fantastic super-beings from the sky come down to interact with human beings, provide them with cultural and techno-logical knowledge, guide them, demand their submission and obedience, have sex with them (often forcefully), and generally terrorize, awe, baffle, and inspire them. This history of religions is the broadest context and grammar of Strie-ber's *Communion*. Nothing anomalous or meaningless there, even if it is all, of course, impossible in *our* modern secular register and assumptions, them-selves all very, very recent and, well, quite anomalous in the human record.

The immediate temporal and spatial contexts of Strieber's *Communion* work similarly against any anecdotal reading. The geographical locale of Strieber's ab-duction experience, the Hudson Valley region, is a well-known hot spot for UFO activity throughout the twentieth century. *Pace* the easy social construc-tivisms, these "things seen in the sky" cannot be accurately read as a piece of Cold War paranoia or pulp fiction projection (although the language of the UFO can be: it originated in the early 1950s in a military context and was probably first coined by an air force captain). The first major "UFO flap" in the US was the Airship Mystery of 1896–97, during which hundreds of sightings of craft fly-ing over major US cities, often with spotlights or "lanterns" no less, were re-ported in the newspapers from California to New York. An airship, for example, floated over San Antonio in May of 1897 and must have flown over Strieber's great-grandmother's house.[53] This was six years before the Wright Brothers managed to get their first dangerous contraption a few feet off the ground in Kittyhawk, North Carolina.

Another major wave of sightings occurred in 1909–10, this time centered in the Hudson Valley region. On July 26, 1909, the *Newburgh Daily Journal* ran this headline: "'Air Ship' Is Seen Again from Washington Heights: She Was Swooping: Too Dark, It Is Said, to Discern Outlines of the 'Ship.'" And here is what *The Sun* of New York City reported a few days later, on August 1: "A mysterious airship which flies only at night is causing considerable excite-ment and keeping the people of Orange county residing between Goshen and Newburgh up nights in their efforts to get a look at it." And here is my favorite piece, under the headline "Human Volcano Erupts," from the *Goshan Demo-crat* of four days later, on August 5:

Otto Pushman, Newburgh's champion cusser, had been sent to jail for thirty days for using sulphurous language. During the nocturnal hours of Tuesday he was discovered on Grand street looking for that ding-blasted airship that the Newburgh papers tell about and cursing fervently at the blanket-blanked moon.[54]

As this precious piece reveals and as Linda Zimmerman emphasizes through an analysis of other newspaper pieces from the same year (one of which featured mocking cartoons and an invocation of Santa Claus), one can see "all the elements of denials, ridiculous excuses, hoaxers, and belittled witnesses already in place, more than a hundred years ago!"[55]

Zimmerman has written two books tracing the UFO phenomenon in the Hudson Valley region from 1909 to the present.[56] What she finds is a dizzying array of apparent technological and patently paranormal phenomena not unlike those we saw in my opening Skinwalker provocations: "airships" and later "spaceships" in the sky ranging from baseball-size glowing balls to huge floating Vs; an immense circular metallic craft with colored lights and symbols that hovered just above the heads of a mother and her twelve-year-old son close enough to hit with a rock; two early abduction reports (from 1929 and 1937) involving things like time standing still, floating humanoids in "diving suits," and a sense of being in two worlds at once; encounters that result in the witnesses developing various psychical capacities, particularly telepathy and precognition (an extremely common pattern in such encounters to this day); a bizarre vision of two immense "wheels" on their side (vaguely reminiscent of Ezekiel's "wheels" and also reported as a spinning "ferris wheel" in the 1980s); an eyeball-to-eyeball encounter with a long-necked green humanoid flying in a circular craft right beside a traveling car; a large pile of sand blown to smithereens with circular landing marks burned into the cement (with attending photographs); UFOs surrounded by helicopters; and numerous stories of scared dogs, cats, and birds. The latter detail is particularly interesting, as it strongly suggests that these events had some kind of biological or physical existence outside the psyches of the witnesses. I think an entire book could easily be written on UFOs and our canine companions.

Moreover, and worse yet for the anecdotal thesis, it was the 1980s that saw the strongest spike in reports of sightings and up-close encounters in the Hudson Valley. The Northwestern University astronomer and air force scientific consultant J. Allen Hynek, the researcher Philip J. Imbrogno, and the journalist Bob Pratt dedicated an entire volume to this subject, with a later edition (after Hynek's death) incorporating some 7,046 reported cases in the Hudson Valley from 1982 to 1995.[57] Particularly important here, since it temporally wraps around the Strieber case, is the three-year flap—beginning on New Year's Eve, 1982, and petering out throughout 1986—that featured something that came to be known as the "Westchester boomerang," basically an immense triangular-shaped craft repeatedly floating over the region. The thing was described variously as "two or three football fields long," "as large as a new cruise ship," as "a flying city," and like "something out of the movie *Close Encounters of the Third Kind.*"[58] It could appear and disappear instantly, vanishing, as one witness put it, "like the Cheshire Cat's smile."[59] It was often described as completely silent. Or in uncanny religious terms: "It just hung there motionless in the sky. It was like seeing a ghost."[60] Squadrons of helicopters were seen in the night skies during some of these sightings, as well as unidentified planes flying in formation, which the witnesses believed were sent up by the military to confuse the matter and provide a bogus explanation to the public.[61] The public was not tricked, or amused.

To underline, in bold red ink, these stable historical patterns, it is worth noting that a very similar case involving a triangular craft occurred in Belgium in 1980 and would occur again, in the summer of 1997, this time over Phoenix. The latter single-night event was featured on the cover of *USA Today*, complete with an artistic rendering of the immense carpenter-square-shaped craft that was witnessed by hundreds, if not thousands, of citizens.[62] A series of flares were dropped near the city an hour *after* the thing floated by, again, many believe, to confuse and provide an easy debunking strategy. The citizens were now openly pissed. Many were now furious with their officials and their gross mishandling and denial of the situation. They knew what they saw, and they knew they were being lied to. Governor Fife Symington attracted much of the wrath. He made fun of the crisis during a press conference, going so far as to walk in a hand-cuffed man in an alien suit. After he was out of office, Symington publicly apologized for his actions, even admitting that he too had seen "a craft of unknown origin" that could not have been flares.[63] This is all a matter of the historical record.

After two books on the Hudson Valley material, Zimmerman's conclusion seems reasonable enough: the Hudson Valley region is "Abduction Alley." And it was *here* that Whitley Strieber had his own abduction experiences over the Christmas holidays of 1985, right smack in the middle of the most active decade of the twentieth century and after at least seventy-six years of similar encounters in the same area. Such a cultural and geographical context does not explain these experiences or offer us any definitive hermeneutic, of course, but it certainly dispels any notion that Strieber must be a kook, or that his honest descriptions and dramatic sufferings can somehow be brushed aside as lacking any meaningful context, as "anecdotal" or "anomalous." They were in historical and contextual fact nothing of the sort.

A STRUCTURE IN THE AIR: THE EARTH-FARM AND THE QUESTION OF OTHER SPECIES

There is one other thing to say about the Hudson Valley context, and it is a biggy in my opinion. It is obvious enough, but no one, to my knowledge, has noted it yet. It is this. Albany, New York, was the birthplace and childhood home of the man who did more than *anyone* to shape the American paranormal: Charles Fort. I have written extensively about Fort elsewhere. Here it is enough to observe that it was Fort who, in four weird and wonderful books between 1919 and 1932 (*The Book of the Damned, New Lands, Lo!,* and *Wild Talents*), first laid down the paradoxical, both-and, real-unreal, mental-material nature of paranormal phenomena, an epistemological structure he named Intermediatism and set against the epistemologies of belief, which he called the Dominant of Religion, and of causal explanation, which he called the Dominant of Science (a "Dominant" for Fort was very close to what Foucault would much later call an "episteme"). It was Fort again who began to speculate about the meaning and purpose of what he called "super-constructions in the sky." It was Fort's speculations that were picked up by the pulp fiction subculture of the 1930s and 1940s, which in turn morphed into modern science fiction literature in the 1950s and 1960s. Fort is the father of all of this.

This strange little man sat in the New York Public Library every weekday afternoon, reading every newspaper and journal in English or French back to 1800 (he had to stop somewhere). He was looking for what he called "the damned," that is, things that happen all the time and appear in the papers but then are immediately forgotten the next day, or ridiculed by the religious and scientific authorities. He found plenty, including, of course, the extensively documented Airship Mystery of 1896–97 and the Hudson Valley wave of 1909–10.

Fort considered some very entertaining, and occasionally very dark, possibilities with respect to all of this. For example, like some future postcolonialist theorist, he often invoked the experience of the Native Americans around 1492, when they first witnessed those immense anomalous ships floating in the bays. It would not go well for them, Fort noted. Then he got darker (and weirder). Earth may not be a "new land" or a galactic colony. It might be a farm. This would certainly explain why the visitors do not establish any open contact or attempt communication with us. Why should they?

Would we, if we could, educate and sophisticate pigs, geese, cattle?

Would it be wise to establish diplomatic relation with the hen that now functions, satisfied with mere sense of achievement by way of compensation?
I think we're property.[64]

This dark thought of a kind of seeding or alien husbandry would have a
long and rich history in the later science fiction, of course, up to and including
Ridley Scott's recent *Prometheus* (2012). But it is not just a sci-fi notion. Francis Crick and Leslie Orgel seriously suggested something similar with a paper
on the "panspermia" thesis, with life on earth the result of some extraterrestrial seeding project.[65] And none other than William James had advanced a
more domestic, less sci-fi version in a related context, that of the spirit world
suggested by his own extensive psychical research with mediums. An important sidenote: the dead are often seen within abduction events (another clear
clue that we are not dealing with simple extraterrestrials here), including the
abductions reported by Whitley and those studied by Anne in the avalanche of
letters that came pouring in, for awhile some ten thousand each week (Strieber, assuming a few dozen responses, had included his address in the back of
the book). More specifically, James wondered if our relationship to the spirit
world was not like that our pets have in relationship to our world. He wrote
the following stunning lines in *A Pluralistic Universe*:

> In spite of rationalism's disdain for the particular, the personal, and the un-
> wholesome [the modern debunker's "anecdotal"], the drift of all the evidence
> we have seems to me to sweep us very strongly towards the belief in some form
> of superhuman life with which we may, unknown to ourselves, be co-conscious.
> We may be in the universe as dogs and cats are in our libraries, seeing the books
> and hearing the conversation, but having no inkling of the meaning of it all.[66]

Such a "superhuman life" is precisely what Fort was writing about. Hence
his affection for the prefix super-, which he attached to pretty much everything: super-constructions, super-vehicles, super-mind, super-imagination,
super-religion, super-sociology. Hence also his extensive focus on the "wild
talents" of paranormal people. Although this is pure speculation on my part,
I cannot help but wonder if behind (or above) all of this super-writing floated
some personal sighting in those haunted Hudson Valley skies, or even some
private "abduction" experience. Charles Fort certainly would have not been

the first to see things in that sky or experience such an encounter in that haunted valley. Nor would he be the last.

This is all highly relevant to our present subject, since much of Strieber's speculations about the meaning of his own experiences is clearly "Fortean" in its both-and, paradoxical structure. This is especially evident in the last chapter of *Communion*, entitled "A Structure in the Air: Science, History, and Secret Knowledge," and in Strieber's new preface to the 2008 edition. It is here that Strieber develops a radically interactive model of the visitor phenomenon. I have written about this model elsewhere. Here it is enough to flag one central aspect of it.

By far, the most difficult aspect of Strieber's "structure in the air," for a traditional academic anyway, is his suggestion that these experiences might represent an encounter with other actual species, invisible life-forms existing in some other dimension of the natural world that overlaps with ours and whose occasional rupture into our dimension is always mediated by our cultural imagination. This, of course, is not simply a theory about the visitors. It is a radical, and deeply critical, theory of religion as well, since it implies that these invisible life-forms have been interacting with us for millennia under various mythical forms that we have traditionally (mis)framed in supernatural terms. In Strieber's elegant phrase, it appears that the visitors "were somehow trying to hide themselves in our folklore."[67]

Others had suggested something similar and in very sophisticated forms, including John Keel and Jacques Vallée in the late 1960s and early 1970s. But there is something more "physical" or "biological" about Strieber's suggestions, something that disturbs the humanist instinct to turn everything into a text or a discourse. Here is how he put the matter in the 2008 preface to *Communion*: "But the visitors are not only real and here. In fact, I don't think they are visitors at all. I think that the truth is that we are embedded in their world in the same way that animal species are embedded in ours. It was hard to accept, but as I got to know some of them, I began to see that their relationship to us was quite similar to ours with, say, chimpanzees."[68]

Shades of Fort's pigs on the farm and James's cat in the library.

Real monsters.

FROM *BODY TERROR* TO *COMMUNION*

Almost. As we have seen, real monsters are not always really monsters, and the demon can quickly turn into an angel. This in fact is the deepest and final message of *Communion*. The book is ultimately not about fear, not about monsters, extraterrestrials, or spaceships. It is about the nature of the human soul and its mutations, not as a metaphor or some abstract spiritual process, but as an actual physical, perhaps electromagnetic, and certainly perfectly historical event.

Strieber's central concept of communion as transformation is fundamentally dialogical and interactive.[69] It is advanced through multiple frames, including that of the triad or triangle in the history of mythology and the epistemological structure of quantum physics, which, as has been amply noted by the physicists and enthusiasts alike, has reintroduced consciousness back into the scientific picture in dramatic and baffling ways that we have yet to understand. Strieber takes this interactive model very far, going so far as to suggest that the visitors may rely on our beliefs to appear. "Thus the corridor into our world could in a very true sense be through our own minds."[70] Strieber is not after simple belief here. He is not a fan of the contactee "eager to see the phenomenon as a dimensionless cartoon of space friends." He is after something much more complex and interesting. Here is how he ends the book, with another version of that call with which I began this essay, the call to create a more sophisticated public culture so that we might have better private encounter experiences. Note that there is no stable subject or object here. There is a communion that brings both subject and object, as potential species, into actualization:

> The visitor experience may be our first true quantum discovery in the large-scale world. The very act of observing it may be creating it as a concrete actuality, with sense, definition, and a consciousness of its own. And perhaps, in their world, the visitors are working as hard to create us. Truly, such an act of mutual insight and courage would be communion. . . . Who knows, maybe really skilled observation and genuine insight will cause the visitor to come bursting to the surface shaking like coelacanths in a net.[71]

There is something else to say here. Although I have never seen anyone comment on this feature of *Communion*, the book is also clearly about joy, humor, longing, and love. It is extraordinary how the motifs of joy and humor run all the way through the text, like a tiny smiling thread. Strieber, for example, notes humor in the feminine being as she teases him with the message that he is "the chosen one," a message he rejects as ridiculous. In other places, he reflects on her "subtly humorous face" and the happiness, even "jollity," of the beings. In one of his hypnosis sessions, he describes the activity of one of the creatures as "kind of a joke." In another hypnotized exchange, he describes the creatures as "impish." And, toward the end of the book, he reflects on their "prankster" quality, linking this in turn, quite correctly, to "our own mystical literature."[72]

Both this mutual co-creation and this joy are encoded, if not explained, in the book's very first word—its main title. Here is how that little one-word poem came about. Toward the end of the book, Strieber relates in detail the transcripts of Anne's own hypnosis sessions and reflects on the "hidden communion" that the couple felt in their marriage through this entire ordeal. The concept of communion, in other words, is built on a steadfast marriage and is a conjugal one at heart, which is to say that it is also sometimes a subtly, or not so subtly, sexual one.[73]

Just after reflecting on the conjugal context of the abduction events, Strieber describes an exchange that he and Anne had in bed sometime in April of 1986. Whitley was explaining to Anne how he wanted to title his new book *Body Terror*, since that was what he had experienced on the night of December 26. But Anne would have none of it.

> Suddenly she said in a strange basso profundo voice: "The book must not frighten people. You should call it *Communion*, because that's what it's about." I looked over at her intending to say why I thought my title was better, and saw that she was totally asleep. Then I realized where I have heard that voice before. I went to my wife and looked down at her sleeping form, my mind full of question and wonder.[74]

Anne thus "channeled" Whitley's most famous book title. This scene speaks volumes about the centrality of their marriage in the whole *Communion* phenomenon. It is a key feature of this hidden communion that Anne did not experience or share in any direct way in Whitley's abduction experiences but rather provided an emotional support system for him and the family unit. In her own hypnotic and generous voice, "Whitley's supposed to go. They came for Whitley."[75]

2017 POSTSCRIPTS

Since writing this essay, I have interacted with Whitley on many levels, including the writing of our book *The Super Natural* and the very difficult death of Anne from brain cancer in August of 2015. I attended the memorial outside of San Antonio on a family ranch. It was the only funeral or memorial I have been to, *ever*, where the formal ritual and the readings focused on personal religious experiences: Whitley spoke openly about the visitors, and one of the readings was Anne's description of a near-death experience that she went through years before she finally passed. Whitley since then has been actively working with Anne toward a book on the nature of the soul. Numerous communications have occurred, from striking synchronicities involving other individuals to deeply meaningful dreams that heal and reveal.

Whitley and I were together again here in Houston in October of the same year. I casually asked him whether he thought the poltergeist phenomena of the early *Communion* manifestations were a function of the cabin or the people in it. He did not hestitate to answer: "It was Anne."

He then told me a bizarre story (I am now used to these). Shortly after Anne and he had gotten married and had moved into an apartment building in New York City, he witnessed a corpse sliding across a hallway of their apartment building—a scene right out of a horror movie. He immediately told Anne about it. She simply took it in stride, as if he were telling her about the mailman. Her response was the same to many of the strange happenings that showed up in their lives. The point of the story, I took it, was this: the spectral phenomena began with Anne, spiked around her, and were, in some sense, about her.[76]

* * * *

Later that same fall, I was engaging in a conversation with Whitley and Jacques Vallée about plasmas in the British *Condign Report*, an official government document that describes plasmas "unknown to science" as a likely influence behind UFO sightings. Anne, recall, had just passed away earlier that same late summer. In the midst of that exchange, Whitley wrote this:

Whitley Strieber
to: Jeff Kripal
cc: Jacques Vallée
Re: Old Air Force document from 1968

Historically, "light beings" and glowing orbs are far more important
than any sort of mechanical-appearing machines. Ezekiel's Wheel was
not nearly as culturally potent as the glowing angel that Mohammed
encountered, or the ball or flash of light that so excited Paul.

In my own life, plasmas, in the form of balls of light have been
quite important. Something that was very obviously a plasma caused

a great deal of suffering and upset in my family as well. This was a violet-purple ball of light that appeared late one night in our living room. I could see a glow coming up from below and ran to look over the balcony above the room. In it I saw the plasma hanging in the air with one of our cats creeping toward it as if she planned to sniff it. As I ran back into the bedroom to get my camera, there was a flash of light that briefly filled the house. The plasma had exploded, apparently right in the cat's face. The next morning, the cat came wobbling down the hall yowling. She had visible tumors in both eyes that were the same color as the plasma. She had to be put down.

A part of Anne's tumor was a gliosarcoma, which is associated almost exclusively with radiation exposure, I am haunted by that incident. So when I saw the discussion of plasmas in the *Condign Report*, I was inclined to take it quite seriously.

Whitley

Meum

> I can think of Jesus only as seated on the wine [cup]—and defecating. And in
> that moment I know that he is God. . . . God—urinating by a fence or wiping
> his sweat. Is this blasphemy? I can't believe it is. God can do this, and not give
> a damn, because he is not bound by anything. . . . Christianity fulfills to the
> highest degree the paradox that has obsessed man since prehistory—of the
> coincidence of the All with a fragment.
>
> MIRCEA ELIADE, *THE PORTUGAL JOURNAL*

Looking back on all of this—from my adolescent dumbbells in the basement and superhero comics in the closet, through my pious suppression
of sexuality and obsessive fasting to become a saint, to my later intellectual interests in erotic mystics and paranormal mutants—I can see
now that I have long been fascinated with "religion" not primarily as a
set of beliefs, a social institution, or a coded political ideology. Others
have done that work, and marvelously so. I have been more interested
in the history of religions for what these literatures and practices can tell
us about *what a human being might yet become.*

I can also better see the original religious inspirations of my thought.
Nowhere are these Origins more apparent than in my recurrent invocation of the Human as Two. I can see now that the secret body sketched
in these pages, particularly in its double insistence on radical immanence and real transcendence, can be understood—there is no better
way to say it—as a kind of Christology of Comparison. Human nature
here, in potential experience if not in actual ontological fact (and certainly not in daily experience), is at once "fully human" and "fully divine,"
to employ the traditional Christian theological expression—"the coincidence of the All with a fragment," to use Eliade's expression, in perfect
sync with the filter thesis.

I am speaking mythically again, of course. I am also speaking hereti-
cally. This is hardly an orthodox position. It does not fetishize a first-
century Jewish wonder worker. I did not arrive at such a double model
through Greek philosophical categories, an obedient submission to religious authority, and an exclusive focus on the Jewish and Christian scriptures. I arrived at this Christology of Comparison through a lifetime of
reading comparative mystical literature from the New Testament and

Nag Hammadi library, through North American guru traditions and the human potential movement, to the parapsychological and ufological literatures. I arrived at it through a long early meditation on the double mystico-erotic nature of Ramakrishna as an *avatara* or Descent of God, the astonishing academic freedoms of the modern research university, up-close and personal encounters with living experiencers or real-world "mutants," and a model of the brain-mind relationship derived from some speculative but increasingly plausible currents within the philosophy of mind.

Certainly it is no accident that, from the opening pages of *Kālī's Child* to the final pages of *Secret Body*, I have been returning to the comparative theme of human deification. My rhetorical trope of the Human as Two has allowed me to take such experiences and claims seriously (as likely manifestations of a universally present cosmic mind), without absolutizing the social ego or person in any single historical instance of such an event (since every person is a receiver or egoic enactment of such mind and *no one* is its producer). I want to make the believer anxious here. Such experiences of human deification or cosmic mind, after all, are not restricted to any culture or religion. They are before and beyond *any* particular religion. But I also want to provoke the nonbeliever. Such experiences of human deification or cosmic mind, after all, are real historical events, and they are sometimes so impactful that they end up shaping the path of entire civilizations by becoming encoded in and as the religions and their countless images of "God."

In a similar autobiographical spirit, I also realize now that there is a particular interpretive principle in New Testament criticism that I first learned in the seminary and that I have been following ever since—the criterion of embarrassment. New Testament critics use the criterion of embarrassment to make good guesses about which passages in the gospels may go back to the actual sayings of the historical Jesus, as opposed to the later faith statements of the early Christian communities, which composed, redacted, and preserved these texts for their own reasons. The logic is a simple one: if the saying would have been embarrassing to the Christian community (say, the one where Jesus encourages his closest male disciples to castrate themselves for the kingdom of heaven), it is probably authentic, that is, the historical Jesus likely said it. Why else would the community feel compelled to remember and record something so outrageous and so problematic?

I certainly followed the criterion of embarrassment in *Kālī's Child*. Indeed, the entire book homes in on precisely those "secret talk" passages that so embarrassed the early Ramakrishna community that they subsequently censored or simply erased them in their translation practices (and continue to erase and deny them by, among other things, demeaning me). But I followed the same criterion again, I realize now, with the paranormal literatures. These, after all, are ultimate embarrassments to good reason *and* good faith. They are so often trickster-like, ridiculous. And that, I have argued in too many words, is why these reports are so often likely authentic, why they probably point to "what really happened" (in the sense of "what was phenomenally experienced or seen"), and why no adequate history of religions can afford to ignore them. Here is my own eccentric version of Tertullian's *Credo quia absurdum*, "I believe because it is absurd."

And so the new comparativism proposed here homes in on the most extreme, embarrassing, and absurd data of the history of religions. The gospels are hardly unique. What, after all, is a miraculous healing, a resurrected body, or a little walking on the water when we have countless cases of similar impossibilities pretty much everywhere we choose to look? Consider the literature on the miraculous or spontaneous cure, or, for that matter, on the modern placebo effect. Consider the historical portfolios of twentieth-century bilocating individuals (yet another kind of Double), like Padre Pio and Mère Yvonne-Aimée de Jésus.[1] And—if the walking on water is what you want—consider an embarrassingly well-documented historical case of actual levitation in the Italian Franciscan priest and friar Joseph of Cupertino.[2] We do not even need to deny the resurrection appearances, which we would see are as common today as they were in first-century Palestine, if we would but take the time to read the literature on physical apparitions of dead loved ones (or just talk to widows who continue to report them). The conclusion is a simple one: to encounter the extraordinary in the present is to take the extraordinary much more seriously in the past, which is not to say naively or literally.

None of this, moreover, need surrender an iota of the power and precision of critical reason, of textual analysis or, if we stick to the case of early Christianity for a moment longer, of contemporary New Testament criticism. Quite the contrary, the same from-the-present-to-the-past method—what I will call in our next chapter the future of the past (gnomon 19)—is actually part of that same intellectual history. At the beginning of the discipline was David Friedrich Strauss (1808–1874), the great nineteenth-century biblical critic who held fast to most of his scandalous conclusions about the historical Jesus but revoked his own simple denial of the miraculous and adopted a "cosmic religion" of evolution when he encountered various occult phenomena through his close-up interactions with a living medium.[3] Here is yet another evolutionary esotericism, at the very beginning of the discipline no less.

A similar move, now enriched by a century and a half of scholarship, can be seen today in the New Testament critic Dale Allison, particularly in his essay "Resurrecting Jesus," in which he destabilizes modern certainties by pointing out the profound resonances between heavily documented modern parapsychological phenomena and the resurrection appearances of the gospels.[4] Similar insights can be seen again in Bertrand Méheust's recent study of Jesus in the comparative light of hagiography and the psychical research tradition, especially the French *métapsychique* school. Méheust moves between and beyond both Christian dogma and rationalist denial in order to see Jesus as a conflicted Jewish thaumaturge, comparable to modern mediums and psychics, like Daniel Dunglas Home and Uri Geller. For Méheust, Jesus "was inhabited by a sense of an Other, of a Source, of a Presence . . . whom he called the Father," but who was finally "an abyss to himself."

Accordingly, Jesus hardly knew himself in some clear and unequivocal way. Rather, he came to, or co-constructed, his own self-understanding through the abiding sense of this powerful Presence through the sacred narratives of Jewish scripture, ethnic memory, and colonial suffering, through the efficacy of his magical works of healing and clairvoyance, and in the mirror of his followers' answers to his own honest question: "Who do you say that I am?" In this reading, at least, Jesus was not asking a question for which he already had the answer. He was co-constructing his identity through the answers of his disciples (and now readers). Ramakrishna does the same in the *Kathamrita*, as I pointed out in "Secret Talk." Like Ramakrishna, it appears that Jesus did not know the limits or boundaries of his own role and identity. He was creating it as he went along. With his disciples, he was reading the "signs" in order to understand "the enigma that was himself."[5] Like so many other historical figures treated in these pages, this Jesus experienced himself as Two.

I dwell on the deified Jewish thaumaturge here at the end not to conclude with a settled faith (I possess none), but to acknowledge and reflect on the religious origins and initial inspirations of my thinking. It
is simply the case that these are inspirations that I can see much more
clearly at fifty-five than I could at thirty-five.

Secret Body, as many a reader has no doubt realized by now, is a free
translation of the Latin expression *corpus mysticum*. This is a technical
phrase taken directly from Roman Catholic ecclesiology and sacramental theology in which I was trained in the seminary by my monastic mentors. Here the "mystical body" refers to both the universal community of
believers, the Church, and the real presence of Christ in the bread and
wine of the Eucharist.

It was the latter notion that blew my young adult mind. *Hoc est enim
corpus meum*. "This is my body." The flesh and fluids of the man-god
consumed in a piece of bread and a splash of wine. I have yet to encounter a more outrageous expression of . . . of *what*? Human deification?
Oral erotic consumption? Human sacrifice and spiritual cannibalism?
Pure unadulterated pantheism? The All in a fragment? It is difficult to
know what the historical Jesus intended when he first allegedly uttered
these scandalous words, probably in the context of a traditional Jewish
seder or Passover meal on the night before his arrest and death.

Whatever he intended, it seems fairly clear that he was at once drawing on his own rich Jewish heritage and turning that heritage upside
down and inside out so that it could express something of his own desires and personal sense of divinity, which, as I have argued throughout
my work, could not be fit into the traditional structures of his own rab-
binic Judaism (or our own conservative Christianities today).

In a similar spirit, I have consciously employed a eucharistic allusion
here to shape and guide these pages, not to reproduce or push my own
relative religious heritage, but to openly acknowledge those religious
roots and to emphasize the ways that my writing practice has always
been responding to a profound sense of *not* fitting into the psychosexual
patterns of this particular tradition and its central ritual expression of
secretly communing with a beautiful man-god over a love-meal. That
has never really worked for me. Hence my writing of *hoc corpus mysticum meum*, this secret body that is secret precisely because it does not
and cannot fit in—because it is mine (*meum*) and not his.

15

The New Comparativism

What It Is and How to Do It

Not only are [many neuroscientists and philosophers of mind] ignoring the progress
in fundamental physics, they are often explicit about it. They'll say openly that quantum physics is not relevant to the aspects of brain function that are causally involved
in consciousness. They are certain that it's got to be classical properties of neural activity, which exist independent of any observers: spiking rates, connections strengths
at synapses, perhaps dynamical properties as well. These are all very classical notions
under Newtonian physics, where time is absolute and objects exist absolutely. And
then [neuroscientists] are mystified as to why they don't make progress. They don't
avail themselves of the incredible insights and breakthroughs that physics has made.
Those insights are out there for us to use, and yet my field says, "We'll stick with
Newton, thank you. We'll stay 300 years behind in our physics."

DONALD D. HOFFMAN, "THE CASE AGAINST REALITY,"

ATLANTIC, APRIL 25, 2016

A few years ago, I stumbled upon the secret criterion of truth in the humanities. Do you want to hear it? Here it is: "If a truth is to be declared in the humanities, it must meet one criterion: it must be depressing."

Try it out. My bet is that if you say something that is deconstructive, reductive, or just simply negative, you might well be challenged, but you will
also be heard. If, on the other hand, you are foolish enough to say something
constructive, positive, even, God forbid, cosmic, you will almost certainly be
labeled a dilettante, an "essentialist," perhaps "pseudoscientific." Maybe, if you
are lucky like me, you will even become a promoter of "New Age woo-woo."
Go ahead. Try it.

I am certain that I will be misrepresented here, so let me be clear. Such an
observation does not obviate the need for critical analysis, deconstruction, or
flat-out reductionism. Much less does it seek to ignore or downplay in any way
the strong "prophetic" strands in the humanities that I emphasized above and
that home in on all those forms of social oppression and injustice via the categories of race, class, gender, and colonialism. It simply observes what I take

to be a very strong professional fact: it is nearly impossible to say anything positive or constructive in the humanities today.

Alas, it is not only the case that humanists are depressing. They are also boring. Louis Menand offered a most potent, and humorous, observation about this.[1] He observed that humanists have surrendered the big ideas to the physicists, who can say any crazy damned thing they want and get away with it. The physicists go on and on about Big Bangs, ghost universes, a multiverse, multiple dimensions, entangled telepathic particles, God particles, nonlocality, retrocausation, even tiny invisible "strings" for which they haven't the slightest empirical evidence. The wilder, the better, it seems.

And us? We allergically avoid all our remarkable stuff, all those religious experiences that strongly suggest that quantum effects *do* scale up into human experience—all that mystical interconnectedness, all those entangled people who somehow instantly know what is happening to a loved one (or a beloved pet) a thousand miles away (nonlocality) or, worse yet, what is about to happen (retrocausation). Instead, we go on and on about how we are all locked into our historical contexts, how religion is only about dubious power, or bad politics, or now cognitive modules and evolutionary adaptations, how these fantastic stories are all just "anecdotal" statistical flukes or perceptual delusions—*anything*, as long as it is depressing and boring.

I am not simply trying to be funny (although I hope you laughed). What we might call this "rhetoric of depression" is especially important to call out and critically query, as I am convinced that it controls some of the deepest, largely unconscious ground rules of academic discourse, that is, what can be said, heard, understood, or imagined. As I have traveled around North America and Europe to lecture over the last quarter century about all of the ideas articulated above, I have witnessed in real time people's reactions to my ideas, so I have seen how quickly and effortlessly these reflex strategies are evoked and immediately come to control the ensuing public conversation. The end result, I have noticed, is *distraction*. "Look away. Just look away. Move on."

The rhetoric can be summarized like this: "Whatever idea or pattern is proposed, pick the darkest and most negative expression of that idea or pattern and respond in a way that implies that this is what the idea or pattern is really about, where it must lead, what you are supporting if you dare think *that*." If, then, I write or speak about Eliade's fascination with paranormal powers, the discussion will immediately go to his early fascist associations in Romania—as if everything Eliade ever thought, including the paranormal, is somehow a function of fascism. If I speak or write about the contactee literature, the discussion will immediately go to sexual trauma or racism, as if that is what all of the literature must be about—people, after all, can't really encounter spectral beings. If I speak or write about sci-fi forms of gnosticism, the conversation will inevitably go to Scientology—as if that is what gnostic science fiction must lead to.

Each of these responses begins with a truth (Eliade's early fascist associations, the key roles of trauma and race in the historical development of the abduction literature, the important case of Scientology). Moreover, the voices that articulate these truths are often sophisticated and collegial ones. I am not questioning the truth of the observations or the intent and integrity of those who articulate them. I am simply observing that the rhetorical result of the response is that, *once such a negative case is invoked, the conversation, in effect, concludes there.* It "concludes" in both senses: it ends or shuts down the conversation, but it also concludes, as if we somehow possess the full truth now. "Move on. Ignore the fantastic. Don't look up. Look down. We have fascism, racism, and a cult now. Really, that's all there is. Move on."

REAL X-MEN

Allow me to give just one positive and very sophisticated example of this phenomenon in order to give the reader a sense of how it works. Consider the blogosphere. Consider Eric Wargo's blog "The Nightshirt" and its review of *Mutants and Mystics*.[2]

I am a big fan of Eric Wargo. He is a model of the kinds of both-and thinking and cosmic imagining I am calling for here (hence I will turn to him again in my concluding comments to help me correct one common misreading of my work). True to the ways of the intellectual gnostic, he contextualizes his review of *Mutants* by confessing one of the existential sources of his own fascination with sci-fi forms of gnosticism: he had two UFO sightings in one month in 2009. No doubt significantly, "The Nightshirt" is also bannered by a painted UFO, closely modelled on a famous flying saucer photograph—so the historical, the photographic and the artistic are already visually fused on the blog.

Wargo is also very funny. His review begins with the original adolescent inspiration of his thought—the 1970s. Think corduroy pants, a wood-paneled rec room in the basement, *Star Trek* reruns, and Leonard Nimoy's series on the paranormal *In Search Of* (an actor who played Spock hosting a television series about real-world paranormal phenomenon: there is that public fusion of the imaginal and the paranormal again). I was *so* there, I mean, in the wood-paneled rec room and coruduroy pants, eating crack-cereal and watching H. R. Pufnstuf.

Wargo sees, quite correctly, that meditating on the anomalies and paradoxes of things like interdimensional beings and machine intelligence resembles the riddles and mind-bending meditations of Zen Buddhism, which he also practices. He is not the first, and he will not be the last, to approach the UFO phenomenon as a "koan in the sky." He even describes a ninth-century Zen master bursting out of his chest, "*Alien* style, to both kill and admonish me one evening as I descended into a Maryland Metro station in the rain. It was a sweet enlightening joke that kicked *me* into a mildly ecstatic state for a few days . . . [and] proved to me that, if only as a line of thinking and inspiration, sci-fi and Fortean realms are truly a *gnosis*." This is one of many reasons that Wargo knows that "secret science-fictional surreality behind the unreasoning mask of consensus reality is where it's at, philosophically and spiritually."

That is the secret of *Mutants*. Like no other reviewer, Wargo just gets it.

But he just can't help himself (and I am teasing him now). He just has to conclude his review with "The Big But" (his words), that is, with the "dark, paranoid as well as elitist aspect of big-G Gnosticism that typically gets downplayed in modern attempts to reawaken interest in this ancient strand of thinking." Enter the case of Scientology. Even here, though, Wargo is careful. He is a both-and thinker. He acknowledges the likely experiential base of some of the most fantastic features of Scientology and its Thetan mythology, including "the apparently genuine religious awakening" Hubbard appears to have had within a near-death experience in a dentist's chair.[3] He even humorously relates this to Philip K. Dick's painful tooth extraction and subsequent "data downloads" in the Valis event. What is it about dentists and sci-fi gnostics?

Nevertheless, his single critique of *Mutants*—that it did not address Scientology—ends up concluding the essay and so leaving the reader with the impression, intended or not, that this is where sci-fi gnosticism must go. Not surprisingly, as with the Q & A sessions after my public lectures on similar topics, the "Comments" section under Wargo's essay review is entirely dominated by a discussion of—what else?—Scientology. This is the odd phenomenon that I am trying to flag and respond to here. This is how the conversation crashes. "Keep moving. Look away from the two UFOs hovering in the sky and above the blog post. Focus on the cultish. Look down, way down, and move on."

My own response is already embedded in Wargo's careful review. He correctly notes that, like Harold Bloom and Elaine Pagels, I have never promoted big-G Gnosticisim. And indeed, from *The Serpent's Gift* on, I have made it crystal clear that I am not promoting or seeking to reproduce any ancient gnosticism, with all of the dualisms and unbelievable mythologies that those ancient systems often carried. Moreover, I have been extremely critical of the military and government conspiracy theories of the UFO mythologies, which do indeed fit the dark, paranoid model of big-G Gnosticism that Wargo is referring to in his review.

I would only add this. Wargo calls Scientologists "the real X-Men," as if, again, this is what real "mutants" look like in the world and so what *Mutants and Mystics* is (or should be) about. No. Scientologists are not the real X-Men. The real X-Men mythology works so well because: (a) it is a conscious, playful mythology and not a religion of belief, authority, and obedience; and (b) it possesses an internal critique of superpowers and their authoritarian and fascist potentials in the central figure of Magneto, a Jewish man who ironically found his electromagnetic powers in a Nazi concentration camp as an imprisoned child. The mythology constantly plays Magneto's fascist instincts off against the liberal universal humanism of Professor Xavier: these are the two poles, the arch-villain and the arch-hero, of the storytelling. Xavier and Magneto, moreover, are *friends*. In short, the mythology is hyper-aware of the dark side of such real-world gifts and treats this tension as the moral driver of its story-telling. Such searching self-criticism is something, as yet, quite foreign to the Church of Scientology. I do not doubt that many Scientologists have extraordinary experiences, nor that their practices often really work, but until they can engage in such open self-criticism, we need to look elsewhere for "real X-Men."

WHAT IT IS

One of the most common questions I am confronted with when I lecture in public or correspond with readers goes, more or less, like this: "What is it exactly you are proposing? How do we *do* it?" As I hope is clear by now, the truth is that I have long been suffering, intuiting, and imagining my way into a new comparativism from below, not declaring one from on high. I do not know how to do it, or perhaps better, I do not know how I am doing it. The plausibility and wholism of the secret body of my thought is confusing to me as well: I often find myself in situations with a text or a person in which the events being reported make way too much sense to me, and I don't know why. I just "get" it. Often I can even predict what the person is going to tell me next ("Here comes the trauma story. Here comes the erotic stuff").

At the same time, I am keenly aware that what I appear to know is deeply problematic, if not actually offensive, to some of the religious communities and individuals in question. It is as if someone in me is inhabiting a mind space that understands these things and considers them both natural and normal, even if I, as an ego now, remain both baffled by the material and fearful of the social consequences of what this Stranger in me is saying and thinking, out loud, no less. Trained in the postmodern and postcolonial denials of the academy, moreover, I know I am not supposed to know anything, particularly about other cultures and subjectivities.

But I do.

Allow me to describe, as best I can, this gnostic mind space.

The "what I know" question, of course, has been our focus all along in the present pages. We need not return to all the lineaments of the secret body. However, we might well observe that the secret body, taken as a whole now, resembles what the philosopher of history Hayden White has called a "metahistory" or an "historical imagination," that is, a set of deep, often unconscious, philosophical assumptions about human nature, the natural world and the nature of time through which a historian selects his or her sources and interprets them to form a particular narrative or set of meanings, that is, *to tell a story*.[4] It is admittedly a bit weirder than that in my own case. This particular mind space—transmitted in that Night and later crystallized in the categories of the Human as Two, the erotic, the gnostic flip, the filter thesis, the super natural, the traumatic secret, and so on—pushes well beyond anything in White's model.

As a way of getting at some of the nuances here, consider for a moment Wouter Hanegraaff's engagement with the historical imagination. Hanegraaff's primary interest is with the historical imagination as an *object* of study, which is to say, with how religious and intellectual communities remember and imagine the past in order to create an identity and culture of their own. As we have seen above, he is particularly interested in how Western esotericism has been remembered and framed by Western intellectuals as the polemical Other of Protestant theology and Enlightenment rationalism, that is, as different forms of "rejected knowledge."[5]

The question is not whether a particular historian is operating with a historical imagination. There are no free passes here. The question is *which* historical imagination is at work in a particular writer. With a chorus of other voices, Hanegraaff points out that there are generally two dominant historical imaginations at work among modern intellectuals.[6]

The first is what he calls the "grand narrative" of rationality and scientific progress. This is the Enlightenment Story of a secularizing rationalism and a promissory materialism that will someday explain everything through mathematical models and causal networks. Its telos or goal is to finally purge Western culture of any and all lingering religious influences and "superstitions" (many have pointed out the vaguely monotheistic or Protestant spirit at work here). In the terms of the philosopher Charles Taylor, the Enlightenment Story is working with a simple (and simplistic) "subtraction story": take away this nonsense, remove that superstition, get rid of that silly belief, and you will eventually arrive at the real truth of things, which looks suspiciously like the worldview of those telling this particular Enlightenment Story.

"Nature" must change to fit this particular tale. After all, in order to accomplish all of this, the Enlightenment rationalist project must prove that everything alive is really, deep down, dead. Hence the famous, or infamous, Deist metaphor of the universe as a giant clock or the biomedical metaphor of the body as a machine. Here, obviously, any serious engagement with paranormal phenomena must be coded as primitive, as "magical thinking," as a falling back to an earlier stage of civilization and thought; in a word, as *regressive.*

There is a second counter-narrative, however, and it is fundamentally positive and hopeful. This is what we might call the Romantic Vision, which does not deny the gifts of reason but works from the conviction in the power of the human imagination to access and mediate other nonrational or superrational truths through symbol, art, poetry, and religion. Things are subtracted here, too, of course (like literal belief and religious exclusivism), but not in order to get to some unvarnished soulless truth. The truth is always a More here, always a matter of *adding,* not subtracting. Excess and overflow are the watchwords.

"Nature" shifts again to fit this particular tale. Indebted to a German movement called *Naturphilosophie,* the Romantic Vision understands nature to be a purposive living Whole and the human being as an expression of this conscious cosmos becoming more and more aware of itself. Here the paranormal and the magical cease to be evidence of regressive thinking and become hints or pointers to the hidden connections and mysteries of the "night side" of nature, as writers like G. H. Schubert in *Views from the Nightside of Natural Science* (1808) and Catherine Crowe in *The Night-Side of Nature* (1849) had it in the nineteenth century.[7] After Darwin, this same night side of nature will brighten and these phenomena and capacities will be reread within a general evolutionary spiritual framework as early signs of a superhuman future; in a word, they will become *progressive.*[8]

WHAT MATTER MATTERS?

What I am proposing with the new comparativism is another kind of historical imagination that clearly participates in both the Enlightenment Story and the Romantic Vision without quite being either, much as my gnostic method as explicated in *The Serpent's Gift* participates in both the modern and the postmodern without quite being either.

Looking back on all of this now, I would say that just about everything appears to hinge, or spin, on "what matter matters" in the different historical imaginations.

Consider again the Super Story. With such a construct, I am proposing that we track a set of modern emergent mythologies as an object of historical study and demonstrate in the process how the discoveries, models, and metaphors of modern science are fundamentally changing how individuals and communities remember and construct the religious pasts and their own presents. I am proposing that we study the Super Story as an *object* of historical inquiry.

But I am also proposing that we treat the implicit mind space of the Super Story as a potential *subject* or legitimate perspective from which to engage in new historical inquiry and new cross-cultural comparisons. I am suggesting that historians of religions should take very seriously the new real of the sciences and rethink their philosophical assumptions and historical practices in this new light.

I simply do not see how we can go on and on about how everything is local, historical, and contextual when the physicists are telling us, with compelling empirical evidence, that deep down none of this is in fact true: in physical and mathematical fact, reality is nonlocal and nontemporal. And it is simply beyond me why we should keep touting various forms of materialism, old *or* new, when the physicists have shown us again and again that *there is no matter*, none anyway as we assume there to be. Put another way, the real nature of matter itself should influence how we imagine and write our so-called material histories. And in the new real of quantum physics, the matter that matters in this particular historical imagination, the weird and the strange are no longer impossible or anomalous. *They are the way things really are.*

THE REALIST IMPULSE

Quantum mechanics, evolutionary biology, and cosmology are not simply about the few measly millennia of texts and artifacts that we fetishize as "history." They are about *everything*. And, regardless of what intellectuals, political ideologues, or religious leaders think in any particular decade or cultural space quantum physical, evolutionary, and cosmological processes continue, with or without their blessing. They simply *are*. Everything that happens or exists—including all the historical events and extreme experiences that are the tiny purview of the history of religions—are in some fashion a result, function, or expression, be it direct or indirect, of these quantum, evolutionary, and cosmological processes.

We are only at the very beginning of understanding this deep history. It is still very unclear whether there is any "direction" in such a cosmic process, although, again, the fundamental forces of matter and their weirdly precise calibration do indeed look "tuned" for the emergence and development of life. In any case, there is no way around the fact: there is immeasurably more complexity now than there was fourteen billion years ago. We may well reject the nineteenth-century modernist, colonial, and racist notions of evolution as "progress," but certainly something in the cosmos has, well, progressed. *A lot*.

What do we make of that indubitable fact? And why do we resist it so? Why can't humanists be cosmic, like the physicists and cosmologists? Are not we an evolved expression of the cosmos itself? So how could we be anything other than cosmic? And why do some intellectuals make fun of modern individuals who know and express their mystical experiences in scientific or parascientific terms, that is, as encounters with the evolutionary impulse of the universe or with the subatomic world of nonlocality and interconnectedness? If such correspondences exist, moreover, cannot these same mystical and paranormal experiences be employed as clues or inspirations for future scientific research? Can we not use the one to inspire and quicken the other?

That is not the normal response, of course. The normal response is the depressing and boring one. The normal response is simply to remove the mystical and paranormal events, that is, deny that they happen at all and brush them aside as statistical flukes or meaningless "anecdotes." Then, of course, there are no correspondences.

Such rhetorical moves (and that is what they are) may work as a polemical propaganda strategy, but they do not work as an honest historical method, as these events do happen, and all the time, *and they are often the single most important historical events in the life of an individual or community*. Denying or ignoring these events and experiences, then, is not just very bad history, since these events drive the history of religions. It is also insufficiently empirical, since these events are a part of our world as well, and no model of that world that does not take them into account is an adequate one.

How, then, to move forward here? How to explore these apparent cosmic correspondences? One way forward here would be to focus on the nature of consciousness, particularly as this nature has been glimpsed in transcendent and traumatic religious experiences. More specifically, I wish to propose that we imagine a new comparativism grounded in a new *realist* philosophy of mind, that is, one that can entertain the possibility that mind is something more than brain; that consciousness is not just culture, cognition, or computer. I propose that we take up David Chalmers's suggestion and think of mind as *real* and as something fundamental to the cosmos itself, like gravity or force.[9]

Chalmers is hardly alone. The Cambridge paleontologist Simon Conway Morris published a book entitled *The Runes of Evolution: How the Universe Became Self-Aware*. After arguing for three hundred (double-columned) pages that consciousness is not unique to humans, that evolutionary convergence is common, and that the evolution of life and mind is likely neither contingent nor random, he ends the book with an afterword that begins with a reference to my own *Authors of the Impossible*. The essay then goes on to tell five extraordinary stories involving the religious inspiration of the Indian mathematical genius Ramanujan (there is the occultism of mathematics again), two apparitions that signaled their otherwise unknown deaths to the visionaries (that is, two telepathic experiences), a British RAF pilot time traveling four years into the future on a strange flight, and a case of apparent levitation in a lunatic asylum. In short, he ends his book with what I have called "the impossible." His very last lines, moreover, playfully suggest that this may well be where the adventure of evolution is heading, that "the journey has only just begun."[10] What we have here, in other words, is another evolutionary esotericism, here advanced by an elite paleontologist.

I think Chalmers and Morris are pointing us in the right direction, which I would reframe as the cosmic and evolutionary nature of embodied consciousness. What would become of the humanities if we were to take up such a realist impulse, take the empirical turn, and reimagine the humanities as the study of (cosmic) consciousness coded in culture within a vast natural history and ecology? What then?

With respect to the study of religion, what if we stopped trying to discipline all of reality into our little depressing nineteenth-century materialist boxes, refigured the sacred as consciousness itself, and looked again to extreme, uncanny, "impossible" experiences as keys to human nature, as Mind winking back from the light through the refractions of body, brain, history, culture, and cognition? In what sense would we be studying ourselves? And in what sense would we be studying someone else, the Wholly Other of our intellectual ancestors? If we were to embrace both this epistemological paradox (the Human as Two) and this realist impulse (Mind is cosmically real), would we not have something crucial to offer the future of knowledge? Let me put the proposal this way:

18. The Realist Impulse of the Cosmic Humanities. Mind is real, a fundamental dimension or nonlocal (and nonhistorical) aspect of the universe. What humanists study—expressions of this mind as embodied forms of subjectivity and their historical expressions—are not simply "subjective" ephemera that can be ignored and wished aside for some imagined "objective" model of reality. No such objectivist knowing can ever be complete, in principle. Humanists, and particularly historians of mystical literature, hold the key to the future of knowledge—consciousness as cosmic.

Such cosmic humanities, it should be admitted up front, do not play by the present rules of the academy. I am not arguing, then, that, "this is what the humanities are." I am arguing rather that "this is what at least some of the humanities might yet become." I am also arguing, in effect, that *the study of the paranormal is the quantum physics of the study of religion.* And I mean this in more than a metaphorical way. I strongly suspect, with figures from Wolfgang Pauli and C. G. Jung to Dean Radin and Bertrand Méheust, that the two very different symbolic systems (the mathematics and the paranormal stories) are formal and narrative expressions of the same real, the "outer face" and the "inner face" of reality, as it were.

Certainly none of the ideas that routinely blow the philosophical circuits of the quantum theorists (nonlocality, the illusion of time, the central role of consciousness in the universe, and retrocausation) are unfamiliar to the historian of mystical literature. Indeed, these ideas are all old news under the old-fashioned theological and historical banners of transcendence, eternity, soul, spirit, and God, and prophecy and divination. But all of these phenomena can also be encountered, up close, in the flesh, and in striking new forms, if only we choose to look.

Again, I think that the imagination, reconceived as a manifestation and medium of consciousness, will become the key to any positive future, if such a future there will be. I also suspect, with Whitley Strieber, that this same imagination, at least in its empowered paranormal modes, is some kind of quantum machine. Somehow, it "scales up" quantum processes into our world as symbolic and mythical experiences of nonlocality (bilocation, clairvoyance), nontemporality (eternity, transcendence), cosmic consciousness (soul, spirit, God), and retrocausation (prophecy, divination, precognition). If we were really serious about understanding these things, we would be talking to the quantum theorists. If they were really serious about understanding their things, they would be talking to us.

HOW TO DO IT

The realist impulse—related to what others have called the "spectral turn" in figures like Jacques Derrida and his followers, or the "ontological turn" in figures like Bruno Latour, Timothy Morton, and Eduardo Viveiros de Castro—is the key move in what I am calling the cosmic humanities and the new comparativism.

Viveiros de Castro is of particular relevance here. His multinaturalism (the notion that "nature" behaves differently within different mental engagements with the material world), his corporeal perspectivism (the related notion that different bodies and sensoriums produce different realities), his language of a "background cosmic humanity," and his framing of the soul (which is always somehow "human") as remaining formally identical across species are all especially close to the dual aspect monism that grounds my comparative practice. Indeed, lines like the following beautifully express a dual aspect monism and its "splitting" of an ontological ground into a subjective and objective epistemological realm, the latter here framed as the realm of myth, where everything metamorphizes into everything else:

> Mythic discourse registers the movement by which the present state of things is actualized from a virtual, precosmological condition that is perfectly transparent—a chaosmos where the corporeal and spiritual dimensions of beings do not yet conceal each other. . . . But spirits are the proof that all virtualities have not necessarily been actualized, and that the turbulent mythic flux continues to rumble beneath the apparent discontinuities between types and species. . . . Myth, the universal point of flight of perspectivism, speaks of a state of being where bodies and names, souls and actions, egos and others are interpenetrated, immersed in one and the same presubjective and preobjective milieu.[11]

This is uncannily close to how I have framed paranormal discourse, which is often, of course, also mythical discourse.

Still, none of this quite captures what exactly this new comparativism is and how it works, that is, *how to do it.*

In some sense, these are unfair questions. We are simply not there yet, and we may never be. I often despair. No wonder that when I am asked what it is I "do," I always trip and tumble. I am, after all, an expert on nothing. That is to say, the historical material I work on and think about is "nothing" to the discipline in which I locate myself. I am laboring in a historical field that has not yet been named, much less established as the object of grants, faculty searches, and doctoral programs. In the playful but apt words of the title of one of the reviews of *The Super Natural,* my interests remains an "Unidentified Scholarly Subject."[12]

Indeed, I think those who are presently working in this Area 51 of the study of religion are laboring at the far edge or boundary of our knowledge. Honestly, I see such thought and the mind space it is trying to articulate as a glowing collective premonition of what is to come. Should the field decide to pursue this glow, I think there are three basic steps through which intellectuals will have to work over the next decades: (1) a deconstructive, suspicious, and critical stage aimed directly at the ideology of physicalism that presently defines our reigning episteme, in all its power and problems, and so locks us into what Taylor has called "the immanent frame"; (2) a realist comparative practice with respect to our historical materials in conversation with the empirical data of the French *métapsychique*, British psychical research and European and American parapsychological literatures; and (3) a speculative positing of new ontologies, sociologies, and ecologies that can replace the conventional materialist and historicist ones and make more sense of all that we encounter, at every turn, in the history of religions.

Allow me to explain more fully each of these three steps.

STEP ONE: IDEOLOGICAL CRITIQUE

As the study of religion stands at the moment, most of the implicit rules of the field are direct or indirect consequences of the same single metaphysical commitment: physicalism. Almost everything we do so well in the humanities and the study of religion—from historical contextualism and constructivism to Marxist, postcolonial, and feminist criticism—demand that we understand the human being as locked down tight to a particular space-time coordinate, to a specific body and to a particular ethnic or religious identity. We are asked to believe that no nonhuman or transhuman agents ("spirits" and "gods") are active in human history: these, after all, are only illusory projections. We are asked to believe that nothing about the human being escapes or overflows the socially constructed body-ego and its local language games. And when we are allowed to think universally (say, in Marxist criticism, cognitive science, or evolutionary psychology), we are allowed to do so only in a baseline materialist mode. Universalism is good only when it is reductive (and depressing).

What we really have here, at the end of the day, is an ideology, that is, an unconscious operating system of assumptions and beliefs that determine everything we can think, feel, or imagine. This ideology needs to be historicized, questioned, and deconstructed, like every other ideology. Why? Because it controls what we put on our academic table and what we keep off of it. It determines *what we consider to be "historical."* Indeed, it even determines *what we think "time" is*—a straight, linear causal arrow. We put things on the table, of course, that support our physicalist ideology, and we keep off the table those phenomena that challenge or subvert this same ideology. This is where the second step comes in.

STEP TWO: REALIST COMPARISON

The second step involves, very simply, putting more things on our academic table. More specifically, it involves the practice of robust comparison between contemporary "impossible" phenomena, whose phenomenological realities are often patently obvious to those who take the time to engage and study them in the present, and past "magical," "supernatural," or "miraculous" phenomena, whose scriptural and mythical expressions have almost always been heavily shaped and exaggerated by all the social and political processes that we know so well.

There is a single, and simple, comparative strategy at the center of the new comparativism. I first introduced it in *Esalen* (2007) and most recently returned to it to introduce the conversations of *The Super Natural* (2016). I would put it this way now:

19. The Future of the Past. The new comparativism works from the present to the past. More specifically, it zeroes in on the anomalous experiences of contemporary individuals and the phenomenology of paranormal or imaginal events (both empirical and symbolic) in order to better understand the anomalous experiences of past individuals and communities and how these were remembered, textualized, disciplined, and so fashioned into the institutions, scriptures, mythologies, and ritual systems that eventually became "religions."

In the end, such a new comparativism is *more* skeptical, not less so, since it is skeptical of everything, including and especially the reigning scientific materialism of the academy. It is also *more* constructivist, since it assumes that the very texture of the real—the way that human beings encounter, sense, and process the physical universe—is constructed, made possible and limited (or made impossible) by our social and linguistic practices, including our professional classification schemes. It is also, as William James called for over a century ago now, *more* empirical, as it refuses to ignore, demean, or deny forms of human experience, which are also historical events, that appear to overflow or violate our present models of reality. It is also, I dare add, *more* sociological, since it imagines forms of sociality (like telepathic communications across space-time or forms of charismatic energy that rewire brains and bodies) that go far beyond anything available in the present social sciences.

Such a realist comparativism from the present to the past is "new" only with respect to the last half century or so of scholarship. Both Bertrand Méheust and Wouter Hanegraaff have pointed out that similar comparative methods can be traced back to the German Romantic magnetic historiographers of the early nineteenth century, who quickly recognized that the trance states and healing and clairvoyant capacities of individuals "magnetized" by the followers of Mesmer, whom they could witness and examine up close, were clearly related to the phenomena of miracle and magic in the historical record.[13] Very similar methods can be seen again in the Scottish folklorist and anthropologist Andrew Lang, who proposed much the same over a century ago in his "Protest of a Psycho-Folklorist."[14] *Psycho-folklore* was his neologism for the project of putting comparative folklore studies (that is, the oral and textual past) in conversation with psychical research (that is, his own present).

The "new comparativism" I am proposing here, then, is neither really new nor especially mine. It is simply one of the many historical strands of the modern study of religion that have been effectively erased by the political and theological histories of the field. It need not be invented. It only need be recovered and developed so that it can take its proper place as one of the many useful tools in our ever-expanding professional toolbox.

STEP THREE: SPECULATIVE ONTOLOGIES

It is not a simple addition without challenge and change, however. It is easy to see why such realist comparisons and impossible historical phenomena are kept off the table either through benign neglect or open hostility: they cannot be reconciled with the physicalist ideology of our present historical imagination. Once we take this stuff seriously, something will indeed have to give, or shift, or—more likely—*flip*. The metaphor implies that nothing is lost, only seen in a radically new or "reversed" way. It is in this way that realist comparison leads inevitably to new speculative ontologies, sociologies, and ecologies, particularly around the nature and scope of mind and its relationship to matter and the larger living cosmos. The matter that matters here appears to be some kind of minded matter or mattered mind. Flippy.

Step three is the crucial one. It is also the step almost no one is ready to take. When intellectuals have not openly sneered at such experienced realities, they have sought to domesticate or disempower them through various sophisticated intellectual strategies. Here is where I would place the traditional "bracketing" of the phenomenological method of the study of religion, the statistical dismissal of the "anecdotal" as unimportant and meaningless in the debunking screeds, the perfectly useful but finally reductive turn to the language of "representation," the philosophical deconstruction of "experience," and, on the most generous end of the scale, the adoption of an open-minded "methodological agnosticism," that is, the position that, whatever one's own ontological commitments, these should not enter or influence one's practice of scholarship.

These responses have all been immunological ones. Whatever their intentions (and I fully recognize that often these intentions are positive and pragmatic ones), *the end result of these various intellectual strategies has been to leave the baseline materialist ideology of the modern academy unchallenged and so unchanged.*

The conclusion is an obvious one: if we do not propose new ontologies, sociologies, and ecologies, the baseline materialist historicism will remain in place. If we do not consistently and constantly turn the dials on our mental radios, the dials will automatically return and "reset" to the physicalist channel. That, after all, is the most obvious and easiest of channels to think out of. This is no one's fault. Materialism simply makes "the most sense" in the modern West because our cultural practices and ideological assumptions have conditioned us to privilege what five senses have evolved to pick up, that is, the material data, and generally only the material data. We are caught in a physicalist interpretive loop of our own cultural software and conditioned sensorium, and we will have to think very critically and very constructively to get out of it (and I doubt thinking alone is sufficient, hence the radiated gnostic intellectual). Criticism, deconstruction, and agnosticism will not be enough. We have to go further.

INTRODUCING THE ESSAY

The following piece has never been published or, for that matter, delivered as a public lecture. There is a reason: it represents the far edge of my thinking, its future perhaps. Accordingly, it should be read more as a thought experiment than a settled position. Having said that, its brief and insufficient engagement with the work of Ian Stevenson is long in coming.

I never met Stevenson, but I have interacted extensively over the years through the Esalen symposia with his successors at the University of Virginia, including the neuroscientist Edward Kelly (lead editor of *Irreducible Mind* and *Beyond Physicalism*), the psychiatrist Bruce Greyson (the doyen of near-death studies), the psychiatrist Jim Tucker (a widely published author on reincarnation memories in children who is now in charge of Stevenson's archives), and the historian of psychology Emily Williams Kelly (an expert on Frederic Myers, deathbed visions, and the history of parapsychology). The Division of Perceptual Studies (DOPS) at the University of Virginia is impressive by any measure. Walls of carefully organized files on Cases of the Reincarnation Type (approaching some 2,700 cases) and Near-Death Experiences (well over one thousand cases), together with the Ian Stevenson archives and library, constitute the richest archive for the study of these particular experiences anywhere in the world.

Transmigration and Cultural Transmission

COMPARING ANEW WITH IAN STEVENSON

(2017)

> Here I need to add and to emphasize that the evidence suggestive of reincarnation imperils no present knowledge. I do not question the findings of genetics or even that environments have some effect on us. . . . I am suggesting that instead of a single line of evolution—that of our physical bodies—we also participate in a second line of evolution—that of our minds, or, if you prefer, our souls.
>
> IAN STEVENSON, "SOME OF MY JOURNEYS IN MEDICINE"

> The history of religions constitutes the point of intersection between metaphysics and biology.
>
> MIRCEA ELIADE, *THE PORTUGAL JOURNAL*

Whatever the ontological reality or irreality of reincarnation, individuals commonly remember previous lives, including individuals in cultures that hold no transmigration beliefs or even find such beliefs religiously dissonant or offensive. Like the content of near-death experiences, past-life memories are not always syntonic with the belief systems of those who possess them. It is highly doubtful that such memories are strictly modern phenomena. It is highly likely that these memories are the deeper sources of transmigration beliefs wherever we find them, from the reincarnation models of ancient Greece, through the countless karma cosmologies of Buddhism, Jainism, Hinduism, and Sikhism, to contemporary Africa and the indigenous cultures of the Americas.[15]

The standard historical imagination of the study of religion cannot, or simply will not, consider the fact that such belief systems possess a strong phenomenological base across cultures and times, much less the possibility that they might also point to some empirical or ontological truth about who or what we are. Indeed, since such scholarship is still hinged to a Protestant one-afterlife model or a materialist no-afterlife model, *it cannot even imagine such possibilities.* But the new comparativism can take all of this in stride, and without taking any presumptive position about the reality, irreality or (ir)reality of reincarnation. In order to demonstrate how, allow me to take the three steps outlined above in conversation with this major comparative pattern in the history of religions.

STEP ONE: MORAL AND IDEOLOGICAL CRITIQUE

The ontological and temporal issues surrounding reincarnation beliefs bear deeply not just on historical methods, but on moral and political questions as well. As a potent example, consider the effects that historical contextualism and postcolonial criticism have had on framing the transmission of Asian religious ideas and practices into Euro-American contexts. I addressed the power and problems of postcolonial criticism above, in chapter 8. Here I want to extend and radicalize that engagement.

The bottom line is this: because the standard historicist and openly anti-comparative methods assume that both the human being and religion are only local, only constructed, only political phenomena, any movement of religious ideas and practices from Asian to Euro-American actors has inevitably been framed as a kind of dubious "appropriation," a sinister "colonial" process, even a cultural "theft" or "raid." Individual religious conversions and human transformations of all sorts are reduced to and dismissed as symptoms of an unconscious colonization of thought and the global hegemony of the Western white subject. More recently, such a model of appropriation has invoked the "neoliberal subject" "shopping" in a "spiritual marketplace." The language of capitalism has replaced the language of colonialism, but the message is a similar one: "This is *bad.*"

Whatever his original intentions might have been (and I recognize that these were nuanced and necessary), Edward Said's *Orientalism* and its reception histories have been absolutely devastating in this regard. After Said and postcolonial criticism, it is nearly impossible for intellectuals to approach doctrines and experiences like the Mind of Clear Light of Tibetan Buddhism, the Self (*atman*) of the Hindu philosophical schools, the Buddha nature and satori of Chinese and Japanese Buddhisms, and the kundalini yoga and *shakti-pat* of Hindu Tantra as universal truth claims potentially applicable to everyone on the planet (which is clearly how they were philosophically argued and why they were propogated by both Asian and Western actors in the first place). After the postcolonial turn, it appears that many intellectuals can only see such culturally inflected truth claims as a kind of positivist possession that can be "owned," "misused," or "stolen." Ironically, it is as if to decolonize thought we must fundamentally deny the gnoseologies we are supposedly no longer colonizing.

Once such Asian forms of gnosis are erased or made impossible by our own (Western) forms of criticism, any and all otherwise insightful academic methods are hauled out to dismiss those individuals who are existentially attracted to such possible truths (just more "appropriations"), who revere or romanticize Asian religious figures or ideas as countless others revere or romanticize Western religious figures (just more "orientalism"), or who actually experience these truths and realizations out of the blue, or at the electric touch of some proselytizing guru (whose missionary impulse is reduced to an imitation of Christian missionary efforts, that is, to more colonialism).

One result of all of this is the preservations of the illusion of cultural essentialism and the fiction of the modern nation-state, and this despite the historical fact that such cultures have *always* been combining and recombining different cultural materials across and between countless borders and bodies. Charles Stang's description of ancient Manichaean theology and mythology could accurately be applied to countless other traditions, including the Asian ones: "omnivorous and accumulative."[16] This *is* the history of religions.

Another dubious result of the postcolonial turn is that we are now repeatedly asked to believe that comparison itself, rather than issuing from an innate universal cognitive hardware and honest (and often highly subversive) observations of similiarites across cultures that we can witness at work from the ancient world to today, is little more than a conservative colonial artifact that should be disposed of as quickly and efficiently as possible. No one seems to remember that the nineteenth-century turn to "the East" was also a modern revisiting of an ancient and extremely stable "Platonic Orientalism," that is, the ancient conviction that philosophical wisdom comes from the East.[17]

Numerous examples of this Platonic Orientalism could be cited. Two will suffice. Consider the gnostic "Hymn of the Pearl" of *The Acts of Thomas* (second to fourth century CE), in which a man travels from the East, commonly and allegorically understood as "from his heavenly origins," in order to recover a pearl from a sleeping serpent in the land of embodiment in the West, in this case Egypt, before he returns home and thereby remembers and recovers his true divine origins with the help of a magical telepathic letter that was inscribed on his heart and a living garment, all over which "the motions of knowledge were stirring."[18] Second, Plotinus actually tried to travel to India, almost certainly to try to find the cultural source of his teachings about the cosmic *nous* or "Intellect." Little wonder that Frits Staal wrote an entire book comparing Neoplatonism and Indian nondualism: they *do* look alike.[19] Clearly, the British colonialists did not invent the Mediterranean world's spiritual reverence for "the East," nor do such convictions have anything necessarily to do with a privileged white subject.

Now enter the heuristic of the Human as Two. All of this talk of "misappropriation" or "theft" (or of a "capitalism" exchanging economic goods, for that matter) makes sense only if persons and cultures are only stable containers or solipsistic boxes exchanging economic goods. Such talk makes half sense, or no sense at all, when we reimagine the Human as Two, that is, as both a local temporary social ego (yes, exchanging economic and cultural goods) *and* a temporarily embodied and historically particularized form of consciousness that likely "reaches down" or "reaches up" into cosmic forms of mind and transtemporal forms of subjectivity.

As a simple thought experiment, consider what all of this looks like if we adopted the mind space of so many of the Asian traditions and took reincarnation as simply a feature of the world. Do not the logics of basic doctrines like reincarnation and the ultimate nature of realized consciousness (the Mind of Clear Light, brahman, the Dao, nirvana, satori, Buddha nature, and so on) imply, indeed demand, that *consciousness precedes culture*? Consciousness is transhistorical and cosmic in these systems, not just some local ethnic epiphenomenon constructed by brain matter, social practice, language and an ethnic group.

If we are really taking seriously the worldviews that we are studying, why are we assuming the absolute truth of the single-life model of Western monotheism and materialism? Why are we fetishizing Protestantism and Karl Marx to study the Buddha and the Tantra? Why not get *really* postcolonial and stop assuming the absolute truth of our own ethnocentric ontologies, sociologies, and ecologies, something along the lines of what Dipesh Chakrabarty or Charles Taylor do, that is, point out that our historical disciplines assume a kind of flat, homogenous model of time and exclude, in principle, nonhuman forms of agency and intervention, and, of course, any kind of nonhistorical form of consciousness or presence.[20] Chakrabarty, of course, would later explode the historical frame even more radically with his lectures and essays on the anthropocene and the emergence of the human as a geological agent of climate change.

Such post-secular, postcolonial, and environmental criticisms are in fact deeply aligned with what I have been trying to do in my later work, particularly on the evolutionary and cosmic nature of the human, the nonduality of para-normal phenomena outside the western Cartesian framework, and modern encounters with "biological gods," that is, with what appear to be conscious energies or plasmas in the environment that possess agency and intervene in dramatic ways. With respect to the biological gods, how exactly does one in-corporate an invisible nonhuman agent into our present materialist historiog-raphies? Or, with respect to the Asian religions and karma models now, how exactly does a person misappropriate something one already is, or someone that one once was or will be?

We are certainly not dealing with some kind of simple sameness or essen-tialism here, nor is this the case in the Asian orders of knowledge. The Asian traditions possess robust contextualist and constructivist insights whose eco-logical claims actually extend well past those of the present academy. Consider the karma cosmologies. These balance sameness and difference in complex and nuanced ways. Something remains the same, and yet the models insist that this something-the-same embeds itself, expresses itself through, *becomes* a dif-ferent social, historical, and psychological self (even a different species) with every new birth. The religious and philosophical schools of a civilization like India have taken a wide range of positions here. There is seldom any stable so-cial ego floating from life to life, as is often imagined, although there is often something that remains, something that survives bodily death—what it is (or is not) has been debated endlessly. Indeed, in many forms of Buddhism, although karma and something like transmigration are affirmed, we might better speak of the "illusion of reincarnation," since these traditions express grave doubts about any stable essence or soul hopping from life to life.[21]

What the soul is (or is not) is not my point. My point is that reincarnation models reimagine both transcendence and history, even as they radicalize the constructivist insights of the modern study of religion. My point is that *karma is constructivism*. My point is that such cosmologies of karma and reincarnation constitute a kind of deep sociality that honors no cultural boundaries or stable identities, and that exposes the orientalist critique as profoundly culture-bound and fundamentally self-contradictory, since you cannot "speak for" these cul-tural systems without taking their models of cultural, historical, and personal transmission seriously, which, in the case of transmigration at least, would need to affirm, not deny, the similar reports and experiences of Westerners.

Let me push this further. We are often told that we cannot share another person's experience, particularly one in another culture or time; that all we have is language, representations, or the text. But this is just another Western assumption, and one that flatly contradicts the experiences of countless human beings around the world (including in Western cultures) that claim the precise opposite, namely, that spirits, that is, the souls of other people, can and do possess others; that people, particularly emotionally bonded or entangled people, commonly receive "telepathic" communications from one another, either in the same room or at a great distance; that people, particularly lovers, often share the same dream; that a spiritual master can transmit his gnosis, mind-to-mind, directly into a disciple; that a Tantric teacher can "zap" another person with the same *shakti* or "energy" that lives and glows in him or her. Just as seriously, much of the world also simply assumes that "you" are in fact "someone else" from a previous life. In these mind spaces, not only can you share another person's experience. You *are* another person. Countless persons, actually.

The anthropologist Bilinda Straight gets this exactly right in her study of the miraculous among the Samburu of northern Kenya. Straight deals with colonialism and postcolonialism when they are relevant, but, in her own words, "these forces are sometimes crucial but often beside the point." What is the point? The point is that we might well be able to share other people's experiences, even and especially their most extraordinary experiences. Consider the universal biological fact of death:

> We anthropologists write death all the time—whether we experientially witness those deaths or not, whether our readers are moved by them or not. We write our own hauntings, the hauntings of others; we write within the spaces of loss not merely because of the specter of death but because of our belief in the singular inability to transcend ourselves, cross the experiential gap, and experience the experiences of another. And yet, there are some traditions that claim to cross precisely that gap—to reincarnate, to inhabit, to possess, to *be* another.[22]

Like Straight, I fully understand the "elusiveness of experience." I am not denying difference. I am simply observing that, in so many cases, *the contextualist and postcolonial models only work as complete models if we deny, a priori, the most basic philosophical claims and extraordinary experiences of the human beings we are supposedly trying to understand.* Of course, such an observation does not establish the truth of such religious claims, nor does it deny the limited utility of the contextualist and postcolonial methods, but it does question the reach of the latter and their right to speak in such absolute and certain terms. *That* is my point. They are tools in the toolbox. They are not the toolbox, and so they should not prevent us from considering other tools, other possibilities—including comparative and cross-cultural ones.

STEP TWO: REALIST COMPARISON

The new comparativist would not stop there. The method is not simply deconstructive. It is also constructive. Accordingly, such a comparative practice would also look for an experiential or empirical base in the present to make better sense of these historical belief systems. And it would find one in the modern CORT literatures, that is, in the Cases of the Reincarnation Type studied for six decades by psychiatrist Ian Stevenson (1918–2007) and his colleagues at the University of Virginia. Such examples, of which there are some 2,700 documented cases now, involve small children from around the world who have claimed to remember previous lives, many of which ended suddenly, unnaturally, and violently (about 70 percent) and many of whom died young: such a "traumatic secret" seems to be one of the catalysts for memories of a past life to carry over into a present one.[23]

Ian Stevenson was a psychiatrist who worked for most of his life at the University of Virginia, where he sat in an endowed chair dedicated to the study of paranormal phenomena.[24] His first trip to India to investigate a case suggestive of reincarnation took place in 1961. It was funded by the English medium Eileen Garrett, who had read an earlier paper on the topic by Stevenson. Later, Stevenson's work would be financially supported by the physicist and inventor Chester Carlson. Carlson was the man who invented electrophotography, which would eventually become the Xerox process. No one seems to think it is funny, but I have often pointed out the implicit humor here: the man who invented the Xerox process funded the man who did more than anyone else to study the Xeroxing or "copying" of human beings from life to life.

Attempted (and failed) humor aside, for over forty years, Stevenson churned out hundreds, and then thousands of elaborate case studies of past-life memories, particularly in Hindu and Buddhist South and East Asia (India, Sri Lanka, Thailand, and Burma), Shiite Lebanon and Turkey, West Africa, Northwest America, Brazil, and Europe.[25] Eventually, Stevenson had collected 2,600 reported cases of past-life memories and had published sixty-five detailed reports on individual cases, including a five-volume collection organized by country and culture.[26] For the last two decades, his successors, and especially the psychiatrist Jim Tucker, have carried on this work, adding more and more cases to the original database.[27] The files now take up two very full walls.

In 1997, Stevenson published what is widely considered to be the jewel of his corpus, his *Reincarnation and Biology: A Contribution to the Etiology of Birthmarks and Birth Defects* (1997). This is a two-volume megawork of 2,268 pages that treats 225 cases. As such, it constitutes the most impressive single text on record with respect to reincarnation memories and their physiological signatures on the body. The book treats what Stevenson calls—as if channeling Eliade in the epigraph above—"the biology of reincarnation," that is, the phenomenon of birthmarks or rare birth defects as physical "marks" from a previous life's violent ending by things like knife, ax, mallet, hanging rope, or bullet wound.[28] The Ian Stevenson Library at the university displays examples of such tools and weapons that Stevenson collected on his travels, which are carefully placed in glass cases near photos of the extraordinary birthmarks and birth defects in question.

Toward establishing these correspondences across lifetimes and bodies, Stevenson was often able to acquire photos of the apparent previous life's wound from coronary or police reports. In one early essay, Stevenson notes that, "in 43 of 49 cases in which a medical document (usually a postmortem report) was obtained, it confirmed the correspondence between wounds and birthmarks (or birth defects)."[29]

The eerie poignant power of these cases is impossible to communicate without a direct reading of the Stevenson corpus and his colleagues. I am certain that power was magnified still more by direct contacts with the people and families involved. I am thinking of moments like the time a four-year-old boy named Joey in Seattle kept talking about his other mother perishing in a car accident. One night at the dinner table, with guests present no less, he turned pale, stood up, and said, "You are not my family—my family is dead."[30]

Debunking stereotypes aside, almost none of the cases involve memories of being someone famous. As Tucker puts it, "almost all describe ordinary lives, often ending in very unpleasant ways."[31] In short, these memories show every sign, even every physical sign down to apparent shovel blows, bullet wounds, and surgery stitches, of being messy *historical* memories. But can history become birthmark and bodily defect? Can memory be written on the body? What kind of historiography is *this*?

Four Themes

Stevenson's lifework deserves generations of nuanced discussion, like those of a Foucault or a Said. The possible (or impossible) implications of his thought and work are vast. One reviewer rightly commented that the psychiatrist was either spectacularly off base, or he would be recognized in the future as a Galileo of the study of the human mind. Allow me to sketch out what I consider to be some of the more fruitful directions for such a future conversation.

1. *Cultural Dissonance.* First, there is the fact that Stevenson commonly commented on how his individual cases often did *not* support the specific models of reincarnation of the cultures in which they occurred, as, of course, one would expect if the cultural production model was sufficient. His biographer Tom Shroder, for example, comments on how the automatic, almost inhumanly cruel nature of some of the Indian cases did not conform to karma theory (with good leading to good and bad leading to bad), and how innumerable Druse cases in Lebanon suggested that the time lapse between death and birth was around eight months, while the Druse system insisted on an immediate rebirth.[32] (The median time lapse between death and rebirth in the cases as a whole is fifteen to sixteen months.[33]) Other cases suggested that the soul and its memories entered the body very late in the pregnancy, or even after the birth of the body, as if the infant organism up to then was a kind of soulless biological automaton or android.[34]

These disjunctions, gaps, and interstices both between cultures but also often between the empirical data and the local cultural models are very important. Emily Williams Kelly hints at the same dissonances toward the end of her edited volume on Stevenson's work, when she quotes a number of reviewers to the effect that serious consideration of these matters might well lead to understandings of the human personality that shock the Western mind even more than the classical reincarnation models, which might simply be more cultural approximations of something far more complex and mind-bending. Kelly also points out that Stevenson's methodology, which lies outside both "science" and "religion" as they are presently construed and so constitute a kind of third way (a "tertium quid" in the classical Latin of the psychical research tradition), clearly engaged any number of classic religious themes and questions but did not support any particular religion.[35]

As I have long argued, this is where careful comparisons often lead (into a religion of no religion), and I suspect it is why the comparative method is so often resisted: its conclusions are just too untraditional, too "nowhere." It is as if we all want to return, as soon as possible, to a local self, a floating stable soul, or a particular cultural framework—be it a religious or secular one. Radical comparison will not allow this. Nor will the complexities of the reincarnation memory literature. So we resist and deny both.

2. Early Theosophical Influences and Paranormal Interests. None of this implies in any way that the standard historical and contextualist methods are inappropriate in engaging these literatures and their authorship. It is important to note, for example, the maternal and textual influences on Stevenson's early development and intellectual interests. As he explains in his autobiographical essay "Some of My Journeys in Medicine," Stevenson was introduced to the power of the mind over the body (of which reincarnation is an extreme case), Asian religions, the comparative study of religion, and the idea of reincarnation itself through his mother's early influence and her occult library, which included a section on sex (on the top shelf[36]) and which was stocked with metaphysical literature, particularly Theosophy. Stevenson clearly recognized the influences here, even if he was also critical of them: like a good postcolonial critic, he would later describe Theosophy as a "potted version of Buddhism."[37] Such books and unorthodox ideas were also a function of the fact that he lived with his mother for two years in Los Angeles, which was a cultural hotbed for such ideas and practices. California again.

Such interests were much broader than reincarnation per se. Stevenson was also very interested in spontaneous ESP or telepathy, wrote an early paper on precognitions of the sinking of the Titanic, was writing about near-death experiences sixteen years before the expression was coined by Raymond Moody, and wrote other papers on paranormal topics as various as mediumship, "drop-ins" (spirits that show up unbidden at a séance), unlearned languages, the mental photography or "thoughtography" of Ted Serios, and metal-bending (a phenomenon that also appeared, by the way, in and around the first Sursem meetings at Esalen, including around the NDE researcher and psychiatrist Bruce Greyson).[38]

It is important to emphasize in this context Stevenson's skepticism and doubt with respect to some of the more gullible literature (with which he no doubt associated Esalen in his refusal to attend the first Sursem meeting). In a blistering short essay on hypnotic regressions to "previous lives" and "books that sell well in 'New Age' bookshops and airports," he lambasts "things too silly to be put in historical novels" that are nevertheless "fobbed off as previous lives." Nearly all such memories are "manifestly bogus" and are simply products of suggestion, although—and here is the tricky part—sometimes "something of evidential value" can emerge from a hypnosis.

Interestingly, what most upsets Stevenson in this essay is not the historical nonsense of the recovered "memories" but the ontological timidity of the hypnotherapists. These are therapists "who try to have it both ways—affecting to be themselves uncommitted and indifferent to the question of whether reincarnation occurs or does not, they yet entice patients with the hope of a cure from remembering a previous life."[39] In my own terms, what most upsets Stevenson is the therapists' refusal to take up the realist impulse of the phenomena in question and take the ontological turn.

3. *Psychedelic Catalysts.* Third, there are the psychedelic catalysts (or revelations) of Stevenson's thought. These should neither be exaggerated nor underestimated. Stevenson wrote more than a dozen papers in which he described his experiments with psychedelics at the University of Virginia, experiments which in fact began in the early 1950s when he was at Louisiana State University.[40] It was probably here that the "gnostic" or knowing element of his research and writing originates. He certainly openly wrote of what he considered to be genuine encounters with a greater reality through these chemical doors. In "Some of My Journeys in Medicine," for example, he describes how mescaline helped him to understand the "subjective element in our sense of the passage of time" (that is, I take it, how temporality is not necessarily a feature of the world "out there" but is produced "in here" by the brain) and how LSD resulted in a "mystical experience by which I mean a sense of unity with all beings, all things."[41]

In a more academic essay entitled "Comments on the Psychological Effects of Mescaline and Allied Drugs," he seems to suggest that, contrary to the assumptions encoded by a word like "hallucination," such chemicals may in fact introduce one to "a new and better vision of external reality." Some psychedelic states might actually grant empirical knowledge about our true cosmic condition: the realist impulse again. Here he explicitly compares the brain to "a great filter" in order to acknowledge the obvious "false perceptions" that such a chemical substance might induce (through the filter of the material brain), but, at the same time, to entertain "the possibility that these drugs may bring us, at least partially, into contact with a world of which we know little and should know a great deal more" (outside that brain filter). In what looks very much like a third-person account of his own psychedelic experiences in the same essay, he also writes of "the separateness of the Self" and of Jung's "objective psyche," which remind him of the Atman or transcendent Self of Hindu philosophy.[42]

This, of course, is exactly what Aldous Huxley thought, even though Huxley's prose was finally much more Buddhist and Tantric in orientation. Stevenson had clearly read Huxley and was informed by the general perennialism of the era, particularly as it was being framed by the Ramakrishna monks, with whom he interacted in India, and *The Gospel of Sri Ramakrishna*, a text that appears a number of times in his writings. Finally—and this is just me—I cannot help but observe that Stevenson's coinage of the "psychophore" (his neologism for the soul or memory collective that enters the body in a reincarnation event) sounds vaguely psychedelic, as in "psychospore," that is, a psychic mushroom.

4. *Sociology of the Impossible.* Fourth and finally, there is what I would call Stevenson's sociology of the impossible. By this phrase, I mean to refer to his keen historical awareness that the modern waning of extreme paranormal experiences and events in Western culture is likely not just a function of disinterest or insufficient reporting. Rather, it is more likely a function of modern secular culture's innate skepticism and fearful rejection of paranormal processes, which somehow suppress the phenomena and prevent them from happening to the same extent. It is as if our modern disbelief is self-confirming, in effect producing the limits on which it insists.

Consider his essay "Thoughts on the Decline of Major Paranormal Phenomena." Stevenson begins by entertaining some delightfully offbeat physical theories about why paranormal experiences are waning. One, which appears in different and contradictory forms in the literature, is that the "electronic smog" of modern civilization—that is, the fact that we are always swimming in an ocean of invisible electromagnetism generated by everything from power lines to automobiles and, now, wi-fi signals—in effect drowns out or scrambles the extremely low electromagnetic waves that allegedly produce paranormal cognitions. This physicalist idea is fascinating, but Stevenson does not really buy it, since his own ontological bets appear to lie with some form of dualism. He seems more convinced that paranormal processes are ultimately functions of mental processes that are not themselves physical. Accordingly, he looks instead to specifically psychological reasons for the eclipse of major paranormal phenomena.

His main answer here is that the primary culprit in the suppression of robust paranormal phenomenon can likely be located in one broad cultural movment: the rise of philosophical materialism. After reviewing the well-known "sheep-goat effect" in the parapsychology laboratory (whereby a subject who is skeptical of psi will generally do worse on psi-related tasks and a subject who is positively disposed to psi will generally do better), Stevenson suggests that "the overall effect of an increased skepticism would be to reduce the number of persons sensitive to apparitions and other paranormal experiences also."[43] In short, there is a kind of all-encompassing but invisible web of doubt and suppression at work in secular culture that in turn instills hesitation, skepticism and fear in people with respect to psi and ends up actually suppressing the phenomena. It is not simply the case that our doubt and materialism do not see what is really there. It is also the likely case that what is really there is no longer appearing to us because of our doubt and materialism.

Stevenson is not just thinking of the letters the president of the University of Virginia received from alumni protesting the subject of his research; nor of the concerns of his wife, who told him that he was "just ruining a promising career."[44] Nor was he thinking of all the cruel reviews his work attracted, with lines like "the Lord have mercy on us all if we have to believe in such rubbish" (an especially odd remark, given that "the Lord" performs such rubbish all the time in the gospels).[45] Rather, he is thinking of a kind of deep collective suppression, of a sociology of the impossible, of an anti-psi psi. He is thinking of "the possibility that spreading materialism has had an inhibiting effect on paranormal phenomena through paranormal causes." He goes on: "An atmosphere of completely unqualified belief appears to facilitate and may indeed be essential for the occurrence of paranormal physical phenomena, and I think this may be equally true of paranormal mental phenomena. If belief facilitates them, disbelief can block them.[46]

Stevenson has a most unusual, and, I think, most insightful side comment at this point. He notes "the current wave of gullibility" around the paranormal in American culture, by which I imagine he was thinking of the New Age literature (which had just peaked at the time this essay was published, that is, in the late 1980s). He knows that intellectuals deplore all of this, but he wonders out loud if such a situation might actually help reignite psi phenomena. I have argued much the same in *Mutants and Mystics* with respect to science fiction, comic books, and film, which I do think are becoming the new media of mystical ideas and occult practices.

Stevenson also has a few more academic responses to the cultural suppression of the phenomena that he wants to study. First, he suggests that we should look for data in cultures that are not so dramatically affected by the materialism of Western secular culture, particularly in Africa and Asia (to which he added in a footnote, the indigenous cultures of the Americas). And why not? Any sociology of the impossible implies that some cultural mind spaces will be better than others in evoking and developing particular human potentials, much as cultures express some linguistic capacities and suppress or wither all the others with which every infant is born.

Accordingly, which cultures we choose to study will be determined largely by what we are looking to study. This certainly played out in Stevenson's ethnographic experience. He found it much easier to find cases of the reincarnation type in cultures that nurtured these sorts of memories and experiences, like India or Burma. He was well aware of the cultural production thesis (that such memories are simply constructions of the culture), but he rejected it as too simple and unconvincing, particularly when it came to all of the empirical data he encountered. It turns out, once again, that India and "the East" really are special, and that it makes perfect sense to go there to look for things one cannot easily find in one's own Western culture.

Second, he suggests that we should look for data in individuals who are particularly gifted with paranormal capacities. In my own terms, we should look for our "mutants." Whether we are looking in other cultures that still nurture such human potentials or at specially gifted individuals in our own who, for whatever reason (from lightning strikes to genetics), have manifested them, the goal is a clear one: "Let us try to seek out again the major paranormal phenomena— wherever they may be."[47] Or, to put it differently: "But it seems to me that it's far better to be ninety percent certain of something *important* than one hundred perent certain of something that is trivial."[48]

Such an earnest request to seek out major paranormal phenomena in Asia, Africa, and the indigenous cultures of the Americas or in specially gifted individuals can only be read within our present intellectual climate as yet another "orientalist" strategy, or as a naive reliance on "anecdotal" experience. That climate, of course, is *precisely* the problem in Stevenson's opinion. And it is a *paranormal problem*, that is, it is a problem driven by unconscious, invisible networks of power, discourse, and suppression that work with the same psi processes that manifest robust paranormal capacities in other cultural and personal contexts.

This speculative suggestion of Stevenson's is Foucault on steroids. Here, "discourse" is literally magical, or anti-magical, and we are all unconscious battling wizards, whether we are blocking or affirming another's magic and power. Bruno Latour had it just right: "Do not trust those who analyze magic. They are usually magicians in search of revenge."[49]

Alternative Readings

The cases Stevenson reports are often rife with motifs that the historian of religions would immediately recognize, including sometimes psychoananalytic ones. The latter motifs are particularly obvious in some of the transgender cases or what Stevenson calls "sex change" cases, that is, those cases in which the gender of the present life of the subject is at odds with the memories of the previous personality: a man in a woman's body or a woman in a man's body, quite literally.

Stevenson would have likely resisted the psychoanalytic readings I will engage in here. He held a well-known and oft-voiced antipathy to psychoanalytic methods, which were extremely dogmatic and reductive when he was trained in them in the 1950s. Such readings, then, are entirely my own. They are designed to remind my reader of one important point, namely, that the realist comparisons proposed here do not preclude, in any way, the use of the standard sociological, psychological, and historical methods. Freud, feminism, and Foucault are all in. So is Said. So is Stevenson. Put differently, I want to insist on the fruitfulness of methodological pluralism and the simple observation that the same case can look very differently when examined through different lenses.

To begin, allow me to observe that from a broad comparative perspective what Stevenson called "paranormal processes" are often also erotic processes. I am reminded here of all of those poltergeist cases that swirl around a pubescent girl or boy, that is, around the manifestation of sexual maturity. I am also reminded of all the stories I have encountered in the literatures or, more dramatically still, in my correspondence: from the couple I know whose lovemaking, they believe, somehow activated the spectral memory or "morphogenetic field" of an angry ghost of a jilted woman who once lived in the house; to a friend in India who described to me a woman whose powers of healing and clairvoyance vanished at menopause. I recognize, of course, that these cases function more as folklore than as ethnographic data. But folklore is data, too, data that tells us that, no, we have not even *begun* to fathom "the point of intersection between metaphysics and biology," that is, between the mystical and the erotic.

As a single example from Stevenson's work, consider the case of Ma Tin Aung Myo, a Burmese woman who identifies as a man and remembers being a Japanese soldier in her previous life.[50] When her mother was pregnant with her future daughter, the mother dreamed three times of a "stocky Japanese soldier, shirtless and wearing short pants," who followed her and said "that he would come to stay with her and her husband." (Such "announcing dreams," as Stevenson called them, are common in the CORT literature.) Ma Tin Aung Myo first began remembering her previous life as such a soldier around three or four (the typical age in the CORT literature). She also began to manifest fear at the sound of airplanes, expressed a deep desire for Japanese culture and cuisine, and began to recount a story about being a cook in the Japanese army that had occupied Burma who had been killed when a warplane flew over and strafed the area. The cook died of severe wounds to his groin area.

Ma Tin Aung Myo did not like the spicy food of her own culture but loved sweet foods and raw fish. She also expressed real anger at American and British people. She insisted on dressing, acting, and playing like a boy, despite the protests of her mother. When this caused problems at her school and its dress codes, she was so insistent that she quit school. When she grew up, she insisted on wanting to marry a woman. During Stevenson's interview with her/him, Mau Tin Aung Myo even told the interview team that they could kill her in any way that they wished if they could promise her that she would be reborn as a man.

Ma Tin Aung Myo did not fit into the gender expectations of her culture, but—and here is the point—she understood this gender dissonance in culturally syntonic ways, that is, through the interpretive framework of reincarnation. Accordingly, her family accepted this explanation with little problem. And why not? Their culture provided them with a perfectly rational reason for why she self-identified as male despite the fact that she lacked the normal genitalia: because in a previous life she was a male who had died from a severe wound in his groin area. That is a fairly abstract description of an intimate wound. Was his penis blown off or mutilated beyond recognition?

The psychoanalytic interpreter, of course, would have a different reading. He or she would restrict the interpretation to a single life and read the reincarnation memories as culturally coded explanations for a transgender identity. Such an interpreter would also point out that the mother's pre-birth dreams would have likely been communicated to the little girl in implicit or explicit ways, and that the "memories" of the Japanese soldier focus on the absence of a penis in the present life, that is, on a kind of castration fantasy. These are not unreasonable readings. The indigenous reincarnation readings and the Western psychoanalytic readings each works just fine within its own ontological framework. Each explains the same psychological and psychosexual facts, but within a different set of assumptions.

STEP THREE: ONTOLOGICAL SPECULATION

Again, proof is not the point. The point is that such memories—whether genuine or constructed, or a bit of both—have played important and key roles in the development of various reincarnation belief systems around the world.

The point is to see that, given the common existence of such memories and apparently empirical confirmations across cultures today, it is very understandable why different cultures would have developed belief systems in the past that feature a separable soul and some form of transmigration. The point is also to read these reincarnation theories as implicit or explicit models of comparison and constructivism, even as implicit models of the cross-cultural transmission of memories, beliefs, and personalities. The point is to employ these acts to question and nuance our own theories, be these of a comparative, psychoanalytic, feminist, or postcolonial sort. The point is to consider the possibility that consciousness precedes culture, history, or person, even if it can only be known in and through culture, history, and persons.

What, for example, would feminist criticism and queer theory look like if they took such reincarnation memories as seriously as they took their own theorists? Psychoanalytic theory? Postcolonial theory? How about philosophy itself? Hegel, we might note, also considered anomalous birthmarks to be of psychic or paranormal origin and traced their symbolic message back as far as his own cultural assumptions allowed, that is, to the thoughts or life experiences of the mother.[51]

If we were to take up such thought experiments, would it not immediately become understandable why a person in one cultural world might experience multiple genders and sexualities, be extremely suspicious of any particular cultural construction, or be drawn to and adopt the religious tradition of another culture? Who, after all, is to say who or what that person "was" in a previous life? If a Thai woman could have been a Japanese soldier and be so drawn to Japanese culture and cuisine in Burma, just what is impossible with respect to crossing gender, sexual, cultural, religious, even temporal boundaries for others? Or should we label Ma Tin Aung Myo an "orientalist" and comment on how she was misappropriating a foreign Asian culture for her own psychosexual and selfish ends?

Obviously, my own answers to these questions are clear enough. I am of the opinion that if we could take such memories seriously, that is, as implicit acts of comparison, constructivism, and cross-cultural transmission, we would stop assuming the absolute truth of our own cultural assumptions about billiard-ball selves and cease fetishizing political identities, cultural practices, and modern nation-state boundaries. We would be more ready, like the Thai man-woman, to transcend and queer them all.

Or Stevenson himself, for that matter. He saw no evidence for some external theistic judge in the reincarnation cases, nor for that matter any reason to accept the often too-clear moral mechanisms of karma theory. Taken together, the cases, after all, bear out the specifics of neither the Western nor the Asian religious worldviews. At the very end of his *Children Who Remember Previous Lives*, the psychiatrist turned away from all of these too-easy certainties to quote Keats's description of this world as a "vale of soul-making," and to suggest that "we are the makers of our own souls." He was making the ontological turn that I am calling for here, but this did not mean that he had landed in some simple essentialism or on an easy religious answer. He had landed in humility and a self-described ignorance, which he wanted to emphasize. His long life study had convinced him that some "may indeed have reincarnated," but it "has also made me certain that we know almost nothing about reincarnation."[52] Like Goldilocks's third bowl of porridge, this conclusion, at once ontologically open and epitstemologically humble, seems "just right" to me.

As do the elegant conclusions of Anita Moorjani. Moorjani is one of the thousand or so case studies in the files of Bruce Greyson at the University of Virginia. She is also a gifted writer and cultural critic in her own right. Consider her memoir *Dying to Be Me* (2012). Here is a most impressive example of what I have called the comparative practices of popular culture, that is, the implicit comparativisms of writers who are not professional scholars but who are clearly advancing comparative-critical visions that are insightful and productive, partly because they are not bound by the usual academic conventions. Indeed, such writers are not even aware of such conventions. As a result, they do not honor them. In some cases, this spells intellectual disaster. In other cases, this produces a kind of creative genius beyond convention. I would put Moorjani in the latter camp.

The book tells the story of Moorjani's upbringing in Hong Kong, advanced cancer, near-death and what can only be called a miraculous healing through a transcendent loving presence and energy influx during a coma. The book is really about more than this still, though. It is very much a model example of what I am calling for above, that is, a realist comparative act and a robust critical critique of religious identity, cultural solipsism, and conservative gender roles. Moorjani, after all, was not just cured of the cancer. She was also cured of her culture. She had to die to all of that to find and be her true Self. She had to die to be Me.

The book begins with a comparative crisis. Moorjani grew up in Hong Kong in an Indian Hindu home, where she had a Chinese Buddhist nanny and was educated in a British Catholic school run by nuns. She grew up, that is, in three different religious cultures among what she calls "distinct and often contradictory beliefs" that "shaped me and fostered the fears that turned out to manifest in disease."[53] These fearful shapings manifested in three primary forms: as painful gender inequity in her home, where she felt inferior as a girl ("gender inequality is rife in my culture"); as dogmatic religious beliefs in the Catholic school that would send her to hell for all eternity for not holding the right religious beliefs; and as the racism of many of her blue-eyed blond classmates at a subsequent English school, who made fun of her darker skin.

Other cultural contradictions were also painfully apparent to her young mind, for example, the different purity codes of Indian and Chinese culture. She noticed that what were held to be profoundly impure and polluting foods in her Indian culture (like pork and beef) were held to be pure and healthy in Chinese culture. At one point in her story, she relates how she effectively ended a prospective arranged marriage simply by innocently ordering a tuna sandwich at a restaurant. Another cultural illusion.

In the spring of 2002, Moorjani learned that she had Hodgkins lymphoma. Four years passed as the cancer spread until she could no longer hold her head up. Her body was now emaciated from months of not being able to absorb any food. On the morning of February 2, 2006, she could not even open her eyes. Her face and body were horribly swollen. Her husband took her to the doctor, who immediately had her rushed to the hospital. She was now in a coma.

Oddly, Moorjani felt fantastic. She could not understand why her family was so upset. For one thing, new kinds of extraordinary abilities kicked in. "I wasn't using my five biological senses, yet I was keenly taking everything in, much more so than if I'd been using my physical organs. It was as though another, completely different type of perception kicked in, and more than just *perceive*, I seemed to also encompass everything that was happening, as though I was slowly merging with it all."[54] A kind of telepathic link was set up between Moorjani and those rushing and worrying around her in the hospital. She now knew what they were thinking and feeling, even if they were not in the room.

Moorjani, by the way, is hardly alone in such experiences. The NDE literature is filled with such clairvoyant scenes, as consciousness, in effect, delocalizes and ceases to identify with the local body-brain. Bruce Greyson shared with me a similar case with which he was intimately familiar. In his professional role at the hospital, he was speaking to a friend of an emergency patient who, it turned out, was having an NDE at that very moment in the hospital. The next day, immediately after the patient was released from the Intensive Care Unit (where no friend or family member was allowed and so where no cues or conversations could have taken place), this woman described in detail to Bruce what he was wearing and what they were saying the day before in the other room. Bruce was understandably stunned, and moved.

The Moorjani case continues in these same delocalizing dimensions. As her NDE developed, Moorjani felt no attachment to her body, which she could now see was not the same as her. "It didn't feel as though it were mine. It looked far too small and insignificant to have housed what I was experiencing. I felt free, liberated, and magnificent." *Magnificent.* That is the word she comes back to again and again. Part of this magnificence was the fact that space and time ceased to have much meaning. She became aware "that I was able to be anywhere at any time. . . . It was as though I were no longer restricted by the confines of space and time." She expanded further and further, becoming everyone and everything, until her emotional attachments dropped away and she felt what she describes as "superb and glorious unconditional love" surrounding her. In a single word (one deeply embedded in her own special Indian culture), she had "awakened."[55]

Not only did she realize the Human is Two within such a traumatic transcendence. She also realized that *Time is Two.* In that other realm, Moorjani describes how she felt "all moments at once." She felt everything that involved her in the past, present, and future as one moment, as spread out as a single space-time sheet, as it were. She knew what Roger Ebert knew just before his own death. Time does not move, she now realized. *We* move through time. She also sensed the presence of multiple lives, but a past life did not feel like it was actually in the past. It was all happening in the present, in the eternal Now. Here was an extreme version of what Ian Stevenson had learned from his psychedelic experiences and described more abstractly as the "subjective element in our sense of the passage of time."

This experience caused her to reflect philosophically on the nature of time and how it appears to be created by our brains and senses. "It's as though our earthly minds convert what happens around us into a sequence; but in actuality, when we're not expressing through our bodies, everything occurs simultaneously, whether past, present, or future." Our senses, she speculates, focus on a single point in time and space, but this is not how reality actually *is.* Time does not move, unless we are using "the filter of our physical bodies and minds."[56] There it is again: the filter thesis.

Through this experience of Time as Two, Moorjani concluded that the reincarnation model she had grown up with was not finally supported by her NDE (this connect/disconnect, recall, is what Stevenson and his colleagues also often found with many of the cases of the reincarnation type). The cultural model was not completely wrong, but it was not completely correct either. She concluded that there really is no sequential or linear soul reincarnating through life after life. Rather, "the concept of reincarnation is really just an interpretation, a way for our intellect to make sense of all existence happening at once." When someone "remembers" a past life, then, she is not really remembering a past life but a parallel or simultaneous one, since "all time exists at once."[57] If I might attempt a translation here, we could say that Moorjani had realized a form of subjectivity that was not simply subjective or historical, that was cosmic and transpersonal. In traditional terms, she had experienced "God."

This was no traditional theism, though, no God "over there" or "up there." She realized that "God isn't a *being*, but a *state of being . . . and I was now that state of being!*" This was a most extreme realization of the Human as Two: "In that state of clarity, I also realized that I'm not who I'd always thought I was: *Here I am without my body, race, culture, religion, or beliefs . . . yet I continue to exist! Then what am I? Who am I? I certainly don't feel reduced or smaller in any way. On the contrary, I haven't ever been this huge, this powerful, or this all-encompassing.*" And then she uses a most traditional word: "I felt eternal, as if I'd always existed and always would without beginning or end."[58] History, as a linear series of events, was effectively relativized or "ended."

Such an ending, of course, had profound consequences on how Moorjani subsequently understood culture and religion. She now saw them as the comparativist might see them: as a relative and anxiously policed set of codes and beliefs. But she saw something else: she saw them as a relative set of codes and beliefs whose conflicting messages and gross gender inequities had literally made her sick, indeed had nearly killed her. All of those hells and judgments, she recognized now, are simply projections of our own fears and our own, very human sense of revenge.[59] Her NDE, on the other hand, was "a state of pure awareness, which is a state of complete suspension of all previously held doctrine and dogma." It was this suspension in turn that allowed her physical body "to 'reset' itself."[60]

Ironically but hardly surprisingly (to the gnostic comparativist anyway), it was an *absence* of belief that was required for her healing. Now that she knew who she really was, not a religious ego but an "infinite self" or a "Universal energy," she could return to her body and heal it, in days. Her emaciated body, the lemon-size tumors, the huge skin lesions, so serious that reconstructive surgery had been planned—all of this began to heal immediately, and at a fantastic rate. She went home five weeks after entering the hospital. The doctors were stunned.

CONCLUDING THOUGHTS

It seems to me that the ethnographic archives of the cases of the reincarnation type (CORT) and the near-death experience (NDE) at the University of Virginia possess serious implications for the comparative study of religion. Foremost among these is the real likelihood that methods like conventional historiography and postcolonial criticism are helpful and necessary but finally insufficient and limited. As I read a book like Stevenson's *Reincarnation and Biology*, I cannot help but think that what these archives really point toward is the very real likelihood that we have been working with a set of far too limiting anthropologies that simply do not match the actual scope, depth, and sci-fi complexity of the human personality. Our methods, based on our own secular materialist anthropologies, then work to some perfectly reasonable conclusions—perfectly reasonable, that is, within those assumed ontological frameworks.

This would all be well and good, *if* the human being were nothing more than a mortal biological unit and a single ethnic ego determined entirely by genetic and local environmental forces—by nature and nurture, as we say. But is this in fact the case? Few, if any, religious cultures would accept such assumptions, including and especially those cultures that postcolonial critics are allegedly speaking for and care about. Moreover, as we have seen here, there is in fact solid and persuasive—which is not to say conclusive—empirical evidence that this is not the full picture. Such literatures and their archives seriously undermine any stable picture of the human personality. They also, I dare add, profoundly destabilize any simply linear notion of time and historical influence. Much like Derrida's telepathy, they deconstruct space and time.

In the end, I think the most reasonable conclusion is that the assumptions around the ethnic ego, the cult of culture, and the linear nature of time that undergird and make possible methods like historiography and postcolonial criticism are not at all obvious, much less established or proven. They are simply a set of materialist and historicist assumptions that generate their own consistency, plausibility, and conclusions, and, consequently, their own cultural worlds and experienced realities.

If my assessment is close to the mark, we might guess that different anthropological and psychological models will in turn generate different forms of consisistency, plausibility, and conclusions, and, consequently, different cultural worlds and experienced realities. A sociology of the impossible again. In the process, the same new realities might also generate new, much more inclusive empiricisms, philosophies of history, and practices of comparison with which to imagine new histories of religions. This is the new comparativism I am calling for, a comparativism in which cultural and historical transmission, like the apparent transmigration of memory and personality, shows every sign of being strange and wondrous beyond measure.

Closing

What the New Sacred Is (Not)

> I say humanity and man are different. Humanity in itself is so noble that the highest peak of humanity is equal to the angels and akin to God. The closest union that Christ had with the Father, that is possible for me to win, could I but slough off what there is of *this* and *that*, and realize my humanity.
>
> MEISTER ECKHART

> The sacred is not a stage in the history of consciousness, it is a structural element *of* that consciousness.
>
> MIRCEA ELIADE, *ORDEAL BY LABYRINTH*

Every historical imagination and accompanying comparative practice needs a base episteme, a way of knowing from which to think and compare across history. The Enlightenment Story privileged the mechanics of discursive reason (*dianoia*) and the base metaphor of the machine. The Romantic Vision privileged intuitive immediacy (*noesis*), the poetics of imagination and the aesthetic experience of beauty and the sublime. Historically, the study of religion has bounced back and forth between these two competing stories as it has moved through a number of comparative strategies over the last two centuries or so: myth, history, psyche, experience, society, institution, the sacred, symbol, art, ritual, power, class, race, sex, gender, sexual orientation, material culture, popular culture, and, now, the brain.

All of these are perfectly legitimate and powerfully productive bases from which to study religion across space and time. The new comparativism I am proposing embraces all of them, even as it suggests another comparative base to "weird" and "wonder" the practice: the nature of consciousness itself. As is patently clear by now, by such a phrase, I do not mean egoic awareness. I do not mean the social self. I do not mean the liberal white subject. I do not mean the computerlike cognitions of the brain. I mean that Other of the Human as

Two that has expressed itself in countless bodies and countless cultures in countless irruptions, omens, revelations, magical acts, precognitive dreams, and mystical experiences. I mean the burning "I Am" bushes, haunting ghosts, egoless enlightenments, lightning struck shamans, possessing spirits, throwing poltergeists, and revealing angels (and aliens) of the history of religions. I mean what I think Ralph Waldo Emerson meant when he uttered these offensive lines in his 1838 Harvard Divinity School Address: "They call it Christianity. I call it consciousness." He would also famously describe this consciousness as a weird all-seeing eyeball. Sounds about right. Notice that, even in our ordinary language games, "consciousness" is required to have the "reason" of the Enlightenment Story or the "imagination" of the Romantic Vision, but that it nevertheless overflows (or underflows) both ways of knowing. Allow me to repeat myself: consciousness is in fact the knower of *all* knowledge, be it philosophical, humanistic, mystical, artistic, mathematical, or scientific. This leads me to my final gnomon:

20. The New Sacred. Consciousness as such is the new sacred.

I have already said much, perhaps too much, about this "consciousness as such." Allow me to add just one nuance here: how one might go about writing a history of consciousness as such, which is to say a new history of religions. Consider, for a moment, what historical writing would look like if we stopped fetishizing the perspectives and concerns of the socialized ego, questioned the secular and very recent understanding of the human experience of time as entirely homogenous and fundamentally meaningless, and took the countless interventions of the fantastic into human historical time as intentionally, if often mischievously, meaningful, which, of course, is exactly how they are commonly described by those who have known (or suffered) them.

Here, at least, "history" would cease to be the flat, arrow-like, completely material process that it is presently assumed to be and would become an immeasurably complicated, still incredibly violent, still often oppressive, almost entirely invisible, mostly unconscious, probably hyperdimensional super-reality that is being influenced and shaped constantly, for better and for worse, by countless forms of consciousness and life-forms, toward what, if any, ends we can only guess.

If we were to take up such a new historiography, how we imagine and write history would change, because our understanding of time itself would change.

Let us be bold. Let us not hold back. Let us work—imaginatively and speculatively—with a whole host of new metaphors.

Let us entertain, for example, the ancient gnostic metaphor of the human, and so human history, as a vast upside-down tree of associations and correspondences growing "down" into time and the material world, from "where" we do not know. Here at least religious experiences might be imagined to be related not only in straight causal, reductive, or historical ways, but also in hyperdimensional, associative, symbolic, and metaphorical ways—so many branches of the same cognitive tree, so many sticky strands in the same neuroweb.[1] Such phenomena might be organized more like information in an internet search, or like correspondences in a magical worldview. Hence the allegedly "wild" comparisons of the older scholarship, which, indeed, often looked like an internet search or a magical act. Turns out that they may well have been onto something important. Turns out that not only is there still magic in comparison, but that comparison may well *be* magic.

In any case, like the nonlocal nature of quantum reality, the new sacred imagined here is not bound to linear or strictly causal models of time in which phenomena like precognition, retrocausal influences, or nonlocal "visions of eternity" are logically impossible. Here time itself warps and twists back on itself, like a snake biting its own tail. The historian of religions who dares take up such a new historical imagination, such a new model of time, would certainly find nothing irrational or implausible about the academic mother who *felt* in her body and saw in her mind, in perfect video-like detail, a car crash with her little boy exactly twenty-four hours before it happened but who mistook it (as a conscious agent or ego) as happening in the present.[2] Nor would she find anything impossible about the deathbed vision of Roger Ebert or the near-death experience of Anita Moorjani, in which past, present, and future were/are/will be happening all at once. The latter Eternal Now, after all, looks a lot like what is sometimes called the "block universe" of the Einsteinian cosmos.

Maybe it is.

Indeed, not only would such a historian of religions find nothing irrational here. She would go to just these sorts of experiences for thought experiments and clues (not proofs) about the nature of time and the nature of consciousness as such. Which is to say, such a new historian would go to these fantastic events for clues about *the actual nature of space-time in relationship to our cosmic humanity*, a relationship that we have, alas, previously shrunken into the near oblivion of a collection of depressing social facts that we now call "history" and "religion."

ASSESSING THE ELIADEAN RESONANCES

A number of colleagues have suggested to me over the years that such thinking echoes, develops, and advances certain classical Eliadean themes. Such individuals include my longtime editor, T. David Brent, who is also the literary executor of Eliade. Sometimes this is observed as a compliment or a hope; sometimes it is advanced as a criticism. I was never consciously working with such an intention, but I have come to see and accept what I would call these Eliadean resonances. Given Eliade's major but contested status in the field, such resonances can function as possibilities or liabilities. The Eliade question, then, seems important to address here at the end.

When I arrived at Chicago in 1985, Eliade was still alive. I never met him. Never even saw the man. I was told that he was retired, that he was suffering from severe arthritis, and that someone had burned a cross in his yard and posted signs accusing him of practicing witchcraft for his recent writings about magic and popular culture, no doubt his *Witchcraft, Occultism, and Cultural Fashions* (1978). Wendy Doniger told me that Mircea and Christinel were both deeply upset by the incident. This is the same book, by the way, in which Eliade expresses his admiration for Teilhard de Chardin and where he briefly explores what I have called the realist impulse of the modern evolutionary esotericisms. In other words, I "met" Eliade in Hyde Park not as a person but as a story about an esoteric thinker and his wife being threatened by a burning symbol deeply implicated in the history of American racism and white Christian terror.

I did not know at that time that Eliade had long been fascinated by what he called "supernormal" capacities (Myers again) like clairvoyance and levitation in the modern world and the "absolute freedom" that they appear to encode; that he wondered in his journals whether he was "an excellent reception post," since he often experienced symptoms in his body (a right palm itch) that appeared to precognitively announce terrible news from his home or the front of the war (the filter thesis again); that he much admired Aurobindo Ghose, which is to say, an evolutionary esotericism heavily inflected by Tantric yoga; or that he once wanted to write a book on the "postmortem problem" to advance a theory of the afterlife very much in line with what I would later propose, namely, in Mac Linscott Ricketts words now, that "each individual finds after death the world in which he has believed." Or, as I would later put it, "We die into our imaginations." He was especially interested in the specific process of depersonalization, that is, how long, in "concrete historical time," a person could "descend" to this plane and appear in apparitions after physical death.[3] In my own terms, he was interested here in the precise historical and psychological relations of the Human as Two as both particularized historical ego and cosmic transtemporal Mind. This, to say the least, is an open question, even with something like the filter thesis, which, after all, neither requires nor excludes the possibility of personal survival of bodily death.

What I did know, or at least heard rumors about, was that Eliade had been reading the quantum mysticism literature with Ioan Couliano, particularly a French philosophical novel entitled *Le Gnosis de Princeton*. I remember reading a few photocopied pages about all of this that was making its way around Swift Hall. But I do not remember what I read, and I really did not understand Eliade's absorption in all of this until much later, when I found myself, like him (because of him?), moving from the study of Indian Tantra to the study of the paranormal roots of science fiction and popular culture, or what he called "cultural fashions." It never occurred to me that I was following in Eliade's footsteps. Honestly, in graduate school, believe it or not, I thought these "cultural fashions" referred to the religious background of the clothing industry, which made no sense to me—*that* is how naive and uninformed I was.

It is not difficult to notice further resonances today. Perhaps most obviously, there are Eliade's well-known early works on yoga and Tantra and his convictions, best expressed in his essay "Spirit, Light, and Seed," around the archaic equations of "divine creativity" and "a seminal iridescence," a definite precedent to what I would later call "the mystical and the erotic" in *Kālī's Child*, which, of course, was all about Indian Tantra. I cannot but also observe the historical facts that we were both existentially "expelled" from India, if not legally then practically, for perceived sexual sins: he, for an alleged affair with the daughter of one of his teachers and a "Tantric experiment" in an ashram with a woman named Jenny; I, for writing about a Tantric saint and his homoeroticism.

The resonances continue. I have already examined above how Eliade's scholarship was informed by his mystical life, as was, of course, my own. In a similar spirit, Eliade also had made a special point to argue that a profound work in the history of religions should "re-create" or "reactivate" the religious worlds that it invokes. This is partly what he meant by the "new humanism" and "creative hermeneutics" he was proposing. In short, although he would not put it this way, there was something fundamentally magical about creative writing for Eliade. Reading and writing here are no neuronal mechanisms designed to process and express "cognitions." Rather, reading becomes a potential occult encounter, interpretation is world-making (as in a quantum measurement), and writing becomes invocation and transmission.

I arrived at nearly identical conclusions in my two theory books, that is, in *The Serpent's Gift*, where I articulated my own "mystical humanism," and in *Authors of the Impossible*, where I argued that the paranormal is a semiotic phenomenon that is deeply connected to the acts of reading and writing, and that, to the extent we take such experiences seriously and engage them in a kind of participatory interpretation, we are rewritten by these events, even as we also write them. Perhaps not surprisingly, it was the writing of *Authors* that forced me to come to terms with my indebtedness to Eliade and his creative hermeneutics.

Finally, there was Eliade's fascination with the *Doppelgänger* or "double goer," a kind of dark divine double that is beautifully and eerily portrayed in Coppola's film adaptation of the scholar's *Youth Without Youth*, which I have already summarized above. This particular Eliadean motif is worth returning to here at the end, since it resonates so powerfully with my own notion of the Human as Two. And more.

It would be quite reasonable, I think, to see in the double of Dominic Matei the esoteric Eliade I posited above in my reading of the comparativist's occult evolutionary notion of a "new humanity" encoded in parapsychological phenomena. Indeed, it would even be possible to hear in the double's voice a fictional precursor of my own call for new ontological speculation, that is, for us "to revise y/our philosophical principles" toward a new comparativism. Listen to Dominic and his (italicized) double whom he hears thinking inside him:

> Such parapsychological phenomena can be the effect of forces we do not know, but which can be controlled by the unconscious. *That's very true*, he heard himself thinking. . . . *But after so many experiences, you ought to revise your philosophical principles. You suspect what I'm referring to.* "Yes, I believe so," he acknowledged, smiling.[4]

Such smiles function in the novel as recognitions or knowings that are never fully articulated. The reader thus must complete or finish the grinning thought of the double, must become Eliade's double in the very act of reading Eliade.

In the same doubled and doubling novel, Eliade has one of his intellectual heroes, the Italian Buddhologist Giuseppe Tucci (1894–1984), investigating a dramatic case of reincarnation memories in a young German woman named Veronica Bühler, who believed that she had been a Buddhist nun living in central India twelve centuries ago. With the financial help of an American foundation called in by C. G. Jung, Tucci engages in an elaborate research trip to India to the physical site of her memories, where Veronica finds the original cave in which "she" died twelve centuries ago: "a clearer demonstration of the doctrine of the transmigration of the soul could not be found."[5] In short, much like Ian Stevenson, Eliade, in this late novel at least, turns to the empirical confirmation of reincarnation memories, even as his main character, Dominic Matei, tries to explain to a very upset Veronica Bühler, who does not believe in transmigration, why "in a sense, you're right" (not to believe). "But, I repeat, only *in a sense*. We'll discuss the problem later."[6] They never do.

It is difficult for me to avoid the conclusion that my later work somehow picked up where Eliade left off, if only in an occult novel where the conversations I want to have are expressed most fully by a kind of haunting and end in knowing smiles and unmet promises to pick up the question later. It seems I picked them up, without quite knowing it. After all, I have discussed, and discuss again above with the Moorjani materials in particular, why a doctrine like transmigration might be correct and incorrect at the same time, since such processes both imply the immortality of consciousness as such (the correct part) and radically destabilize any simple notion of a permanent human subject or social self (the incorrect part)—Dominic's (and Eliade's) mysterious and never fully explained "only *in a sense*."

Still, I also do not want to make too much of these resonances or smiles, and I am certainly drawing no equation, although I suppose one *can* compare a lion and a house cat. Moreover, there is much in the Eliadean corpus with which I simply cannot identify. I am thinking here of moments like his moral allergy against the use of psychoactive plants in *Shamanism*, or his generally insufficient engagement with reductive and suspicious forms of criticism, particularly psychoanalysis. Moreover, I am persuaded by much of the scholarly literature around his early Iron Guard associations. I do not gloss over or deny these early influences, as some have implied or claimed. But neither do I fetishize them or focus on them out of context. If the charge here is that I do not make these early troubling political associations the end-all of reading and interpreting the Eliadean corpus, then call me guilty. I simply do not see how these early political associations irreparably taint his body of scholarship, which stands on its own merits and whose ideas and conclusions are reflected and shared in literally hundreds of other thinkers with no such political associations.

With respect to my own work, it is important to understand that I learned my Eliade at Chicago primarily through Wendy Doniger, a major Jewish intellectual who firmly rejects the simplistic readings of her former colleague and friend, who always spoke admiringly, even lovingly, of him, and who taught me to think with another Jewish intellectual—Sigmund Freud, an Austrian Jew exiled from Vienna to London by a Nazi occupation.

I also learned my Eliade through Joseph Kitagawa, Eliade's longtime colleague and Dean for whom I acted as research assistant for about two years in the late 1980s. Kitagawa was a specialist on Japanese religions, an Episcopalian priest, and a Japanese American who had been rounded up and imprisoned in an American prison camp during WWII. I still remember the day that I delivered a letter to him from President Reagan. The letter was an official apology for this appalling act of American xenophobia and racism. The letter also included a fairly large reparation check. Mr. Kitagawa (for some reason, that's what we called him) adored Eliade.

This was the academic culture, the *Sitz im Leben*, in which I received Eliade's person and scholarship. This is how Eliade was perceived and experienced in his maturity and conclusions by a major Jewish intellectual and a Japanese American formerly imprisoned by the US government.

I must also observe in this context that there are irrationalities and inconsistencies apparent in this kind of complete conflation of thought and politics. I have Jewish colleagues who read and appreciate Martin Heidegger, a known Nazi. Such Jewish intellectuals understand the historical situation perfectly well, but they have little problem separating the philosophical genius from the political commitment, and here such a commitment is beyond question and extended well beyond any youth.

And where exactly does this kind of thinking stop? How much of the scholarly canon was written by white men with openly colonialist or racist views? Do we throw all of them out, too? Ever read David Hume's famous essay "On Miracles" in *An Inquiry Concerning Human Understanding* (1748)? This text functions as a kind of holy grail for contemporary debunkers and academics dismissive of the anomalous and fantastic, as if it somehow answered all the questions almost three centuries ago. It didn't. More to my present point, it opens with a snotty anti-Catholic riff and is rife with openly racist views about "savages" and such (you know, only savages believe this nonsense; civilized white Europeans never do).[7] Does such religious prejudice, ethnocentric arrogance, and simple ignorance (no, Europeans experience the miraculous all the time) render the entire Humean corpus irrelevant? Of course not.

So, again, why here? Why must every topic with which Eliade was fascinated get impaled on the stake of his earliest political leanings? One suspects ideological motives here. I do anyway. Certainly, the logic in the Eliade bashing is often one of casual association and dark insinuation with little or no reference to the larger historical picture in which Eliade's ideas were embedded and of which they were simply one of numerous expressions.

Consider how the paranormal interests of Eliade that now interest me so are inevitably read as nothing more than occult echoes of his early Iron Guard or fascist associations. Evolutionary esotericism equals fascism. End of story. That sort of thing.

Echoes, of course, there certainly are, as Doniger herself has observed with respect to "Eliade's most autobiographical work of fiction," *Youth Without Youth*, in which the main protagonist, a historian of religions and of ancient languages now endowed with all sorts of precognitive, telekinetic, and telepathic powers, worries that "someone might mistake him for a member of the Iron Guard."[8] I have no trouble with these observations or these worries. They are *worries*, after all; I see no denials, affirmations, or justifications. I see a struggle.

Now it is perfectly true that sometimes occult ideas are connected to authoritarian and fascist regimes, as we saw above in chapter 12. It is also perfectly true, as I have repeatedly reminded my parapsychological colleagues, that there are deep historical reasons that their laboratory work on psi is literally demonized by Evangelical Christians. It is demonized because Christianity, really monotheism in general, has had a long, sometimes violent, battle with magical spiritual orientations and ritual techniques designed to harness and use paranormal powers. More difficult still, psi is also demonized because much of the history of magic is in fact "black magic," that is, ritual techniques and spells designed to hurt, harm, or control others. From a traditional monotheistic or Christian perspective, then, to bring such forces into the lab and attempt to operationalize them for scientific, corporate, or military projects is not good science; it is a veritable conspiracy of occult wizards and black magicians, the dark forces of Satan himself at work in the world.

I have also emphasized the indubitable "trickster" elements, those evasive or deceptive forms of what I have called "the paranormal-screwing-with-us" that render any clear moral position on the subject difficult, if not actually impossible, to maintain.[9] Here is another version of my early insistence that there is no necessary relationship between the mystical and the ethical, or, if you prefer, between the sacred and the good (gnomon 4 again).

So can paranormal phenomena be experienced or framed in destructive, authoritarian, cultish, or politically phobic ways? And can related occult ideas be used for dangerous or even deadly ends? Yes. Are paranormal or psychical phenomena and their study or practice necessarily or commonly connected to authoritarian political systems or violent moral positions? No. Often, indeed, the exact opposite is the case, as we saw above with the central founding figures of Frederic Myers working for the education of women and Henri Bergson refusing to accept the title "Honorable Aryan."

So, I ask again, why are those stories not the ones being told? Why does it always go back to Nazis? The answer, I think, is fairly obvious: because such positive origin stories would not serve the ideologies being advanced in the criticisms. These ideologies, I think, tend to take two different, but related forms: one is monotheism, which still drives so much of our modern intellectual sensibilities; the other is scientific materialism, the successor of monotheism and the new jealous god on the block. Put those two forces together—monotheism and materialism—and magical worldviews that display pluralistic, panpsychic, pantheistic, or openly polytheistic dimensions stand little chance of serious and sustained consideration. This is the deeper reason, I think, why they are roundly condemned by both fundamentalist Christians and elite intellectuals, that is, by people who would not agree about almost anything else except *this*.

Eliade, of course, aligned his work with all of the "wrong" historical actors here—he was neither a good monotheist nor a good materialist. As he wrote in his Portugal journal, "Basically, the tragedy of my life can be reduced to this formula: I am a pagan—a perfect, classical pagan—trying to make a Christian of myself. For me, cosmic rhythms, symbols, signs, magic, sexuality—*exist* more largely and more 'immediately' than the problem of salvation."[10]

Having said all of that, it also remains true that I do not need Eliade's precedent or authority for the convictions expressed in these pages. Indeed, many of what are considered Eliadean themes—from the centrality of comparativism, the privileging of the polytheistic over the monotheistic historical imagination, the dream of a "new humanity" inspired by the ontologies of non-Western religious traditions, the camouflaging of the sacred in the sciences, and an intellectual fascination with magnetic, occult, or paranormal phenomena—were all popular tropes among major intellectuals well before and after Eliade arrived on the scene. The works of Thomas Hakl vis-à-vis the Eranos group and Jason Ānanda Josephson-Storm with respect to the esoteric dimensions of the rise of the human sciences in Europe have more than established this historical fact. To emphasize the comparative, pluralistic, humanistic, evolutionary, or paranormal dimensions of modern thought is not to be Eliadean, much less fascist. It is simply to be modern.[11]

THE SECRET HISTORY OF CONSCIOUSNESS

Then there is the antihistorical charge. Critics of Eliade and his particular vision of comparativism have often pronounced his scholarship "unhistorical," even "antihistorical." To be cute, or just plain mean, they have dubbed him an "anti-historian of religions." I am certain the same will be written about me and this book.

As with most stereotypes, there is some truth in such cruel phrases. It is perfectly fair to observe that the history of religions as imagined by Eliade (and, again, as reimagined here) is not "history," not at least as professional historians have generally imagined and practiced it within the rationalist, positivist, and social scientific modes of Enlightenment thinking. But—and here is where such critics are mistaken—this does not mean that such a comparative project is not a form of historical consciousness.

Quite the contrary. The accent has simply shifted. Or, better, now we have a double accent. Such a history of religions is a form of "*historical* consciousness," for sure, but it is also a "history of *consciousness*." It is the latter move that changes everything, without surrendering an iota of historical detail. All of the advances of the rationalist critical methods remain as they are, but their meaning and reach have changed, shifted, and become much more reasonable and humble.

The result is an esoteric history of religions to the extent that such a practice focuses on the nature of consciousness as the defining, if entirely invisible or "secret," factor in the history of human civilization, perhaps, as we have seen, even in the evolution of the cosmos itself—a secret factor that is looking more and more like it is not entirely located in space or time. What we have here, of course, is not some "anti-history," but another historical imagination, another way of putting the factual elements of historical research (a lot more of them) on the table and then arranging them through the gestalt of a particular set of narratives: in this case, the secret history of consciousness as revealed in the mystical and parapsychological literatures, the history of science, and the cutting edge of the philosophy of mind.[12]

ANSWERING THE PERENNIALIST CHARGE
(WITH A SCIENCE FICTION NOVEL)

I have been called a "perennialist" for such speculative commitments. The name feels more like an immunological response than an accurate label, as if the field's materialist and historicist constitution needs to fight off an oh-so-familiar cancer—an exaggerated, runaway mutation of its own unacknowledged comparative implications. Putting aside my serious polytheistic insistence that the history of religions may also give witness to the human species' interaction with "biological gods" or invisible non-carbon species in the environment (hardly a perennialist notion), my employments of the filter thesis and what Huxley called Mind at Large do in fact imply some sort of psychic universalism. This universalism or sameness, however, is of a much more reflexive, critical, culturally relative, and participatory sort than is usually imagined when people invoke the dreaded label of "perennialism."

This reflexive relativism can be seen in public contexts, for example, in my engagement with the Evangelical audience through "The Chess Game" and its trippy notion of climbing up mountains of religion that arose out of the earth of us.[13] It can also be seen in more intellectual and esoteric forms, for example, in my invocation, in *Vishnu on Freud's Desk*, of the cultural anthropologist Richard Shweder's "ontological polytheism" and "a realism and rationality . . . compatible with the idea of multiple worlds," as well as in my reflections, in *Authors of the Impossible* now, on Ernesto de Martino's magical anthropology and Eliade's history of religions, both of which suggested that reality may well behave differently in different cultural zones and through different linguistic screens and accompanying mental sensoriums. De Martino even wrote of a "paranormal phenomenology" that could demonstrate this astonishing (im)-possibility.[14]

Such a "culturally conditioned nature" is certainly borne out in my close interactions with individuals like Whitley Strieber and Elizabeth Krohn. They simply interact with levels or dimensions of reality that the rest of us do not. Their cognitive and sensory capacities are *different*. Accordingly, so too is the "nature" they know and experience on an almost daily basis.

There are better metaphors and terms than the "filter" or the worn-out whipping boy of "perennialism" for the difference-in-sameness I am trying to get at here, and, once again, it is my super-readers who have seen them, not me. Consider Jules Evans of Queen Mary College, University of London, and his blog "Philosophy for Life." Evans has invoked a classic science fiction novel to understand and explain my thought to his readers: Polish sci-fi master Stanislaw Lem's *Solaris* (1961). In Evans's words, what I am proposing with my work on categories like the imaginal and the paranormal is that "our relationship with Being is reciprocal, it responds to how we relate to it, manifesting in the attitudes or stories we project, playing with them, making them real." This in turn reminds him of Solaris, "the magical force that projects our dreams back to us."[15]

What Evans is referring to here is the title character of Lem's novel (a novel which clearly played into Philip K.Dick's self-understanding of the Valis event). Solaris is not exactly a character. It is a sentient, probably supercon-scious planetary ocean-planet that churns up extremely elaborate, mountain-like architectural forms on its seething surface. Weirder still, it materializes the thoughts, desires, and dreams of the human scientists who attempt to en-gage it in an orbiting satellite research station. It can even re-create their tech-nology and living breathing biological organisms, perfect human clones essen-tially, that match precisely the emotional and personal histories of those on the station: think the dead wife of the main protagonist, Kris Kelvin. These humanoids do not know that they are replications of an original. They are not aware of their own secondary nature. Interestingly, Lem calls these artificial human forms that haunt the satellite research station "the visitors," a phrase that will echo precisely into the later nonfiction work of Whitley Strieber, be-ginning with *Communion* in 1987.

Lem spends much of the book describing in detail the history of research on Solaris and what the human scientists know about its finally unfathomable mysteries. He calls Solaris a "Metamorph" and the mimetic mountain-like forms and "cartilaginous cities" that it constantly produces on its surface "mimoids" and "symmetriads."[16] Neologisms aside, the reader is left with the impression that Solaris can produce *any* form it wishes, even technological machines and former lovers, like some planetary meta-medium in an infinite cosmic séance.

In a beautiful blog essay entitled "The Solaris Mind," Eric Wargo compares Solaris to the most fantastic reaches of hypnagogia, that liminal both-and realm between waking and sleeping that occasionally produces fantastic imagery, seeming materializations, and stunning intellectual insights from the noctur-nal metabolization of our daily experience in the unconscious. The sheer imag-ination and pure creativity of the human unconscious revealed in such twilights is an autopoetic marvel: one thinks of Theodore Flournoy marveling at the fantastic serial "memories" of Élise Müller, the Hindu Princess from Mars; or of the astonishing visitors of Whitley Strieber's abduction experiences, hyp-notically induced memories, and subsequent physical encounters.

Such a Mind behind the mind appears to create endlessly, effortlessly, and entirely outside our conscious control. Sometimes, it might even produce em-pirical scientific knowledge, as in the famous case of August Kekulé, who dreamed a solution to a problem he was working on: the structure of the benzene ring.

What was his scientific dream or, in Wargo's reading, hypnagogic realization? A snake biting its own tail, which, it turned out, mirrors nicely the actual molecular structure of benzene.

Okay, that's just a little too much.

Then Wargo goes further. Drawing on his own personal experience with Zen meditation and satori moments involving things like the suchness of his coffee cup, Wargo blames the mimetic phantasmagoria of the same creative imagination "for the foremost obstructions of spiritual vision: the arising of the idea of self, and with it the constant fading of *presence* (that is, 'being here now') that has been the bane of meditators and mystics for millennia." In other words, if I read him correctly, the ultimate mimetic production of the Solaris-like mind in us all is the second-to-second reproduction of the separate self and its sensory objects (the "subject" and its "objects"), all of which the imagination is constantly doubling in a never-ending series of dioramic representations and lightning-quick replacements in our heads—the internal 3-D movies of our second-to-second experience. We never see reality as it is this way: we only see an immediate reproduction of the ego and the senses just after the fact—in essence a recent memory, a split-second projection, an *absence* between the projector "at the back" and the internal screen of our external sensory interactions.

But there is hope. Like the scientists orbiting Solaris in hopes of finally making "contact with the 'reasoning monster,'" human beings occasionally stumble or awaken into the Mind behind the mind. Suddenly, they *know*.[17] They realize that we as egos, like the materialized visitors on the satellite station, are unaware of our own secondary nature as representations. We also do not realize that we have it exactly backward. We do not realize that our sense of absence is actually a projection of pure presence: "The least of us contains infinities, and genius, that are really unimaginable, if we only bother to peer into this seething Solaris-like realm and recognize it as belonging to us—or perhaps, realize *us* as belonging to *it*."[18] There is the gnostic "reversal" or "flip" again (gnomon 7). There is the filter thesis (gnomon 10).

I believe that bloggers like Jules Evans and Eric Wargo are very close to the truth of things. We are all special-effects masters and expert filmmakers. We are all watching the movies of ourselves in every egoic state, every cognition, every sensory display. As little selves, we are all visitors, androids, walking forms of living machine intelligence that do not know what we in fact are: repetitions, memoids, simulacra *of something else*. While some of us androids, by hook or by crook, enter into direct or indirect contact with this Something Else, others spend their lives in what Lem calls "Solaris Studies" or "Solaristics," a seemingly hopeless academic project that disguises itself as a purely scientific endeavor but in fact is "the expression of mystical nostalgias which men are unwilling to confess openly."[19] But, alas, despite centuries of effort and countless essays and books, Solaris studies appears to have gotten no closer to the truth of things on the weird monster planet of Lem's novel.

I am more hopeful about our own Solaris studies on this weird planet, which is to say our religious studies on planet Earth. We already know way more than we are willing to admit, either to the public (probably for good reasons) or to ourselves (probably for not so good reasons). Such a project, at least the version of it proposed here, would predict that particular historical individuals in any culture, for a variety of psychological, physiological, and environmental reasons, will accidentally or intentionally tap into the Metaphorph or Mind at Large at some point in their lives, experience this contact in the shapes of their own cultural and individual imaginations, subsequently experience their subjectivities as both dual and divine (or as a channel for the divine), and then return from such states with new revelations and teachings about "God," the nature of ultimate reality or, in many cases, their own deification or special powers. Unfortunately, they will often confuse the projective shapes of the Metamorph for the universal truth of things, or, worse yet, they will fail to distinguish between themselves as social egos and the Mind or Metamorph constantly reproducing and projecting them. This, of course, is precisely what we find in the history of religions.

Obviously, then, I do not think that all the religions are pointing to the same mountaintop or stable core of perennial wisdom. I may well think that they are expressions of some shared planetary Mind at Large (that, and all those posited biological gods or secret species), but I do not claim to know what this irreducible Other is or how it creates all of these mimetic forms. If, then, I speculate about the sui generis nature of consciousness as a real and central constituent of the cosmos (and I do), I do not claim to know what this consciousness is, nor do I imagine it in any stable or essentialist terms. This new sacred remains an undetermined mystery that has been shaped into countless forms in the mirrors of our embodied minds and historical bodies, very much like Philip K. Dick's Valis or Stanislaw Lem's Solaris.[20]

HOW TO THINK LIKE A WHIRLPOOL

In the end, the truth is that what I have called the Human as Two is a *poetics* or *heuristic device*, not a dogmatic conclusion or traditional perennialist conviction.

Such a heuristic device shifts and changes, as the Other or Two of its gaze changes. The Freudian unconscious is not the channeled voice of the inspired poet, prophet, or sci-fi gnostic, and neither of these are the alien light (*sphinther*) of the ancient gnostic texts, the spherical subtle body or spiritual vehicle (*ochema*) of the Neoplatonic materials, or the luminous orbs of the modern ufological materials. The Human is Two *in relationship to the human ego*, but that Two or Other is phenomenologically multiple and many, not one or singular. The Human is Three in Jungian depth psychology (ego, personal unconscious, collective unconscious). The Human is Twenty-Four in Indian Samkhya philosophy, or just Two again (*purusha/prakriti* or "witness mind"/"material nature"). The Human is Trillions in the modern bionome of contemporary genetics, where each of us is a living ecosystem, a vast invisible living jungle that we so simply and foolishly call "the body."

Such a shifting, flexible poetics allows us to work with countless historical materials. It also encourages us to employ all of our most robust critical methods, to see and to better understand our own present cognitive dilemmas, and then to speculate about some possible resolutions. It does not provide us with any clear conclusions of a metaphysical sort. Those may well come someday, particularly if we can put our scientific and humanist methods together. I do not rule this out, and I do not consider such a project to be some kind of moral monster or philosophical impossibility.

I first explained my understanding of the Human as Two in the conclusion of *The Serpent's Gift*, but it seems appropriate to try to do so again, this time under the moniker of an apophatic anthropology, a phrase I have borrowed from the historian of early Christianity Charles Stang, who, not coincidentally, has written a book on what he calls "our divine double," a rich historical and theological exploration of the human as mirrored, twinned, wed, and deified in Platonic thought, the Gospel of Thomas, Manicheanism, and Plotinus.[21] The Human as Two.

We might observe that one half of this divine double is fairly easy to define and is already massively described and theorized, and that the other half (it is not really a half) cannot be, as both the history of apophatic mystical thought and the recent postmodern turn have taught us in different ways. Consciousness is the ultimate foundation of all knowledge and experience *that is itself beyond or before all knowledge and experience.*

As rational embodied egos, we are *way* out of our league here, like the cat in James's library. It is not that we do not know our actual cosmic condition. It is that, as embodied rational egos, we *cannot* know that cosmic condition. Our feline-like brains and sensory systems cannot read the books. Our cognitive and intellectual capacities simply evolved for different pragmatic purposes. To "make sense" of things, that is, to frame everything through the prism of our senses, is precisely to misapprehend our actual situation.

And, alas, we appear to be getting duller and duller in some ways. As modern embodied egos, we have made immeasurable gains in our science, technology and cosmological understandings, but we have paid heavy spiritual costs for these gains. In the process, we have become excessively "buffered selves," as Charles Taylor has put it.[22] Indeed, we have become so buffered from our cosmic context that we now honestly and sincerely think that we are nothing but those buffered selves, or, worse yet, that we do not exist at all. We are locked in Weber's rationalized "iron cage," incarcerated in Philip K. Dick's "Black Iron Prison" of mechanism and materialism, buffered into near oblivion within Taylor's "immanent frame" without an outside and without any hope of transcendence.

It is not difficult to define and describe the buffering. This is the first half of the Human as Two, the socially constructed ego or social self, with *all* of its historical, linguistic, cultural, religious, political, anatomical, biological, neurological, and evolutionary structures and conditionings. This first half of the human is the object of historical, contextualist, deconstructionist, reductionistic, and scientific forms of the study of religion, and rightly so. This half of the human, after all, *is* contextual, constructed, enculturated, socialized, physical, genetic, local, and so eminently reducible to what Meister Eckhart called the *diz und daz*, the "this and that."

But, if the history of religions means anything at all, we are not all *diz und daz*. Such a history, and particularly the history of comparative mystical literature, gives ample witness to the fact that there is another half to our shared humanity, a field of consciousness that cannot be reduced to social context or even the physical body and brain, that really and truly *transcends* all of these local historical and biological factors. In many forms of mystical literature, the claim is a remarkably simple one: this field of consciousness exists in a realm beyond space and time and so cannot be reduced to anything involving locality, causality, or temporality.

How, after all, can a conventional historicist method capture an order of experience that erupts from a dimension of the real that is not in time? Or how can a conventional sociological method capture an order of experience that erupts from a dimension of the real that has no social location? Indeed, precisely because the reported source of such experiences lies outside the objectivist structures of human sensory perception and binary logic, such events cannot be fully captured as a "something" at all. They are not simple objects to measure or locate.[23] To employ the common mystical codes, such an event is precisely a Nothing, an emptiness that cannot, by virtue of its own indeterminacy, be captured by any either-or logic or objectivist mode of knowing. In Samhkya terms, it is the nonmaterial Witness behind all forms of knowledge that can never be known as a material object. In Eckhart's medieval Christian cultural code, this is "the highest peak of humanity" that "is equal to the angels and akin to God."

Both of these arguments—the historical/contextualist/reductive argument and the apophatic/deconstructive/mystical argument—are familiar ones to the historian of religions. What is not common is the attempt to bring these two modes of knowing together into a dynamic whole toward a future robust comparativism. This has been my project here.

The imagination naturally looks for metaphors. I fear that the reader will be left with some very false image of a ghost in a machine, a traditional ego-soul or an unchanging Hegelian Absolute floating from civilization to civilization. As my invocations of Valis and Solaris have made clear, I am imagining no such things. First, my thought is radically humanistic, even if the limits of "the human" are not at all clear (because they are not), and even if I often write of superhumans (because they are). I have never encountered a religious experience of transcendence, however extreme, that was not finally the experience of a human being. Whatever else religious experience might point to, it is finally and obviously an expression of the human. Hence my central trope of *the Human* as Two. I really cannot emphasize this enough. The accent falls there.

Moreover, the mind-matter relationship between the new sacred and material history I am imagining here is much loopier, much more paradoxical, than any simple dualism or theistic transcendence can capture. Again, that relationship is much closer to how Philip K. Dick experienced and subsequently struggled with Valis; or how the contemporary computer engineer and philosopher Bernardo Kastrup has imagined a new idealist philosophy of mind. Since both men engage our present digital obsessions, both are worth dwelling on before we close.

Dick, as we have already seen, realized through an encounter with the Logos or Cosmic Mind that "reality *is* a giant brain." He even thought that such a reality appears to work like a binary computer code network.[24] But there is no computer quite like Dick's Valis. Valis is not a machine. It is a living being of cosmic proportions. It is a kind of "animal," but an "animal" whose body is the entire universe. It is a vast biological god. Valis is also paradoxical, reflexive, ouroboros-like—in short, enacted. Here is a typical passage from Dick's *Exegesis*:

> All that I could fathom was that the conventional picture that we normally get—and seem to share—is not in fact what is there; what is there is not even in time or space, nor is causation involved. There seems to be a mind and we are in it. . . . "We are all but cells in a colossal mad brain that both makes and perceives reality"—something like that, the main thrust being that there is some relationship between the creating of reality and the perceiving of it . . . the percipient is cosmogenitor ["creator of the universe"], or conversely, the cosmogenitor wound up as unwilling percipient of its own creation.[25]

There "is some relationship between the creating of reality and the perceiving of it." There is the hermeneutical key again. There is the enactment. There is the snake biting its own tail. There is the Parmenidean "One" of the German quantum theorist Carl von Weizsächer in which "knowing" (*noein*) and "being" (*einai*) are the same thing.

Dick's weird thought eerily reflects the more precise and calmer books of Kastrup. Both share a digital or computer-based model of cognition, but both also understand that *consciousness is not the same thing as cognition.*

Kastrup has argued in multiple books now that the conventional picture of material reality that we assume to be the case is simply false. As in Ebert's deathbed vision, this ordinary view of things is an extremely elaborate hoax (indeed, I got the Ebert story from one of Kastrup's books). Like many idealist thinkers and texts, he often invokes the metaphor of the dream to explain the at once real/unreal nature of our situation. More specifically, he thinks of the material world as a kind of dream in which God incarnates in order to reflect back on itself and come to know itself inside the dream. For Kastrup, we are all living inside God's brain.

As such, as egos now, we are embodied forms of cosmic mind, split off "alters" in some vast multiple-personality (dis)order—something like Dick's "colossal mad brain." These alters have entered God's dream through sexual reproduction and evolutionary biology (note that eros becomes the energy and portal of divine incarnation here) in order to wake up within the dream, look around the physical universe as the interior of God's brain, and reflect on our own cosmic nature within this same neural galactic network. Here is how

Kastrup summarizes our cosmic condition: "Put in another way, *the universe is a scan of God's brain*; except that you don't need the scanner: you're already inside God's brain so all you have to do is look around. Your perceptions of the sun, rainbows, thunderstorms, etc., are as inaccessible to God as the patterns of firing neurons in your brain—with all their beauty and complexity— are inaccessible to you in any direct way."[26] Note the materialism *and* idealism implied here.

Kastrup explores a set of suggestive metaphors for the relationship between the ego-alters and cosmic mind, images that I personally find much more satisfying than the "filter" metaphors of the earlier literature. Among these are the whirlpool, the knot, the ocean of quicksilver, and the vibrating membrane.

For Kastrup, the brain can be thought of as a kind of neurological whirlpool swirling in a river or ocean of mind. Such a whirlpool localizes or particularizes the flow of water but does not, of course, produce the water: "to say that the brain *generates* mind is as absurd as to say that the whirlpool generates water!"[27] The brain and enacted individual mind are all "water," although they are water behaving, moving in very specific ways. And a whirlpool, of course, is a very fragile process, like us. It can be interrupted, and it will always, eventually, flow back into the deeper currents of the larger body of water of which it is a local expression. This larger body of water Kastrup compares to an ocean of quicksilver or mercury, whose spinning cones create a mirroring effect within themselves, a kind of infinite recursivity whose amplification within the whirlpool blocks everything else out until the localized cone imagines that it is separate from everything else.

One can also think of the brain as "a knot of mind, with the very neurological branching structures of the brain suggesting complex knots that somehow capture mind and localize it within a closed tangle,"[28] not unlike, by the way, what one sees in those computer models of the universe, with the galaxy clusters looking remarkably like neuronal pathways (Dick's giant cosmic brain again). Or, now invoking the further reaches of contemporary physics (string theory and M-theory), Kastrup speculates that all of reality might be imagined as a single membrane vibrating in multiple dimensions, with all of our experiences now refigured as so many vibrations of mind in a hyperdimensional medium or empty void. The Indologist in me cannot help but notice that this latter metaphor looks *a lot* like Kashmiri Shaivism and its witness to a kind of Cosmic Mind expressing itself through "vibrations" (*spanda*) in and as the universe.

We need not pursue any of these metaphors here to realize one thing: each resists any conventional materialist or dualist interpretation, even as they also relate the two fields of consciousness that define what I have called the Human as Two. The whirlpool remains a whirlpool, but it is also finally no different than the river or ocean of which it is a localized and particularized expression. Difference and sameness are both preserved, as are immanence and transcendence, localism and universality, personality and the void.

RESTORING A BALANCE
(OR BECOMING TWO AGAIN)

As is probably more than obvious by now, it is my own conviction that the study of religion, and the humanities in general, have generally swung much too far toward the otherwise perfectly true facts of difference—really to the point of a dysfunctional relativism or nihilistic solipsism—and have inappropriately ignored the other half of the data, that is, a universally shared humanity, sameness or (non)ground. Or, if you prefer, we have ignored and denied the Other of all others, the Difference of all difference, the Stranger in us—consciousness as such. We are thus lost in the swirling of the little whirlpools and seem to have forgotten the river or ocean in which they appear and to which they always return.

This extreme swing has carried with it immense professional, moral, social, and political costs. Humanists are more or less ignored now by our colleagues in the social and natural sciences, and, of course, by the public and the media.

And for good reason. Why should anyone listen to the truth claims of a set of disciplines whose central arguments boil down to the claim that truth itself is a constructed chimera; that the only truth to have is that there is no truth; that all efforts toward truth are nothing more than power grabs; and, finally, that all deep conversation across cultural and temporal boundaries is essentially illusory, that we are all, in effect, locked into our local contexts, constructs, and language games? Little wonder we are ignored. By these rules, no one can know anything beyond his or her own local conditionings. We are locked down tight to the cave floor. We are only *diz und daz*.

I know exactly how I will be (and have been) misread here, so let me underline, one last time, that nothing above denies in any way the advances and importance of contextualism, historical criticism, reductionism, and ideological critique. Such repeated claims are no simple rhetorical bows on my part, no vacuous gestures toward the other side. I mean it. A deep abiding suspicion of all traditional images of "God" is present and active in my work, burning like the bush that Moses saw and the refusal to be named that spoke from it.

Please also remember: I was the poster boy of the dreaded Freudian reductionist for years. I was hated, hounded, and blacklisted for my public thoughts. So, no, I am not the least bit interested in swinging the pendulum back toward some kind of simple sameness, much less to any compromise of critical reason in its various historical, sociological, and psychological modes. I also do not look away from the ideological and the political. I remain to this day a gnostic critic of religion, by which I mean an intellectual who privileges consciousness over culture; who understands the "intellect" (*nous*) in both cognitive and cosmic ways; and who thinks and writes out of the (im)possibility that there is an alien principle in the human being, a spark or light that is not finally reducible to brain, body, or society nor answerable to *any* religious authority or scriptural text.

NOTHING NOW

Not reducible or answerable, but also not measurable or fully speakable. In the end, such a gnosis is groundless, without foundation, as the postmodern philosophers like to say. It is a great Nothing and Now, as Eckhart said much better. It is not a *diz* or a *daz*.

And so, in the end, we cannot say what this other Other, Alien, or Stranger is. And it is a serious philosophical mistake to think that we can, since such a looming presence is not an object or "thing" of any sort, and our "sayings" (including our secret sayings, or gnomons) are always local and constructed. I certainly do not know what (or who) this is telling us. The one event of my little life that imploded this myth of "me" into the other half of human being was marked by a profound sense of the abysmal, not by any certain ontological knowledge. The little whirlpool flowed back into the ocean. I was not certain. I was gone.

I do not write here or anywhere else, then, to pretend some knowledge that I do not possess. I write to illuminate our present materialist commitments, suggest how limiting these are, and finally demonstrate how once we imaginatively posit a double apophatic anthropology, many of the conundrums of the study of religion cease to be conundrums and become indirect expressions, even promises of what I have hymned as the Human as Two. Here is the mere sketch of a new historical imagination and a new comparativism, a comparativism unbound from a half century of denials and depressions. It is now for others to fill in the lines, to bolden and brighten them, to erase them, or to take them in entirely new directions. Who is to say how we will author, draw, and so become ourselves?

In any case, I have done my best to explore *la pensée surhumaine* and its understanding of the human being as doubled, as an embodied historical social being that is also an evolving filter, reducer, transmitter, portal, or spinning whirlpool of some larger cosmic presence or Ocean of Mind. In the process, I became a myth. Stranger still, I became a theory of religion. I began as a boy and morphed through millions of events called words into a proposal about how to compare religions anew.

Of course, I cannot say for sure if any of this points toward something of our future humanities, be these disciplines or species, or disciplines that play some humble role in the enactment of new species (Eckhart's "If I had not been, there would have been no God" . . . or Dick's "there is some relationship between the creating of reality and the perceiving of it"). What I do know is that any vision short of something so fantastic is simply too small. Any story smaller is not worthy of who and what we already are.

Airport Afterword

The symbols of the divine show up in our world initially at the trash stratum.
PHILIP K. DICK, *VALIS*

They haven't come here to read our stories. They've come here to be a story.
WHITLEY STRIEBER IN PRIVATE CONVERSATION

As I was finishing this book in the fall of 2015, I attended my discipline's annual professional meeting, the American Academy of Religion. It happened to be in Atlanta that year. There I had one of those encounters that mark a new direction on one's life path. This one was a conversation with one of my longtime editors about a project that I had proposed to the press earlier in the year. I had proposed to archive, map out, and interpret a prominent new historical field, which I suggested we call "paranormal currents in the history of religions." I would focus on these currents in North America over the last two centuries. That seemed like enough.

It was not a humble proposal. Quite the contrary. What I was really suggesting is that I could help do for the study of the American paranormal what Gershom Scholem did for the study of Jewish Kabbalah, what Mircea Eliade did for the study of Indian Tantra and shamanism, what Antoine Faivre and Wouter Hanegraaff did for the study of European esotericism, and what Elaine Pagels did for the study of gnosticism. Each of these topics, I observed, was considered to be gross superstition, obscene nonsense, mental illness, pure stupidity, or dangerous heresy before these writers took up their histories and helped transform them into some of the most quoted and generative areas in the study of religion. These new fields of historical study in turn spawned vast ripple effects in different public cultures, from Indiana to Israel to India.

I now proposed to do the same for that ridiculed American fantastic—the paranormal.

Practically speaking, what I was actually proposing was a "Super Story Trilogy," a three-volume work of historical scholarship that would read like an immense science fiction novel ("You should write fiction"). I have been moving toward such a vision for quite some time, as the last half of the present book gives witness. The Super Story Trilogy would extend and complete all of this. It would take up the filter thesis, the realist impulse, the cosmic humanities, and the new comparativism traced in these pages in order to show we can use this new historical imagination to locate, read, and understand the secret histories of evolutionary biology, mathematics and physics, and modern cosmology, or, as I had it in *Mutants and Mystics*, the emergent mythemes of Mutation, Radiation, and Alienation. The evolutionary esotericisms that I had come to know so well, "from Esalen to the X-Men," would lead off and define the trilogy as a whole. The quantum esotericisms, altered states of energy, hyperdimensional thought experiments, entangled particles, and paraphysics of consciousness literatures would take it further. The extraterrestrial esotericisms and ufological eschatologies in the sky would end it.

To my delight, the meeting in Atlanta about the project went extremely well. We planned to proceed with negotiations in the New Year. On my way back home, I took a long walk through the Atlanta airport, partly to get some exercise, partly to wind down. I was thinking about nothing in particular. Suddenly, the Super Story Trilogy popped into my head. Then, a minute or so later, something caught my eye, something bright and golden on the airport floor. I stopped and looked down. There was a piece of cheap costume jewelry. I am guessing it was a brand logo of a woman's handbag or purse that had fallen off its proper leather or vinyl. It was an "L" and a "V" stylishly joined, but upside down, which is how it caught my eye after the thought of the Super Story. The two letters formed a perfect and unmistakable "X." Laughing out loud, I picked it up.

Of course, this bizarre little synchronicity speaks back to the previous X in the X-Men movie parking lot that marked the definitive beginning of *Mutants and Mystics*. It *is* that X all over again. It is about the past, then—a little physical memory. But it is also about the future—the Super Story Trilogy.

This second X does not declare or prove anything. I am sure the debunker can come up with some explanation for the physical events that conspired to produce this special effect, but that, like all such "explanations," misses entirely the meaning and punch of such events.[1] In the end, the point of the second X was, exactly like the first, not to prove, but to prod and to point. This divine piece of trash shimmers and shines in a little aluminum shadowbox in my study now, reminding me of what has already been written—in the past? in the future?—so that I can write it out now in the present. Another weird loop. Another snake biting its own tail. Another future of the past.

Appendix: The Gnomons

The simplest rudiment of mystical experience would seem to be that deepened sense
of the significance of a maxim or formula which occasionally sweeps over one.

WILLIAM JAMES, *THE VARIETIES OF RELIGIOUS EXPERIENCE:
A STUDY IN HUMAN NATURE*

What would it mean, however, to *write* rather than to read the divine double? What
would it mean to take on authorship of our own "I" and not-"I," to become, in Kripal's words, an "author of the impossible . . . who knows that the Human is Two *and*
One?" . . . Who are our impossible authors of the divine double, past, present, and,
most crucially, *future*? Might we be?

CLOSING LINES OF CHARLES STANG'S *OUR DIVINE DOUBLE*

I sincerely hope that this secret body is not just mine. I began this book with the
intuition that there is an unconscious secret body at work behind and within
my various and sundry projects; that these four decades of spiritual struggle
and all those words are somehow coming into focus to form a more and more
clear picture, perhaps even a vision worthy of other people's attention and consideration. But is this true? Has something "popped" for you? Or are these ideas
more akin to personal ghosts that I have exorcised onto the page but that have
little or no relevance outside my own little psyche and its multiple neuroses
and obsessions? More ghost stories to entertain, perhaps, but certainly not to
believe, much less to take seriously as buds of some future theory of religion.

You will no doubt not be too surprised to learn that I think it is most likely
a bit of both, that there is a very thin line between an intellectual vision and a
personal haunting, between a revelation for the public and a private dream. An
individual, after all, is in some sense a dream of a culture, just as a culture is in

some sense the shared dream of a collection of individuals. It's *all* enchanted fiction.

So what can I say now, here at the end of a volume that claims to speak for the whole of a lifework, which is not yet over? What does the still-evolving secret body look like at this juncture of space-time? It looks something like my gnomons. I have historically contextualized, explained, and qualified each of these above. Here they are in one place, in more or less the order in which they first wrote me:

1. *Heretical Heterosexuality.* Whereas male heteroerotic forms of the mystical generally become heterodox or heretical, sublimated male homoerotic forms generally become orthodox.

2. *The Human as Two.* Each human being is two, that is, each person is simultaneously a conscious constructed self or socialized ego and a much larger complexly conscious field that normally manifests only in nonordinary states of consciousness and energy, which the religious traditions have historically objectified, mythologized, and projected outward into the sky as divine, as "God" or introjected inward into the human being as nirvana, brahman, or located in some sort of experienced paradoxical state that is neither inside nor outside, as in the Chinese Dao or the American paranormal.

3. *The Erotic Mystic.* There is a profound connection between the mystical and the erotic.

4. *The Amoral or Transmoral Mystic.* There is no necessary or simple connection between the mystical and the ethical.

5. *The Tantric Transmission.* In terms of the twentieth-century American translation of Asian religions, we can see a fairly clear "flip" around 1950. Before that date, the Asian systems and practices that drew the most attention tended to be ascetic and dualistic in practice (think Advaita Vedanta and Theravada Buddhism). After 1950, with the rise of Beat culture and the subsequent counterculture, they tended to be much more Tantric and erotic in practice (think Tibetan Buddhism, kundalini yoga, Shakta Tantra, Kashmiri Shaivism, and a general Daoism).

6. *Resonant Comparisons.* The works of scholars of comparative mystical literature are often catalyzed by the mystical or anomalous experiences of the intellectuals themselves. These autobiographical roots set up intuitively obvious resonant patterns between the interpreter and the interpreted, patterns which are then camouflaged in their texts and secreted in their theories of religion.

7. *The Gnostic Reversal and Reflexive Rereadings.* The study of religion possesses both Enlightenment and Romantic roots. Both together can form gnostic episte-

mologies that employ robust rational models to "reduce" the religious back to the human only to "reverse" or "flip" the reduction back toward theological or mystical ends. These are what we might call reflexive rereadings of religion.

8. *Comparative Mystics.* The deepest roots of critical theory in the comparative study of religion lie in apophatic mystical literature, which is to say that they lie in the nature of consciousness itself before and beyond any local cultural shaping of that same consciousness.

9. *It's about Counterculture, not Colonialism.* The most significant and immediate historical roots of critical theory in the comparative study of religion do not lie in colonialism; they lie in counterculture and its insistence on the primacy of consciousness over culture.

10. *The Filter Thesis.* Mind exists independently of the brain, into and by which it is filtered, transmitted, reduced, particularized, and translated through all of the neurological, cognitive, linguistic, cultural, and social processes that we have identified in the humanities, sciences, and social sciences. The filter thesis does not require that we deny any of these hard-won knowledges—only that we "flip" our interpretive perspective and see these processes as reductions rather than complete productions of consciousness.

11. *The Humanities Are the Study of Consciousness Coded in Culture.*

12. *Sometimes the Imagined Is Not the Imaginary.* The category of the imaginal draws attention to those moments of energetic influx or empowerment in which the imagination appears to have become a cipher of the real either as the empirical historical world of events toward some adaptive or survival advantage (as in a precognitive or clairvoyant event) or as some other dimension of being (as in a visionary or revelatory event). We might refer to the former as the empirical imaginal and to the latter as the symbolic imaginal.

13. *The Paranormal Is a Kind of Story.* Paranormal experiences tend to organize themselves around narrative, language, even playful puns and metaphors. They are, as such, expressive, goal-oriented, and inherently meaningful phenomena within which we are both authorial agents and fictional characters.

14. *The Paranormal Is a Nondual Signal.* A paranormal event is one in which a material event corresponds more or less precisely to a subjective event or mental state, thereby collapsing the assumed subject-object dualism of our ordinary cognitive and sensory experience and suggesting some deeper super-reality that is neither simply mental nor material but somehow both.

15. *The Super Story.* Modern science (willing or not) has inspired and guided in an intimate and secret dialogue with the anomalous experiences of individuals (including and especially those of scientists) a new narrative of where we have come

from, who we are, and where we are going, in short, a new evolutionary or cosmic humanism. This future humanism takes a strikingly empirical and experimental approach to what were once considered to be "religious" or "supernatural" experiences.

16. *The Super Natural.* The paranormal is the super natural not yet fully understood or sufficiently modeled. It is the natural world behaving in a "super" way, that is, beside or before our sensory and cognitive capacities split and so reduce it to a human experience.

17. *The Traumatic Secret.* The paranormal event or altered state of consciousness appears to be "let in" through the temporary suppression or dissolution of the socialized ego, which was opened up or fractured (either at the moment of the event or earlier in the life cycle) through extreme physical, emotional, and/or sexual suffering, that is, through what we would today call trauma. The trauma here is the trigger, but not necessarily the cause.

18. *The Realist Impulse of the Cosmic Humanities.* Mind is real, a fundamental dimension or nonlocal (and nonhistorical) aspect of the universe. What humanists study—expressions of this mind as embodied forms of subjectivity and their historical expressions—are not simply "subjective" ephemera that can be ignored and wished aside for some imagined "objective" model of reality. No such objectivist knowing can ever be complete, in principle. Humanists, and particularly historians of mystical literature, hold the key to the future of knowledge—consciousness as cosmic.

19. *The Future of the Past.* The new comparativism works from the present to the past. More specifically, it zeroes in on the anomalous experiences of contemporary individuals and the phenomenology of paranormal or imaginal events (both empirical and symbolic) in order to better understand the anomalous experiences of past individuals and communities and how these were remembered, textualized, disciplined, and so fashioned into the institutions, scriptures, mythologies, and ritual systems that eventually became "religions."

20. *The New Sacred.* Consciousness as such is the new sacred.

All that we saw was owing to your metaphysics.

BLAKE TO AN IGNORANT ANGEL IN *THE MARRIAGE
OF HEAVEN AND HELL* BEFORE THE ANGEL ABDUCTS
HIM INTO OUTER SPACE, LIKE AN ALIEN, AND LEAPS
"INTO THE VOID BETWEEN SATURN AND THE FIXED STARS"

The Method of All Methods

Colleagues and readers often ask me how I write so much. I have tried to rebuff the question out of a sense of embarrassment. My common answers have been "coffee" and "neurosis" (preferably working in tandem). But those are dodges, not the real truth (although they *have* helped, and I highly recommend the former). The fuller truth crystallizes down to two basic life events, and in this order: my marriage, and the energizing empowerment of that Night.

I have said enough about the latter, that Night, herein and elsewhere. The former, my marriage, is not some abstract, dutiful invocation. The simple truth is that I could not have written the books I wrote without Julie's constant companionship, emotional support, and domestic labor. I have done my best to help in and around the home, but it is Julie who has carried the vast brunt of all of this, and that, in truth, is one major reason why I have been able to write so much. There are other more esoteric reasons. I am convinced, for example, that the erotics of that Night had something to do with the erotics of our marriage. I have also learned a great deal from Julie's hands floating over my body during the "energy work" that she practices. These fields of intelligent force are as palpably obvious to me as holding a magnet to a steel refrigerator door. Clearly, Mesmer was onto something very real and important.

There are other deep debts to recognize. I have had a simply astonishing editor in T. David Brent of The University of Chicago Press. This book is dedicated to David, as well it should be: David guided book after book through the conceptual development, peer review, contractual, and production processes. The *corpus mysticum* exists as it exists because of him. Alan Thomas has also been a constant source of support, encouragement, and editorial advice, particularly around my future projects. In a book designed to crystallize all of the other books, these two men stand out as the writers behind the writer. I really ımilar long-term debt to Nicolas Shum-

ıes here at Rice over the last seven years

e has been an intellectual leader, a trusted

stic dean who has supported my work, and

ıstantive ways.

ery first pages, there were many colleagues

e to terms with this project and then helped

with close readings of this manuscript, criti-

ıgement. In many ways, this entire book is a

ıel Murphy, as always, provided spiritual sup-

port ann   e at Esalen to explore these ideas and meet so
many of the authors wh.. ... e influenced me. The following individuals have
all played important roles as well, in some cases providing detailed, page-by-
page criticisms and commentary: Dale Allison, Harald Atmanspacher, Loriliai
Biernacki, Ralph Blumenthal, Nathan Carlin, Bernard Carr, Rajagopal Chatto-
padhyaya, Peter Chemery, Paul Courtright, April DeConick, Wendy Doniger,
Stephen Finley, Norman Girardot, Bruce Greyson, Wouter J. Hanegraaff, Nick
Herbert, Marsha Hewitt, Andrea Jain, Scott Jones, Bernardo Kastrup, David
Litwa, Glenn Magee, Paul Marshall, Benjamin Mayo, Diana Walsh Pasulka,
Gregory Perron, Erin Prophet, Lynn Randolph, Bryan Rennie, Mark Ryan,
Gregory Shaw, Christine Skolnik, Kenny Smith, Charles Stang, Whitley Strie-
ber, Jacques Vallée, and Eric Wargo. These are some of the human mirrors in
which I glimpsed the outlines and shape of the secret body. These are the friend-
ships that, together, constitute the method of all methods.

37. Kathleen Taylor, *Sir John Woodroffe, Tantra and Bengal: "An Indian Soul in a European Body?"* (London: Curzon, 2001).

38. For this correspondence, see Robert Forte, ed., *Timothy Leary: Outside Looking In* (Rochester, VT: Park Street Press, 1999), 108–9.

39. Such Western actors, of course, often missed the ascetic and conservative orthodoxies of these ancient cultures, and their engagements with the Tantric traditions were filled with their own psychocultural projections and defined largely by their own historical needs. But they also found something very real and very important there; they found the Asian countercultures.

40. Roszak, *Making of a Counter Culture*. Roszak did not quite initiate the expression. It was probably J. Milton Yinger who first used a similar term (*contraculture*, which he adapted from Talcott Parsons) in 1960 as a marker of moral opposition to dominant cultural forms. See Peter Braunstein and Michael William Doyle, "Historicizing the American Counterculture of the 1960s and 1970s," in *Imagine Nation: The American Counterculture of the 1960s and 1970s*, ed. Braunstein and Doyle (New York: Routledge, 2002).

41. Roszak, *The Making of a Counter Culture*, 135–36. Roszak almost certainly got the phrase "the tantric tradition" from the Austrian anthropologist, Hindu monk, and American Tantric mystic Agehananda Bharati (born Leopold Fisher), who published *The Tantric Tradition* in 1965 with the same press (in a later edition) that would publish Roszak's *The Making of a Counter Culture* (another textual link between "counter culture" and "tantric").

42. Christoph Bochinger has argued that Blake was the first to use the expression "the New Age" in the sense that it became popular at the end of the twentieth century (*"New Age" and Moderne Religion: Religionswissenschaftliche Analysen*, revised ed. [Güterslow: Chr Kaiser, 2005]). For a balanced discussion, see Daren Kemp, *New Age: A Guide, Alternative Spiritualities from Aquarian Conspiracy to Next Age* (Edinburgh: Edinburgh University Press, 2004), 41–42.

43. Roszak, *Making of a Counter Culture*, 239.

44. Ibid., 240.

45. I first told this story in Roy Thomas's classic fanzine *Alter Ego*. See "Esalen and the X-Men: The Human Potential Movement and Super-Hero Comics," *Alter Ego* 84 (March 2009): 50–59.

46. I have engaged the remote viewing literature in a number of venues, but my fullest statement is probably the essay Antoine Faivre translated as "Les vies secrètes des superpouvoirs: La littérature de la vision à distance, et l'imaginal," in *Techniques du corps et de l'esprit dans les deux Ameriqués: Continuités et discontinuités culturelles*, ed. Antoine Faivre and Silvia Mancini (Paris: Éditions Imago, 2012).

47. Wendy Doniger O'Flaherty, *Dreams, Illusion and Other Realities* (Chicago: University of Chicago Press, 1986).

9: THAT OTHER NIGHT

1. This story is most fully told in Kurt Leland, *Rainbow Body: A History of the Western Chakra System from Blavatasky to Brennan* (Lake Worth, FL: Ibis Press, 2016).

2. Probably the fullest display of a Reichian approach to the UFO phenomenon is Trevor James Constable, *The Cosmic Pulse of Life: The Biological Power behind UFOs* (Santa Ana, CA: Merlin Press, 1976).

3. Again this piece was eventually published in Roy Thomas's fanzine as "Esalen and the X-Men: The Human Potential Movement and Superhero Comics," *Alter Ego* 84 (Spring 2009).

4. This makes it a species of panentheism. See Michael Murphy, "The Emergence of Evolutionary Panentheism," in *Panentheism across the World's Traditions*, ed. Loriliai Biernacki and Philip Clayton (New York: Oxford University Press, 2013), 177–99.

5. I am thinking in particular of Wouter Hanegraaff, Olav Hammer, and Kocku von Stuckrad. As will become apparent, my approach is less neutral and much more interested in engaging with ontological questions than their historical-critical, sociological, and discursive approaches. This is not a criticism. It is simply an observation, and a confession.

6. See https://www.youtube.com/watch?v=9D05ej8u-gU.

7. Kimberly A. Hamlin, *From Eve to Evolution: Darwin, Science, and Women's Rights in Gilded Age America* (Chicago: University of Chicago Press, 2014).

8. Adrian Desmond and James Moore, *Darwin's Sacred Cause: Race, Slavery, and the Quest for Human Origins* (Chicago: University of Chicago Press, 2009).

9. Here is the originating phrase: "what the Gñáni ["Gnostic"] sees and obtains is a new order of consciousness—to which, for want of a better we may give the name *universal* or *cosmic* consciousness, in contradistinction to the individual or special bodily consciousness with which we are all familiar." Edward Carpenter, *From Adam's Peak to Elephanta* (New York: E. P. Dutton & Co., 1904 [1892]), 154. My thanks to Mark Ryan for pointing this passage out to me. For the use of "cosmical consciousness" before this meeting, see Paul Marshall, *Mystical Encounters with the Natural World: Experiences and Explanations* (New York: Oxford University Press, 2005), 123.

10. David J. Hess, *Science in the New Age: The Paranormal, Its Defenders & Debunkers* (Madison: University of Wisconsin Press, 1993); Olav Hammer, *Claiming Knowledge: Strategies of Epistemology from Theosophy to the New Age* (Leiden: Brill, 2004); Kocku von Stuckrad, *The Scientification of Religion: An Historical Study of Discursive Change, 1800–2000* (De Gruyter, 2014).

11. Arthur C. Clarke, *Childhood's End* (New York: Del Rey, 1990), 200; for Clarke's use of Myers's "supernormal," see, for example, 87, 89, 95.

12. Hammer, *Claiming Knowledge*, 254–55.

13. Joscelyn Godwin, Foreword to Basarab Nicolescu, *Science, Meaning & Evolution: The Cosmology of Jacob Boehme* (New York: Parabola Books, 1991), 3.

14. Wouter J. Hanegraaff, *New Age Religion: Esotericism in the Mirror of Secular Thought* (Albany: State University of New York Press, 1998), 159–61.

15. For a description and analysis of the Hindu side of the story, see C. Mackenzie Brown, *Hindu Perspectives on Evolution: Darwin, Dharma and Design* (New York: Routledge, 2012).

16. See, for example, Abdullah Ucman, "The Theory of the *Dawr* and the *Dawriyas* in Ottoman Sufi Literature," in *Sufism and Sufis in Ottoman Society*, ed. Ahmet Yasar Ocak (Ankara: Turk Tarih Kurumu, 2005), 445–75.

17. Rebecca Stott, *Darwin's Ghosts: The Secret History of Evolution* (New York: Spiegel & Grau, 2012).

18. For a summary of these and a proposal of a model of holism, discontinuity, nonlocality, synchronicity, and convergence that is more reflective of the actual paleontological record, see the Italian paleontologist Roberto Fondi, "The Holistic Factor in Biological Evolution," in *Octagon: The Quest for Wholeness*, ed. Hans Thomas Hakl, 177–206.

19. Thomas Nagel, *Mind and Cosmos: Why the Materialist Neo-Darwinian Conception of Nature Is Almost Certainly False* (New York: Oxford University Press, 2012).

20. Wouter J. Hanegraaff, *Esotericism and the Academy: Rejected Knowledge in Western Culture* (Cambridge: Cambridge University Press, 2014).

21. Wouter J. Hanegraaff, ed., Introduction to *Dictionary of Gnosis & Western Esotericism*, in collaboration with Antoine Faivre, Roelef van den Broek, and Jean-Pierre Brach (Leiden: Brill, 2005), vii.

22. Hanegraaff, *Esotericism and the Academy*, 106.

23. Wouter J. Hanegraaff, *Swedenborg, Oetinger, Kant: Three Perspectives on* The Secrets of Heaven (West Chester, PA: Swedenborg Foundation, 2007), xvii.

24. Hanegraaff, Introduction, viii.

25. Gopi Krishna, *Kundalini: The Evolutionary Energy in Man* (Boulder, CO: Shambhala Press, 1974), 213.

26. Krishna, *Kundalini*, 207.

10: THE FILTER THESIS

1. For a history of the Sursem group and some reflections on the "sociology of the impossible" apparently at work in its interpersonal interactions, see my "Mind Matters: Esalen's Sursem Group and the Ethnography of Consciousness," for *What Matters? Ethnographies of Value in a (Not So) Secular Age*, ed. Ann Taves and Courtney Bender (New York: Columbia University Press, 2012).

2. Each of these metaphors gives us something different. The "filter" metaphor works well with all of the constructivist methods of the study of religion. The "transmission" metaphor is less dualistic and works well with the emanationist ontologies of so many of these traditions. The "reduction" metaphor invokes those transformers on our power line poles that "step down" the energy of the power line so that it can be fed into a human home.

3. Stang, *Our Divine Double*, 34–35.

4. William James, "A Suggestion about Mysticism," *Journal of Philosophy* 7, no. 4 (1910).

5. See Immanuel Kant and Gregory R. Johns, *Kant on Swedenborg: Dreams of a Spirit-Seer & Other Writings* (West Chester, PA: Swedenborg Foundation, 2003); and Wouter J. Hanegraaff, *Swedenborg, Oetinger, Kant: Three Perspectives on* The Secrets of Heaven (West Chester, PA: Swedenborg Foundation, 2007).

6. I am indebted to Whitley Strieber for this way of framing the problem.

7. See, for example, Harald Atmanspacher, "20th Century Variants of Dual-Aspect Thinking," *Mind & Matter*, vol. 12, no. 2 (2014): 245–88. Diagram used with permission.

8. Charles Darwin, *The Origin of Species* and *The Voyage of the Beagle*, with an introduction by Richard Dawkins (New York: Alfred A. Knopf, 2003), 913.

9. Quoted in Friedrich von Hügel, *The Mystical Element of Religion as Studied in Saint Catherine of Genoa and Her Friends*, 2 vols. (New York: E. P. Dutton, 1927), 1: 265.

10. Glenn Alexander Magee, *Hegel and the Hermetic Tradition* (Ithaca, NY: Cornell University Press, 2008), 9–10.

11. Ibid., 38.

12. Quoted in ibid., 39.

13. See ibid., 4–8, but also the historian of religions Ernst Benz, *The Mystical Sources of German Romantic Philosophy*, trans. Blair R. Reynolds and Eunice M. Paul (Allison Park, PA: Pickwick Publication, 1983).

14. See Cyril O'Regan, *The Heterodox Hegel* (Albany: State University of New York Press, 1994), 18–19.

15. For Hegel's equation of the "speculative" with the earlier "mystical," see Magee, *Hegel and the Hermetic Tradition*, 86 (including n. 10), 88.

16. Ibid., 2; Magee interprets the famous triangle drawing at 104–19.

17. Ibid., 256.

18. Kripal, *Esalen: America and the Religion of No Religion* (Chicago: University of Chicago Press, 2008), 343–44.

19. Glenn Alexander Magee, "Hegel on the Paranormal: Altered States of Consciousness in the Philosophy of Subjective Spirit," *Aries: Journal for the Study of Western Esotericism* 8 (2008): 28.

20. Quoted in ibid., 31–32.

21. Magee, *Hegel and the Hermetic Tradition*, 213–22; and Magee, "Hegel on the Paranormal." See also "The Dark Side of Subjective Spirit: Hegel on Mesmerism, Madness, and Ganglia," in *Essays on Hegel's Philosophy of Spirit*, ed. David Stern (Albany: State University of New York Press, 2012).

22. Quoted in Magee, *Hegel and the Hermetic Tradition*, 85, 87.

23. Quoted in ibid., 25.

24. See Leigh Eric Schmidt, *Restless Souls: The Making of American Spirituality* (New York: Harper Collins, 2005); and Michael Robertson, *Worshipping Walt: The Whitman Disciples* (Princeton, NJ: Princeton University Press, 2008).

25. Quoted in Alan Gauld, *The Founders of Psychical Research* (New York: Schocken, 1968), 64.

26. I am indebted in these two paragraphs, and for so much more in all things Huxley, to conversations with Dana Sawyer.

27. Aldous Huxley, *Island* (New York: Bantam, 1971), 199. One interesting question here is, Why? What changed Huxley? Dana Sawyer offers three interlocking answers: (1) according to Huxley's son, Aldous had made real progress in noetic insight or awakening and so had a genuine confidence about what he was saying late in life; (2) his love and attraction for his second wife, the young and beautiful (read: "sexy") Laura Huxley; and (3) psychedelics, which revealed to him the astounding beauty of the physical universe. Film interview with Dana Sawyer for *Supernature: The Story of Esalen*, dir. Scott Jones.

28. Ibid., 52–53. Hence the figures of the pious Queen Mother Rani, that "clutching and devouring mother" (ibid., 54), and her homosexual son, Murugan, who was especially fond of a military dictator (Colonel Dipa), the Sears catalog, and weaponry. The novel, however, has no trouble embracing unrepressed bisexual and homosexual expressions as perfectly legitimate and entirely natural (ibid., 73).

29. Ibid., 169. See 73–79 for Huxley's fullest treatment of this central theme.

30. Ibid., 73.

31. Ibid., 76.

32. This is precisely what Will Farnaby realizes at the end of the novel, at ibid., 274.

33. Ibid., 149.

34. Ibid., 37.

35. Ibid., 205.

36. Ibid., 184.

37. Ibid., 94.

38. Aldous Huxley, Preface to Krishnamurti, *The First and Last Freedom* (London: Victor Goolancz Ltd., 1954), 10–13.

39. Letter to Reid Gardner a few months before his own death, quoted and discussed by Milton Birnbaum, *Aldous Huxley: A Quest for Values* (New Brunswick, NJ: Transaction, 2009), 25.

40. By this clumsy phrase, I really mean apophatic mysticism, that is mystical forms of thought and experience that "say away" (*apo-phasis*) any and all naive realist objectivist *or* sub-

jectivist modes of knowing, opting instead for models that are broadly "nondualist" in orientation. Think Meister Eckhart's "God beyond God" or Divine Nothingness, the Buddhist models of "emptiness," and so on.

41. Amarnath Amarasingham, *Religion and the New Atheism: A Critical Appraisal* (Leiden: Brill, 2011).

42. See his blog: http://www.samharris.org/site/full_text/response-to-controversy2.

43. Taylor, *My Stroke of Insight*, 45–46.

44. David Eagleman, *Incognito: The Secret Lives of the Brain* (New York: Pantheon, 2011), 1–2.

45. Ibid., 221–22. Nor, by the way, am I suggesting that the brain is like a radio. And I am certain the simple duality that the metaphor of the filter implies is false.

11: THE RISE OF THE PARANORMAL

1. I am thinking of the evolutionary biologist Jerry Coyne's rant against my *Chronicle of Higher Education* piece, "Visions of the Impossible." Go look.

2. "Changed in the Blink of an Eye: Near-death Experiences and Other Transformations of Consciousness," October 29, 2015, Institute for Spirituality and Health, Houston.

3. Mircea Eliade, *Youth Without Youth* (Chicago: University of Chicago Press, 2007), 36. Dominic's first precognitive dream is of an unknown car he will get into the next day.

4. Jess Hollenback, *Mysticism: Experience, Response and Empowerment* (University Park, PA: Penn State University Press, [1996] 2007). Jess deserves the credit for definitively reintroducing the paranormal back into the comparative study of religion, in 1996, with this remarkable book.

5. Henry Corbin, *Creative Imagination in the Sufism of Ibn 'Arabi* (Princeton, NJ: Princeton University Press, 1969), 42, 47–48, 68, 222–24. The Sufi lore around teleportation (not named as such, of course) occurs at 237–38.

6. The next four paragraphs on Flournoy are adapted from my *Mutants and Mystics*, 64–68.

7. Théodore Flournoy, *From India to the Planet Mars: A Case of Multiple Personality with Imaginary Languages*, with a new introduction by Sonu Shamdasani (Princeton, NJ: Princeton University Press, 1994), 250.

8. Corbin, *Creative Imagination*, 224.

9. For more on this historical development, see my chapter "What Evolution Looks Like," in Strieber and Kripal, *The Super Natural*; and Kripal, *Mutants and Mystics: Science Fiction, Superhero Comics, and the Paranormal* (Chicago: University of Chicago Press, 2015), 75–85.

10. Bertrand Méheust, *Jésus Thaumaturge: Enquête sur l'homme et ses miracles* (Paris: InterEditions, 2015), 246–47.

11. "Receive the Hero," Foreword to Paul Selig, *The Book of Mastery* (New York: Tarcher/Penguin, 2015). For a decent introduction to Paul's person and work, see the case of the rock star Sammy Hagar and his wife in the ABC Nightline piece "Love Psychic" at http://abcnews.go.com/Nightline/video/psychic-claims-couples-work-relationship-problems-41790758. Hagar's description of Paul perfectly dramatizing the hand gestures of his wife, whom he had never seen, is exactly the kind of thing I experienced.

12. Chris Jones, "Oral Histories of 2013: Roger Ebert's Wife, Chaz, On His Final Moments," *Esquire*, December 24, 2013. http://www.esquire.com/blogs/news/roger-ebert-final-moments.

13. This "sociology of the impossible" was first announced in my *Authors of the Impossible: The Paranormal and the Sacred* (Chicago: University of Chicago Press, 2011). I have since honed my thinking here with the help of Philip Wexler and Eric Ouellet.

14. I am relying here and in the paragraph immediately above on the French clinical psychologist Renaud Évrard and his *La folie et paranormal: Vers une clinque des experiences exceptionnelles* (Rennes, France: Presses Universitaries de Rennes, 2014), 12–32. I briefly explored the same therapeutic dimensions with a psychologist and psychiatrist in "Perspectives on 'Sacred Moments' in Psychotherapy," with James W. Lomax, M.D., and Kenneth I. Pargament, Ph.D, *American Journal of Psychiatry* 168, no. 1 (January 2011): 1–7.

15. I first came to this idea in conversation with an admired colleague on a conference panel, Ivan Strenski. I told this story in "Secrets in the Seat: The Erotic, the Paranormal, and the Free Spirit," in *Teaching Mysticism*, ed. William B. Parsons (New York: Oxford University Press, 2011).

16. Robert Moss, *The Secret History of Dreaming* (Novato, CA: New World Library, 2009), 195.

17. See the entry "Mental Telepathy/Extrasensory Perception," in *The Mark Twain Encyclopedia*, ed. J. R. LeMaster and James D. Wilson (New York: Routledge, 1993), 511, which links Clemens's interest in such things to both the era's fascination with psychical research and the author's "own quest for the sources of his creative powers." See also the entry on "De Quille, Dan."

18. The respective issues are *Harper's New Monthly Magazine*, no. 84 (December 1891), 95–104; and no. 92 (September 1895), 521–24. I am employing the reprint of "Mental Telegraphy" in Twain, *Tales of Wonder*, 96–111. For more from Twain on mental telegraphy, see the recently published *Autobiography of Mark Twain*, Vol. 1, ed. Harriet Elinor Smith (Berkeley: University of California Press, 2010), 429, 465.

19. Twain, "Mental Telegraphy," in *Tales of Wonder*, 101–6.

20. Ibid., 99–100. This was no minor eccentricity of the author. Twain suspected that whatever processes this mental telegraphy named had some deep relationship to the sources of his own literary powers. And he acted on this conviction. He was an enthusiastic member of the London Society for Psychical Research. Appropriately enough, he served on the society's Committee on Thought Transference. See Clemens's humorous letter of October 4, 1884, to William Barrett published in the *Journal of the Society for Psychical Research* (October 1884), 166–67, in which he relates another instance of mental telegraphy involving, of all things, his iconic cigars *while he was writing the letter to Barrett.* The letter is available here: http://www.twainquotes.com/Mental_telegraphy.html.

21. John Blake, "Do Loved Ones Bid Farewell from Beyond the Grave?" at http://www.cnn.com/2011/09/23/living/crisis-apparitions/index.html?hpt=hp_c1.

22. William James, *The Works of William James: Essays in Psychical Research*, introduction by Robert A. McDermott (Cambridge, MA: Harvard University Press, 1986).

23. For more on Wallace, see Alan Gauld, *The Founders of Psychical Research* (New York: Schocken, 1968), 83, 137, 214–15.

24. My sincere thanks to Carlos S. Alvarado and Renaud Évrard for their help on this history. All of the textual references for Maxwell below are the work of Évrard in correspondence.

25. For a fuller lexical history, see Leigh Penman, "The History of the Word *Paranormal*," *Notes and Queries* 62, no. 1 (March 2015): 31–34.

26. J. Maxwell, *Les Phénomènes Psychiques: Recherches, Observations, Méthodes*, Préface de Charles Richet (Paris: Félix Alcan, 1903), 90, 102, 104, 105, 111, 113, 114, 158, 161, 201, 207, 208, 211, 267, 298, 299, 300, 301, 305.

27. Ibid., 298.

28. Ibid., 299. According to Évrard, since the work of the Polytechnique administrator colonel Albert De Rochas D'Aiglun, the French researchers had divided these phenomena into

those that "exteriorized" perceptual capacities (like telepathy or clairvoyance) and those that "exteriorized" motor or physical capacities (like psychokinesis or poltergeist phenomena). In both cases, the human being and the human body somehow extended itself well into the physical environment, sometimes at fantastic lengths.

29. Ibid., 57, 69, 99 for the synonyms; 267 for the defining characteristic.

30. Christopher Laursen, "The Poltergeist at the Intersection of the Spirit and the Material: Some Historical and Contemporary Observations," in *Religion: Super Religion*, ed. Jeffrey J. Kripal (New York: Macmillan, 2016), chap. 20.

31. Such "souls of purgatory" are actually one of the keys to the whole story. Often seen as brilliant balls, flames of light, handprints or burns in the historical literature, such luminous soul spheres will also later be linked to the UFO phenomenon (more light balls and bodily burns) by Diana Walsh Pasulka in *Heaven Can Wait: Purgatory in Catholic Devotional and Popular Culture* (New York: Oxford University Press, 2015).

32. A. R. G. Owen, *Can We Explain the Poltergeist?* (New York: Helix, 1964), 129–70. Owen suggests two contributing factors: "very rapid pubescence" and "mental or emotional turmoil" (134). He also claims "conclusive proof" of two classes of poltergeist phenomena: the production of strange noises and the moving of objects by paranormal means (130).

33. King, *On Writing*.

34. Nicholas Royle, *The Uncanny* (Manchester, UK: Manchester University Press, 2003), chap. 19, "The 'Telepathy Effect': Notes Toward a Reconsideration of Narrative Fiction." See also Royle's earlier book, *Telepathy and Literature*.

35. Derrida, "Telepathy," 253.

36. Ibid., 236.

37. Ibid.

38. Ibid., 250–52. In another place, Derrida relates a case not of cross-correspondence, but cross-telephony or "telepathy-calls," that is, a case in which he called a woman just as she was putting her hand on the phone to call him (241). He then refers to the "terrifying telephone," plays on the tele- of telepathy and telephone, and even wonders about a future *tekhne telepathike*, that is, a telepathic technology. Recall Elizabeth's experience of a phone call from the dead.

39. Ibid., 236. Derrida tells us that he derived this time-transcending *koan* from a Zen text.

40. Ibid., 227.

41. Derrida, "Telepathy," 244.

42. For Derrida, it is "difficult to imagine a theory of what they still call the unconscious without a theory of telepathy" (ibid., 237), and yet telepathy remains "the speaking scar of the foreign body" within psychoanalysis, never truly integrated, never ever resolved (261).

43. Ibid., 243.

44. Ibid., 254.

45. Robert A. Orsi, "Abundant History: Marian Apparitions as Alternative Modernity," *Historically Speaking* (September/October 2008): 16.

12: *LA PENSÉE SURHUMAINE*

1. Robert Lanza, with Bob Berman, *Biocentrism: How Life and Consciousness are the Keys to Understanding the True Nature of the Universe* (Dallas: Benbella Books, 2009), 7.

2. A true skeptic would be as skeptical of materialist interpretations of science as any other.

3. The fullest treatment of this particular phenomenon is in Jean-Pierre Jourdan, *Deadline: Dernier Limite* (Paris: Pocket, 2010). But see also Robert J. Brumblay, "Hyperdimensional Perspectives in Out-of-Body and Near-Death Experiences," *Journal of Near-Death Studies* 21, no. 4

(Summer 2003): 201–21; and F. Gordon Greene, "At the Edge of Eternity's Shadows: Scaling the Fractal Continuum from Lower into Higher Space," *Journal of Near-Death Studies* 21, no. 4 (Summer 2003): 223–40. My thanks to Bruce Greyson and Bernard Carr for help here.

4. Clarke, *Childhood's End*, 176.

5. Ibid., 67.

6. Clarke's Buddhism is apparent in the novel. All religions must end, except some form of Buddhism.

7. Ibid., 210.

8. Ibid., 175–76.

9. For a fuller treatment of this history and some other physicists, including James Jeans, Arthur Eddington, David Bohm, and especially Fritjof Capra, see Hammer, *Claiming Knowledge*, particularly the section "Quantum Metaphysics," 271–303. I treated Capra at some length in *Esalen* as well.

10. Heinrich Päs, *The Perfect Wave: With Neutrinos at the Boundary of Space and Time* (Cambridge, MA: Harvard University Press, 2014).

11. Hammer, *Claiming Knowledge*, 279.

12. Ibid., 279.

13. "Mind by its very nature is a *singulare tantum*. I should say: the overall number of minds is just one." Ernest Schrödinger, *What Is Life?* and *Mind and Matter* (Cambridge: Cambridge University Press, 1969). 145; see also 139.

14. George Gamow, *Thirty Years that Shook Physics: The Story of Quantum Theory* (New York: Dover, 1985), 164.

15. Back cover-flap bio of Carl Friedrich von Weizsächer, *The Unity of Nature*, trans. Francis J. Zucker (New York: Farrar, Straus & Giroux, 1980).

16. Von Weizsächer, 383. Von Weizsäcker has "to see" for *noein* instead of the more accurate "to know," probably to bring the verse in line with the Copenhagen interpretation, whereby a quantum particle does not come into being until it is "seen" or observed.

17. This argument appears on the last two pages of *The Unity of Nature*, 399–400, but I am relying here on Päs's reading and explanation in *The Perfect Wave*, 28. I hope I have both men right, as I am no quantum theorist, and I don't stand outside the universe.

18. For another Neoplatonic reading of quantum physics, again by a quantum physicist, see Simon Malin, *Nature Loves to Hide: Quantum Physics and the Nature of Reality, a Western Perspective* (New York: Oxford University Press, 2001).

19. Loren Graham and Jean-Michel Kantor, *Naming Infinity: A True Story of Religious Mysticism and Mathematical Creativity* (Cambridge, MA: Belknap Press at Harvard University Press, 2009).

20. Robert Kanigel, *The Man Who Knew Infinity: A Life of the Genius Ramanujan* (New York: Washington Square Press, 1992), 36.

21. Ibid., 7, 67; see also 65–66.

22. Ibid., 31, 66.

23. David Kaiser, *How the Hippies Saved Physics: Science, Countrculture, and the Quantum Revival* (New York: Norton, 2011).

24. Scott Jones, dir., "Supernature: Esalen and the Human Potential" (in production).

25. Nick Herbert, *Elemental Mind: Human Consciousness and the New Physics* (New York: Dutton Adult, 1993).

26. For an elegant example of how something like Bell's Theorem "makes the impossible possible," see Dean Radin, *Entangled Minds: Extrasensory Experiences in a Quantum Reality* (New York: Paraview Pocket Books, 2006).

27. The phrase occurs in *Ecce Homo: How One Becomes What One Is*. See *Basic Writings of Nietzsche*, translated and edited with commentaries by Walter Kaufmann (New York: Modern Library), 681.

28. I borrow the "Preterhuman," as in "preternatural," from Arthur C. Danto, who considered it accurate but too "eccentric." See his *Nietzsche as Philosopher* (New York: Columbia University Press, 1965), 197. The "most scientific" line is also cited and discussed there, at 203. For what it is worth (and in even more eccentric spirit), I read Nietzsche's revelation of the eternal return, the core of his Sils Maria revelation and so of Zarathustra's teachings, as a nineteenth-century expression of the block universe, that is, the cosmological notion that all time—past, present and future—already exists and is always happening or, if you will, "repeating" itself. I think Nietzsche actually *experienced* a vision of our block universe, much like the film critic Roger Ebert and the near-death author Anita Moorjani discussed in the present book (see the index for references). Here, too, I would place Nietzsche's famous *amor fati* or "love of fate" (not to mention the whole parapsychological realm of precognition). The future, after all, is "already written" in such a block universe. Better to accept and embrace such a present future than to fear it, or to call it impossible.

29. *Ecce Homo*, 744, 751.

30. Ibid., 715. See also 721.

31. Ibid., 757.

32. Ibid., 751.

33. Ibid., 756–757. I am indebted for these passages and leads to my Ph.D. student, Benjamin Mayo, who is working on the mystical and occult dimensions of Nietzsche's thought and reception history and knows more about Nietzsche in his little pinky than I ever will know in my whole body and life.

34. *Ecce Homo*, 737.

35. Quoted in Julian Young, *Friedrich Nietzsche: A Philosophical Biography* (Cambridge: Cambridge University Press, 2010), 10.

36. Bertrand Méheust, ed., Aimé Michel's *L'Apocalypse Molle: Correspondance adressee à Bertrand Méheust de 1978 à 1990 (texts inédits)* (Meyrin, Switzerland: Aldane Editions, 2008); and Aimé Michel, *La Clarté au Coeur du Labyrinthe: Chroniques sur la science et la religion publiées dans France Catholique 1970–1992*, Textes choisis, presents et annotés par Jean-Pierre Rospars, Préface de Oliver Costa de Beauregard (Cointrin, Switzerland: Aldane Editions, 2008).

37. See Michel's essay "Une société secrete mondiale" in Michel Picard's *Aimé Michel ou la Quête du Surhumain: de l'Homme intérieur au Cosmos Pensant: l'Humanité au seuil du prodige* (Agnieres, France: JMG Editions, 2000).

38. As Michel puts it: "la réflexion sur des faits non prouvés circulant clandestinement a guidés et inspirés" (Picard, *Aimé Michel*, 57).

39. I first made this point in "The Future Human: Mircea Eliade and the Fantastic Mutant," in "Remembering, Reimagining, Revalorizing Mircea Eliade," ed. Norman Girardot and Bryan Rennie, special issue in *Archaevs: Studies in History of Religions* 15 (2011).

40. Eliade, *Youth Without Youth*, 68.

41. Ibid., 74.

42. Ibid., 90.

43. Ibid., 3. In another place, the fact that the lightning struck "in the center of the cranial cap" is described as a "significant detail" (125).

44. I made this case in "The Future Human: Mircea Eliade and the Fantastic Mutant," for Norman Girardot and Bryan Rennie, eds.

45. Wendy Doniger, "Introduction II: Life and Art, or Politics and Religion, in the Writings of Mircea Eliade," in *Hermeneutics, Politics, and the History of Religions: The Contested Legacies of Joachim Wach and Mircea Eliade*, ed. Christian Wedemeyer and Wendy Doniger (New York: Oxford University Press, 2010), xxvii.

46. Nicholas Goodrick-Clarke, *The Occult Roots of Nazism: Secret Aryan Cults and Their Influence on Nazi Ideology* (New York: New York University Press, 1993).

47. G. William Barnard, *Living Consciousness: The Metaphysical Vision of Henri Bergson* (Albany: State University of New York Press, 2012), xxi.

48. As a counter-example, Vallée appreciatively referenced the psychoanalytic classic of Robert Lindner, *The Fifty-Minute Hour* (New York: Other Press, 1999).

49. Much of this paragraph is indebted to an email letter from Ralph Blumenthal, September 13, 2016.

50. Keith Thompson, *Angels and Aliens: UFOs and the Mythic Imagination* (New York: Ballantine, 1993).

51. http://www.vanityfair.com/unchanged/2013/05/americans-alien-abduction-science.

52. I am grateful to David Halperin, Diana Walsh Pasulka, Brent Landau, and Troy Tice for their help with this essay.

53. We do not know who painted it. Art historians attribute it to Sebastiano Mainardi, Jacopo del Sellaio or Filippo Lippi. The original provenance was a convent of Sant' Orsolo in the district of San Lorenzo in Florence. I am relying on D'Amico below.

54. See http://www.florenceinferno.com/madonna-of-ufo-painting-palazzo-vecchio/.

55. See http://www.sprezzatura.it/Arte/Arte_UFO_5_eng.htm.

56. The Hebrew word here is *hashmal*. Considered to textualize the highest and most dangerous holy mystery by the ancient rabbis and Jewish mystics, the word was translated into the Greek as *elektron*, into the Latin as *electrum*, and is now the basis of modern Hebrew words for "electricity." It only appears three times in the Bible, all in Ezekiel. See Michael Lieb, *Children of Ezekiel Aliens, UFOs, the Crisis of Race, and the Advent of End Time* (Durham, NC: Duke University Press, 1998).

57. David Halperin, email communication, October 19, 2015.

58. The same phenomenon is claimed in the biblical book of Exodus, of course, where a column or pillar of cloud and lightning is described guiding the Israelites through the desert, but this would take us too far afield.

59. Lieb, *Children of Ezekiel*, 17.

60. I am indebted to Diana Walsh Pasulka for this language and insight.

61. Barbara Ehrenreich, *Living with a Wild God: A Non-believer's Search for the Truth about Everything* (New York: Twelve, 2014), xii–xiii. More on Erhrenreich below, in chapter 13.

62. J. Z. Smith, "Close Encounters of Diverse Kinds," in *Relating Religion: Essays in the Study of Religion* (Chicago: University of Chicago Press, 2004).

63. Brent Landau, "The Coming of the Star-Child: The Reception of the *Revelation of the Magi* in New Age Religious Thought and Ufology," *Gnosis* 1, no. 1 (2016); and Landau, *Revelation of the Magi: The Lost Tale of the Wise Men's Journey to Bethlehem* (New York: HarperCollins, 2010), 90–91.

64. For a modern account, see American evangelist William Marrion Brahnham's vision of a ball of light or "great star" that transforms into an angelic messenger in David Edwin Harrell, Jr., *All Things are Possible: The Healing and Charismatic Revivals in Modern America* (Bloomington: Indiana University Press 1975), 27–28. My thanks to Dale Allison for pointing out this consistent motif and this particular text.

13: COMPARING RELIGIONS IN PUBLIC

1. I summarize my position and tell this story in "Mysticism Disputed: Major Debates in the Field," in *Secret Religion*, ed. April De Conick (New York: Macmillan, 2016).

2. A documentary, "Let Me Be Frank," captures all of this especially well. See http://www.letmebefrankmovie.com/#home.

14: THE SUPER NATURAL

1. Martin Riesbrodt, *The Promise of Salvation: A Theory of Religion*, trans. Steven Rendall (Chicago: University of Chicago Press, 2010), 74–75.

2. For the written account, see Kary Mullis, *Dancing Naked in the Mind Field* (New York: Pantheon, 1998). The event was "Future Technologies, Emergent Mythologies," Earthrise Retreat Center, Institute of Noetic Sciences, Petaluma, California, September 2–5, 2016, sponsored by Esalen Center for Theory and Research.

3. For another expression of this third discursive space with respect to Strieber, see David G. Robertson, "Transformation: Whitley Strieber's Paranormal Gnosis," *Nova Religio* 19, no. 2 (2015). Robertson's expression could also well function as a crystallization of my own corpus and its secret body, with the accent on "gnosis" in the first half of that corpus and the accent on "paranormal" in the second.

4. Whitley Strieber, Foreword to Jacques Vallée, *Dimensions: A Casebook of Alien Contact* (Chicago: Contemporary Books, 1987), vii.

5. Recall John Mack's alleged postmortem communication recounted above, about the alien and/or death.

6. See the Kim Arnold interview in Paola Leopizzi Harris, *UFOs: How Does One Speak to a Ball of Light?* (San Antonio: Anomalist Books, 2011), 1–32.

7. Ehrenreich, *Living with a Wild God*, xii–xiii.

8. Ibid., 114.

9. Ibid., 116–17.

10. Ibid., 226.

11. Ibid., 197.

12. Ibid., 228.

13. Ibid., 229.

14. We need to be careful here, as Dick in fact moved through dozens of mystical systems to explain his metaphysical opening. He usually landed on some form of gnosticism, pantheism, or panentheism, with the latter (the position that everything is in God, but God overflows physical reality) probably being his consensus conclusion. Although she does not realize it, this both-and panentheistic model is very close to Ehrenreich's language of realizing that, as a form of consciousness, she was both "a part of" the universe and "apart from" it (ibid., 50).

15. Ibid., 229.

16. Ibid., 215.

17. Stephen Jones, ed., *A Ghostly Cry: True Encounters with the Paranormal* (New York: Fall River Press, 2009).

18. Paul Davids, "The Life after Death Project" (2013). This film is an excellent treatment (and example) of the nitty-gritty details of the phenomena of synchronicity.

19. Jeffrey J. Kripal, "The Traumatic Secret: Bataille and the Comparative Erotics of Mystical Literature," in *Negative Ecstasies: Georges Bataille and the Study of Religion*, ed. Jeremy Biles and Kent Brintnall (New York: Fordham University Press, 2015).

20. For these details, see Taylor's famous TED talk, "My Stroke of Insight" (now at almost twenty million views): http://www.ted.com/talks/jill_bolte_taylor_s_powerful_stroke_of _insight.

21. McGilchrist, *Master and His Emissary.*

22. See Anthony B. Pinn, *Terror and Triumph: The Nature of Black Religion* (Minneapolis, MN: Augsburg Fortress, 2003).

23. Ytasha L. Womack, *Afrofuturism: The World of Black Sci-Fi and Fantasy Culture* (Chicago: Chicago Review Press, 2013).

24. Stephen Finley and Margarita Guillory, eds., *Esotericism in African American Religious Experience: "There Is a Mystery"* (Leiden: Brill, 2014).

25. Ouellet, *Illuminations*, 133–48.

26. Ibid., 139.

27. Stephen C. Finley, "Hidden Away: Esotericism and Gnosticism in Elijah Muhammad's Nation of Islam, in *Histories of the Hidden God: Concealment and Revelation in Western Gnostic, Esoteric, and Mystical Traditions*, by April D. DeConick and Grant Adamson (Durham, NC: Acumen, 2013).

28. Michael Lieb, "Above Top Secret: The Nation of Islam and the Advent of the 'Mother Plane,'" *Criterion* 43, no. 1, 4–5. For Lieb's fuller argument and its many nuances, see Lieb, *Children of Ezekiel.*

29. Lieb, "Above Top Secret," 5.

30. Ibid., 6.

31. Louis Farrakhan, *The Announcement: A Final Warning to the U.S. Government* (Chicago: FCN Publishing Co., 1989), 5–6.

32. Lieb, "Above Top Secret," 8.

33. Ibid., 6.

34. Stephen Finley, "UFOs: A Position Paper," for "Beyond the Spinning: Shifting the Conversation around the UFO Phenomenon," a symposium sponsored by the Center for Theory and Research, Esalen Institute, at Institute of Noetic Sciences, Petaluma, California, September 11–13, 2015.

35. For three examples, see Andy Sixkiller Clarke, *Encounters with Star People: Untold Stories of American Indians* (San Antonio: Anomalist Books, 2012); Clarke, *Sky People: Untold Stories of Alien Encounters in Mesoamerica* (Pompton Plains, NJ: New Page Books, 2015); and Colm A. Kelleher and George Knapp, *Hunt for the Skinwalker: Science Confronts the Unexplained at a Remote Ranch in Utah* (New York: Paraview Pocket Books, 2005).

36. *The Complete Books of Charles Fort*, with a new introduction by Damon Knight (New York: Dover, 1974), 471.

37. Joscelyn Godwin, *Upstate Cauldron: Eccentric Spiritual Movements in Early New York State* (Albany: State University of New York Press, 2014).

38. Greg Mogenson, *A Most Accursed Religion: When a Trauma Becomes God* (Spring 2005).

39. Jacques Derrida, "Telepathy," in his *Psyche*, 254.

40. Carl Raschke, "UFOs: Ultraterrestrial Agents of Cultural Deconstruction," in *Cyberbiological Studies of the Imaginal Component in the UFO Contact Experience*, ed. Dennis Stillings (Archaeus Project, 1989), 25, 28, 29.

41. Philip K. Dick, *The Exegesis of Philip K. Dick*, ed. by Pamela Jackson and Jonathan Lethem, annotations ed. by Erik Davis (Boston: Houghton Mifflin Harcourt, 2011), 107.

42. The next two paragraphs are condensed revisions of material appearing in Jeffrey J. Kri-

pal, "On the Mothman, God, and Other Monsters: The Demonology of John A. Keel," in *Histories of the Hidden God:* ed. DeConick and Adamson.

43. Kelleher and Knapp, *Hunt for the Skinwalker*, 270.

44. Personal communication, October 18, 2010.

45. Whitley Strieber, *Evenings with Demons: Stories from 30 Years* (Grantham, NH: Borderlands Press, 1997), 192, 176, 184.

46. Personal communication, August 11, 2014. The erection, minus the ejaculation, is discussed in the hypnosis session at Strieber 2008, 77.

47. Whitley Strieber, *Communion: A True Story* (New York: Harper, 2008), xix.

48. Ibid., 4.

49. Ibid., 14.

50. Ibid., 16.

51. Ibid., 18.

52. Ibid., 175.

53. Personal communication, August 11, 2014.

54. Linda Zimmerman, *Hudson Valley UFOs: Startling Eyewitness Accounts from 1909 to the Present* (New York: Eagle Press), 1, 4, 7.

55. Zimmerman, *Hudson Valley UFOs*, 2.

56. Zimmerman, *Hudson Valley UFOs*; and *In the Night Sky: Hudson Valley UFO Sightings from the 1930s to the Present* (New York: Eagle Press, 2014).

57. J. Allen Hynek, Philip J. Imbrogno, and Bob Pratt, *Night Siege: The Hudson Valley UFO Sightings* (St. Paul, MN: Llewellyn Publications, 1998).

58. Zimmerman, *Hudson Valley UFOs*; Hynek, Imbrogno, and Pratt, *Night Siege.*

59. Hynek, Imbrogno, and Pratt, *Night Siege*, 81.

60. Ibid., 39.

61. Ibid., 56–57.

62. "Skies, Phone Lines Light Up Az.," *USA Today*, June 18, 1997, front page.

63. Leslie Kean, *UFOs: Generals, Pilots, and Government Officials Go on the Record* (New York: Harmony Books, 2010), 253.

64. Charles Fort, *The Book of the Damned: The Collected Works of Charles Fort*, introduction by Jim Steinmeyer (New York: Penguin Tarcher, 2008), 163.

65. Franics H. Crick and Leslie E. Orgel, "Directed Panspermia," *Icarus* 19 (1973): 341–48.

66. William James, *A Pluralistic Universe*, introduction by Henry Samuel Levinson (Lincoln: University of Nebraska Press, 1996), 309.

67. Strieber, *Communion*, 90.

68. Ibid., xv–xvi.

69. Ibid., 5, 216, 222, 282–85, 301.

70. Ibid., 300.

71. Ibid., 301.

72. Ibid., 104, 163, 172, 200, 205, 298.

73. For some sample erotic passages, both graphic and symbolic, see ibid., 76–79, 99, 247–48, and 282.

74. Ibid., 216.

75. Ibid., 208.

76. This is a well-known feature of poltergeist phenomena in parapsychology. Such a person is called a "focal agent."

MEUM

1. The latter case, largely unknown in the English literature, is particularly striking, as it involves reports of *physical* encounters with the bilocating nun around extreme trauma, in this case, physical beatings and imprisonment during the Nazi occupation of France in World War II. See Bertrand Méheust, *Jésus Thaumaturge: Enquête sur l'homme et ses miracles* (Paris: Inter-Editions, 2015), 130–35.

2. Michael Grosso, *The Man Who Could Fly: St. Joseph of Copertino and the Mystery of Levitation* (Lanham, MD: Rowman & Littlefield, 2015).

3. See Thomas Fabisiak, *The "Nocturnal Side of Science" in David Friedrich Strauss's* Life of Jesus Critically Examined (Atlanta: SBL Press, 2015).

4. Dale Allison, *Resurrecting Jesus: The Earliest Christian Tradition and Its Interpreters* (New York: T & T Clark, 2005).

5. Méheust, *Jésus Thaumaturge*, 197–99.

15: THE NEW COMPARATIVISM

1. Louis Menand, "Dangers Within and Without," *Profession* (2005): 10–17.

2. "Mutants, Mystics and Scientologists (Thoughts on Jeffrey Kripal, Gnosticism, and Sci-Fi Spirituality)" at http://thenightshirt.com/?p=1367.

3. Lawrence Wright, *Going Clear: Scientology, Hollywood, and the Prison of Belief* (New York: Vintage, 2013), 35–36.

4. Hayden White, *Metahistory: The Historical Imagination in Nineteenth-Century Europe* (Baltimore: Johns Hopkins University Press, 2014). For much more on these historical imaginations and metahistories, see my "The Mythologies of Scholarship: The Deep Narratives of the Study of Religion and Some Possible Futures," in *Religion: Narrating Religion*, ed. Sarah Johnston (London: Macmillan, 2016), 353–72.

5. See Wouter J. Hanegraaff, "Religion and the Historical Imagination: Esoteric Tradition as Poetic Invention," in *Dynamics of Religion: Past and Present*, ed. Christoph Bochinger and Jörg Rüpke (Berlin: DeGruyter, 2016).

6. Another important voice here is Bruce Lincoln in *Theorizing Myth: Narrative, Ideology, and Scholarship* (Chicago: University of Chicago Press, 2000).

7. I am relying here on Lachman, *The Secret Teachers*, 353–56.

8. With respect to the brightening, I have been inspired by the work of Victoria Nelson in books like *The Secret Life of Puppets* and *Gothicka*.

9. This is likely an allusion to Giulio Tononi's claim that "consciousness is a fundamental part of the universe—just as fundamental as mass, charge, and so forth" (quoted in Kelly, BP, 118). http://www.ted.com/talks/david_chalmers_how_do_you_explain_consciousness.

10. Simon Conway Morris, *The Runes of Evolution: How the Universe Became Self-Aware* (West Conshohocken, Pennsylvania: Templeton Press, 2015), 301–3.

11. Eduardo Viveiros de Castro, *Cannibal Metaphysics: For a Post-Structural Anthropology*, ed. and trans. Peter Skafish (Minneapolis, MN: Univocal, 2014), 65–68.

12. http://www.texasmonthly.com/the-culture/unidentified-scholarly-subject/.

13. For Méheust, see my chapter study of his corpus in *Authors*. For Hanegraaff, see his section on "Magnetic Historiography: German Romantic Mesmerism and Evolutionism" in *Esotericism and the Academy*, 260–77.

14. *Folklore* 6, no. 3 (September 1895): 236–48.

15. See, for example, Gananath Obeyesekere, *Imagining Karma: Ethical Transformation in*

Amerindian, Buddhist and Greek Rebirth (Berkeley: University of California Press, 2002); and Alma Gottlieb, *The Afterlife Is Where We Come From: The Culture of Infancy in West Africa* (Chicago: The University of Chicago Press, 2004). Obeyesekere's corpus, with its astonishing fusion of anthropological comparison, psychoanalytic sophistication, and ontological openness, is a beautiful example of the new comparativism I am trying to imagine here. See especially his *The Awakened Ones: Phenomenology of Visionary Experience* (New York: Columbia University Press, 2012).

16. Stang, *Our Divine Double*, 184.

17. I am inspired here by Hanegraaff, "Religion and the Historical Imagination."

18. Quoted in Stang, *Our Divine Double*, 140. There is something vaguely sexual and sublimating, even "Tantric," about recovering a "pearl" from a sleeping serpent in the land of flesh and embodiment. As I have pointed out elsewhere, the ritually aroused phallus can create a pearl of lubricatory fluid if ejaculation is suppressed, that is, if the serpent is not fully aroused (*Kālī's Child*, 161).

19. Frits Staal, *Advaita and Neoplatonism* (University of Madras, 1961).

20. See Dipesh Chakrabarty, *Provincializing Europe: Postcolonial Thought and Historical Difference* (Chicago: University of Chicago Press, [2000] 2008); and Charles Taylor, *The Secular Age* (Cambridge, MA: Harvard University Press, 2007).

21. For a potent reminder of this historical fact, see Giuseppe Baroetto, "The Illusion of Reincarnation," in Hakl, ed., *Octagon*, 265–73.

22. Bilinda Straight, *Miracles and Extraordinary Experience in Northern Kenya* (Philadelphia: University of Pennsylvania Press, 2007), 7–8.

23. Jim B. Tucker, *Return to Life: Extraordinary Cases of Children Who Remember Previous Lives* (New York: St. Martin's Griffin, 2015), 200.

24. A sidenote, but perhaps a relevant one: Stevenson liked the adjective "paranormal" and used it often but disliked the expression "parapsychology," because he felt it ghettoized researchers and prevented fruitful cross-disciplinary correction and conversation.

25. A special issue of the *Journal of Scientific Exploration* was dedicated to Stevenson: vol. 22, no. 1 (Spring 2008). An excellent biography also exists, Tom Shroder's *Old Souls: Compelling Evidence from Children Who Remember Past Lives* (New York: Simon & Schuster, 2001). Significantly, the book is partly inspired by a massive synchronicity the author experienced in college in 1976: "For some reason, I was given this gift, this weird, irrefutable demonstration that there is more to the world than its surface. That whatever we're all about, whatever the universe is, it is far more than just some empty, mechanical material machine" (237).

26. *Cases of the Reincarnation Type*, 4 vols. (Charlottesville: University Press of Virginia, 1983), which was then supplemented by a fifth volume on European cases: *European Cases of the Reincarnation Type* (Jefferson, NC: McFarland and Company, 2003).

27. Jim B. Tucker, *Life Before Life: A Scientific Investigation of Children's Memories of Previous Lives* (New York: St. Martin's Press, 2005); and *Return to Life*. The latter book concludes with Tucker's own speculative ontology.

28. Ian Stevenson, *Reincarnation and Biology: A Contribution to the Etiology of Birthmarks and Birth Defects* (Westport, CT: Praeger Publishers, 1997).

29. For a short and accessible example, see Stevenson, "Birthmarks and Birth Defects Corrpsonding to Wounds on Deceased Persons (1993)," in *Science, the Self, and Survival After Death: Selected Writings of Ian Stevenson*, ed. Emily Williams Kelly (Lanham, MD: Rowman & Littlefield, 2013), chap. 25, pp. 263–78.

30. Tucker, *Life Before Life*, 12.

31. Ibid.

32. Shroder, *Old Souls*, 173.

33. Tucker, *Life Before Life*, 12.

34. Private conversation with Bruce Greyson, University of Virginia, April 30, 2016.

35. Emily Williams Kelly, "Conclusion: Toward a Tertium Quid," in *Science, the Self, and Survival after Death*, ed. Kelly, 387.

36. Kerr L. White, "Ian Stevenson: Recollections," *Journal of Scientific Exploration* 22, no. 1 (2008): 13.

37. Stevenson, "Some of My Journeys in Medicine (1989)," in *Science, the Self, and Survival after Death*, ed. Kelly, 18.

38. For the ESP material, see Carlos S. Alvarado and Nancy L. Zingrone, "Ian Stevenson and the Modern Study of Spontaneous ESP Experiences," *Journal of Scientific Exploration*: 44–53. For the metal-bending scene at the first Sursem meeting, see Kripal, "Mind Matters."

39. Ian Stevenson, "A Case of the Psychotherapist's Fallacy: Hypnotic Regression to 'Previous Lives,'" *American Journal of Clinical Hypnosis* 36, no. 3 (January 1994): 188–93.

40. See "The Heretic," in Shroder, *Old Souls*, 96–110. For the near-death material, see Bruce Greyson, "Ian Stevenson's Contribution to Near-Death Studies," ibid., 54–63.

41. Stevenson, "Some of My Journeys," 17.

42. Stevenson, "Comments on the Psychological Effects of Mescaline and Allied Drugs" (1957), in *Science, the Self, and Survival after Death*, ed. Kelly, 99. For a similar description about how LSD and mescaline "increased my conviction of the dual natures of mind and body," see Stevenson, "Some of My Journeys," 17.

43. Stevenson, "Thoughts on the Decline of Major Paranormal Phenomena," in *Science, the Self, and Survival after Death*, ed. Kelly, 137.

44. Schroder, *Old Souls*, 106–7.

45. Quoted in Kelly, ed., *Science, the Self, and Survival after Death*, 383.

46. Stevenson, "Thoughts,"138.

47. Ibid. 141.

48. Shroder, *Old Souls*, 107.

49. Quoted in Randall Styers, *Making Magic: Religion Magic, and Science in the Modern World* (New York: Oxford University Press, 2004), 3.

50. Ian Stevenson, M.D., *Children Who Remember Previous Lives: A Question of Reincarnation* (Charlottesville: University Press of Virginia, 1987), 59–61.

51. See Magee, "Hegel on the Paranormal."

52. Stevenson, *Children Who Remember Previous Lives*, 259–60.

53. Anita Moorjani, *Dying to Be Me: My Journey from Cancer, to Near Death, to True Healing* (Carlsbad, CA: Hay House, 2012), xiv.

54. Ibid., 60.

55. Ibid., 64–65.

56. Ibid., 142.

57. Ibid., 142–43.

58. Ibid., 68–69.

59. Ibid. 144.

60. Ibid., 137.

CLOSING

1. This is more or less what Ioan Couliano was trying to do, I think, with his "morphodynamic" view of history in *The Tree of Gnosis: Gnostic Mythology from Early Christianity to Modern Nihilism* (New York: HarperCollins, 1992).

2. For this story, from a scholar of religion who chose to remain anonymous, see the opening of the final chapter of *Comparing Religions*.

3. All of these points are discussed and referenced in Mac Linscott Ricketts, "Glimpses into Eliade's Religious Beliefs as Seen in his *Portugal Journal*," in Hakl, ed., *Octagon*.

4. Eliade, *Youth Without Youth*, 70. For what it is worth, I suspect Eliade's "knowing smiles" are inspired by the similar knowing grins of Krishna in the Bhagavad Gita.

5. Ibid., 101.

6. Ibid., 103.

7. For more on this postcolonial reading of Hume, see my "Introduction: Reimagining the Supernatural in the Study of Religion," in *Religion: Super Religion*, ed. Kripal (New York: Macmillan, 2016).

8. Doniger, "Introduction II," xxvii. For the passage, see Eliade, *Youth Without Youth*, 22.

9. I have spoken to the Parapsychological Association twice now on these difficult subjects. For one such lecture, see my J. B. Rhine Plenary Address, "Authors of the Impossible: What the Humanities Have to Offer Parapsychology," *Mindfield* 6, no. 3 (Fall 2014): 55–63, particularly the section entitled "Why You Are So Scary."

10. Quoted in Ricketts, "Glimpses into Eliade's Religious Beliefs," in Hakl, ed., *Octagon*, 225.

11. I play this out with respect to Hakl and Eranos in my review of Hakl's book in *Aries: Journal for the Study of Western Esotericism* 15, no. 2 (2015): 8–16. For Josephson-Storm, see *The Myth of Disenchantment*.

12. I borrow the phrase "the secret history of consciousness" from the learned bard of the esoteric Gary Lachman in books like *A Secret History of Consciousness* (Great Barrington, MA: Lindsifarne Books, 2003) and *The Secret Teachers of the Western World*. I also have in mind the storied program in the history of consciousness at the University of California, Santa Cruz.

13. This mountain metaphor was an intended allusion to Walt Whitman's *Leaves of Grass* and its understanding of scriptural texts that, like leaves on a tree, have grown out of us, will be shed by us, and will grow out of us again (*Comparing Religions*, 63).

14. See T. G. Vaidyanathan and Jeffrey J. Kripal, *Vishnu on Freud's Desk: A Reader in Psychoanalysis and Hinduism* (New Delhi: Oxford University Press, 1999), 438–39; and Kripal, *Authors of the Impossible*, 13, 19, 244–45.

15. Evans is commenting on my own work on the imaginal in conversation with the writings of Jorge Ferrer and Tanya Luhrmann. See http://philosophyforlife.org/exploring-the-multi verse-of-spiritual-pluralism/.

16. Stanislaw Lem, *Solaris*, trans. Joanna Kilmartin and Steve Cox (San Diego: Harcourt, 1970), 165.

17. Ibid.

18. See "The Solaris Mind: Hypnagogia, Meditation, and Insight" at http://thenightshirt .com/?p=2218.

19. 172–73. Lem reflects on the history of religions and the belief in "an imperfect god" whose imperfection "represents his essential characteristic" and who "would like to free himself from matter, but . . . cannot," a "very old mimoid," at 197–99.

20. I draw the language of enactment and indeterminacy from a public lecture of Jorge Ferrer, March 21, 2015, for the conference "The Spiritual but Not Religious: Past, Present, Future(s)," Rice University.

21. Charles Stang *Apophasis and Pseudonymity in Dionsyius the Aeropagite: No Longer "I"* (New York: Oxford University Press, 2012); and Stang, *Our Divine Double*. Stang in turn borrowed the phrase from Bernard McGinn.

22. Taylor, *Secular Age*.

23. I fully understand that the reductionist will step in here and point out that the *representations* of such experiences are indeed always local, contextual, constructed, and so on. This is true. This is also an example of the conflation of cognition and culture with consciousness that I referred to above as the fundamental limiting factor of our present order of knowledge.

24. Jackson and Lethem, eds., *The Exegesis of Philip K. Dick*, Davis, annotation editor, 588.

25. Ibid., 717–18.

26. Bernardo Kastrup, *More than Allegory: On Religious Myth, Truth and Belief* (Winchester, UK: Iff Books, 2016), 212.

27. Bernardo Kastrup, *Why Materialism Is Baloney: How True Skeptics Know There Is No Death and Fathom Answers to Life, the Universe, and Everything* (Winchester, UK: Iff Books, 2014), 81.

28. Ibid., 89.

AIRPORT AFTERWORD

1. One of the more open-minded skeptics, Michael Shermer, gets this key point about meaning outside of cause, but only after he and his bride experienced such a paranormal event on their wedding day. See his "I Just Witnessed an Event So Mysterious It Shook My Skepticism," *Scientific American*, October 2014.

Index of My Brain

This index is another act of clarification and crystallization. I have included the names and subjects that one might look for in a typical search. Even here, though, the list is selective, as the point of the index is not exhaustion or some pointless expansion of detail but a coming-into-focus of the whole, of the vision, of the secret body within the corpus.

I imagined the index a bit like a neuroscientist imagines the brain's hyperconnected neurons and their intricate branchings. My general rule was to look for names, subjects, and terms that would spark the most associations or meanings in my mind (and so also, I assume, the most connected neurons in my brain). I then expanded on the most densely connected of these branches with short phrases or descriptions in the subheadings to connect them further. Nothing is unintentional here. It is no accident, for example, that the thing begins with a British theologian (with a quasi-monastic surname) writing about the fourth dimension, gender relations, and occult phenomena and ends with a Japanese contemplative tradition of paradoxical riddle, the complete collapse of the sacred and the profane in the ordinary, and the "Aha!" of enlightenment in the Now.

It was in this way that I sought to tighten and strengthen the spider's web one last time and, in some cases, foreground ideas that were present but relatively undeveloped or unconscious and may well be still "future" for me (the entries on "conscious energies," "myth," and "science fiction" are good examples). These final pages thus become another way of becoming more conscious of the outlines of my thought, of sensing the invisible spider that spun these webs. Here that sticky weave is expressed as a series of brief summary codes and page numbers—not exactly your most literary approach, but efficient and helpful, I hope.

Unless, of course, you happen to be a fly.

Abbott, Edwin, 263
abortion, 31, 438n1, 438n5
Ackerman, Forrest J., 322
Adam and Eve myth, 119–21, 174–75, 261
Adidam, 70
Afrofuturism, 326
Akhenaton, 283
Albanese, Catherine, 185
al-Hallaj, 107–9
alien abduction literature: and Atlantic slave trade, 329; bilateral brain and phenomenology of, 324–25; horror and sci-fi film expression of, 337; insectoid theme, 235; possible racial background of the "gray," 327; presence of the dead in, 287, 317; role of trance induction in, 285; sexual violence of, 338; in William Blake, 431. *See also* esotericism, extraterrestrial; UFO
Allison, Dale, 37, 38, 356
Alpert, Richard. *See* Dass, Ram (Richard Alpert)
American Academy of Religion, 69, 297–98, 423
anorexia, 30, 35, 39, 46, 165
anti-intellectualism, 298
Arnold, Ken, 317–18
Atmanspacher, Harald, 198, 239, 267
Authors of the Impossible: attempt to "cross over" into broader readership, 166; emergent mythologies as implicit focus, 271; history of paranormal in, 238–39, 403; and methodology of this book, 1–2; relationship to teaching of Nietzsche's *Zarathustra*, 272; "science mysticism" coinage in, 315; Simon Conway Morris employment of, 368; superhumanism of Aimé Michel and students in, 273; treatment of Jacques Vallée, 282

Barnard, G. William, 80–81
Baum, Frank, 23–25
Beat poets, 86
Bell, Rudolf, 39
Benjamin, Walter, 15
Bergson, Henri, 154, 216, 279
Bernard of Clairvaux, 65
Big Bang, 261
Bigfoot, 240
biological gods: defined and discussed, 318–19; "feeding off" of human beings, 319, 322; as non-carbon based life forms, 410; as nonhuman agents in human history,

380; as participating in posited shared planetary Mind, 413; relationship to categories of animism, panpsychism, and polytheism, 319, 410. *See also* conscious energy; plasmas
Blake, William, 42–43, 44, 97, 98, 100, 140, 141–59, 215, 221, 431
block universe, 401, 455n28
Bloom, Harold, 362
Blumenthal, Ralph, 284–87
Boas, Antonio Vila, 338
Boehme, Jacob: and dual aspect monism, 200; exemplar of heretical heterosexuality thesis, 42–43; as Hermetic, 207; as implicit exemplar of evolutionary esotericism, 177, 207–8
Bohm, David, 198
bracketing, 374
brahman, 36, 161, 194, 379, 428
brain, bilateral: and academic eclipse of the imagination, 6–8; and "being right," 10; light on phenomenology of the alien, 324–25; universe as giant brain in Philip K. Dick, 416–18; universe as literally God's brain in Bernardo Kastrup, 417–18. *See also* Taylor, Jill Bolte
Brent, T. David, 402, 433
bridal chamber, 42, 43, 131–32
Broad, C. D., 192, 216
Brooks, David, 212–13
Buber, Martin, 113
Bucke, Richard Maurice, 116, 119
Butterfield, Stephen, 89–92, 96

Campbell, Joseph, 156
Campbell, Virginia, 252
Capps, Donald, 36–39
Capps, Walter, 143
Capra, Fritjof, 197
Carlin, Nathan, 36, 39
Carpenter, Edward, 175
Carpenter, Karen, 30
Carrington, Hereward, 251–52
castration, 41, 354, 391
Catherine of Genoa, Saint, 203
celibacy, 41, 46, 133–34
Chakraborty, Dipesh, 379
chakra systems, 50, 62, 170, 447n1
Chalmers, David, 198, 368
channeling, 237, 348
Chardin, Teilhard de, 43, 119, 176, 193, 402
charisma, 82–83

Chattopadhyaya, Rajagopal, 59–60

Christology, 7, 353–54

Clarke, Arthur C., 176; and *Childhood's End*, 262–64, 312, 321

Clemens, Samuel. *See* Twain, Mark

coincidentia oppositorum: and the erotic in my thought, 68; in Indian Tantra and the thought of Mircea Eliade, 110–13, 114; of Nicolas of Cusa, 110, 113; in structural anthropology, 133–34. *See also* paradox

comparativism, new: appearance and place in this book, 19; and consciousness, 399; and cosmic humanities, 370; and criterion of embarrassment, 355; and cultural transmission, 397–98; filter thesis as philosophy of mind of, 195, 368; first use of phrase in, 280, 293–95; and gnomon 19 on the future of the past, 372–73; ideological and moral critique of, 371–72; imagining from below, 363; and Mircea Eliade's esoteric or "fictional" double of Dominic Matei, 404; as more capacious and critically inclusive historical imagination, 364–65, 376, 399, 420–21; ontological turn in, 370; realist comparisons of, 368, 372–73; rooted in "universal" body, 142; speculative ontologies of, 373–74; and Super Story trilogy project, 424. See also *Comparing Religions* (2014); comparison

Comparing Religions (2014): attempt to "cross over" into broader readership, 166; the humanities defined in, 206; origins of initiatory model at Westminster College after Bryan Rennie, 305–6; "super natural" coinage in, 315; treatment of the mystical experiences of G. William Barnard, 81. *See also* comparativism, new; comparison

comparison: as art, 103–4; as associative, Internet-like magic, 401; Christology of, 353–54; exclusivism, 308; inclusivism, 308–9; initiation into, 305; as justice, 306–7; living, as correspondence between subjective states and objective events within paranormal experience, 1; origins in mystical literature and thought, 124–25, 170; pluralism, 309; of quantum mystical literature, 264–68; secret humanism implied in, 310–11. *See also* comparativism, new; *Comparing Religions* (2014)

conscious energy: as altered states of energy, 6, 8, 424; "electricity" of charisma, 373;

and electromagnetism of physics, 100; as energy species or biological gods, 292, 333; as evolutionary, 182–83; fundamental unity of consciousness and energy, 36, 50–51, 56, 61, 63, 100; as "God," 393, 396; and the imagination, 232; in Jill Bolte Taylor, 225; and kundalini yoga, 50, 92, 93, 182–83, 277; and that Night, 51, 53, 55, 99; and paraphysical esotericism, 200–201, 232; and poltergeist phenomena, 251–53; relationship to sexuality, 62, 93, 123, 134, 158, 251–53, 417; as *shakti*, 50, 62, 86, 92–95, 169, 377, 381; as soul, 253; source of genius, 182; source of *siddhi*s or paranormal powers, 182, 231, 243; in William Blake as foundation of reason, 97, 145. *See also* biological gods; plasmas

consciousness: as antisocial or antinomian, 149–50; base of *all* human knowledge, 206, 400, 414; as cosmic, fundamental or "primitive," 149–50, 175, 368, 448n9; as countercultural, 150; in dual aspect monism, 197–200; eternal, 149, 367, 370, 396, 401; and filter thesis, 193–200; as fundamentally exotic, 139, 166; historiography of, 409; and the humanities, 206; illusory in conventional neuroscience, 255; is the new sacred, 400; as non-human, 196; (not) always intentional, 196; prior to culture, 137, 379; as Subjective, Objective and Absolute in Hegel, 208–11; as subversive and counter to religion, 190–91; sui generis, 206, 256, 413; terrifying beyond belief, 154; transconsciousness in thought of Mircea Eliade, 7, 194. *See also* gnomon 10

CORT (cases of the reincarnation type), 192, 382–91, 397

counterculture: and American reception of Indian Tantra, 50; as more influential than colonialism on the study of religion, 137–40; and reception of William Blake, 145–59; and Tantric transmission, 85–86. *See also* gnomon 9

Crookes, Sir William, 248–49

Crowe, Catherine, 251, 365

Daoism, 36, 86, 124, 217, 265

Darwin, Charles, 166, 171, 174–75, 178–79, 190, 193, 201, 202, 214, 278–79, 298, 365

Dass, Ram (Richard Alpert), 153–54

Da Vinci Code, The, 43–44

Dawkins, Richard, 175, 212

Day, Dorothy, 31

Dean, James, 160

debunkers, 83, 241, 247, 262, 318, 340, 345, 406, 424, 448n10

DeConick, April, 132

deification: and Adam and Eve myth, 122; dialectic of in the thought of Elliot Wolfson, 102; and Eucharist, 357; and filter thesis, 203, 413; and gnosis, 181; in Indian Tantra, 50; as major motif of my corpus, 19, 354; of Master Fard Muhammad, 329; reading as, 64, 70–71; in Saint Catherine of Genoa, 203; in William Blake, 147

de Martino, Ernesto, 410

Derrida, Jacques, 15, 208, 241, 243, 253–54, 255, 256, 332, 370, 397

de Santo, Nina, 247, 256–57

Dick, Philip K., 1, 15, 167, 207, 210, 254, 319, 321, 331, 332, 362, 411, 413, 415–18, 421, 423, 457n14

Dilthey, Wilhelm, 205

Dimock, Edward, 48

docetism, 233

Doniger, Wendy: as artist, 143; clairvoyant dream of, 64, 77, 236; influence on my work, 48–49, 141–43; intellectual generosity of, 140; on Mircea Eliade, 277, 402, 405–6; as object of censorship campaigns, 57; and structuralist anthropology, 133–34, 239; success in remote viewing experiment at Esalen, 159–61

Douglas, Mary, 87–88, 133, 239

dreams: clairvoyant, 64, 77, 236; precognitive or premonitorial, 108, 112, 231–32, 245–47, 273; in seminary psychoanalysis, 141; and symbolic imaginal, 236–37

dual aspect monism: of Barbara Ehrenreich, 320; and cosmic history, 205; defined and discussed, 197–200; echoed in my category of the super natural, 316; implicit in Jacob Boehme, 200; model for antistructure and nonduality of the paranormal, 239, 241; Pauli-Jung variant, 198–200, 267; relevance to comparative practices of the quantum mystical literature, 267; relevance to contemporary critique of epistemological value of religious "experience," 199; and Viveiros de Castro, 370. See also Atmanspacher, Harald; gnomon 16

Du Bois, W. E. B., 312, 326

Durkheim, Émile, 298, 334

Eagleman, David, 225–27

Ebert, Roger, 237, 395, 401, 417, 455n28

Eckhart, Meister: as apophatic mystic, 450–51n40; Eckhartian allusion of "Kali's child," 46, 52; formative influence on my thought at Chicago with Bernard McGinn, 48; and Hegel's Hermeticism, 192, 210; on the Human as Two, 399, 415–16, 420–21; in thought of Aldous Huxley, 222

Ehrenreich, Barbara, 176, 292, 319–22

Einstein, Albert, 108, 269, 271, 401

Eliade, Mircea: camouflaged sacred, 312; countercultural context of career and reception history, 137–38; creative hermeneutics of, 205–6, 403; dialectic of the sacred, 112–13, 315–16, 376; diurnal/nocturnal modes of thought, 54; esoteric self as double in Youth Without Youth, 404–5; fascism charges against, 278–79, 360–61, 406–8; hierophany, 315–16, 444n66; Human as Two in thought, 7; intellectual transformation from new humanism to new humanity, 276–78, 403–5; on Jesus, 353; John Mack's employment of in his study of abductions, 281; legitimation of shamanism, Tantra and yoga, 423; mystical origins of thought, 103, 109–13, 117–18, 403; polytheism of, 406; premonitorial dreams of, 112; on reincarnation memories, 405; resonances in my work, 402–9; resonant with that Night, 101–2; on the sacred as a structural element of consciousness, 399; on the supernormal, 402; terrorizing of in Hyde Park, 402; transconsciousness of, 7, 194

Emanation, 169, 177, 180–83, 201–3, 449n2

Emerson, Ralph Waldo, 184–85, 189–91, 213, 400

emptiness (Buddhism), 90–91, 124, 199, 416, 450–51n40

energy. See biological gods; conscious energy; plasmas

erotic (category in my thought): dialectic misunderstood, 57; hydraulic model of in Freud and Tantra, 61–62; as key to out-of-body flight, 100; from Plato, 61; and Ramakrishna, 68; resonance model of, 62–63. See also gnomon 3

Esalen: attempt to "cross over" into broader readership, 166; bodies of, 171; coinage of the "future of the past" in, 372; exemplary of thesis of *Roads of Excess*, 170; origin in late-night phone call, 169–70; as origin of Tantric Transmission thesis, 85; relation of project to *Kali's Child*, 171; treatment of secret remote viewing programs, 209; "X" found while finishing, 258–60. *See also* gnomon 5

Esalen Institute: citizen diplomacy with Soviet Union and in Middle East, 186, 188; collaboration with Wouter Hanegraaff at, 125; and counterculture, 187; evolutionary esotericism of, 190–91; and John Mack, 286–87; "impossible" conversations at, 160; in "Mad Men" finale, 183; metal bending at, 385; and natural world, 189; not too dodgy for Wendy Doniger, 159–60; and quantum mystical literature, 197, 270; as real-world mystical tradition of the X-Men mythology, 172–73, 257, 258–59, 424; teaching with Paul Selig at, 237; too dodgy for Ian Stevenson, 192, 385; Whitley Strieber at, 315, 337. See also *Esalen*; Huxley, Aldous; Murphy, Michael

esotericism: as countercultural, 147; emanationism of, 169, 180–83; of scientists, 275–76; and Wouter Hanegraaff, 170, 180–81

esotericism, evolutionary: agnosticism about of Théodore Flournoy, 235; of Aimé Michel, 273–75; of Arthur C. Clarke, 176; David Friedrich Strauss, 356; defined and discussed, 175–76; and deification, 203; emanation models of, 180–81; of Esalen Institute and X-Men mythology, 172–73, 187, 190–91, 258–59; and extraterrestrial esotericism, 316; fascism charges against, 278–79, 296, 407–8; and filter thesis, 200–204; in heart of modern science, 276; and Hegel, 204–11; as Hermetic, 207; and Indian Tantra, 50; of Jacob Boehme, 207; of Mircea Eliade, 276–77; Neoplatonism as early implicit exemplar, 177; as "New Agey," 174; origins in Alfred Russel Wallace, 174, 191, 249; and panentheism, 207; and the paranormal, 250; and reincarnation beliefs, 177–78; replacing trope of mystical marriage, 13; and sex, 43; of Simon Conway Morris, 368; of Whitley Strieber, 316. *See also* biological gods; Eliade, Mircea; Ghose, Aurobindo; Krishna, Gopi; Murphy, Michael; superhumanism; supernormal

esotericism, extraterrestrial: in African American religion, 326–30; in Afrofuturist literature, 326; of Aimé Michel, 273–75; of Arthur C. Clarke, 176, 263–64, 321; of Barbara Ehrenreich, 322; and biological gods, 319; and the dead, 287, 317; defined, 316–17; distorted by Cold War invasion mythologies, 317–18; naïve literalism of, 241, 291; in Renaissance art, 288–95; role of hypnosis and trance induction in, 234; signaled early (1899) in work of Théodore Flournoy, 234; in Super Story trilogy project, 424; in thought of Jacques Vallée, 279, 281–87; in thought of Terence McKenna, 288. *See also* alien abduction literature; Dick, Philip K.; Strieber, Whitley

esotericism, paraphysical: of Barbara Ehrenreich, 321–22; defined and discussed, 262–64; emanationist and "pagan" pedigree of, 180–81; expression borrowed from Arthur C. Clarke's *Childhood's End*, 176, 262–64; as generator of new forms of plausibility, 268; of Gopi Krishna, 182–83; of Mircea Eliade, 208, 403; and quantum mystical literature, 264–68. *See also* gnomon 18; quantum physics

eternal return (Nietzsche), 272, 455n28

ethnocentrism, 135, 138, 175, 176, 205, 209, 278, 379, 406

Eucharist, 357

Evangelical Christianity: debates with, 307; "family values" of, 41, 298; and homosexuality, 77

Evans, Jules, 410–11

evolutionary humanism, 193

Évrard, Renaud, 250–51

Faivre, Antoine, 423

Farrakhan, Louis, 330

fate, 455n28

Fatima, Our Lady of, 290–91

feminism, 10, 123, 145, 174, 187, 292, 320, 338, 371, 390, 392

film: and evolutionary esotericism, 176; the fiction of my life, 2; gnostic, 131; horror, 331; impact of my work on, 12; and invasion mythologies of the UFO, 284; "loop" between abduction experiences and, 337; metaphor for consciousness and projected ego-world, 4–5, 8, 13, 183, 412–13; metaphor for sensory processing, 237; religion as "legitimate form of science

film (*cont.*)
  fiction," 312–13; as site of the camouflaged sacred, 312; as site of the paranormal, 159–60, 388. *See also* Ebert, Roger; science fiction
filter thesis. *See* gnomon 10
Finley, Stephen, 326, 327–30
Flournoy, Théodore, 233–35, 411
Fodor, Nandor, 252
Fort, Charles, 251, 273, 319, 330, 344–46
Foucault, Michel, 10, 123, 332, 334, 383, 389, 390
Freud, Sigmund, 7, 10, 32–33, 35–36, 39, 46–47, 59–60, 62–63, 68, 89, 123, 141–43, 165, 174, 188, 217, 218, 221, 235, 252, 256, 339, 406, 414, 420. *See also* gnomon 1

gay rights movement, 40, 187
Geller, Uri, 356
Ghose, Aurobindo, 50, 171–72, 176, 182, 186, 402
Ginsberg, Allen, 137, 148–51
Girard, Réne, 296, 304
gnomon, 9, 35
gnomon 1, Heretical Heterosexuality: antinomian nature of homosexuality vis-à-vis heteronormative society, 151; and Bengali Vaishnavism, 48; defined and discussed, 36, 43; exile from sanctioned male sanctity, 141; and Jesus, 37–45, 129–30, 440n1; and Ramakrishna, 60; and "secret body" of this book, 48
gnomon 2, The Human as Two: and Christology, 35; and Christology of Comparison, 353–54; and consciousness, 4–5; and creative process, 167; defined, 36; and deification, 203; as "divine double," 14; and "double consciousness" of being black in America, 325; and gnomon 4 on the Amoral or Transmoral Mystic, 84; in Hindu thought, 7; and historical/constructivist epistemologies of the humanities, 414–16; in Mircea Eliade, 7, 402; in Nietzsche, 272; as a poetic device or shifting heuristic, 413–14; and postcolonial theory, 379; and psychoanalysis, 7, 35
gnomon 3, The Erotic Mystic: and mythology of Shiva, 133–34; and psychedelics, 155; as sexual expression of the reversal method of gnomon 7, 123–24; in the thought of Mircea Eliade, 403. *See also* erotic

gnomon 4, The Amoral or Transmoral Mystic: and gnomon 2 on the Human as Two, 84; and gnomon 17 on Traumatic Secret, 82; informed by Elliot Wolfson, 81; partial origins of idea in sexual-spiritual traumas of my readers, 84–85; and Plato, 81
gnomon 5, The Tantric Transmission: in Aldous Huxley, 215–17; defined and discussed, 85–86, 156–57; Tantra as Asian counterculture, 50; in Theodore Roszak, 156–58. *See also* gnomon 9
gnomon 6, Resonant Comparisons: defined and discussed, 98–101; Hegel and remote viewing, 209; and that Night, 54
gnomon 7, The Gnostic Reversal: defined and discussed, 122–24; intuited in *Kali's Child*, 123–24; origins in that Night, 123; as ouroboric, 126, 128–29, 133, 425; William Blake on the nature of Christ, 147
gnomon 8, Comparative Mystics: defined and discussed, 124–25; Esalen origins as perfect example of, 170; example of Frederic Spiegelberg, 189; example of Gershom Scholem, 113–17; example of Louis Massignon, 105–9; example of Mircea Eliade, 109–13. *See also* Night, that
gnomon 9, It's about Counterculture, not Colonialism: and American reception of Hinduism, 49; coinage of contraculture, 447n40; defined and discussed, 137–39; paranormal phenomena in times of social upheaval, 238–39, 240; vs. the Religious Right, 221; role of Aldous Huxley, 193, 223; shortcomings of counterculture, 223; Tantra as Asian counterculture, 50; and William Blake, 144–45, 158–59. *See also* gnomon 5; gnomon 8
gnomon 10, The Filter Thesis: of Aldous Huxley, 152–53, 216, 219–20; of Allen Ginsberg, 154; of Anita Moorjani, 395; in Arthur C. Clarke, 264; of Bernardo Kastrup, 417–19; defined and discussed, 193–200; and deification, 202–3; and dual aspect monism, 197–200; and Elizabeth Krohn, 231; and the erotic, 62; of Erwin Schrödinger, 265; and evolutionary esotericism, 200–204; of Gopi Krishna, 182–83; of Hegel, 204, 208–11; of Henri Bergson, 154; of Ian Stevenson, 386; and metaphor of Plato's Cave, 196; metaphors of, 449n2, 451n45; of Mircea Eliade, 353, 402–3; as neurobiological, 275–76; and neurotheologian,

223–27; of Nick Herbert, 370; possible in David Eagleman, 225–27; and psychic universalism, 410; and religion, 309–10; suggested in Jill Bolte Taylor, 225; and the traumatic secret, 323–34

gnomon 11, The Humanities Are the Study of Consciousness Coded in Culture, 205–6. *See also* hermeneutics

gnomon 12, Sometimes the Imagined Is Not the Imaginary: discussed and defined, 237–38; empirical imaginal, 235–37, 269; the imaginal and the paranormal, 238, 361, 372; the imaginal defined, 233; the imaginal in Frederic Myers, 235, 261; the imaginal in Henri Corbin, 233–34; the imaginal in Théodore Flournoy, 234–35; the outrageous nature of the imaginal, 240; symbolic imaginal, 235–37, 269

gnomon 13, The Paranormal Is a Kind of Story, 238–39, 245–47. See also *Authors of the Impossible*

gnomon 14, The Paranormal Is a Nondual Signal, 241. *See also* dual aspect monism

gnomon 15, The Super Story: defined and discussed, 271; and the new real, 366; and superhumanism, 272–75; and trilogy project, 423–25. See also *Mutants and Mystics*

gnomon 16, The Super Natural: defined and discussed, 315–16; as gloss on Eliadean hierophany, 444n66; as gloss on Michael Murphy's evolutionary vision, 173; and horror writing, 322; and L. Frank Baum, 24; transition from the supernatural seen in history of the poltergeist, 251–53. *See also* biological gods; plasmas; Strieber, Whitley

gnomon 17, The Traumatic Secret: and Elizabeth Krohn, 231; as explanation for honest skepticism, 324; and gnomon 4, 82; and Ramakrishna, 60–61, 323; and reincarnation memories, 382; and trance induction, 285; and ufological literature, 279; and Whitley Strieber, 323

gnomon 18, The Realist Impulse: defined and discussed, 366–70; in email of Whitley Strieber, 349–50; and empirical imaginal, 236; of evolutionary esotericisms, 402; and psychedelic states, 386; of Teilhard de Chardin, 402

gnomon 19, The Future of the Past: in David Friedrich Strauss, 355–56; defined and discussed, 372–73; example of comparing resurrections, 256–57; materialized in "X" found in airport, 425

gnomon 20, The New Sacred, 399–401. *See also* consciousness

gnosis: in Aldous Huxley, 193; as countercultural, 147; and esotericism, 181; paranormal, 457n3; as refashioned modern intellectual epistemology, 121–23, 130; and structuralist anthropology, 133–34

go-kart racing, 27

Gould, Stephen Jay, 175, 316

Greyson, Bruce, 375, 385, 394–95

Hanegraaff, Wouter J.: creating new field, 423; defining esotericism, 180–81, 182; on evolutionism, 177; and genesis of this book, 125–26; on historical imagination, 364–65; on realist comparison, 373; "religionist" criticism, 129; response to, 125–32

Hansen, George, 239–41

Harrison, George, 138

Harvard Divinity School, 49, 64, 170, 184, 282, 400

Hatcher, Brian, 76

Hegel, G. W. F., 204–11, 416; and *Geist*, 205–6; Hermetic dimensions of thought, 192, 206–11; and history, 204–5

Heisenberg, Werner, 264–66

Herbert, Nick, 270

hermeneutics: about subjects caught in and freed from stories, 5; creative hermeneutics of Mircea Eliade, 403–4; criterion of evaluating, 95; and gnosis, 104; hermeneutical union, 109, 149; hermeneutics of suspicion, 154; the Hermetic radicalization of, 210; and that Night, 52; and paranormal potentials of reading and writing, 64, 148–49, 166, 417; and participation in text, 70–71; played Hermes in grade school play, 24; and resonant comparisons, 98–101; and secret readers, 13; self-identified as hermeneut, 126; sexual-spiritual dialectic of, 57, 58; and the text as coded consciousness, 208; and UFO phenomenon, 286; and Wilhelm Dilthey, 205. See also *Authors of the Impossible*

Hermeticism, 206–7

Hill, Barney and Betty, 326–27

History of Religions (Chicago school): and alien abduction literature, 281; countercultural context of development, 138;

History of Religions (Chicago school) (*cont.*) as form of art, 143; hermeneutics of suspicion and Huston Smith, 154–55; and myth, miracle and magic, 247. *See also* Doniger, Wendy; Eliade, Mircea; University of Chicago Divinity School

History of Religions (journal), 276

Hitchens, Christopher, 212

Hollenback, Jess, 451n4

Home, Daniel Dunglas, 248, 356

homoeroticism: and apocalypticism, 41; of Jesus, 37–45, 80, 129–30, 440n1; of Kabbalah, 80; of Ramakrishna, 68–69; of seminary, 33–34, 46–47, 141; of traditional male Christian mystical literature, 13, 36, 43, 48, 65, 141, 151. *See also* gnomon 1

homosexuality: and black churches, 40; and celibacy, 217; as civil rights issue, 40, 76–77; and genesis of King James Bible, 39; of Louis Massignon, 106–7; Roman Catholic Church teaching on, 34, 43–44; and suicide attempts, 34. *See also* gnomon 1

Hopkins, Budd, 283–85

Hopkins, Jeffrey, 46, 56

horror, 322–23, 329–30, 331

"H. R. Pufnstuf," 25, 362

humanities: conventional epistemology of, 243–44; conventional historiography of, 257; conventional ontology of, 243–44; conventional philosophy of mind of, 255; cosmic, 366–70; exclusive emphasis on difference, 419–20; fundamental principles of, 300–301; in Germany, 205; after Hegel, 210–11; and historical consciousness, 303; potential prophetic function, 98, 297; secret criterion of truth in, 359–60; understanding of religious identity, 301–2, 310–11

human potential movement, 85, 165–66, 170–71, 172–73, 185–88, 193, 207, 217

Hume, David, 406

Huxley, Aldous: and *Brave New World*, 214, 217, 220–21; and *The Doors of Perception*, 215–16; early Advaita Vedanta of, 215; and homosexuality, 450n28; influence on Esalen, 193; interest in Asian religions, 137; and *Island*, 155–56, 212, 220–21; mescaline trip of with Humphrey Osmond, 151–55, 193; notion of Mind at Large, 152, 193, 216; and *The Perennial Philosophy*, 214–15, 217, 218; privileging of or con-

version to Tantra, 156, 450n27; role in human potential movement, 186–87; and William Blake, 221

Huxley, Julian, 193, 214

Huxley, Laura, 216

Huxley, T. H., 193, 214

imaginal: in C. G. Jung, 233; empirical, 236–37; as evolutionary, 235; in Frederic Myers, 235, 261; in Henry Corbin, 233–34; as insectoid, 235; symbolic, 236–37; in Théodore Flournoy, 233–35. *See also* imagination

imagination: "black box" or "X-factor" of the study of religion, 232–33; as organ of this book, 5–6; as quantum machine, 369. *See also* imaginal

imperialism, 144–45

insider-outsider problem, 86, 87–88, 94–96, 126. *See also* hermeneutics; paradox

invisible colleges, 174, 275–76

Jacobs, David, 283–85

Jain, Andrea R., 138

James, William: academic framing of mysticism, 213; antinomianism, 143; empiricism of, 373; inspiration of Sursem Esalen group, 192–93; on psychical phenomena, 248–49, 274; superhumanism, 273, 345; teacher of W. E. B. Du Bois, 326; understanding Hegel on nitrous oxide, 208; understanding of filter thesis, 194–95, 216

Jesus: apocalypticism of, 41; criterion of embarrassment, 354–55; depiction on crucifix in home church, 38; divinity, 147, 283, 307; dream of ithyphallic, 38; and Eucharist, 357; and Freud, 35; frustration with home town, 296–97; and imagination, 37; miracles, 355–57; and Mircea Eliade, 353; and the poor, 299; and psychical research, 356; resurrection, 256–57; right-wing distortions of, 299; self-understanding, 356; sexual orientation of, 37–45, 47, 80, 129–30, 151, 184, 190, 228; teaching of "sun" shining on good and bad alike, 81; teaching on castration, 41, 354; as thaumaturge, 356–57. *See also* Christology

John of the Cross, 65

Jordan, Mark, 76

Josephson-Storm, Jason, 15

Jung, C. G., 108, 121, 198, 233–34, 265, 267, 369, 386, 404–5, 414, 444n66

Kabbalah: reliance on absolute authority of Torah, 116; and UFOs, 328–29; and William Blake, 147, 159; in work of Gershom Scholem, 113–17, 423. *See also* Wolfson, Elliot

Kaiser, David, 269–70

Kakar, Sudhir, 66, 67, 73, 142, 211, 282

Kali's Child: alleged translation errors, 58–60, 75–76; alleged translation errors answered by Rajagopal Chattopadhyaya, 59–60; censorship campaigns against, 57–58, 68–78, 84, 128, 140; countercultural roots, 137–39; criterion of embarrassment, 355; as early intuition of the "flip" or reversal method of gnomon 7, 123–24; example of Tantric Transmission or gnomon 5, 85; "exoticizing" charge, 139; extreme nature of reception, 11–12; historical and social context of book, 79–80; History of Religions Prize, 69; and human deification, 354; mystical origins in that Night, 52–54, 123; phallic foot controversy, 59–60; place in total corpus, 19, 35; positive "secret" reception of, 69, 84–85; postcolonial criticism and "orientalist" charges against, 73–74, 134–36; reading of Michael Murphy, 169; role of sexual trauma in one American censor activist, 84; transference phenomena of "colonial" charge, 72–73

Kant, Immanuel, 195–96, 209

Kastrup, Bernardo, 416–19

Keel, John, 346

Kelly, Edward, 192–93, 375

Kelly, Emily Williams, 192–93, 375

King, Stephen, 15, 253

Kitagawa, Joseph, 406

Kripal (surname), 72

Krishna, Gopi, 50, 182–83, 194, 195, 277

Krishnamurti, Jiddu, 66, 222

Krohn, Elizabeth, 230–33, 236

Kundera, Milan, vi, 14

Lachman, Gary, 6–7

Landau, Brent, 294

Lang, Andrew, 373

Last Temptation of Christ, The, 43–44

Latour, Bruno, 370

Leary, Timothy, 137, 154–56

Lévi-Strauss, Claude, 133, 239

Lieb, Michael, 290, 328–29

Lincoln, Bruce, 298

LSD, 138, 155, 215–16, 270, 386, 462n42

Luhrmann, Tanya, 54–55

Luther, Martin, 42, 251

Mack, John, 279, 281–87

Magee, Glenn Alexander, 206–11

magnetism, phenomenology of, 99–100, 209

Manning, Matthew, 243

Marriage of Heaven and Hell, The, 97, 98, 144, 153, 431

Mary Magdalene, 42–44

Maslow, Abraham, 186–87

Massignon, Louis, 101, 103, 105–9, 115, 117–18

masturbation, contemplative, 148–51, 158

materialism: as automatic "reset" position, 374; critique of Bernardo Kastrup, 417–19; and Darwinism, 201–2; as denial of consciousness, 139, 166, 212, 234; and ethnocentrism, 276; and the humanities, 126, 243–44, 319, 373; as inadequate to our questions, 130; as new intolerant monotheism, 408; as oh-so nineteenth-centuryish, 368–69; as polemical rhetoric, 181; promissory, 226, 365; and quantum physics, 179, 198, 262, 366; reasonableness of, 200, 374; and resistance to the paranormal, 387–88; of Robert Monroe, 100; and the super natural, 316; writing against as most radical intellectual transgression, 127, 131, 179; and zaniness of extreme religious experience, 7. *See also* consciousness; dual aspect monism

McCarthyism, 152, 187

McGinn, Bernard, 48

McKenna, Dennis, 176

McKenna, Terence, 176

McLean, Malcolm, 75–76

Méheust, Bertrand, 236, 273–74, 356, 373

Merton, Thomas, 31

metal bending, 385

métapsychique tradition (French), 14, 250, 274, 356, 371. *See also* Michel, Aimé

methodological agnosticism, 374

Michel, Aimé, 273–75, 279

Miller, Henry, vi, 15, 187

Moench, Doug, 254

Monroe, Robert A., 99–100

monster, 24, 104, 133, 239–40

monster theory, 332–33

Moorjani, Anita, 393–97, 401, 405

Mormonism, 330

Morrison, Grant, 176

Morton, Timothy, 370

Muhammad, Master Fard, 327–29

Muktananda, Swami, 47, 50, 66, 80, 92–94

Mullis, Kary, 313–14

Muow, Richard, 397

Murphy, Michael: co-founder of Esalen, 185–86; coining of "human potential," 186; evolutionary esotericism, 190, 207; and John Mack, 286–87; and mystical comparativism of Frederic Spiegelberg, 170, 182, 189; as "Nightcaller," 169; origin call of relationship and mentorship, 169; reading of *Kali's Child* through Tantric lens of Aurobindo Ghose, 171; and *siddhi*s or paranormal powers, 171–72; and X-Men mythology, 169, 172–73, 258–59. *See also* Esalen Institute

mutant: Dominic Matei in Eliade's *Youth Without Youth* as, 228, 276–78; as privileged objects and subjects of humanistic and scientific research on the paranormal, 389; readers as, 2–3; in real-world, 2, 228–33, 253, 361–63; and Scientology, 361–63

Mutants and Mystics: as attempt to "cross over" into broader readership, 166; extraordinary reception of, 12; origins in finding of X in parking lot, 424; origins in that Night, 55; out-of-body experience of a reader, 99; as study of emergent mythologies, 271. *See also* Dick, Philip K.; mutant; science fiction; Strieber, Whitley

Myers, Frederic: coinage and understanding of telepathy, 249–50, 252; education reformer, 279; influence on William James, 248; inspiration for Sursem meetings at Esalen, 192–93; use of "subliminal," 250. *See also* supernormal; telepathy

mysticism: apophatic, 450–51n40; as countercultural, 147; and mathematics, 268–71; as object of rationalist/Protestant polemic, 180; on possibility of modern or secular non-institutional forms, 116–17, 119, 444n91; relationship to William James on filter thesis, 194–95; science mysticism, 315; in understanding of David Brooks, 213

myth: Adam and Eve as gnostic, 120; of biological gods, 319; Bruce Lincoln on myth as coded ideology, 298; Darwin and Adam and Eve, 174–75; and dual aspect monism, 198; emergent mythologies, 12–13, 271, 366, 424; as expression of mystical experience, 207; as the genre of this book, 1–8, 420–21; and the imagination, 233–34; of invading extraterrestrials, 317; and Jacques Vallée, 279–80, 281, 282–86; mythical transformation of the mystical marriage into the mutant, 13; in Nation of Islam, 329; Native American, 22–23; and that Night, 123; and the paranormal, 238–39, 240–41, 245, 247, 255, 257, 327; physical expressions of, 327; and quantum physics, 369–70; scholar living, 103; in Scientology, 362–63; structuralist understanding of paradox in, 133–34; and Super Story, 271, 424; of the trickster, 240; and Viveiros de Castro, 370; and Whitley Strieber, 314–15, 346; of the X-Men, 172–73, 258–60. *See also* gnomon 13; gnomon 19

Nagel, Thomas, 179

nationalism, 153, 221, 298, 299. *See also* imperialism

Native American cultures of Nebraska, 21–22

nature, 364–65, 410

near-death experience (NDE), 230–31, 240, 263, 349, 362, 393–97, 455n28

Nelson, Victoria, 127, 131, 167

Neoplatonism: emanationist theology of, 180–81; and the erotic, 68; etheric body in, 2; as example of implicit evolutionary esotericism, 177, 202; and Hermeticism, 207; and history of out-of-body experience, 99; and Indian nondualism, 378–79; and mystical origins of comparativism, 124; and reincarnation beliefs, 178; spiritual vehicle (*ochema*) and ufological orbs, 414; and William Blake, 147

neurotheologian, 212–13, 219–20, 223–27

New Age: loss of political edge, 159; origin of expression in Blake, 157; and UFOs, 290, 294

New Atheists, 128, 212, 316

Nietzsche, Friedrich, 3, 171, 176, 272–74, 278, 296, 455n28

Night, that: as creative origin of corpus, 12, 228, 420, 433; illustrated in graphic novel pages, 55; as out-of-body experience, 99–100; resonant with Eliade's *The Secret of*

Doctor Honigberger, 101–2; as *shaktipat*, 86; unpublished preface of, 51–54
Nussbaum, Martha, 57

Obeyesekere, Gananath, 66–67, 73, 142
OCD (obsessive compulsive disorder), 30, 34
orientalism: challenge of reincarnation memories for, 392; in Edward Said, 377–78; and *Kali's Child*, 72–74, 134–39; Platonic, 378–79
Orsi, Robert, 257
Ouellet, Eric, 83, 327, 451n13

Pagels, Elaine, 362, 423
panentheism: in Barbara Ehrenreich and Philip K. Dick, 457n14; in Jacob Boehme and Michael Murphy, 207
paradox, 133–34, 200, 233, 239, 334
paranormal: in academy, 229, 238, 244–45, 261, 292–93, 451n4; as anti-structure, 239–40; and bilateral brain, 7; bilocation, 355; coinage and definition by Joseph Maxwell, 250–51; and criterion of embarrassment, 355; as dangerous, 263; definition, 233; and Derridean deconstruction, 240–41; and Eliadean hierophany, 444n66; in Hegel, 208–11; in Ian Stevenson, 461n24; and intellect or *nous*, 14; in Jess Hollenback, 451n4; levitation, 355; and meaning, 239; and Michael Shermer, 464n1; mythical dimensions, 1, 239; as the "quantum physics" of the study of religion, 369; and reading and writing, 13–14; rhetorical trick of the "anecdote," 367, 374; and sexuality, 209, 252–53; and *siddhi*s or superpowers, 50, 171–72; as social, 238–39, 240, 385–86; as story, 1, 238–39; "super natural" gloss, 316, 444n66. *See also* gnomon 13; gnomon 14; poltergeist; psychical research tradition (British); telepathy
parapsychology (American), 14, 371
parasociology, 14, 83
Parmenides, 266
Pasulka, Diana Walsh, 453n31
Paul (apostle), 42, 65, 228
Pauli, Wolfgang, 198, 233, 265–66
perennialism, answering charge of, 409–13
Pinn, Anthony, 325–26
plasmas: as biological gods, 380; in British *Condign Report*, 349; of lightning bolt

initiating near-death experience, 231; in mystical thought of Philip K. Dick, 332; in that Night, 51; as paraphysical basis of "soul," 263; in thought and experience of Whitley Strieber, 314, 319, 349–50. *See also* biological gods; conscious energy
Plotinus, 148–49, 181, 183, 202
poltergeist, 251–53, 452–53n28, 453n32
postcolonial theory, 377–82. *See also* orientalism
posthumanism, 273
postmodernism, 66, 71–75, 89, 122, 131, 272, 300–301, 332, 364, 366, 414, 420
Powers, Barclay, 55
precognition: in Aurobindo, 170; and block universe, 455n28; of Derrida, 241; of Elizabeth Krohn, 231–32; in Hegel, 209; in Hudson Valley UFO events, 342; as mixture of symbolic and empirical material, 237; and the new sacred, 401; plausible in retrocausation in physics, 370, 401; and sinking of the Titanic, 385. *See also* dreams: precognitive or premonitorial
Price, Richard, 170, 185–86
Proudfoot, Wayne, 81
Pseudo-Dionysius, 124
psychedelics, 462n42. *See also* Herbert, Nick; Huxley, Aldous; McKenna, Dennis; McKenna, Terence
psychical research tradition (British), 14, 171, 173, 186, 188, 190, 192–93, 215, 216, 248–49, 263–64, 274, 279, 345, 356, 371, 373, 384, 452n17, 452n20
psychoanalysis: and Buddhism, 88–89; and crucifix of home church, 38; and failed remote viewing experiment, 160; posterboy for Freudian reductionism, 420; and reincarnation memories, 389–91; in seminary, 32–33, 34–35
psychokinesis, 449n1, 452–53n28, 462n38. *See also* poltergeist
purity/impurity, 88, 96, 217
Pythagoras, 268

Quakers, 190
quantum biology, 179
quantum physics: and Bell's Theorem, 269–71; comparisons with mystical literature, 262, 264–68; implications ignored by conventional neuroscientists, 359; and new plausibility structures, 267–68,

quantum physics (*cont.*)
270–71; in reading of Mircea Eliade, 403. *See also* dual aspect monism; esotericism, paraphysical
Quispel, Gilles, 121

race: centrality in the study of religion, 325–26; and doubling of consciousness in American culture, 326; key critical category of radicalization, 97, 325–26; related moral issue of homosexuality, 40; systemic racism in American culture, 303; in UFO literature, 326–30
Radin, Dean, 159–60
Rajneesh, Bhagwan, 47, 66
Ramakrishna Paramahamsa: coded criticism of in Aldous Huxley's *Island* (1962), 219, 450n28; dissertation research, 49; and gnomon 17, 323; in that Night, 52, 54. See also *Kali's Child*
Ramanujan, Srinivasa, 269, 368
Ratzinger, Joseph, 34, 43–44
reductionism, 54, 123, 224, 226, 239, 359, 419. *See also* materialism
reflexivity: birth of in scrupulosity, 31; birth of in suicide pattern of seminary, 34; as ouroboric, 126, 128, 129, 131, 166, 417; as structure of gnosis, 122–24. *See also* hermeneutics
Reich, Wilhelm, 145, 171, 445n11
religious intolerance, 301–3, 307, 314
remote viewing, 160, 209, 447n46
Riesbrodt, Martin, 312
Roads of Excess, Palaces of Wisdom: Blakean inspiration of, 98, 140, 143–45; and Catholic clerical scandals of 2002, 80; early thesis on mystical origins of comparativism, 125; exoticizing scholars of religion, 137–39; Frederic Spiegelberg as exemplary model of thesis, 170; narrative of seminary experience and awakening to unconscious, 31–37; origins in resonant comparisons of anomalous experiences, 100; place of book in larger corpus, 19, 64; relationship to *The Serpent's Gift*, 119, 129; as strategy to answer critics of *Kali's Child*, 134–35
Romero, Óscar, 31
Rospar, Jean-Pierre, 274
Roszak, Theodore, 137, 155–58
Roy, Parama, 76
Royle, Nicolas, 15, 253

Rubin, Jeffrey, 88–89, 94–95
Russell, Bertrand, 198

sacred: as dialectical or paradoxical, 334–35; Eliadean, 7, 112–13, 315–16; and horror, 331; as "legitimate form of science fiction," 312–13; as performance or theatre, 313. *See also* gnomon 20
Said, Edward, 377–78. *See also* orientalism
Sarkar, Sumit, 76
Sawyer, Dana, 222
Schaeffer, Frank, 307
Schindler, William, 58
Scholem, Gershom, 101, 103, 113–18, 423
Schrödinger, Erwin, 265
science fiction: actual human potential weirder still, 2; as adequate resource for thinking about complexities of reading and writing, 14, 253; and alien husbandry or seeding of planet, 345; as camouflaged sacred or new mode of mystical literature, 312, 388, 403; and Charles Fort, 344; as dialectical influence on alien abduction experiences, 337; as gnostic, 131, 361–62; influence on Nation of Islam, 327; in Michael Murphy's *The Future of the Body*, 173; in Mircea Eliade's *Youth Without Youth*, 228, 230–33; and the paranormal at Esalen symposium, 159–61; paranormal experiences of major sci-fi artists and authors, 12; religion as legitimate form of, 312–13; Super Story trilogy project as, 424; treatment of cosmic Mind in Philip K. Dick's *Valis*, 15, 167, 207, 319, 321–22, 332, 362, 411, 413, 416–17, 423; treatment of morphing Mind in Stanislaw Lem's *Solaris*, 410–13; treatment of paranormal in Arthur C. Clarke's *Childhood's End*, 262–64. *See also* Clarke, Arthur C.; Dick, Philip K.; mutant; Strieber, Whitley; UFO
Scientology, 361–63
scrupulosity, 30–31
secrecy, 70–71, 103–5
Secret Gospel of Mark fragment, 80, 440n1
secret humanism, 310–11
Secret of Doctor Honigberger, The, 101–2, 111–12
Selig, Paul, 237, 451n11
Serpent's Gift, The: Blakean inspiration of, 98, 140; as closure on the sexual questions, 165; example of intellectual gnosticism,

315; exoticizing the study of religion, 139; mystical humanism of, 404; as mystical literature, 119; on mystical origins of comparativism, 125; place in corpus, 19, 35; relationship to *Roads of Excess*, 119; as strategy to answer critics of *Kali's Child*, 134–35

sexual-spiritual orientation, 13, 19, 129–30, 228, 357. *See also* gnomon 1

shaktipat, 86, 92, 93–94, 95, 381

Sharf, Robert, 199

Shiva, 51, 133–34

Shweder, Richard, 410

Siddha Yoga, apology to scholars of, 86

Skinwalker ranch, 333–34

Smith, Huston: criticisms of *Kali's Child*, 154–55; psychedelic revelations, 137, 154; sighting of five flying saucers, 137–38

Smith, Joseph, 330

Smith, J. Z., 293

Sophia, 43, 44

space-time: in block universe, 401; and the historiography of the new comparativism, 401; hyperdimensional modeling and NDEs, 263; transcendence of in near-death experience of Anita Moorjani, 395–96, 401; transcendence of in near-death experience of Roger Ebert, 237, 401; transcendence of in quantum physics, 268; transcendence of in thought of Louis Massignon, 108–9; transcendence of in thought of Mircea Eliade, 111

Spiegelberg, Frederic, 170, 182–83; intellectual refugee from Nazi Germany, 189; mystical origins of his "religion of no religion," 189

Spiritual But Not Religious, 185, 213, 219

Stang, Charles, 14, 194, 414, 427

Staubach, Roger, 27

Stevenson, Ian: critique of New Age, 385, 387; on cultural dissonance of reincarnation memories, 384; Esalen too dodgy for, 192; on evolution of souls, 376; and Mircea Eliade, 405; paranormal interests, 385–86; personal interactions with his colleagues, 375; promotion of filter thesis, 386; psychedelic catalysts of thought, 386–87; study of reincarnation memories and birthmarks, 383; Theosophical influences through mother, 385

Straight, Bilinda, 381

Strenski, Ivan, 452n15

Strieber, Anne, 348, 349–50

Strieber, Whitley: and *Communion*, 313–14, 335–48; early trauma "cracking open" the psyche, 323; and history of hypnosis, 411; implant, 337; radiation or plasma theory, 314, 349–50; reductive self-hypotheses, 337; superhumanism of, 314; on terror, 329–30, 348; and trance, 336; the visitors and story, 423. *See also* *Super Natural, The*

Struck, Peter, 14

subliminal, 250, 252

superhumanism: of Aimé Michel, 273–74; black, 329; as evolutionary esotericism, 273–75; of Nietzsche, 272–73; and Super Story, 271; of Whitley Strieber, 314; of William James, 345

Superman (Nietzsche), 272, 274, 278, 455n28

super natural. *See* gnomon 16

Super Natural, The: as attempt to "cross over" into broader readership, 166; as exoticizing, 139; origin of project, 315; use of the "future of the past," 372. *See also* Strieber, Whitley

supernormal, 233, 250–51, 252, 261, 402

symbol, 5, 14, 339, 342, 365, 369

synchronicity: of bridal chamber symbolism, 132; and Eliadean hierophany, 444n66; in evolutionary biology, 448n18; and Forrest J. Ackerman, 322, 457n18; Pauli-Jung model, 265; and reading and writing, vi, 2; of Tom Shroder (biographer of Ian Stevenson), 461n25; of Whitley Strieber, 349; of "X" found, 424

Tantra: in Aldous Huxley's *Island*, 217–19; defined and discussed, 49–51; discovered in seminary library, 47, 66, 73–74; as example of the reversal method in sexual frame, 123–24; as precolonial, 135–36; privileged by Mircea Eliade, 110–12; and William Blake, 144, 147. *See also* gnomon 5

Taoism. *See* Daoism

Targ, Russell, 160

Taves, Ann, 54, 81

Taylor, Charles, 379

Taylor, Jill Bolte, 224–25, 325

telepathy: coined by Frederic Myers, 235; expressive of human love and deep sociality, 279; in French science, 452–53n28; as insectoid, 235; in Jacques Derrida, 208, 241, 243; as "mental telegraphy" in Mark Twain, 245–47; as mixture of empirical and symbolic material, 237; possible

telepathy (*cont.*)
  expression of entanglement, 270–71; in psychedelic states, 240; and study of religion, 255–57; as text, 253–54; traumatic technology of, 248–53; in UFO events, 240
Teresa of Avila, 65
Thompson, Keith, 286–87
Thompson, Marianne Meye, 307
transgression, 41, 146
transhumanism, 193, 273
Trump, Donald, 299
Trungmpa, Chogyam, 90–91
Tucker, Jim, 375, 382
Turner, Victor, 133, 239, 305
Twain, Mark, 15, 245–47, 452n20
Tyagananda, Swami, 58–59
Tyson, Neil DeGrasse, 174

UFO: as agent of cultural deconstruction, 332; appearance over Hudson Valley and Burned-Over District, 330, 340–44; as biological god, 318–22; coined as "flying saucer," 317; in contemporary Native American lore, 330; and dogs, 288–89, 333; and earth farm theory, 344–45; as expression of dual aspect monism, 199; and Ezekiel, 289–90, 328–29, 456n56; "falling-leaf" pattern, 290; and Indian Tantra, 49; invasion mythology of Cold War America, 11, 284, 292, 317–18; the Madonna of the, 288–95; as metaphor for hermeneutics, 165; and Nation of Islam, 327–29; in New Age, 290, 294; Oz factor, 24; and purgatory, 453n31; radiation or plasma theory, 349–50; role of Christian fundamentalism in invasion mythologies of, 317; as seen by Jacques Vallée as a teenager over Paris, 101; sexual violence of, 338; on Skinwalker ranch, 333; space animal theory, 318–19, 344–46; and superhumanism, 273
Underhill, Evelyn, 213
University of Chicago Divinity School, 48–49, 56, 64, 66–67, 69, 77, 134, 154, 204, 205, 208, 278, 309, 402, 405–6. *See also* Doniger, Wendy; Eliade, Mircea

Vallée, Jacques: in *Authors of the Impossible*, 282; and biological gods, 346; and Invisible College, 275; mentoring me, 279; sighting of flying saucer over Paris as a teenager, 101; student of Aimé Michel, 273
"vibration," phenomenology of, 99–100, 183
virgin for Christ, 42, 65
Virgin Mary: apparitions and UFO phenomenology, 288–95; oedipal dimensions of in my life, 38
virgin soul, 107
Viveiros de Castro, Eduardo, 261, 370
Vivekananda, Swami, 52, 54, 74, 76
Vrajaprana, Pravrajika, 58

Wallace, Alfred Russel, 174, 190–91, 249
Wargo, Eric, 323, 361–63, 411–12
Watts, Alan, 47, 137
Weizsächer, Carl von, 182, 265–67
Wexler, Philip, 451n13
White, David Gordon, 49
White, Hayden, 364–65
Whitman, Walt, 116, 119, 175, 213, 463n13
Wizard of Oz, The, 23–25. *See also* UFO: Oz factor
Wolfson, Elliot: on human deification, 102; indebtedness to, 126; nuanced dialectic of "reversing" thought, 102; thesis of transmoral mystic, 81–82
Woodroffe, Sir John, 50, 156

X, found: in airport, around negotiations for Super Story trilogy project, 424–25; in parking lot, as mistaken Christian cross for synchronistic mutant X, 14–15, 258–60
Xavier, Professor, 2–3, 228–29, 230, 363
X Club, 193
X-Men, 2, 169, 172–73, 253, 259, 424

Yeltsin, Boris, 188

Zen Buddhism, 89, 156–57, 217, 362, 412, 453n39